VOLUME ONE

The Illustrated History of Humankind

PEOPLE
OF THE
PAST

THE EPIC STORY OF HUMAN ORIGINS AND DEVELOPMENT

VOLUME ONE

The Illustrated History of Humankind

PEOPLE
OF THE PAST

THE EPIC STORY OF HUMAN ORIGINS AND DEVELOPMENT

GENERAL EDITOR GÖRAN BURENHULT

FOG CITY PRESS

Published by Fog City Press
814 Montgomery Street
San Francisco CA 94133 USA
Copyright © 2003 Weldon Owen Pty Ltd and Bra Böcker AB
Reprinted 2004

Chief Executive Officer: John Owen
President: Terry Newell
Publisher: Lynn Humphries
Editorial Coordinator: Jessica Cox
Production Manager: Caroline Webber
Production Coordinator: James Blackman
Sales Manager: Emily Jahn
Vice President, International Sales: Stuart Laurence

Project Coordinator: Annette Carter
Copy Editors: Jo Avigdor, Roderick Campbell, Carson Creagh, Glenda Downing,
Gillian Hewitt, Jacqueline Kent, Margaret McPhee
Picture Editors: Anne Burke, Jenny Mills, Ann Nichol
Art Director: Sue Burk
Illustration Editor: Joanna Collard

ISBN 1 877019 30 5

Color reproduction by Colourscan Co. Pty Ltd
Printed by Kyodo Printing (Singapore) Co. Pty Ltd
Printed in Singapore

A WELDON OWEN PRODUCTION

Page 1
Neanderthal Skull found at La Ferrassie, France.
DAVID L. BRILL, 1985

Pages 2–3
A Bushman on the lookout for springhares in
the Kalahari Desert.
PETER JOHNSON/NHPA

↪ Magnificent weapons of flint and bone,
about 11,000 years old, found in Montana,
in the United States.

◄ Carved Venus figure from Laussel, in France,
dating from the Upper Paleolithic period.

JEAN VERTUT/MUSEE D'AQUITAINE, BORDEAUX

CONTENTS

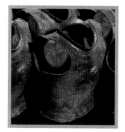

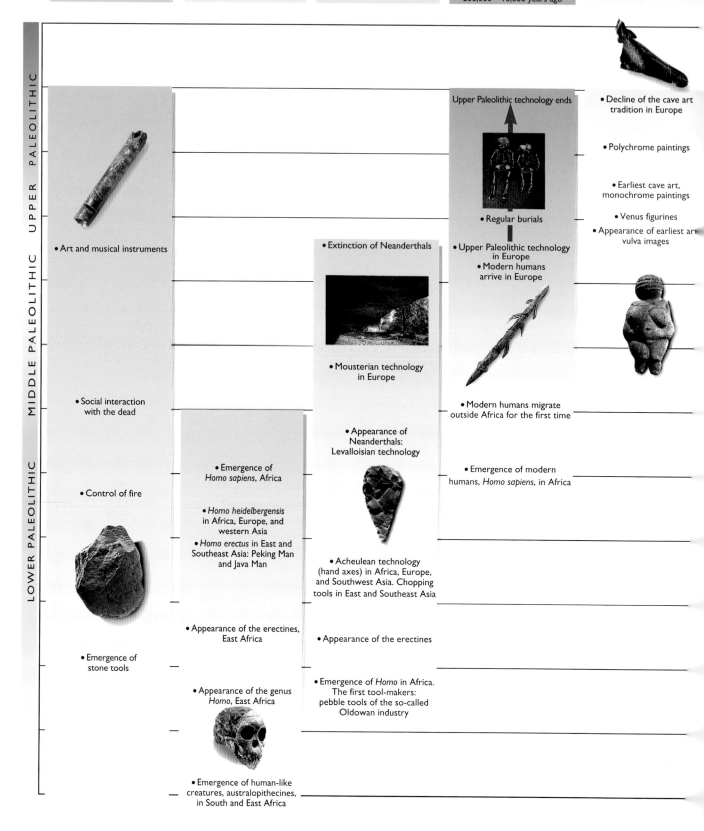

UPPER PALEOLITHIC

MIDDLE PALEOLITHIC

LOWER PALEOLITHIC

Upper Paleolithic technology ends

• Decline of the cave art tradition in Europe

• Polychrome paintings

• Earliest cave art, monochrome paintings

• Venus figurines

• Appearance of earliest art, vulva images

• Regular burials

• Art and musical instruments

• Extinction of Neanderthals

• Upper Paleolithic technology in Europe
• Modern humans arrive in Europe

• Social interaction with the dead

• Mousterian technology in Europe

• Modern humans migrate outside Africa for the first time

• Appearance of Neanderthals: Levalloisian technology

• Emergence of Homo sapiens, Africa

• Emergence of modern humans, Homo sapiens, in Africa

• Control of fire

• Homo heidelbergensis in Africa, Europe, and western Asia
• Homo erectus in East and Southeast Asia: Peking Man and Java Man

• Acheulean technology (hand axes) in Africa, Europe, and Southwest Asia. Chopping tools in East and Southeast Asia

• Appearance of the erectines, East Africa

• Appearance of the erectines

• Emergence of stone tools

• Emergence of Homo in Africa. The first tool-makers: pebble tools of the so-called Oldowan industry

• Appearance of the genus Homo, East Africa

• Emergence of human-like creatures, australopithecines, in South and East Africa

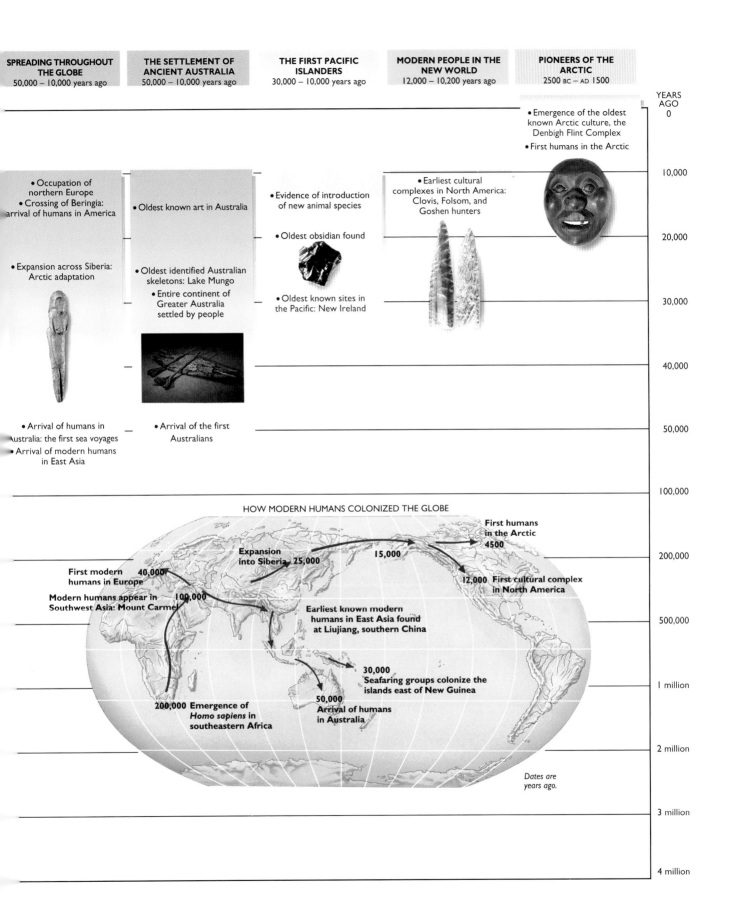

| SPREADING THROUGHOUT THE GLOBE 50,000 – 10,000 years ago | THE SETTLEMENT OF ANCIENT AUSTRALIA 50,000 – 10,000 years ago | THE FIRST PACIFIC ISLANDERS 30,000 – 10,000 years ago | MODERN PEOPLE IN THE NEW WORLD 12,000 – 10,200 years ago | PIONEERS OF THE ARCTIC 2500 BC – AD 1500 | YEARS AGO |

• Emergence of the oldest known Arctic culture, the Denbigh Flint Complex

• First humans in the Arctic

0

10,000

• Occupation of northern Europe
• Crossing of Beringia: arrival of humans in America

• Oldest known art in Australia

• Evidence of introduction of new animal species

• Earliest cultural complexes in North America: Clovis, Folsom, and Goshen hunters

• Oldest obsidian found

20,000

• Expansion across Siberia: Arctic adaptation

• Oldest identified Australian skeletons: Lake Mungo
• Entire continent of Greater Australia settled by people

• Oldest known sites in the Pacific: New Ireland

30,000

40,000

• Arrival of humans in Australia: the first sea voyages
• Arrival of modern humans in East Asia

• Arrival of the first Australians

50,000

100,000

HOW MODERN HUMANS COLONIZED THE GLOBE

First humans in the Arctic 4500

Expansion into Siberia 25,000

15,000

200,000

First modern humans in Europe 40,000

Modern humans appear in Southwest Asia: Mount Carmel 100,000

12,000 First cultural complex in North America

Earliest known modern humans in East Asia found at Liujiang, southern China

500,000

30,000 Seafaring groups colonize the islands east of New Guinea

1 million

200,000 Emergence of *Homo sapiens* in southeastern Africa

50,000 Arrival of humans in Australia

Dates are years ago.

2 million

3 million

4 million

13

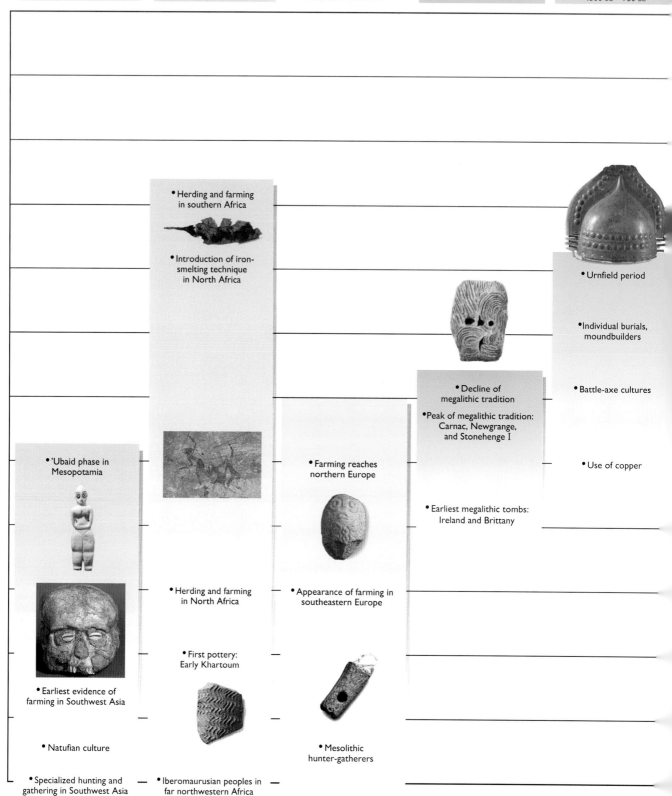

THE GREAT TRANSITION
10,000 BC – 4,000 BC

HUNTER-GATHERERS AND FARMERS IN AFRICA
10,000 BC – AD 200

STONE AGE HUNTER-GATHERERS AND FARMERS IN EUROPE
10,000 BC – 3000 BC

THE MEGALITH BUILDERS OF WESTERN EUROPE
4800 BC – 2800 BC

BRONZE AGE CHIEFDOMS AND THE END OF STONE AGE EUROPE
4500 BC – 750 BC

• Herding and farming in southern Africa

• Introduction of iron-smelting technique in North Africa

• Urnfield period

• Individual burials, moundbuilders

• Decline of megalithic tradition

• Battle-axe cultures

• Peak of megalithic tradition: Carnac, Newgrange, and Stonehenge I

• 'Ubaid phase in Mesopotamia

• Farming reaches northern Europe

• Use of copper

• Earliest megalithic tombs: Ireland and Brittany

• Herding and farming in North Africa

• Appearance of farming in southeastern Europe

• First pottery: Early Khartoum

• Earliest evidence of farming in Southwest Asia

• Natufian culture

• Mesolithic hunter-gatherers

• Specialized hunting and gathering in Southwest Asia

• Iberomaurusian peoples in far northwestern Africa

STONE AGE FARMERS IN SOUTHERN AND EASTERN ASIA 6000 BC – AD 1000	PACIFIC EXPLORERS 10,000 BC – 0 BC	FARMERS OF THE NEW WORLD 10,000 BC – AD 1492	WHY ONLY SOME BECAME FARMERS 11,000 BC – AD 1500	AUSTRALIA: THE DIFFERENT CONTINENT 10,000 BC – AD 1800	
			• Qilakitsoq mummies		AD 1500
		• Peak of Chaco culture		• First contacts with outside world?	AD 1000
		• Mogollon, Hohokam, and Anasazi cultures	• Thule culture in the Arctic		AD 500
					0
		• Hopewell culture: first farmers in eastern North America		• Appearance of X-ray paintings	1000 BC
• Wet-rice agriculture reaches Korea and Japan	• Stone quarries for axeheads in the Wahgi Valley				
	• Earliest Lapita pottery	• Establishment of agriculture in the North American southwest; drained field agriculture in Mexico		• Development of backed blades	2000 BC
• Rice cultivation reaches Southeast Asia from southern China	• First pottery		• Pitted-ware culture	• Appearance of finely shaped spear points and hatchets with ground stone heads	3000 BC
• Yangshao period in northern China		• Earliest known remains of corn			
• Arrival of agriculture on the Indian subcontinent				• Seas rise to present-day level: shell middens common	4000 BC
			• Earliest burials in Scandinavia		5000 BC
• Early millet and rice farming in China					6000 BC
	• Gardens and drainage systems at Kuk				7000 BC
		• Early domesticated plants in the Andes	• Komsa and Fosna hunters in Scandinavia		8000 BC
			• Jomon fishermen and potters in Japan		10,000 BC

WHAT IS HUMANKIND?

The Evolution of Human Behavior

ROLAND FLETCHER

HUMAN BEHAVIOR HAS EVOLVED over the past three to four million years. Beginning with walking upright, in combination with the usual camping and tool-using behavior of the higher primates, successive generations of hominids have developed the capacity to control fire, to interact socially with their dead, and to represent the universe in art. We are a unique species because we have these characteristics. They are readily visible in the archaeological record, and this has allowed us to date their appearance as habitual features of our behavior.

We also have less tangible characteristics, such as our distinctive sexual behavior, a remarkable capacity for persistence, the power of speech, our elaborate moral beliefs, and, combined with a ready tendency to kill other humans, an extraordinary ability to care for the helpless and the aged. Quite when these aspects of our nature evolved is less obvious, and is subject to considerable dispute.

◄Ə The early hominids were rare and scarcely visible on the East African savanna, which teemed with herbivores such as zebras and buffaloes. A remnant of those great herds can still be seen in the Ngorongoro Crater, in Tanzania.

⬧ Oldowan "chopper", 1.5 to 2 million years old.
DAVID L. BRILL. © 1985

⟳ Humans and other primates have a very similar skeletal structure. The key difference is that humans (right) habitually walk with the upper body held upright above the pelvis. By contrast, gorillas (left) occasionally walk upright but do not maintain an upright posture for very long.

Primates have a general, though not universal, pattern of periodic sexual accessibility (the estrus cycle). However, like the tree-climbing, solitary orang-utan, we can be sexually active at any time, regardless of whether conception is possible. Nor is our tendency to kill each other unique. Lions, for example, sometimes kill other lions. But we are unique in lacking the behavioral controls found among many other species that would normally prevent such incidents. Caring for each other is not unique, either. Reciprocal altruism is not uncommon among animals, playing a straight-forward evolutionary role by helping closely related individuals with similar genes to survive. True, humans attach moral values to caring for each other, but morals are probably a very recent development.

To transmit moral values, we need language, and there is no evidence that our current form of language is much more than 50,000 years old. We were becoming human long before that, and our humanness is founded in our distant past, not uniquely created by our most recent forms of behavior.

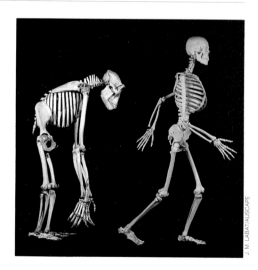

Creating tools requires the ability to remember actions. Humans have long made simple tools and continue to do so, but we have developed the ability to carry out the increasingly complex sequences of actions required to make more and more elaborate stone tools. Similarly, while we made only the simplest windbreaks a million or more years ago, by the end of the most recent Ice Age, about 15,000 years ago, we were able to build elaborate huts from hundreds of interlocked mammoth bones. Within the last half-million years, the action sequences became complex enough for us to make and sustain fires. By remembering actions, we began, within the last 100,000 years, to recall the movements and gestures associated with our dead, turning meaningless corpses into remembered relatives. And within the last 50,000 years, our capacity to make such associations and to retain mental images has led to the ability to represent the outside world and the content of our minds in art. What we must strive to understand is how long all these things took. Our evolution began very slowly, and the majority of the changes and elaborations we recognize as distinctly human are, in archaeological terms, very recent.

Stand Up and Be Human

Once we stood up and began to walk on two legs (or, in other words, became bipedal), important physical changes began to occur. Our new stance altered the position of our sexual organs and made the frontal surface of the body conspicuously visible. Sexual signaling had to change as a result. In ground-dwelling primates, the onset of estrus is marked by a distinctly visible alteration to the external genitalia. But when humans stood up, the female genitalia were concealed between the legs, and a variety of different adaptations may have resulted. Estrus disappeared, a distinctly female form evolved, and females became capable of sexual activity at any time. As humans became

⬧ The earliest stone tool assemblages, between about 2.6 and 1.5 million years old, consisted of numerous small flakes of varied shapes and a few larger pieces usually referred to as "choppers", although they were probably the cores from which flakes were struck to make tools. The production of stone tools results in large amounts of debris.

Towards a Human Culture

Over the past two to three million years, human cultural behavior has become considerably more complex. As our ability to make things, using progressively longer sequences of actions, has evolved, we have also developed a much greater range of distinctively human behavior. The capacity to retain information in our mind and to retrieve this information has increased enormously over this time, and at some point allowed us to consciously know who we are. Our evolving culture creates new opportunities but also complex problems.

bipedal very early in their evolution, our distinctly human sexuality probably evolved at an early stage, too.

Durable Tools

We did not have to walk upright in order to be able to make and use tools, but it did free the hands to carry and manipulate objects much more readily. Primates are very dexterous. They are also playful and inquisitive. The making and use of tools by early hominids is not in itself surprising, since our nearest primate relatives possess this ability. What is different with hominids is that they began to manipulate durable materials. We might expect this from a creature living in less wooded country and camping on open ground by streams and lakes. The search for food in shallow water, scrabbling among pebbles for lizards and insects, or pushing aside dead branches and bits of rock to define a camping space brought hominids into habitual contact with durable materials. This ability is what sets us apart. Inevitably, the camp sites became marked by fragments of stone and food debris as hominids began to use naturally fractured rock, and then started to smash rocks to obtain sharp pieces. Eventually, the ability to repeatedly produce tools of similar form evolved. The earliest known tools of this kind have been found at Hadar, in Ethiopia. But we should not assume that stone tools gave us an immediate adaptive advantage. For a million years, hominids were no more successful as a species than monkeys or apes had been.

This relationship with durable materials, whether in the form of tools or debris on camp sites, began a profound transformation of our behavior. Several new factors were introduced into our social life. Significantly, territorial control could be signaled by inanimate objects, such as abandoned camp sites. These not only indicated the location of hominid groups throughout the landscape, they also served as a warning to newcomers that they might be trespassing. An inanimate, durable, cultural geography appeared, signaling the way in which hominids were spread across the landscape even when the individuals were no longer present. While this signaling was not at first deliberate, it would gradually have become so under selective pressure. Here, too, our behavior sets us apart from the higher primates, who mark territory primarily by active confrontation between individuals.

➲ At Laetoli, in Tanzania, Mary Leakey found the footprints of a hominid adult and child preserved in volcanic ash. This is the earliest evidence for bipedalism. About 3.5 million years ago, they walked northwards across the ash fall from a nearby volcano, the child walking in the footsteps of the adult. Small antelope passed by, and a brief rainstorm splattered across the landscape, before further eruptions buried the footprints.

OLDUVAI GORGE: A WINDOW ON THE PAST

Roland Fletcher

OLDUVAI GORGE cuts across the Serengeti Plain, in Tanzania, close to the Ngorongoro Crater. Long before the gorge began to develop, the area was occupied by a lake, which periodically expanded and contracted. Hominids lived around the shore and near the small rivers that flowed into it. When the lake flooded, layers of mud buried these sites, along with any skeletal remains that lay there.

From time to time, great deposits of volcanic ash covered the region. These are especially valuable to archaeologists, because they create a natural sequence of layers within a site, and the sequence can be dated. The gorge exposes a sequence of layers nearly 90 meters (300 feet) deep. At the bottom, in Bed I, are layers dated to 1.8 to 1.6 million years ago. The upper layers, in Bed IV, date to 200,000 to 100,000 years ago. Because of its depth, the gorge provides an extraordinary opportunity to study human evolution.

⚒ An Acheulean hand axe made about 400,000 years ago by *Homo erectus*. Each tool was made in at least two stages and required about 50 actions. Such tools are more elaborate than those of the earlier Oldowan type.
MARY JELLIFFE/ANCIENT ART & ARCHITECTURE COLLECTION

📍 View over Olduvai Gorge and the Serengeti Plain to Ngorongoro Crater.

R.I.M. CAMPBELL/BRUCE COLEMAN LTD

R.I.M. CAMPBELL/BRUCE COLEMAN LTD

☝ Looking into the gorge.

❮❯ Oldowan tools were found in Bed I and may be associated with *Homo habilis*. The assemblage included small flakes of stone as well as large cores, or "choppers".
MARY JELLIFFE/ANCIENT ART & ARCHITECTURE COLLECTION

❯ Louis and Mary Leakey began work at Olduvai in the 1930s. They soon found stone tools made from basalt and other kinds of volcanic rock, associated with concentrations of animal bone. Only after 30 years' work, however, did they discover the hominid fossils for which they and Olduvai are famous.

Mary Leakey is shown here meticulously excavating a hominid site. When *Australopithecus boisei* was found in 1959, it took 19 days of excavation just to free the face and teeth.

R.I.M. CAMPBELL/BRUCE COLEMAN LTD

❯ The Leakeys' research involved the whole family, especially one of their sons, Richard, seen here measuring hominid fossils. Richard Leakey later became Director of the Kenya National Museum.

R.I.M. CAMPBELL/BRUCE COLEMAN LTD

❮❯ *Australopithecus boisei* (top), found in 1959, and *Homo habilis* (bottom), found in 1961, both from Bed I.
TOP: R.I.M. CAMPBELL/BRUCE COLEMAN LTD
BOTTOM: MARY JELLIFFE/ANCIENT ART & ARCHITECTURE COLLECTION

FROM SOUNDS TO SPEECH: A HUMAN DISCOVERY

William Noble and Iain Davidson

L ANGUAGE IS A SYSTEM of symbols, consisting of either visible patterns (such as written or sign language) or audible sounds (such as speech), which represent things other than themselves. Not all visible patterns or audible signs, of course, amount to language. Those who make and perceive these signs must know what they represent, so the signs must be both consistent and easily recognizable. For example, all people who understand and recognize the English word *cat* can relate it to the domestic animal. But, while language must be used consistently, in another sense it is arbitrary: the written or spoken word *cat* bears no resemblance to the animal it refers to.

🔊 Statuette of a mammoth from Vogelherd, southwest Germany, dated to about 32,000 years ago.
STAATLICHE MUSEEN ZU BERLIN/PREUSSISCHER KULTURBESITZ, MUSEUM FÜR VOR- UND FRÜHGESCHICHTE

🔊 This statuette with human body and feline head from Hohlensteinstadel, southwest Germany, is about 32,000 years old. Statuettes with similar parallel markings on the shoulders have been found in neighboring sites.
K.H. AUGUSTIN/ULMER MUSEUM

From Signaling to Signs

Animals cannot be said to use language, although they do respond to visible and audible signals. Vervet monkeys in eastern Africa make different sounds in response to the presence of different kinds of predators, such as snakes, leopards, and eagles. Other monkeys in the area respond immediately and appropriately when they hear these calls. They look up when an "eagle" call is made, around when they hear a "leopard call", and down in response to a "snake" call. These animals, however, show no sign of realizing that the sounds they make and the postures they adopt signify the predators in question. They utter these signals only in the presence of predators. For these vocal calls to be considered linguistic, the monkeys would need to use and respond to them when predators were not present.

We believe that language emerged when our ancestors realized that the sounds or signals they made were a means of referring to features of the environment. Once this happened, then and only then could these sounds or signals be used, altered, and multiplied to refer to more and more such features. In this way, early humans discovered the symbolic possibilities of gestures used for communication. As a result, their behavior became more complex. They could remark upon their current behavior, conceive of other ways of behaving, recite past events, and plan future ones—and were thus able to bring their environment, including their social environment, under increasing control.

Hominid evolution is said to have involved an increasing capacity for visual control of the arms and hands, and thus improvement in one-handed, aimed throwing. This, of course, would have enabled hominids to point in order to indicate features of the environment—such as prey or predators. In turn, this could have led to tracking the movements of animals, and characteristic features of the animal being tracked could

also have been signaled by hand and arm movements tracing or mimicking the animal's gait or outline. These silent maneuvers would have communicated the necessary information to other group members without alerting the prey to the group's presence.

From Signs to Symbols

The next step in the emergence of language-like behavior could have occurred when, in the act of making such signs, our ancestors left marks in mud or sand. The marks would have become visible as objects in the external world. The gesture as a visible record could then be seen as an independent entity, conveying information by itself. When this happened, the way was open for signs, both visible and audible, to be seen and exploited as symbols. In Europe, evidence of such symbols is not found earlier than about 36,000 to 32,000 years ago, in the form of three-dimensional figures which were clearly created using common conventions of representation and reference.

The arrival of humans in Australia, which has been reliably dated to at least 50,000 years ago, is our earliest evidence for the use of language. The people who came to Australia would have to have crossed open seas, and to do this they obviously had to build seagoing craft. To have conceived, planned, and carried out such activity without the use of language would clearly have been impossible.

🔊 A python approaches a group of vervets. The monkeys show alarm when they hear one of the group calling in response to the approach. The call is specific to this source of danger.
RICHARD WRANGHAM/ANTHROPHOTO

Aggression at a Distance

Stone tools would also have become a part of the signaling behavior within each group. Some primate signaling is very aggressive. Chimpanzees and gorillas, for example, recognize status hierarchies among both males and females. A dominant male, the most powerful in the group, may be challenged by another male in a contest for control of sexual access to females. These fights usually involve a great deal of face-to-face posturing, noise, and the displaying of teeth, but rarely cause serious injury. When one of the contestants acknowledges defeat, the contest stops. Chimpanzees also throw sticks during fights, and when they are tense or insecure. Because the contestants are usually very close to each other, facial and bodily gestures of submission are easy to see, serving to switch off the victor's aggressive drive.

But throwing or hitting with lumps of stone or other hard objects is much more drastic than bodily posturing. Hominids who kept their distance from their opponents and aimed straight would have been at a distinct advantage. This, in turn, would have made facial and bodily gestures less necessary and less effective. The most useful defense was the ability to predict a competitor's next move and to pre-empt it. Individuals who could do this were more likely to avoid injury and therefore more likely to produce offspring with the same aptitude. The advent of hard tools may help to explain why human aggression is not tied to overt display and why gestures of submission do not necessarily control violence among humans.

The Persistent Human

Being able to remember and to predict actions would have led to the development of the characteristic human trait of persistence. Clearly, the more information a hominid could remember as a basis for its actions—whether in making tools, social competition, or the search for food— the more advantaged it would be. For instance, between one and two million years ago, we may

J-P VARIN/JACANA AUSCAPE

have hunted, but we were certainly opportunistic scavengers. At least 100,000 to 50,000 years ago, we were successfully hunting big game, perhaps even in a coordinated way. Modern humans continue to hunt even when the prey is out of sight for many hours. The more information we have stored in our brains, the more persistent we are likely to be in order to achieve our end.

Fire Power

Alone among the animals, humans are attracted to fire and can control it. But we should not suppose that savanna animals are unfamiliar with fire or always avoid it. Grassland fires are frequent and extensive. Numerous insects and small animals die. Scavengers move in behind the fires to obtain food, and early hominids would presumably have sought food in the same way, picking through the ashes and moving charred sticks to get at food. They might well have carried a smouldering stick as a tool. But actually maintaining fires and having the capacity to create fire require quite elaborate

⬧ When chimpanzees are frightened or become aggressive, they sometimes run bipedally and can carry a stick to threaten an intruder or a predator. Vigorous facial gestures and vocal signaling are a feature of attacks and status fights, which take place at close range.

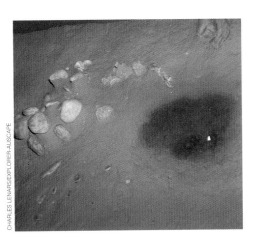

CHARLES LENARS/EXPLORER-AUSCAPE

◄ Traces of fire and occupation debris dating back to between 300,000 and 200,000 years ago have been found at Terra Amata, in France, at camp sites on the sand near the former shore of the Mediterranean. Some of the hearths are in shallow pits, while others are on patches of pebbles.

🐾 In the Gombe Reserve, in Tanzania, Jane Goodall and Hugo van Lawick saw a chimpanzee mother carrying her dead baby around for a day or so. After a while, she began to hold the corpse negligently. Eventually, she put it down, went for a drink, and did not pick the dead baby up again.

☞ There is intense debate as to whether the Neanderthals buried their dead—and if so, why they did. The recent discovery of a Neanderthal at Kebara Cave, in Israel, dated to 60,000 years ago, has added a further example for discussion. Part of the reason for the debate is the new claim for an African origin for modern humans that would exclude the Neanderthals from our direct ancestry. But we need not envisage a simple continuity of behavior. Neanderthal bodies are found in very varied contexts and in a variety of positions, and we should not assume that this behavior can be explained in terms familiar to us.

sequences of actions. Near the underground lake of Escale, in France, possible remains of fires have been found, along with the debris of human occupation, dating back as far as 700,000 years ago. Most evidence of hearths, however, is found within the last 300,000 years.

The control of fire has several consequences. Food can be cooked, and wooden tools shaped and hardened. Controlled burning of grassland helps to drive animals toward hunters. Accidental, repeated fires in woodland increase the extent of open pasture, encouraging larger populations of herbivores, such as deer. Fires also signal the presence of humans. When Captain James Cook first approached the eastern seaboard of Australia, he knew the country was inhabited because he could see plumes of smoke from numerous camp fires. At night especially, a fire can indicate where people are living. By using fire, humans inadvertently provided additional signals, visible over considerable distances, about their location in the landscape. Meetings no longer depended entirely on chance, and the social world became more complex. Just as stone tools gave humans a new means of signaling, so too did fire, adding to their capacity to predict and control their world.

Remembrance of Things Past

The next major change in human behavior was the ability to recognize that the dead body was once human. Up to 100,000 years ago, there is no evidence that hominids perceived their dead any differently from other kinds of dead meat. Hominid bones have been found scattered and broken among the rubbish of camp sites. This is consistent with the way other primates neglect the dead. A chimpanzee mother will carry her dead baby around for a day or two, but becomes increasingly less aware of it. At first she cuddles the corpse, but she is then likely to carry it by one leg or drag it along, until eventually she puts it down and forgets it. The body no longer emits signals indicating that it is a chimpanzee, and the mother does not have the conceptual capacity to remember the actions once associated with her offspring.

After about 100,000 years ago, the Neanderthals began to interact with their dead, which they treated in many different ways. But we should beware of inferring that they thought as we do. The Neanderthals may be fascinating precisely because they perceived their dead in ways entirely beyond our experience. What if memory span varied among Neanderthals, as intelligence does among modern humans? The Neanderthal bodies found at Krapina, in the Balkans, were elaborately defleshed and burned, yet in the cave of Hortus, in the Pyrenees, they were just dumped in with the rubbish. In the cave of La Chapelle-aux-Saints, in southern France, an old man was buried in a deep pit.

MICHAEL NICHOLS/MAGNUM PHOTOS

◄○ Threat display of a male chimpanzee: characteristics of this expressive behavior are the bristled hair, which enlarges the silhouette, the exposed teeth, and the threatening stare. Staring and displaying the teeth as though in readiness to bite are also basic to human expressions of anger. The bristling of the fur exists in vestigial form in the "shiver" we experience when the hair erector muscles contract—and, as we say, our hair stands on end.

AGGRESSION AND WAR: ARE THEY PART OF BEING HUMAN?

IRENÄUS EIBL-EIBESFELDT

AGGRESSION OCCURS WHENEVER a person or a group of people attempts to dominate another by the use of physical force or threat. It is very common among animals, arising out of competition for limited resources such as food, mates, and territory. It may also be used as a means of defense—for example, when mothers protect their young. Within species, aggressive behavior is often ritualized, so that the opponents reduce the risk of physical harm. The loser can end the fight by assuming a submissive posture, which switches off the victor's aggressive drive.

Individual aggression needs to be distinguished from aggression between groups. The sort of intergroup aggression we could consider to be a precursor of war occurs only among nonhuman and human primates and some species of rodents, such as the Norwegian rat. Jane Goodall observed intergroup aggression among chimpanzees who live in fairly close proximity to other groups. The males of such groups patrol the borders of their territory and attack members of other groups, mauling and often killing them. Humans, too, exhibit aggression individually and collectively—for example, in disputes over rank, territory, and rivalry for mates.

IRENÄUS EIBL-EIBESFELDT

☞ Bushmen fighting: rock painting from South Africa copied by D. F. Bleek, 1930.

The basic expressions of threat, in the form of facial expressions and posturing, are universal among humans, and similar behavior is found among chimpanzees and other nonhuman primates. Humans have also evolved other patterns of behavior that serve, among other things, to dampen aggression. Crying, for example, generally elicits a sympathetic reaction. It is significant that newborn babies respond to tapes of crying by themselves crying in sympathy, but not to tapes with different human sounds. Another effective strategy is to threaten to cut off social contact with the aggressor (see the sequence of photographs).

External and Internal Triggers

Contrary to what some of the more romantic anthropologists think, human beings do not necessarily grow up to be peaceful when raised in a warm family environment with affection and body contact. Nor do they necessarily become aggressive when these are lacking. In contemporary warrior cultures, both mothers and fathers treat their children with great affection and love, yet the children grow up to become fierce fighters. This is because children who grow up in a loving environment identify with their parents and their group and are prepared to accept their values, whether warrior-like or pacifist. Until the late 1960s, it was believed that hunter-gatherers were nonterritorial and peaceful, living in open societies. Investigations carried out over the last decades, however, have revealed this to be a myth. Warriors in combat have been a theme of rock paintings from the Stone Age to the present day—as evidenced by contemporary paintings of the Bushmen of southern Africa.

Aggressive behavior is not just a response to external stimuli. It can result from a number of internal factors. One of these is male hormones. Success in real or symbolic fights (such as sports or examinations) leads to an increase of testosterone in men, but this is not automatically switched off when the goal is reached, as is the case with such consummatory acts as eating and sex. This may explain why the drive for power and military superiority runs wild in some men. The spontaneous activity of certain neurons in the brain can also trigger aggression, but cultural factors can override this, of course.

Negative and Positive Aggression

Aggression in humans, as in animals, serves several different purposes. It can lead to destructive behavior and cause enormous difficulties, but sometimes it has a positive aspect. For example, we overcome physical and mental problems—any goal-directed activities blocked by an obstacle—by taking an aggressive approach to them. This point needs to be emphasized, for aggression is often considered solely as a negative force. Some people have even proposed that children should be brought up in such a way that they would lack any aggressive tendency at all. This would do great harm to the individuals concerned, rendering them defenseless. Among other things, aggression is necessary if people are to rebel against injustice and dictatorship.

War as Organized Aggression

War is, of course, an organized form of human aggression. Despite the biological precursors to be found in chimpanzee behavior, it must be considered as a product of cultural evolution, as it involves strategically planned and concerted effort, is carried out with weapons that kill at a distance (thereby reducing the likelihood of personal contact), and is aimed at destroying a common enemy. Apart from aggression, war depends on feelings of group loyalty, which are often promoted by propaganda that dehumanizes the enemy. In this way, conflict is shifted to a moral plane, where killing becomes sportive and virtuous, if not positively heroic—a tactic that has worked fairly well throughout history.

To understand group aggression in human beings, it is important to realize that people have fundamentally ambivalent feelings toward their fellow humans. They respond with friendly behavior (particularly towards acquaintances), but also with fear. They fear domination, but often attempt to dominate when they perceive weakness.

War, as such, is certainly not in our genetic make-up, but it has always been a very efficient way of acquiring and defending limited resources. As increasingly destructive weapons have been developed, it has become a very much riskier undertaking, although certain conventions and rituals have arisen to lessen this risk. Clearly, we must strive to resolve the large-scale problems that confront our species not by aggression and war but by social and political contracts that respect others' rights.

☞ Threatening to cut off social contact is one of the ways in which humans ward off aggression. A Yanomami boy is threatened by another boy, who attempts to push him aside. The attacked boy initially smiles appeasingly, but this tactic is ineffective. After being hit, he averts his gaze (contact avoidance), lowers his head, and pouts—a very effective way of counteracting aggression from another individual. The aggressor then leaves.

➔ *Opposite page:* Some of the earliest art in Europe, about 25,000 to 30,000 years ago, consists of simple engravings on the walls of caves in France. The engravings on this boulder at La Ferrassie have been interpreted as vulvas—roughly triangular shapes with a line bisecting the narrowest angle.

➔ This smoothed plaque of ivory from Tata, in Hungary, colored with ocher, is about 50,000 years old. Opinions are sharply divided as to whether it is a product of natural processes or was made by humans.
HUNGARIAN NATIONAL MUSEUM/ANDRAS DABASI

⚱ Dated to the Upper Paleolithic period, this bone plaque from Abri Blanchard, in France, has been studied in great detail by Alexander Marshack. It is marked with rows of gouged holes arranged in groups. Each group was usually made by the same tool and may represent some form of tallying procedure.
JEAN VERTUT/MUSEE DES ANTIQUITES NATIONALES, ST GERMAIN-EN-LAYE

When hominids began to bury their dead, we have the first indication that they were able to connect past actions with an inert body. No great memory capacity was required, probably no more than a few weeks. The Neanderthals usually interred complete bodies, presumably within a few days of death. We should not conclude from this that these early burials are evidence of a belief in an afterlife. That surely requires the combination of a developed capacity for memory and the ability to envisage a future stretching beyond one's own lifetime.

The Meaning of Art

Once humans could consciously link past actions with an object, they possessed the basic capacity needed for artistic behavior. Linking an observed object with remembered characteristics leads to the ability to recall the characteristics of a person or animal without direct observation. Instead of seeing an object and merely remembering the past, humans could remember versions of the past and represent them as objective shapes, or see an object and shortly after immediately recall it to produce an image. This was probably an unusual aptitude— even today many people cannot do it well.

At first these shapes and images were vague, uncertain, or simple. There is much dispute as to what constitutes the earliest recognizable art, such as a few pieces of polished and scratched ivory from Tata, in Hungary, and some scratches on a bone from La Ferrassie, in southern France, dating back to 50,000 years ago. By 30,000 years ago, we find small carvings of horses and simple engraved shapes which have generally been interpreted as

images of vulvas. Over the next 10,000 to 15,000 years, art became more elaborate, both in technique and content. Among the cave art discovered at Lascaux, also in southern France, there are even images of fictitious creatures combining features of several animals.

As well as trying to understand what the art meant, we can ask what purpose it served. Just as fire signaled location over great distances, so art allowed detailed messages to be transmitted through time. We no longer needed to remember all we had learned—we simply needed to know where to find the required information in the material records we could create.

The Rhythms of Life

Art also provided us with the means to represent periodicity. In paintings and carvings, this took the form of repeated rows of marks. It also appeared in the first known musical instruments, which consisted of bone tubes with holes drilled in them to produce different sounds. Both the signs and the musical instruments take a continuum and divide it up. This is the essential logical device for imposing human order on the natural phenomena of time and sound. Simple though they are, each represents a fundamental development of human thought. Once humans had the concept of periodicity, time could be divided up and patterns of change,

➔ This flute made from bird bone, from Grotte de Placard, France, is about 10,000 to 15,000 years old.
MUSEE DE L'HOMME, PARIS/ M. DELAPLANCHE/COLLECTION MUSEE DES BEAUX ARTS D'ANGOULEME

such as lunar cycles and the breeding habits of herd animals, could be recognized. Prediction no longer depended upon our capacity to remember. Instead, we gained a material means of understanding and managing our otherwise unpredictable world.

What our ancestors did two to three million years ago was to commit us to a complex relationship with artifacts made of hard materials. In a myriad ways, these objects created social stresses and new signals and have successively affected the way we interact with other human beings in our communities, across space and time. Not only did these artifacts help to shape our behavior, developing our ability to predict and persist, they eventually gave our finite brains the material means to store, organize, and analyze potentially unlimited knowledge.

SEX ROLES IN PREHISTORY

MICHELLE LAMPL

SEX ROLES REFER TO the prescribed ways in which men and women relate to each other and behave in their daily life. All human societies have defined roles for men and women that are both overt or active roles and passive roles that are learned by imitation and instruction as children. Scientists continue to debate the nature of biological and cultural contributions to sex roles, and often turn to the study of human evolution for insights into the origins of modern sex roles.

Our knowledge of our prehistoric ancestors comes from the archaeological record, which reveals details of settlement patterns, food habits, and other aspects of our ancestors' way of life. The fossil record provides information on physical features, health status, and life span. Unfortunately, neither form of evidence can provide us with definitive answers as to how and why modern human sex roles evolved.

Males and females differ in their reproductive biology. Women have larger amounts of body fat in proportion to the rest of their body mass, broader hips to permit the passage of the infant at birth, and mammary glands to nurture the young after birth. Men, in contrast, tend to have more muscle in proportion to their body mass. Together with body size differences, these differences between the sexes are known as sexual dimorphism.

Although in many human populations men are usually somewhat bigger than women, modern humans are not especially sexually dimorphic, in contrast to some of our closest primate relatives. Sexual dimorphism is an often debated characteristic in the human fossil record, because primate researchers have noted that few primates living in social groups where males and females are highly dimorphic live in male–female, monogamous units.

The earliest fossil evidence of creatures directly ancestral to humans belongs to the genus *Australopithecus*, who lived in East and South Africa two to four million years ago. Although this continues to be debated, some scientists studying these fossil bones note a marked difference in the body size of males and females. An adult female individual (named "Lucy" by her discoverers) has been reconstructed as about 1.1 meters (3 feet, 7 inches) tall and some 27 kilograms (59 pounds) in weight. A presumed male individual was reconstructed to perhaps 1.6 meters (5 feet, 3 inches) tall and about 50 kilograms (110 pounds) in weight.

On the basis of this evidence, it has been suggested that early in our evolutionary history, the pair-bonded, monogamous nuclear family common to many modern human societies, and the sex roles associated with it, had not yet evolved. During subsequent human evolution, the fossil evidence shows a gradual reduction in dimorphism, so that by the time individuals who looked like modern humans appear on the scene, some 100,000 years ago, dimorphism is similar to that in living humans. None of this tells us precise details about sex roles; but if our understanding of skeletal and social relationships is accurate, it implies that male–female relationships were different in our earliest prehistory. What the situation was, we do not know.

The second kind of evidence, archaeology, does not tell us much, either. The oldest information, the stone tool record from some 2.5 million years ago, does not provide information about sex roles. Personal ornaments are found about 30,000 years ago in Europe: shells with holes drilled in them, probably to be strung as bracelets and body

◄❯ In contrast to modern humans, some of our closest primate relatives are very sexually dimorphic. The gorilla female (left) is only some 60 percent of the size of the male. Sexual dimorphism appears to be greatest where males compete for sexual access to females, and least in those species whose males and females often pair-bond for life.

ornaments, found in the graves of both sexes. Not long after, also in Europe, are found some of the remarkable remains of the plastic art of the time: incised or, sometimes, sculptured images of women on bone and ivory, and clay sculptures such as the well-known Venus of Willendorf. While some images of males are found in the famous cave art paintings or engraved on rock faces, most images are of women with exaggerated anatomical features in the form of pronounced breasts and buttocks. Scholars debate the significance of these objects. Were they simply accurate images of local women? Did they represent fertility images? Or were they intentionally erotic? By the time agriculture appeared, some 10,000 years ago, humans were living in organized groups that we would not find unusual.

Lacking specific evidence, scholars speculate about the ways by which male–female sex roles evolved in our evolutionary history. These conjectures have often projected modern notions onto the past and have followed our own social trends. For example, many scholars believed until recently that the evolutionary history of human social groups involved male and female division of labor, whereby males hunted and brought back the spoils to so-called home places, where they shared this food with the females, who waited for them, nurturing and caring for infants and young. A modification of this view proposed that males and females initially had separate feeding strategies and that a monogamous pair bond was not only a way of sharing resources and maximizing the survival potential of each sex but also had the benefit of ensuring paternity. The dietary preferences and concerns of many modern societies can be identified in these scenarios.

By contrast, recent researchers have pointed to the importance of women in modern, egalitarian hunting and gathering societies and have suggested this as a model for our prehistoric past. Here, men and women have overlapping activities and spheres of influence, in which the basic food items (vegetables,

seeds, nuts, insects, small animals) are supplied by women, with men supplying much less material of daily importance. Other contemporary accounts not only focus on gender roles but also look at aspects of sexual behavior and emotion. Recognizing nonmonogamous lifestyles and reconsidering the nature of male and female sexuality, some investigators have suggested multiple sexual partners for both sexes, in the form of mild polygyny or serial pair-bonding, as a pattern accompanying our

evolutionary history.

Thus, the concerns of modern American and European society as to the place of monogamy and the nuclear family, and division of labor in terms of power relations, sharing, and cooperation in daily life, have all contributed to reconstructions of prehistoric sex roles. The accuracy of these notions when applied to prehistory is unclear. It may be that instead of looking down the long corridor of the past, we have been looking in the mirror.

J.M. LABAT/AUSCAPE

Female figures appear in the Upper Paleolithic period across Europe. Both the figurines emphasizing sexual anatomy, with indistinct heads and legs, and the detailed, graceful head from Brassempouy, France (bottom, right), reflect an image of female form we can only aspire to see through the eyes of that time.

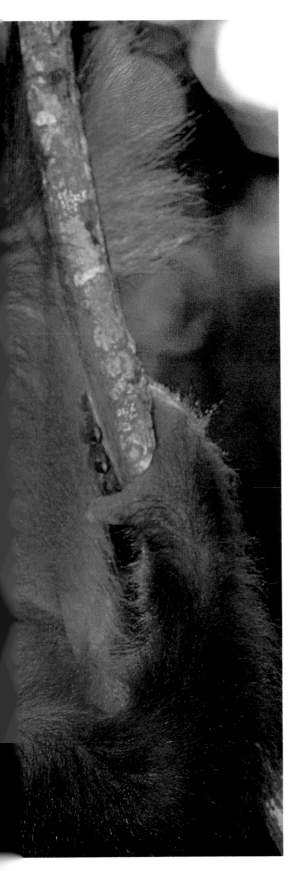

HUMAN ORIGINS

20 MILLION YEARS AGO – 100,000 YEARS AGO

Our Earliest Ancestors

COLIN GROVES

DURING THE EIGHTEENTH CENTURY, European intellectuals became fascinated by apes. What kind of creatures were they? Monkeys were already a familiar sight: Madame de Pompadour owned a pet marmoset from Brazil; two centuries earlier, Dürer had painted a pair of mangabeys from West Africa; while the Barbary macaque from North Africa (often mistakenly called an ape) had been well known since Roman times. But real apes—at that time called "orang-utans"—were different: tailless, upright creatures, almost human in form but covered in hair, their eyes shining with intelligence, their faces so expressive that they seemed to need no speech to make themselves understood. Indeed, many wondered whether, with a little training, they might actually learn to speak. Others were convinced that they had their own language, and that it was only a matter of time before they would be able to communicate in fashionable society.

It is rather surprising that so much speculation was based on so little careful observation. It was not until near the end of the eighteenth century that it dawned on such naturalists as Johann Friedrich Blumenbach, in Germany, and Georges Cuvier, in France, that the young apes that had been brought to Europe from time to time (and soon died for want of proper care) were of two kinds. The big red ones—the real orang-utans—as well as the little gibbons came from the East Indies, while the big black ones, which came to be called chimpanzees, were from Africa.

◄ Orang-utans were the first of the Great Apes to become well known to scientists. This Southeast Asian ape is our third closest relative, after the chimpanzee and the gorilla.

♦ This skull from Sterkfontein has usually been classified as *Australopithecus africanus*, but it has recently been suggested that it may in fact be a very primitive specimen of *Paranthropus*.
DAVID L. BRILL, 1985

➤ The intelligence that seems to shine out of the eyes of this chimpanzee is no illusion. Chimpanzees are our closest living relatives: they make and use tools in the wild, have a complex social organization, and even have a rudimentary self-awareness.

By the time that a third ape, the gorilla, was made known to science, in 1847, the differences between chimpanzees and orang-utans were becoming better known. But it was that conceptual bombshell of 1859, Charles Darwin's *The Origin of Species*, that finally put them into perspective. The apes are like us because they are related to us.

As early as 1863, in an essay entitled "Man's Place in Nature", Thomas Huxley had concluded that the African apes—the chimpanzee and the gorilla—are more closely related to us than is the orang-utan. In his *Descent of Man*, published in 1872, Darwin argued that if the African apes are

and, eventually, analysis of the DNA itself. The answer was always the same. Chimpanzees, gorillas, and humans are very closely related indeed, orang-utans are more distantly related to us, gibbons are further away, and monkeys still further off. There is still disagreement as to whether chimpanzees are closer to humans or to gorillas (or whether all three are equally closely related), but there is no longer any doubt about the closeness of all three.

Many now believe that, taken overall, changes in the protein structure and DNA of living organisms occur fairly regularly over long periods of time. If it is known how different two species are in terms of one of their proteins, or in parts of their genome (the complete genetic material for any cell, which determines heredity), it is possible to calculate how long ago they shared a common ancestor. This concept is known as the molecular clock, and although it does not keep perfect time, it does set limits—and it tells us that our evolutionary line must have separated from the chimpanzee's between about seven and five million years ago.

DAVID L. BRILL, 1985

☝ An almost complete skeleton of *Proconsul nyanzae*, a hominid that lived in East Africa 18 million years ago. Medium-sized apes like this flourished in rainforests at that time, amid a primitive primate fauna that included the ancestors of monkeys as well as of apes.

COLIN GROVES

☝ A skull of *Afropithecus turkanensis*, a recently discovered contemporary of *Proconsul*, and probably closer to the ancestry of humans and apes.

indeed more closely related to us than the Asian ones, our own origins are likely to have been in Africa. Though a number of authorities have from time to time argued otherwise, since the 1940s the consensus has been that Huxley and Darwin were right: the chimpanzee and gorilla are closer to us than is the orang-utan, and it is in Africa, not in Asia or elsewhere, that we should look for remains of our earliest ancestors.

Traditionally, apes have been classified as belonging to a zoological family, Pongidae, separate from our own family, Hominidae. Increasingly, however, specialists have been inclined to include the Great Apes as well among the Hominidae, putting the orang-utan in one subfamily and humans, chimpanzees, and gorillas in another.

Tracing Our Family Tree

By the early 1960s, analytical techniques were available that allowed us to compare different primate groups in terms of their biochemistry. Immunological techniques were used at first, but these were gradually superseded by the more sophisticated techniques of protein sequencing

The Early Apes

The taxonomic group that includes humans and apes—the superfamily known as Hominoidea, or the hominoids—was established by about 20 million years ago. In the Early Miocene period (19 to 18 million years ago), there were at least 10 different species of apes in East Africa, large and small. The best-known belong to the genus *Proconsul* (named after a popular zoo chimpanzee of the 1890s called Consul), discovered in 1933 and now known from a nearly complete skeleton (and several partial ones) and dozens of jaws, teeth, and skull fragments. Studies of the remains have shown that *Proconsul* lived in trees, walked on all fours, lived on fruit, was probably tailless, and had large canine teeth. One species was smaller than a modern chimpanzee, another nearly as big as a gorilla.

Many authorities considered *Proconsul* a good candidate for the common ancestor of the Hominidae, the family comprising humans, chimpanzees, gorillas, and orang-utans (but not gibbons, whose evolutionary line was already separate). Others were unsure, pointing to features of the teeth, the jaw, and the limb bones that were not what we would expect to see in such a common ancestor. In the mid-1980s, a new fossil ape was discovered, contemporary with *Proconsul*. Named *Afropithecus*, it is still less well known than *Proconsul* but seems much more like what we would expect the common ancestor to have looked like. In a sense, it is a fossil that had to be invented before it was discovered.

Another large ape, *Kenyapithecus*, has been identified from the Middle Miocene period (14 million years ago). Like its probable ancestor,

➲ Despite appearances, the giant ape, the gorilla, is usually a gentle, family-oriented, near-human ape. Males weigh about 150 kilograms (330 pounds) on average, females only 70 kilograms (154 pounds). Today, deforestation, hunting, and human population pressures threaten the continued existence of this remarkable creature.

D. PARER AND E. PARER-COOK/AUSCAPE

LÁSZLÓ KORDOS

🦴 *Dryopithecus* has been known since the mid-nineteenth century, but a skull found recently in Hungary gave us new information about it. One specialist has recently proposed that it is close to the direct ancestor of the Great Apes and humans.

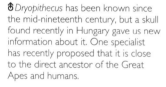

LOUIS DE BONIS

🦴 *Ouranopithecus macedoniensis* is known by many skull, jaw, and skeleton specimens from 10 million-year-old sites in Greece. It is likely to be on the common ancestral line of humans, chimpanzees, and gorillas.

➲ Until comparatively recently, almost nothing was known of the evolution of the Great Apes. But in 1980, this magnificent fossil of a proto-orang-utan was discovered in Pakistan. Known as *Sivapithecus indicus*, it is about 10 million years old.

DAVID L. BRILL, 1985

Afropithecus, it had large canine teeth, but the face was shorter, and in other respects, too, it was more "advanced" in evolutionary terms towards the living Hominidae, whose last common ancestor it may well have been.

The earliest fossils of other hominoid species so far found outside Africa date from about the same time: *Dryopithecus* in Europe and, a little later, *Sivapithecus* in South and West Asia and *Lufengpithecus* in China. Well-preserved fossils, mainly skulls, from the Siwalik Hills, in Pakistan, and Sinap, in Turkey, have shown that *Sivapithecus* is almost certainly the ancestor of the orang-utan. (Some fragmentary remains from the Siwaliks were at one time thought to be human ancestors and dignified with the name *Ramapithecus*, but it is now clear that they belong to a small species of *Sivapithecus*.) Fossils of later representatives of the orang lineage have been found in China and Indonesia.

But if we have now traced the orang-utan's ancestors, the same cannot be said of the chimpanzee or the gorilla. We know nothing of their evolution after their ancestors separated from ours, and very little of what happened to the common stock between the time the orang line split off, between 12 and 10 million years ago, and the time the gorilla, chimpanzee, and human lines separated, between 7 and 5 million years ago.

There are, in fact, only two serious candidates for this intermediate phase: a maxilla (upper jaw) from the Samburu Hills, in Kenya, dating to 9 million years ago; and a series of fossils from Rain Ravine, in northern Greece, dating to about 10 million years ago, which have been named *Ouranopithecus*. Parts of a facial skeleton of *Ouranopithecus* discovered recently at another Greek site, Xirochori, strongly suggest that this fossil is part of the non-orang lineage. If it is, it is clear that this line ranged outside Africa from time to time.

Enter the Australopithecines

From about four million years ago, it is as if a curtain has suddenly been lifted. Instead of a few frustrating scraps of bone, we are confronted with an abundance of fossils. Key sites are Laetoli, in Tanzania, dating to between 3.75 and 3.5 million years ago; Hadar, in Ethiopia, dating to between 3.3 and 2.9 million years ago; and two sites in South Africa, Sterkfontein and Makapansgat, both between 3 and 2.5 million years old.

The fossils found at these sites belong to the genus *Australopithecus* (meaning "southern ape"). Like apes, they had a small cranial capacity and a protruding jaw (a feature known as prognathism), but their canine teeth were much shorter and they walked upright. The first specimen was an infant, discovered by Raymond Dart in 1924 at Taung, in Cape Province, South Africa. Robert Broom discovered the rich site of Sterkfontein, while Dart himself excavated Makapansgat, and Mary Leakey, Tim White, Don Johanson, and others were involved in the discoveries further north.

The earliest of these fossils, from Laetoli, have been given the name *Australopithecus afarensis*. They consist of the jaws and teeth of some 24 individuals, the partial skeleton of a juvenile, and some fossil

footprints. The jaws show canine teeth much smaller than those of apes, but rather larger and more pointed than our own, and the dental arcades are neither parabolic like those of modern humans nor rectangular like those of apes. The footprints are contentious, but they seem, on most assessments, to indicate creatures that walked on two legs, but had slightly divergent great toes and lateral toes that are long relative to humans but somewhat shortened relative to apes.

✦ The famous Taung child, discovered by Raymond Dart in 1924, was the first known specimen of *Australopithecus*. It is a tribute to Dart's anatomical expertise that, from this very young skull and brain endocast, he was able to recognize its status as an intermediate between ape and human—an insight abundantly confirmed by later discoveries.
DAVID L. BRILL, 1985

JOHN READER/SCIENCE PHOTO LIBRARY/THE PHOTO LIBRARY

♂ An australopithecine footprint from Laetoli, 3.75 to 3.5 million years old, shows that bipedal walking—if not of a fully modern type—had developed by that time.

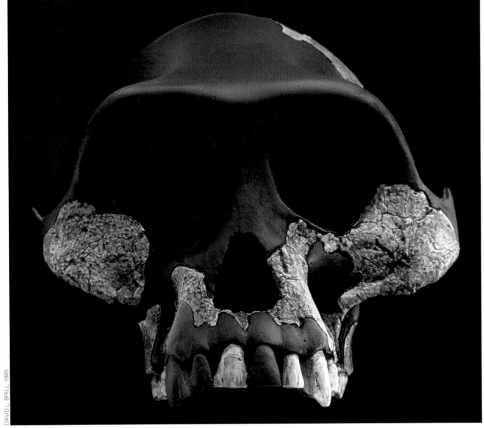

DAVID L. BRILL, 1985

✦ The reconstructed skull of a male from the "First Family", at Hadar, is generally classified as *Australopithecus afarensis*, although controversy persists. But there is no controversy about its position on or close to the human lineage, and all agree that it is more primitive than *Australopithecus africanus*, *Paranthropus*, or any species of *Homo*.

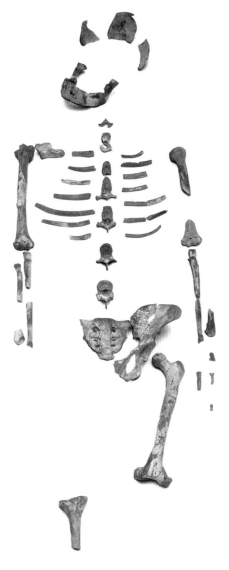

◄ Here at Hadar, a joint United States–French team discovered australopithecine remains in the 1970s, including the famous "Lucy" skeleton and the "First Family". Since that date, further finds have been made here by Berhane Asfaw, an Ethiopian anthropologist.

◄ Lucy, the two-thirds-complete skeleton from Hadar, is 3.2 million years old. Should it be included in the same species, *Australopithecus afarensis*, as other Hadar and Laetoli remains? There is no agreement on this question.
JOHN READER/SCIENCE PHOTO LIBRARY/ THE PHOTO LIBRARY

The abundant fossil remains from Hadar include a two-thirds-complete skeleton nicknamed "Lucy"; a group of fossils that, from their context, most likely represent a single social group (known as the "First Family"); and sundry other specimens. Lucy is only about a meter (3 feet, 7 inches) tall and has long arms and short legs, a funnel-shaped (ape-like) chest, and a V-shaped jaw, but a pelvis that indicates an upright (but not fully human) gait. The members of the First Family are mostly larger than Lucy, and it is claimed that their limb bones indicate a more human-like gait than Lucy's. Are they two different species? One school of thought thinks so. Others think that they are all the one species, *Australopithecus afarensis*, the same as that from Laetoli.

↑ There is no doubt that "Lucy" stood and walked upright, but she did not have the long legs of modern humans.

⚓ The most complete known skull of *Australopithecus africanus*, known as "Mrs Ples", is part of the rich trove of finds from Sterkfontein. Discoveries continue to be made at this site in the Transvaal highveldt. *Australopithecus* and the other animals whose bones were found here were probably the victims of a large carnivore, perhaps a sabertooth cat.

☞ A partial skeleton of *Australopithecus africanus* from Sterkfontein, South Africa. Although clearly an upright biped, *Australopithecus* did not have a modern, striding gait and was also adept at climbing trees.

JOHN READER/SCIENCE PHOTO LIBRARY/
THE PHOTO LIBRARY

The South African fossils are of a different species, known as *Australopithecus africanus*, which had a broad, heavily built face, with prominent cheekbones and a prominent muzzle. The average cranial capacity of seven specimens studied was 450 cubic centimeters (27 cubic inches), ranging from 420 to 500 cubic centimeters (25 to 31 cubic inches). The canine teeth were smaller than Lucy's—like those of modern humans, although more pointed—but the molars were very large, and the face was obviously buttressed to withstand the stresses of vigorous chewing.

Their gait was not simply halfway between that of apes and humans, but unique, though mainly upright and bipedal; they obviously also spent a good deal of their time in trees. They had not developed the striding motion of humans. The legs were short, the pelvis was poorly buttressed (indicating that it was not required to bear much weight), and the shoulders and arms were powerful, as if for climbing. The foramen magnum, the hole underneath the skull where the spinal cord enters it, was far forward on the skull base, indicating that the head was balanced on top of the spine, as would be expected in creatures with an upright posture, rather than far back, as it is in apes.

Arguments as to whether *Australopithecus africanus* was directly ancestral to the human line, or an offshoot from it, have raged ever since the first specimen was discovered at Taung in 1924—and they are still raging!

SEXUAL DIMORPHISM:
COMPARATIVE AND EVOLUTIONARY PERSPECTIVES

WALTER LEUTENEGGER

In most mammals, males and females differ somewhat in size and sometimes also in aspects of shape or color. This is referred to as sexual dimorphism. Usually, the males are bigger than the females, but sometimes the reverse is the case. Most species that are polygynous tend to be more sexually dimorphic than those that are monogamous.

Sexual differentiation in humans leads to more or less pronounced sexual dimorphism in a number of structural, physiological, and behavioral features. This phenomenon is not unique to humans but also occurs in other sexually reproducing animals and plants. We can gain valuable insights into the ultimate nature of human sexual dimorphism by analyzing it from comparative and evolutionary perspectives. How do humans compare to nonhuman primates, in particular the apes, in the magnitude of sexual dimorphism?

Since neither behavior nor physiology is preserved in the fossil record, the focus here is on structural differences. Among nonhuman primates, structural sexual dimorphism occurs in a wide range of features, including body size, the size of canine teeth, and skull characteristics, and varies considerably between species. The degree of body weight dimorphism in apes, for example, ranges from species in which males on the average are twice as heavy as females (gorillas, orang-utans) to those in which males and females weigh about the same (gibbons, siamangs).

How do modern humans fit within the range of nonhuman primates? Clearly, modern humans show considerable variation in the magnitude of sexual dimorphism both within and between populations. At the species level, modern *Homo sapiens* can be considered mildly dimorphic in the majority of physical features. For example,

average males are about 15 to 20 percent heavier, and 5 to 12 percent taller, than average females. Similarly, differences in the size of teeth, skulls, and skeletal parts also tend to be slight.

Fossil evidence for human evolution spans almost the last four million years. There is evidence for at least two evolutionary lineages: *Australopithecus* and *Homo*. The australopithecines, with an ancestral–descendant sequence of *Australopithecus afarensis–Australopithecus africanus–Paranthropus robustus/boisei*, represent the initial adaptation to an open-country habitat: vegetarianism associated with habitual terrestrial bipedalism. *Homo*, with a sequence of habilines–erectines–*Homo sapiens*, represents the second phase: hunting-gathering associated with evidence of systematic material culture. There is ongoing debate as to which *Australopithecus* species represents the immediate ancestor of *Homo habilis*: *Australopithecus afarensis* or *Australopithecus africanus*. This issue, however, has no direct bearing on questions related to the evolution of sexual dimorphism.

Skeletal Parts

The pattern of sexual dimorphism in the jaws, skulls, and other skeletal elements of the australopithecines and early *Homo* is quite different from that of modern humans. Variation in the size and shape of the lower jaws of *Australopithecus afarensis* equals that of gorillas, suggesting strongly developed sexual dimorphism in this respect. So great is the variation, in fact, that many authorities refuse to accept that it is due to sexual dimorphism. It is often believed that the "species" actually contains more than one single species. Lower jaw material from the other australopithecine species suggests strongly developed sex differences similar to those of *Australopithecus afarensis*. Marked

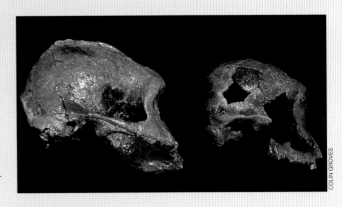

COLIN GROVES

to moderate lower jaw dimorphism is also characteristic of habilines and erectines, and first reduces substantially in archaic forms of *Homo sapiens* and the Neanderthals. Similarly, sex differences in the size and shape of the skull and the skeletal parts used for walking, such as the thigh bone, are considerable in australopithecines and early *Homo*.

Body Weight

By the standards of nonhuman primates, body weight dimorphism in the earliest species, *Australopithecus afarensis* and *Australopithecus africanus*, seems to have been very marked, comparable to that of gorillas and orang-utans. The habilines show moderate body weight dimorphism. Regardless of one's opinion as to their immediate ancestor, *Australopithecus afarensis* or *Australopithecus africanus*, there is evidence that reduction during this phase was largely due to a decrease in male weight—from 65 to 50 kilograms (143 to 110 pounds); while females essentially remained the same— about 30 kilograms (66 pounds). *Homo erectus* maintained moderate body weight dimorphism, with both sexes increasing in weight by about the same amount—12 to 14 kilograms (26 to 31 pounds). The latest phase of human evolution leading to *Homo sapiens* brought a further small reduction in body weight dimorphism. Most important,

A comparison of male (ER-406) and female (ER-732) skulls of *Paranthropus boisei*. Note the marked differences in both size and shape. Such a degree of sexual dimorphism equals that of gorillas and orang-utans, and was also common in early hominids.

the reduced body weight dimorphism in *Homo sapiens* seems to be solely due to a further increase in female weight—from 42 to 55 kilograms (92 to 121 pounds); while males have tended to stay the same since the *Homo erectus* stage—about 65 kilograms (143 pounds).

Several hypotheses have been proposed to account for the evolution of human sexual dimorphism. Reduction of body size dimorphism has traditionally been explained in terms of competition among males for access to females becoming less intense—that is, a lessening of polygyny. While this hypothesis cannot be refuted, it is important to note that changes in body weight dimorphism, in particular from the erectines to *Homo sapiens*, seem to have been the principal result of an increase in female size. This finding supports Katherine Ralls's hypothesis that a "bigger mother is often a better mother"—in other words, larger females tend to produce a greater number of surviving offspring.

OUR EARLIEST ANCESTORS

COLIN GROVES

T HE EARLIEST KNOWN primate lived in Africa 60 million years ago. Known as *Purgatorius,* it had a long, slender snout and four premolar teeth—more than any living primate. Other undisputed primates from this period include the Petrolemuridae (members of the suborder Strepsirrhini, to which living lemurs and lorises belong), from China, and a few, difficult to classify, fossils of Haplorrhini, the suborder to which modern tarsiers, monkeys, apes, and humans belong.

The Adapiformes and Omomyiformes, which include most of the earliest strepsirrhines and haplorrhines, were abundant during the Eocene period, and many skulls and partial skeletons are known. The Omomyiformes lingered on in North America until the Early Miocene period, while Adapiformes survived in India until the Middle Miocene.

The earliest known platyrrhine, or New World monkey, *Branisella,* lived 26 million years ago in Bolivia, while the catarrhines—the group that includes Old World monkeys, apes, and humans—are known from about 40 million years ago in Egypt and perhaps 50 to 40 million years ago in Algeria. Fossil catarrhines are easy to recognize, having only two premolars in each half of each of their jaws, and long canine teeth that hone against the first lower premolar.

Early Old World monkeys, Hylobatidae (ancestral gibbons), and Hominidae (ancestors and cousins of humans and Great Apes) are known from several East African sites dated to 20 to 17 million years ago. *Kenyapithecus,* from East Africa, and *Dryopithecus,* from Eurasia, represent a stage before modern hominid lines had begun to separate from other Great Apes. *Sivapithecus,* from India, Pakistan, and Turkey, is, at 8 to 12 million years old, the earliest member of the orang-utan lineage. *Ouranopithecus,* a contemporary species from Greece, may be on the human–chimpanzee–gorilla line.

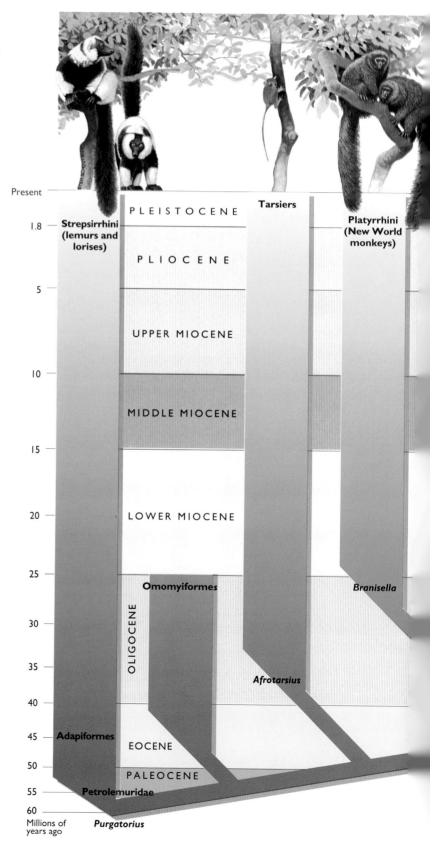

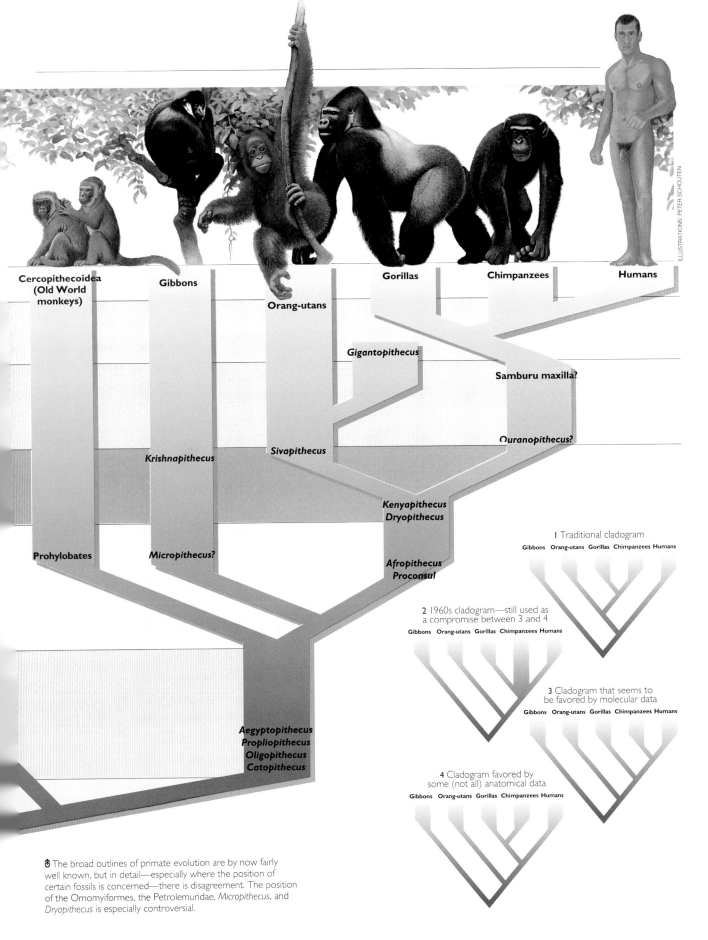

Cercopithecoidea (Old World monkeys)

Gibbons

Orang-utans

Gorillas

Chimpanzees

Humans

Gigantopithecus

Samburu maxilla?

Ouranopithecus?

Krishnapithecus

Sivapithecus

Kenyapithecus
Dryopithecus

Prohylobates

Micropithecus?

Afropithecus
Proconsul

Aegyptopithecus
Propliopithecus
Oligopithecus
Catopithecus

ILLUSTRATIONS: PETER SCHOUTEN

1 Traditional cladogram

Gibbons Orang-utans Gorillas Chimpanzees Humans

2 1960s cladogram—still used as a compromise between 3 and 4

Gibbons Orang-utans Gorillas Chimpanzees Humans

3 Cladogram that seems to be favored by molecular data

Gibbons Orang-utans Gorillas Chimpanzees Humans

4 Cladogram favored by some (not all) anatomical data

Gibbons Orang-utans Gorillas Chimpanzees Humans

☝ The broad outlines of primate evolution are by now fairly well known, but in detail—especially where the position of certain fossils is concerned—there is disagreement. The position of the Omomyiformes, the Petrolemuridae, *Micropithecus*, and *Dryopithecus* is especially controversial.

⊙ Olduvai Gorge, in present-day Tanzania, cleaves the Serengeti Plain. In the Early Pleistocene period, it was the site of a lake.

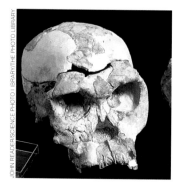

☝ A skull of *Homo habilis* from Olduvai—nicknamed "Twiggy". Despite its general resemblance to *Australopithecus*, anatomical details show that it is more "advanced" in the human direction.

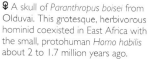

♀ A skull of *Paranthropus boisei* from Olduvai. This grotesque, herbivorous hominid coexisted in East Africa with the small, protohuman *Homo habilis* about 2 to 1.7 million years ago.

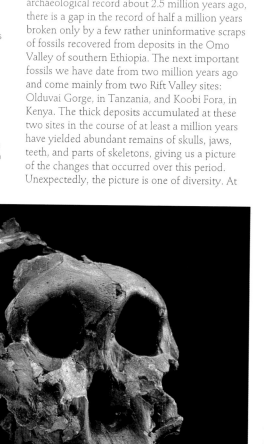

Ancestors and Cousins

After *Australopithecus africanus* disappears from the archaeological record about 2.5 million years ago, there is a gap in the record of half a million years broken only by a few rather uninformative scraps of fossils recovered from deposits in the Omo Valley of southern Ethiopia. The next important fossils we have date from two million years ago and come mainly from two Rift Valley sites: Olduvai Gorge, in Tanzania, and Koobi Fora, in Kenya. The thick deposits accumulated at these two sites in the course of at least a million years have yielded abundant remains of skulls, jaws, teeth, and parts of skeletons, giving us a picture of the changes that occurred over this period. Unexpectedly, the picture is one of diversity. At both sites, two different prehuman species lived side by side from at least 2 to about 1.5 million years ago, and at the lower levels of Koobi Fora (known as the Upper Burgi Member), there is a third contemporary species as well.

The two Olduvai species are quite distinct. There is a small, lightly built one and a larger one with enormous premolar and molar teeth. The small one has a higher, more rounded braincase, with an average cranial capacity of 650 cubic centimeters (40 cubic inches), ranging in four specimens from 590 to about 700 cubic centimeters (36 to 43 cubic inches); a lightly built face with smaller, narrower cheekteeth; and the beginnings of a protruding nose. The large one has a smaller braincase—the average cranial capacity is 515 cubic centimeters (31 cubic inches), ranging in five specimens from 500 to 530 cubic centimeters (30 to 32 cubic inches)—and a foreshortened but heavily buttressed face, with tiny front teeth but huge cheekteeth and enormously developed chewing muscles, commonly giving rise to a crest on top of the head where they attached (known as the sagittal crest). Both walked upright, with the foramen magnum even further forward than in *Australopithecus*—as far forward as in modern humans—but both still had short legs and long arms.

There is no doubt that the small, lightly built one is *Homo*. In every respect it is more "modern" than *Australopithecus*, more like ourselves. The very earliest specimen of *Homo* is a scrap of skull from Chemeron, near Lake Baringo, dated as being 2.5 million years old. The Olduvai species is known as *Homo habilis*. The large, robustly built type has traditionally been considered to be a late survival of *Australopithecus*, but most authorities now recognize it as something rather different and call it *Paranthropus* (sometimes, affectionately, "the Nutcracker"). The Olduvai species is called *Paranthropus boisei*.

There are abundant remains of *Paranthropus boisei* at Koobi Fora, and they are accompanied by not one but two species of *Homo*. One is small and short-faced, the cranial capacity of the two specimens found being 510 and 582 cubic centimeters (31 and 36 cubic inches). The other is larger, with a muzzle-like face, one specimen having a cranial capacity of 770 cubic centimeters (47 cubic inches) and two others a slightly larger capacity.

Opinion is divided over their relationship to each other and to *Homo habilis*. The large species is generally thought to be a distinct species, called *Homo rudolfensis*. Some think the small one is *Homo habilis*, while others think it is a different species. They are in some respects rather like each other, though only because they are both very primitive representatives of the human lineage. To avoid arguments over taxonomy, we can lump them together informally as "the habilines". As to which habiline is ancestral to later forms of *Homo*—that is another controversy!

Remains of *Homo habilis* have been discovered further south in Africa, at Sterkfontein, in more recent deposits than those in which *Australopithecus* was found. The nearby sites of Swartkrans and Kromdraai have yielded remains of the Nutcrackers, though of a different species (*Paranthropus robustus*) from the East African one. Some authorities consider that only the Kromdraai species is *Paranthropus robustus*, and that the Swartkrans species is different, calling it *Paranthropus crassidens*.

Where did these new species, the habilines and the Nutcrackers, come from? We still do not know where the habilines came from. Many anthropologists think they are directly descended from creatures like the "First Family" of Hadar, while others think they derived from *Australopithecus africanus*. The scrappy fragments that have survived from intervening time periods simply do not allow us to decide. But a magnificent skull from West Turkana, Kenya, dated to 2.5 million years ago, solves the problem of the Nutcrackers. Very like *Paranthropus boisei* in its general features, it has a long, muzzle-like face and large front teeth like *Australopithecus*. This early, primitive species has been named *Paranthropus walkeri*, after the famous paleoanthropologist Alan Walker.

There seems little doubt that the habilines made simple stone tools. The earliest stone tools were found at Hadar and are 2.6 million years old. From two million years ago, artifacts are found in the archaeological record in their thousands, and wherever we find traces of their makers, they are members of the genus *Homo*—beginning with the habilines.

The Road to Homo sapiens

Where did our own direct ancestors come from? Many people believe that a key fossil is a well-preserved skull from Koobi Fora known as ER-1813, one of the habilines. It has a very small braincase—the cranial capacity is only 510 cubic centimeters (31 cubic inches)—but its facial modeling and other aspects of the skull are just what we would expect in a direct ancestor of later human beings. It is certainly more "modern" in this respect than the other habilines, *Homo habilis* and *Homo rudolfensis*, which have larger cranial capacities. If this is so, it means that different species evolved large brains independently. Parallel evolution is well known among animals and plants, but somehow it is unexpected in the brain—the very feature we regard as making us superior to all other animals!

DAVID L. BRILL 1985

⚜ Skull 1470 from Koobi Fora, northern Kenya. Formerly considered to represent *Homo habilis*, this specimen and others like it have recently been shown to belong to a separate species, *Homo rudolfensis*. There were probably several closely related species of early *Homo* living in Africa at this time, about two million years ago.

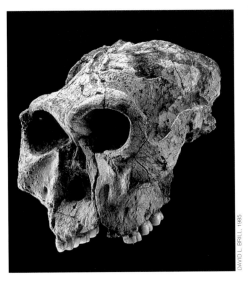

DAVID L. BRILL 1985

NATIONAL MUSEUM OF KENYA

⚜ The Black Skull, from West Turkana, 2.5 million years old, is the earliest, most primitive representative of *Paranthropus*.

◄ *Paranthropus crassidens*, from Swartkrans, South Africa, was a smaller but closely related contemporary of the East African *Paranthropus boisei*.

WHEN DID LANGUAGE BEGIN?

IAIN DAVIDSON AND WILLIAM NOBLE

We find it almost impossible to imagine what it would be like to "think" about the world without language—either spoken or signed. As language is one of the things that distinguishes the behavior of humans from that of other animals, however, it clearly must have emerged at some time during the course of our evolution. The question is when.

Some scientists believe that language evolved at a very early stage in human development, basing their view on two pieces of evidence: our ancestors' brain size and the shape of stone tools.

Language and the Brain

Over the course of the last two million years, the hominid brain has become bigger. Although the brain does not fossilize, it leaves some blurred indications of the convolutions of the cortex on the inside of the skull. By making a latex endocast, it is possible to study something of the shape of the cortex. It has been suggested that the cortex of australopithecines was very similar to that of chimpanzees, while the earliest habiline skull, known as KNM ER-1470, which is at least 1.8 million years old, already shows signs of some of the distinctive features of the human brain, particularly in the regions said to be associated with speech. But this theory does not attempt to explain how or why spoken language became distinct from the noises made by other apes. The suggestion is simply that language appeared as a result of the human brain becoming bigger.

Did We Need Language to Make Tools?

A second theory that has been put forward is that language was necessary for early hominids to have organized their actions sufficiently to make stone tools. But others have pointed out that the earliest tools that have been found,

from the Oldowan period, did not require any more organization or technical skills than tools made by modern chimpanzees.

Still another theory is that the symmetrical and apparently standard dimensions of Acheulean hand axes, dating back to between 1.5 million years ago and 150,000 years ago, indicate that early hominids had a mental image of the desired end product, which must have been communicated through language. But the dimensions of the axes found in Africa that were cited in support of this theory were

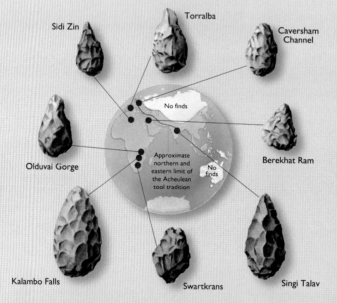

Sidi Zin

Torralba

Caversham Channel

Olduvai Gorge

No finds

Approximate northern and eastern limit of the Acheulean tool tradition

No finds

Berekhat Ram

Kalambo Falls

Swartkrans

Singi Talav

similar to those of axes found in Europe and Asia, so it is unlikely that they result from any deliberate attempt to produce an object of a particular shape. Even if hominids did have mental images of ideal axe shapes, these are unlikely to have been the same over such widespread areas. The similarities could have resulted from similar physical limitations in early hominids' ability to manipulate objects of particular sizes and shapes, and from their learning by imitation to make flakes from standard cores by using a restricted set of hand and arm movements.

The shape of Acheulean hand axes around the world suggests species-specific behavior rather than individual planning.

Human Behavior?

Shelter, the use of fire, and meat-eating are often considered fundamental to early hominids' ability to move out of Africa and successfully colonize new territory in more temperate and seasonal parts of the world. But much of the claimed evidence for these aspects of behavior has recently been brought into question. For instance, a stone circle dated to about 1.8 million years ago at Olduvai Gorge, in present-day Tanzania, said to be the remains of a human shelter, was in an area

where crocodiles would most likely have eaten any hominids who rested there. Similarly, claims for the existence of a bough hut at Terra Amata, in southern France, 230,000 years ago rest on the evidence of nothing more than four stains in the sand. And although evidence of fire has been claimed from sites such as Chesowanja, dating back to 1.4 million years ago, and Zhoukoudian, dating back to 500,000 years ago, a recent

assessment suggests that none of the claims earlier than Terra Amata is reliable—and even 230,000 years ago, it is doubtful whether hominids could regularly make fire. Furthermore, although meat has probably been an important part of the hominid diet since the genus *Homo* began to emerge, it is not clear how early hominids obtained meat. Early sites such as Torralba and Ambrona, in Spain, where large deposits of animal bones have been found, seem more likely to have been scavenging areas than places where hunted animals were butchered. There seems to be no good evidence that hominids built shelters, regularly made and used fire, or hunted systematically earlier than 125,000 years ago.

Claims for "modern"-seeming behavior among Neanderthals are exaggerated. The cave bear cult has been dismissed as wishful thinking inspired by nothing more than the accidental survival of a few bones of the many bears that died while hibernating in caves. The romantic story of the burial of a Neanderthal with flowers at Shanidar, in modern-day Iraq, does not stand up in the light of evidence that the Shanidar hominids died in, and were buried by, rock falls. In fact, most of the objects that have been interpreted as indicating that Neanderthals were capable of symbolic behavior prove to have simpler explanations in the physical world.

It seems, then, that language is not necessary to account for a number of early features of the archaeological record. It is necessary, however, to account for events that occurred around the world from about 60,000 years ago: the colonization of Australia and later of the Arctic and the Americas; the beginnings of art; the fact that ritual and convention became regionalized and localized; the beginnings of gender roles and power structure; and the start of agriculture. More than this we cannot say at present.

DAVID L. BRILL, 1985

The Turkana Newcomer

About 1.6 million years ago, a new species appeared in East Africa. The first specimen discovered was a complete skull, ER-3733, from Koobi Fora (KBS Member). Other, less complete skulls, as well as other bones, have been found there since. In the mid-1980s, a nearly complete skeleton, WT-15000, was discovered at Nariokotome, on the other side of Lake Turkana from Koobi Fora. So we now know a good deal about this new species, which for the moment we can call simply the Turkana Newcomer. Bernard Wood has proposed that the species should be called *Homo ergaster*, and this is probably correct.

The two measurable specimens found had a cranial capacity of 848 and 908 cubic centimeters (52 and 55 cubic inches): bigger than ER-1813, but not bigger than some of the other fossils similar to *Homo habilis*. They had projecting brow ridges, a short face, a rather angular skull, and the merest

beginnings of a projecting nose. They also had long legs and a much more modern skeleton than the australopithecines or habilines. The skeleton known as WT-15000 was that of a boy about 12 years old. If he had survived into adulthood, he would have been 180 centimeters (6 feet) tall. Very clearly, the Turkana Newcomers were directly ancestral to later members of the human stock. Equally clearly, they were descended from the habilines—in fact, there is one habiline specimen, ER-1805, that some authorities prefer to place along with the Newcomers.

These people made stone tools, at first not very different from those made by *Homo habilis*. Did they make fire, hunt big game, speak? We do not know—the evidence is equivocal. What they did do is replace the habilines. In some way, they were just that much better at—what? At being human, or "nearly human", we suppose.

☝A new phase in human evolution: *Homo ergaster*, the Turkana Newcomer. The brain was only a little larger than in the habilines, but the shape of the skull is more like *Homo erectus*, as which it was classified until very recently.

SITES WHERE OUR FOSSIL FOREBEARS HAVE BEEN FOUND

Earlier members of the human group have been found only in Africa. About a million years ago, *Homo* spilled out of Africa and populated the entire Old World. They did not reach Australia until about 50,000 years ago, and arrived in the Americas later still.

I	Laetoli, Olduvai, Ndutu, Natron, Eyasi
2	Hadar, Bodo, Belohdelie, Maka
3	Koobi Fora, Omo, Nariokotome, Lothagam, Tabarin, Baringo
4	Sterkfontein, Swartkrans, Kromdraai, Taung, Makapansgat
5	Sangiran, Trinil, Mojokerto, Ngandong, Kedung Brubus, Sambungmacan, Wajak
6	Gongwangling, Jenjiawo
7	Zhoukoudian, Jinniushan
8	Hexian, Dali, Maba, Liujiang
9	Hathnora
10	Petralona
11	Mauer, Steinheim, Bilzingsleben, Neanderthal, Hahnöfersand, Ehringsdorf
12	Montmaurin, Arago, La Ferrassie, Biache, Cro-Magnon, Dordogne sites, St Césaire
13	Swanscombe
14	Gibraltar, Atapuerca
15	Monte Circeo, Saccopastore
16	Jebel Irhoud, Casablanca, Rabat, Salé
17	Tighenif
18	Yayo
19	Zuttiyeh, Tabun, Skhul, Qafzeh, Amud
20	Shanidar
21	Teshik-Tash
22	Klasies, Saldanha
23	Kabwe

➤ Exactly which Lower and Middle Pleistocene fossils should be classed as *Homo erectus* is controversial, but the Zhoukoudian fossils belong to this species. So-called "Peking Man" lived in North China 450,000 to 250,000 years ago.

From Homo erectus . . .

The earliest traces of humans found outside Africa appear a little more than a million years ago. The best-known fossils of this period belong to a species called *Homo erectus*. In Java, the earliest specimens are about a million years old, the youngest only 100,000 years old. In China, they range from at least 800,000 to 230,000 years old.

Like the Turkana Newcomers, *Homo erectus* have large brow ridges, but they are different in form: straight and thick, flaring out to the sides. The cranial capacity is larger, ranging from 750 to 1300 cubic centimeters (46 to 79 cubic inches), with some evidence from both Java and China that it increased over time. The braincase was low, flat, and angular, with thickened bone along the midline and at the back. There are some differences between fossils found in Java and China: the Java skulls have a flat, receding forehead, while the Chinese skulls have a convex forehead, and there are other slight differences. They are generally considered to be two different subspecies: *Homo erectus erectus* (Java) and *Homo erectus pekinensis* (China). The forehead shape of the Java fossils is the more primitive type, and the earliest of the China fossils, from Gongwangling, is, in fact, similar to the Java type.

The earliest subspecies of all was excavated

from levels at Olduvai dating to about 1.2 million years ago, and this primitive race, *Homo erectus olduvaiensis*, is held by some to be the only record of *Homo erectus* in Africa. If so, it evolved in Africa, then migrated elsewhere, and died out in its homeland. Others consider the Turkana Newcomers to be early representatives of *Homo erectus*, and others again include later African fossils in the same species.

Fossils from the same period have been found in Africa, and even Europe. Specimens from Tighenif (Ternifine), in Algeria, may be 900,000 years old. The most recent of these "contemporaries" with an agreed date is from Bilzingsleben, in Germany, and is more than 300,000 years old. Both the African and European fossils differ from the *Homo erectus* fossils found in Java and China in characteristic ways: the brow ridges are more curved and do not flare out at the sides; the braincase is less flattened and angular, without the thickening along the midline and at the back; and there are differences in other features, including the shape of the mandible and the ear region.

Should these, then, be classified as *Homo erectus* or as a different species? Those who believe they are a different species call them *Homo heidelbergensis*, after the earliest discovered specimen, a jaw found in 1908 near Heidelberg, in Germany. Those who believe they are a subspecies of the same species call them *Homo erectus heidelbergensis*. This may seem to be nothing more than a question of semantics, but it is important. If they were all one species, they could all have been in some way ancestral to modern humans—a view known as the regional continuity hypothesis (or, sometimes, the

"candelabra" model). If they were two different species, because by definition different species do not interbreed to any significant extent, only one of them could have been our ancestor, and it or its descendants must have replaced the other— a view known as the replacement hypothesis (or the "Noah's Ark" model).

. . . *to* Homo sapiens

The earliest representatives of our own species, *Homo sapiens*, are known from two sites in Israel. Fossils found at Qafzeh have been dated by the thermoluminescence technique to 91,000 years ago, although a technique known as electron spin resonance analysis (ESR) suggests an even earlier date. Those found at Skhul are dated by ESR to 80,000 years ago. However, two sites in South Africa, Border Cave and Klasies River Mouth, may be equally old. Like modern humans, they have a high, rounded, shortened braincase, a rounded forehead, and a straight face with a chin. The brow ridges are smaller than in more primitive species, and the limb bones are long and straight.

Even older fossils found in Africa seem to indicate that *Homo sapiens* developed from *Homo heidelbergensis*. Two specimens from the Kibish Formation on the Omo River, in Ethiopia, as well as one from Ngaloba, in Tanzania, have been dated by the uranium–thorium method to 130,000 years ago; two from Jebel Irhoud, in Morocco, are about 120,000 years old; and there are a few others. They are all intermediate between *Homo heidelbergensis* and modern humans, but the two Omo skulls are particularly interesting. One, of which only the braincase has survived, resembles *Homo heidelbergensis* but has a higher braincase and

🔻 In Skhul Cave, at the foot of Mount Carmel, in Israel, 10 human skeletons were found in the 1930s. It is now known that they are 80,000 years old— older than many fossils of Neanderthals found in the same region.

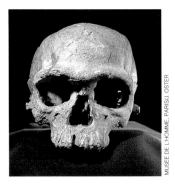

🔻 Jebel Irhoud I is one of a group of fossils from various parts of Africa, some 120,000 to 130,000 years old, that document the transition between an ancestral, primitive species, often called *Homo heidelbergensis*, and its descendant species, *Homo sapiens*.

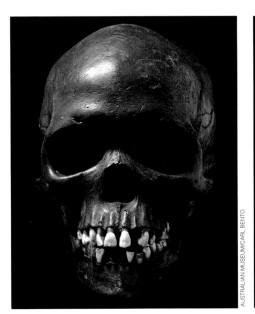

🔻 The skull of the orang-utan (right) has tall, narrow orbits (eye sockets), with no brow ridges above them, unlike that of the chimpanzee and the gorilla. Despite this superficial similarity, the fossil evidence shows that our ancestors are descended from quite different-looking apes, with large, projecting brow ridges.

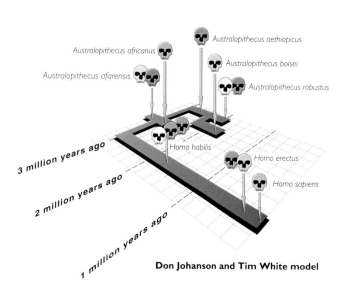

Don Johanson and Tim White model

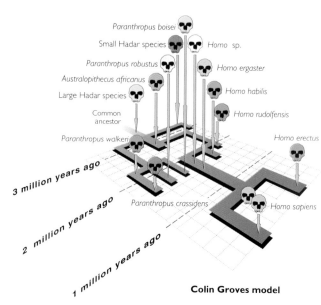

Colin Groves model

Laetoli fossils, and larger fossils from Hadar, typified by the "First Family"

Smaller fossils from Hadar, typified by "Lucy"

The Black Skull from Lomekwi, West Turkana

Swartkrans fossils of "robust australopithecines"

Kromdraai fossils of "robust australopithecines"

East African "robust australopithecines"

Australopithecus africanus from Sterkfontein, Makapansgat, and Taung

Large-brained Turkana *Homo*, typified by ER-1470

Olduvai *Homo habilis*

Small-brained Turkana *Homo*, typified by ER-1813

"Turkana Newcomer" fossils

Homo erectus from Java and China

Middle and Upper Pleistocene fossils from Africa and Europe—Kabwe, Bodo, Arago, Petralona, Steinheim, Neanderthal—and people of modern type

smaller brow ridges. The other, more complete, is much more modern and resembles one of the Skhul skulls. These transitional populations evidently varied a good deal.

If *Homo sapiens* evolved in Africa between 130,000 and 120,000 years ago, they had probably begun to spread out into Eurasia by about 90,000 years ago, or a little earlier. By 68,000 years ago,

our species was in China. By 50,000 years ago, they were in Australia (which they had to reach by crossing open water, as Australia was never connected to Asia by dry land). And by 36,000 years ago, they were in western Europe, where we know them as the Cro-Magnon. It seems, however, that they did not reach the Americas until 15,000 to 12,000 years ago, although there is much controversy about this. If the regional continuity model, rather than the replacement model, is correct, then these dates simply record when modern humans evolved independently in different areas.

Wherever *Homo sapiens* were found—in Africa, Europe, East or Southeast Asia, or Australia—the earliest people tended to resemble present-day peoples of the same region, but with one difference: they were bigger and more "robust". At the end of the Pleistocene period, people everywhere rapidly became slightly smaller-boned, with smaller teeth. This is puzzling. It was at one time suggested that once people began to practice agriculture, they did not need such big teeth, but the same development took place even in people who remained hunter-gatherers, as in Australia. Perhaps, as the climate became warmer, more succulent foods became available, and it was simply easier to exist with smaller teeth and less chewing effort. The changes were small, but we simply do not know why they occurred.

What Makes Us Human?

The Great Apes are not only closely related to us anatomically, they also have very similar bio-chemistry to ours. A study carried out in the 1970s showed that humans and chimpanzees have nearly

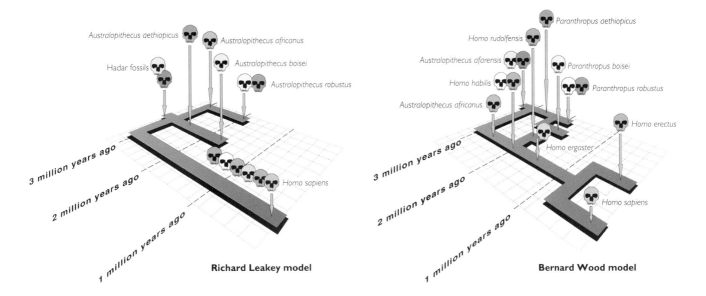

Australopithecus aethiopicus
Australopithecus africanus
Hadar fossils
Australopithecus boisei
Australopithecus robustus
Homo sapiens

Richard Leakey model

Paranthropus aethiopicus
Homo rudolfensis
Australopithecus afarensis
Paranthropus boisei
Homo habilis
Paranthropus robustus
Australopithecus africanus
Homo erectus
Homo ergaster
Homo sapiens

3 million years ago
2 million years ago
1 million years ago

Bernard Wood model

99 percent of their DNA (the material of heredity) in common—a pretty amazing statistic. Given that they are so similar to us in terms of both anatomy and genetics, might we not expect them to be similar psychologically as well—particularly in terms of those features we think of as being uniquely human, such as tool-making, intelligence, self-awareness, and even language? Should we not expect to find these qualities at least in a rudimentary form?

The use of stone tools has characterized human (or, at first, protohuman) activity from 2.6 million years ago. It has been known for a long time that Great Apes in zoos and laboratories show a certain inventive flair in regard to mechanical aids. During the First World War, Wolfgang Koehler found that the chimpanzees in his laboratory on the Canary Islands could not only use sticks to get food that was out of reach, but could join different-sized sticks together, and pile boxes on top of each other, to reach food that was high up. Though gorillas are less dexterous, some orang-utans have developed extraordinary tool-making skills. In the London Zoo, an orang-utan manufactured a wooden replica of the key to its cage and let itself out. Another, in the 1960s, was shown how to work stone, and made itself a sharp-edged flake to cut the string around a box containing food.

In the 1970s, the intriguing discovery was made that chimpanzees learn to recognize themselves in mirrors. Monkeys, in contrast (like dogs and even elephants), react to their reflection as if it were another individual, even though they can come to understand the general concept of a mirror and use it to find hidden objects, as well as recognizing

cage mates in it. Like chimpanzees, orang-utans and gorillas can also learn to recognize their own reflection. Does this mean that, like humans and unlike other animals, the Great Apes have a concept of self?

The first language experiments were performed in the 1950s, when a home-reared chimpanzee was taught, with extraordinary time and effort, to say "Mama", "Papa", "cup", and "up". Watching a film of this laborious experiment, psychologists Allen and Beatrice Gardiner noticed that the chimpanzee seemed to be using its hands to express itself, and they decided to try and repeat the language experiment using hand signs instead of words. The success of this sign-language experiment with a young female chimpanzee named Washoe encouraged a number of other researchers to do similar work with orang-utans and gorillas and to use other linguistic modes such as computer language.

But too much was claimed for much of this early work—even, at one point, that the apes were using elementary syntax. When Herbert Terrace analyzed videotaped ape-language sessions in 1979, he found that the hand signs the apes made were often not spontaneous, but depended on inadvertent cues from their trainers. He also found that multiword utterances were not like sentences but consisted mostly of important words repeated, and that most of the apes' signs were techniques for requesting food or other things. There was little evidence that they understood words or signs as symbols. As a result, language researchers reconsidered their methods as well as their earlier findings.

The most significant language work with apes since then has been done by Sue Savage-Rumbaugh

☙ Why do the specialists disagree? There are many reasons. One is that it is difficult to recognize what are different species in the fossil record. Another is differences of opinion as to the meaning of some anatomical features. But the outlines of the evolutionary story remain the same.
ILLUSTRATIONS: COLIN BARDILL

☙ Kanzi, a young bonobo (pygmy chimpanzee), learned simply by watching how to interpret "lexigrams" as symbols—a very crude approach to language. He and his trainers take the lexigram board with them on their visits to the woods near Atlanta, and he indicates where he intends to go and what he will do.

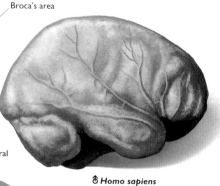

Parietal   Frontal   Broca's area

➤ Brains increased in size stage by stage along the path from australopithecine to modern human. What is more difficult is to read the bumps and folds on the surface, as they are very poorly reproduced on the inside of the skull, from which these endocasts are made. So it is not clear whether, for example, any of our ancestor species could speak.

ILLUSTRATIONS: OLIVER RENNERT

Occipital

Temporal

Cerebellum

🜨 **Homo sapiens**
130,000 years ago to the present
1,040–1,595 cubic centimeters
(63–97 cubic inches)
(normal range: 90 percent of individuals)

900–2,000 cubic centimeters
(55–122 cubic inches)
(extreme range)

➤ **Homo erectus erectus** (early)
1 million to 700,000 years ago
815–1,059 cubic centimeters
(50–65 cubic inches)

Homo erectus erectus (late)
100,000 years ago
1,055–1,300 cubic centimeters
(64–79 cubic inches)

♀ **Paranthropus robustus**
1.8 million years ago
500–530 cubic centimeters
(31–32 cubic inches)

🜨 **Homo habilis**
2 to 1.6 million years ago
590–700 cubic centimeters
(36–43 cubic inches)

◄ **Australopithecus africanus**
3.3 to 2.9 million years ago
420–500 cubic centimeters
(26–31 cubic inches)

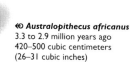

🜨 **Chimpanzee**
305–485 cubic centimeters
(19–30 cubic inches)

And Our Big Brains?

Did life on the savanna become so complex that we developed big brains to cope with it? Did early humans' way of life—the cooperation needed to hunt big game, or the need to outsmart lions to scavenge their prey, or the need to calculate where the most productive plants were likely to be ripening, or the requirements of food sharing, or the need to make tools—require us to have greater intelligence?

Before speculating on such things, it is as well to recall that the Great Apes are already more intelligent than other primates, including gibbons and monkeys, and to ask ourselves why this should be so. Chimpanzees and orang-utans, and some populations of gorillas, live on fruit, and because they are all very large, they have an energy conservation problem. They certainly make calculations, both about the likelihood of fruiting in particular parts of the forest and about each other's motives. Their high intelligence also seems to enable them to be physically lazy. Is this what brainpower is really all about?

Perhaps, then, the question is not why are we so intelligent, but what is it that apes do that our ancestors did more of? In addition, there is certainly a great deal of serendipity involved, different aspects of our ancestors' anatomy and psychology seeming to pre-adapt us for full humanity. By the evolutionary process known as neoteny, the head remains juvenile in appearance (small jaws, large brain) but continues to grow. Upright posture: the hands are freed for tool use. Head balance: the larynx is repositioned, as if ready for articulate speech. Mobile shoulder: the arm is already adapted for throwing. Intelligence and sociability: social traditions develop into culture. Humans could not have evolved from any creatures other than apes.

and her colleagues, who taught a sort of computer language to chimpanzees. Using a special technique, they managed to teach apes to name objects, and not merely request them; to "converse" with each other using computerized symbols; and to announce by this means what they were going to do next. Most recently, a young pygmy chimpanzee spontaneously learned the computer "language" just by watching—without having to be taught.

All this work on the mentality and intelligence of apes reminds us that we, as members of the human species, are part of the natural world. Even our special abilities (those we think of as being uniquely human) are not qualitatively but quantitatively different from those of our nearest nonhuman relatives. When we start speculating on the origin of various characteristically human forms of behavior, we have to remember that we did not evolve directly from animals that acted purely by instinct and lacked all traces of a human-like intellect.

SO SIMILAR AND STILL SO DIFFERENT: THE GREAT APES AND OURSELVES

WULF SCHIEFENHÖVEL

His mother had been ailing before she died. The child, old enough to be cared for by his relatives, became more and more depressed. It was obvious that he had lost the will to live. Three and a half weeks later, he, too, died.

This and similar cases were documented by Jane Goodall in her ground-breaking studies of mother–child relationships among chimpanzees (*Pan troglodytes*)—with their cousins, the bonobos (*Pan paniscus*), most probably our closest relatives. In the last decades, clinical research has confirmed that traumatic events in our lives, such as the loss of a beloved person, can trigger our own death. This is an extreme example of the psychosomatic effects that can result from emotions such as deep depression. If chimpanzees react to such events with the same grief, the same loss of joy and will to live, as we do, where do we draw the line between these creatures and ourselves?

The Great Apes are surprising in many ways. Bonobos engage in sexual acts for various apparently non-reproductive purposes, as Frans de Waal has demonstrated. This behavior acts as a kind of social lubricant—for example, to console, to appease, or to achieve goals. The biggest of all the Great Apes, gorillas (*Gorilla gorilla*), sometimes display astoundingly human-like behavior in the films Dian Fossey made during the time she spent with them. In one case, a powerful male can be seen watching her intensely while she writes notes in her scientific diary. She holds her pen in his direction, he slowly takes it, looks and sniffs at it, and hands it quietly back to her. He seems to respect the principle of ownership, returning to her what he recognizes as her property.

Neurobiologists have compared the brains of humans and chimpanzees and have found no structural differences between the two species. There seem to be no nuclei (the foci where neuroelectric impulses are generated), no tracts connecting the various brain parts with each other, and no areas (the sections responsible for specific perceptions or actions) in a chimpanzee's brain that cannot be found in our own brain. So why do we speak, count, calculate, write, travel to the moon, and wear business suits? Not all these things are typical of our species, of course. Sophisticated counting, calculating, writing, and all the achievements of our impressive technology are quite recent events in the time scale of our evolution.

It was thought for a long time that the real difference between the "animals" and us was the fact that we have developed culture and they have not. However, we now believe that monkeys and apes are able to "teach" things to their young, which they, in turn, pass on to their own young, or which are imitated by the whole group: one animal picks up a technique or habit from the next. For instance, in studying a group of Japanese monkeys (*Macaca fuscata*, which do not belong to the Great Apes), Michael Huffman and other primatologists

WULF SCHIEFENHÖVEL

♦ Members of a group of *Macaca fuscata*, living in semi-wild conditions near Kyoto, Japan, have developed the habit of playing with small stones. As this behavior has been passed on through a number of generations, many scientists view it as a precursor of "culture".

♣ A young chimpanzee catching termites with a specially modified twig—another example of behavior passed on from mother to children.

discovered that they have developed the custom of playing with stones in a specific way. Other Japanese monkeys now, have developed custom of washing sweet potatoes in a stream before eating them. Certain groups of chimpanzees use stone hammers to open hard nuts, while others do not. Clearly, these achievements are at least equivalents or precursors of culture, forms of behavior passed on by tradition.

Chimpanzees, bonobos, and gorillas live in groups and have social hierarchies. The orang-utan (*Pongo pygmaeus*), on the other hand, seems to be mostly solitary, except at mating time. In gorilla harems, the females are not related to each other and must therefore have migrated into the group. The same pattern seems to operate among chimpanzees: young females may leave the group to find partners outside. In most human societies, young women are required by custom (which may be genetically based) to leave their parents' family and to live with their husband.

We cannot, of course, conclude from such single behavioral and social traits that human beings are shaped after the model of a particular species of Great Apes. In so many ways, the apes are very different from each other and from us in their preferences, their characteristics, their behavior, and their social structure. But by studying the Great Apes and the other nonhuman primates, scientists can trace probable evolutionary connections between such variables as habitat, social structure, behavior, cognitive abilities, and capacity for culture. By continued study of these creatures, preferably in the wild in groups, we will not only learn more about their own fascinating lives, but will also come to a better understanding of our own species' history. But this will only be possible if we, as a species, stop encroaching on their habitat and threatening their very survival as a species.

PETER DAVEY/BRUCE COLEMAN LTD

TOWARDS *HOMO SAPIENS*

2.5 MILLION YEARS AGO – 35,000 YEARS AGO

Habilines, Erectines, and Neanderthals

GÖRAN BURENHULT

ABOUT 2.5 MILLION YEARS AGO, a series of crucial events were to influence the human family tree. In Africa, different species of *Australopithecus* and *Paranthropus* lived side by side, and recently, at Chesowanja, in Kenya, the existence of very early *Homo* has been confirmed at this age. This early *Homo* was named *Homo habilis* ("clever human"), but many now believe that more than one species is represented in this phase.

These events resulted in a number of anatomical changes that mainly occurred during the period that preceded the erectines—that is, about 1.5 million years ago. Brain size increased, hips and thigh bones became more and more adapted to bipedalism, and there was a reduction in sexual dimorphism—that is, size difference due to sex. The oldest fossils of *Homo* have a brain size of little more than 500 cubic centimeters (30 cubic inches), but apart from that the difference between the new genus and *Australopithecus* was not particularly striking. They all grew to roughly the same height, 1 to 1.3 meters (3 to 4 feet), and weighed 40 kilograms (88 pounds) on average. All of them were bipedal and thus moved freely on two legs. Early *Homo* had a slightly more rounded skull and were probably less ape-like than other hominids. The greatest anatomical difference was the appearance of the teeth, especially the reduced premolar and molar width, but the signs of wear on preserved teeth show that all species fed mainly on seeds and plants, especially fruits. Moreover, anatomical studies indicate that early *Homo* probably spent a great deal of time in the trees and for this reason was less "human" than previously assumed. It has turned out that the greatest difference was the mental capacity. Habilines were the first hominids to make stone tools.

The erectines were the first humans to leave the African homeland. By 700,000 years ago, they had occupied much of the Old World and had spread as far east as China and Southeast Asia. The volcanic soils of East and central Java, in Indonesia, have produced a number of *Homo erectus* fossils.

A hand axe—the typical tool of the Acheulean phase.
DAVID L. BRILL. © 1985

Defining the use of tools is not a simple matter. Californian sea otters fetch mussels on the seabed and, swimming on their back, crush the shell against their chest with a suitable stone to be able to reach the food. This behavior is remarkable but does not mean that a stone tool has been manufactured, or that the sea otter becomes a human. Chimpanzees, our closest relatives among the apes, not only use tools such as stones, branches, or slips of wood, but, by using their teeth and hands, they often also improve objects of wood or fibers to make them more efficient. Although an obvious manufacturing process, not even this kind of tool can be ranked in the same category as the tools made by habilines. The greatest difference lies in the mental functions—in the decision-making process. The chimpanzee is manufacturing a suitable slip of wood as a result of an instantaneous, intelligent idea, whereas the human action was characterized by a more advanced foresight, a deliberate manufacturing of an object with a particular appearance and for a certain purpose. A picture of the final product and its range of uses was already projected in the brain before the individual started to collect the raw material in the form of stones of suitable kinds and sizes. Furthermore, the knowledge of the manufacturing process could be transmitted to other members of the group as well as to succeeding generations.

The Habilines: The First Tool-makers

The first tool-making technique—which, as far as we know at present, is entirely linked to early *Homo*—existed between 2.5 and 1.5 million years ago and is distinguished by the use of pebbles from riverbeds as raw material. By means of another, smaller stone, flakes were struck off from both sides of the core. This bifacial flaking procedure is usually called the chopping-tool technique and was named the Oldowan industry after the site of its first discovery—Olduvai. Even though this technique sometimes has been considered simple, it nevertheless reveals a sound knowledge of the nature of the raw material, how to strike the stone to get a suitable flake, and, not least, the final result after a long series of strokes in a given succession.

For a long time, the general opinion was that the shaped core in itself represented the final product—the tool—and that the flakes were to be regarded as waste or leftovers from the manufacturing procedure. Close examination has shown, however, that much of the variation among chopping tools was the result of a deliberate production of flakes, which then could be used as knives, scrapers, or other tools for cutting meat, woodwork, and gathering plants. Many of the chopping tools found have probably been used for rough jobs, such as crushing animal bones, to be able to reach the much sought-after marrow, or digging up edible tubers and bulbs.

The chimpanzee may begin to gather materials for tools while still not in sight of the objective;

⚲ More than two million years ago, early *Homo* began to make stone tools from pebbles collected from riverbeds. The chopping-tool technique used by these early tool-makers is called the Oldowan industry, after Olduvai, in Tanzania, the site where such tools were first discovered.

ILLUSTRATION: JOHN RICHARDS

in Gombe National Park, for example, where chimpanzees modify grass stems and thin twigs to "fish" for termites in their mounds, they collect stems and take them to the termite mounds, where they are modified as and when necessary. If Richard Potts is right, that the accumulations of pebbles found at Olduvai represent "caches" of stone placed conveniently for future use by *Homo habilis*, then we can attribute to our early ancestors, of two million years ago, a degree of foresight considerably greater than that shown by modern chimpanzees. But we must not make the mistake of thinking of these primitive forebears as already human. Thomas Wynn has analyzed samples of their pebble tools and found no evidence that they modified them in anything but an ad hoc manner, striking off one flake after another until a usable tool resulted.

However, the findings from Koobi Fora and Olduvai also show that stone tools were carried considerable distances. This is yet another piece of evidence that habilines planned a future use for their tools, that they were able to think in the future tense. "Culture" was born.

Any Time but Not with Anybody

Why, then, did this new branch on the human family tree suddenly evolve some 2.5 million years ago? Today, most experts agree that human evolution resulted from the same sorts of pressures as the evolution of other animal species, and very often it is obvious that these processes of evolution occurred at the same time. Clearly, global climatic alterations, and the ecological changes that followed, played a crucial part in these processes.

About five million years ago, the Antarctic ice sheet started to grow substantially, whereas the corresponding glacial period of the Arctic did not begin until about 2.5 million years ago. During these two Ice Ages, the average temperature on Earth dropped markedly. In Africa, as in other parts of the world, this meant great changes in both flora and fauna. Vast tropical rainforest regions disappeared and were replaced by savanna, and parts of the fauna became extinct or changed owing to the adaptation to the new environment. These great ecological changes can be traced back to both of the glacial periods. The first one resulted in the development of the australopithecines— perhaps the separation of the human line itself— and it was surely not an accidental occurrence that the latter Ice Age coincided with the appearance of the genus *Homo* and the rise of tool use.

As we have seen, a number of different proto-human species lived side by side during this period, but, as far as we know at present, australo-pithecines never manufactured or used stone tools. While australopithecines in the course of time became extinct, the *Homo* groups survived and evolved into modern humans. But what was the biological difference between nonhuman

JOHN READER/SCIENCE PHOTO LIBRARY/THE PHOTO LIBRARY

hominids and early humans? This is a controversial issue, but one of the basic differences is human females' total lack of estrus periods—that is, mating seasons. They are, unlike many other mammals, always sexually receptive, almost independently of the menstrual cycle, although chimpanzees, especially pygmy chimpanzees (bonobos), also have very little sexual cyclicity. This evolution of human sexuality can perhaps be linked to a gradual reduction of body hair, resulting in increased skin sensitivity and a strengthening of female sexual signals. For example, the growth of the breasts is not necessary for the production of mother's milk or for breastfeeding, but is instead related to a visual, sexual stimulation for males. A change in the food composition, with a changeover to a diet consisting of more meat, and accompanying changes in the social organization, has been suggested as one reason for this evolution.

Far-reaching studies of baboons and chimpanzees show these considerable differences between different mammal species, and the interpretations can, with caution, be transferred to the study of early hominids. Among baboons, old males possess absolute dominance over food and mating, and they defend this position with extremely aggressive behavior. Sexual dimorphism is con-siderable—for example, males are twice as big as females. The dominant males and females lay their hands on most, and the best, of the food, and apart from the fact that a mother and her young sometimes share food, a systematic distribution never occurs among the different members of the group.

◄ This habiline skull discovered at Koobi Fora, on the eastern shores of Lake Turkana, in Kenya, in 1972 is believed to be about 1.9 million years old. Known as no. 1470, it has a relatively large braincase—nearly 800 cubic centimeters (49 cubic inches)— and was reconstructed from 150 pieces of fossil bone found scattered over a large area.

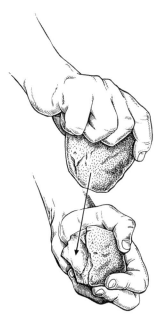

The Oldowan industry represents the simplest form of tool-making. The raw material consisted of pebbles collected from riverbeds at Koobi Fora and Olduvai. By means of a small stone, flakes were struck off from both sides of the core. Each core could yield a large number of flakes, and probably both the flakes and the remaining core were used as tools.
ILLUSTRATIONS: KEN RINKEL

The reverse is the case among chimpanzees. These lack a hierarchic division, and all males have free access to the receptive females—any time and with anybody. There are no mating seasons, but female receptivity varies. Furthermore, chimpanzees have a much less strict organization in terms of territorial control. Ethologist and primatologist Pierre van den Berghe described the agreeable life of chimpanzees in the following way: "Chimpanzees, it seems, successfully achieve what *Homo sapiens* radicals only dream of: peaceful, non-competitive, non-coercive, non-possessive, egalitarian, jealousy-free, promiscuous, non-tyrannical communes."

Of course, this must not be taken too far. Dominant males often do monopolize fertile

⊕ Olduvai Gorge, in northern Tanzania, is one of the world's most important archaeological sites. Its many fossil finds of australopithecines, habilines, and erectines, as well as modern humans, have added immensely to our knowledge of our distant prehistoric past.

females, although free consortships are often formed as well; and the males of a community patrol the territory boundaries, and one case is known where the males in one community apparently set out (successfully) to exterminate the small neighboring community. Maybe, after all, we are being a bit romantic: chimpanzees may be more like us than we care to admit.

It seems clear, then, that hunting behavior, the lack of mating seasons, the distribution of food within the group, as well as family structure, are factors that are intimately associated with each other and that probably were of crucial importance in the subsequent evolution of humans. An increasingly marked disposition toward living in couples, or perhaps small polygamous groups, which also created a basis for a more rigid distribution of work between the sexes, may have helped to reduce conflict within groups. Any time but not with anybody became typically human behavior.

Hunters or Scavengers?

The use of stone tools made possible the exploitation of foodstuffs previously inaccessible to hominids. When taking care of meat, entrails, and hides, sharp-edged flakes were a great advantage, especially in competition with predators such as hyenas and lions. Large amounts of meat could be cut loose from a dead animal in a short time, something that would have been impossible if only hands, teeth, and wooden objects were used. But detailed knowledge of the eating habits of early *Homo* is still very limited. (See the feature *Mighty Hunter or Marginal Scavenger?*)

Inevitably, the archaeological record gives us a very incidental and selective picture of prehistoric reality. Preserved food remnants are rare, and, when found, they almost always consist of animal bones. This means that stone tools, which are always well preserved, represent the most important source of information in our attempt to establish the modes of subsistence and the preparation of food of early humans. These tools thus become overrepresented in the interpretation of what once took place on the site in question. Scattered remnants of animal bones are often found together with large numbers of chopping tools and flakes, and these concentrations have usually been interpreted as sites of activity or even occasional home bases where animals were brought in, quartered, and eaten.

The problem is, however, that we do not know to what extent habilines made use of meat in their diet, nor if they, in that case, only grabbed the prey of predators by scaring off the true hunters, or were themselves actively engaged in big-game hunting. The use of stone tools has often been associated with big-game hunting and

thereby with a rapidly changing economic and social organization, but modern analyses have shown that early *Homo* may never actually have hunted big game and may to a very small extent only have depended upon any form of hunting. Still, great numbers of stone tools are found together with the bones of large animals such as hippopotamuses, buffaloes, or gnus, and unquestionably the tools have been transported there over considerable distances. The facts indicate that these kinds of sites represent locations where quartering and possibly scavenging took place, and where predators were frightened away after having brought down their prey. These sites can by no means be looked upon as more or less permanent settlements or home bases where humans stayed for some time, but in some cases it cannot be excluded that pieces of meat were carried to safe spots and consumed out of reach of wild beasts. Without fire and advanced weapons such as spears or bows and arrows, this kind of subsistence must have been a risky business in an open savanna environment with few or no possibilities to seek shelter or take flight. Many of the examined animal bones show traces

of both stone tools and teeth of predatory animals, clear evidence of the prevailing competitive situation. Marks of animal teeth that superimpose those of stone tools may, of course, indicate that animals consumed leftovers from habiline meals, but in many cases marks of tools superimpose those of animal teeth, and this surely indicates scavenging on predator kills.

Finds of bones of many different animal species on these sites have, however, led many experts to believe that early *Homo* actually, to some extent, used hunting as part of the subsistence—a part that certainly became more important as time went on—and that a combination of hunting and scavenging is the most probable explanation. Yet most experts agree that vegetable foodstuffs such as plants, bulbs, roots, and fruits formed an overwhelming part of the diet, and that animal products such as birds' eggs, larvae, lizards, and small game played a much more important role than big game. This is the case among chimpanzees, and the same kind of food constitutes an important part of the diet of present-day hunter-gatherers. Nothing in the find material indicates that early *Homo* differed from this pattern.

MAJOR ERECTINE SITES

It is generally believed that the erectines migrated outside Africa more than 700,000 years ago and settled southern Asia and much of Europe. Coastlines and ice sheets are shown as they are assumed to have been during the peak of one of the extensive glacials that preceded the last Ice Age. European sites are shown in the detail map at left.

CARTOGRAPHY: RAY SIM

MIGHTY HUNTER OR MARGINAL SCAVENGER?

PETER ROWLEY-CONWY

What was life like for our earliest hominid relatives? How did they live? Archaeologists have been seeking to answer these questions ever since 1924, when Raymond Dart identified the Taung skull as that of a hominid he named *Australopithecus africanus*. In the process, they have produced some of the most interesting archaeological work of recent years.

The Australopithecines of South Africa

The australopithecine group known as the Nutcrackers has been studied in detail in South Africa, where several important fossil sites have been excavated, including Makapansgat. As well as hominid remains, these sites have yielded numerous bones of other large mammals, including buffalo and various species of antelopes and carnivores. Should we conclude that these bones are the remains of animals hunted and eaten by the australopithecines? Dart's answer was a decided "Yes", for several reasons.

No stone tools were found in these sites, but Dart believed that the australopithecines at Makapansgat used tools made of bone, teeth, and horn instead. He argued that evidence of pitting and breakage on some of the animal bones showed that they had been used for hammering or pounding, and that some pieces of bone had been sharpened to a point for use as weapons. In other words, Dart claimed that these hominids were using a whole range of bone tools in their daily lives, some of them intended to hunt and kill their prey, and perhaps other hominids, too.

Recent work by C.K. Brain and others has largely demolished this theory. In a book entitled *The Hunters or the Hunted?*, published in 1981, Brain argues that all the bones at these sites, including those of hominids, result from the hunting behavior of large carnivores, especially leopards. Hominids

SHAH ANUP/JACANA-AUSCAPE

⊷ Leopards often carry their prey into trees. As they consume their victims, bones fall to the ground, where some are gnawed by scavenging hyenas. Sites such as Swartkrans were deep fissures that trapped and preserved such bones, including those of early hominids.

would have been one of the animals leopards preyed upon, and after a leopard had eaten its fill, hyenas would have moved in to scavenge the remains of the carcass. This explains the bone finds much better than Dart's theory did. Bones collected from present-day hyena dens are pitted and broken in very much the same way as those from the South African sites, and the same sharp points are also found.

In fact, there is no evidence that the South African australopithecines used bone for any purpose at all. And as their own bones were gnawed and broken like those of the other animals, they must have suffered the same fate—they were

the hunted rather than the hunters.

This theory has been given further support by recent geological work showing that the sites where these bones have accumulated were not caves but vertical cracks or fissures in the ground. These would have retained water in the otherwise dry landscape, leading to the growth of isolated groups of trees. Leopards today can be seen to carry their prey up into trees in order to escape the hyenas attracted by a fresh kill. As the leopard eats, parts of the carcass fall to the ground. The hyenas set upon these, and the discarded bones are likely to end up in any natural fissures in the vicinity. This is the best explanation of

the South African sites: they are natural fossil traps. No one ever lived there, and they have preserved the evidence of leopard kills made as far back as two or three million years ago.

Early Homo *in East Africa*

By the time *Homo habilis* appears in the archaeological record in East Africa, some two million years ago, many differences are immediately apparent. Accumulations of animal bones are still found, but there are two crucial differences. First, they are found scattered in horizontal layers, not down deep fissures; and second, they are found together with stone tools. They look, in fact, very like habiline camp sites.

But are they? In such key areas as Olduvai Gorge and Koobi Fora, collections of stones and bones have often been found on the shores of ancient rivers or lakes. It is therefore possible that floods washed the various items together by chance. Just because the bones and stones are found together now, it does not necessarily mean that they started that way. Sometimes, however, various fragments of stone found within a short distance of each other have been able to be fitted back together again. This must mean that someone made a tool on that very spot, because the various pieces would have become separated if the area had later been flooded. Similarly, several pieces of animal bone have sometimes been able to be fitted back together.

The animal bones provide a vital clue to habiline behavior. Many leg bones bear impact marks, where they were struck with stone

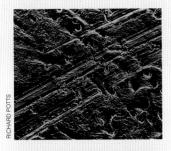

⚫Cut marks on prehistoric bones (top) can look similar to gnaw marks made by carnivores (bottom) to the naked eye, but can usually be distinguished by microscopic examination.

years back into the past, all on the basis of the division of labor implied by hunting. The hunting hypothesis has a lot to answer for.

So how well founded is it? More recently, archaeologists including Lewis Binford and Richard Potts have re-examined the evidence. Clearly, the origin of modern forms of behavior is of key importance for our understanding of ourselves. It is something we should try to discover, not something we should have preconceived ideas about.

Interest has focused on the evidence of the animal bones. Some, as mentioned, have cut marks. Others, however, have gnaw marks made by carnivores, and where cuts and gnaw marks are found on the same bone, the gnaw marks were usually made first. This shows that, in some cases at least, the habilines were getting their hands on these bones only after the carnivores had finished with them. There is only one way to explain this: the habilines were in such instances demonstrably

scavenging from carnivore kills, not killing their own prey.

This casts a new light on many things. First, scavenging requires no division of labor and does not imply sharing or any other social behavior approaching our own modern forms of behavior. Second, this may explain the early use of sharp stone tools. Habiline scavengers would have been competing with other scavengers such as hyenas, which are biologically much better equipped for the job and, indeed, could easily have killed and eaten the habilines if the opportunity had arisen. For the habiline scavengers, the crucial thing was probably to get away from a carcass as quickly as possible. Lacking their competitors' sharp teeth, they may have used sharp stone tools to cut quickly through the tough skin and sinew, fleeing with edible portions before the hyenas arrived.

According to this theory, the "home bases" would have been places to which the habiline scavengers

took their food to eat it in safety. Paleoecological work has provided further information about such sites. As mentioned, they have often been found on the banks of former streams or lakes, under what would once have been stands of trees. This might seem to be a perfectly reasonable place to live—but not for early habilines, and not in tropical Africa. Even modern hunter-gatherers do not camp under trees along waterways, because at night lions prowl these locations, killing animals that come down to drink.

This is a crucial point, because it suggests that habilines did not sleep at the sites that have yielded evidence of their presence. We do not know where they slept. If they were similar to other primates, they might have done so on cliffs or rocks some distance from the water. The so-called "home bases" were therefore no such thing, but rather places visited during the daytime to eat food scavenged from the kills of large carnivores. Habilines do not appear to have operated from bases as modern humans do. It is more likely that they ranged over considerable areas during the daytime, much as baboons do.

The evidence now suggests a pattern of movement from the sleeping site across the open savanna, via abandoned carnivore kills, sources of plant foods, and caches of stone suitable for making tools, to a daytime waterside site under the trees—and back again before nightfall. This is hardly recognizable as specifically human behavior. As Lewis Binford puts it, our earliest ancestors were really not very like us.

tools to break them open for marrow, and some have cut marks, indicating that flesh was cut from them with sharp stone flakes. The inference is clear: habilines brought animal bones to these sites, using stone tools to get at the flesh and marrow.

It would be tempting to conclude that these sites were regular home bases, to which hunters brought back their kill, but it would also be premature. Archaeologist Glynn Isaac came to this conclusion some years ago, and it is instructive to see what followed from this. If animals were hunted, Isaac postulated, there would have been a division of labor. Males would have been the hunters, while females, encumbered by children, would more likely have gathered plant foods and small animals in the vicinity of the camp site. This would mean that food was shared between the sexes, implying a reasonably complex social structure.

This scenario is instantly recognizable—it is a simplifed version of the behavior of modern hunter-gatherers at their base camps. What the theory does is to project a form of modern behavior two million

⚫Two injuries on the skull of an australopithecine child from Swartkrans were formerly thought to have been inflicted with a pointed club. However, the injuries exactly match up with the canine teeth of a leopard, suggesting that the child was a hunting victim.

⚬➤ The Great Rift Valley—the cradle of humanity—is the most extensive rift in the Earth's surface. It extends from southwestern Asia southwards through East Africa to Mozambique. The section of the valley shown here is in Kenya.

The period between 2.5 and 1.5 million years ago was a crucial and formative phase in the evolution of humans—mentally, technologically, and economically, as well as socially. The pressure from the ecological competition enforced early human characteristics in early *Homo* and at the same time led to the extinction of other proto-hominid species. The number of hominids in central East Africa may have been equivalent to the number of baboons living in the same region today—in other words, a very large number of individuals in mutual competition. The ever-increasing brain size led to considerably smaller brains in infants than in adults, which facilitated childbirth. This in turn resulted in a considerable prolongation of the period in which children were dependent on their mothers, which involved important changes in the social organization and the division of work between the sexes.

Habilines probably lived in small groups or bands, much like present-day hunter-gatherers, but the social organization was more similar to that of chimpanzees. Only with the appearance of *Homo erectus* some 1.6 million years ago did a more human social structure develop.

The Homo erectus Phase: "Apeman Who Walks Upright"

When the erectines came on the scene, entirely new characters in human evolution appeared, with abilities and driving forces that made our ancestors spread outside Africa for the first time. This demanded totally different ways of ecological adaptation. The cold climate and trying environment further north implied that humans used fire and wore well-adapted clothing to be able to keep warm during the winter. Above all, the migration of *Homo erectus* into northern regions shows that people now were able to adjust themselves to considerably harsher ecological situations, where the supply of food varied markedly during the different seasons and where hunting became increasingly important, especially during the winter. Many of the edible plants withered in the autumn, and it was necessary to store nonperishable foodstuffs such as nuts, bulbs, and tubers.

Physically, the erectines were more similar to modern humans than to habilines. The greatest difference was probably the shape of the head and face, which still had strikingly primitive features— a sloping forehead, very heavy brow ridges, and a receding chin. The muscles at the nape of the neck were extremely well developed. Brain size increased over time from 775 to 1,300 cubic centimeters (47 to 79 cubic inches), which on average is equivalent to 70 percent of that of modern humans. Fully adapted to an upright gait and equipped with a muscular and stocky body of between 1.5 and 1.8 meters (about 5 and 6 feet) in height, *Homo erectus* must have made the impression of being very strong and powerful.

MICHAEL DENIS HUOT/JACANA-AUSCAPE

Today, most experts agree that the erectines slowly evolved from the habilines in central East Africa, from where they spread north across the Old World. The oldest fossils have been found in East Turkana, in Kenya—sometimes referred to as the "Turkana Newcomers"—and date back some 1.6 million years. A million years later, *Homo erectus* and its sister species, *Homo heidelbergensis*, occupied all of Eurasia, from the Atlantic coast in the west to China and Java in the east.

It was never really a matter of migration. Hunter-gatherers move across vast areas in search of food, and an increasing population implied that groups split up and new territories were occupied. At a pace of 20 kilometers (12 miles) per generation, a distance of 14,000 kilometers (9,000 miles), or roughly the distance between Nairobi and Beijing, was covered in 20,000 years. Even with much shorter movements, this natural, successive spread was enough for the erectines to occupy these vast areas in just a few hundreds of thousands of years. As colder and darker regions of Europe and Asia became populated, skin color became lighter to allow the rays of the sun to penetrate the skin to produce vitamin D, and the protecting fat layer, as well as the sweat glands, adapted to the new climatic situation. The big question is why these groups of people were forced to leave the always well-laid African table.

As we have seen, *Homo* itself, and, later, the erectines, evolved on the savannas of tropical Africa. The great climatic fluctuations that prevailed

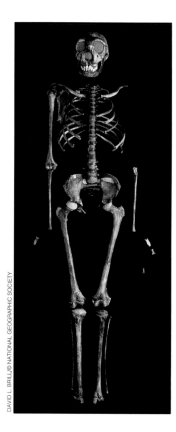

DAVID L. BRILL/© NATIONAL GEOGRAPHIC SOCIETY

⚬⬆ A well-preserved, 1.6 million-year-old erectine skeleton discovered near Lake Turkana, in Kenya, in 1984 is believed to be that of a 12-year-old boy. The skeleton measures almost 1.7 meters (5 feet, 6 inches) in length, suggesting that adult erectines grew as tall as 1.8 meters (about 6 feet).

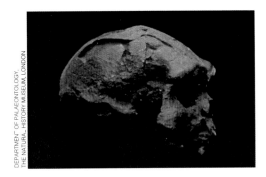

DEPARTMENT OF PALAEONTOLOGY,
THE NATURAL HISTORY MUSEUM, LONDON

oldest date in Southwest Asia has been obtained at Ubeidiya, in modern-day Israel, at an age of 700,000 years, although there are no diagnostic human remains from there, while the oldest known find in western Europe has been uncovered in Italy, at Isernia La Pineta, southeast of Rome; stone tool finds show that humans lived there some 730,000 years ago. However, on the basis of a recent find of a lower jaw beneath the city of Dmanisi, southwest of Tblisi, in the former Soviet republic of Georgia, it has been claimed that humans had already spread outside Africa 1.8 million years ago.

◄ This *Homo erectus* skull found at Sangiran, in central Java, Indonesia, is believed to be about 800,000 years old.

♀ The famous Zhoukoudian Cave, outside Beijing, in China, was first excavated by Davidson Black in the early 1920s. So far, the remains of some 40 *Homo erectus* individuals have been uncovered here, together with more than 100,000 stone tools such as scrapers and chopping tools, making it one of the most important erectine sites in the world. Its layers date back to between 460,000 and 230,000 years ago.

between five and one million years ago intensified about 900,000 years ago, and the global climate was influenced by glacial periods alternating with warmer interglacials. Consequently, the African vegetation was characterized by savanna alternating with rainforest. To be able to survive these freaks of nature, humans had to adapt in different ways, either by moving or by occupying new climatic zones. The latter implied, among other things, the ability to alternate vegetable foodstuffs with a meat diet.

Obviously, the Sahara Desert played an important role in this process. During periods with higher rainfall, populations from the south entered the virgin soils in the north, and during drier periods they were forced to leave. In some cases, the retreat southwards may have been cut off, and for that reason a northward expansion toward the Mediterranean coast and southwestern Asia was necessary. Demonstrably, a heavy increase in the number of big land animals took place in Europe about 700,000 years ago, when elephants, hoofed animals, hippopotamuses, and a series of predators such as lions and leopards migrated north from Africa. It is probable that the causes that lie behind these migrations are also behind the contemporary appearance of humans outside Africa.

To sum up, the erectines—of which *Homo erectus* is the best known species—first appeared in Africa, and a number of finds from Lake Turkana, Chesowanja, and Olduvai date back to between 1.6 and one million years ago. The Asian finds, on the other hand, are all of a later date. Ban Mae Tha, in Thailand, is one of the oldest known sites in Southeast Asia, at an age of 700,000 years, whereas the *erectus* finds from Zhoukoudian, in China, date back to between 460,000 and 230,000 years ago. Other Chinese finds from Lantian, Jenjiawo, and Gongwangling have proved to be somewhat older than the earliest layers of Zhoukoudian, and have been dated to 600,000 years ago. For the Java humans, there are potassium–argon dates of between 900,000 and 600,000 years ago, and these are supported by fission-track dates which go back to a little over a million years ago.

Erectine groups, it seems, entered Europe at roughly the same time as they entered Asia. The

ROBERT RAYMOND

ROBERT RAYMOND

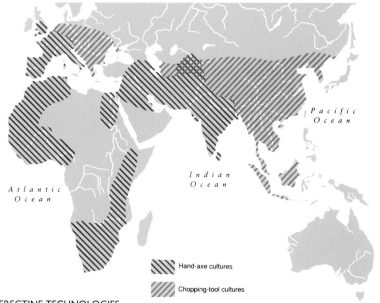

Hand-axe cultures

Chopping-tool cultures

CARTOGRAPHY: RAY SIM

ERECTINE TECHNOLOGIES

During the erectine phase, two technologically distinct regions can be distinguished in the Old World. The technology of the populations in Africa, western Europe, and Southwest Asia was characterized by the hand axe, and is usually called the Acheulean tradition. In East and Southeast Asia, as well as in eastern Europe, however, chopping tools dominated.

This magnificent hand axe, the characteristic tool of the Acheulean period, was found at the site that gave the period its name—St Acheul, in northern France.
GÖRAN BURENHULT

Acheulean: Period of Hand Axes

During the erectine era, bifacially worked hand axes became the dominant tool type in many parts of the Old World. This tool tradition is called the Acheulean and was named after the site of its first documentation—St Acheul, in France. The subtriangular hand axe probably had a wide range of uses, such as cutting, digging, and scraping, and was often shaped into a neat but very efficient tool. Wynn's analysis of Oldowan pebble tools has shown clearly that the makers of hand axes must have had, before they started, a clear mental picture of the finished object, and worked towards achieving it as they flaked. Presumably, hand axes were never hafted, but were instead used by hand, and some experts have even suggested that they were used during hunting as a kind of missile or discus. The extent of big-game hunting at this period is, however, a most controversial issue.

During the long erectine period, the Old World gradually split up into two technologically distinct regions. The reason for this split is still unclear. The tool assemblage of one region, which embraced Africa, Europe, and parts of western and southern Asia, was dominated by the hand axe, whereas that of East and Southeast Asia lacked hand axes and was dominated by local chopping-tool industries. It is interesting that the East/Southeast Asian area was the domain of *Homo erectus* itself, while many specialists consider that the western region was occupied by the species *Homo heidelbergensis*.

Acheulean technology was extremely long-lived. In Africa, it existed from 1.5 million until between 200,000 and 150,000 years ago, when it was replaced by the more complex stone technology of the so-called Middle Stone Age. This was characterized by scrapers and points manufactured out of flakes. In Europe, the hand-axe tradition survived much longer, until more modern humans appeared some 100,000 years ago.

The appearance of hand axes has led most experts to believe that big-game hunting constituted an important part of the erectine subsistence, and a number of sites have been pointed out as evidence of this. At Olorgesailie, southwest of Nairobi, in Kenya, Glynn and Barbara Isaac have excavated a kill site with the remains of large mammals such as hippopotamuses, but, above all, also the remains of 63 giant baboons, a now extinct species, which were found together with more than 10,000 beautiful hand axes. The area was no bigger than 12 meters by 20 meters (40 feet by 65 feet). The excavators interpreted the spot as a kill site where the baboons had been hemmed in, probably at night, frightened, and then clubbed to death when they tried to escape; others are more convinced that the site represents a longer time span, over which giant baboons were favored prey.

American anthropologist Lewis Binford has, however, called not only Olorgesailie in question, but even the whole idea that the erectines were big-game hunters. In his opinion, there is presently no way of determining whether a site is the result of butchering or if there are other explanations of the accumulated find material. The deposits of animal remains may very well be leftovers from scavenging on predator kills. According to Binford, the same applies to other classic sites that have been pointed out as "proof" of big-game hunting in Europe and Asia in Middle Pleistocene times—Torralba, in Spain, and Zhoukoudian, in China.

Terra Amata, in Nice, on the French Riviera, is another important European site from this period that has been under intense discussion. The site contained the remains of 10 large, oval-shaped huts 8 to 10 meters (26 to 33 feet) long and equipped with centrally situated hearths and longitudinal stone arrangements along the postholes and walls. The excavator, Henry de Lumley, considered the 300,000-year-old find to be a seasonal settlement, where its inhabitants during parts of the year supported themselves on fishing and gathering, particularly sea mussels, oysters, and limpets. Terra Amata, too, has been questioned by many experts, but the claimed remains of postholes and stone tools are not easily explained away. Although the original layer may have been disturbed—by landslides and freezing, for example—it is still very likely that the site was used in some way by human groups. Pollen analyses show that the settlement in that case was used especially during late spring.

WHAT DO THE ZHOUKOUDIAN FINDS TELL US?

PETER ROWLEY-CONWY

Imagine a huge cavern. Imagine it existing for hundreds of thousands of years, and consider a few of the things that would take place there through this colossal span of time. From time to time, hyenas inhabit the cave. They bring in their prey and gnaw the bones, they rear their young, they defecate, and they die. At other times, wolves live there. Huge cave bears occasionally hibernate in the cave, some of which die and add their bones to the debris inside. Owls roost in suitable crannies, regurgitating pellets of indigestible fur and bones, the remnants of the small animals they prey upon. Sand, dust, and mud are continually blown and washed inside by wind and rain, gradually building up into thick layers.

From time to time, pieces of rock break loose from the roof, crushing anything beneath, to lie on the cave floor until covered by the rising deposits. Sometimes a roof fall blocks an existing entrance or creates a new one, changing the appearance of the cavern. Plants grow near the entrances. Their seeds are blown inside or are carried in by the rodents that live in rock crevices round about. These rodents sometimes perish inside the cave, or fall victim to owls or wolves. All the while, the various deposits and objects inside the cave are being worked upon by the unceasing processes of nature that erode, break, move, redeposit, change, and destroy. And finally, people sometimes enter the cavern —to do what?

This is the archaeological problem in such caves—disentangling all the agents of accumulation to find out what the humans did. And let us build in a few additional problems. The cave is not excavated as part of a single coherent campaign, but in a series of excavations led by many directors over many years. Some of these excavations do not meet modern archaeological standards, not because of any shortcomings on the part of the various

PETER ROWLEY-CONWY

directors, but simply because the science of excavation was less advanced than it is today. The vicissitudes of civil war, world war, and revolution also pass over the site during the various excavations. In the confusion, many of the most important finds go missing in mysterious circumstances which many international experts still consider to be highly suspicious.

All this describes the situation at one of the most famous archaeological sites in Asia: Zhoukoudian (formerly spelt Choukoutien), where the richest fossil finds of a local group of *Homo erectus* known as Peking Man have been made. More bones of these people have been found here than anywhere else in Asia, along with many quartz tools.

But working out how Peking Man lived is extremely difficult. We certainly cannot assume that everything in the cave was brought in by people just because stone tools have been found there. Clearly, caves act as traps for all kinds of materials and bear witness to many different activities. Many early researchers—notably the great Chinese excavator Pei Wenzhong— were aware of this, but others have published accounts of Peking Man's life that go far beyond the evidence.

The Cannibalism Theory

All the *Homo erectus* skulls found at Zhoukoudian have the faces and undersides missing. This has excited much discussion of cannibalism, some people claiming that the brains were extracted and eaten by other humans. Moreover, many more skulls have been found than other human bones, leading to the suggestion that corpses were ritually dismembered outside the cave and that only the heads were brought inside—in other words, that some kind of religious ceremony took place there. If true, this would be of enormous significance, because it would be by far the earliest indication of such ritual behavior.

However, there is a less dramatic explanation of these finds. The parts of the skulls that are missing are the weakest parts, those most likely to be destroyed by natural means, so not too much can be concluded from this. Furthermore, we know that hyenas often carry the head of their prey to their den and break into the skull through the weakest parts. Human brains may well have been eaten at Zhoukoudian—but by hyenas. Most of the other animal bones were probably carried in by hyenas as well. Many are complete (whereas humans would have

Homo erectus skullcaps from Zhoukoudian all have missing faces and undersides. Formerly thought to indicate cannibalism, this is now believed to have resulted from gnawing by hyenas or natural breakage.

broken them for marrow), and there are also numerous skulls of other species. The fact that hyena feces are commonly found in the excavation layers also points to this explanation.

The Evidence for Fire

Black layers several meters deep and many meters long have been interpreted by some as evidence that humans built fires here, but this, too, is unlikely. These areas are far too extensive to have been fireplaces. Many tiny groups of rodent bones were found throughout these layers, indicating that owls had roosted above and regurgitated pellets. The black deposits could, in fact, be thousands of years' worth of owl droppings, which may even have ignited spontaneously. But while no regular fireplaces have been found, people probably did use fire. The upper teeth and skulls of some animals are burned, and this must have been done by people, presumably to cook the brains. Whether people hunted the animals is doubtful. No spearheads or arrowheads were found among the stone tools, and animal heads are at least as likely to have been scavenged from the kills of other carnivores.

What, then, does Zhoukoudian tell us? It tells us that people entered the cave, left some bones and tools there, and used fire—but that is about all it tells us. Humans used the cave much less frequently than hyenas did, and the various complexities should make us cautious in drawing any conclusions. This is not to diminish the importance of the site. As a source of hominid fossils, it is immensely important, and the problems it poses have given rise to new analytical methods that have revolutionized our approach to such sites.

Homo sapiens *in the Making*

The period between 300,000 and 40,000 years ago was an important transitional period between erectine and sapient stages and was characterized by a series of physical and technological changes. Brain size increased from 1,100 to about 1,400 cubic centimeters (67 to 85 cubic inches), and at the same time, face and bodily constitution more and more resembled those of modern humans. The tool technology was refined, and during the Neanderthal era the first signs of ritual life and religious beliefs appeared. In addition to the hand-axe technology of the Acheulean tradition, a typical flake technology arose, which is named the Clactonian, after the site of its first discovery—Clacton-on-Sea, east of London.

The finds of fossil humans from this important transitional period are still few, but in Europe some remains have been found that seem to document the emergence of Neanderthal features. A young adult woman found at Swanscombe, in England, lived about 225,000 years ago and had a brain volume of 1,325 cubic centimeters (80 cubic inches). Another woman, found at Steinheim, in Germany, is slightly older. However, the most important finds from this period so far discovered are from Arago, in the French Pyrenees, and date back at least 200,000 years. Undoubtedly, these were precursors of the classic European Neanderthals, who appeared for the first time

about 130,000 years ago. Similar fossils have been uncovered at Bilzingsleben, in eastern Germany (more than 300,000 years old), and at Petralona, close to Thessaloniki, in Greece.

The finds from Swanscombe, Steinheim, and Arago show that people with an almost modern brain capacity lived in Europe and probably also in large parts of Asia and Africa between 300,000 and 200,000 years ago. In South and East Asia, populations of the same type replaced *Homo erectus* at about the same time: remains from Dali and Jinniushan, in China, and Hathnora, in India, are clearly like Steinheim or Petralona. But *Homo erectus* lingered on in Southeast Asia until 100,000 years ago. Their European/West Asian descendants, the enigmatic Neanderthals, were just round the corner.

The Neanderthal Enigma

Ever since the first fossil was found in 1856 at Neanderthal, close to Düsseldorf, in Germany, the relationship between Neanderthals and modern humans has been under constant discussion. New finds of Neanderthal fossils have resulted in recurring changes of opinion as to which role they actually played in the evolution of *Homo sapiens sapiens*. Recently, results from a series of African sites have once more overthrown established and universally recognized theories on the course of events. The Neanderthals are once again in the limelight.

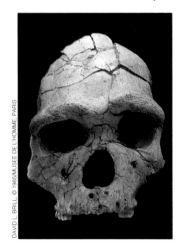

⬥ This skull from Arago, in the eastern Pyrenees, in France, is considered by many to represent a transitory stage between erectines and Neanderthals.

NEANDERTHAL SITES

The major Neanderthal sites in Europe and Southwest Asia. The Neanderthals evolved during a warm phase and persisted in Europe well into the last glacial, eventually disappearing about 33,000 years ago. Coastlines and ice sheets are shown as they were during the peak of the last glacial.

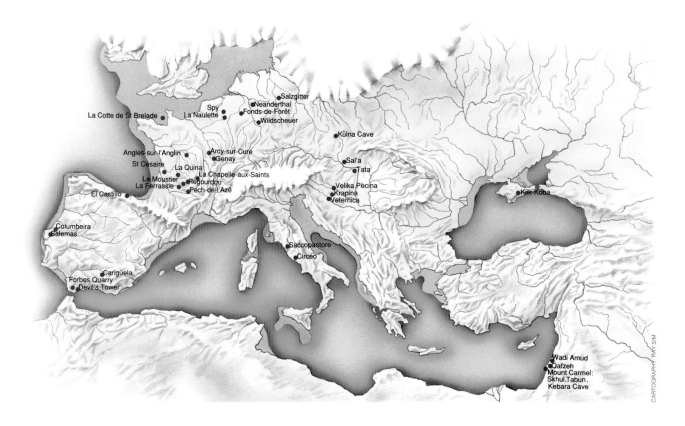

For a long time it has been clear that the physical appearance of European Neanderthals in particular strongly differed from that of anatomically modern humans. Their brain was actually larger than ours on average. They had a considerably bigger face, with a heavy brow ridge and a remarkably robust nose. Their lower jaw was massive, and they had a receding chin. Even the teeth were considerably larger and were placed in a U-shaped curve, not in a parabola shape, like ours. Their head was supported by short and very robust muscles at the nape of the neck. The Neanderthals reached only about 1.6 meters (5 feet, 3 inches) in height, but were extremely muscular. (See the feature *The Neanderthals*.)

In spite of the physical differences, modern humans were for a long period of time considered to be lineal descendants of the Neanderthals. Only with the work of French paleontologist Marcellin Boule at the beginning of the twentieth century was it suggested that these differences were too great for the Neanderthals to be the ancestors of modern humans.

The Neanderthals evolved between 200,000 and 100,000 years ago and are usually associated with the so-called Mousterian culture, named after a site at Le Moustier, in the Dordogne, in France. Since anatomically modern humans made their appearance in Europe about 40,000 years ago, there clearly was no time for a transition from *Homo neanderthalensis* to *Homo sapiens sapiens*. Boule, instead, suggested that the Neanderthals became extinct during the last Ice Age and were replaced by the new immigrants. We now know that the last of the Neanderthals lingered on until 35,000 years ago, so that there was a brief period of coexistence.

However, a series of new discoveries led to conclusive reinterpretations of the relationship between Neanderthals and *Homo sapiens sapiens*. On Mount Carmel, close to Haifa, in Israel, and situated on the Mediterranean coast, several caves have been known for some time to contain important finds of fossil humans—for example, Mugharet es-Skhul, Mugharet et-Tabun, Kebara, and Jebel Qafzéh. In Qafzeh, a primitive form of modern humans has been found which already lived in the area some 92,000 years ago, whereas Tabun contained the remains of a Neanderthal form from about 120,000 years ago, and Neanderthals at Kebara lived only about 60,000 years ago—in other words, spanning the period of the modern people at Qafzeh. In Skhul, remains at an age of about 80,000 years have been found. All of these Levantine humans can be linked to the Mousterian tradition of the Middle Paleolithic, even those with modern traits.

If Neanderthals and people of modern type actually coexisted in the Middle East for some 60,000 years, and overlapped for about 5,000 years in Europe, then, obviously, one cannot be descended from the other. Most likely they both evolved from *Homo heidelbergensis*: the Neanderthals in the temperate zone of Europe and/or the Middle East, from ancestors such as Petralona or Arago; *Homo sapiens* in Africa, from precursors such as Kabwe or Bodo. In fact, a whole series of transitional remains from *Homo heidelbergensis* to *Homo sapiens* is now known, in the range of (approximately) 130,000 to 120,000 years ago: Omo, Ngaloba, Jebel Irhoud, and Eliye Springs. The earliest representatives of our species emerged from Africa about 100,000 years ago and coexisted with Neanderthals for many millennia, until something—perhaps the chance invention of the Upper Paleolithic stone technology—gave them an advantage and they were able to spread further and replace the unfortunate Neanderthals altogether.

Thinking about the Neanderthals has gone through several phases. In the 1860s, they were regarded as our ancestors. Boule then exaggerated the differences between them and us, not realizing that the skeleton he studied, known as the "Old Man of La Chapelle-aux-Saints", was deformed with arthritis. William Straus and A.J.E. Cave pointed this out in 1952, and once again the Neanderthals were given a place in our family tree, though perhaps as ancestors of modern Caucasians (Europeans, Middle Easterners, and Indians) only. Now, with new dating methods such as thermoluminesence and electron spin resonance, we have a fresh perspective, and they are preferably seen as our cousins rather than our ancestors, though very like us in many features. (See the feature *Dating the Past*.) The discussion is once again directly linked to the original home of humans—Africa.

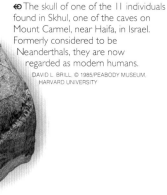

The skull of one of the 11 individuals found in Skhul, one of the caves on Mount Carmel, near Haifa, in Israel. Formerly considered to be Neanderthals, they are now regarded as modern humans.
DAVID L. BRILL, © 1985/PEABODY MUSEUM, HARVARD UNIVERSITY

This Neanderthal skull found in Amud Cave, near the Sea of Galilee, in Israel, had a brain volume of 1,800 cubic centimeters (110 cubic inches).

The skull of one of the individuals found in Qafzeh Cave, Israel. Like those in Skhul Cave, the humans found at this site are regarded as archaic forms of *Homo sapiens*.

THE NEANDERTHALS

COLIN GROVES

I F THERE IS ONE FOSSIL human type everyone has heard of, it is the Neanderthals. For tens of thousands of years, scattered groups of these people roamed the tundras and forests of western Eurasia. European specimens are known from as early as about 60,000 years ago, at Saccopastore, in Italy, and as late as 35,000 years ago, at St Césaire, in France. In Southwest Asia, the earliest specimen, from Tabun Cave, in Israel, is 120,000 years old; the latest, from Shanidar, in Iraq, is about 45,000 years old. The Neanderthals are sometimes regarded as just a race of *Homo sapiens* that happens to be extinct, sometimes as a distinct human species, *Homo neanderthalensis*. In Southwest Asia, they overlapped for tens of thousands of years with modern humans, while in Europe, they coexisted for only a few thousand years. We do not know what the two peoples thought of each other, whether they normally traded or were at war, or even occasionally interbred. At any rate, the Neanderthals are no longer with us. Their disappearance remains a mystery, but it is generally thought that our own species gained some advantage, maybe technological or cultural or both, and the Neanderthals, unable to compete, died out.

ILLUSTRATION: JOHN RICHARDS

WAS THERE A NEANDERTHAL RELIGION?

PETER ROWLEY-CONWY

I t is a common archaeological joke that any finding that cannot be explained in practical terms is labelled "ritual"—and the joke contains more than a grain of truth. The main text of this chapter refers to a number of finds that have often been thought to reflect ritual behavior of some kind among Neanderthals. Recently, these finds have come under renewed scrutiny. Here is a brief summary of three of the best-known claims, with the case against accepting them as fact.

The Cave Bear Cult

Popularized by Jean Auel's novel *The Clan of the Cave Bear* some years ago, this theory now has few, if any, supporters. It was based on the fact that quite a large number of caves have been found containing Neanderthal artifacts and thousands of bear bones. All this shows is that these early people occasionally visited a cave in which the huge bears hibernated and sometimes died. It does not show that Neanderthal people killed any of these bears, and still less that any ritual was involved.

There was also a reported finding from Drachenloch cave, in Switzerland, of several bear skulls set inside an arrangement of stone slabs—clear proof, it was claimed, of ritual behavior. But two mutually contradictory drawings of this were published at different times, no photographs exist, and it was recently established that the excavator was not even present on the day that the find was made. The whole thing, in fact, was reconstructed from the descriptions of the unskilled workmen who had carried out the excavation. Slabs of stone often fall from cave roofs and lie at unusual angles on the floor below, where the bones of dead cave bears would also lie. Verdict: a chance arrangement magnified by wishful thinking.

Cannibalism

Even if Neanderthals did eat each other, this of itself need indicate nothing more than hunger or greed.

In a cave at Monte Circeo, in Italy, a Neanderthal skull was found in what was said to be a circle of stones, but, again, no photographs were taken before the skull was removed. Drawings made later by the person who found (and removed) the skull show a rough heap of stones rather than a regular circle, and nothing to suggest that the stones were deliberately arranged. The skull has no marks made by cutting tools, but appears to have been gnawed by a carnivore. Hyenas commonly carry animal skulls into their dens, and this is a more likely, if more prosaic, explanation of the presence of the skull. Verdict: a hyena settled on top of a rock fall to eat a grisly meal.

Neanderthal Burials

These are less easily dismissed. Certainly, some are doubtful, including the often quoted burial of a boy inside a circle of ibex horns at Teshik-Tash, in Uzbekistan. This in fact comprises a few bones (not the whole skeleton) of a 12-year-old Neanderthal boy found in close proximity to a few ibex horns. There is no evidence that the horns were ever in a circle, there is no sign of a grave pit, and we have already seen that hyenas commonly take skulls into their dens. Verdict: another hyena meal.

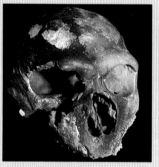

There are also strong doubts about the famous "flower burial" from Shanidar, in Iraq. Not only is no grave pit visible, but the cause of death was a large roof slab that fell and crushed the Neanderthal man beneath it. Only a concentration of flower pollen suggests ritual activity: the heaping of flowers on the corpse, a scene reconstructed in many textbooks and films. Given the complexities of cave deposits, however, the pollen could have got there in various ways—indeed, even during the archaeological excavation. Verdict: an unfortunate Neanderthal who stood in the wrong place at the wrong time.

But at least two burials do seem to stand up to scrutiny. A skeleton from La Chapelle-aux-Saints, in France, was found in a steep-sided

⬆ Kebara Cave, in Israel, has provided definite evidence of a Neanderthal burial. The grave pit is clearly visible, and must have been deliberately excavated, implying planned disposal of the corpse. However, most other finds of Neanderthals do not appear to result from deliberate burial.

◄ The hole in this Neanderthal skull found at Monte Circeo was probably caused by a hyena breaking into the skull and eating the brain.
CHRIS STRINGER/MUSEO NAZIONALE PREHISTORICO EO ETNOGRAFICO "L. PIGORINI", ROME

pit, and the findings were published in 1908. The pit seems too regular to be a natural depression into which the Neanderthal man simply crawled and died. It has been suggested that the hole may have been formed by floodwater, but it looks so square-cut that it appears to be a regular grave pit. The clearest grave pit found from this period is that in which a Neanderthal skeleton from Kebara, in Israel, was buried. This must have been deliberately dug. Verdict: these two Neanderthal men were buried, certainly, but does this prove that the Neanderthals had a religion or believed in an afterlife? It is not impossible that what we see is the simple disposal of dead bodies, and that nothing more complex than this was ever involved.

The Mousterian: Time of the Neanderthals

The Neanderthals were the first humans to really adapt to the cold northern climate. On the whole, their evolution took place during a warm period, the last interglacial. However, the classic tool technology of the Neanderthals—the Mousterian, named after the legendary rock shelter at Le Moustier, in the Dordogne—did not appear in Europe until the last Ice Age, about 70,000 years ago, although Mousterian-like industries were being used in the Middle East as early as about 120,000 years ago. They became an Ice Age people with all that this implied in terms of arctic survival and economic flexibility.

Like their predecessors, the Neanderthals roamed over extensive territories and used seasonal settlements during different times of the year. Presumably, big-game hunting (mainly deer and reindeer) played an increasingly important part in their subsistence. But above all, the cold climate forced people to adapt their diet to the cycle of the seasons, and the increasingly rich assemblages of different kinds of stone tools with different functions may be looked upon as a result of this. Storage of food was a vital necessity during parts of the year. Cave openings and rock shelters, so-called *abri*, were commonly used as dwellings, and although open-air settlements are known in many places, it is not unfounded to apply the term "cave people" to the Neanderthals.

About 130,000 years ago, the tool technology developed with great strides. For the first time, cores were preshaped in order to give the planned flake a certain look and size. This manufacturing process is called Levalloisian technology, after a site outside Paris. Furthermore, it was easier to make better use of the raw material, and several more flakes could be struck off from the same core. The top surface of the core was trimmed and shaped into a striking platform from which flakes were struck off. Owing to their appearance, the prepared cores have been named tortoise cores.

The new technique made possible the production of a series of new tool types with varying ranges of uses—particularly, different kinds of scrapers and points. During the Mousterian period, the technique was further refined and the new tools were equipped with effective and durable edges. The objects were sharpened by fine trimming, which created a toothed edge.

The Mousterian technology had a series of regional differences, where sets of tools varied greatly. Some experts have suggested that this shows that different European "Neanderthal cultures" lived side by side, whereas others suggest that the function of the tools had created the differences or simply that they were the result of a gradual, time-related change. In any case, the new tool

technology of the Neanderthals was more varied and functionally adapted than ever before. The Mousterian technique was a result of the Neanderthals' vital ability to meet and adjust to the demands of the environment.

As we have seen, there was great anatomical variation within the Neanderthal population. Remains of classic Neanderthals are limited to western Europe, while those of Southwest Asia show less extreme features. It is believed that this physical diversity was the result of climatic adaptations, since the European Neanderthals really were the only ones living in typically Ice Age surroundings. Supposed Neanderthal-like humans in Africa and Southeast Asia were very different, and the sites of Kabwe (formerly Broken Hill), in Zambia (the so-called "Rhodesian Man"), Hopefield (Saldanha), near Cape Town, in South Africa, and Ngandong, by the Solo River, in Java, have provided some of the fossils that were formerly thought to represent Afro-Asian parallels to the European Neanderthals. Kabwe and Saldanha, however, are now recognized as belonging to *Homo heidelbergensis*, while the Ngandong fossils are late survivors (100,000 years ago) of *Homo erectus*.

⬥ Making a Levalloisian flake: a suitable stone is trimmed on the edges and top surface, and a striking platform is then made in one end of the core. A large flake (right), the final product, is then struck off from the core (left).
ILLUSTRATIONS: KEN RINKEL

⬥ The classic Neanderthal rock shelter at Le Moustier, by the Vézère River, in the Dordogne, France, has given its name to the Mousterian period. A skeleton of a Neanderthal boy was unearthed here in 1908.

GÖRAN BURENHULT

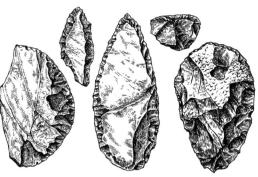

⬥ Examples of Mousterian points and scrapers. The Mousterian tool tradition is closely linked to the Neanderthals, being found at Neanderthal sites across Europe, western Asia, and northern Africa. Related technologies are found in Africa and in South and East Asia.
ILLUSTRATIONS: KEN RINKEL

It was thought for a long time that the Quaternary period was dominated by three or four distinct Ice Ages. Research in recent decades, however, has revealed a much more complex picture of climatic fluctuations through time. The left-hand side of the diagram shows global climatic change as revealed by deep-sea cores from the equatorial Pacific. By establishing the ratio between oxygen isotopes at different depths of such cores, it is possible to record the fluctuating global temperature. The traditional terminology used for the different glacials and interglacials is shown at right.

The remarkable circumstances surrounding the findings of the Ngandong, or Solo, humans have led to speculations about possible cannibalism. The 11 skulls found consisted only of braincases, with the rest of the head and face missing. As all the material was found within a limited area, the remains have been interpreted as leftovers from ritual feasting on human flesh. Also, the remains of some 20 individuals at Krapina, in Croatia—men, women, and children with their heads and bones smashed and split—have been interpreted as evidence that Neanderthals engaged in cannibalism, but other experts have called this evidence into question. If so, is there any other evidence that may strengthen the theory that Neanderthals were the first humans to perform rituals and have religious beliefs? The appearance of the first burials seems to point in that direction.

The Origins of Burial and Religious Belief?

Death is inescapable for all of us. The deposition of the mortal remains, in some way or another, is thus an action that is common to all human beings, in prehistory as well as in recent times. The appearance of the first burials shows that humans' ability to think in the abstract and to communicate orally had reached an advanced level. Whether a burial reflected notions of a "kingdom" of the dead or whether it was just a way to show regret at the loss of a family member, the burial ceremony reveals the presence of ritual conceptions and long-term thinking that previously had been impossible. Burial customs, such as sprinkling the dead with red ocher or depositing grave goods, bear witness to a world of magic thinking that lies behind the most definite of manifestations—that of dying. (See the feature *Was There a Neanderthal Religion?*)

It has long been accepted that Neanderthals buried their dead, and several important sites are known in Europe and Southwest Asia, most of them in caves. A teenage boy has been found in a pit at Le Moustier, in the Dordogne. His head rested on a collection of flint flakes and one arm was placed under his head, as if he were in a reclining position. Similar finds have been made in several other Neanderthal settlements in France—for example, at La Ferrassie and La Chapelle-aux-Saints. A small burial ground has been uncovered at La Ferrassie, where two grown-up individuals and four children had been buried in tightly placed pits. Many of the French burials had been sprinkled with red ocher, and large amounts of animal bones have been found in or nearby all of the graves.

On the western slopes of the Himalayas, a remarkable Neanderthal burial has been unearthed. At Teshik-Tash, in Uzbekistan, a young child had been buried together with the horns of six wild goats, which had been placed in a ring around the grave. Marks on the skeleton indicate that the flesh had been cut off before the body was buried, perhaps for ritual reasons. Other conspicuous burials have been found at Shanidar, in the Iraqi Zagros Mountains, where, according to the excavators, a 30-year-old man had been placed on a bed of flowers. Pollen analyses have shown the presence of yarrow (milfoil), horsetail, thistle, cornflower, grape hyacinth, and hollyhock, among other plants.

Lately, however, many experts have questioned the Neanderthal burials and the validity of the evidence. Excavations of Paleolithic sites are difficult enterprises, and the stratigraphy is generally hard to interpret. Later activities at the site, as well as falling debris, often make

Years ago	Climatic fluctuations ← Colder	Stages Warm / Cold	Traditional terminology		
			Central Europe	**Northern Europe**	**North America**
50,000			Würm	Weichsel	Wisconsin
100,000			Riss/Würm interglacial	Eemian interglacial	Sangamon interglacial
150,000			Riss	Saale	Illinoian
200,000					
250,000					
300,000					
350,000					
400,000			Mindel/Riss interglacial	Holstein interglacial	Yarmouth interglacial
450,000					
500,000					
550,000			Mindel	Elster	Kansan
600,000					
650,000					
700,000					

CURVE BASED ON DATA FROM SHACKLETON, N.J. AND OPDYKE, N.D. (1973): 'OXYGEN ISOTOPE AND PALAEOMAGNETIC STRATIGRAPHY OF EQUATORIAL PACIFIC CORE V28–238'. QUATERNARY RESEARCH 3, 39–55.

it impossible to determine what actually took place at the time of the depositing of the body. Some have even stated that there is, in fact, no evidence whatsoever that Neanderthals buried their dead and that the finds are the result of coincidences and later disturbances. Contrary to this, it may be said that there is no evidence that they didn't.

In all scientific debate it is necessary to question and to present new hypotheses to, in that way, be able to force new and even more critical examining of the materials in question and, as far as archaeology is concerned, in which context they were found. Obviously, archaeologists previously accepted uncritically many of the finds of Neanderthal skeletons as true burials, and these must therefore be re-examined. But it is also important to point out that we at present cannot dismiss the majority of them as nothing but coincidences. Perhaps the recently excavated Neanderthal burial in Kebara Cave on the slopes of Mount Carmel, in Israel, can bring this issue to

☝ Clusters of pollen found by the skeleton of this 30-year-old Neanderthal man in Shanidar Cave, in northern Iraq, have been interpreted by some as suggesting that he had been buried on a bed of flowers. Recently, however, others have questioned the validity of the evidence for a deliberate burial.

☚ The huge Shanidar Cave, in Kurdistan, in northernmost Iraq, has yielded Neanderthal finds dating from between 60,000 and 44,000 years ago. Nine Neanderthal individuals have been uncovered, among them the much debated burial of the 30-year-old man shown above, as well as bones of such animals as wild goats and boars.

a conclusion. It seems as if the burial structures, which are more distinct here than in any other Neanderthal site so far excavated, clearly indicate a deliberate burial.

Similar doubts about the ritual life of Neanderthals have been raised concerning findings from two other classic European sites: Regourdou, in the Dordogne, and Monte Circeo, south of Rome, in Italy. At Regourdou, a rectangular pit covered with a large stone slab was found which contained the skulls of at least 20 cave bears. A complete bear skeleton as well as an incomplete Neanderthal one was found nearby. This find has been

considered an example of a Neanderthal bear cult, a form of cult that has been practiced until recently by many arctic peoples. The circumstances surrounding the find are unclear, though, and today many experts feel dubious about this interpretation.

As far as the archaeological material is concerned, it is extremely difficult to interpret notions of the supernatural or the presence of magical or religious systems. In any case, however, it is no exaggeration to say that all these finds indicate that the Neanderthals developed complex ideological and social behavior which later on was also to become characteristic of modern humans.

DATING THE PAST

Colin Groves

Fossils that are more than a few tens of thousands of years old contain no material that can be dated directly. It is the deposits that contain them that are dated, not the fossils themselves. Dating methods can be broadly divided into absolute and relative methods.

Absolute Methods
URANIUM–LEAD DATING

Uranium is radioactive, which means that it decays, changing its atomic nucleus into other elements at a regular rate through a series (known as the U-series) and ending up as lead. The two main atomic forms (isotopes) of uranium, U_{235} and U_{238}, decay at different rates, through different intermediate stages, into different isotopes of lead. As we know what these rates of decay are (they do not change under conditions normally occurring on Earth), we can calculate how long ago it was since the decay began and thus the age of the deposit containing the uranium—including any fossils the deposit contains. The fact that the two isotopes have different decay series acts as an internal check on the date obtained, to make sure nothing has been lost or gained in the deposit since it was laid down. Uranium dating can be used to measure deposits as old as the Earth itself—4.5 billion years.

Particular parts of the decay series, such as that from uranium to thorium, can be used to date much shorter periods of time.

POTASSIUM–ARGON DATING

Many minerals in the Earth's crust contain the element potassium (K). A tiny proportion of all potassium consists of its radioisotope, potassium-40 (K_{40}). Like uranium, this decays at a known rate and becomes the gas argon (Ar).

When a volcano erupts, it spews forth molten lava, which includes potassium-containing minerals, and the argon that has

DAVID L. BRILL/© NATIONAL GEOGRAPHIC SOCIETY

been forming by decay of K_{40} is released into the atmosphere. As the lava cools, crystals are formed, and the argon that is formed subsequently is trapped in them. By measuring the relative proportions of K_{40} and argon in the crystals, we can work out how long ago the lava cooled—that is, when the volcanic eruption occurred. (There are ways of checking whether any argon has been lost from the crystals.) Lava flows are easy to date by this method.

Within a short time, volcanic lava and ash deposits start to erode. They are swept away by running water and deposited as sediments elsewhere, mixed in with sediments of different origin. Sediments containing material of recent volcanic origin are called tuffs. In a tectonically active area such as the East African

Rift Valley, the fossil-containing sediments are interspersed as layers with tuffs, and so we can calculate a series of dates at intervals throughout the formation. Like uranium-series dating, potassium–argon dating can be used for extremely ancient deposits as well as for some surprisingly young ones—provided that there has been volcanic activity in the region concerned.

RADIOCARBON DATING

This is one of the few methods based on the fossils themselves, but it can only be used over the past 50,000 years or so (70,000 years with the use of special techniques). Plants take in carbon from the atmosphere, and this carbon contains a tiny proportion of a radioisotope, C_{14} (formed in the atmosphere by cosmic radiation).

◄● Potassium–argon dating is still the most important method used to date the rock in which fossil hominids are found. Here, a geophysicist analyzes a rock sample to calculate the amount of radioactive potassium that has decayed into argon, and so the length of time that has elapsed since the volcanic eruption that produced the rock occurred.

Once the plant dies, it no longer takes in carbon, and so C_{14} is progressively lost from the remains. (It decays into nitrogen.) We can calculate the amount of C_{14} remaining, and thus the time that has elapsed since the plant died, but the decay rate is so rapid that all the C_{14} will be gone in a few tens of thousands of years.

The animals that eat the plants take in the plants' carbon, too, so their remains can also be dated in this way.

We now know that the amount of C_{14} in the atmosphere fluctuates, presumably in relation to the amount of cosmic radiation, so radiocarbon dates have to be calibrated against some known standard, such as annual growth rings in trees.

THERMOLUMINESCENCE DATING

When certain types of sediments are exposed to sunlight, or heated in some other way, they become bleached, and electrons are trapped. When the sediments are buried, the trapped electrons are progressively released. We can measure the light emitted by residual electrons, and so, when we have ascertained the original light dose, we can calculate the length of time that has elapsed since the sediments were first buried. Thermoluminescence (TL) dating covers the same time span as C_{14} dating (and more, as it can be used to date deposits more than 100,000 years old), so the two methods can be used to check each other. This method is now increasingly being used to date deposits in the formerly undatable range of 50,000 to 100,000 years.

A recently developed method, electron spin resonance (ESR), measures trapped electrons directly, and can be used to date biological materials such as tooth enamel.

FISSION-TRACK DATING

As well as undergoing radioactive decay, U_{235} sometimes undergoes spontaneous fission, and the subatomic particles emitted leave tracks through the mineral. These tracks can be revealed by etching with hydrofluoric acid and counted. As we know the rate at which fission occurs, we can calculate the time that has elapsed since the mineral was cooled and laid down. Volcanic glass yields excellent fission tracks, so this method can be used to cross-check potassium–argon dating.

Relative Methods
FAUNAL DATING

As new dating methods are discovered, relatively few sites remain that cannot be dated by one of the absolute methods. As far as human evolution is concerned, the only important sites that are still not directly datable are those on the highveldt in South Africa: Taung, Sterkfontein, Makapansgat, Swartkrans, and Kromdraai (although there has been a preliminary trial of ESR in the case of Sterkfontein). Here, faunal dating is used.

Long-lived species—for example, certain types of pigs, monkeys, and antelopes—have evolved in distinct stages. At some sites, such as Koobi Fora and Olduvai, in the East African Rift Valley, potassium–argon and fission-track methods can be used to date their remains, so that we know these species to have had characteristic shapes and measurements at certain dates. The animal fossils in sites such as Sterkfontein are then compared with fossils of the same species in the dated East African sites to determine their evolutionary stage. The limitation is, of course, that a more archaic stage in a species' evolution might have survived in South Africa when a more advanced form was already present in East Africa.

PALEOMAGNETISM

Another method is based on the fact that the Earth's magnetic field has swung back and forth during geological time. At present, it is centered on magnetic north, but before 700,000 years ago it was centered near the South Pole. A few hundred thousand years before that, it was north-centered again, and so on. A remnant magnetic orientation often remains in deposits, so a paleomagnetic column, showing the alternation between "normal" (north-pointing) and "reversed" (south-pointing), can be built up for some sites. This can then be compared with the standard column (based on the results of hundreds of magnetic determinations of levels of known date throughout the world); and other evidence—the presence of key fossils, or any stray absolute dates that have been made somewhere in the sequence—may help to line up, or "position", the magnetic reversals on the standard.

CHEMICAL METHODS

Chemical methods are sometimes used, as well. In many areas, the chemical composition of fossils changes; for example, the older a fossil is, the more fluorine it may contain. This method can only be used across very limited regions, where soil conditions do not vary much. Another method is based on the fact that a living organism's amino acids, the building blocks of proteins, rotate polarized light to the left. When the organism dies, polarization slowly alters until there are equal proportions of left-rotating and right-rotating amino acids. But the rate at which this occurs varies with temperature and, especially, humidity, so the method, which is known as amino acid racemization, can only be used under certain strict conditions (such as in sealed cave deposits).

↪ Over geologic time, the Earth's magnetic field has reversed itself many times. During long periods (chrons), the prevailing magnetism would be either normal or reversed, with shorter periods (subchrons) of the opposite magnetism. This chart shows in detail the paleomagnetic column for the last five million years.

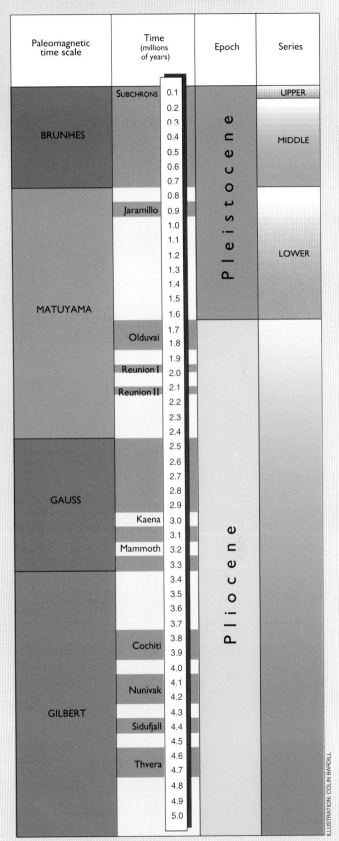

MODERN PEOPLE IN AFRICA AND EUROPE

200,000 YEARS AGO – 10,000 YEARS AGO

Out of Africa: Adapting to the Cold

GÖRAN BURENHULT

WHATEVER VIEW WE TAKE of the relationship between modern humans and Neanderthals, it is clear that *Homo sapiens sapiens* migrated into Europe about 40,000 years ago, carrying with them new technological and intellectual skills. There are significant differences between the tool technology of the Neanderthals in Europe during the Middle Paleolithic period, known as the Mousterian tradition, and that of the Upper Paleolithic period, known as the Aurignacian tradition. These changes can be directly linked to the arrival of modern humans in Europe.

One of the fundamental changes was that from flake tools to blade tools. Neanderthal scrapers are sidescrapers, having a retouched edge on one side of the flake, whereas the blade-scrapers that appeared in Europe during the Upper Paleolithic period are endscrapers. In addition, many new types of tools appeared, including burins and points of different kinds.

◄● Situated on the border between South Africa and Swaziland, Border Cave is one of a number of South African sites that have recently thrown new light on the origin of our species. Its oldest occupation layers date back to about 200,000 years ago.

⚑ An Aurignacian split-base spear-point from Gorge d'Enfer, in the Dordogne, France.
J. M. LABAT/AUSCAPE

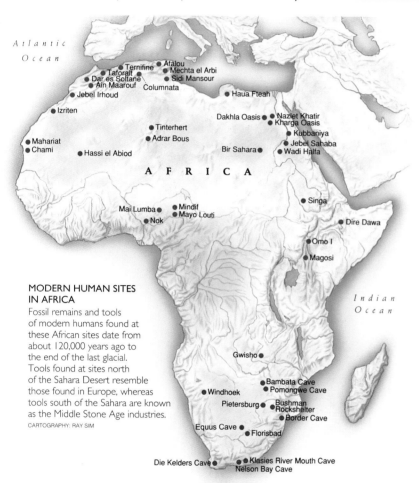

MODERN HUMAN SITES IN AFRICA

Fossil remains and tools of modern humans found at these African sites date from about 120,000 years ago to the end of the last glacial. Tools found at sites north of the Sahara Desert resemble those found in Europe, whereas tools south of the Sahara are known as the Middle Stone Age industries.

CARTOGRAPHY: RAY SIM

☞ Klasies River Mouth Cave, situated at the southernmost tip of Africa, has proved to be of immense importance to our understanding of the evolution of *Homo sapiens*. Fossil remains of modern humans found here date to between 115,000 and 80,000 years ago, and from the fossil evidence of mussels, limpets, and seals, we know that marine foods were important to the early modern humans at this site.

H.J. DEACON

☚ Ocean view at the mouth of the Klasies River. Evidently, the sea provided a considerable part of the food supply for the early modern humans at this site.

While the Neanderthals almost never fashioned their tools from antler, bone, or ivory, these new raw materials formed an important part of the tool traditions during this period. They were shaped and polished into valuable articles for everyday use, as well as beautifully decorated works of art and adornments. And soon after these new types of tools were introduced, regional differences developed in the way they were used and decorated, in sharp contrast to the conservative and homogeneous tool technology of the Neanderthals.

But the most obvious differences between modern humans and Neanderthals are much more profound than the way they made and used tools. American anthropologist Richard Klein summarizes them as follows: "Initially, their behavioral capabilities differed little from those of the Neanderthals, but eventually, perhaps because of a neurological change that is not detectable in the fossil record, they developed a capacity for culture that gave them a clear adaptive advantage over the Neanderthals and all other nonmodern people." In other words,

they developed new, more flexible forms of social organization. They built new types of settlements, developed a rich ceremonial and ritual life, and began to express themselves through the medium of art. Richard Klein adds: "The result was that they spread throughout the world, physically replacing the nonmoderns, of whom the last to succumb were perhaps the Neanderthals of western Europe." The fact that these people simultaneously and rapidly replaced the Neanderthals all over Europe indicates, according to Klein, that we are dealing with a rapidly expanding population that can only be explained if modern humans migrated to Europe from elsewhere.

This theory is strongly supported by new finds in South Africa. Five notable sites—Klasies River Mouth Cave, Border Cave, Equus Cave, Florisbad, and Die Kelders Cave—have yielded evidence that is vital to our understanding of the origins of modern humans. Richard Klein considers Klasies River Mouth Cave, about 160 kilometers (100 miles) east of Cape Town, to be the most significant of these sites. Large numbers of fossilized human bones have been found there, some between 115,000 and 80,000 years old, and they have a strikingly modern appearance. These relatively modern humans, therefore, lived in Africa at the same time as the Neanderthals flourished in Europe. Although the differences in tool technology between the Middle and Upper Paleolithic periods were as great in Africa as they were in Europe, the humans who inhabited South Africa during the Middle Paleolithic period looked much more like modern humans than the European Neanderthals did.

The South African finds indicate that modern humans evolved in Africa over a very long period of time, perhaps more than 200,000 years. To the older and more archaic stage of this course of events belongs, for example, the find of "Rhodesia Man" (*Homo heidelbergensis*) from Kabwe (formerly Broken Hill), in Zambia, while the above-mentioned South African fossils represent a more advanced stage of human evolution. But if the cradle of *Homo sapiens* is to be found in Africa, who was the ancestor? *Homo erectus*? Many experts don't think so, suggesting that another, as yet unclassified, human species existed in Africa. Others are of the view that this species was the 1.5 million-year-old Turkana Newcomer, *Homo ergaster*.

The evolutionary process was probably slow and steady. The African savanna landscape probably provided ideal conditions for humans, and the tropical environment offered plentiful supplies of good-quality food. This might have brought humans together to live in larger groups, with a more selective diet.

These modern human beings, according to Richard Klein, did not migrate outside Africa until fairly late, and they subsequently replaced other,

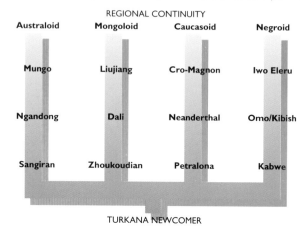

REGIONAL CONTINUITY

Australoid	Mongoloid	Caucasoid	Negroid
Mungo	Liujiang	Cro-Magnon	Iwo Eleru
Ngandong	Dali	Neanderthal	Omo/Kibish
Sangiran	Zhoukoudian	Petralona	Kabwe

TURKANA NEWCOMER

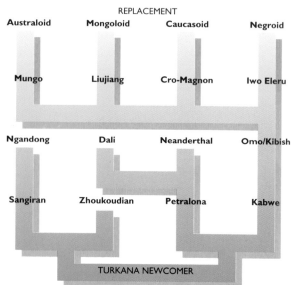

REPLACEMENT

Australoid	Mongoloid	Caucasoid	Negroid
Mungo	Liujiang	Cro-Magnon	Iwo Eleru
Ngandong	Dali	Neanderthal	Omo/Kibish
Sangiran	Zhoukoudian	Petralona	Kabwe

TURKANA NEWCOMER

🔥 Two main theories have been put forward to explain the origin of our own species: regional continuity (the candelabra model) and replacement (the Noah's Ark model). The latter is supported by the finds from Klasies River and other sites in southern Africa, as well as recent DNA studies.

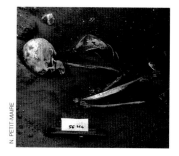

N. PETIT-MAIRE

🔥 Burial found at the site of Hassi el Abiod, in Mali. This and several other North African sites have yielded remains of Cro-Magnon-like humans, and it has been suggested that the first modern Europeans originated here.

more archaic human types all over the so-called Old World. Anthropologist William Howells has named this the "Noah's Ark" hypothesis, because it implies that *Homo sapiens sapiens* originated in one single area of Africa. The opposing, more traditional view of human development is called the "candelabra" model. (These models are also known as the replacement theory and the regional continuity theory, respectively.)

Recently, the replacement theory has been strongly supported by modern genetic research, which has been able to tell us for how long the various human races have been separated from each other and how they are mutually related. Using the mitochondrial DNA technique (mt DNA), Allan Wilson and Mark Stoneking, of the University of California, at Berkeley, and Rebecca Cann, of the University of Hawaii, have concluded that all now-living humans are descended from a common first mother in South Africa who lived about 200,000 years ago. This is known as the "Eve" theory. It has been calculated that the descendants in the female line of all other mothers became extinct over the course of 50,000 generations, leaving only one set of matrilineal descendants. These results are consistent with the archaeological finds at such sites as Klasies River Mouth Cave. The same DNA technique shows that as modern humans spread across the globe, they rarely interbred with existing, but more archaic, human beings, such as the Neanderthals.

The "Eve" theory has not remained unchallenged, of course, but most evidence does indicate that modern humans spread rapidly from Africa to the rest of the world. If Africa is indeed the original home of modern humans, how and why did they spread into Europe and Asia? Finds from the caves of Mount Carmel, in present-day Israel, indicate that this migration occurred somewhat before 100,000 years ago. The only previous obstacle had been the Sahara Desert, but higher rainfall during this period transformed it into an area of verdant plains, with lakes and streams. A plentiful supply

of game and edible plants would have made northern migration not just possible but very attractive. Southwest Asia was a natural first stopping place, and this explains the Mount Carmel finds. But during the last Ice Age, which began about 75,000 years ago, this Levantine area became much drier. Food would have become scarce, and this may well have forced the humans who had settled there further north, towards the richer tundra and steppe regions of Europe. At the same time, modern humans were also spreading across Asia.

During the Middle and Upper Paleolithic periods, two tool traditions that are quite different in a number of important respects developed in North Africa and the part of Africa south of the Sahara Desert. That of the North African region, logically enough, had much in common with the tool tradition of Europe and Southwest Asia and developed about the same time. For example, excavations in Haua Fteah Cave, in Cyrenaica, northern Libya, show that the tool technology characteristic of the Upper Paleolithic period began there, as in Europe, about 40,000 years ago. This North African culture is known as the Aterian culture, after the site of Bir el Ater, in Tunisia. The Aterian culture extended from Libya in the east to the Atlantic coast in the west and as far south as the Lake Chad basin. A number of important sites in the region, including Mechta el Arbi, in Algeria, and Dar es Soltan, in Morocco, have yielded bones of Cro-Magnon-like humans.

Paleobotanical research at Tihodaine, in Algeria, among other places, has shown that at this time the North African region was steppe-like, with patches of forest near lakes. The area teemed with such animals as elephants, buffaloes, rhinoceroses,

GÖRAN BURENHULT

◄● Lakes, streams, and verdant plains once characterized what is now the Sahara Desert, making it an ideal area for human habitation. What is not generally known is that the Sahara still has large amounts of subsoil water, which sometimes reaches the surface in the form of so-called gueltas, like this one at Tinterhert, in Tassili n'Ajjer, southern Algeria.

♀ This huge carving showing the North African aurochs (*Bubalus antiquus*) at Tinterhert, at the foot of Jebel Efehi, in Tassili n'Ajjer, southern Algeria, measures about 5 meters (16 feet) in length and is filled with carved lines, spirals, and circles. Belonging to the so-called "Bubalus period", it represents the earliest art in the Sahara. It may be as old as 12,000 years.

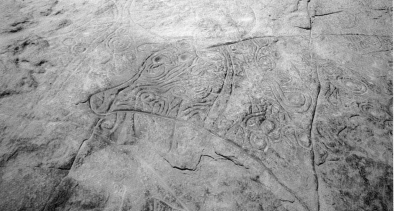

GÖRAN BURENHULT

and antelopes. Aterian people were the first to make points with tangs—that is, a retouched area at the base of the point to which a handle could be attached. These spear-like weapons were an important technological innovation, making it possible to bring down animals from a distance.

For natural reasons, the climatic and environmental changes that occurred at the end of the last Ice Age were much less dramatic in North Africa than in Europe. About 20,000 years ago, the Aterian tradition was replaced by a series of so-called epipaleolithic cultures (which means simply that they were related to Paleolithic cultures and existed around the same time). Finds of microliths —that is, very small points, edges, and barbs of flint—indicate that these people developed the bow and arrow. This was their only technological innovation of note, but it was a major one. Among the most important of these groups were the Quadan people of Upper Egypt, who existed between about 13,000 and 11,000 BC. They lived by hunting and fishing and also gathered seeds from wild grasses and other plants, and were among the few peoples of the Upper Paleolithic period who used grinding stones.

In the part of Africa south of the Sahara Desert, people were using much the same tools between 200,000 and 40,000 years ago, at much the same periods, as they were in Europe. In other words, the Middle Paleolithic period—in Africa, the Middle Stone Age—corresponds fairly closely in both these parts of the world. The Upper

Paleolithic, or Late Stone Age, differs markedly from the previous period, but finds from 40,000 to 20,000 years ago are few. More recent finds, dating from 20,000 years ago or less, are much more common, and these show that people were hunting big game, especially buffalo and wild pig, to a greater extent than in earlier times and that scavenging had become much less important. Fishing had also become very important, which it had not been during the Middle Paleolithic. The appearance of microliths indicates that bows and arrows were in use, and from finds of microliths suitable for mounting in rows on sickles made of bone, antler, or wood, we know that plant gathering was also becoming more important.

ICE THROUGH THE AGES

BJÖRN E. BERGLUND AND SVANTE BJÖRCK

Lⁿ ONGER OR SHORTER PERIODS of glaciation are a natural part of our planet's history. The most recent Ice Age epoch, called the Pleistocene, began about 2.5 million years ago. During the Pleistocene, there was a fluctuating pattern of cold, glacial periods, known as glacials, interrupted by warm periods, known as interglacials. The impetus behind these ice-sheet rhythms appears to have been the three solar insolation cycles, governed by the Earth's tilting and its orbit around the sun.

⏚ This East Greenland landscape shows an arctic environment with inland ice in the background much as we would imagine the situation to have been in mid-latitude and high-latitude parts of the world 18,000 years ago.

Paleotemperatures and paleo-ice volumes, deduced from oxygen isotope records in deep-sea cores, reveal that the first 1.8 million years of the Pleistocene were characterized by glacial–interglacial cycles of about 41,000 years. During the last 700,000 years, the dominant cycle has been about 100,000 years, including interglacials lasting 10,000 to 15,000 years. The most recent Ice Age began about 115,000 years ago and ended about 10,000 years ago, when the present interglacial was initiated. It was in this period that *Homo sapiens*, or modern human beings, developed. They had to adapt to quite rapid climatic changes which had a huge impact on the geological and other features of this planet.

Forty thousand years ago, we were in a milder part of the last glacial period. But Europe had already experienced three cold spells since the last

interglacial, and the world looked very different from today. The sea level was 50 meters (nearly 200 feet) lower, the mountainous parts of North America and Eurasia were glaciated and surrounded by windswept tundras, and the vegetation and climate zones were much farther south than they now are. And the Big Chill was still to come!

The Big Chill

Twenty-five thousand years ago, the ice caps started to accumulate so much snow that large parts of northwest Europe, North America, and alpine areas such as the Andes, the Alps, and parts of central Asia gradually disappeared under huge sheets of ice. These continental ice sheets reached their greatest extent 20,000 years ago, when the sea level dropped to 120 meters (400 feet) below the present level and parts of today's continental shelf areas were dry land. Land bridges were formed in many areas where today there are sounds, including the English Channel, Bering Strait, and some of the sounds between Southeast Asia and Australia.

Most of Europe that was not actually under ice was virtually barren, with only tundra or steppe vegetation, and exposed to wind and cold. The average temperature was about 8 degrees Celsius (14 degrees Fahrenheit) lower than today. Trees

⊙ Global climate curves for the last 30,000, 150,000, and 900,000 years. Curves **a** and **b** are based on changes in oxygen isotopes in deep-sea sediments (the dotted line indicating where information is uncertain), and curve **c** on pollen data and alpine glacier variations.

FROM WEBB, T. III 1990: "THE SPECTRUM OF TEMPORAL CLIMATIC VARIABILITY: CURRENT ESTIMATES AND THE NEED FOR GLOBAL AND REGIONAL TIME SERIES". IN BRADLEY, R.S. (ED.): *GLOBAL CHANGES OF THE PAST*. UCAR/OIES, BOULDER, COLORADO, 61– 81.

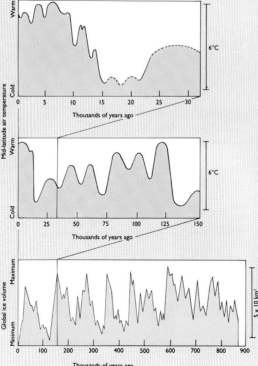

⏚ Changes in the position of the oceanic polar front between 20,000 and 9,000 years ago.

FROM RUDDIMAN, W.F. AND MCINTYRE, A. 1981: "THE NORTH ATLANTIC OCEAN DURING THE LAST DEGLACIATION". *PALAEOGEOGRAPHY* 35, 145–214.

**VEGETATION
18,000 YEARS AGO**

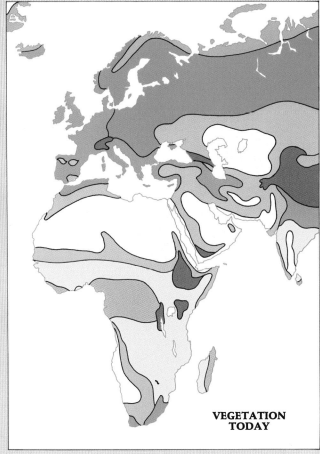

**VEGETATION
TODAY**

and woods were restricted to the Mediterranean peninsulas and some sheltered mountain areas. The tundra zone, however, was much narrower on the North American continent than in Europe, and from low lake levels and fossil sand dunes we know that low-latitude and mid-latitude areas were much drier than they now are. With no Indian monsoon, Southeast Asia was generally drier. In tropical regions, lower temperatures meant that mountain tree-belts grew between 1,000 and 2,000 meters (3,000 and 7,000 feet) lower than they do today.

The Start of the Thaw

About 15,000 years ago, temperatures began to rise throughout the globe. The melting ice caused the oceans to expand, drowning former land bridges. Forests grew in areas that had been tundra—earlier in North America than in Europe—and the highly productive grasslands and half-open woodlands that developed supported a wide range of animals. In low latitudes, such as in North Africa, the climate became moister. Here, former deserts changed into savannas and woodlands, not only supporting a diverse range of plants and animals but also being very favorable for humans.

A Mini Ice Age

About 11,000 years ago, the solar insolation reached a peak in the temperate regions, and a new interglacial was in sight. But in Europe and parts of North America, a glacial climate suddenly took hold. During this so-called Younger Dryas event, which lasted about 500 years, the North Atlantic polar front migrated from Iceland to the Bay of Biscay; summer temperatures dropped by 5 to 10 degrees Celsius (9 to 18 degrees Fahrenheit); the ice sheets that had started to melt began to increase and advance; the tundra and permafrost extended once again; and many animals and plants were forced southward.

This rather enigmatic period ended almost as abruptly as it began, about 10,000 years ago. Its ending marks the division between the Pleistocene and Holocene eras. With the start of this new interglacial, vegetation once again spread to the north. At high latitudes, this meant a change from glacial and periglacial tundra to temperate woodlands, while at low latitudes, it meant a change from arid desert steppe to humid, tropical woodlands. It was a period of dramatic environmental changes to which humans had to adapt.

◑Vegetation and climate zones in Europe and Africa 18,000 years ago (left) and today (right).

BASED ON LILJEQUIST, G.H. 1970: *KLIMATOLOGI* (GENERALSTABENS LITOGRAFISKA ANSTALT, STOCKHOLM), AND MCINTYRE ET AL. 1976, IN *GEOLOGICAL SOCIETY OF AMERICA MEMOIR* 145 (BOULDER, COLORADO).

☐ Humid tropical: rainforests
☐ Tropical wet-dry: savannas
☐ Arid: deserts
☐ Semi-arid and dry-continental: steppes
☐ Humid, warm temperature: evergreen and deciduous forests
☐ Humid, cold temperature: coniferous forests
☐ Mountains
☐ Polar: tundra
☐ Polar: inland ice

CARTOGRAPHY RAY SIM

• Settlement sites
• Burial sites

Sites shown on map:
Sungir, Robin Hood's Cave, Pin Hole, Paviland, Gough's Cave, Kent's Cavern, Halling, Fonds-de-Forêt, Hengistbury Head, Spy, Obercassel, Gönnersdorf, Lommersum, Engis, Pincevent, Entzheim, Klause, Vogelherd, Brno, Kulna, Prědmostí, Arcy-sur-Cure, Brillenhöhle, Dolní Věstonice, Pavlov, Petersfels, Willendorf, Châtelperron, St Germain, Solutré, Le Rond du Barry, Les Hoteaux, Camargo, El Castillo, Bruniquel, Le Figuier, Arene Candide, Duruthy, Grimaldi, Pushkari, Mezin, Kostenki, Mezhirich, Molodova, Escoural, Paglicci, Parpalló, Barranc Blanc, Romanelli, San Teodoro

UPPER PALEOLITHIC BURIALS AND SETTLEMENTS IN EUROPE

Major Upper Paleolithic settlement and burial sites in Europe. The Dordogne region in France is shown in the detail. Coastlines and the extent of the ice sheet as they were at the peak of the last glacial, some 18,000 years ago, are indicated.

Inset sites: Le Fourneau du Diable, Laugerie-Haute, Chancelade, La Madeleine, Solvieux, Cro-Magnon, Font Robert, La Gravette, Laugerie-Basse, Le Cap Blanc, Combe Capelle, Abri Pataud

Europe—The Backwater Country

These new theories about the origins of modern humans have changed the way we look at Europe in the context of evolution. Once considered a center of physical and cultural development, it must now be regarded as a backwater, a marginal, stagnating region without further importance.

The classic finds of human fossils dating from the interglacial period that occurred between 300,000 and 200,000 years ago, at Swanscombe, in England, and Steinheim, in Germany, have recently been supplemented by new finds. These include the Petralona skull from Greece, dated to between 400,000 and 300,000 years ago, and the Arago skull from the French Pyrenees, which is about 200,000 years old. All are now classified, along with their African contemporaries, as *Homo heidelbergensis*. Although the earlier finds were considered to be the ancestors of modern humans and were called "pre-*sapiens*", these new finds indicate that they are most likely the ancestors of the European Neanderthals. It was these "pre-*sapiens*" finds that provided the framework of the traditional "candelabra" model of human evolution.

When *Homo sapiens sapiens* appeared in Europe about 40,000 years ago, during the last glacial,

they did so in the form of the Cro-Magnon people, who were named after a site in Les Eyzies, in the Dordogne, in France. They found the climate considerably harsher than the North African one they had come from, but, gradually, they adapted. Little by little their skin color became lighter to facilitate the absorption of the necessary vitamin D from the weak sunshine of the north. The arctic climate meant totally different requirements for human survival.

At that time, Europe was very different from the continent of today. The whole Scandinavian peninsula, as well as large parts of northern Germany, England, and Ireland, was covered with ice sheets a kilometer (3,000 feet) thick. As a result, the sea level was much lower than it is today. South of the ice edge lay widespread tundra plains with a rich variety of animals, including reindeer, horses, aurochs, bison, deer, mammoths, and rhinoceroses. Lions, leopards, and wolves competed with humans for the game. England and Ireland were part of the continental landmass, and large parts of the Bay of Biscay and the North Sea were drained. The climate was more hospitable in southern France and the Iberian

peninsula, with summer temperatures close to 15 degrees Celsius (59 degrees Fahrenheit). Here, food was more varied and plentiful, with a range of plant foods as well as fish and other marine foods.

The remains of Neanderthal-like individuals excavated at Hahnöfersand, near Hamburg, in Germany, and St Césaire, in France, may indicate that surviving Neanderthals lived side by side with the new immigrants. The fossils at both these sites have been dated to 36,000 years ago, and thus postdate the appearance of *Homo sapiens sapiens* in Europe. Neanderthals and modern humans may have interbred in some places, and so the original population may have been assimilated to some extent. But basically the newcomers took over completely. Time simply did not allow for any evolution from Neanderthals to *Homo sapiens sapiens*, since the physical differences were too great. As Richard Klein says, "compared to their antecedents, Upper Paleolithic people were remarkably innovative and inventive, and it is this characteristic more than any other that is their hallmark".

Tools and Traditions

The Upper Paleolithic period was a time of intense development and innovation. The Cro-Magnon people made many new tools, with a wide range of quite specialized uses. In contrast to the Neanderthals, the Cro-Magnon had a clear concept of style, of what the "ideal tool" should look like. A wide range of scrapers, burins, spear-points, and knives appeared, all made of flint, using the new blade technology. Styles varied according to function, region, period, and, presumably, social conditions.

For the first time, bone, antler, and ivory were widely used to make everyday articles as well as ceremonial objects and symbols of status. The latter were often decorated with elegantly carved patterns or shaped like animals. Many specialized kinds of burins have been found, indicating that these people enjoyed working with these new plastic, organic raw materials. By carving a deep incision on each side

of an animal bone, they split it into two halves to provide the raw material for beautifully worked bone tools such as harpoons, fish spears, points, and adornments. Needles have also been discovered, indicating that the Cro-Magnon people were the first to sew clothes and tents, of animal hides. Stag antlers were shaped into efficient spear-throwers, the advanced weapon of the age.

When the Paleolithic period was first studied, all these new tools were grouped chronologically and geographically within a series of archaeological periods. We still use these classifications to identify stages within the Upper Paleolithic period. Because most of the research was carried out in France, these

phases were named after important French sites. Their relationship, however, is only partly understood. Some coexisted, and it is reasonable to assume that different styles resulted as much from different regional traditions as from time-bound evolution.

The first appearance of Upper Paleolithic technology in Europe can be linked to two cultural phases, the Aurignacian and Chatelperronian, named after the sites of Aurignac and Châtelperron. Both existed in different regions between 35,000 and 30,000 years ago. The Aurignacian tradition dominated much of western and southern Europe.

◄● Neanderthal skull from La Ferrassie, in the Dordogne, France (left), compared to the skull of an anatomically modern human found at Cro-Magnon, in the same area. Neanderthal skulls are characterized by a receding forehead, a long, low braincase, and heavy brow ridges.
JOHN READER/SCIENCE PHOTO LIBRARY/THE PHOTO LIBRARY

◄● Barbed harpoons of bone became one of the characteristic tools of the Magdalenian phase, towards the end of the Upper Paleolithic period. A series of different types indicates that they were developed for highly specialized purposes.
DAVID L. BRILL, © 1985

◑ Typical of the Solutrean phase, this beautifully worked spear-point of flint, in the shape of a laurel leaf, was found in the cave of Placard, at Vilhonneur, in Charente, France.
J. M. LABAT/AUSCAPE

ANIMALS OF ICE AGE EUROPE

RONNIE LILJEGREN

DURING THE LAST GLACIATION, middle Europe—from the Atlantic coastal fringes to the Urals—formed part of an extensive steppe tundra commonly known as the mammoth steppe. This steppe stretched across Asia to the Pacific, and was at times even connected with the North American steppes via the land bridge of Beringia. The boundaries of the steppe shifted periodically with climatic changes, but its central area remained the same throughout the last glacial. The steppe had a cold, dry climate, often with strong winds, and a maximum summer temperature of 15 degrees Celsius (59 degrees Fahrenheit).

Different soils and varying exposure to wind, sun, and water produced a range of local environments, which supported many species of animals. Grasses, sedges, wormwoods, and other resistant species

The woolly mammoth (*Mammuthus primigenius*), once perhaps the commonest animal of the steppe, could stand as high as 3 meters (10 feet) at the shoulder but was usually a little smaller. It disappeared from Europe at the end of the last glacial, although it may have survived for another thousand years in arctic Asia.

The cave bear (*Ursus spelaeus*) was common during the early phase of the last glacial but disappeared towards the final phase. About the size of the present-day brown bear of Alaska, it was almost exclusively vegetarian. The remains of thousands of these bears have been found in European caves.

The wild horse (*Equus ferus*) was quite small, having a shoulder height of 115 to 145 centimeters (47 to 57 inches). A common inhabitant of the steppe, especially during the later part of the last glacial, it was heavily hunted by humans. Despite this, it survived in eastern Europe and Asia until quite recently.

The wolf (*Canis lupus*) is a successful survivor and can still be found in some of the wilder parts of Europe, as well as in Asia and North America.

The cave lion (*Panthera leo spelaea*) was about a third bigger than African lions but was probably closely related to them. Its relationship to more recent lions in Asia and the Balkans, however, is unknown. It disappeared from Europe at the end of the last glacial.

The wolverine (*Gulo gulo*) was considerably larger than present-day specimens and was found only in small numbers on the steppe. Today it inhabits the northern parts of Europe, Asia, and North America.

The willow grouse (*Lagopus lagopus*) is known from Pleistocene deposits and still exists. Fossil bird bones are rare but include many species.

Wild horse

Wolf

Cave lion

Woolly mammoth

Wolverine

Cave bear

Willow grouse

PETER SCHOUTEN 92

provided irregular cover. There were few trees, but woods of pine, spruce, juniper, and birch grew in sheltered areas.

With the end of the glacial, about 10,000 years ago, the climate rapidly became warmer and wooded areas increased. Some animals adapted to the new conditions or migrated to other areas, but many others died out. Many species disappeared earlier, in the later stages of the glacial. Such extinctions were even more marked elsewhere, notably in the Americas.

No evidence exists for a similar pattern of extinctions from previous glacials, and no one theory has yet emerged that satisfactorily explains it. Humans alone could not have caused these extinctions on such a vast scale. Nor is it likely that so many species simply failed to adapt to the new conditions, given that they appear to have survived similar changes following previous glacials. Many other theories founder on misinterpretations of fossil evidence.

The reasons for these extinctions remain mysterious. We can only speculate that they were caused by some as yet unknown combination of factors, including climatic change and human activity.

Steppe bison
Reindeer
Musk ox
Woolly rhinoceros
Cave hyena
Irish elk (giant deer)
Suslik
Saiga antelope

ILLUSTRATION: PETER SCHOUTEN

The steppe bison (*Bison priscus*), once common, became extinct at the end of the last glacial. A powerful animal, it was about 3 meters (10 feet) long and stood more than 2 meters (6 feet) at the shoulder. Its relationship to the modern European bison is unclear.

The reindeer (*Rangifer tarandus*) was one of the commonest animals of the steppe, especially during the later phase of the last glacial. It is today found in northern Europe and Asia.

The musk ox (*Ovibos moscatus*) was another characteristic inhabitant of the steppe. It disappeared from Europe at the end of the last glacial and is today found only in Canada and Greenland.

The woolly rhinoceros (*Coelodonta antiquitatis*) disappeared about 12,000 years ago. It had two very prominent nose horns.

The cave hyena (*Crocuta crocuta spelaea*) was probably the same species as the present-day spotted hyena of Africa but was considerably larger. It disappeared from Europe towards the end of the last glacial.

The Irish elk (*Megaloceros giganteus*), also known as the giant deer, was almost the size of the American moose. Its huge antlers probably served both to signal dominance to males and to attract females. It disappeared at the end of the last glacial.

The suslik (*Citellus citellus*), a type of ground squirrel, favored loess areas of the steppe. It is now found in eastern central Europe.

The saiga antelope (*Saiga tartarica*) was another characteristic animal of the steppe. It now inhabits southern Russia and the Asian steppes.

This was the culture of the Cro-Magnon people, and most finds of human fossils, including burials, date from this phase. The more local Chatelperronian tradition is also linked with modern humans, with the exception of one Neanderthal skull dating from the early Chatelperronian phase found at St Césaire. As noted previously, this shows that Neanderthals lived side by side with the Cro-Magnon for a time. It also shows that, at least to some extent, they adopted their technology.

About 27,000 years ago, the Gravettian tradition appeared (named after the site of La Gravette), followed by the Solutrean (named after the site of Solutré). The Gravettian is characterized above all by the emergence of artistic expression, particularly in the form of small, stylized female figures known as Venus figurines. When they arrived in Europe, the people of the Aurignacian culture had already developed the ability to express themselves symbolically through the medium of art. Sexual symbolism was dominant, in the form of images of vulvas, but the elegant Venus figurines, with their exaggeratedly swelling breasts and buttocks, strongly indicate that ritual and ceremonial systems were becoming established over vast distances. Very similar figurines appear south of the ice edge throughout a continuous area extending from the Atlantic coast in the west to Siberia in the east. For the first time, we can see that people had a need to be in regular contact with other groups over extensive areas. Exotic raw materials were transported and interchanged all over Europe, particularly shells from the Mediterranean and the Atlantic, as well as amber. Everything indicates that recurrent meetings with other groups played an increasingly important role in the social system.

In this connection, a series of important sites stands out as being particularly interesting. At Dolní Věstonice, in the Czech Republic, a couple

↥ Well-preserved burials unearthed at Dolní Věstonice, in Moravia, in the Czech Republic. Two of the skulls were adorned with ivory beads as well as teeth of wolf and arctic fox. The left-hand skeleton reaches toward red ocher on the ground.

↩ Dolní Věstonice, in Moravia, in the Czech Republic, is one of the most famous and important Upper Paleolithic sites. Excavations have revealed the remains of several huts dating back to about 28,000 years ago, one of which contained an oven in which clay figurines had been fired.

🔥 Reconstruction of a mammoth bone dwelling excavated at Pushkari, in Ukraine. It measured 12 by 4.5 meters (40 by 15 feet), and consisted of three circular huts joined together.
ILLUSTRATION: STEVE TREVASKIS

of extensive open-air settlements dated to about 27,000 years ago have been excavated. People of this area lived in pit houses, the floor countersunk a meter (about 3 feet) into the ground to facilitate sealing between the roof and the floor against the winter storms. The walls were built of wooden posts and covered with animal hides. The constant need of fire required large amounts of solid fuel, and since wood was scarce, mammoth bones were used instead. It has been estimated that at least 100 to 125 people lived in one of these settlements.

A similar series of settlements and gathering places dating from about 25,000 years ago has been excavated at Kostenki, in Russia, on the shores of the River Don. With no wood available, the houses were built entirely of mammoth bones—a spectacular sight indeed. The ground plan is difficult to interpret but seems to indicate that the houses were longhouses about 12 meters (40 feet) long.

The most important region during the Upper Paleolithic period was, however, southern France. Although traces of open-air settlements have been found in this region, most people lived under the protection of the natural rock shelters, or *abri*, that are so characteristic of this limestone area.

◀ Unearthing mammoth bones at Kostenki, near Voronesh, in Russia. About 20 Upper Paleolithic sites have been discovered in this area, and several huts, as well as numerous art objects, have been found. Kostenki has yielded more Venus figurines than any other site in Europe.

UPPER PALEOLITHIC CULTURAL TRADITIONS OF EUROPE

YEARS AGO	CLIMATE	CULTURES	MAJOR SITES
10,000	End of last glaciation		
15,000	Increasingly warmer after 14,000	**MAGDALENIAN** Peak of cave art, with polychrome paintings. Skillful bone and antler work, including harpoons and spear-throwers. Highly specialized burins.	SEGEBRO FINJA LE MAS D'AZIL MEIENDORF MEZHIRICH SOLUTRÉ LA MADELEINE
20,000	Peak of last glaciation: very cold	**SOLUTREAN** Heat treatment of raw material. Leaf-shaped spear-points. Pressure flaking technique.	
25,000	Increasing cold	**GRAVETTIAN** Smaller, more delicate backed blades. Venus figurines. Earliest cave art from about 24,000 years ago. Strong regional variation among the cultural traditions of central Europe.	SUNGIR KOSTENKI DOLNÍ VĚSTONICE WILLENDORF
30,000	Somewhat warmer	**AURIGNACIAN** Earliest blade technology. Bone points with split base for hafting. Sharpened backed knives and blades. Burins. Earliest art.	GRIMALDI
35,000	Cold	**CHATELPERRONIAN** Earliest blade technology. Bone points with split base for hafting. Curved, backed blade points. **MOUSTERIAN** Surviving late Middle Paleolithic (Levalloisian/Mousterian) tradition, with flake technology. Retouched sidescrapers.	ST CÉSAIRE HAHNÖFERSAND CRO-MAGNON
40,000			

Hunters of the North: The Magdalenian Period

About 18,000 years ago, the Solutrean tradition was swept away by the wave of technological, intellectual, and cultural developments that characterize the Magdalenian tradition. Named after the famous *abri* settlement of La Madeleine, on the shores of the Vézère River, close to Les Eyzies, in the Dordogne, the Magdalenian is the most intense period of change in the whole of the Upper Paleolithic period. It was to last until about 10,000 years ago.

The people who ushered in this new phase had adapted perfectly to their Ice Age environment. Over a period of 8,000 years, both craftsmanship, in the form of artifacts made of bone, antler, and flint, and art, in the form of portable art objects and cave art, reached a peak. More than 80 percent of known cave art was created between 15,000 and 12,000 years ago—during the latter part of the Magdalenian phase.

The fact that gathering places were becoming more important is also very evident in this region. Four settlements in the Dordogne, including La Madeleine, have yielded about 80 percent of all the known portable art from the Magdalenian phase in this region. Many of the large caves containing paintings and carvings, such as Lascaux, Pech-Merle, and Niaux, in France, and Altamira, in Spain, were probably used as communal ceremonial places.

The site that has most to tell us about social organization at the end of the last Ice Age is the enormous cave of Le Mas d'Azil, in the Pyrenees. It was used seasonally as a meeting place for neighboring groups of people from a very wide area. As deep as a 20-storied building, the thick occupation layers inside the cave have yielded thousands of examples of portable art and other decorated objects, including beautifully carved spear-throwers. The cave was important as a dwelling, gathering, and ceremonial place well beyond the end of the Paleolithic period, in recognition of which the name Azilian has been given to the transitional period between the end of the Paleolithic period and the rise of the hunter-gatherer cultures that developed in the postglacial period known as the Mesolithic.

The Earliest Herders?

The people of the Magdalenian phase were predominantly big-game hunters. They mostly hunted horned animals, especially reindeer, which became the most important game animal—to the extent that 99 percent of all animal bones found on many sites of this period are those of reindeer. Reindeer migrate seasonally in search of pasture over very large areas, sometimes thousands of kilometers (many hundreds of miles). Hunters who rely on reindeer all year round obviously have to follow these migrating herds.

♦ Beneath these cliffs at Solutré, near Lyon, in France, huge quantities of horse bones have been found, indicating that this was a major kill site during the Upper Paleolithic period.

◄ Aerial view of the Vézère River at La Madeleine, in the Dordogne, France. This site was a major gathering place for the nomadic groups of big-game hunters that roamed the surrounding area during the last glacial.

⚜ The halter-like engravings on this horse's head of bone, found at St Michel d'Arudy, Basses-Pyrénées, France, have been interpreted by some as evidence that horses were domesticated during the Upper Paleolithic period.

MUSEE DES ANTIQUITES NATIONALES. ST-GERMAIN-EN-LAYE/R.M.N.

⚜ The wild horses of Ice Age Europe were similar to Przewalski horses, a species that until recently roamed the steppes of central Asia. Horses were an important source of food at this time and may also have been domesticated to some extent.

British archaeologist Paul Bahn has suggested that the way of life of the Upper Paleolithic people in southern France and the Pyrenees was probably very similar to that of present-day reindeer hunters and herders in Siberia. These people are seasonally nomadic, and as well as hunting, they keep domesticated animals to provide milk and to use as beasts of burden. Bahn suggests that the reindeer would have moved to pastures in several different directions during their seasonal migrations from the Dordogne: toward the Atlantic coast on the Bay of Biscay, the Pyrenees, and perhaps also the Alps. Analysis of the bone material from the *abri* settlement of Abri Pataud, in Les Eyzies, has shown that this settlement was occupied exclusively during late autumn, winter, and early spring. Abundant finds of cockle and mussel shells in almost every inland settlement lend support to the theory that humans followed the herds as they headed for the Atlantic coast.

Bahn is therefore open to the suggestion that Magdalenian hunters may have tamed part of the reindeer herds. It has long been wondered whether they may have tamed another important herd animal—the horse.

At the end of the nineteenth century, French researcher Edouard Piette suggested that the big-game hunters of the Upper Paleolithic period controlled or even domesticated some animals, in particular reindeer and horses. In support of this, he drew attention to carvings and paintings depicting animals apparently equipped with halters or harnesses of some kind—for example, a reindeer bull at the *abri* site of Laugerie-Basse and a horse in the cave of La Pasiega. The most striking example, however, was found in 1893 in the cave of St Michel d'Arudy—a carved horse's head equipped with something that could only have been a halter made of twisted rope. Piette's theories were heavily criticized, notably by the legendary and very influential Abbé Breuil, and after his death in 1906 the matter was more or less forgotten.

Sixty years after Piette's death, two French researchers found a carving of a horse's head wearing a halter at La Marche, in southwestern France. According to Paul Bahn, the halter was added after the head had been completed. This may indicate that horses were used for riding or as beasts of burden. Researchers who have studied finds of horses' teeth dating back to 30,000 years ago have claimed that many show distinct signs of so-called crib-biting—the wear pattern that results when a horse develops a habit of biting its stall—which was thought not to occur among wild horses. Recently, however, other researchers have strongly disputed this, claiming that it is more likely to be a natural wear pattern.

Notwithstanding this, there is some evidence to suggest that the big-game hunters of the Upper Paleolithic period did exercise some degree of control over horse and reindeer herds, and

perhaps also mountain goats. How is this to be reconciled with the large-scale drives and mass killings considered so characteristic of the period? These hunting methods would have required a joint effort by a very large number of hunters, who would have had to force the herds over a precipice or into a narrow gorge where the animals could be easily brought down. But to drive a galloping herd of horses on foot is clearly no easy task. Perhaps these Upper Paleolithic hunters were indeed the first horsemen.

One of the sites often cited as evidence of this large-scale hunting strategy is a precipice at Solutré, in the Rhône Valley. Excavations at the foot of the cliffs have uncovered the remains of tens of thousands of horses, dated to 17,000 years ago—that is, the early Magdalenian phase. More recently, it has been pointed out that the site is not particularly suitable for drives but ideally suited to a strategy of encirclement. The precipice was more likely used as a barrier to hedge the animals in, allowing them to be separated and slaughtered—or possibly, in the case of young animals, to be kept for future use, thereby ensuring a continuing food supply.

Whatever future research may tell us about Ice Age humans' control over animals, there was clearly great variation in living conditions and the availability of food across Eurasia. While big-game hunting was crucially important across the extensive tundra along the ice edge, the milder climate of southwestern Europe produced a plentiful and reliable supply of a variety of foods. As noted earlier, cockle and mussel shells have been found in most settlement sites in this area,

GERARD LACZ/NHPA

BRYAN AND CHERRY ALEXANDER/HPA

indicating that marine foods were eaten, at least during some parts of the year. The numerous images of salmon, sole, and other saltwater species found among cave art would seem to suggest that fishing was an important means of subsistence. In some areas, fish may even have been the staple food, encouraging people to adopt a more settled way of life. Plant foods were readily available in western Europe, though lacking further east. All these factors were vitally important in promoting population growth, which, in turn, led to new forms of social organization and ceremonial life.

The Birth of Inequality

In southern France in particular, the rich food resources led to a substantial increase in population during the Magdalenian period. It has been estimated that between 2,000 and 3,000 people lived in this area 20,000 years ago. Ten thousand years later, at the end of the Ice Age, this figure must have tripled. During the later stages of the Magdalenian period, *abri* settlements were becoming much larger. Some of them, such as Laugerie-Haute, Laugerie-Basse, and St Christophe, by the Vézère River, close to Les Eyzies, may have sheltered several hundred people at the same time for part of the year. Some groups, or parts of groups, probably lived in this region all year round.

How was society organized within and between different groups of people during this period? Within modern traditional societies, the two main factors determining group size are the ability to survive and the ability to live in peace. The ability to survive is drastically reduced if the group is too small. A lone individual rarely survives for more

than a year, whereas a group of five can continue for up to a generation (about 30 years). A group of about 25 has a good chance of surviving for perhaps 500 years, assuming it is in regular contact with other groups, not least for intermarriage.

On the other hand, the risk of conflict within groups increases with the number of people. Again, it turns out that 25 is a reasonable average number, and ethnographic studies among present-day hunter-gatherers have shown that most of them live in groups of between 20 and 70. This is true of the Australian Aborigines, the Kalahari Bushmen, and the Andamanese, as well as the Birhor of northern India. American anthropologist Robert Carneiro has observed that when the Yanomami Indians of South America form a group of more than 100 people, aggressive tendencies become so great that the group has to split into two halves.

For survival, a number of groups or bands must be organized in larger units or tribes, and here there are always certain limits. To avoid the problem of inbreeding, there must be at least 475 in the larger group. In fact, most known tribes of hunter-gatherers have about 500 people, with a maximum of about 800. It seems likely that similar conditions prevailed in southwestern Europe during the Magdalenian phase.

By studying the food supply within present-day areas that have the same climatic conditions as the various ecological zones of the Paleolithic Ice Age, we can estimate the likely productivity of each area in terms of hunting, fishing, and food-gathering—in other words, we can estimate its carrying capacity. The poorest regions, such as the tundra zone close to the ice edge, could have

🔥 Judging by the quantities of bones found at settlements, reindeer were one of the main sources of food for the Ice Age hunters, who followed the seasonal migrations of the herds.

GÖRAN BURENHULT

🔥 This life-size reconstruction of a mammoth bone hut is on display at the Thot Museum, near Montignac, in the Dordogne. The original was excavated at Mezhirich, in the Ukraine.

RADIOCARBON : A KEY TO THE PAST

Göran Burenhult

No other method has had such a revolutionary influence on modern archaeology's possibilities to establish absolute chronology as the radiocarbon or Carbon-14 method—the dating of radioactive carbon. This dating technique has been constantly refined, and a new revolution came about when the obtained C_{14} values could be calibrated into calendar years—that is, historically comparable dates. And right now we are in the middle of a third radiocarbon revolution—accelerator dating.

In 1949, an American physical chemist, Willard Libby, discovered that organic materials could be dated by measuring the amount of radioactive charcoal they contained. All living plants absorb small amounts of radioactive C_{14} from the atmosphere when they build up organic matter by photosynthesis and by using atmospheric carbon dioxide. There are three main isotopes of carbon, $C1_2$, C_{13}, and C_{14}. C_{12} and C_{13} are stable; C_{14} is radioactive and decays at a known rate. C_{14} is also continuously being produced in the upper atmosphere. Constant decay of C_{14} is balanced by constant production, which means that this radioactive isotope is in constant proportion to the common stable isotope C_{12}, the same as in carbon dioxide in the air. By consuming plants or herbivorous animals, all other animals and humans ingest and accumulate the radioactivity. When a human dies, or a tree is felled, the accumulation of radioactivity ceases and the measurable amount disintegrates at a known rate. The term "half-life" denotes the time it takes for radioactive matter to halve its number of atoms. For C_{14}, the half-life is 5,568 years. By measuring the remaining amount of C_{14}, it is thus possible to determine the time that has elapsed since the accumulation of radioactivity ceased. The obtained values are given in radiocarbon years BP (Before Present = before AD 1950), and can then easily be converted

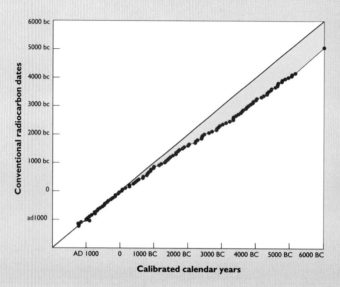

Diagram showing the deviation between conventional radiocarbon dates (bc/ad) and calibrated calendar years (BC/AD). The latter are based on C_{14} samples of tree-rings.
AFTER HANS E. SUESS

into radiocarbon years BC or AD. Deviation is given as a plus or minus factor—for example, 4,600 ± 100 years, which means with a possible deviation of plus or minus 100 years. The sample in this example can thus be dated in between the span of 4700 and 4500 BP. More exactly, there are 2 chances in 3 that this is the correct time span, but 19 chances in 20 that 4800 to 4400 BP is correct.

As the content of radioactivity constantly decreases over the years, the radiocarbon method has its limitations and is restricted to materials younger than about 70,000 years. The method is most effective on materials between 50,000 and 500 years old. Radiocarbon datings can be carried out on most organic materials, such as wood, charcoal, resin, hair, skin, bone, or peat. The margins of error vary, depending on material and quantity, and, as a rule, resin, wood, or charcoal provide more reliable dates than bone or peat, owing to their resistance to secondary influence.

When the radiocarbon method came into use, it was generally assumed that the absorption of atmospheric radioactivity had been relatively invariable over the millennia, and that radiocarbon years therefore on the whole corresponded

with calendar years in the historical sense. However, during the 1960s, two scientists, Hans E. Suess and H.L. de Vries, showed independently of each other that this was not at all the case. Fluctuations as a result of variations in the Earth's magnetic field and alterations in solar activity and in the balance between atmosphere and oceans were proved to exist. Recently, too, exhaust fumes from cars, power stations, and the like, as well as nuclear tests, have influenced the C_{14} curve. By radiocarbon-dating the tree-rings of very old trees in the western United States—primarily giant sequoia (*Sequoiadendron giganteum*) and bristlecone pine (*Pinus longaeva*), which reach an age of more than 4,000 years—it was possible to check the C_{14} values and calibrate them into calendar years. By means of dendrochronology (the study of the annual growth rings on trees), it was possible to extend the sequence back to about 5300 BC, and today we can give very accurate archaeological dates in calendar years. In other words, these correspond exactly to historically known dates, such as the building of Cheops' pyramid in the Old Kingdom of Egypt, or later events in the classical world, in Greece and Rome.

To avoid confusion, and as the calibrated dates are still subject to adjustment, experts have agreed to give all C_{14} values in conventional radiocarbon years as well in the future, and to clearly state calibrations into calendar years.

The established deviation is at its greatest between about 4000 and 3000 BC. The calibrated C_{14} dates therefore greatly influenced the understanding of, for example, the important and complex cultural situation of Neolithic Europe. The timing of the appearance of agriculture was particularly important in this respect, as it was backdated nearly a thousand years. The Stone Age peoples of Europe could no longer be looked upon as passive recipients of cultural advances from the Mediterranean area and Southwest Asia.

The C_{14} method took a great leap forward when the accelerator mass spectrometric (AMS) technique was introduced, both in terms of exactness and applicability. The amount of material needed for a radiocarbon dating has been drastically reduced, and nowadays only a few milligrams will suffice to obtain reliable datings. In future, the method will become an extraordinarily important dating instrument to archaeologists, and a number of spectacular datings have already been carried out on, for example, the domestication of plants and the first appearance of humans in the New World. Moreover, the famous Shroud of Turin has been dated with the AMS technique: on no account can it be the authentic shroud of Jesus Christ—the linen was made about AD 1300.

supported only one person per 200 square kilometers (77 square miles), but in southern France and Spain, this might well have been one person per 20 square kilometers (8 square miles). A tribe of about 500 people would have had to use more than 100,000 square kilometers (39,000 square miles) in the former area, but only 10,000 square kilometers (3,900 square miles) in the latter. This great variation in population density explains the differences in social and ceremonial systems among Paleolithic peoples, clearly indicating the need for extensive networks over large areas. In southern France, where so much activity was centered in this period, regular, communal ceremonies were held in several important gathering places—for example, in connection with mating.

A study of 76 skeletons from the Upper Paleolithic period in Europe and Asia has shown that less than half the people reached the age of 21, only 12 percent were more than 40, and not one single woman reached 30 years of age. Many skeletons showed signs of malnutrition, rickets, and other deficiency diseases. Significantly, many bore traces of injury resulting from physical violence. Life during the Ice Age was undoubtedly a relentless struggle for survival, and the evidence of social organization and ceremonial life that has survived from this period reflects a society under heavy pressure as people competed for limited resources.

During the later part of the Upper Paleolithic period, large settlements became gathering places for people from surrounding areas, where goods were exchanged and rituals observed. The many examples of portable art that have been found from this period may have served as personal status symbols on such occasions. One of the most remarkable examples has been excavated at Mezhirich, on the Dnepr River, southeast of Kiev, in the Ukraine. Five houses were found here, built of about 70 tonnes (just under 70 tons) of mammoth bones.

There is a good deal of evidence to show that certain people had higher status than others, and these people—possibly in the form of shamans—probably conducted rituals and ceremonies. Finds of a number of magnificently ornate burials provide, perhaps, the most persuasive evidence of status in this period. At Sungir, near Moscow, remains have been found of two adults and two children, the man and children buried in clothes decorated with thousands of beads of ivory and animal teeth and accompanied by ornately carved weapons and other objects suggesting a high status. The remains of magnificently adorned children have also been excavated from a site known as Grotte des Enfants, on the Italian Riviera.

Because these children were aged between 7 and 13, they cannot have attained high rank in their society by their own efforts. Their elaborate adornments have been interpreted as the first

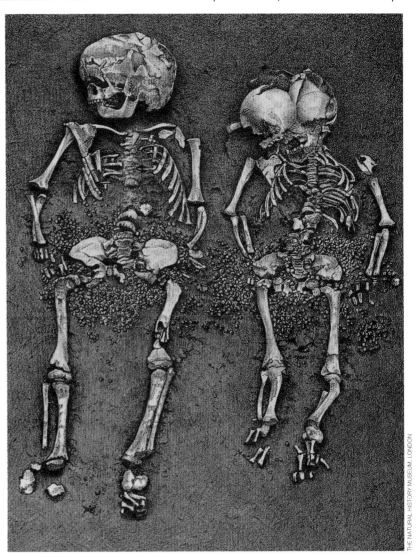

examples of hereditary status, evidence that some families in Paleolithic society were ranked higher than others. American writer John Pfeiffer summarizes: "A great deal of effort went into these burials, and into the appropriately elaborate ceremonies that must have accompanied them. Such honors are not for everyone, only for special people, indicating the beginnings of formal social distinctions. The burying of young children suggests further developments. A leader who earns his position by actual deeds needs time to win recognition as hunter or shaman. He must keep proving himself and when he can no longer do so he is replaced by someone else who can. But the existence of children buried with high honors before they are old enough to do anything out-standing raises the possibility of status by heredity rather than achievement."

⚱ Richly adorned child burials excavated in Grotte des Enfants—one of the Grimaldi caves—at Balzi Rossi, Italy. Their elaborate adornments, in the form of clusters of perforated shells, are one of the earliest examples of what may be hereditary status symbols.

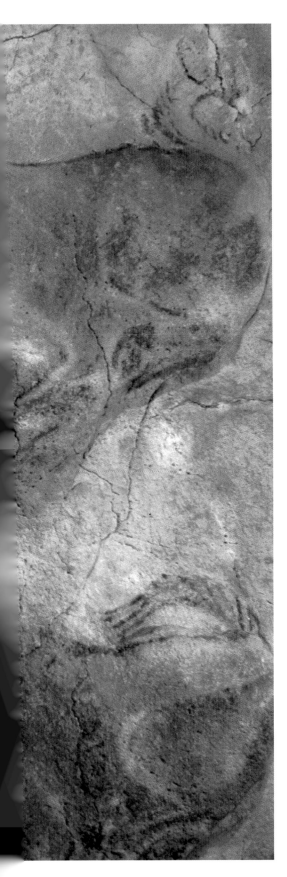

THE RISE OF ART

Image-making in Europe during the Ice Age

GÖRAN BURENHULT

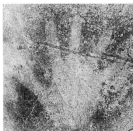

EVER SINCE A DAY in 1879 when Don Marcelino de Sautuola's five-year-old daughter happened to look up at the roof of a cavern and discover the painted bison of Altamira Cave, in northern Spain, the magnificent art of the Paleolithic hunters has been a source of fascination. No other remains from our prehistoric past have been found in such a remarkable location, deep inside dark, damp, and narrow limestone caves.

To encounter the world of beliefs of Upper Paleolithic people is an experience marked by awe, anxiety, excitement, and wonder. Often it involves an expedition of a kilometer or more (about half a mile) into the depths of a mountain—walking, crawling on one's knees and elbows, and sometimes swimming across underground lakes and rivers. The remote location is characteristic of cave art. The experience itself, of isolation, darkness, and unnatural timelessness, must have been of vital importance to the people of that age when selecting a sanctuary. The explorer is overwhelmed by a sense that secret rites and ceremonies of great mystery must have taken place in these unreal surroundings.

◄● The painted bison in the cave of Altamira, in northern Spain, are some of the most elaborate and well-known examples of Paleolithic art in the world. Painted some 12,000 years ago, they represent the highlight and also mark the end of a several-thousand-year-old artistic tradition in Europe.

♂ Hand stencils—a dramatic and personal message from the Ice Age.

RONALD SHERIDAN/ANCIENT ART AND ARCHITECTURE COLLECTION

GÖRAN BURENHULT

⚓ The famous rock shelter (or *abri*) of La Madeleine, which has given its name to the Magdalenian phase, is situated on the banks of the Vézère River, in the Dordogne, France. This site has yielded some of the finest pieces of portable art known, and appears to have been an important ceremonial gathering place.

➣ A magnificent horse-shaped spear-thrower made of bone from Bruniquel, Tarn-et-Garonne, France. The spear-thrower (also known as a throwing stick or atlatl) is well known among many hunter-gatherers in more recent times, including the North American Indians and the Australian Aborigines. The technique is ingeniously simple. The spear-thrower has a hook on one end which engages with a hollow at the end of the spear, and the effect of this extension of the throwing arm is to improve both penetrating power and accuracy quite dramatically. A skilled hunter can bring down a deer from a distance of more than 30 meters (30 yards), and kill an animal with a direct hit from a distance of 15 meters (15 yards).
DAVID L. BRILL, ©1985/MUSEE DES ANTIQUITES NATIONALES, ST GERMAIN-EN-LAYE

De Sautuola was an amateur archaeologist, and at first no one believed that his finds were unique art treasures from Paleolithic times. The elegant, vividly painted animals were thought to be too perfect—too naturalistic and technically advanced—to have been created by a Stone Age man or woman. They were believed to be a hoax of recent origin. Don Marcelino died before the sensational age of the paintings was confirmed. It was only much later that new finds of cave art in or together with datable strata convinced the scientific world of their great age. These new finds consisted mainly of small, three-dimensional animals carved in antler and bone—examples of so-called portable art—and were crafted with the same remarkable skill to create astonishingly life-like images.

The time perspective alone is dizzying. The earliest images found are more than 30,000 years old. As far as we know at present, the Neanderthals never expressed themselves in art. The image as a means of expression belongs exclusively to modern humans, *Homo sapiens sapiens*, who appeared in Europe about 35,000 years ago in the form of the people we know as the Cro-Magnon. There is nothing to indicate that Neanderthals were less able to express abstract thought in the form of imagery, but for some reason they never did.

What happened at the start of the Upper Paleolithic? Why did Ice Age humans suddenly need to express themselves in images? And why did they find their way, with the evident danger of being killed, through extremely difficult passages to the deepest parts of caves? Why are these caves to be found almost exclusively within an area in southern France and northern Spain? Were the cave paintings created by one person, or did entire communities find their way into the silent sanctuaries to perform their cult ceremonies? Who created the paintings? Were they men or women, or perhaps children?

No preliminary stages of paintings or carvings have been found, and this has been interpreted to mean that the cave art was created by a limited group of selected individuals—a sort of priesthood, in the form of medicine-men or shamans. Another possible explanation is that people trained on perishable materials, such as hides or wood, outside the caves.

A Time of Changes

To understand what led up to the beginnings of art, we have to look far beyond the art itself. The Upper Paleolithic period was a time of dramatic changes. The appearance of a new human species in Europe is sensational enough, but these newcomers were to introduce a number of social and technological innovations that radically changed conditions of life within a short period. The population grew markedly, and nomadic family groups began to gather in larger units and for longer periods than in earlier times. The archaeological record shows that goods were interchanged over greater distances, indicating a growing network of relationships between groups.

The most conspicuous change that occurred at this time was the development of a new and stylistically more complex tool technology. The stone tools of the Neanderthals consisted of a few similar types. Prepared, tortoise-shaped pieces of flint provided the raw material, from which flakes were struck off. These flakes were then retouched to make scrapers and points of different kinds. (This is known as Levalloisian technology.) *Homo sapiens sapiens* developed a more advanced blade technology, and were able to produce long, thin tools, such as blades in the shape of a laurel leaf. Many new types of tools were developed, including flint tools with double functions, such as retouched flakes where one end was shaped as a scraper, while the other served as a burin. The large variety of burins that have been found from this period clearly indicates that they served a range of specialized purposes.

The new tools were largely developed to enable people to work with bone and antler. Burins in particular were mainly used for this purpose. By the end of the Paleolithic period, during the Magdalenian phase, most artifacts—both those with a practical function and those that appear to have been ornaments or ritual objects—were made of these materials. Tens of thousands of portable works of art have been found in Europe, most of them in southern France. A large number of different kinds of harpoons and fish-spears, each with a specialized function, have also been found from this period, indicating that hunting small game and fishing were becoming more sophisticated and much more important as a means of subsistence.

Spear-throwers made of antler, often beautifully carved, were another addition to hunting weapons at this time.

But tools and works of art are not the only evidence of profound social change in the Upper Paleolithic period. New needs and traditions are reflected even more clearly in a series of spectacular finds which indicate that the people of this time had developed a rich ceremonial life based on complex concepts and rituals.

For the first time, evidence of regular burials appears, the bodies dotted with red ocher, many dressed in magnificent clothing and adornments, and accompanied by sets of tools. At Sungir, some 200 kilometers (125 miles) northeast of Moscow, four well-preserved burials dated to between 25,000 and 20,000 years ago have been found—a man, a woman, and two adolescent children. The man had been buried together with blades of ivory, and was dressed in a headband and a number of necklaces carrying some 3,000 beads of mammoth ivory. The cranium of a female had been placed on the grave in the course of his burial ritual. In a double grave in which a girl and boy were buried head to head, more than 10,000 ivory beads were found, together with rings, ornaments, the teeth of arctic fox, and 16 weapons in the form of spears, spear-throwers, and daggers. Similar burials from this period have been found at a number of other European sites, including Grimaldi, in Italy, and La Madeleine, in France.

Carving of an animal head from Le Mas d'Azil, one of the most important Paleolithic sites in the French Pyrenees. The enormously rich finds of portable art as well as cave art at this site suggest that it was one of the main ceremonial gathering places in the Franco-Cantabrian region. The site has also yielded small pebbles with painted red dots.

JEAN VERTUT/COLLECTION DE SAINT-PERIER

Ibex carved in a piece of bone from the cave of Isturitz, Basses-Pyrenées, France.

JEAN VERTUT/COLLECTION DE SAINT-PERIER

Together with the different kinds of art, both portable art objects and cave art, these burials clearly indicate that the people of this time felt the need to communicate abstract information by means of symbols. In the whole history of human evolution, this is the first evidence we have of the need to show group affiliation and social status—while the child burials are the first indication that status may have been hereditary. For this reason, it has been suggested that the Upper Paleolithic period may mark the beginning of the end of the totally egalitarian society.

As the population grew and these new and more complex patterns of social organization emerged, people clearly had a greater need to communicate both within their own group and with outside groups. The development of images and symbols can be directly linked to this growing need for communication, and it has been suggested that language may have undergone a parallel development at this time.

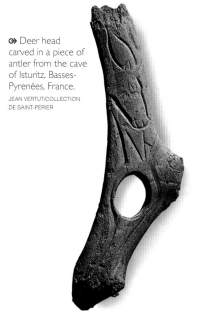

Deer head carved in a piece of antler from the cave of Isturitz, Basses-Pyrenées, France.

JEAN VERTUT/COLLECTION DE SAINT-PERIER

Bison carved in a piece of bone found in Magdalenian layers in the cave of Isturitz, Basses-Pyrenées, France.

JEAN VERTUT/COLLECTION DE SAINT-PERIER

⚥ Carving depicting a vulva at La Ferrassie, in the Dordogne.
DAVID L. BRILL, ©1985/MUSEE NATIONAL DE PREHISTOIRE, LES EYZIES DE TAYAC

☛ *Opposite:* Head of a Venus figurine from Brassempouy. This exquisite piece of craftsmanship, one of the earliest depictions of a human face, dates from the Gravettian phase, between 29,000 and 22,000 years ago. The checked pattern on the head has been interpreted as a hairnet.

The Artistic Revolution

Cave art, with its naturalistic images of animals, arose during a later stage of the Upper Paleolithic period. The first expressions of art in Europe consist of symbols of female sexuality. As early as 35,000 years ago, Cro-Magnon people carved images of vulvas on rock and other surfaces. Some millennia later, about 29,000 years ago, the first portable art appeared in the form of the famous Venus figurines, small female figures with a characteristically stylized form. They were to dominate artistic expression for nearly 10,000 years.

Most of these female figures have exaggeratedly swelling breasts and buttocks, while the head and legs taper off into a less defined shape, clearly being seen as of minor importance. They have been found over extensive areas, indicating widespread contacts and a common system of rituals throughout widely scattered communities during this period. Similar-looking Venus figurines have been found in great numbers from southern Russia in the east to the Atlantic coast in the west, a distance of more than 2,000 kilometers (1,200 miles). The most important sites include Dolní Věstonice, in the Czech Republic, Kostenki, in Russia, Willendorf, in Austria, and Brassempouy and Lespugue, in France.

Two possible explanations have been put forward to explain this emphasis on female genitals in the artistic and ritual life of the Cro-Magnon people and the distinctive characteristics of the Venus figurines. First, we know from the skeletons of this period that Cro-Magnon women were generally less robust than their predecessors, the Neanderthals, and had a considerably narrower

pelvic opening. This may have resulted in more difficult childbirth and, as a result, a high death rate among mothers and babies. Second, it is not unlikely that the rapidly growing population led to increasing conflict, and conflict within traditional societies usually involves competition for women. In any case, women's vital role in ensuring the continued existence of a society whose survival was coming under increasing pressure may very well have given rise to a cult centered on women.

We can trace the growth in population by the number of sites that have been discovered from different periods. At present, we know of only six sites from the Neanderthal era in the Russian region—the area between the Black Sea and the ice edge in the north—while the same area has more than 500 settlements from the Cro-Magnon period. As people have more frequent contact with outside groups, they have a greater need to show who they are and what position in society they hold. In all traditional societies, this is done by wearing adornments and other objects indicating personal status, and also by different kinds of body decoration, in the form of tattoos or body painting. The beautifully carved ivory spear-points and spear-throwers, as well as many of the other portable art objects made of bone and antler, could have marked out individuals of high status in Upper Paleolithic society, while other artifacts might have been protective amulets.

It was not until about 23,000 years ago that cave art appeared. When it did, it was concentrated in one main area—the Franco-Cantabrian region of southern France and northern Spain.

☛ Elegantly stylized, headless female figures from Lalinde, at La Roche, in the Dordogne. Their buttocks are heavily marked. About 10 to 15 centimeters (4 to 6 inches) high, these carved figures date back to the Magdalenian phase.

JEAN VERTUT

THE VENUS FIGURINES

GÖRAN BURENHULT

Thirty-thousand-year-old fertility symbols, the Venus figurines are among the most fascinating and enigmatic works of art of the Upper Paleolithic period. They bear witness to beliefs in magical power and to advanced ritual ceremonies, to long-term planning and to a clear knowledge of the importance of fertility for survival. These magnificent works present the first glimpse into the world of beliefs of Ice Age hunters and mark the prelude to the use of images as a means of establishing contacts between people and the supernatural.

The appearance of the first human expressions of art is one of the most evident signs of the fact that *Homo sapiens sapiens* possessed mental capacities superior to those of their predecessors—the ability to communicate through symbols. But this abstract world of symbols also reveals the modern human's need of religious and ritual systems, emanating from a changed subsistence and thus a changed social organization.

⊙ Venus figurine made of mammoth ivory from Des Rideaux, at Lespugue, in Haute Garonne, France, dating back to about 23,000 years ago. According to some, this figurine may indicate that steatopygia occurred among Ice Age women. Marija Gimbutas, on the other hand, has suggested that the exaggerated buttocks are a metaphor for the double egg or pregnant belly—a symbol of intensified fertility.
MUSÉE DE L'HOMME, PARIS/J. OSTER

DR LIDIO CIPRIANO, 1932/NATIONAL MUSEUM OF ETHNOGRAPHY, STOCKHOLM

◐ It has been suggested that the swelling buttocks of some of the Venus figurines indicate that steatopygia occurred among Ice Age women—that is, an extreme accumulation of fat at the hips which is used as a reserve during times of food shortage. Steatopygia still exists among the females of some traditional societies, including the Bushmen of the Kalahari, among whom it is also considered to have great aesthetic value.

◄ⷪ This well-known Venus figurine of limestone was found in layers of Gravettian age at Willendorf, near Krems, in Austria.
NATURAL HISTORY MUSEUM, VIENNA

One might expect that the first symbols of the Upper Paleolithic big-game hunters would be linked to the most essential part of Ice Age survival—the game animals that constituted the main source of food across much of the European tundras. Instead, the world of images was centered on sexuality and fertility—another vital part of the struggle for survival: securing the continuity of the group.

The oldest known figures consist of carved vulva depictions, which may be linked to the Aurignacian tradition and which date back about 30,000 years. They have been found on rocks at, for example, Abri Blanchard, Abri Castanet, and La Ferrassie, in the Vézère Valley, in the Dordogne. But the famous Venus figurines, which have been found over a very large area, became the most characteristic kind of object in this world of beliefs. They were made out of a number of different kinds of materials, such as mammoth ivory, antler, bone, stone, and clay, and they all share the same standardized design: exaggeratedly swelling breasts and buttocks, and many of them appear to be pregnant. Most of them are naked and equipped with marked genitals. With a few exceptions, their heads are rudimentary and most often shaped only as little knobs, and, likewise, the swelling thighs taper off to poorly marked

feet. The fertility symbolism is evident—the important thing was reproduction, fertility, and pregnancy.

But not all of these little fertility goddesses—perhaps even depictions of the Mother Goddess herself—have been depicted pregnant. American archaeologist Marija Gimbutas has pointed out that probably not even the classic Venus figurines from Willendorf, in Austria, and Lespugue, in France, are pregnant. Breasts and buttocks are the focus of attention, and, moreover, their hands are placed over their breasts. Others, like those from Kostenki, in Russia, and the famous limestone bas-relief from Laussel, in France, have their hands placed over their abdomen and may be interpreted as being pregnant. Consequently, breasts and buttocks are not particularly marked in these figures.

The remarkable Venus tradition belonged primarily to the Gravettian phase, between 29,000 and 22,000 years ago, a period of increasing cold and advancing glaciers and ice sheets. The figurines had a standardized appearance over a distance of more than 2,000 kilometers (1,200 miles), from the Atlantic Ocean in the west to Russia in the east, and this bears witness to far-away contacts and intensive communication between the Upper Paleolithic big-game hunters along the Eurasian ice edge.

◄ⷪ Found at the Upper Paleolithic site of Dolní Věstonice, in Moravia, in the Czech Republic, this Venus of burned clay is about 26,000 years old.
RONALD SHERIDAN/ANCIENT ART AND ARCHITECTURE COLLECTION

◄ⷪ A 22,000-year-old Venus made of serpentine marble (steatite) from Savignano, in northern Italy. Her head has been interpreted as a phallus symbol.
MUSEO NAZIONALE PREHISTORICO EO ETNOGRAFICO "L. PIGORINI", ROME

◄ⷪ This Venus, with both hands placed on her genitals, was found at the famous Upper Paleolithic burial site of Grimaldi, on the French-Italian border.
J. M. LABAT/AUSCAPE

◄ⷪ This beautiful, amber-colored limestone Venus from Sireuil, in the Dordogne, France, dates back to about 23,000 years ago.
MUSEE DES ANTIQUITES NATIONALES, ST-GERMAIN-EN-LAYE/R.M.N.

DETAIL OF VÉZÈRE VALLEY

CARTOGRAPHY: RAY SIM

UPPER PALEOLITHIC ART SITES
The major Upper Paleolithic art sites in France and on the Iberian Peninsula. The region along the Dordogne and Vézère rivers, in south central France, shown in the detail, is particularly rich in cave art. Coastlines as they were during the peak of the last glacial, some 18,000 years ago, are indicated.

The Franco-Cantabrian Heartland
At present, we know of more than 200 European caves with Paleolithic paintings and carvings. Of these, no fewer than about 180, or 85 percent, are located in southernmost France and northern Spain, in what is usually called the Franco-Cantabrian heartland. If we look at the spread of cave art outside this area, this concentration becomes even more striking. The remaining part of the Iberian Peninsula has another 20 or so caves with Paleolithic art, while about 10 have been found in Italy and only one in eastern Europe—Kapova Cave, in the Ural Mountains.

The fact that more than 90 percent of cave art is found in France and Spain cannot be explained by the lack of suitable caves in other regions. Very similar areas with cave systems are to be found in many other places in Europe, including the Carpathians, the Alps, and the Urals. Neither can we attribute it to insufficient research or accidental discoveries. During the present century, speleologists have penetrated and mapped most known cave systems in these regions. In the extensive area south of the ice edge, from France in the west all the way to the Urals in Russia in the east, a long series of Upper Paleolithic sites has been found, and almost all have yielded considerable quantities of portable art. This serves to make the concentration of cave art even more surprising.

Research indicates that the reasons for this concentration were demographic, economic, and social. There were great differences in population density over the vast tundra regions, reflecting equally great differences in climate and, therefore, subsistence systems. The warmer climate close to the Atlantic coast in southwestern Europe obviously led to an ecology significantly different from that of the permafrost steppes farther east. People in the southwest had less need to be nomadic, because fish and plant foods were abundant.

This is reflected in the archaeological record by a long series of settlements that can be interpreted as important meeting places and ceremonial centers. Some of these had complex stone structures, some of which may have served ritual purposes. At Solvieux, near Bergerac, in the Dordogne Valley, no fewer than 16 occupation levels dating from about 30,000 to 14,000 years ago have been unearthed. In the Dordogne, four sites dating from the Magdalenian period have yielded 1,400 portable works of art made of bone or antler— 80 percent of those so far known. This clearly indicates that people were concentrating in particular areas.

It has been estimated that about 20,000 years ago, between 2,000 and 3,000 people lived in what is now France, while the population of the rest of Europe, including Spain, cannot have exceeded 10,000. In the heart of the French area, at Les Eyzies, on the Vézère River, between 400 and 600 people lived side by side, at the same time, under the protection of four or five rock shelters known as *abri*. Similar gathering places located much farther apart are known further east—for example, at Dolní Věstonice, in the Czech Republic, and at Sungir and Kostenki, in Russia.

The evidence of increased mass killings of single species of animals also suggests that the population was growing substantially during this period—although it is usually difficult to determine whether the bone deposits in these kill sites are the result of a single hunt or have accumulated over a longer period from regular killings. Some sites in eastern Europe have yielded the remains of close to 1,000 mammoths. At Solutré, in eastern France, a kill site has been found with the bones of perhaps as many as 100,000 horses, which were either driven to their death over the cliffs or herded into the natural trap formed by the narrow pass below to be slaughtered.

A food resource often overlooked previously, salmon fishing, may have drawn people to the Franco-Cantabrian heartland during the Upper Paleolithic period. Images of salmon have long been known in several caves, particularly in the Pyrenees. The known temperature range between 20,000 and 10,000 years ago suggests that the rivers of the Franco-Cantabrian heartland would have provided ideal conditions for salmon. Even as late as the nineteenth century, the rivers in this area were among the best salmon-fishing areas in Europe. People may have settled in one place for longer periods to exploit the regular seasonal migrations and spawning time of salmon, and as the numbers of horses, mammoths, bison, and reindeer declined as a result of mass killings, fishing and food gathering would have become even more important. And, like the meat from mass killings, fish could be dried and stored.

While portable art is clearly associated with the nomadic big-game hunters of the extensive tundra area south of the ice edge, cave art is concentrated in an area that offered much more varied ways of subsistence and therefore encouraged a more settled way of life. It is in the context of these major social changes that we must understand the developing ceremonial world reflected by the remarkable works of art created in the dark of the caves.

⚲ The valley of the Vézère River, an area of unmatched natural beauty and charm, boasts the highest concentration of Paleolithic art in the world. The rich environment provided ideal conditions for human habitation during the last Ice Age, and the area seems to have been an important center for social and ceremonial activities.

A. BORDES/EXPLORER-AUSCAPE

➤ One of the main characteristics of Paleolithic art was the artists' habit of using pre-existing natural formations on walls as an integral part of their images. Most parts of this magnificent horse's head at Commarque, in the Dordogne, including the eye, the ear, and the forehead, are natural irregularities in the rock surface. Only the nostril, the muzzle, and the mouth have been carved by human hands.

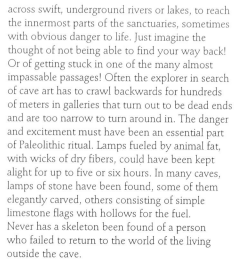

JEAN VERTUT

➤ *Opposite page*: Paleolithic art in Europe developed over a period of 25,000 years. The earliest works of art consisted primarily of carved vulva images. Cave art appeared about 24,000 years ago, but the true flowering of mural art did not begin until the end of the Upper Paleolithic period, between 20,000 and 12,000 years ago.

AFTER ANDRE LEROI-GOURHAN'S DATINGS OF FRANCO-CANTABRIAN CAVE ART

⚲ Depictions of salmon, such as this one from Gorge d'Enfer, in the Dordogne, indicate that fishing may have been an important part of the Magdalenian hunters' subsistence. Interestingly, depictions of purely salt-water species, such as different kinds of flatfish, have been found far within the central areas of the Dordogne and the Pyrenees. This may indicate that people spent parts of the year by the sea.

Encountering the Supernatural

As we have seen, the cave art tradition developed over a very long time and can be linked to social and demographic conditions as well as economic conditions and climate. Most works of cave art, more than 80 percent, were created between 17,000 and 12,000 years ago, and it is easy to forget that we ourselves are closer in time to the heyday of the Magdalenian artists than they were to their ancestors who created the first cave art and the first sculptures more than 30,000 years ago.

To encounter the works of art created by the big-game hunters is to encounter the supernatural. The meeting is in itself a fascinating experience. The almost inaccessible location of cave art is one of its most characteristic features. The images never or very seldom appear at the cave entrances, where people lived. Instead, we have to walk and crawl on our knees and elbows, or even swim

across swift, underground rivers or lakes, to reach the innermost parts of the sanctuaries, sometimes with obvious danger to life. Just imagine the thought of not being able to find your way back! Or of getting stuck in one of the many almost impassable passages! Often the explorer in search of cave art has to crawl backwards for hundreds of meters in galleries that turn out to be dead ends and are too narrow to turn around in. The danger and excitement must have been an essential part of Paleolithic ritual. Lamps fueled by animal fat, with wicks of dry fibers, could have been kept alight for up to five or six hours. In many caves, lamps of stone have been found, some of them elegantly carved, others consisting of simple limestone flags with hollows for the fuel. Never has a skeleton been found of a person who failed to return to the world of the living outside the cave.

Deep inside the least accessible galleries, these Paleolithic artists created their works of art. But even here, not on the obvious surfaces. Instead, they often chose an out-of-the-way location in a narrow passage, not immediately visible from the obvious vantage points.

Clearly, these artists, with their flickering lamps, sought a very special vision of the wall surfaces, one that brought life to the image from the real world they had in their mind's eye— a running horse or a charging bison. Among the irregularities of the rock surface, they searched for natural formations they could use as an integral part of the image. This is a distinctive feature of much cave art, including the magnificent mammoths of Rouffignac and the suggestive lioness of Les Combarelles, whose eyes consist of natural cores of flint embedded in the limestone.

It is often difficult to determine the angle from which the artist intended a particular image to be seen—or rather from which he or she would have seen it. Often it seems that the artist wanted to build in an element of surprise for the observer, who must crouch in an awkward position to see the image come to life. We find it hard to conceive how these artists were able to produce life-size images in correct proportion without being able to stand back and view the work as a whole.

Paleolithic art has sometimes been called "animal art", and it is true that the vast majority of paintings, carvings, and reliefs depict game animals, such as reindeer, horses, mammoths, bison, woolly rhinoceroses, deer, ibex, and aurochs (wild cattle). Occasionally, cave lions, bears, fish, and birds appear. But there are also some images of humans, often dressed in animal hides and equipped with hooves, horns, or other animal attributes. These probably depict shamans during cult ceremonies. There are many images of genitals, mainly vulvas, with or without the female body. In some caves, there are numerous

JEAN VERTUT

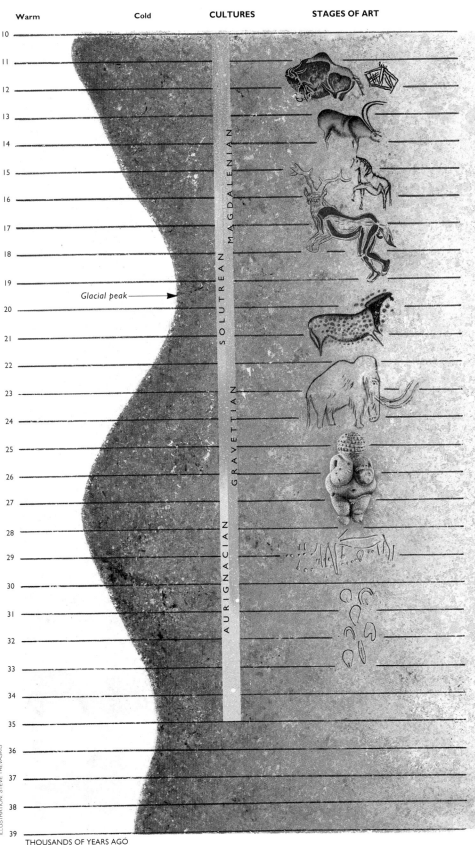

Warm   Cold   **CULTURES**   **STAGES OF ART**   **TYPICAL SITES**

10
11
12
13
14
15
16
17
18
19
20
21
22
23
24
25
26
27
28
29
30
31
32
33
34
35
36
37
38
39

Glacial peak ➤

M A G D A L E N I A N

S O L U T R E A N

G R A V E T T I A N

A U R I G N A C I A N

THOUSANDS OF YEARS AGO

ALTAMIRA AND FONT-DE-GAUME
The 12,000-year-old bison paintings in Spain's Altamira cave and the hut-like signs from caves such as Font-de-Gaume mark both the high point and the end of Ice Age art in Europe.

FONT-DE-GAUME
Cave art peaked about 13,000 years ago with the naturalistic carvings and monochrome and polychrome paintings found in such caves as Font-de-Gaume, Niaux, and Les Combarelles.

LE PORTEL
A more mature style of cave art started to appear some 15,000 years ago. The paintings in Le Portel and some of those in Lascaux belong to this period.

LES TROIS FRERES
The first polychrome cave paintings appeared about 18,000 years ago. These early images include the famous sorcerer from Les Trois Frères and the earliest depictions of animals in Lascaux.

PECH-MERLE
There was a marked proliferation of Ice Age art about 20,000 years ago, at the peak of the last glacial. The first evidence of ceremonies in cave sanctuaries, notably in Pech-Merle, dates from this time.

ROUFFIGNAC
The earliest cave art consists of carvings and monochrome paintings created between 24,000 and 22,000 years ago. Many of the images are of mammoths and woolly rhinoceroses, perhaps the most famous being those in the spectacular cave of Rouffignac.

WILLENDORF
Between 28,000 and 24,000 years ago, portable art in the form of carved Venus figurines appeared. These figurines are found over a vast area, from western Europe to Siberia. Among the most famous are the Venuses found at Willendorf, Lespugue, Brassempouy, and Kostenki.

LA FERRASSIE
During the early phases of the Gravettian period, schematic signs and images of archaic animals and vulvas appeared in such caves as La Ferrassie and Arcy-sur-Cure.

LA FERRASSIE
The earliest art consists mainly of vulva signs. It appeared about 33,000 years ago, and is found at a number of sites in the Dordogne, including La Ferrassie, Abri Cellier, and Castanet.

⚘ The main gallery of the famous cave of Lascaux—often called the Hall of Bulls. The cave with the remarkable paintings remained dark and unknown for several millennia, until a day in 1940, when four teenagers happened to discover it.

JEROME CHATIN/GAMMA/PICTURE MEDIA

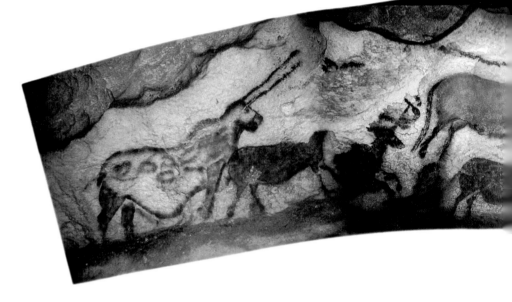

⚭ Images of vulvas in the cave of El Castillo, Santander Province, northern Spain. Their exact age is unknown, but they were probably created during the middle of the Magdalenian phase.

JEAN VERTUT

⚭ This carving of a human figure dressed as a bison, in Le Gabillou, in the Dordogne, may depict a shaman during a cult ceremony. Others have suggested that these figures with combined human and animal features represent spiritual beings in the form of "protectors" of animals and forests.

JEAN VERTUT

schematic symbols or signs, often in the form of standardized, geometrical figures. Different types of figures predominate in different regions. Schematic symbols, for instance, are much more common in the southern region—the Pyrenees and the caves of southern Spain, such as La Pileta, near Malaga.

Among the most dramatic cave art images are negative hand stencils, created by spraying color through a blowpipe over a hand placed on the rock surface. Many of these hands have mutilated fingers, a feature that has been interpreted differently in different caves. It may be that Paleolithic people deliberately amputated fingers, a practice known among many traditional cultures of recent times. This has a magical or religious purpose, being performed during times of severe

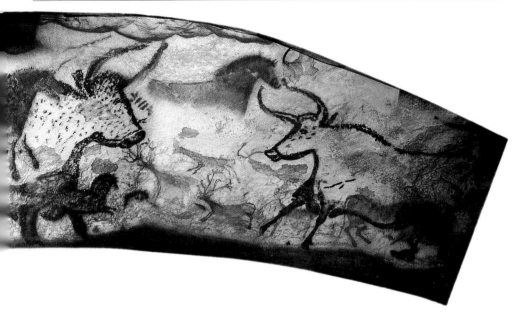

◄● Panorama of one of the two friezes in the main gallery of Lascaux, considered by many to be the finest Paleolithic paintings found to date. The small herd of galloping black horses is one of the few examples of composition in Paleolithic art.

adversity to appease the spirits. But many of the mutilated hands, such as those in the "cave of a hundred mutilated hands" at Gargas, in the Pyrenees, have been interpreted as depicting unintentional injuries such as frostbite, and it has also been suggested that the fingers may have been bent in a sort of sign language.

The range of images in cave art differs from region to region. Many caves have a unique character, and this must clearly be taken into account in any attempt to interpret the different groups of images. In certain caves, such as Rouffignac, images of mammoths and woolly rhinoceroses predominate. In others, such as Niaux and Lascaux, most images are of horses, aurochs, and bison.

The paint used by Paleolithic artists was made of pulverized rock—mainly iron oxide, which gives the red color, and manganese oxide, which gives the black—mixed with animal fat. Paintbrushes of different kinds and blowpipes have been found in numerous caves. In many cases, such as in Lascaux, holes have been found in the cave floor from scaffolding erected to enable the artists to reach suitable surfaces further up on the walls or on the roof of the cave. This, too, strongly suggests a systematically performed cult.

One of the great areas of debate in the interpretation of cave art has been whether the different images should be seen as parts of compositions, or whether each constitutes an individual, self-contained ritual. A problem is posed by the fact that there are many instances of images painted or carved over an earlier image. These superimposed images can be interpreted in a number of different ways. The new image may

◄● A remarkably realistic depiction of a Przewalski horse in Gallerie Noir (the Black Gallery) of the cave of Niaux, southern France. Parts of the image are now covered by white deposits of calcite.

♀ A bison painting in Gallerie Noir, the main gallery of Niaux. This huge sanctuary, situated more than 1,000 meters (3,000 feet) inside the mountain, mainly contains monochrome paintings of horses and bison.

♦ Depictions of the mysterious woolly rhinoceros are rare and limited to the very earliest phases of Paleolithic art. This one is from the cave of Rouffignac, in the Dordogne.

♀ The spectacular cave of Rouffignac is dominated by very early monochrome paintings of mammoths and woolly rhinoceroses. The strange formations in the rock surface are natural cores of flint embedded in the limestone.

have been placed over the old one to make use of the existing supernatural power or, equally likely, to destroy it. Alternatively, the earlier image may have been regarded as unimportant and only happened to be at the site of a later ceremony. The same difficulties apply when trying to interpret the many puzzling signs and symbols which most often appear on or alongside the animals.

The animals are depicted in greatly varying sizes, even on the same section of rock surface, and are placed among each other in a seemingly formless muddle, with no perspective or horizon line. With the notable exception of the famous galloping black horses of Lascaux, it would seem that the concept of composition, in a traditional artistic sense, cannot be applied to Paleolithic art. However, modern research has revealed that cave art reflects a much more sophisticated understanding and use of symbolism than previously thought to be possible among the hunters of the Upper Paleolithic.

Interpretations and Reinterpretations

As is always the case with archaeological research, interpretations of cave art have changed as new findings have emerged. For a long time, Paleolithic art was thought to reflect the big-game hunters' need for decoration and beauty in their everyday surroundings—art for art's sake. No one was inclined to believe that "the primitive savage" would have had a religious or ceremonial life. Little attention was paid to the fact that almost none of the works of art were found in settlements and almost all were located in remote parts of caves.

It was not until the beginning of the twentieth century, when ethnographic studies made the world aware of the remarkable complexity and variety of beliefs that exist within traditional cultures, that researchers began to realize that the cave images probably had a more profound significance. The Australian Aborigines in particular excited much interest. Their rock paintings were shown to be ceremonial expressions of a complex

mythology. For the first time, the concept of totemism was discussed. This refers to a system of social organization based on tribes or clans in which each tribe or clan is distinguished by a totem—an object from the natural world, most often an animal—with which it considers itself to have a special, usually a blood, relationship.

The researcher who dominated the discussion of Paleolithic cave art from the 1930s to the 1950s was Abbé Breuil. He strongly supported the then current view that cave art was an expression of sympathetic hunting magic: by depicting the game animal and then injuring it symbolically by placing a feather-like symbol over it, supernatural powers were released and successful hunting was assured. This interpretation, however, left many aspects of the art unexplained.

First, why did the artists often depict hunting weapons as feather-like signs, particularly since most of these signs were placed outside the images of the game animals? Second, why do the most common game animals very seldom appear in cave art? This applies particularly to reindeer, which, judging by the enormous numbers of bones found in the settlement layers throughout this region, must have been one of the main sources of food during the Magdalenian period. Nor does it fully explain the dominating element of sexual symbolism in cave art, even if the many images of seemingly pregnant animals can be linked to the concept of fertility—perhaps within both the clan and the species.

Modern research began with André Leroi-Gourhan, whose important studies in the 1960s focused on the placing of the different images and their relationships to each other. By means of comprehensive statistical analysis, he revealed previously unsuspected patterns.

⬥ This historic photograph records the first investigation of Lascaux, in 1940. Standing third from right is the legendary cave art researcher Abbé Breuil. The boys sitting on the floor are two of those who discovered the cave.

PECH-MERLE:
A 20,000-YEAR-OLD SANCTUARY

Göran Burenhult

MUSEUM FÜR VOR- UND FRÜHGESCHICHTE/BILDARCHIV PREUSSISCHER KULTURBESITZ

DEEP INSIDE THE CAVES of the Franco-Cantabrian region, Stone Age hunters left behind a remarkable testimony to their cult ceremonies, and to the magical beliefs and complex social systems that gave rise to them. What took place when these images were created is one of the most fascinating issues in the study of the Paleolithic period.

⚲ Thanks to its many stalagmites and stalactites, the huge cave of Pech-Merle, near Cahors, in Lot, France, is one of the most beautiful caves with cave art. Its famous dotted horses, painted on a fallen rock, occupy a prominent position. There is evidence that ceremonies took place in these unreal surroundings.

RENE DELON/CASTELET

Among the many such caves known, a small number are exceptional, partly because of their size, and partly because of the way in which the artists used the natural features of the cave walls to enhance their images. They include such classic caves as Lascaux, Font-de-Gaume, and Rouffignac, in the Dordogne region; Niaux, in the Pyrenees; and Pech-Merle, near Cahors, in Lot, in southwestern France. The evidence from a number of caves strongly suggests that these magnificent underground halls were the site of recurring ceremonies—probably rites of passage—and that the images were created successively, never on just one occasion. Clearly, such ritual gathering places were an important part of Stone Age people's encounters with the supernatural.

Pech-Merle is one of the oldest known caves containing Paleolithic art. In contrast to most of the other caves, it is a dripstone cave, its forests of stalagmites and stalactites making it one of the most beautiful underground galleries. The startling paintings of dotted horses for which it is famous are prominently displayed in a huge hall, painted on a fallen rock surrounded by a large flat area that might have been used for dances and ceremonies.

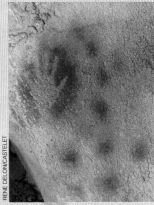

☜ I was here! The personal stamp of those who participated in the ceremonies, the hand stencils in Pech-Merle are eloquent evidence that rites of passage once took place here.

⚲ The footprints left behind in Pech-Merle, as in many other Paleolithic caves, are our closest and most immediate point of contact with the people who performed their cult ceremonies in the depth of the caves more than 20,000 years ago.

RENE DELON/CASTELET

RENE DELON/CASTELET

With the help of infrared light, we now know how these paintings were created. The red and black dots consist of different mixtures of paint and were placed on the horses on different occasions. The first figure represented a red fish and was placed slightly to the right of center on the rock surface. The outline of the first horse was then painted. Its head is inspired by the contour of the rock but is small and rudimentary—painted, with the neck, in black. The red and black dots were then sprayed onto the body through a blowpipe. When the body outline had been created, additional dots were placed outside the animal. The second horse was then created in the same way. Finally, hand stencils were placed on the rock, their obvious message being: I was here.

☗ The two dotted horses for which Pech-Merle is famous are mono-chrome, and represent a rather early stage of Paleolithic art. Analyses of the dots have revealed important information about the cult ceremonies that lie behind the paintings—each dot was formed from a different mixture of paint, indicating that they were created on different occasions.

☞ Several monochrome paintings of the now extinct woolly mammoth have been found in secluded parts of the cave of Pech-Merle. These belong to the very earliest stages of cave art, and add to the mysteriousness of this remarkable underground gallery.

MUSEUM FÜR VOR- UND FRÜHGESCHICHTE/BILDARCHIV PREUSSISCHER KULTURBESITZ

☛ The famous sorcerer from Les Trois Frères, Ariège, southern France. About 75 centimeters (30 inches) high, the image is partly painted and partly carved and has combined human, horse, deer, bird, and bear features. It probably depicts a shaman. The sketch was made by Abbé Breuil.

⚥ Two remarkably well-preserved bison sculptures of clay from Le Tuc d'Audoubert, southern France. A number of footprints of children, forming circular dance patterns around a group of sculptured clay phalluses, have been found in an adjoining chamber.

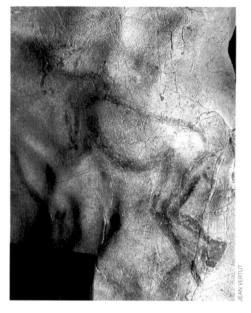

It was established that the figures in all Paleolithic caves appear in a dualistic relationship, with some species always appearing together, while others are never depicted on the same wall. More than half of the animal images depict horses and bison, two of the species that are always shown together.

The location of the images in the caves also shows a remarkable pattern. About 90 percent of all images of bison, aurochs, and horses appear in the central sanctuaries or main galleries, while all other animals are relegated to other, less prominent, locations in the caves.

Leroi-Gourhan interpreted the pairing of the animals as representing the relationship between masculine and feminine. In doing so, he also took into account the placing of the images in relation to the genital and schematic figures. He considered that horses were male symbols, while bison, aurochs, and mammoths were female symbols. Interestingly, another researcher, Annette Laming, came to the same conclusion independently at about the same time, except that she reversed the sexual symbolism, seeing the horses as female.

Details of Leroi-Gourhan's interpretations have been strongly criticized, but there is no doubt that his work raised a new set of questions and changed forever our perception of Paleolithic cave art. It is now accepted that this art was part of a deliberate and complex ritual system that was itself an integral part of the Paleolithic world of belief.

Ceremonies for Survival

Our new knowledge of the social and economic background to the rise of Paleolithic art does not, however, satisfactorily explain the individual peculiarities of the various groups of images, with their elements of sexual symbolism, fertility cult, hunting magic, shamanism, and totemism. The total picture is far too complex for a single explanation, and much of the substance of the rituals no doubt changed during the many thousands of years the cave art tradition persisted. However, recent research has revealed that many caves were used as ceremonial gathering places. A number of pieces of evidence clearly point to this.

Images of humans are comparatively rare in cave art, but a striking number of them combine human and animal features, and often the features of several animals. The most famous example is the "sorcerer" from Les Trois Frères, in the Pyrenees, a male figure with the antlers of a stag, a nose like the beak of a bird of prey, and staring, owl-like eyes. The figure also has a horse's tail and unnaturally short forelimbs ending in bear-like paws, with claws. His genitals are abnormally placed, under the tail. This strangely hunched, or crouched, figure seems to be engaged in a ceremonial dance.

Shamanism is the dominant element in the religion of most known arctic and subarctic hunter-gatherers, including the present-day Inuit (or Eskimos) and the reindeer hunters of northeastern Asia. Shamans are men or women who have a special relationship with the spiritual world and are called upon in times of sickness and other troubles to mediate with the spirits on the community's behalf. For example, when a shortage of game animals threatens the community's survival, the shaman enters a trance and sends out his or her soul to find out why the spirit who controls the animals is withholding them, and to persuade the spirit to send more animals. Shamans are also called upon to cure sickness (which in many such societies is believed to result from the

breaking of a taboo rather than from natural causes). It seems likely that similar beliefs were important to the big-game hunters of the Ice Age, and that shamans—or some equivalent—may have conducted ceremonies in the caves. What might these ceremonies have been?

Discussions of cave art have long been centered on the content and meaning of the images themselves, and in the process some important evidence indicating that ceremonial dance and other cult ceremonies took place inside the caves has been largely overlooked. For understandable reasons, this evidence has survived at only a few sites. In their eagerness to study paintings or carvings in a newly discovered cave, early researchers walked around on the moist and often soft floor surface, unwittingly destroying for all time the unique information that had remained untouched for tens of thousands of years: the footprints of the people who performed their ceremonies in the sanctuaries. A few sites where such evidence has been preserved have been known for a long time. The classic example is the cave of Le Tuc d'Audoubert, known for its well-preserved bison modeled from clay, where the footprints of six people have been found in an adjacent chamber. They are all those of children, and six rows of footprints reveal a distinct dance pattern.

In recent years, a number of cave chambers with well-preserved Paleolithic footprints have been discovered. The most spectacular example is in a previously unknown section of the big cave of Niaux, in the Pyrenees. More than 1,000 meters (3,000 feet) farther into the mountain than the famous sanctuary known as Gallerie Noir, with its black outline drawings of horses and bison, there are more than 500 footprints, the largest number so far discovered in any cave. The way in is extremely difficult, as three large underground lakes must first be negotiated.

The footprints have proved to be those of children between 13 and 15 years old. But, as in all known caves where footprints have survived, they are mingled with the tracks of adults. Flutes and the remains of what may have been other musical instruments have been found in many caves, indicating that the ceremonial dancing was accompanied by music.

Abbé Breuil, André Leroi-Gourhan, and others had earlier suggested that at least some Paleolithic cave art could be related to initiation rites of different kinds, but this was overshadowed by attempts to unlock the meaning of the images themselves. Within all traditional cultures, rites of passage are a crucial part of ritual and ceremonial life. They are related to birth, puberty, marriage,

Deep inside the cave of Niaux, more than 500 footprints of 13 to 15-year-old children, as well as those of adults, have been found, indicating that ceremonies once took place here.

The numerous rock shelters (or *abri*) in the Dordogne area were ideal dwelling places for people during the Paleolithic period, providing excellent protection from the elements.

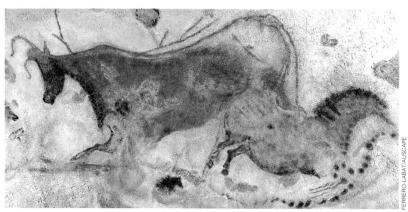

⚮ Polychrome paintings of a cow and a horse in one of the main friezes of the famous cave of Lascaux, in the Dordogne.

and death. Male initiation rites—when young boys, under the direction of a master, are initiated into the mysteries of the adult world—are often associated with isolation, darkness, and frightening experiences. Painful tests of manhood, such as tattooing and, sometimes, circumcision, are often an important element of these prolonged ceremonies. Dancing often accompanies such rituals, and among many traditional peoples today, including Australian Aborigines and the Bushmen of southern Africa, rock art is directly related to puberty rites of this kind. Nearly always, the rites are also used to impart knowledge of the mythological world. Animals play an important part in the mythology of most traditional peoples, particularly within totemistic societies, and often serve as sexual and fertility symbols.

As is the case with many archaeological findings, we may never understand the precise significance of cave art, with its many different images. Mythological symbols cannot simply be read like a book. Nevertheless, we are closer than ever before to understanding its function within Paleolithic society. The images in the caves are unique social documents, a kind of prehistoric encyclopedia, in which the different entries together reflect the need for communication, identification, and cohesion within a rapidly expanding and changing society. Contemporary evidence of ceremonial gathering places in the open as well as in caves suggests that some communities in this period had developed more accessible forms of ritual. Perhaps the most famous is the ceremonial center at Mezhirich, southeast of Kiev, in the Ukraine, built of 70 tonnes (almost 70 tons) of mammoth bones from 200 animals.

Art and ritual as forms of human expression would seem to represent one of the key ways in which people came to terms with a new, more demanding, and socially more complex way of life. The world of beliefs, and the ceremonies and rituals this engendered, were a means of binding the society together, protecting it, and preserving its values—ultimately, a strategy for survival.

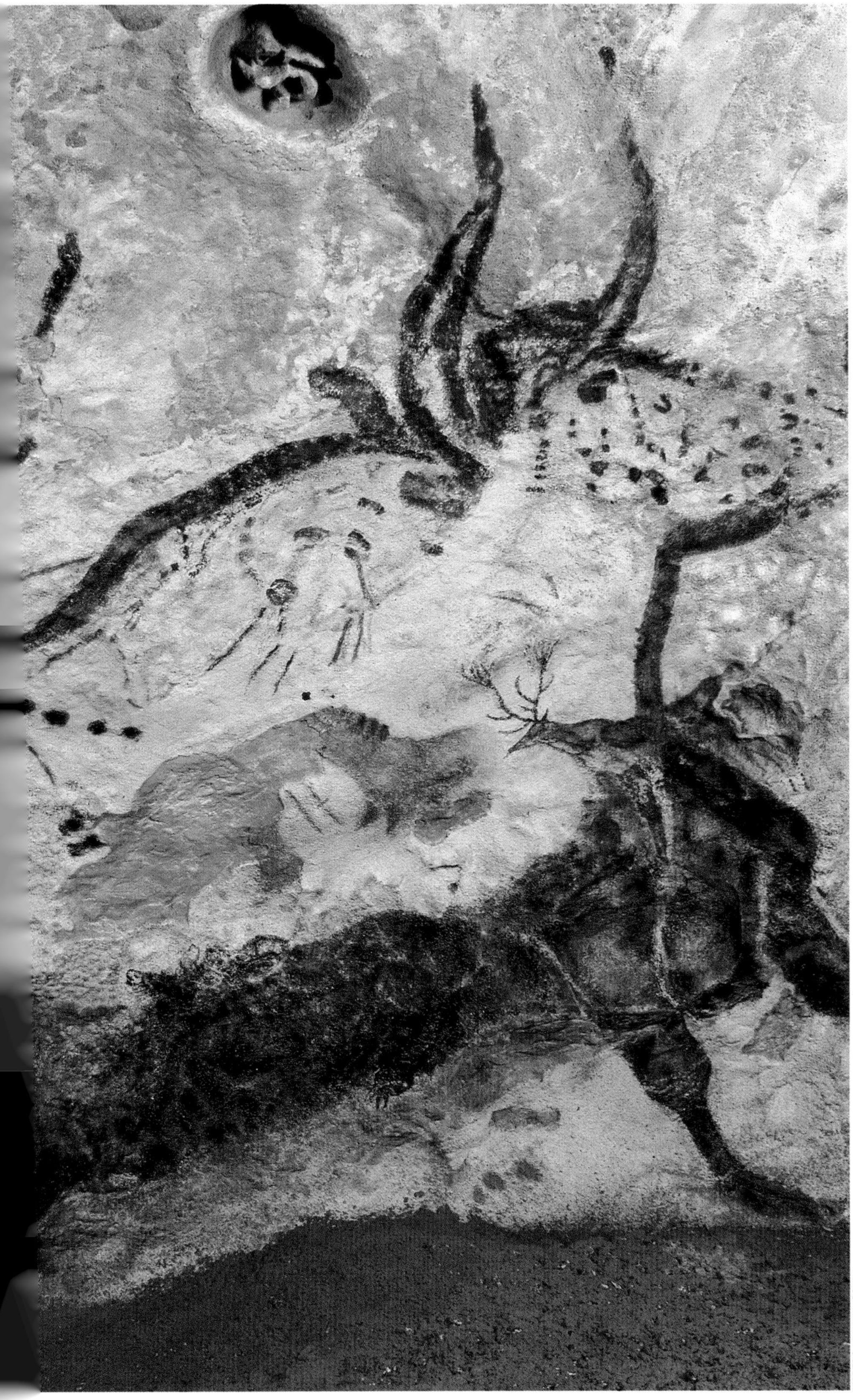

Challenged only by Altamira, Lascaux cave contains some of the finest examples of polychrome painting yet discovered. These paintings represent the peak of the 20,000-year-old tradition of Ice Age art in Europe, a tradition that died out about 12,000 years ago.

COSQUER CAVE:
AN ANCIENT SUNKEN GALLERY

JEAN CLOTTES AND JEAN COURTIN

E ARLY IN SEPTEMBER 1991, professional undersea diver Henri Cosquer informed the French Ministry of Culture that he had discovered prehistoric paintings and engravings in a cave deep under the sea off Cape Morgiou, near Marseilles. At about the same time, three amateur divers, who had probably heard about the discovery, swam into the cave, became lost in its murky galleries, and drowned when their air supply ran out.

◈ Henri Cosquer, who discovered the cave, beside a large bison painted black, its head shown in three-quarter view while the horns are represented frontally and the body in profile.

☛ The entrance to Cosquer Cave lies at the base of a limestone cliff, 37 meters (120 feet) below sea level, at Cape Morgiou, between Marseilles and Cassis, in the south of France.

Four black horses were painted over numerous finger tracings dating from an earlier period. An ibex, its horns depicted from the front while its body is in profile, and many other lines were then engraved over the horses (middle of the photograph).

The Ministry of Culture responded swiftly to these events. With the help of Henri Cosquer, whose name was given to the cave, it organized a series of dives from 16 to 25 September. The other members of the expedition were combat divers from the French navy and Jean Courtin. We examined the cave closely, took many photographs, collected samples for analysis, and made a preliminary survey of the galleries. The entrance was later blocked with rock and railings to secure the cave and its contents and to deter would-be explorers.

Hidden Chambers under the Sea

The tiny cave entrance is at the bottom of a cliff, 37 meters (120 feet) under the surface of the Mediterranean Sea. A narrow passage slopes upwards for 160 meters (525 feet), opening into several huge chambers. Only the upper half of the chambers is above sea level, and it is here that a number of wall paintings and engravings were found.

The cave opening was flooded at the end of the last Ice Age, when the sea level rose 120 meters (400 feet)—probably about 10,500 years ago. The lower part of the main chamber must have remained above water for a long time, because it contains a number of large stalagmites, which could not otherwise have formed. Cosquer Cave is only one of a number of caves in the area—some of them

These large stalagmites in the lower part of the main chamber are now entirely underwater. As calcite cannot deposit under such conditions, this proves that the chamber was free of water for millennia before it was flooded.

⬧ One of the many stenciled hands discovered on the walls of the cave. This one and several others are exceptional in showing part of the forearm. Like the finger tracings, these stenciled hands are several thousands of years older than the animal paintings and engravings.

known for a long time—that could have sheltered groups of people who were living by the sea in Paleolithic times.

There were no traces of art in the long gallery leading up to the chamber. Any images on its walls would long since have been destroyed by the salt water, which has deeply corroded the limestone walls. The same applies to the flooded part of the main chamber.

Where the cave is above water, it expands into a chamber 50 meters by 60 meters (165 feet by 200 feet). The ground is covered with stalagmites and huge fallen rocks. There are numerous charcoal fragments scattered about, many of them covered with calcite (the mineral from which stalagmites are formed).

Two small hearths, about 30 centimeters (12 inches) in diameter, may have been used to light the cave, as no bones, flints, or other artifacts were discovered. This is a place where people came but did not stay long.

A Unique Gallery

The cave has not yet been fully surveyed, and many images undoubtedly remain to be discovered. So far, the following have been recorded. On the walls and parts of the roof, there are paintings of at least 23 animals. Two are indeterminate (not unusual in cave art), but all the others are recognizable. They include 10 horses, 5 bison, an ibex, a red deer, and the head of a cave lion. There are also three paintings

of the extinct great auk (*Alca impennis*), a flightless relative of the razorbill, which was hunted to extinction during the nineteenth century— the only images of these birds known in Paleolithic art.

Among the many engravings, there are 21 animals: 4 horses, 2 bison, 6 ibexes, 5 chamois, 2 seals, and two that can't be determined. Long, spear-like lines with a barbed top have been engraved over the top of a number of them. In addition, thousands of lines crisscross the walls, many of them obviously traced or scraped by human fingers.

There are also 26 negative hand stencils on the walls and calcite draperies (wide, thin sheets of stalactites), 19 black and 7 red. (These were created by placing

⬥ This stag was painted on the roof of a very low passage, where there are only 40 centimeters (16 inches) between the roof and the floor, so the artist must have lain on his back. An ibex and two horses were also painted on the same ceiling. Bright white patches of calcite and a few stalactites have developed in this area and have covered parts of the animals.

One of the three black great auks—the only images of these birds known in an Upper Paleolithic cave. Like all the other animal paintings and engravings in this cave, they can be dated to between 18,000 and 19,000 years ago. The images of marine creatures—seals, fish, and possibly jellyfish or squid, as well as the auks—are one of the unique features of Cosquer Cave.

a hand on the wall and outlining the shape with paint blown through a blowpipe.) Most have incomplete fingers, as in the cave of Gargas, in the Pyrenees. The most likely explanation for this is that the fingers were bent in a sort of sign language.

As is to be expected, the images are very weathered. The lines of the paintings are eroded on the sides, and many are partly covered with calcite, which deposits slowly over decades. A random sample of charcoal taken from the ground was radiocarbon-dated at 16,490 BC plus or minus 440 years—that is, about

18,500 years old. This makes Cosquer Cave some 15 centuries older than Lascaux. Many other charcoal fragments were identified as belonging to two species of pine known to have grown in the area during the last Ice Age (*Pinus silvestris* and *Pinus nigra*), providing further confirmation of the date.

The conventions the artists followed in depicting the animals—showing the horns and antlers front on, when the bodies are drawn in profile; always omitting the hoofs; the stiff postures, with shortened, stick-like legs—are fully consistent with the radiocarbon date. The

Provence painters who came to this cave used the same artistic conventions as those who painted the cave of Ebbou, in the Ardèche Valley, about 150 kilometers (90 miles) to the northwest.

Cosquer Cave is the first cave containing mural art to be found in Provence. It is a find of great significance, adding much to our knowledge of Paleolithic art. The images are abundant and varied, and the seals and great auks are unique. Our only regret is that the sea, which has preserved the cave over millennia, has also destroyed so much of what it once contained.

SPREADING THROUGHOUT THE GLOBE

50,000 YEARS AGO – 10,000 YEARS AGO

Towards New Continents

GÖRAN BURENHULT

W E KNOW THAT MODERN humans first appeared in Africa between 200,000 and 150,000 years ago. From there they spread outward to the rest of the continent, to Europe, and to parts of Asia. Southwest Asia seems to have provided a natural passage for these pioneers.

Human remains have been found in the Levantine area dating to about 100,000 years ago, whereas Europe was first populated by *Homo sapiens sapiens* only about 40,000 years ago. These modern humans spread into unknown territory slowly but steadily. It was never a question of deliberate migration. Scattered groups extended their hunting grounds by only a few kilometers (2 or 3 miles) per generation, but this was enough for them to populate the world in some tens of thousands of years.

↩ Between 50,000 and 10,000 years ago, anatomically modern humans spread across the world. In pursuit of game, people gradually settled the vast and previously uninhabited tundras of Siberia and North America. Reindeer and, in North America, caribou were the favored game animals of these early pioneers.

⚘ An Upper Paleolithic Venus figurine from southern Siberia.
MUSEE DE L'HOMME, PARIS/J. OSTER

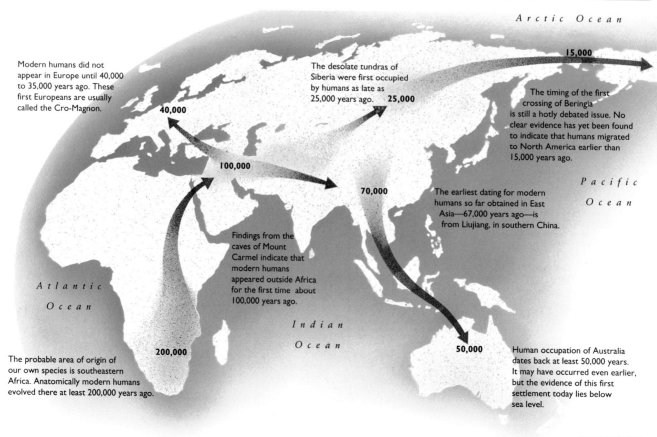

Modern humans did not appear in Europe until 40,000 to 35,000 years ago. These first Europeans are usually called the Cro-Magnon.

Arctic Ocean

The desolate tundras of Siberia were first occupied by humans as late as 25,000 years ago.

The timing of the first crossing of Beringia is still a hotly debated issue. No clear evidence has yet been found to indicate that humans migrated to North America earlier than 15,000 years ago.

Pacific Ocean

The earliest dating for modern humans so far obtained in East Asia—67,000 years ago—is from Liujiang, in southern China.

Findings from the caves of Mount Carmel indicate that modern humans appeared outside Africa for the first time about 100,000 years ago.

Atlantic Ocean

Indian Ocean

The probable area of origin of our own species is southeastern Africa. Anatomically modern humans evolved there at least 200,000 years ago.

Human occupation of Australia dates back at least 50,000 years. It may have occurred even earlier, but the evidence of this first settlement today lies below sea level.

CARTOGRAPHY: RAY SIM

THE SPREADING OF MODERN HUMANS

About 100,000 years ago, anatomically modern humans began to spread outside Africa. The arrows indicate their assumed routes of expansion, and approximate dates of arrival are given.

The characteristics these modern humans acquired were to influence cultural evolution throughout the world. They were remarkably adaptable, which meant that they could inhabit areas that had been inaccessible to earlier hominids. For the first time, people settled in the arctic regions of Eurasia, adapting to the most difficult ecology on Earth. Ten to fifteen thousand years before Cro-Magnon humans entered Europe, their cousins in Southeast Asia had crossed 90 kilometers (56 miles) of open water by some form of sea-craft and reached present-day Australia and New Guinea. Some millennia later, groups of people took advantage of the low sea level during the last glacial to walk or paddle across present-day Bering Strait, entering the continent of North America. In the space of a few tens of thousands of years, modern humans opened up new worlds—in the north, the northeast, and the southeast.

Asian Anomalies

While cultural evolution in western Asia generally corresponded with that in Europe, East Asia developed characteristics of its own. Human fossils found there, dated to between 200,000 and 100,000 years ago—the period during which the

Neanderthals were evolving—look very different from those found in the west. As American anthropologist Richard Klein says, "At a time before 50,000–40,000 years ago when western Asia was variably occupied by Neanderthals perhaps derived from Europe or by very early moderns arguably derived from Africa, eastern Asia seems to have been occupied by a distinctive human type(s) that was neither Neanderthal nor modern".

The lack of modern excavations makes this period in East Asia difficult to evaluate. We have known for a long time that the blade tools that appeared in Europe with *Homo sapiens sapiens* were apparently not introduced or developed in East Asia. Instead, the flake and chopper tools used by *Homo erectus* survived there for more than 300,000 years, to as late as about 10,000 BC. Correspondingly, there seemed to be no evidence in eastern Eurasia of the cultural developments that took place in Europe during the Upper Paleolithic period—a wider and more sophisticated use of antler and bone, the rise of art, and evidence of a rich ritual life, with complex burial practices.

A number of important new finds indicate, however, that modern humans who had developed advanced stone and bone tools and a complex ritual and artistic life settled the southern, eastern, and southeastern parts of Asia during the very early phases of the Upper Paleolithic period. The remarkable fact that *Homo sapiens sapiens* populated Australia and New Guinea at least 50,000 years ago certainly points to this, but this is not the only evidence. Fossils of modern humans found at Liujiang, in China, have been dated to 67,000 years ago. At Batadomba Iena, a cave in the southwestern part of Sri Lanka, settlement layers dating back to about 29,000 years ago have yielded the remains of modern humans, together with small, technically sophisticated stone tools (so-called geometric microliths) and bone tools. Apparently, sophisticated stone tools existed in Southeast Asia, but they were not widespread and not as standardized as those found further west. Because they existed side by side with more traditional tools, it would appear that they were developed locally. Consequently, the big, as yet unanswered, question is why *Homo sapiens sapiens* took new technology with them to the west but not to the east.

Between 35,000 and 20,000 years ago, Upper Paleolithic big-game hunters spread over the vast tundras of northeastern Siberia for the first time and soon became the first humans to set foot in America. Siberian stone tools differed from their contemporary European equivalents, being made from different raw materials and influenced by the blade cultures of the west and the flake cultures of the southeast. As time went on, this Siberian cultural tradition spread south and east to Mongolia, China, Korea, and Japan.

During the last glacial, northeastern Siberia had such low levels of rain and snow that ice sheets and glaciers like those in northern Europe never formed. The hunters who inhabited these immense, frozen, and treeless expanses had to cover vast territories in pursuit of game and other food. There were few caves and rock shelters for protection, so they had to build huts that could withstand the severe cold. They also needed effective fireplaces that would allow them to maintain fires almost continuously, and close-fitting clothes of fur and hide. Antler and bone implements were crucial aids to these enterprises. The mammoth became a sought-after game animal, because it provided food, hides, and large quantities of bones that could be used as fuel, building material, and tools.

Towards New Horizons

Some time between 50,000 and 40,000 years ago, groups of people in today's Indonesia became the first seafarers, paddling some 90 kilometers (56 miles) in canoes or on rafts across the Sunda Strait to present-day Australia and New Guinea. The lack of reliably dated material in Southeast Asia still makes it difficult to chart the appearance of modern humans in this region in any detail. The best-documented material has been found in

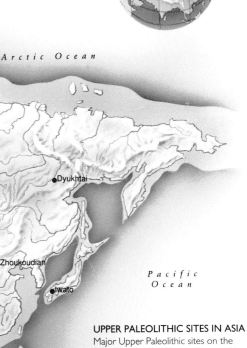

CARTOGRAPHY: RAY SIM

UPPER PALEOLITHIC SITES IN ASIA
Major Upper Paleolithic sites on the Asian continent, with coastlines and ice sheets as they were during the peak of the last glacial, some 18,000 years ago. Exposed land bridges facilitated expansion into America and Japan, and towards Australia.

Australia, and we now know that *Homo sapiens sapiens* had reached Tasmania, the southernmost part of the continent, before 30,000 years ago.

In tracing the stone tool cultures of Southeast Asia during the Upper Paleolithic period, two sites in Vietnam have long been important: Son Vi and Hoa-Binh. Modern excavations and radiocarbon datings have confirmed that the Sonviian tradition is the older of the two, suggesting that it existed between 18,000 and 11,000 years ago. The Hoabinhian tradition, which appeared about 14,000 years ago, became much more widespread, extending south to Sumatra and east to the Philippines. It survived in many different forms well into the Neolithic period. Pottery from Spirit Cave, in Thailand, for example, has been dated to

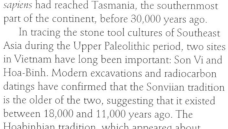

View from inside one of the Niah Caves, situated in the Gunung Subis limestone massif, in Sarawak, East Malaysia. This famous and spectacular site was used both for habitation and burial, and has yielded a human skull believed to be about 40,000 years old.

HANS HÖFER/APA PHOTO AGENCY SIN

PETER BELLWOOD

Excavation at the rock shelter of Hagop Bilo, one of the Baturong sites, in Sabah, East Malaysia. The site was occupied between 17,000 and 12,000 years ago.

this period, and in Vietnam, the bearers of this tradition were making pottery as early as 8000 BC.

The finds at Son Vi and Hoa-Binh are clearly much too recent to shed any light on the first Australians. However, newly found sites in Southeast Asia dated to earlier than 25,000 years ago may in time tell us much more about cultural development in this part of the world during the Upper Paleolithic period. Lang Rong Rien, in southern Thailand, is a particularly important site, the tools in its oldest layers dating back to about 40,000 years ago. Other important sites are Leang Burung and Wallanae River, in South Sulawesi, Indonesia; Tabon Cave, on the island of Palawan, and Cagayan Valley, in Luzon, both in the Philippines; Tingkayu, in Sabah; and Niah Cave, in Sarawak, East Malaysia. (See the feature *Tools and Cultures in Late Paleolithic Southeast Asia.*)

The closest fossils that could possibly be the ancestors of the Australian Aborigines and the Papuans of New Guinea are the classic skulls found at Ngandong and Wajak, in Java, Indonesia. These are almost certainly more than 60,000 years old, although they cannot yet be accurately dated. On this evidence, it seems likely that further finds of modern human fossils, considerably older than

those so far discovered, will soon be made in southern Asia.

At certain times during the last Ice Age (the Upper Pleistocene period, which extended from about 115,000 years ago to about 10,000 years ago), the sea level dropped as much as 120 meters (400 feet) as large amounts of water were frozen in the immense land glaciers in the north. During such periods, the area that today comprises Australia, New Guinea, and the Sahul Shelf was exposed as one landmass, known as Sahul or Greater Australia. Water-craft would still have been needed to cross the narrow straits separating the Sunda Shelf (of which Java, Sumatra, and Southeast Asia formed part) from Sahul.

◑ Modern humans reached the steaming jungles of Southeast Asia at least 60,000 to 50,000 years ago. Fossil finds of early settlers in this region are, however, still very few.

TOOLS AND CULTURES IN LATE PALEOLITHIC SOUTHEAST ASIA

Ian C. Glover

I N THE 1940s, the American prehistorian Hallam Movius characterized the Paleolithic cultures of Southeast Asia as being a part of the "East Asian Chopper and Chopping Tool Complex", a tradition dominated by large flint-core tools showing little refinement and few specialized types. This tradition was thought to have survived throughout the Middle and Upper Pleistocene periods and to have persisted, with little change, into the early Holocene period as the Hoabhinian culture, which was largely replaced from 4000 BC by Neolithic cultures brought by intrusive southern Mongoloid populations expanding into the region from South China.

Recent excavations in several parts of Southeast Asia have shown that there was much greater variability, change, and specialization in the stone tool assemblages of the late Upper Pleistocene than was previously appreciated, and this period now promises to overthrow many previously held assumptions about cultural adaptations and processes in Southeast Asia. However, very little is yet known about the late Upper Pleistocene cultures of this part of the world.

IAN C. GLOVER

⚒ Excavating in Leang Burung 2.

⚑ The Tingkayu Plain, in Sabah, was covered by a lake from 28,000 to 18,000 years ago, and hunters left many bifacially flaked chert points by its shores.

⚒ In South Sulawesi also, excavations in 1975 revealed a Levalloisian point and blade industry at the rock shelter site of Leang Burung 2 (Bird Cave 2) which can be dated to between 30,000 and 19,000 years ago. The abundant animal remains from the cave show that the environment was little different from that of today. The rich flake assemblage includes some fine points with prepared platforms, and blades, scrapers, and flakes with edge gloss. The few cores confirm a knowledge of Levalloisian technology.
IAN C. GLOVER

✏ Hagop Bilo, a rock shelter in the Baturong limestone massif in Sabah, in the Malaysian part of the island of Borneo, was occupied by humans some 17,000 to 12,000 years ago and shows a typical island South East Asian Late Stone Age flake and blade industry. Flakes with a silica gloss are known, together with remains of modern animals including pigs, deer, monkeys, rats, snakes, lizards, tortoises, porcupines, and some birds, as well as three species of freshwater gastropods.

♀ Tabon Cave, on the island of Palawan, in the Philippines, has long been known for its long sequence through the Late Pleistocene period. Here, too, the assemblage is dominated by a flake tradition, although the coarse nature of the quartzite used limited the range of specialized tool types in comparison with other sites further south in the islands of Southeast Asia.

PETER BELLWOOD

PETER BELLWOOD

PETER BELLWOOD

⚒ Vietnam's Stone Age prehistory has been more extensively researched than that of any other Southeast Asian country, and yet a previously totally unknown Levalloisian flake industry dated to before 23,000 years ago has recently been found at Nguom Cave, in the limestone mountains of North Vietnam's Bac Thai Province, below a Hoabhinian assemblage, from which it was separated by layers of rock fall and breccia.
IAN C. GLOVER

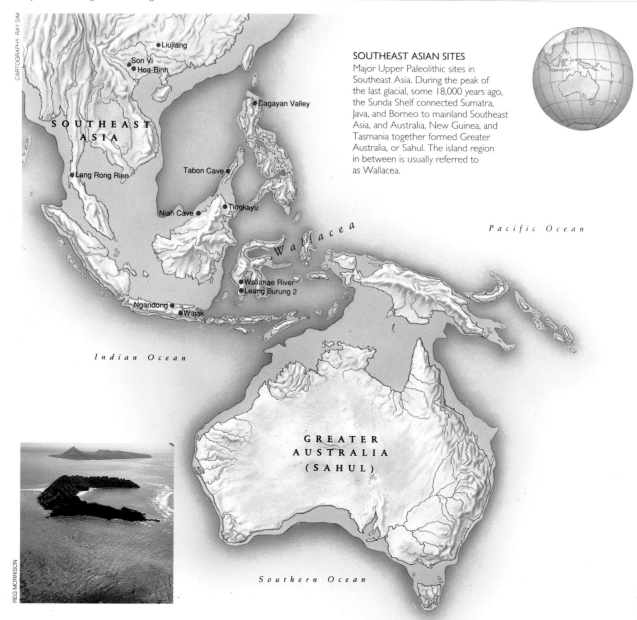

CARTOGRAPHY: RAY SIM

SOUTHEAST ASIA

Liujiang
Son Vi
Hoa-Binh
Cagayan Valley
Lang Rong Rien
Tabon Cave
Niah Cave
Tingkayu
Wallanae River
Leang Burung 2
Ngandong
Wajak

Indian Ocean

Wallacea

Pacific Ocean

SOUTHEAST ASIAN SITES
Major Upper Paleolithic sites in Southeast Asia. During the peak of the last glacial, some 18,000 years ago, the Sunda Shelf connected Sumatra, Java, and Borneo to mainland Southeast Asia, and Australia, New Guinea, and Tasmania together formed Greater Australia, or Sahul. The island region in between is usually referred to as Wallacea.

GREATER AUSTRALIA (SAHUL)

Southern Ocean

REG MORRISON

⚓ The Mer Islands in Torres Strait—isolated remains of the land area that once connected Australia to New Guinea. Some 8,000 years ago, the land bridge was drowned, thereby separating the populations of Australia and New Guinea.

↪ Eastern Java, Madura, Bali, and Lombok, in Indonesia, as seen from space. It was in these waters that people conquered the sea for the first time, making possible human occupation of the Australian continent.

The fact that sea journeys were necessary to cross between the islands in Wallacea—the island region between the Asian mainland and Sahul—suggests that the early peoples who lived along the coasts would have developed some sort of sea-craft.

About 53,000 years ago, and again about 35,000 years ago, the sea level dropped considerably, making Sahul more accessible. Reaching Sahul through Timor 53,000 years ago, however, still involved a sea voyage of about 90 kilometers (56 miles). In view of this, it seems likely that Sahul was originally settled by accident. The first occupants were probably small groups of people landing in different places. Significant physical differences between the New Guineans and the Australian Aborigines suggest that separate groups landed in different parts of Sahul and established viable populations. The physical differences have become more and more marked as these peoples have adapted to vastly different environments over a very long period.

Most of the settlements dating from the first occupation of Sahul will never be found, as they are now at least 100 meters (300 feet) below sea level. The fact that no early materials have yet been found may indicate that these earliest settlers lived mainly on the coast. They gradually spread throughout the continent, reaching the southernmost parts of Australia before 30,000 years ago. By 20,000 years ago, they inhabited all environmental zones, including the central desert.

Mammoth ivory carvings depicting flying waterbirds have been found at the Upper Paleolithic site of Mal'ta, near Lake Baikal, in Siberia. Some of these bird figurines have female features, and it has been suggested that they represent a Bird Goddess.
SISSE BRIMBERG

The Arctic Challenge

In Europe, Neanderthals had occasionally ventured into the extensive tundra steppes of the north during the summer months, but they did not settle there permanently. To survive in a region where it was winter for nine months of the year required a quite different technology, and it was *Homo sapiens sapiens* who developed this technology. Many of the tools that made it possible for them to adapt to this harsh environment were made of antler and bone. The many perforated bone needles that have been found suggest that sewn leather clothing was common, and their sophisticated, often richly decorated spear-throwers made of antler made it possible for them to bring down animals from greater distances than previously—a necessity for hunters in this open, treeless landscape.

A series of more or less spectacular settlements stretching from the Czech Republic in the west to Siberia's Chukchi Peninsula, on Bering Strait, in the east indicates that the northern tundra steppes were settled between 30,000 and 15,000 years ago. The oldest of these settlements so far excavated is at Dolní Věstonice, in the Czech Republic, dating back to about 28,000 years ago, where a couple of large houses with central fireplaces were found.

On Russia's River Don, about 470 kilometers (290 miles) south of Moscow, lies the settlement of Kostenki, which has given its name to the Kostenki–Bershevo culture. Most sites from this tradition have been dated to between 27,000 and 13,000 years ago. The houses at Kostenki are known as pit dwellings, because the floors were dug about a meter (3 feet) into the ground to make the house as draftproof as possible. The rib-like frame of the arched roof was made out of mammoth tusks, and this was then covered with hides. The size of these houses, as well as the large number of fireplaces inside them, suggests that a number of families lived there at the one time.

Many of these magnificent settlements appear to have been places where large groups of people gathered for ceremonies and other social activities. The ritual function of these places is most obvious in the most remarkable of them all: Mezhirich, situated on the banks of the Dnepr, southeast of Kiev, in Ukraine. Dating back to 15,000 years ago, the five houses that have been excavated here were made entirely of ingeniously interlocked

More than 30 mammoth ivory figurines have been found in the remains of a dwelling at the Upper Paleolithic site of Mal'ta, in Siberia. Many of them, like this one, depict stiff-looking female figures.
MUSEE DE L'HOMME, PARIS/J. OSTER

mammoth bones and tusks, and the settlement covered more than 10,000 square meters (17,000 square yards). The houses were very large, each enclosing an area of 80 square meters (100 square yards). At least 50 people probably lived here at the one time. Finds of amber and shells, which must have been carried over distances ranging from 160 to 800 kilometers (100 to 500 miles), also strongly suggest that Mezhirich was a rendezvous for ceremonial activities and the interchange of commodities. (See the feature *Mammoth Bone Huts.*)

The famous and well-preserved graves discovered at Sungir, outside Moscow, allow us an even more telling glimpse of the ritual life and social organization of the Paleolithic big-game hunters. Here, both children and adults were buried with remarkably rich grave goods, dressed in magnificent clothes and headdresses, with decorations of thousands of pierced animal teeth. These burials have been interpreted as indicating the beginnings of social stratification among arctic hunter-gatherer societies of the Ice Age. (See the feature *Sungir: A Stone Age Burial Site.*)

◄► The first immigrants in Alaska discovered a land of breathtaking vistas. The previously uninhabited continent was abundant in big game and must have been a land of milk and honey for the early Americans.

⚭ Siberian figurines, like some of those found at sites near Lake Baikal, represent the easternmost examples of the widespread and long-lived Venus tradition. Very similar carvings were created all the way to the Atlantic coast, nearly 8,000 kilometers (5,000 miles) away, indicating intensive contacts between the big-game hunters of Ice Age Eurasia.
SISSE BRIMBERG

Southeast of Samarkand, in central Asia, lies Shugnou, another riverside site and one of the world's highest Paleolithic sites. Bone deposits reveal that the most common game in this region were horses, aurochs, wild sheep, and goats. The oldest layers at Shugnou date back to about 20,000 years ago, and the location of the site indicates that the growing population was forcing people to settle further north and higher in the mountains.

During the Upper Paleolithic period, Siberia and northeastern Asia were inhabited by two entirely different cultural groups. The Mal'ta Afontova, which is probably the older, is named after two sites in the valley of the Yenisey, near Lake Baikal. People had settled in this arctic environment by about 22,000 years ago, living in longhouses and hunting big game, including mammoths and horses, locally and on the plains further south. Apart from retouched stone tools such as spear-points, scrapers, and burins, they made tools of bone, antler, and ivory, and female and bird figurines. Clearly, this group had close ties with contemporary cultural groups in the west, particularly those of eastern Europe.

The second group who had settled in this arctic region of northeastern Asia were the Dyukhtai, who lived largely around the rivers of Lena and Aldan, east of the Yenisey. They existed between 18,000 and 12,000 years ago, although there is some unconfirmed evidence of older occupation. Their tools were very different from those of the Mal'ta–Afontova tradition. Among other things, they made very effective tools from small chips of stone, known as microblades. We do not know where this practice originated, but similar tools have been found in northern China, dating from about 22,000 years ago, and also in Japan, although the latter finds have not as yet been reliably dated.

Unlike the Mal'ta people, the Dyukhtai were clearly orientated towards the east, and this is crucially important in tracing the first migration across Bering Strait into America. As time went on, the Dyukhtai proved adept at adjusting to climatic and environmental conditions very different from those traditional tundra hunters were accustomed to.

MAMMOTH BONE HUTS

ROLAND FLETCHER

AFTER THE END of the period of extreme
cold between 20,000 and 18,000 years
ago, people began to move back into the
central Russian plain. In the winter and spring,
they lived in huts made of mammoth bone.
One such settlement, discovered at Mezhirich,
in Ukraine, was occupied some time between
15,000 and 14,000 years ago. It lay a short distance
from the junction of two rivers, on the higher,
western bank of the main river. The hills were
covered with grass. Pine trees, birch, and alder
grew on the floodplains below. The community
hunted mammoths (quite how we do not know),
bison, horses, and reindeer. They also caught
birds and a few fish, such as pike, and hunted
arctic foxes and hares for their pelts. Between
30 and 60 people may have lived here. Each
hut had a hearth, fueled by bone. Around
the dwellings were fireplaces, storage pits
for meat and bone, and areas where flint
and bone tools were made.

☝ This engraved piece of mammoth ivory found at Mezhirich may be a picture of the huts—perhaps the oldest known map. Images of landscapes are very rare in Upper Paleolithic art.

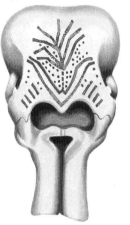

☚ A mammoth skull elaborately painted with red ocher was found in one of the huts. Similarly decorated mammoth bones have been found at Mezin, 200 kilometers (120 miles) to the north. Small ivory figurines and beads made of amber from the Kiev area were also found.

♀ Mezhirich was excavated by I. Pidoplichko, N.L. Kornietz, and M.I. Gladin in several stages between 1966 and 1983. Olga Soffer, on whose work much of this description is based, analyzed the animal remains.

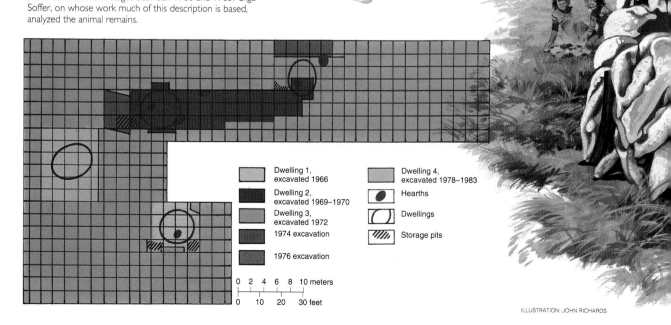

Dwelling 1, excavated 1966	Dwelling 4, excavated 1978–1983
Dwelling 2, excavated 1969–1970	Hearths
Dwelling 3, excavated 1972	Dwellings
1974 excavation	Storage pits
1976 excavation	

0 2 4 6 8 10 meters

0   10   20   30 feet

ILLUSTRATION: JOHN RICHARDS

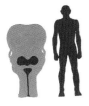

➤ Each hut had a solid base of large mammoth bones and a lighter superstructure. The bones were carefully interlocked, often in symmetrical patterns. Different bones predominate in each hut.. The base of one was built of mandibles; that of another, mainly of long bones. Some of the large bones have holes cut in them, probably to support a timber frame. Large tusks were fitted together to form the roof arch. The frame was presumably covered by skins and turf.

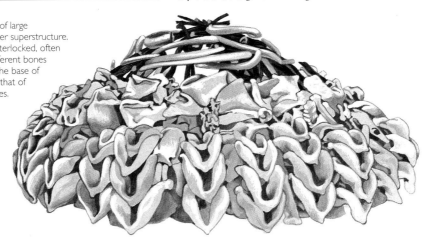

♀ It would have taken 10 people about 15 days to build the settlement. The storage pits, which are about a meter (3 feet) deep, could only have been dug in warmer weather, when the ground was not frozen, so building would have started in the autumn. Between 150 and 650 bones were used for each hut—a total of 97 crania, 109 mandibles, 92 tusks, and several hundred other large bones. The biggest of the huts was made of 20 tonnes (just under 20 tons) of bone, including 46 crania, 95 mandibles, and 40 tusks. A single cranium weighs 100 kilograms (220 pounds), and a tusk can be as heavy as 200 kilograms (440 pounds). Most parts of the mammoth were used, and bones of the same animal are found in different huts. The bones probably came from a nearby natural "cemetery".

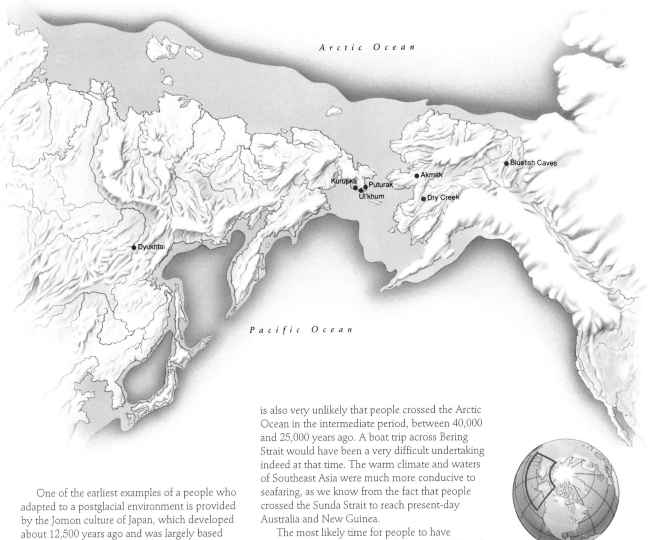

Arctic Ocean

Bluefish Caves

Akmak

Kurupka Puturak
Ul'khum
Dry Creek

Dyukhtai

Pacific Ocean

One of the earliest examples of a people who adapted to a postglacial environment is provided by the Jomon culture of Japan, which developed about 12,500 years ago and was largely based on fishing and other marine resources. The rich resources along the coasts allowed the Jomon people to become sedentary, which, in turn, led to their becoming one of the first peoples in the world to make pottery. Dating back to 12,000 years ago, their pots were probably used for cooking mollusks and plants. In some areas, the Jomon culture survived unaltered right up to the beginning of the first century AD.

During two phases of the last Ice Age—from 50,000 to 40,000 years ago, and again from 25,000 to 14,000 years ago—the present Bering Strait was drained, as were large parts of the Arctic Ocean in the north and the Bering Sea in the south. This territory, often called Beringia, connected Alaska with Siberia's Chukchi Peninsula, making it possible for humans and animals to cross from one continent to the other. It is unlikely that humans migrated into North America during the first phase, as there is no evidence of human set-tlement in northeastern Asia from this period. It

is also very unlikely that people crossed the Arctic Ocean in the intermediate period, between 40,000 and 25,000 years ago. A boat trip across Bering Strait would have been a very difficult undertaking indeed at that time. The warm climate and waters of Southeast Asia were much more conducive to seafaring, as we know from the fact that people crossed the Sunda Strait to reach present-day Australia and New Guinea.

The most likely time for people to have crossed Bering Strait is clearly between 25,000 and 14,000 years ago. This corresponds with the known spread of modern humans into the arctic regions of Europe and with the earliest finds of big-game hunters' settlements within the Mal'ta and Dyukhtai traditions of northeastern Siberia, which date back to between 18,000 and 15,000 years ago. The oldest known tools on both sides of Bering Strait exhibit a similar microlithic blade technique: those within the Dyukhtai tradition, in Siberia, and those found in sites such as Bluefish Caves (c. 13,000 BC), Dry Creek (9000 BC), and Akmak (c. 8000 BC), in Alaska. In spite of intensive efforts to find older signs of human occupation in Alaska, there are at present no reliable finds older than those from Bluefish Caves, going back 15,000 years. Tools of a similar age have been excavated from several Upper Paleolithic sites in the Chukchi Peninsula, including Kurupka, Puturak, and Ul'khum, which undoubtedly housed the ancestors of the first Americans.

THE ICE AGE LAND BRIDGE OF BERINGIA
Between 25,000 and 14,000 years ago, eastern Siberia and Alaska were connected by a land bridge usually referred to as Beringia. The timing of the first crossing of people into North America is the subject of intense debate. Coastlines and ice sheets are shown as they were during the peak of the last glacial, some 18,000 years ago.
CARTOGRAPHY: RAY SIM

◄► Only some 80 kilometers (50 miles) of icy waters today separate Russia's Chukchi Peninsula from Alaska. During the last Ice Age, Bering Strait was drained, allowing humans to cross by land from Asia to the New World. Shown here are the Diomede Islands, situated in the middle of the strait.

SUNGIR: A STONE AGE BURIAL SITE

OLGA SOFFER

THE SITE OF SUNGIR, containing the richest Upper
Paleolithic burials found in the world to date,
is located on the outskirts of the city of Vladimir, some
200 kilometers (125 miles) east-northeast of Moscow,
in Russia. The site was discovered in 1955 during brick
quarrying and was excavated between 1956 and 1977.

The cultural layer of the site, 15 to 90 centimeters
(6 to 35 inches) thick, was situated on a 50 meter
(164 foot) promontory formed by the banks of the
Klyazma River and those of its tributary, the Sungir.
It was found some 3 meters (10 feet) below the
present-day surface and lay on top of soil formed
during a somewhat warmer period that occurred
between about 29,000 and 25,000 years ago.
Radiocarbon dates obtained on wood charcoal
from the site put its age between some 25,500 and
22,000 years ago, with the former age probably
being the more accurate one.

Although people occupied Sungir during a warmer
spell of the last Ice Age, they were nonetheless living
in a tundra environment when climatic conditions
were severe enough to produce permafrost
(permanently frozen ground). Climatic conditions
worsened after the site was abandoned, and the
cultural layer was significantly disturbed by repeated
freezing and thawing of the deposits.

Sungir measured some 10,000 square meters
(108,000 square feet) in area, of which 4,500 square
meters (about 48,500 square feet) were excavated.
The opened area contained five concentrations of
cultural materials, consisting of the remains of surface
dwellings; numerous hearths and pits of various sizes;
work areas where stone and bone implements were
manufactured; and remains of at least six burials, three
of which were undisturbed. The nature of the animal
remains (reindeer, horses, mammoths, arctic foxes,
and a few wolves, bears, wolverines, arctic hares,
and bison) and the transitory nature of the dwellings
indicate that people occupied Sungir during the
summer to early autumn, while the distribution of
cultural remains suggests that the site was visited
repeatedly over a number of years.

MUSÉE DE L'HOMME, PARIS/O. BADER

☙ More than 3,000 ivory beads were sewn onto the clothing of the older male
buried at the Upper Paleolithic site of Sungir.

Tools and Ornaments

Sungir's stone tool inventory consisted of more than 50,000 pieces made from locally available cobbles. The stone tools (3.6 percent of the total inventory) include bifacially retouched triangular points, Aurignacian pieces, and archaic Mousterian forms, and point to the site's early Upper Paleolithic age. Scholars disagree on its cultural affinity. Some assign the inventory to an Aurignacian tradition with leaf points, while others see it as a younger stage in the development of the local Kostenki–Streletskaia culture.

Sungir also produced a very rich inventory of worked bone, ivory, and antler pieces shaped into a variety of implements; remains of jewelry made of stone, bone, ivory, shell, and belemnites; and perforated arctic fox canine teeth fashioned into beads, bracelets, pins, pendants, and rings. Carved decorative objects found included two animal figurines (a horse or saiga antelope and a mammoth) and perforated ivory and stone disks. Most of these objects were found in the graves described below.

Double burial of an adolescent boy and girl at the Upper Paleolithic site of Sungir with a rich inventory of ivory spears, lances, and jewelry. Close to 6,000 beads were sewn onto the clothing, but these were removed before the photograph was taken.
MUSEE DE L'HOMME, PARIS/ARLETTE LEROI-GOURHAN

The Human Evidence

Although remains of nine anatomically modern people (*Homo sapiens sapiens*) have been found at Sungir to date, two intact burials of three bodies found in the southwestern part of the site have made it world famous. These, consisting of a single grave of a 45 to 60-year-old male (burial 1) and a double grave where a 13-year-old boy was interred head to head with a 9 to 10-year-old girl (burial 2), were found some 3 meters (10 feet) apart. Both graves, measuring 2.05 by 0.7 meters (6 feet, 9 inches by 2 feet, 3 inches) and 3.05 by 0.7 meters (11 feet, 6 inches by 2 feet, 3 inches), respectively, were situated inside dwellings and had been dug into permafrost to a depth of 65 to 75 centimeters (26 to 30 inches). The bottom of the graves was covered with a layer of black charcoal, then white limestone, then red ocher.

The bodies were laid out extended on their back, with arms folded across their pelvis, and all three burials were liberally sprinkled with red ocher. The placement of thousands of beads sewn on their hide and fur clothing suggests that all three were clad in shirts, long pants with attached footwear, over-the-knee fur boots, and short outer cloaks. The males were wearing fur hats, and the girl wore a hood.

The man's clothing was decorated with some 3,000 ivory beads, his hat or cap was circled with perforated arctic fox teeth, and his forehead and biceps were bedecked with ivory bracelets. Just under 5,000 beads were sewn onto the boy's clothing, and he wore a belt made of more than 250 drilled arctic fox canines and a bracelet and pendant made of ivory. An ivory sculpture of a mammoth had been placed underneath him. A spear measuring 2.4 meters (nearly 8 feet) and weighing more than 20 kilograms (44 pounds) lay beside him, along with assorted ivory spears and lances and a perforated ivory disk with a latticework design. At his left side, near the edge of the grave, lay a human femur with broken epiphyses which was filled with red ocher.

The girl's burial was the most elaborate. The grave contained 5,274 beads and bead fragments; numerous ivory lances, including one 1.6 meters (5 feet, 3 inches) long; two perforated and decorated pieces of antler known as *bâtons de commandement* (sometimes called shaft straighteners); and four carved round ivory disks with a latticework design, one of which was inserted into an ivory shaft.

While both the single and the double burials were dug down from the same cultural layer into the underlying loess–loam stratum, microstratigraphic observations suggest that the two children were buried earlier than the adult male, who may have been interred a few seasons after them. The children's grave was superimposed by the burial of another adult, whose almost totally decomposed remains, minus the head, were interred in the upper part of the grave. The top part of the adult male's grave, on the other hand, was covered with a large ocher stain on which sat a sizable boulder and the poorly preserved cranium of an adult female. The headless adult must have been buried some time after the children, but the cranium of the

female was placed over the interred adult male in the course of his burial ritual.

What Was the Social Structure?

The stylistic similarity in the burial features and associated inventories indicates that the man and the children belonged to the same social group. The wealth of the burial inventory, measured by the labor invested in the making of the grave goods found, suggests that these individuals may have had special status in their community. Since the children were too young to have achieved high status through their skills or talents, some scholars believe the abundance of goods buried with them to indicate that they may have been related to people of high status and thus inherited their important social position. If this were so, then the Sungir burials show us that some Upper Paleolithic groups lived in complex social units. But messages from the grave can be equivocal, and the wealth of these burials may simply reflect the high status these individuals achieved in death itself, the wealth buried with them bearing no relationship to high status in life.

⊙ At Matanuska Glacier, in Alaska, one can get a feeling of what it was like to live along the ice edges of glacial Eurasia and North America.

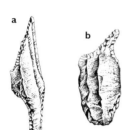

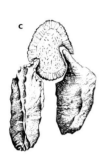

⊙ Typical tools of the Hamburg culture include coarse points with tangs—so-called *kerbspitze* (**a**)—and a very specialized gimlet called a *zinken* (**b**), both made of flint. The latter was used for splitting bones (**c**). The *riemenschneider* (**d**), a crescent-shaped tool probably used for leatherwork, consists of a coarse flint point mounted in a piece of reindeer antler.

ILLUSTRATIONS: RAY SIM

The Settling of Northern Europe

At the end of the last Ice Age, between 15,000 and 8,000 years ago, the climate changed dramatically throughout the world. These changes decisively altered the patterns of human life and, in time, led to the birth of agriculture. As the climate in western Europe improved rapidly and the ice edge retreated, the herds of reindeer and horses, so important to the big-game hunters of the Magdalenian period, moved north. With the spreading forests came totally different forms of subsistence. Some groups of people followed the animals north, while others adjusted to the new conditions where they were. This meant a change from big-game hunting to fishing, beachcombing, hunting small game, and—an activity that was to become increasingly important—gathering plants. For the big-game hunters, the desolate tundras of Scandinavia provided a short-lived refuge for their several-thousand-year-old way of life.

Towards the end of the Ice Age, groups of reindeer hunters related to both the European Magdalenian tradition of the west and to more eastern cultural groups appeared in northern Germany, Holland, and Belgium.

Among the earliest was the so-called Hamburg culture, named after the Hamburg area, in which a number of sites dated to between 17,000 and 12,000 years ago have been found. These include Meiendorf, Stellmoor, Borneck, and Poggenwisch. The oldest sites, such as Meiendorf, appear to have been summer hunting grounds, whereas the more recent ones also show traces of winter settlement. These people were predominantly reindeer hunters, but they also hunted wild horses, hares, foxes, and wildfowl. Some settlements were very close to the ice edge, where the harsh tundra climate allowed only birch and willow to take root in the frozen ground.

The tools of the Hamburg culture are very distinctive. They include coarse spear-points with tangs for hafting (known as *kerbspitze*); knives with handles of reindeer antler (*riemenschneider*), probably used for leatherwork; and bent gimlets (*zinken*), used for splitting bones. Many more hunting sites dating from about 10,000 BC have been found in northern Europe—for example, Usselo and Tjonger, in Belgium and Holland, and Wehlen and Rissen, in northern Germany. These are all known as Federmesser cultures, after a feather-like spear-point characteristic of them all.

These big-game hunters gradually spread into the vast tundras of northern Europe, ranging of necessity over large areas. Population was sparse, and large areas in the west which today are covered by the North Sea were part of the reindeer hunters' territory. About 13,000 years ago, reindeer hunters from the Federmesser cultures were the first to move into the ice-free regions of southern Scandinavia. Reindeer skeletons and antlers have been found in Denmark and southern Sweden,

but the age of the bones indicates that these kill sites resulted from short visits, perhaps of only a few weeks. This is almost certainly why so few settlements from this time are known: Bromme, on the island of Zealand, in Denmark, and Segebro and Finja Lake, in the province of Scania, in Sweden. All have been dated to about 10,000 BC. Similar blade tools have been found at Bromme and Segebro, including scrapers, burins, borers, knives, and points with tangs. A bent gimlet, or *zinken*, of the Hamburg type has also been found at Finja Lake. No organic material has survived at these sites, but as well as reindeer, the people probably ate elk and wildfowl, and also some fish.

Since the vast majority of people in western and northern Europe hunted reindeer, a similar range of tools is found throughout these areas until about 10,000 BC, when, in response to climatic changes, the forests spread north. This led to an increase in both big and small game and also made plants a more important source of food, and new tools were gradually developed to suit local conditions and the new subsistence patterns. With a vastly richer ecosystem, smaller areas of land were able to support larger groups of people, leading to rapid population growth, and clear seasonal settlement patterns developed within different regions. Coastal

LATE GLACIAL SITES IN NORTHERN EUROPE

Important sites in northern Europe at the end of the last glacial, some 13,000 years ago. At this time, Scandinavia was the only part of Europe still under ice. By about 6000 BC, the ice sheet had melted away completely.

CARTOGRAPHY: RAY SIM

Atlantic Ocean

Komsa

Fosna

Finja Lake
Segebro
Bromme

Meiendorf Ahrensburg
Poggenwisch Stellmoor

As early as 10,000 years ago, small groups of people from the east settled the barren but ice-free coasts of Europe's northern outposts. In Norway's Nordland, they established the so-called Komsa culture.

settlements became more common, although we know very little about these, as most coastlines that existed during the late Ice Age, like those of the early postglacial period known as the Holocene, have long since been submerged by the rising seas.

A northern German culture known as the Ahrensburg, after a village north of Hamburg, is an important example of a culture that changed in response to changing conditions. Existing between 9000 and 8300 BC, these people had most of the tools characteristic of the Paleolithic world, none of the clearly Mesolithic ones—notably axes and microliths (having no need of axes in the tundra landscape)—but a series of tools showing the transition from one subsistence pattern to another. As the climate improved and hunting small game, fishing, and plant gathering gradually became more important, they tended to make smaller tools for these new purposes—not yet microliths, but what might be called precursors

of microlithic technology. These included small, bifacially trimmed points with tangs (known as *stielspitze*), indicating that bows and arrows were in use in the north. The Ahrensburg culture thus represented the end of the late glacial tundra economies in northern Europe.

Big-game hunting did not, of course, disappear entirely as a way of life. The hunters who spread to southern Scandinavia probably moved further north along the ice-free coastal areas of western Scandinavia, where they established various hunting-gathering economies that survived un-altered for thousands of years in the form of the Fosna culture. In the extreme north, scattered groups of reindeer hunters from the tundra steppes of eastern Europe reached the ice-free coasts of the Kola Peninsula and Nordland, establishing the so-called Komsa culture, which survived until about 2000 BC—well into the late Neolithic period.

In most of Europe, however, a new era was just around the corner. Mesolithic peoples were showing a remarkable ability to adapt to a diverse range of environments and ecosystems, and in time these successful hunter-gatherers would adopt herding and farming as an increasingly necessary part of their subsistence.

The tools of the first Scandinavians are very similar to those of other late glacial reindeer hunters in northern Europe, consisting mainly of scrapers, burins, and points with tangs. The examples illustrated here are from Segebro, in southern Sweden.
ILLUSTRATIONS: RAY SIM

Huge rock carvings depicting reindeer have been found at the water's edge at Sagelven, in Norway's Nordland, in northernmost Europe. These works of art are attributed to the Komsa people, who arrived in the area some 10,000 years ago.

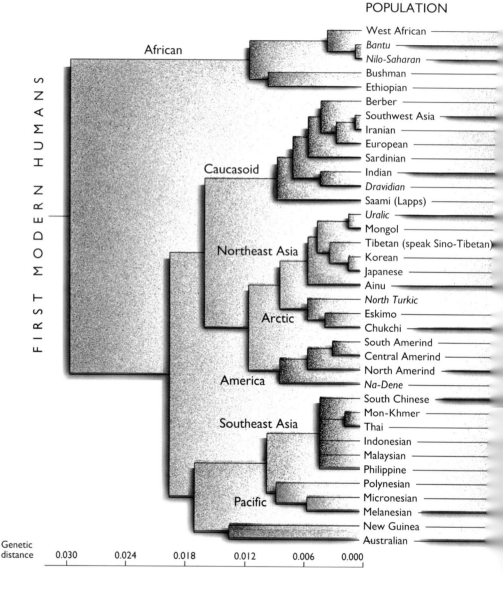

POPULATION

↪ Revolutionary new evidence suggests that language may be linked to our genetic origins. The "family tree" shown here is controversial, but reflects some of the latest research in this fascinating area.

Closeness of relationship is indicated by how far to the left one has to go to find a line connecting two populations. Thus, in the Caucasoid group, the two closest groups are the Iranian and Southwest Asian populations. Next closest are Europeans, and next after them come Berbers—and so on, until the Saami are included as the most distantly related population within the Caucasoid group.

Higher-order groups are connected still further to the left: the Caucasoid, Northeast Asian, Arctic, and American groups form one such higher-order group, which is still more distantly related to the Southeast Asia–Pacific–Australia– New Guinea higher-order group. African populations are more distantly related to the other groups, a factor supporting an African origin for all living humans. If modern humans evolved elsewhere, diverged, and later spread into Africa, then modern Africans and their closest non-African relatives should form a linked higher-order group, but no such group exists.

Italics indicate populations that are defined linguistically rather than ethnically.

Genetic distance is calculated from the average frequencies of 120 genes in the various populations studied.

GENES, LANGUAGES, AND ARCHAEOLOGY

Peter Rowley-Conwy

RECENT GENETIC EVIDENCE indicating that all living humans trace their descent to a single hypothetical woman ("Eve") who lived in Africa less than 250,000 years ago is of immense importance. Even more recently, several new lines of work have come together to support this picture and are beginning to give us a revolutionary new insight into our origins.

Genetics have provided one "family tree". The various human populations are not characterized by the simple presence or absence of particular genes, but have different *frequencies* of different genes. By analyzing a huge body of genetic data, L.L. Cavalli-Sforza has recently produced the family tree shown in the chart. The populations he studied are listed down the middle. Most are ethnically defined, but a few are linguistically defined, and these are shown in italics. The interrelationships are shown at left, calibrated against the scale of genetic distance (or difference) between the various populations (see the caption). African populations are distantly related to all the other groups, a factor that supports an African origin for all living humans.

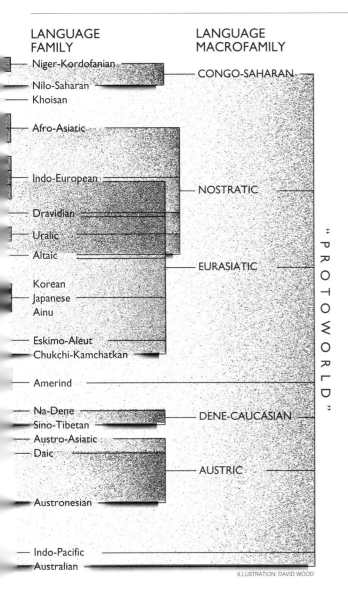

LANGUAGE FAMILY

- Niger-Kordofanian
- Nilo-Saharan
- Khoisan
- Afro-Asiatic
- Indo-European
- Dravidian
- Uralic
- Altaic
- Korean
- Japanese
- Ainu
- Eskimo-Aleut
- Chukchi-Kamchatkan
- Amerind
- Na-Dene
- Sino-Tibetan
- Austro-Asiatic
- Daic
- Austronesian
- Indo-Pacific
- Australian

LANGUAGE MACROFAMILY

- CONGO-SAHARAN
- NOSTRATIC
- EURASIATIC
- DENE-CAUCASIAN
- AUSTRIC

"PROTOWORLD"

ILLUSTRATION: DAVID WOOD

Languages have only recently been brought into this debate, and their role is highly controversial. The right-hand side of the chart shows the language families corresponding to the genetic populations Cavalli-Sforza studied. Clearly, many populations that are genetically quite closely related also speak closely related languages.

The extent to which languages reflect ancestry is currently under debate. People cannot change their genetics, but they can obviously change their language. For example, black Americans are genetically like Africans but

linguistically like Europeans. The chart shows more problems of this kind. Ethiopians are genetically Africans but speak an Afro-Asiatic language.

These problems aside, some scholars are beginning to believe that languages may reflect ancestry and population movements, such as when early farmers spread out, replacing hunter-gatherers in other regions. This is plausible but difficult to prove, because the various agricultural dispersals took place long before writing was developed. Very recently, a minority of linguists have gone even further,

proposing language groups bigger than those labeled "language family" in the chart. If these groups are valid, the implications are enormous. Vladislav Illich-Svitych has proposed a "Nostratic" macrofamily, while Joseph Greenberg has suggested a different but overlapping "Eurasiatic" macrofamily. This would imply that, at some time, perhaps 15,000 to 10,000 years ago, a "proto-Nostratic" or "proto-Eurasiatic" language was actually spoken somewhere. As people dispersed, this branched out into distinct regional languages, which themselves later split into the languages that are now spoken.

Other such higher-level groups are currently being suggested, and these, too, are indicated in the chart. But considerable difficulties remain. The proposed Dene–Caucasian macrofamily would link not only American and Southeast Asian populations, but also the Basques. These people live in the border region between France and Spain and speak a language usually thought to be unrelated to any other in the world, so this seems a most unlikely grouping. Merrit Ruhlen has suggested, however, that even these macrofamilies have links. In other words, they may all descend from a single language, for which the term "protoworld" has been coined. It has been suggested that this language may have been spoken in Africa.

Are distant echoes of a linguistic "big bang" still reverberating? Could it be that the speech of all of us reflects, however distantly, a single original "protoworld" language, spoken by the first modern humans in Africa? Most linguists believe that such a language existed, but do not accept that any trace of it persists to this day.

Archaeology is also coming up with evidence, in two main ways. First, it is obviously not possible to excavate a language, but it may be possible to detect in the archaeological record the type of symbolic thought processes without which a spoken language of modern complexity could not exist. Art and other evidence of

symbolic thought appear only about 35,000 years ago, and tool types start to become stylized at about the same time. There is also some (controversial) evidence, derived from studies of the lower parts of skulls, that Neanderthals would not have been able to make all the complex sounds we can make. William Noble and Iain Davidson have recently suggested that language as we know it is no more than about 50,000 years old—an unexpectedly short time span. If this is so, it seems just possible that linguistic traces of a "protoworld" language could have survived into the present.

Second, archaeology can provide fossil evidence of our origins. New finds, and new dating methods, currently support the hypothesis that modern humans originated in Africa. The earliest dated finds of modern humans are African, going back more than 100,000 years. These people were living at the same time that Neanderthals were living in Europe. Dates from finds in Israel show that modern humans were present there 90,000 to 100,000 years ago. The next dates we have for modern humans are 67,000 years ago, for human remains found at Liujiang, in China, and about 50,000 years ago, when Australasia was colonized. Europe was colonized about 35,000 years ago, the Americas about the same time or later. This pattern indicates that humans did indeed originate in Africa and spread from there to the rest of the world.

These three lines of evidence—genetics, linguistics, and archaeology—*can*, therefore, be brought together to tell a single, coherent story. All three are controversial and need much more detailed testing before the story can be accepted as fact. Only two things are certain. First, by the time you read this in print, significant new developments will have taken place. And second, if these three lines of evidence are not disproved by future work, we are on the threshold of a colossal breakthrough in our understanding of ourselves.

146

THE SETTLEMENT OF ANCIENT AUSTRALIA

50,000 YEARS AGO – 10,000 YEARS AGO

The First New World

J. Peter White

EVERY SOCIETY HAS its own ways of explaining how it came to be. Australian Aborigines trace their own and their country's origins to the great Spirit Ancestors of the Dreamtime. These beings, the Aborigines believe, created the world and determined the pattern of life as Aborigines know it. They remain a vital influence on Aboriginal life today, particularly through the medium of ceremonies during which stories and song-cycles telling of the events of the Dreamtime are recited and enacted. Parts of two creation accounts are given here, to introduce Aboriginal ways of looking at Australia's past—and present. For "Dreamtime" is an English translation of a term that doesn't refer to a past or a future, but to an eternal present. We translate these stories into a time frame, but for most Aboriginal people, creation is a continuing process.

Our own industrial society's version of Australia's history comes from recent scientific research. It is less personal than the Aboriginal accounts, and chronology, or when things happened, is given greater prominence.

The common element in both the Aboriginal and the scientific accounts is that they seek to explain the emergence of a new world. The humans who settled Australia were the first people to break the sea barriers that had previously kept humans in the Old World. Australia was *Homo sapiens'* first New World.

◄◐ On the shores of Lake Mungo, people camped, fished, and buried their dead more than 35,000 years ago. As the eastern margins of these lakes were built up by wind and water, the evidence of these activities was buried. Today, these sandy shores are eroding, exposing ancient relics.

⊕ THE NATURAL HISTORY MUSEUM, LONDON

Sun Mother and the Creation

Once the earth was completely dark and silent; nothing moved on the barren surface. Inside a deep cave below the Nullarbor Plain slept a beautiful woman, the Sun. The Great Father Spirit gently woke her and told her to emerge from her cave and stir the universe into life. The Sun Mother opened her eyes and darkness disappeared as her rays spread over the land; she took a breath and the atmosphere changed, the air gently vibrated as a small breeze blew.

The Sun Mother then went on a long journey, from east to west and from north to south she crossed the barren land and wherever her gentle rays touched the earth, grasses, shrubs and trees grew until the land was covered in vegetation. In each of the deep caverns in the earth, the Sun found living creatures which like herself had been slumbering for untold ages. She stirred the insects into life in all their forms and told them to spread through the grasses and trees, then she woke the snakes, lizards and many other reptiles and they slithered out of their deep hole. Behind the snakes mighty rivers flowed, teeming with all kinds of fish and water life. Then she called for the animals, the marsupials and many other creatures to awake and make their homes on the earth. The Sun Mother then told all the creatures that the days would from time to time change from wet to dry and from cold to hot, and so she made the seasons. One day while all the animals, insects and other creatures were watching, the Sun travelled far in the sky to the west and as the sky shone red, she sank from view and darkness spread across the land once more. The creatures were alarmed and huddled together in fear. Some time later, the sky began to glow on the horizon to the east and the Sun rose smiling into the sky again. The Sun Mother thus provided a period of rest for all her creatures by making this journey each day.

Karraru Tribe

The Origin of Lake Eyre

An old woman was out hunting when she saw a huge kangaroo in the distance. From her belly a young boy, Wilkuda, jumped out and chased the kangaroo west, hoping to spear it. He chased it until his spear finally reached its mark and, thinking it was dead, he threw it over his fire to cook and went to sleep. When he awoke the kangaroo had jumped off and escaped him. Wilkuda followed that kangaroo from sunrise to sunset for many days, until finally he grew weary. An old man with a dog came across their path, and with the aid of his dog, killed the kangaroo. Wilkuda said the old man could have the meat from his kangaroo, but he needed the skin.

Then Wilkuda travelled back east and threw the skin down east of Anna Creek, where it changed into a huge lake, Lake Eyre. Wilkuda is today seen as a boulder by the shores of the lake.

Arabana Tribe

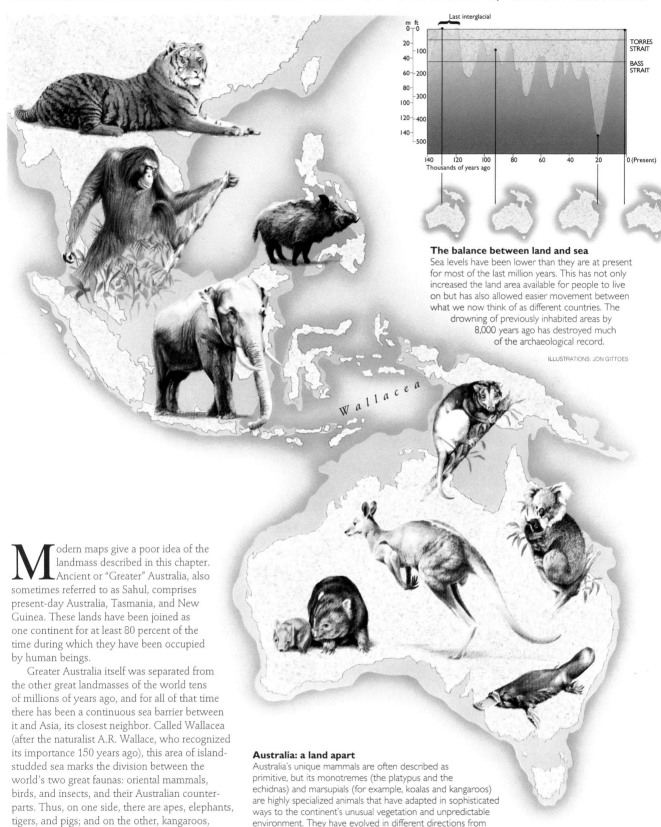

The balance between land and sea

Sea levels have been lower than they are at present for most of the last million years. This has not only increased the land area available for people to live on but has also allowed easier movement between what we now think of as different countries. The drowning of previously inhabited areas by 8,000 years ago has destroyed much of the archaeological record.

ILLUSTRATIONS: JON GITTOES

M odern maps give a poor idea of the landmass described in this chapter. Ancient or "Greater" Australia, also sometimes referred to as Sahul, comprises present-day Australia, Tasmania, and New Guinea. These lands have been joined as one continent for at least 80 percent of the time during which they have been occupied by human beings.

Greater Australia itself was separated from the other great landmasses of the world tens of millions of years ago, and for all of that time there has been a continuous sea barrier between it and Asia, its closest neighbor. Called Wallacea (after the naturalist A.R. Wallace, who recognized its importance 150 years ago), this area of island-studded sea marks the division between the world's two great faunas: oriental mammals, birds, and insects, and their Australian counter-parts. Thus, on one side, there are apes, elephants, tigers, and pigs; and on the other, kangaroos, koalas, and wombats.

Australia: a land apart

Australia's unique mammals are often described as primitive, but its monotremes (the platypus and the echidnas) and marsupials (for example, koalas and kangaroos) are highly specialized animals that have adapted in sophisticated ways to the continent's unusual vegetation and unpredictable environment. They have evolved in different directions from animals in other parts of the world for millions of years.

◆◆ This single-outrigger canoe was observed by Abel Tasman off New Ireland in 1643. It was being used for shark fishing, as the propeller-like floats between each man indicate. It would have been quite seaworthy, but have taken a great deal of effort to paddle between islands.

⚓ Outrigger canoes propeled by paddles are now found throughout the tropical Pacific and are both stable and seaworthy. John Forrest observed islanders near New Guinea hunting pigs from such a canoe in 1775.

◑ A raft and paddles made of mangrove wood, hibiscus bark, and twine. Used by the Kaiadilt people of Mornington Island to cross rivers and as spearing platforms, this example was made in 1987. Craft like this would not be used to travel between distant islands.

♀ Tasmanian Aborigines observed in 1802 made canoe-rafts consisting of three bundles of tied bark or dried reeds lashed together with grass string. Being very buoyant, these handled well in rough water, but they became waterlogged on voyages of more than 10 kilometers (6 miles).

AUSTRALIAN NATIONAL MARITIME MUSEUM

AUSTRALIAN NATIONAL MARITIME MUSEUM

Greater Australia looked very different from the Australia of today. Where now the roaring forties blow uninterrupted across Bass Strait, 10,000 years ago there was a broad, flat plain with several isolated hills. Between Australia and New Guinea stretched a similar but tropical plain, the sea covering the last spit of Torres Strait only about 8,000 years ago. And until the sea finally rose to its present level about 6,000 years ago, the coasts extended further than they do now, sometimes by only a little, sometimes by several hundred kilometers (about 200 miles), as we can judge from the offshore contours. This means that today's sea boundaries are not a good guide to cultural boundaries in the past. Obviously, some resources that would have been available in the Pleistocene period were not available more recently, while almost all evidence of life in shoreside areas more than 6,000 years old has long since been submerged by the rising seas.

The First Settlers

The people who settled in Greater Australia unquestionably came from Southeast Asia. Several different lines of evidence point to this. First, we may be certain that *Homo sapiens* did not evolve in Greater Australia. No primates (apes, monkeys), or even more distant human relatives, are found east of Java, Sumatra, and Borneo. The permanent water barrier of Wallacea kept early people out, as it did other recent mammals. All human remains found in Australia belong to *Homo sapiens sapiens,* our own modern species. No earlier forms have been found. This suggests that only modern people developed the cultural ability to cross water barriers by means of boats or rafts.

Second, Southeast Asia is the closest landmass from which people might have come. There were no sophisticated sailing craft 50,000 years ago, and people could not have paddled in bark canoes or on bamboo rafts from India, China, or Africa and survived. The most likely craft would therefore be outrigger canoes or single-log hulls with outriggers. The island chains of what is now Indonesia offered a pathway. Indeed, the tropical, generally calm, waters of these areas would have provided a kind of sheltered nursery, where, for the first time in human history, people could learn safely to exploit the sea and its resources.

Finally, humans have been in Southeast Asia for at least the last million years. Skeletal remains of earlier hominids, *Homo erectus*, have been found in Java, as well as the remains of more modern, but still ancestral, humans. We do not know the precise routes people followed when they came to Greater Australia. Every move from island to island was probably made by a few people traveling to the next piece of visible land, or land they inferred to exist from bushfire smoke, clouds, or bird movements. Almost certainly, there was no large-scale, deliberate migration. On the other hand, it seems likely that different parts of Greater Australia (New Guinea and Australia, for instance) were settled by different groups of people. Today, New Guineans and Australians are more closely related than either is to anyone else in the world, but they are still two identifiable groups, although similar enough to suggest a common origin. Although it is unlikely, each group may have descended from a single boatload of people, whose descendants inter-married relatively little and whose gene pool was little affected by later comers.

We cannot say exactly when people came to Greater Australia. Because people of the time could not make long sea voyages, they probably traveled when sea levels were lower, island areas were more extended, and sea crossings were shorter. One period when the sea level was lower was between about 55,000 and 50,000 years ago. At these ages, the reliable tool of radiocarbon dating is stretched to its limits. The fact that many human sites throughout Greater Australia have been dated to between 28,000 and 37,000 years ago, but that there are very few older sites, may mean only that we are at the limits of the technique. Or it could mean that by that time the population had grown large enough to leave traces in the archaeological record. Other radio-metric dating techniques (most of which involve measuring the ratios of certain radioactive isotopes in specimens) are being used, and if we accept current scientific claims, they show that humans came to Greater Australia at least 50,000 years ago. Two sites, both in the north of the continent, have been dated by the thermoluminescence technique as slightly younger than this date. (See the feature *Thermoluminescence Dating.*) We are never, of course, likely to find the very first site!

The Oldest Sites

Bobongara is a hillside that rises out of the sea on the north side of New Guinea's Huon Peninsula. Unusually for New Guinea, it is in a rainshadow area and covered with grass, so the series of horizontal terraces making up its surface can be seen clearly. Each terrace is formed by an old coral reef. At some time in the past, the flat top was a lagoon. The terraces have been gradually lifted out of the sea by the steadily rising rock base on which they are built. Scattered across the hillside are scores of large and heavy stone artifacts, up to 2 kilograms (between 4 and 5 pounds) in weight, made of big flakes knocked off river boulders. They look like axeheads and have a notch on either side in the middle, which seems to have been intended for some kind of handle.

⚲ Scores of waisted tools have been found in the raised reefs of Bobongara Hill. They are made of very large flakes struck from water-rolled boulders, and the side notching (or "waist") was clearly intended for hafting. These tools are usually thought of as axes, but they are not very sharp, and it seems likely that they were used as wedges or digging tools.
J. PETER WHITE

⚲ Raised coral reefs extend up Bobongara Hill like a series of steps from sea level to a height of more than 1,000 meters (3,300 feet). The youngest reef was lifted out of the sea some 6,000 years ago. Each reef once comprised a flat lagoon, with waves breaking against the steep front. Artifacts more than 40,000 years old have been found here.

ROBERT RAYMOND

THERMOLUMINESCENCE DATING

Richard G. Roberts

Archaeologists use a variety of dating techniques, each suited to different materials. Radiocarbon dating can be used on organic materials, such as charcoal and bone, while inorganic materials, such as quartz and feldspar crystals, can be dated by thermoluminescence (TL). These crystals occur in most soils (clay, silt, and sand), as well as in flint and volcanic ash. The TL method can date materials up to about 200,000 years old (or more in favorable circumstances), and dates are usually accurate to within about 10 percent.

The method relies on the fact that there is a low level of radioactivity within the crystals themselves and in the surrounding soil and rock. During the process of radioactive decay, small quantities of radiation (alpha particles, beta particles, and gamma rays) are regularly released, producing free electrons within the crystals. These electrons eventually become trapped at defects but can be released if the crystals are heated to 500 degrees Celsius (932 degrees Fahrenheit) or exposed to sunlight for several hours. The TL method exploits this fact.

Dating Pottery

TL was used originally to date pottery that has been fired in a kiln or open fire to make it hard. This firing causes all the trapped electrons to be released and thus sets that pot's TL "clock" at zero. Once the pot (or a fragment of it) is buried in the ground, electrons once again start to become trapped within its crystals. This continues until the pot (or fragment) is reheated. When this is done in a darkened laboratory, the release of electrons is visible as a quantity of light, which can be measured. The greater the quantity of light, the greater the number of electrons released, and so the older

the pot. The method is widely used to authenticate pottery and ceramics for museums and art sales.

Dating Sediments

TL dating can also be used on flint artifacts that have been heated, and buried sediments that have been exposed to sunlight at some time in the past. For example, excavated soil containing stone tools can be dated. The method in this case relies on the fact that the TL clock was set at zero when the soil was last exposed to sunlight. Using TL in this way is trickier, since sunlight rarely releases all the electrons, and so the clock is not truly set at zero. Some allowance must be made for the number of trapped electrons remaining since the sediment was last exposed, and this is done by measuring the number of electrons retained by similar sediment in an exposed area. A closely related technique, known as optical dating, is currently being developed to avoid this problem of incomplete zeroing by sunlight.

Because electrons are trapped at different rates in different samples, the rate of electron trapping is determined for each sample. This is done

in the laboratory by exposing separate portions of each sample to different amounts of radiation and then measuring the quantity of light released by each portion when heated. To calculate the amount of radiation that the pot has accumulated since it was buried (the paleodose), the quantity of light released by the "as collected" portion of the pot is compared with the light from the irradiated portions. The same procedure is used to date flints and sediments.

Establishing the Date

To finally obtain an age for a sample of pottery, flint, or sediment, it is necessary to know not only the paleodose but also the amount of radiation that the sample received, on average, each year that it was buried (the annual dose). The sample age is equal to the paleodose divided by the annual dose. In the case of pottery, the annual dose results mainly from the radioactive decay of uranium, thorium, and potassium, which are present in the clay from which the pot is made and in the soil surrounding the buried pot. In the case of sediment, the sample and the surrounding soil often have the same mineral composition and hence the same radioactivity. For pottery, it is important to measure the radioactivity of the soil as well as that of the pot itself to obtain an accurate date. Consideration must also be given to the water content of the sample, averaged over the period it was buried, because the annual dose is reduced by the presence of water in pottery and soil.

ZALEHO TASVILLO/MUSEUMS DEPARTMENT OF MALAYSIA

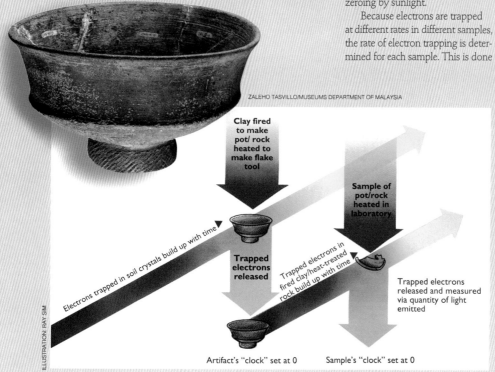

Clay fired to make pot/ rock heated to make flake tool

Sample of pot/rock heated in laboratory

Electrons trapped in soil crystals build up with time

Trapped electrons released

Trapped electrons in fired clay/heat-treated rock build up with time

Trapped electrons released and measured via quantity of light emitted

Artifact's "clock" set at 0

Sample's "clock" set at 0

ILLUSTRATION: RAY SIM

◄● The TL clock is reset when a pot is fired in a kiln or open fire. When the pot is later reheated in the laboratory, the quantity of light emitted is related to the number of electrons released, and hence the time elapsed since the pot was fired.

While most of these tools have been found on the surface, three have been found stratified between the weathered volcanic ash that blankets the surface of reef IIIA and the front of reef IV. Reef IIIA is dated to between 45,000 and 53,000 years ago. Reef IIIB, where there is no ash, is dated to 40,000 years ago. The ash surrounding the waisted axes has been dated by the thermoluminescence technique to more than 40,000 but less than 60,000 years ago. It seems probable, therefore, that the tools are about 45,000 years old, or possibly a little older.

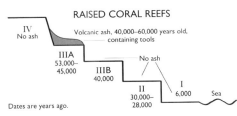

RAISED CORAL REEFS

Volcanic ash, 40,000–60,000 years old, containing tools

IV No ash

IIIA 53,000–45,000

IIIB 40,000

No ash

II 30,000–28,000

I 6,000

Sea

Dates are years ago.

Of the three tools found embedded in the ash, two were waisted in the usual way but one has a groove over both faces, showing even more clearly that these tools were meant to be hafted. Scientists have speculated that they were axes used to clear small spaces in the forest that would have grown there at a time of higher rainfall. These clearings might have been made to allow edible fruit trees or other plants more room to grow, or to get wood for houses. Such explanations, however, are difficult to test.

Another site with evidence of human occupation going back 50,000 years is Malakunanja II, a large rock shelter near the Arnhem Land escarpment. It consists of more than 4 meters (13 feet) of sand deposit, the upper 2.6 meters (8 feet 6 inches) of which contain stone artifacts. These are less distinctive than the waisted blades, consisting only of flakes and chunks with sharp edges. But there are many more of them: more than 100 have been collected from the lowest 20 centimeters (8 inches) of the occupation deposits in a pit only a meter (just over 3 feet) square. It is significant that artifacts have not been found below 2.6 meters (8 feet, 6 inches), suggesting that the site was not occupied before this time.

Some researchers have claimed that humans came to Greater Australia much earlier than 50,000 years ago, but none of these claims has so far been generally accepted. The two main reasons for this are that the material alleged to prove early occupation, such as an increase in charcoal in a lake bed or an accumulation of shells on a seashore, cannot be proved to have resulted from human actions, and that the association between the dated material and artifacts made by humans could also result from more recent events. Despite considerable research in likely areas, such as old lake shores, no human remains or artifacts have been found that are older than about 50,000 years.

RICHARD G. ROBERTS

Depth of sample below surface		TL date
in cm (in)		given as most likely range
STONE ARTIFACTS PRESENT	149–155 (59–61)	12,000–18,000
	190–209 (75–82)	19,000–29,000
	230–236 (91–93)	36,000–54,000
	241–254 (95–100)	41,000–48,000
	254–259 (100–102)	48,000–74,000
NO STONE ARTIFACTS	295–315 (116–124)	51,000–79,000
	339–362 (133–143)	65,000–97,000
	452–458 (178–180)	86,000–128,000

The large rock shelter known as Malakunanja II sits at the base of the spectacular sandstone escarpment of northwest Arnhem Land. The site faces onto a flat, sandy plain and has been occupied for some 50,000 years.

TL dates for Malakunanja II. The upper (younger) levels of this site have also been dated by the radiocarbon method, and the correlation between these two techniques, along with normal scientific caution, suggests that the younger end of each TL age range should be used at present. (That is, stone artifacts were present at least 12,000 to 48,000 years ago.)

Colonizing the Continent

From what is known of past climates, people who arrived in the north of the continent would have found climatic conditions very little different from those they had left. People coming from Asian tropical coastal environments would not have found their new home particularly strange, except for the animals. Most of the fish and shellfish would have been similar, and so would the plants, including the edible ones. It thus seems highly probable that settlers would most rapidly have occupied tropical areas: the coasts and lowlands of New Guinea and northern Australia; the land between; and the large, visible islands of New Britain and New Ireland.

A real contrast existed further south. Temperate Australia (see map) was not only climatically different, it was also the home of different plants and animals, whose habits, availability, and usefulness to humans needed to be learned before the country could be occupied permanently. Temperate Australia 50,000 years ago has been called a "land of lakes", indicating the effect of an increased rainfall on the country around the arid core, then much smaller than it is today. But these lakes did not last. Gradually the rainfall decreased, temperatures declined, and the arid core of the continent expanded. By about 25,000 years ago, temperate Australia was as dry as it is now; and by 20,000 years ago, much drier, colder, and windier.

The theory that the continent may have been colonized in two stages is supported by the types of stone artifacts that have been found: notably waisted, sometimes stemmed, blades and stone axe (or hatchet) heads, with working edges sharpened by grinding. The technique of grinding tough stone to create and sharpen artifacts is a relatively recent invention. In Europe and other parts of the Old World, it goes back about 10,000 years (thus falling within the Holocene period), and is usually found within farming communities. But there is now widespread, if not extensive, evidence that this technique was used in the north of Greater Australia at least 25,000 years ago.

Ground-edge tools like modern Australian hatchet heads have been found at the Nawamoyn and Malangangerr sites of Arnhem Land and dated to about 20,000 years ago, as have similar tools found in Cape York and the Kimberleys, while one found at Nombe in the New Guinea Highlands has been dated to 26,000 years ago. The waisted blades, which are generally flaked, not ground, are older still, being the main tools found at Bobongara. Other, younger, or surface (and therefore undatable), finds of waisted blades have been made throughout New Guinea and in Cape York.

The relationship between these two groups of tools is not clear. Most researchers are inclined to think of both as axes or hatchets, or something similar, but why there were two forms in the Pleistocene period when one served the full range

♀ Many of Australia's temperate landscapes have a sandstone base, most often either flat or steeply scarped. As soils are commonly thin and acidic, the vegetation is highly specialized. People lived along the river valleys in areas such as Grose Gorge, in the Blue Mountains of New South Wales, using the ridge tops for their ceremonies and as a route to other areas.

PHILIP QUIRK/WILDLIGHT

of (presumably) similar functions in the Holocene in both areas is not known. The significant point is that both groups of tools are found only in the tropics and that there is no evidence of them in temperate Australia until less than 5,000 years ago (with the possible exception of a few examples on Kangaroo Island, off the coast of South Australia). This indicates cultural differences between the two areas during the Pleistocene period, a difference that continues—underlined by the physical separation of New Guinea and Australia—until the present. The rock engravings found in the tropical and temperate areas of Greater Australia (discussed below) similarly suggest such a cultural division.

Once people learned how to use the country of temperate Australia, perhaps more than 40,000 years ago, there is evidence that they expanded into it quite rapidly. Early dates from Tasmania, southwestern Australia, and inland regions—though not the central desert—are all around 35,000 to 40,000 years ago. After that time, the most extensive climatic change, which affected the whole continent except for some coastal regions, was at the peak of the cold, dry period that occurred about 18,000 years ago, when few or no people lived in large parts of the inland.

More local environmental effects occurred at other times, however. In Tasmania, people stopped using all the known southwestern sites about 12,000 years ago. The warmer climate caused the forests to increase, apparently making the landscape unfit for certain animals and plants and therefore unfit for the humans who depended on them for food. As a result of such changes, people moved gradually to other parts of the country which generally did not support such large populations. As the sea level rose, local changes certainly occurred in some coastal

REG MORRISON

⚹ Today, at least two-thirds of Australia is arid or semi-arid, and even more of the continent was dry in the Pleistocene period. Despite appearances, these environments support a diverse range of plants and animals, but because rainfall is low and unpredictable, few people can live in them.

♦ A grindstone from the lower levels of Malakunanja II, excavated in 1989. At about 50,000 years old, it is currently one of the oldest grindstones in the world. It was probably used for preparing ochers for painting on bodies, artifacts, or walls.
D. MARKOVIC

locations, but we have no record of these changes before the sea reached its present level about 6,000 years ago.

We cannot accurately estimate the number of people who might have lived in the country at a particular time: our archaeological records are too sparse. We can say, however, that there are unlikely to have been more than a million in Australia or 1.5 million in New Guinea, which is a generous estimate of the numbers at the beginning of European colonization in AD 1788. But once the entire Greater Australian continent had been occupied, there are unlikely to have been fewer than 250,000 people, or we would not have the kinds of archaeological records we have. There must always have been enough people to sustain an organized social system, with appropriate marriage and other networks. Families cannot live in isolation for very long.

The population was not, of course, spread evenly over the country. Many people would have lived along the coast, as they did in more recent times, but the remains of their settlements have long since been drowned by the rising seas. Within Australia, they also settled around rivers and lakes. Traces of occupation during the last 35,000 years have been found at sites along the Darling River, and on the shores of the Willandra and other overflow lakes in western New South Wales. The population in different areas of Australia has always been closely related to rainfall and the availability of water, for obvious reasons.

The distribution of people in what is now New Guinea is harder to determine. Apart from the coasts, people certainly used the highlands from early on, although few areas were completely free from tropical disease. It is unlikely that many lived in the inland lowlands, with their high rainfall, malaria, yaws, and other tropical diseases.

The People of Australia

Many anthropologists have attempted to show not only that Australian Aborigines and New Guineans are genetically different but that modern Aborigines have developed from different races which came here at different times. Early anthropologists either classified mainland Australians and Tasmanians separately, or divided the people of these two islands into three groups—basically, northern, central and southern, and rainforest (Queensland and Tasmania). The data on which these judgments were based were either literally superficial, relying on such surface features as skin color and hair form, or consisted of a few skull measurements. It was assumed at the time that such factors were not subject to selection pressure or random change and that they reflected the original differences between groups, preserved for tens of thousands of years. We now know that this is a false assumption.

A more reliable source of information about

D. ELFORD/WESTERN AUSTRALIAN MUSEUM

ancient populations is provided by remains of human skeletons dating from prehistoric times. Some of the largest and best preserved accumulations of these in the world have been found in Australia, especially the southeast. These records of the Aboriginal past can tell us a great deal about the history of both individual peoples and human settlement in Australia.

The study of human bones has been controversial in Australia for the last 20 years. While some Aborigines are interested in learning what scientists can add to their knowledge of the past, many think the dead should not be disturbed. Until recently, most scientists—like most white Australians—were prepared totally to ignore the affront that digging up bones and putting them in museums gives to Aborigines. Many now understand, however, that once Aboriginal control of the Aboriginal past is accepted, cooperative research may be possible.

The oldest Australian skeletons so far identified come from three burials on the shores of Lake Mungo, in western New South Wales, dated to more than 20,000 years ago. Many more date from 15,000 to 10,000 years ago, when people along the Murray River Valley,

in particular, buried their dead in riverside sands at Kow Swamp, Coobol Creek, and other locations. Analysis of these skeletons has shown conclusively that all are of modern humans, *Homo sapiens sapiens.* Beyond that, there are two schools of thought.

Some physical anthropologists have contrasted the very thick skulls, large teeth, and heavy brow ridges of some skeletons with the much thinner, lighter, and more gracile build of others, and on this basis have divided the skeletons into two groups. The more robust group they compare with ancient Indonesian skeletons, and the more finely built group with some ancient Chinese skeletons, suggesting that there were two migrations to Australia, from different places and at different times. They believe the robust group to be the older but have not yet been able to demonstrate this.

Others have re-examined the finds and concluded that no sharp distinction can be drawn between "robust" and "gracile" skeletons and that there is no significant demonstrable difference in their age. Rather, they claim that most larger skeletons are male, while most smaller, lighter skeletons are female. The fact that the two oldest skeletons are relatively gracile they attribute to chance, given the small sample represented by these finds. On this view, the skeletons simply show that some Pleistocene Australians were bigger than those of the Holocene and that the population as a whole was physically more varied than in the later period, but that is true of many human populations in the world at that time.

◄ This necklace of sea shells was recently excavated from a rock shelter in the northwest of Australia. It is more than 30,000 years old—which roughly corresponds to the time humans all over the world began to decorate themselves.

⚲ Pits of this kind are found in tropical areas from 20,000 years ago. They seem to be the result of many years of cracking nuts and pounding ocher to use as pigment. This series of pits in Kakadu National Park, in Arnhem Land, is particularly extensive.

ART OF THE LAND

PAUL TACON

AUSTRALIAN ABORIGINAL PEOPLES have been marking their rocky landscapes with engravings and paintings for tens of thousands of years. Archaeologists using a variety of experimental dating techniques may not agree on the age of the oldest rock art, but they are convinced that many forms have survived for at least 15,000 years. These include some petroglyphs, such as macropod or bird tracks and circular designs, that are covered by a thick silica skin or rock varnish, and some pictographs from the escarpments of northern Australia. The painted images are of immense interest, as they show perishable objects and aspects of life of which there is no other record.

❧ Boomerang stencils are among the oldest stencil forms of Arnhem Land, in the Northern Territory. Boomerangs have not been used as weapons in Arnhem Land for more than 6,000 years, but many of the older styles of painting include depictions of figures fighting and hunting with boomerangs.

❧ A large, barbed spear protrudes from the breast of an emu painted in the Pleistocene "dynamic figure" style of Arnhem Land. The dashes near its open beak may be an early visual symbol of sound. Dynamic human figures are also shown with such dashes when they are chasing or in opposition to each other.

❧ Macropod (kangaroo and wallaby) and bird (often emu) tracks are common in the oldest petroglyphs of Australia. These examples from Kakadu National Park have a thick silica skin covering them. Much current research is devoted to dating these skin formations more precisely.

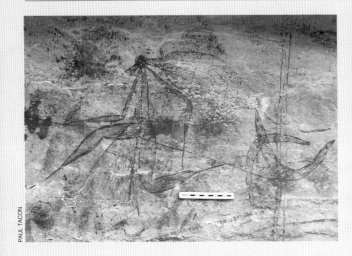

PAUL TACON

PAUL TACON

♂ Male dynamic figures often carry large spears and boomerangs and are often shown in combat, hunting, or carrying out domestic activities. They depict a way of life that has not been seen in Arnhem Land for more than 10,000 years.

♂ Female dynamic figures are rare, but they, too, are animated and painted along with their material artifacts, such as digging sticks and baskets. Sometimes, they are shown interacting with males, animals, or beings with animal heads.

REG MORRISON

♂ So-called Bradshaw figures, similar to the dynamic figures of the Northern Territory, were painted in the Kimberley region in the far north of Western Australia. They, too, are shown with boomerangs, spears, grass skirts, and elaborate headdresses. Investigations currently focus on whether the two have a common age and origin.

It does not mean that there was more than one founding group.

There is less evidence from New Guinea. Only a few small fragments of Pleistocene skeletons have been found, but at present we believe that the first inhabitants were of the same stock as the original Australians. Australians and New Guineans look very different from each other now as a result of many factors, including climate, isolation, selection, and genetic drift. But the differences are mostly only skin deep: genetically, the two groups are quite close.

Caves and Shelters

Remains from Pleistocene times are found throughout Greater Australia. Where they are found depends on two factors: where people lived in the past and where their debris has survived until the present. Caves and rock shelters are good places to look for evidence: the rubbish people left behind in the course of repeated visits is protected

from the weather, and from the layers that build up over the years we can construct an historical sequence. Malakunanja II (see map) is one such site. In many places, however, stone tools and charcoal are the only evidence to have survived, since local conditions, such as acid ground water, often destroy organic materials. Tasmania is a notable exception. (See the feature *Hunters on the Edge of the Tasmanian Ice*.)

Rock shelter and cave sites often yield evidence of long-term changes in human occupation. At Lawn Hill station, in northern Queensland, for instance, Peter Hiscock has shown that when the site was first occupied about 20,000 years ago, people made their tools from various kinds of stone, some found only on the plains to the north, others on the plateau to the south. Then, at the peak of the cold, dry period that occurred about 18,000 years ago, local rock shelters close to permanent water were used more intensively, and people made stone tools mainly from material close at hand. After about 13,500 years ago, when the climate improved, they reverted to the earlier pattern. What we can see here, then, is the long-term impact of environmental change on human behavior—changes that were probably not obvious to those living at the time.

But most Pleistocene sites are not found in protected locations. Consistent with the fact that most people lived in the open air, making only temporary shelters, the majority of sites consist of scatters of material resulting from short-term stays in one place.

Riverside Middens

Jane Balme and Jeanette Hope recently carried out research in western New South Wales showing both the impact of environmental change on human behavior and how changes in the local environment determine the nature of the archaeological record. They researched the 15,000 square kilometers (5,800 square miles) of the lower Darling River basin, an area of very flat country through which run the current river channel and a string of anabranches (Talyawalka, Tandou, and Redbank creeks) representing the course of the river before 9,000 to 7,000 years ago. There are also two sets of overflow lakes created by the flooding of present and past rivers.

Balme and Hope found middens of freshwater shellfish along the river and anabranch banks and the lake shores, usually consisting of small concentrations of shells and freshwater crayfish carapaces surrounding a small fireplace. The middens were preserved only if they had almost immediately been covered by slow-moving river or lake silt. Once the material had been uncovered by wind erosion, it soon deteriorated. Clearly, we cannot judge settlement patterns in prehistoric times simply from surviving sites. Most sites will long since have been destroyed by the elements.

GREATER AUSTRALIA

Eighteen thousand years ago, the sea level dropped about 150 meters (500 feet) as glaciers spread across the northern hemisphere, locking up sea water. In the Pleistocene period, this created the landmass of Greater Australia. People lived throughout the continent, but the only surviving records are from areas that are above the modern-day sea level. During the Pleistocene, all of modern-day Australia was in the temperate zone, and much of it was quite cold and arid.

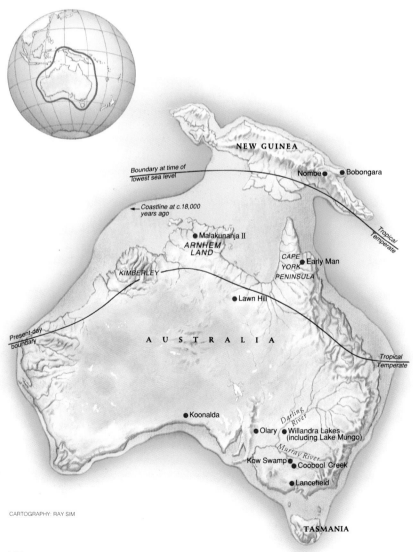

CARTOGRAPHY: RAY SIM

REG MORRISON

⬅ Freshwater shellfish, usually the bivalve *Velesunio* sp., inhabit many rivers and lakes throughout temperate Australia and have long been part of the Aboriginal diet. The discarded shells are often found in archaeological sites, such as here at Lake Mungo. As well as giving an insight into the environment of the time and people's eating habits, shells can be radiocarbon-dated and thus help to establish the age of sites.

As the map shows, however, carbon dates of shell middens in this area reveal a clear pattern of settlement. Pleistocene dates are found only along the anabranches and around the adjacent overflow lakes. Sites less than 7,000 years old are found along the modern river and its lakes, such as Lake Menindee. In the period between 9,000 and 6,000 years ago, very high river flows clearly filled Ratcatchers Lake and other lakes, and for a short time provided conditions favorable to both Aboriginal settlement and the preservation of midden sites.

Research on the shell middens of this area showed Balme and Hope that Aborigines were present in some part of the area almost continuously from about 27,000 years ago. Combined with data from another set of middens and hearths found around overflow lakes from the Lachlan River, about 100 kilometers (60 miles) south, the record shows that people have lived in this general area continuously for about 35,000 years. No single set of archaeological materials, however, provides a complete and reliable picture of how humans related to their environment over this period.

The Lake Mungo Burials

More dramatic but rarer finds give us an insight into the day-to-day lives of ancient people. The most famous of these are the burials at Lake Mungo. Mungo I is the burial of the remains of a cremated woman. The body was burned while

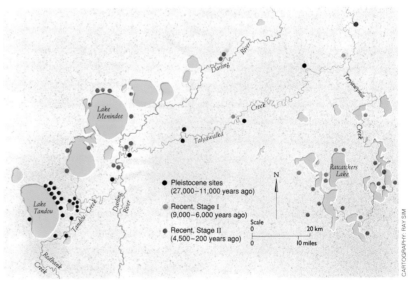

CARTOGRAPHY: RAY SIM

- **Pleistocene sites** (27,000–11,000 years ago)
- **Recent, Stage I** (9,000–6,000 years ago)
- **Recent, Stage II** (4,500–200 years ago)

Scale
0   20 km
0   10 miles

N

lying on its left side, after which the bones were gathered up, broken into small pieces, and placed in a pit near or perhaps under the pyre. Mungo III is the burial of an adult man, who is lying on his back. Pink ocher powder was sprinkled over the upper part of his body before he was buried. We do not know whether the differences between these burials stem from time, sex, totem, or some other cause. But these complex burial practices show that Pleistocene Australians, like people

MODERN AND FOSSIL LAKES

The lakes of western New South Wales are mostly dry today, but at various times in the past they have been filled. People in Australia have always settled around rivers and lakes, water often being a scarce resource.

⚱ This 26,000-year-old bone bears the tooth marks of the extinct carnivore *Thylacoleo*, a relative of modern possums.

⚱ Lower jaws (mandibles) of the extinct kangaroo *Sthenurus*, which lived in the more forested parts of eastern Australia.

⚘ Many of the prehistoric engravings in the rock walls of Early Man Shelter, in Cape York, appear to be symbolic.

elsewhere in the world at the same time, had some kind of relationship with a spiritual world. (These Mungo remains were recently returned to the local Aboriginal community.)

Humans and the Environment

One of the major puzzles in the archaeology of early Greater Australia concerns the relationship between humans and their environment. We know that in recent times much of temperate and arid Australia was regularly burned, a practice its Aboriginal owners described as "cleaning it up". The long-term effect of this method of land management is difficult to evaluate, as is the interaction between Aborigines and the animals that used to inhabit the country. One account of the animals involved, and one view of their relationship, is given in the feature *The Lost Animals of Australia*. Here is another.

Prehistoric people have certainly hunted animals to extinction elsewhere in the world. Where this has happened, many bones of extinct animals have been found at human sites. This is not the case in Greater Australia. The evidence to date does not show a great deal of interaction between humans and animals.

Excavations at Lancefield Swamp, in southern Australia, have revealed a large bone bed, some 2,000 square meters (2,600 square yards) in area, resting on green clay and sealed in by about 70 centimeters (27 inches) of black clay. Below the bone bed, which consists of thousands of bones of all sizes, a small channel has been eroded into the green clay. It contains bone fragments and charcoal. This charcoal has been dated to about 25,000 years ago, and the bone bed that seals it in must be younger than this, although not much. Most bones are of one species of extinct kangaroo,

but there are a few pieces of diprotodon and of extinct bird species. These bones are not cut or burned, so they did not accumulate as a result of the animals being hunted, butchered, or cooked. They are more likely to be the remains of *Thylacoleo* prey, because some bones bear tooth marks fitting the pattern of this animal's sharp carnassial teeth. (*Thylacoleo* was a large carnivore closely related to possums—a meat eater similar to a panther or a leopard, rather than a bone crusher such as a hyena or, the Australian equivalent, *Sarcophilus*. Both are now extinct.)

The Lancefield findings show that at least some animals that are now extinct lived long after people arrived. This is also shown at Nombe in the New Guinea Highlands, where diprotodon bones and the bones of three different macropods (animals from the kangaroo family), which were apparently killed by humans, were found with stone tools and material of human origin in levels dated to between 25,000 and 15,000 years ago. None of the animals is very big: the diprotodon is about the size of a pig.

If people were responsible for the extinction of these animals, the process was different from that in other parts of the world. Elsewhere, many species of birds and mammals disappeared rapidly after humans arrived. As with more modern examples from our industrialized world (the dodo, the passenger pigeon, and some whales, seals, and bears), large animal populations were wiped out in only a few centuries. This is not the case in Australia, and given that we have no good evidence of large-scale killing, climatic change has been suggested as the most likely cause of these extinctions.

But is this feasible? We know that there have been many climatic changes during the last two million years, and we have no reason to believe that the most recent changes were more extreme or wide-ranging in their impact than earlier ones. To claim that climatic change during the last 50,000 years caused so many extinctions would seem to require evidence of a large-scale catastrophe, such as an extreme drought and consequent dust storm—and even then, such an event is highly unlikely to have affected the whole of Greater Australia. What does seem likely is that both climate and humans have been involved in these extinctions, each contributing differently in different areas. Humans probably played a bigger part in the tropics, and climate in the arid zone, but with local variations.

Art in Early Australia

Recent developments in dating techniques show that during the Pleistocene there was a wide range of decoration on rock surfaces. The best-documented of these is at Early Man Shelter, in Cape York, where Andrée Rosenfeld found engravings on a rock wall against which were

banked 13,000-year-old archaeological deposits. The figures included spirals, "bird tracks" and other three-pronged shapes, and meandering lines—none directly representational and some appearing to be symbolic.

Very similar figures have been found engraved on rocks throughout nontropical Australia. Known as the Panaramitee style, after a site in central Australia, their distribution has been cited as evidence for a kind of "community of culture" throughout Pleistocene Australia and Tasmania. Certainly, it is interesting to note that this engraving style has not been found in New Guinea or in Arnhem Land. It may, in fact, help to demarcate the temperate province of Greater Australia.

Direct dating of some engravings by the new cation-ratio method, however, puts the age of many in dispute. This technique, which involves correlating mineral ratios with radiocarbon dates, is not yet totally accepted, but seems to give consistent results when used in various parts of the world. According to this, the lowest levels of desert varnish (a deposit made by microorganisms that oxidize manganese and iron) covering rock engravings in the semidesert of South Australia's Olary region range between 1,500 and perhaps 30,000 years old, but the older dates are less reliable with this technique. If confirmed, these dates would suggest that such engravings were being made from the time humans first came to Australia, as well as at the same time as a whole range of rock paintings, nearly all of which are thought to date from the last few thousand years. Too little is known of the reasons behind engraving and painting to say that such a range of ages is impossible, but an artistic tradition that continued unchanged for 30,000 years would be surprising. Other radiocarbon-based dating techniques suggest that the more recent dates are more probably correct.

There are other examples of Pleistocene art. Deep inside South Australia's Koonalda Cave, many hands have traced multiple lines on the soft

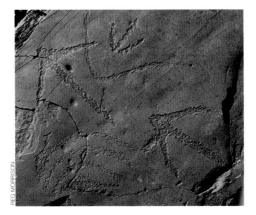

Engravings such as these have been found in several areas of Australia. Known as the Panaramitee style, they look like kangaroo and emu footprints and sometimes occur in a line. Although they are usually called engravings, they are actually pecked into the rock surface. When paintings are found at the same site, the engravings always appear below them and are presumably older.

Elaborate "rayed" circles of this kind have been found together with Panaramitee-style art at some sites. This particular symbol has not yet been dated.

Peckings found in the Olary region include a wide range of Panaramitee-style motifs. They were probably done in the course of ceremonies and used to transmit traditional knowledge and law. In time, they became covered with desert varnish, a layer of predominantly organic material which can be dated.

REG MORRISON

PAUL TACON

☞ This rock painting in Arnhem Land depicts the thylacine (commonly known as the Tasmanian wolf), which has been extinct on the Australian mainland for more than 3,000 years.

REG MORRISON

☜ Naturally occurring red and yellow ochers, usually oxides of iron, were mined for use as pigments to decorate bodies, tools, weapons, and rock walls.

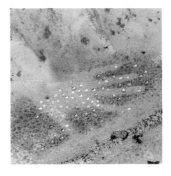

cave walls when the cave was used at least 15,000 years ago. Hands stenciled in red paint have been found in Tasmanian caves last occupied 12,000 years ago, while lumps of ocher found near the Mungo burials suggest that the practice of painting bodies or artifacts is very old indeed. There have even been serious attempts to show that a few paintings of some extinct large animals survive, but the evidence for this is much more disputed. The only good examples are of the Tasmanian "wolf", *Thylacinus*, which became extinct on the Australian mainland between about 3,000 and 4,000 years ago. Our present knowledge of Pleistocene art suggests that it was much more restricted in range of motif, use of color, and elaboration of design than more recent art, but whether this is because it was used for different purposes, or whether it only appears to be so because so little has survived, has yet to be determined. (See the feature *Art of the Land*.)

How Much Do We Know?

By 30,000 years ago, the entire continent of Greater Australia had been settled by descendants of Asian tropical foragers, who crossed sea barriers and discovered and settled environments ranging from the familiar to the subtemperate, from rainforest to near-desert. Even the desert core was probably occupied, although sparsely. These people were the direct ancestors of most of today's Aborigines.

🜨 Aboriginal paintings have been found in several Tasmanian caves. Most are hand stencils, made by blowing red paint through a pipe around a hand held against a rock wall. The organic material—perhaps saliva or blood—mixed with the paint to make it stick has been dated to about 10,000 years ago.
JOHN VOSS FOR TASMANIAN DEPARTMENT OF PARKS, WILDLIFE AND HERITAGE

♀ Koonalda is one of many sinkholes that dot the Nullarbor Plain. Today, many people visit the site, as the tracks indicate, but few are allowed to descend into this ancient mine.

🜨 From deep underground in Koonalda Cave, Aborigines mined flint to make tools. The charcoal deposits from the fires they lit to work by have been dated to between 15,000 and 20,000 years old. The soft limestone walls near the mining areas are covered with engravings made with sharp stones or sticks, and with fingers.

REG MORRISON

HUNTERS ON THE EDGE OF THE TASMANIAN ICE

RICHARD COSGROVE

T he colonizing of Tasmania in late Pleistocene times represents a surprising and important chapter in the story of the spread of anatomically modern humans throughout the globe. Archaeological evidence now being won from limestone caves in southwest Tasmania shows that humans had traversed the vast continent of Greater Australia, from the tropical north and the islands of Melanesia to the glacial south, at least 35,000 years ago, demonstrating a remarkable ability to exploit the entire range of ecological habitats.

⚑ A small artifact made of Darwin glass, recovered from Nunamira Cave.

R. COSGROVE/SOUTHERN FORESTS ARCHAEOLOGICAL PROJECT

Over the past five years, the Southern Forests Archaeological Project at La Trobe University, Melbourne, has recorded more than 100 radiocarbon dates for material excavated from seven widely dispersed cave and open sites in southwest Tasmania (see map). These cover a period from 35,000 years ago to 11,000 years ago. The oldest of these dates has significantly changed our thinking about the people of the Late Stone Age. We now know that hunter-gatherers did not survive and thrive solely on coastal, lake, and river resources, but were able to exploit subantarctic inland and upland environments previously thought to have been too harsh for settlement. The finds are of particular interest, because they mark the southernmost appearance of humans on the planet at this time.

An Ancient Land Bridge

Until recently, it was thought that humans arrived in Tasmania only about 23,000 years ago, when the world was entering a period sometimes referred to as the Big Chill. At this time, so much water froze that the sea level was 60 meters (200 feet) lower than at present. About 20,000 years ago, it dropped to a maximum of 120 meters (400 feet), exposing the land under what is now Bass Strait. We now know, however, that people arrived some 12,000 years earlier, in a milder part of the last Ice Age, when the sea was at its previous lowest level.

LATE PLEISTOCENE SITES IN SOUTHWEST TASMANIA

Scale
0 10 20 30 40 50 km
0   10   20   30 miles

Launceston ■

Mersey R.
▲ Warragarra Shelter
(9,750–3,500)

▲ Mackintosh 90/1
(17,000)

*CENTRAL
HIGHLANDS*

T A S M A N I A   Great Lake
Arthurs Lake

● King River   Lake St Clair

Queenstown ■

Darwin Crater

Flying Fox site
(c. 19,000)

Kutikina Cave
(14,840–19,770)

● Acheron Cave
(13,410–29,800)
● Warreen Cave
(18,630–34,780)
▲ Ballawinne
Cave

● Nunamira Cave
(11,630–30,420)

Lake Gordon

● ORS7
(2,500–30,840)

▲ Bone Cave
(13,700–29,000)   Hobart ■

Lake Pedder

▲ Judds Cavern
(10,730)

AUSTRALIA

40°

145°

▲ Cave sites occupied by Ice Age people. (*Dates are years ago.*)
● Open sites with artifacts. (*Most sites are unnamed.*)
→ Movement of Darwin glass from Darwin Crater

CARTOGRAPHY: RAY SIM

At this time, temperatures were declining, reaching their lowest level in Tasmania 18,000 years ago, when the annual average temperature was between about 2 and 4 degrees Celsius (35 and 40 degrees Fahrenheit). During this cold period, glaciers developed above many of the western valleys occupied by humans. Trees could not flourish at heights above 250 meters (820 feet), and patches of grassland and

herb fields developed in their place, attracting such animals as wallabies and emus. Because of the rain-shadow effect of the western mountains, the drier eastern part of the island had a much lower rainfall. Destabilized soils and cold northwesterly winds inhibited plant growth. Summers were probably short and cool. Although rainfall was reduced by about half, south-west Tasmania probably did not suffer the fluctuating drought conditions of the east, so its resources were more predictable than those in the southeast of the island.

Subantarctic Hunter-gatherers

Despite the bleak conditions, most of the cave sites in southwest Tasmania have yielded exceptional quantities of human food remains. At Nunamira Cave, in the Florentine Valley, more than 200,000 pieces of bone, amounting to 30 kilograms (66 pounds), have been excavated from less than a cubic meter (about 35 cubic feet) of deposits. Of this, 90 percent are remains of the red-necked wallaby. Large quantities of emu shell found at some sites indicate that these sites were occupied in late winter and early spring. This is important, because it is the most difficult time of the year for hunter-gatherers and their prey, especially in a subantarctic environment.

The human occupants of these caves were able to exploit a range of animals according to their needs.

☝ These thumbnail scrapers, from Nunamira Cave, are 23,000 years old.
R. COSGROVE/SOUTHERN FORESTS ARCHAEOLOGICAL PROJECT

Numerous stout bone-points made from the lower leg of the wallaby have been found, indicating that these people were making clothes at least 26,000 years ago. Many have polished ends, suggesting that they were used to work hides, and some have been shaped into fine needle-like forms. Others were probably used as spear-points.

At all these sites, a range of small tools, or thumbnail scrapers, has been found. These have been dated to between 23,000 years old (in Nunamira and Bone Caves) and 18,500 years old (in Warreen Cave), while some found outside the southwest zone at Cave Bay Cave, in northwest Tasmania, are about 19,000 years old. They are made from a variety of raw materials, including fine-grained chert, silcrete, hornfels, quartz, and, most important, glass from Darwin Crater, which was formed by the impact of a meteorite some 700,000 years ago. This glass material has been found at all sites, and was used over a long period, between 27,000 and 13,000 years ago. It has been found up to 100 kilometers (60 miles) from its source, indicating that these hunter-gatherers traveled long distances throughout the region, almost certainly seasonally.

A recent find of cave art has given us a new insight into the life of these Stone Age people, suggesting that it had an intellectual and spiritual dimension beyond the realm of mere day-to-day survival. More than 30 human hand stencils have been discovered in two of the caves, Ballawinne Cave, 60 meters (196 feet) underground, and Judds Cavern, 60 meters (196 feet) underground.

Significantly, at the same latitude (43 degrees North) and throughout this glacial period, on the other side of the world—in France, Spain, and Russia—people were also creating art deep inside caves and hunting a range of animals including bison, reindeer, horses, and ibex under similar glacial conditions. This suggests that modern humans had similar ways of adapting to their environment and exploiting physically inhospitable landscapes.

What Drove Them Out?

The combined archaeological evidence shows that these Tasmanian Ice Age people had developed a technology and a social system that allowed them to exploit the southwest region for more than 25,000 years. Clearly, they were no mere puppets of environmental change. But about 12,000 years ago, almost all the caves were abandoned. Why this happened we don't know, but it has been suggested that with the rapid change in climate at the end of the Pleistocene period the zone was covered in unproductive temperate rainforest, which drove out the game animals—and the humans who had hunted them for more than a thousand generations.

☝ Bone and stone tools excavated from Bone Cave.
R. FRANK/SOUTHERN FORESTS ARCHAEOLOGICAL PROJECT

◀ A selection of points, made of wallaby leg bones, excavated from Warreen Cave.
B. DOUGLAS/SOUTHERN FORESTS ARCHAEOLOGICAL PROJECT

⚲ Nunamira Cave, Florentine River valley.

THE LOST ANIMALS OF AUSTRALIA

TIMOTHY FLANNERY

THE HISTORY OF AUSTRALIA'S ANIMALS over the past 50,000 years has been largely one of extinction. The time has been far too short for new species of large animals, such as mammals and birds, to evolve. Yet over this period nearly one-third of Australia's mammal species have become extinct, along with nearly all the large reptiles and many of the flightless birds. The cause of these extinctions is still hotly debated. One school of thought suggests that humans caused the extinctions, and the other that they were due to changes in climate.

The greatest problem in evaluating these theories is that we do not know precisely when these animals became extinct. Fossils from a number of well-dated cave and lakeside sites suggest that all the now-extinct species had vanished by 35,000 years ago—but a few other sites suggest that giant marsupials might have survived until 25,000 years ago, or even as late as 6,000 years ago. We know that Australia's climate has changed greatly over the past 40,000 years. Between 25,000 and 15,000 years ago, the sea level dropped by more than 100 meters (320 feet), and the

continent experienced an extremely arid phase. Clearly, the timing of the extinctions is of critical importance. If they can be shown to coincide with the arrival of humans, about 50,000 years ago, then circumstantial evidence would point to humans as the cause. If, however, the giant marsupials survived until 25,000 years ago, then the increased aridity would seem to be the more likely cause.

Australia's Ancient Giants
Before these great extinctions, Australia was a very different place. Fires were probably less frequent

ILLUSTRATIONS FROM KADIMAKARA, EXTINCT VERTEBRATES OF AUSTRALIA, 1991, PRINCETON UNIVERSITY PRESS. BY P. V. RICH AND G. F. VAN TETS. DRAWINGS BY FRANK KNIGHT. © MUSEUM OF VICTORIA

☝ The size of a large rhinoceros, diprotodons were the largest land mammals ever to have existed in Australia. The trunk shown here is conjectural.

than they are now, because large, now-extinct marsupial herbivores (of which there were about 40 species) reduced the standing crop of vegetation. Rainforest plants were more widespread in the drier parts of Australia. (Today, their distribution is limited not by lack of water but by bushfires, which kill them.)

The largest marsupial species was the diprotodon, which, like other Australian marsupial giants, was about one-third the weight of its ecological equivalent elsewhere. It probably weighed between 1,000 and 2,000 kilograms (2,200 and 4,400 pounds), while the elephant of Afro-Eurasia weighed about 5,000 kilograms (11,000 pounds). The relatively small size of the Australian marsupial giants has been attributed to Australia's extraordinarily poor soils and

◄● The marsupial lion was Australia's largest warm-blooded carnivore. Closer to a leopard than a lion in size, it evolved from herbivorous ancestors.

erratic climate, both factors that inhibit plant growth.

Judging by the teeth of extinct species, there were many specialist grazers and browsers, paralleling the great mammal communities of Africa today. But the Australian carnivores were very different. For example, there was no equivalent of a lion (the Australian marsupial lion, *Thylacoleo carnifex*, was only about the size of a leopard), and no equivalent of the vast number of cat-like and dog-like carnivores of Africa. Among the larger carnivorous mammals, Australia had only one cat-like species (the marsupial lion), one dog-like species (the thylacine, *Thylacinus cynocephalus*), and one scavenger (the Tasmanian devil, *Sarcophilus harrisii*). The larger Australian carnivores were all reptiles. The gigantic snakes of the genus *Wonambi* were more than 6 meters (20 feet) long and were the major predators throughout Australia, while over the warmer three-quarters of the continent, the 7 meter (23 foot) long goanna

Magalania prisca, and the 3 meter (10 foot) long land crocodile *Quinkana fortirostrum*, were the main predators.

There were never vast numbers of most species. Large, warm-blooded creatures were at a disadvantage, their prey being limited by the continent's poor soil and erratic climate. The cold-blooded reptilian carnivores, which required less energy, were therefore able to dominate.

The Impact of Humans

Humans had evolved in their Afro-Eurasian homeland as a medium-sized member of a very large community of mammalian carnivores and omnivores. By 40,000 years ago, they were taking an extraordinarily broad range of prey, including mammals much larger than themselves. They had thus become highly successful and generalized predators. Studies have shown that when humans or other predators arrive in areas where there have previously been no ecologically equivalent species, they invariably have a profound impact. For example, over the last thousand years, Polynesians in Hawaii have destroyed more than 70 percent of the island's bird species; during the nineteenth century, sealers on Macquarie Island severely depleted many seal species; and after rats (*Rattus rattus*) were introduced on Lord Howe Island in 1918, nine species of birds became extinct.

Australian animals were particularly vulnerable to the impact of humans. Marsupial herbivores were adapted only to avoiding predation by large but relatively unintelligent reptiles. Although there were many species of large animals, their numbers were probably quite small. Humans, then, are the most efficient and largest warm-blooded predators that have ever existed in Australia.

From the upper mountain rainforests of Irian Jaya to Australia's desert center, extinctions emptied landscape after landscape, until finally the largest remaining mammals were humans them-

selves. The medium-sized species, weighing between 10 and 100 kilograms (22 and 220 pounds), either became extinct or shrunk in size over thousands of years. Gray kangaroos are now half the weight they were, while koalas, Tasmanian devils, and the larger wallabies weigh on average one-third less than formerly. In general, the larger the species, the more it has reduced in size—with the exception of humans, and possibly wombats (which might have been protected

because of their burrowing habits). This, too, may be attributable to human hunting practices. If hunters claimed the largest individuals of these species, fast-maturing dwarfs would have been more likely to survive to maturity. Increasingly, they would then have produced smaller offspring.

Only the smallest mammals, those weighing less than 10 kilograms (22 pounds), survived largely unaltered, although some may have been restricted to fewer

areas. This changed with the arrival of Europeans towards the end of the eighteenth century. Over the course of the following century, 21 medium-sized species of mammals and one large species—the sole remaining native carnivore, the thylacine—became extinct.

♀ The thylacine, Australia's only dog-like carnivore, had vanished from mainland Australia by 3,000 years ago but survived in island Tasmania until the 1930s.

THE FIRST PACIFIC ISLANDERS

Pioneers of the Oceans

J. PETER WHITE

EAST OF AUSTRALIA and New Guinea in the Pacific Ocean lie a number of islands that gradually decrease in size. The largest are New Britain and New Ireland, close to New Guinea and each other. Manus and the other Admiralty Islands to the north, as well as Bougainville and the other Solomon Islands to the southeast, are much smaller, and cannot be seen from the larger islands. Some of the Solomon Islands are no more than the hills remaining from a larger Pleistocene landmass. All these islands can be called Near Oceania, and this chapter is about the people who lived there. They developed skills and technologies that allowed them, ultimately, to visit almost all the islands in the Pacific and to settle on many of them.

The settlement of Near Oceania involved sea crossings of more than 100 kilometers (60 miles), some out of sight of land. Nowhere else in the world has sea travel of this kind been known until the last few thousand years, when islands such as Cyprus and Crete were first visited. Seafaring developed much earlier in the Pacific region, because the sea and climate are warm and there are many intervisible islands stretching east from Southeast Asia. So the people who entered Near Oceania were already accustomed to traveling by sea.

◀● The Solomon Islands were the first large islands to be reached by people who had to voyage out of sight of land to find them. Thirty thousand years ago, when people first arrived here, many of the present islands were the mountainous interior of a much larger island.

⚓ RAY SIM

171

THE FIRST PACIFIC SITES

All the Pleistocene sites of Near Oceania, shown here, have been discovered within the last decade. Their antiquity, which matches that of Australia and New Guinea, is a surprise, since early people would have to have made a long sea voyage to reach some of these islands. Even now, only a handful of sites is known—enough to establish their great age, but too few to do more than hint at the area's history. It seems likely that most sites have not survived, since they were in the open air. Logging, plantation development, and resettlement during this century have also destroyed many sites.

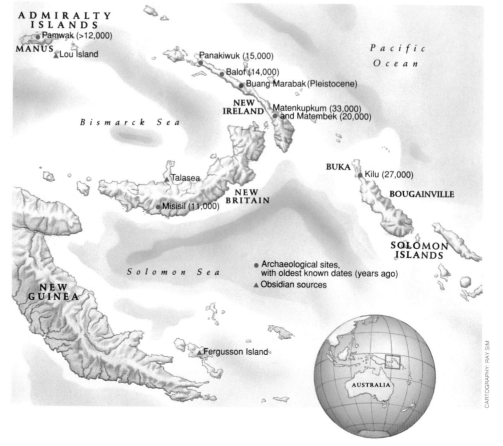

↪ Rainforests are the most diverse ecosystems in the world, housing an enormous variety of vegetation. They are also very fragile, since all available nutrients are constantly in use by plants and animals, rather than some being stored in the soil, as occurs in temperate climates. Much rainforest life is found in the upper canopy, and only along streams, where sunlight penetrates to the forest floor, is there a profusion of ground-level plants.

↑ At the long-occupied cave site of Balof 2, excavated animal bones—each pile from a different excavation square and level—are set out to dry after being washed. All are remnants of human meals eaten thousands of years ago.

We do not know what kinds of craft were used on such voyages, since none have survived. They must have been more than simple rafts or small canoes, but whether they were paddled or had sails as well, we cannot tell. Both kinds have been used in the last few centuries of Pacific travel, although paddling canoes were used for shorter voyages and in more protected waters. Sailing vessels seem more likely for longer journeys, as do boats big enough to carry several adults and some supplies. Single-hulled outrigger canoes with a riding platform, the all-purpose craft of recent Pacific peoples, had probably already been developed. Moreover, a boatload of people would have had a much better chance of establishing themselves than would any castaway couple.

Given the location of these islands and our knowledge of climate change, it is likely that these islands were as covered with rainforest throughout the Pleistocene period as they are today.

In the last decade, traces of occupation during the Pleistocene period have been discovered on four of the main island groups. Two sites from New Ireland and one from the northern Solomons have been radiocarbon-dated to about 30,000 years ago. (No sites of this age have been discovered in New Britain, but because it is the closest island to New Guinea, they probably exist.) All the

oldest sites are in the rock shelters or limestone caves of old reefs now raised above the sea. (See the feature *Relics of the First New Ireland Settlers*.) Because of their alkaline properties, these have preserved bone, shell, and some other organic materials, as well as providing protected locations for the accumulation of debris. They have, therefore, played an important part in preserving evidence of human occupation.

Food Sources: Animals and Plants

Being seafarers, the people were accustomed to using the ocean as a source of food, especially its shellfish and fish. It is surprising to find, however, that early sites show no evidence of trolling or other techniques used to catch large, open-sea fish. The surviving fish bones have proved to be of reef-dwelling species that can be caught by trapping or spearing.

Our best information about the animals of the area comes from New Ireland, where all five known Pleistocene sites have yielded the remains of animals that were cooked and eaten. At Balof 2, for example, 5 cubic meters (180 cubic feet) of deposits have produced the bones of between 250 and 300 possums, along with those of rats, bats, lizards, snakes, and, in more recent layers, wallabies. Other sites have produced similar quantities of bones.

often carried around today for later use as food and decorative fur, and also as pets. Because these animals were introduced so long after human settlement, I believe that they were most likely introduced by accident. (See the feature *Moving Animals from Place to Place* for a different view.)

The situation in New Britain—which covers an area of about 37,000 square kilometers (14,300 square miles)—and the Admiralty Islands is less clear, as there are fewer sites, with fewer animal remains, and no prehuman deposits known so far. But both islands have a very small range of marsupials today. New Britain has two phalanger species, one wallaby, and one bandicoot, while the Admiralties have one phalanger and one bandicoot. This contrasts strongly with the main island of New Guinea—820,000 square kilometers (317,000 square miles) in area—where there are 53 species of larger marsupials, including at least 9 bandicoots, 8 phalangers, and 14 wallabies and kangaroos. The differences can be explained to some extent by the fact that the islands are smaller than New Guinea, with less diverse environments. But if animals migrated there naturally, we would expect them to have done so over many millennia. We would then see both greater evolutionary differences between animals on different islands and considerably more species on large than on small islands. Since we find the same few species on each island, it seems likely that they are all recent arrivals, brought deliberately or accidentally by humans.

🔶 *Pteropus temincki ennisae* is a newly discovered subspecies of bat so far known only from the northern part of New Ireland. Its close relatives live in New Britain and some small islands nearby. It is one of only two New Ireland mammals (the other being a rat) to have evolved sufficiently to be different from animals elsewhere in the Bismarck archipelago.

ILLUSTRATION: PETER SCHOUTEN/AUSTRALIAN MUSEUM

↪ The dusky pademelon (*Thylogale brunii*) is widely found throughout the eastern two-thirds of New Guinea, in forest and upper alpine grasslands. It does not inhabit lowland savanna. It probably breeds throughout the year and is thus able to adapt fairly easily to new habitats.

Particularly interesting is the vertical distribution of these bones within the deposits, indicating when they were thrown away. In the lowest levels of each site, both in the natural soil and in the early human deposits, there are no marsupials at all: the only animal remains belong to two species of rats, many species of bats, and several species of reptiles. Then, between 14,000 and 10,000 years ago, possum bones first appear, and in considerable numbers. Wallaby bones occur later, from about 7,000 years ago at the earliest. As it is highly unlikely that people would not have hunted them if they had been present, we must assume that these animals, so common elsewhere, were introduced. We cannot tell whether this happened deliberately or accidentally, but we know that "wild" animals of this kind, especially phalangers (a family of tree-dwelling marsupials which includes cuscuses and brush-tailed possums), are

JEAN-PAUL FERRERO/AUSCAPE

MOVING ANIMALS FROM PLACE TO PLACE

TIMOTHY FLANNERY

Human beings are the only vertebrate predators that relocate some of their prey species in order to establish new populations. This is very unusual behavior, and we have to look to certain ant species, which are known to relocate sap-sucking insects such as aphids, to find anything similar in the animal world. Like music and mathematics, this is one of the things that set us apart from other vertebrates. It is of particular interest, because it may represent the first step towards domesticating animals.

The history of moving, or translocating, animals in this way is difficult to trace, because there is rarely any clear evidence in the fossil record. For example, if early humans moved a herd of deer from one valley to another where they were not naturally found, there would be no way of judging this from fossils alone. The evidence would be the same if the deer had migrated there of their own accord. For this reason, the clearest evidence for animal translocation comes from islands, especially in areas where animals differ markedly from island to island and island animals are different again from those of nearby continents. Obviously, if an animal is clearly out of place on an island, it must have been brought there.

The Earliest Evidence

The islands of Melanesia are ideal for studying animal translocation. Not surprisingly, they have yielded the earliest evidence of this practice. New Guinea, the largest island in the region, has more than 200 indigenous species of mammals, including 2 species of monotremes, 63 species of marsupials, 59 species of rat-like and mouse-like rodents (including some very large ones), and 79 species of bats. Before humans arrived, there were also some giant marsupials, weighing up to 300 kilograms (660 pounds). This extraordinary diversity of species is in marked contrast to the

JEAN-PAUL FERRERO/AUSCAPE

☝ An inhabitant of the lowland rainforests of northern Melanesia, the northern common cuscus (*Phalanger orientalis*) spends the day hidden in epiphytes in the treetops and becomes active at dusk, when its loud snarls and dog-like, yapping calls are often heard in the rainforest.

situation on nearby islands, such as Halmahera, which has only 27 indigenous mammal species, all but two of which are bats, and New Ireland, which has 29 indigenous species, again all bats except two.

We know more of New Ireland's prehistory that we do of that of any other island in Near Oceania, and it is here that the earliest evidence of animal translocation has been found. The species in question is the northern common cuscus (*Phalanger orientalis*), brought to New Ireland between 19,000 and 10,000 years ago.

The Adaptable Cuscus

Over the last 20,000 years, the northern common cuscus has been translocated repeatedly, making it one of the most widespread marsu-

pials. The reason for this is found in its biology. There is good reason to believe that the translocated animals were "back young"—that is, young that have developed fur and no longer depend on the mother's milk, but, for a brief period, are carried around on her back. Younger animals are susceptible to hypothermia and starvation, and older, less tractable animals are liable to be injured on capture and often suffer from "capture myopathy", a debilitating form of shock that is sometimes fatal.

Moreover, the northern common cuscus is unique among northern New Guinea's larger marsupials in that it usually bears twins. Because of this, a single female with back young could quite easily found a new population.

This would be much less likely in the case of any of the other marsupials, which bear only one young at a time. Most New Guinean mammals do not breed seasonally, so, assuming that the young are carried on the mother's back for only one month out of the 12 in the breeding cycle, the chance of obtaining back young is 1 in 24. (On average, half the animals captured will be males.) The likelihood of capturing two females, one with a male and one with a female back young, at the right time (shortly before a trading voyage), is very remote indeed.

If the northern common cuscuses in New Ireland do indeed descend from a brother and sister, there should be considerable evidence of inbreeding. Preliminary studies suggest that this may be the case, particularly among those found on the Solomon Islands (which most likely derived from New Ireland).

If a species is to be translocated successfully, two vital conditions must be met. It must be able to exist on whatever food its human captors offer it, and it must be able to survive at its release site, which may not have been very carefully chosen. Obviously, adaptable animals will do better than those with very precise food and habitat needs. The little that is known of the northern common cuscus's diet and habitat requirements suggests that it is such a generalist.

Animal translocation is similar to animal husbandry in important ways. In both cases, only a few species are suitable, and in both, animals and humans must live in close contact. It seems remarkable that prehistoric people did not take that small step further and domesticate the northern common cuscus. Perhaps it does not reproduce readily in captivity, or there may be other biological reasons why it was not domesticated. It may also be that the early Melanesians' way of life was simply not conducive to keeping domesticated animals.

1 Selecting the stone
Stone for tools is taken either from seams of good rock or, as here, from river gravels. Pebbles and cobbles are smashed by throwing them down so that the newly broken surfaces can be inspected and their quality assessed.

HEAT TREATMENT:
A 50,000-YEAR-OLD TECHNOLOGY

J. Peter White

2 Building an oven
As direct contact with fire will cause the stone to shatter and split, the rocks are buried in sand to a depth of 4 or 5 centimeters (1 or 2 inches) and a fire lit over the top. Modern researchers use a sand bath in an oven.

For the last two million years, people have flaked stone to make tools and other artifacts. The stone used has usually been brittle and fine-grained, without large crystals, rather than tough or very crystalline. This is because brittle rocks such as flint, chert, and obsidian flake cleanly, giving a sharp edge. More crystalline rocks, such as quartzite and silcrete, are more difficult to flake, because the force of the flaking hammer must travel around all the tiny crystals, resulting in an edge that is less sharp.

Heat treatment makes stone flake more readily by driving water out of the interstices between the crystals and increasing the number of internal microfractures. The flaking force can thus travel through the crystal lattice rather than around it. This makes the rock more brittle, reducing its tensile strength by about half. Heat treatment, therefore, allows a wider range of rocks to be flaked more precisely, and also produces sharper, though more brittle, edges. The procedure is shown in the illustrations.

Heat-treated rocks usually have a glossy appearance when flaked, since the flaked surfaces are flatter. They may also change color, either on the surface or all through, becoming redder as a result of the oxidation of microscopic quantities of iron.

Heat treatment appears to have been invented within the last 50,000 years. Flakes struck from heat-treated stone have been recovered from Late Pleistocene sites in Siberia, the Americas, and Australia.

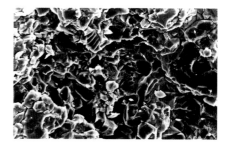

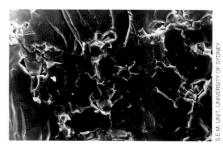

🔥 Scanning electron microscope photographs of the surface of a flake from the same piece of stone (magnified 2,500 times) made before (top) and after (below) heat treatment. The force of a blow can travel through most rock grains after heat treatment.

3 Slow heating, slow cooling
The fire needs to be small but maintained continuously. The temperature of the rock is raised over several hours to around 275 degrees Celsius (527 degrees Fahrenheit) and held for about 8 hours. The rock is then allowed to cool gradually, to avoid thermal shock.

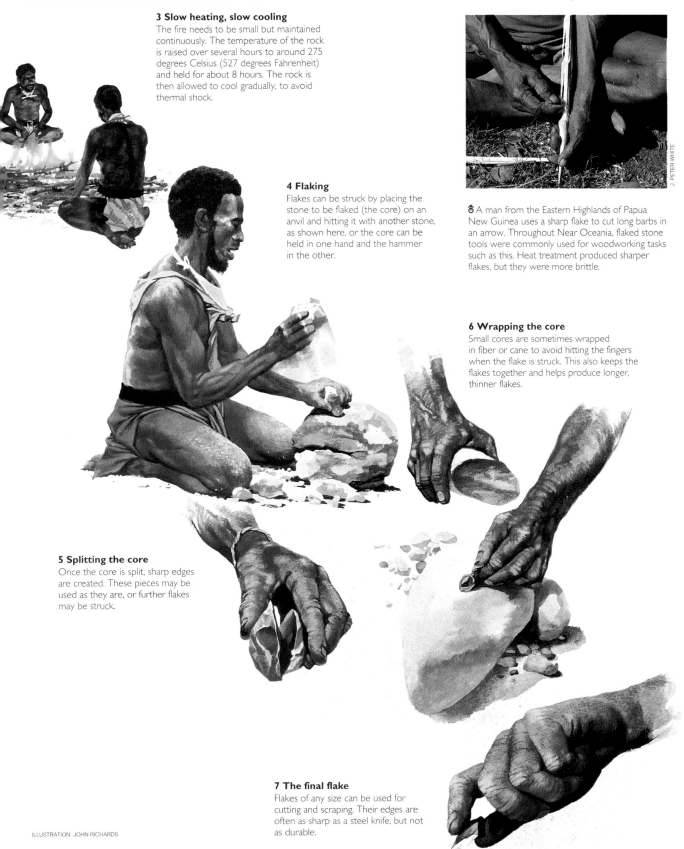

J. PETER WHITE

🔥 A man from the Eastern Highlands of Papua New Guinea uses a sharp flake to cut long barbs in an arrow. Throughout Near Oceania, flaked stone tools were commonly used for woodworking tasks such as this. Heat treatment produced sharper flakes, but they were more brittle.

4 Flaking
Flakes can be struck by placing the stone to be flaked (the core) on an anvil and hitting it with another stone, as shown here, or the core can be held in one hand and the hammer in the other.

6 Wrapping the core
Small cores are sometimes wrapped in fiber or cane to avoid hitting the fingers when the flake is struck. This also keeps the flakes together and helps produce longer, thinner flakes.

5 Splitting the core
Once the core is split, sharp edges are created. These pieces may be used as they are, or further flakes may be struck.

ILLUSTRATION: JOHN RICHARDS

7 The final flake
Flakes of any size can be used for cutting and scraping. Their edges are often as sharp as a steel knife, but not as durable.

FROM STONE TO TOOLS: RESIDUE ANALYSIS

Tom Loy

Blood residue

mm 0   10

☙ The dark discoloration from the blood residue can be seen on the cutting edge, at left.
TOM LOY

A hundred thousand years ago, an artisan who lived at Barda Balka, along a river in northwestern Iraq, picked up a small grey nodule of flint, with a few blows created a tool, used it, and threw it away. With hundreds of others, this tool was excavated and analyzed by a research team from the Oriental Institute in Chicago. They found nothing unusual about the artifact, and on the evidence of shape and flaking patterns decided that it had been a scraper or a knife. But some years ago, traces of blood were discovered on its surface. Microscopic and biochemical analysis of the organic residues has since been able to tell us a surprising amount about how the tool was used.

Traces of woody tissue with characteristic pits in the cell walls

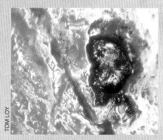

☙ Photomicrograph showing the blood residue from the Barda Balka tool at 600 times' magnification. The reddish brown and brown areas are where the blood residue is very thick, the yellowish areas where it is much thinner. The flint itself is light grey.

were found along the working edge of the Barda Balka tool, indicating that it was used, probably only once, to scrape a coniferous softwood. While scraping, the artisan was cut, but continued to work. Analysis of serum albumin, hemoglobin, and immunoglobin G molecules removed from the reside has shown that the blood is human. Wood fragments were preserved in the blood film as it dried. No human skeletons were excavated from the Barda Balka site, but the date suggests that the person who used the tool was probably a Neanderthal. The DNA contained in the white blood cells found in the blood residue may eventually be used to study the genetic relationship between the tool user and ourselves, and ultimately indicate the user's sex.

Evidence through the Ages

Such residues are often found. They have been discovered on artifacts from open-air and cave sites, arctic regions, the desert, tropical jungle swamps, and most environments lying between these extremes. Biochemical analysis of preserved residues indicates that blood molecules may survive throughout the millions of years that human beings have been using and making tools.

This analysis does not only tell us about human beings. Far removed from Barda Balka, 11 chert knives were found at a site known as Toad River Canyon, near the northern end of the Rocky Mountains in western Canada. (They were eventually deposited in the Royal British Columbia Museum in Victoria, Canada.) The acidic, subarctic soils in this region do not preserve animal bones, but analysis of the tool residues has revealed that mountain sheep and caribou were among the animals butchered by the prehistoric hunters. More significantly, many traces of blood tissue and hair from North American bison

were found on the tool surfaces. Bison are no longer found in the region, and were not thought to have been among the animals slaughtered for food at that time.

Because the site was destroyed after the tools were collected, conventional methods could not be used to date the collection. However, advances in the radiocabon dating of minute amounts of carbon have allowed 50 micrograms (or 1/500,000 of a gram) purified from blood proteins on one of the tools to be dated at about 3,000 years ago. This collection of tools has given us the first animal DNA from blood residues. With our current methods, which can detect DNA from a single cell, the way has now been opened to directly analyzing a variety of animal species in terms of their taxonomy and evolutionary relationships.

New Insights into Ancient Lives

Blood and tissue are not the only materials that have survived. Starch grains and plant tissue preserved on 27,000-year-old tools from the Kilu Cave site in the north Solomon Islands, in the Southwest Pacific, document the oldest known use of root vegetables. The starch grains have been identified as taro, *Colocasia esculenta*, a staple food throughout Southeast Asia and the Pacific. Preserved seeds or plant tissue are rarely found at archaeological sites, but the direct analysis of plant remains on stone tools will fill in many gaps in our knowledge of the long history of gathering and cultivating wild and semiwild plants that culminated in the development of Neolithic farming methods.

The scientific methods developed to study these microscopic and molecular remains are able to provide much greater detail than traditional methods of classification. They represent a major advance in archaeological research, allowing us a vastly greater insight into the lives of ancient peoples.

Sample for DNA analysis

Sample for radiocarbon dating

Hairs

mm 0   10

☙ Abundant hairs can be seen slightly to one side of the tip of this tool excavated from the Toad River Canyon site in northern British Columbia, Canada. For the purposes of radiocarbon dating and DNA analysis, blood residues were taken from the areas indicated.
TOM LOY

☙ Low-power photomicrograph showing the hair and blood residue found on the Toad River Canyon tool. The hairs have been identified as belonging to the North American bison (*Bison bison*), and analysis of DNA extracted from the blood residue has confirmed this.

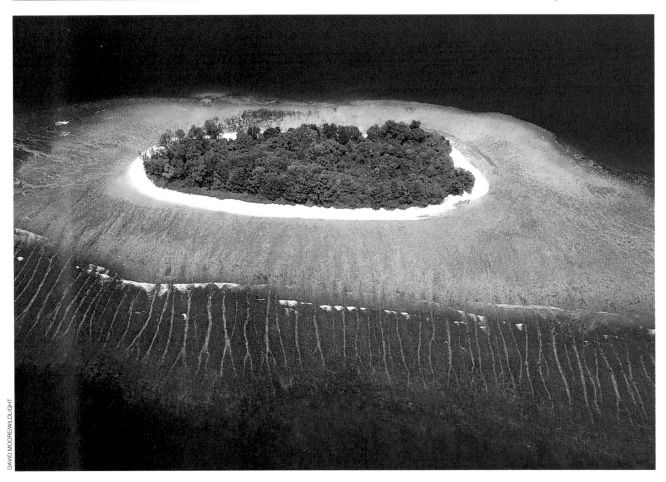

DAVID MOORE/WILDLIGHT

On the Solomon Islands—39,000 square kilometers (15,000 square miles) in area—the picture is different. The earliest levels excavated at the Kilu site (see map) contain the remains of five species of rats, as well as of bats and two lizard-like reptiles. The rats are all highly distinctive, ranging up to 2 kilograms (between 4 and 5 pounds) in weight. They are clearly not recent introductions. Two of these species disappeared in the course of human settlement, presumably because they were hunted to extinction or because their habitat changed. Remains of nonnative animals do not appear after 3,000 years ago, with the exception of one piece of phalanger jaw found in a 10,000-year-old level, which may be a relic of trade in smoked meat or an introduced animal that did not escape into the wild.

These studies of human–animal relationships have broad implications, showing not only that hunters and gatherers can cause animals to become extinct, but also the extent to which they alter the natural environment to their own advantage. In the light of the archaeological evidence, theories of island biogeography that suggest a direct and simple relationship between numbers of animal species and island size, environmental diversity, and distance from a potential population source, such as a continental landmass, need to be reconsidered. The present "wild" fauna of the Pacific islands is in large part the result of human action.

MICHAEL McCOY

A classic Pacific island, with dense vegetation, golden sands, an extensive reef, and the sea—an island one might visit to catch fish, shellfish, and perhaps birds, but one not likely to have fresh water or soil good enough for gardens.

The king rat, *Uromys rex*, is one of the large, mosaic-tailed rats of the Solomon Islands—so called because the tail scales do not overlap but fit together, like a mosaic. It is about 60 centimeters (2 feet) long, half its length being the tail. A tree dweller, it is still found on some islands, but is now rare.

MICHAEL McCOY

🔸 *Canarium indicum* trees are native to the New Guinea area and have been transplanted to other Pacific islands, being valued for their plentiful crop of edible nuts and also their bark, which can be used to treat burns. The trees are sometimes grown near villages, as shown here, but more commonly, trees growing naturally in the forest are owned and looked after by villagers, who harvest the nuts.

MICHAEL McCOY

🔸 Canarium nuts have a high protein content. They can be eaten raw, either alone or used as flavoring for sago or taro, and can also be dried over a fire, after which they can be stored for many months.

As well as useful animals, useful plants were being transported across the sea. At the Pamwak site on Manus Island—about 2,100 square kilometers (800 square miles) in area—the nuts of *Canarium indicum* ("galip" nuts), which are native to mainland New Guinea, have been found. These shiny black nuts are about the size of a golf ball and grow on a large, easily propagated tree. The nut kernels are high in protein and are good to eat, as well as being easily stored, particularly when smoked. Canarium nuts have also been found in levels 10,000 years old at the Kilu site in the Solomons, while taro starch residues have been found on stone tools from the earliest levels. (See the feature *From Stone to Tools: Residue Analysis*.) Whether these taro were simply wild plants that were collected and scraped before they were cooked, or whether they were cultivated, has not been determined.

This plant evidence suggests that islanders were looking after wild plants in the Pleistocene period. These people would not have had large fenced gardens, but rather a formal system whereby people owned, cared for, and harvested food plants growing naturally in the tropical jungle.

Artifacts

All the cave and shelter sites contain a range of artifacts, either discarded tools or manufacturing waste from tools. Surviving materials are stone and bone, although some organic residues, mainly plant tissues and blood, cling to the used edges.

In New Ireland, the stone artifacts consist solely of sharp flakes and the cores from which they were struck, both of which were used as tools. Many were made from local stone, including partially marbled limestone and coarse-grained volcanic rocks collected as cobbles from stream beds. In their lower levels, all sites contain tools made from hard, fine-grained rocks such as variously colored cherts. But the sources of these rocks are problematic. At Balof, neutron activation analysis of 102 specimens showed that they belonged to two groups. A few, found in the lowest levels and about 14,000 years old, were calcium–aluminium silicates of volcanic origin, while the rest were cherts and quartzites, which form in marine environments. The volcanic group must have originated at least 30 kilometers (18 miles) from where they were found, as there are no closer volcanic sources, but no precise source has been determined. They might even have come from another island. (Sources of this kind are often very small, and are unlikely to be found unless local people remember them.) Cherts and quartzites have not been found in the local limestone, which was, of course, formed under water or as pebbles in local stream beds. In this case, an offshore source seems likely, in the form of a layer of limestone long since drowned by the rising seas during the Holocene period. None of

J. SPECHT/AUSTRALIAN MUSEUM

these fine-grained rocks were used more recently than 8,000 to 10,000 years ago.

The other major rock type used for tools is obsidian, a type of volcanic glass. This is found in only three small areas of New Guinea and Near Oceania: Fergusson Island, several outcrops around Talasea in New Britain, and one small island in the Admiralties (see map). All the obsidian more than 3,000 years old found in New Ireland derives from a source known as Mopir, near Talasea. The oldest obsidian has been found at Matembek, which is about 400 kilometers (250 miles) from Mopir, in levels dated to about 19,000 years ago, suggesting that people over a wide area have valued this material for thousands of years.

In the Holocene period (the last 10,000 years), obsidian was carried much further out into the Pacific. What it was exchanged for we do not know, but a whole range of local goods, such as feathers, food, and wood carvings, may have been involved. We might surmise that this extensive distribution network was organized by specialized traders, but this seems unlikely among earlier hunters and gatherers. More loosely organized group-to-group trading, as takes place today, is more probable.

The presence of obsidian on New Ireland has puzzled archaeologists. It appeared at Matembek about 19,000 years ago, but was first found at Balof and Panakiwuk less than 10,000 years ago.

These sites are on the same island, and not far apart, so such a difference is unlikely to have resulted from lack of contact between them. It is possible, of course, that the dating is inaccurate, but this too seems unlikely, because each site has yielded a set of internally consistent radiocarbon dates taken from different materials. Perhaps the activities carried out at Balof and Panakiwuk more than 10,000 years ago did not require the use of obsidian, but nothing else points to this—indeed, there seems to have been very little difference in the ways these cave sites were used. There might have been some kind of cultural barrier, or a prohibition on the use of obsidian in the northern part of the island, but research to date has yielded

☝ The volcanic landscape of Willaumez Peninsula, New Britain. Obsidian from some of its volcanoes was distributed widely throughout the western Pacific, but living in this volcanically active area was risky.

no evidence of this either, and such propositions are in any case difficult to test.

How were stone artifacts used? Again, this is often hard to judge, as their form is not always a reliable guide. However, recent research in two areas—the microscopic analysis of the wear patterns on artifacts, which are then compared with those resulting from various known uses, and organic residue analysis—has given us new insights into the lives of ancient peoples. At Balof, for example, Huw Barton has found that all artifacts made from fine-grained rocks, including obsidian, were used on wood or other parts of plants, including the starchy parts (possibly tubers used as food). He also found a few fragments of bird feathers but little blood, indicating that very few tested tools were used on animals. The bones of many complete animals were found at the site,

including burned and chewed bones, which clearly indicate that the animals were cooked on a fire and eaten there. Perhaps wooden tools were used to skin and butcher them.

The Pamwak site on Manus Island contains stone tools made from local chert that has been heat-treated to make flaking easier. (See the feature *Heat Treatment: A 50,000-year-old Technology*.) Obsidian, presumably from outcrops on nearby Lou Island, first appears at the site about 12,000 years ago. And in New Britain, where only one clearly Pleistocene site has been discovered, levels dated to 11,000 years ago contain five small flakes of obsidian and some charcoal. This island is an important link in the settlement of Near Oceania, although given the high level of volcanic activity in the last 20,000 years, it remains to be seen how many of its Pleistocene sites will be accessible.

Kavachi volcano erupting in the Solomon Islands. Once the eruption ceases, this lava cone will be slowly colonized by plants and insects. If the final eruption consists of ash, which makes good soil, it will be colonized more rapidly.

RELICS OF THE FIRST NEW IRELAND SETTLERS

CHRISTOPHER GOSDEN

The site known as Matenkupkum, on the southeast coast of New Ireland, close to Papua New Guinea, is a dry limestone cave 18 meters (59 feet) long by 10 meters (33 feet) wide. It sits just above present-day sea level on an uplifted limestone terrace, and its mouth faces southeast, looking out over the Pacific Ocean.

This cave was first excavated in 1985, a year after archaeologists discovered it. The excavation team consisted of myself, Pru Gaffey (another archaeologist from the Australian National University), and five people from the local village of Hilalon, where we stayed. We had two aims: to find out when the cave was first occupied, and to gain an understanding of the lives of the people who used it. We thought it likely that the light would have influenced the nature of the activities carried out in the cave, and so we decided to excavate a trench 10 meters by 1 meter (33 feet by 3 feet) from the mouth of the cave back to the center.

Our decision turned out well. We stripped the soil off one layer at a time along the whole trench, and in the middle found a series of hearths, which we later dated to between 14,000 and 12,000 years ago. These hearths consisted of pits, sometimes lined with limestone blocks, which had been redug and reused over 2,000 years. The hearths and their associated piles of rubbish provide a remarkably consecutive record of how people have used the cave over 80 or so generations.

Laboratory analysis showed that much of the soil we excavated was, in fact, ash from the hearths. Behind the hearths, in the darker part of the cave, we found a pile made up of shell taken from the nearby reef, the bones of rainforest animals (the northern common cuscus, *Phalanger orientalis*, rats, bats, birds, lizards, and snakes—all potential food sources), and large pieces of flaked stone from a local

♦ The cave of Matenkupkum had its first human visitors some 33,000 years ago. Obsidian found here in 12,000-year-old deposits had been brought by sea a distance of 350 kilometers (220 miles).
CHRISTOPHER GOSDEN

river. There were also pieces of obsidian, a type of volcanic glass which has a sharp cutting edge. This came from volcanoes on the island of New Britain, about 350 kilometers (220 miles) away. It must have been transported by sea, showing that people who used the cave were in contact with people on other islands.

From Distant to Recent Past

Evidence unearthed at the front of the cave dated from quite a different period. During the Second World War, Japanese soldiers had occupied the cave to prevent the sabotage of a telephone line running along the coast. They dug a trench across the front to protect themselves from attack, and when they left they filled it with rubbish. The trench destroyed most of the prehistoric deposits at the front of the cave, and contained a range of everyday objects—saucepans, beer bottles, shoes, and so on—which provided an interesting insight into an ordinary soldier's life and the nature of jungle war.

Beneath the levels where the hearths were found, there was evidence that the cave was used between 21,000 and 18,000 years ago. Here we found fine layers of sand and ash, hard to distinguish

in excavation, which probably resulted from sporadic occupation of the cave over a long period. The fact that there was no obsidian or cuscus bones in these levels may indicate that the people of this time were not in contact with groups from outside. The base of the deposit was sand from an old beach, formed before the cave was uplifted to its present position. In this, we found evidence of the first use of the cave some 33,000 years ago: tools made from local stone and large shells picked from previously untouched reefs, as well as some bones of bats, rats, snakes, lizards, and birds.

These lowest deposits contained no trace of hearths, and rubbish appeared to have been scattered at random. If only small numbers of people had visited the cave infrequently, they would not have needed to clean up. The fact that rubbish was piled up in a more orderly way in later years, from about 12,000 years ago, indicates that more people lived on New Ireland at that time and visited the cave more frequently.

Although it is only one point in a landscape over which people may have ranged widely, the cave of Matenkupkum can tell us a great deal, both about the initial colonization of a large Pacific island and the changes that took place on it over 20,000 years.

♦ These limestone blocks may have been used as a hearth base 12,000 years ago.

mm 0 10

♦ For 20,000 years, people used stone tools like these, made from local river cobbles.

◄● Shells harvested from the local reef 33,000 years ago.

MODERN PEOPLE IN THE NEW WORLD

12,000 YEARS AGO – 10,200 YEARS AGO

The Clovis Mammoth Hunters and the Goshen and Folsom Bison Hunters

GEORGE C. FRISON

FOR MORE THAN HALF A CENTURY, archaeologists have been probing the geological deposits of the late Pleistocene period in their quest to identify the first humans to set foot in North America. These efforts have been both frustrating and rewarding. Although much information has come to light, the identity of the first migrants and their Old World ancestors, the entry route they used, and the conditions under which they arrived are still vigorously debated. (See the feature *Who Were the First Americans?*)

To date, the earliest cultural complex in North America that all archaeologists recognize is known as Clovis. (A cultural complex refers to a group of distinctive cultural artifacts found in association with each other and presumably used by a single population, perhaps over several generations.) It appeared somewhere between 12,000 and 11,000 years ago, just before the last of the large mammals (or megafauna) of the Late Pleistocene period became extinct. Two other cultural complexes, Folsom and Goshen, appeared not long after Clovis, and the surviving evidence of these three cultures constitutes our knowledge of the early North American Paleoindian hunters.

◄● Present-day herd of bison (*Bison bison*). Although bison are naturally gregarious, herd size changes as small groups split away and other groups join. Mature males may be solitary or form small separate groups, except during the breeding season. Late Pleistocene bison were larger and were the mainstay of the Plains Paleoindian economy.

⬆ A Clovis point from the Colby site, in northern Wyoming.
GEORGE C. FRISON

At the time of the last glacial maximum, about 18,000 years ago, huge ice sheets covered nearly all of Canada and extended south of the present-day Great Lakes in the eastern United States. So much water from the oceans was frozen in glaciers around the world that sea levels dropped, exposing a continental shelf that included a large, unglaciated landmass known as Beringia connecting northeast Asia and present-day Alaska. Beringia was a flat, well-vegetated landmass capable of supporting not only the giant animals of the late Pleistocene era but also human predators crossing into the area from the west.

As the glaciers melted, sea levels began to rise, gradually submerging the exposed continental shelf. By 12,000 years ago, the Laurentide ice sheet had retreated to the east and the Cordilleran ice sheet to the west, resulting in an open corridor between them that stretched south from present-day Yukon across Canada to Montana. Usually referred to as the "ice-free corridor", this is believed by many prehistorians to have been the route the earliest big-game hunters took to reach the Great Plains of North America. Others think they entered from Alaska, south along the northwest coast.

A New Environment

Significant climatic and environmental changes took place between 12,000 and 10,000 years ago. When the Clovis Cultural Complex first appeared, between 12,000 and 11,000 years ago, winters were warmer and summers were cooler, so

seasonal extremes of temperature were less marked than at present. Vegetation was different: tall grasses, for example, covered the short-grass plains of today. The giant animals of late Pleistocene times were on the edge of extinction. They included mammoths, mastodon, horses, camels, and giant sloths. Large bison would survive for another 3,000 years. Perhaps even more impressive were the carnivores, such as the short-faced bear—twice the size of a present-day grizzly bear—and the American lion and American cheetah—again, both bigger than their present-day African counterparts. There were many small animals as well. The collared lemming, for example, a tiny creature that can survive only in cold environments, lived around the margins of the glaciers. It can still be found today in arctic glacial environments.

Some time after about 11,000 years ago, another environmental shift occurred. Seasons became more marked, with long periods of sunlight and warmer temperatures, while snowfall and annual rainfall declined. These changes culminated about 10,000 years ago, at the beginning of the Holocene period, when climatic conditions were similar to those we know today.

Although many archaeologists are convinced that humans were present in North America during pre-Clovis times, all agree that Clovis tools and weapons are the earliest found to date that would have enabled people to hunt the large animals present at that time. This strongly suggests that the Clovis hunters were related to the Upper Paleolithic hunters of the Old World, who had pursued and killed mammoths, bison, reindeer, and other large animals for many thousands of years previously.

The First Paleoindian Finds

Early this century, it was generally believed that humans had arrived in North America relatively recently in prehistoric terms. Then, in the 1920s, a black cowboy, George McJunkin, made an historic discovery when he noticed some large bones exposed in the earthen bank of an arroyo (a steep-sided channel) while herding cattle near the small town of Folsom, in northeast New Mexico. The find was brought to the attention of the Colorado Museum of Natural History, and in 1926 paleontologists from the museum found stone weapons of a type later to become known as the Folsom projectile point, along with butchering tools, among the bones, which proved to be those of an extinct species of bison. But archaeologists were not convinced that the tools and weapons were associated with the bones, and several eminent scientists of the time, including Barnum Brown, a paleontologist from the American Museum of Natural History, and Frank H.H. Roberts Jr, of the Smithsonian Institution, were called in to view a projectile point in place

JOSEPH H. BAILEY/© NATIONAL GEOGRAPHIC SOCIETY

☞ The mammoth stood no taller than a modern Asian elephant but was unique for its massive tusks. It was a grazing animal adapted to the open grasslands, while the mastodon was more of a browser adapted to forested areas.

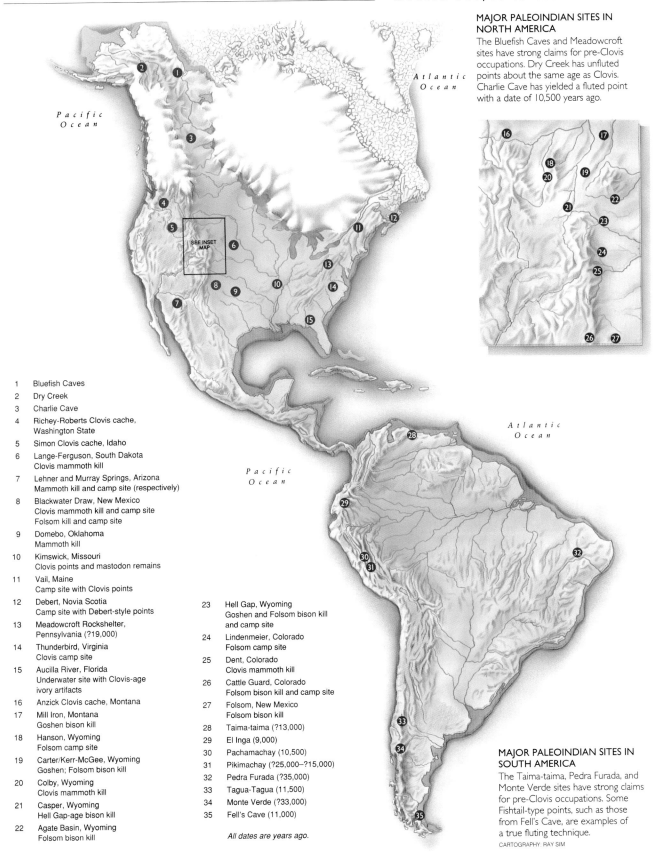

MAJOR PALEOINDIAN SITES IN NORTH AMERICA

The Bluefish Caves and Meadowcroft sites have strong claims for pre-Clovis occupations. Dry Creek has unfluted points about the same age as Clovis. Charlie Cave has yielded a fluted point with a date of 10,500 years ago.

1   Bluefish Caves

2   Dry Creek

3   Charlie Cave

4   Richey-Roberts Clovis cache, Washington State

5   Simon Clovis cache, Idaho

6   Lange-Ferguson, South Dakota
    Clovis mammoth kill

7   Lehner and Murray Springs, Arizona
    Mammoth kill and camp site (respectively)

8   Blackwater Draw, New Mexico
    Clovis mammoth kill and camp site
    Folsom kill and camp site

9   Domebo, Oklahoma
    Mammoth kill

10 Kimswick, Missouri
    Clovis points and mastodon remains

11 Vail, Maine
    Camp site with Clovis points

12 Debert, Novia Scotia
    Camp site with Debert-style points

13 Meadowcroft Rockshelter,
    Pennsylvania (?19,000)

14 Thunderbird, Virginia
    Clovis camp site

15 Aucilla River, Florida
    Underwater site with Clovis-age
    ivory artifacts

16 Anzick Clovis cache, Montana

17 Mill Iron, Montana
    Goshen bison kill

18 Hanson, Wyoming
    Folsom camp site

19 Carter/Kerr-McGee, Wyoming
    Goshen; Folsom bison kill

20 Colby, Wyoming
    Clovis mammoth kill

21 Casper, Wyoming
    Hell Gap-age bison kill

22 Agate Basin, Wyoming
    Folsom bison kill

23 Hell Gap, Wyoming
    Goshen and Folsom bison kill
    and camp site

24 Lindenmeier, Colorado
    Folsom camp site

25 Dent, Colorado
    Clovis mammoth kill

26 Cattle Guard, Colorado
    Folsom bison kill and camp site

27 Folsom, New Mexico
    Folsom bison kill

28 Taima-taima (?13,000)

29 El Inga (9,000)

30 Pachamachay (10,500)

31 Pikimachay (?25,000–?15,000)

32 Pedra Furada (?35,000)

33 Tagua-Tagua (11,500)

34 Monte Verde (?33,000)

35 Fell's Cave (11,000)

All dates are years ago.

MAJOR PALEOINDIAN SITES IN SOUTH AMERICA

The Taima-taima, Pedra Furada, and Monte Verde sites have strong claims for pre-Clovis occupations. Some Fishtail-type points, such as those from Fell's Cave, are examples of a true fluting technique.

CARTOGRAPHY: RAY SIM

⊕ Excavations at the Dent site, in Colorado, during the summer of 1933. In 1932, large bones discovered near Dent, along the South Platte River, proved to be the remains of several mammoths. Father Conrad Bilgery, of Regis College, Denver, directed excavations at the site, and on 5 November a Clovis projectile point was recovered close to the bones. In 1933, the Colorado Museum of Natural History continued the excavations, and a second Clovis point was found.

⚒ Removing a cast block of bison bones from the arroyo at the Folsom site, in northeast New Mexico.

among the bones. It was only after a third year of excavation that all archaeologists and paleontologists agreed that the evidence was overwhelming: humans had indeed inhabited North America much earlier in prehistory than was previously believed to be possible and had successfully hunted long-extinct animals.

In 1932, a flood along the North Platte River, in northern Colorado, exposed the remains of several mammoths. When the site was excavated, two projectile points were found among the mammoth bones and later confirmed to be Clovis fluted projectile points. But it was a concentration of finds from a site known as Blackwater Draw Locality No. 1, near the town of Clovis, in eastern New Mexico, that gave the Clovis Cultural Complex its name. As the town of Clovis is on the western edge of the Llano Estacado, the complex is also sometimes known as Llano.

Blackwater Draw is a drainage channel that, during a much earlier geological period, was a stream flowing southeast across the Llano Estacado. By Clovis times, because of climatic changes, all that remained was a series of shallow seasonal ponds that collected sediment during runoff periods. These ponds were natural gathering places for large animals such as mammoths and bison. Hunters either killed the

animals at the waterholes or followed prey wounded elsewhere back to the water, where the animals sought to alleviate their suffering. Tools and weapons preserved in stratigraphic sequence in the continually accumulating sediments attest to several thousand years of Paleoindian hunting and butchering activities around Blackwater Draw. There can be no doubt that Clovis hunters were killing mammoths and bison some 11,000 years ago. Immediately above the Clovis level is evidence of the Folsom hunters, who, a short time later, were killing bison, but not mammoths.

The Blackwater finds came about because the culture-bearing sediments were buried under gravel, a scarce commodity on the Llano Estacado. As the gravel was being excavated for road building, mammoth and bison bones were exposed, along with human tools and weapons. However, the site was turned into a gravel pit, and archaeologists had to salvage what they could (although the operator of the gravel pit deserves credit for cooperating with them). In 1956, an attempt was made to have an area of 2 hectares (5 acres) set aside for future research, but this was unsuccessful. As a result, what was possibly the major part of the most significant Paleoindian site in North America was lost to posterity.

With the discovery of Clovis and Folsom

remains, most archaeologists believed that Clovis was the oldest culture, followed closely by Folsom. This view was challenged in the 1960s by excavations at Hell Gap, in southeast Wyoming, one of the earliest and largest Paleoindian sites in North America. Being a deeply stratified site, Hell Gap helped to establish a reliable chronology for the Paleoindians of the Northern Plains. A small number of chipped stone artifacts discovered beneath a Folsom level at Hell Gap were at first believed to be Clovis. More detailed analysis soon showed that they were neither Clovis nor Folsom but included projectile points closely resembling a type recovered from the Southern Plains and known as Plainview. However, because the Plainview culture was believed to be more recent than Folsom, and the Hell Gap finds were clearly older than Folsom, the new finds were given the new name of the Goshen Cultural Complex, after the county in which they were found. Although further Goshen artifacts have since been discovered, Goshen's relationship to both Clovis and Folsom remains unresolved.

The Clovis Cultural Complex

When the people we now know as the Clovis Cultural Complex began to spread south of the continental ice sheets, they emerged into an area populated by large animals that had not previously been exploited by human predators. Clovis people developed superior types of tools and weapons and became efficient hunters. There was no competition for food resources, so they had little, if any, need to defend their hunting territories. They lived in small bands, and when

resources diminished, they could simply move on to a new area. This could explain why the Clovis culture spread so rapidly and widely over the ice-free areas of North America, and why similar tools and weapons are found over vast distances. In contrast to later Paleoindian groups, the Clovis hunters were not forced to adopt specialized subsistence strategies that would have restricted their mobility and required them to modify their tools and weapons to suit local and regional conditions.

Evidence of Clovis occupation—in the form of their distinctive fluted projectile points and variations of these weapons—has been found in mammoth kill sites across the whole of North America. In the 1950s, the search shifted to the San Pedro Valley area of southern Arizona.

⊙ Location of the deeply stratified Hell Gap site, in southeast Wyoming, which has provided a reliable chronological sequence of Paleoindian cultural complexes in western North America.

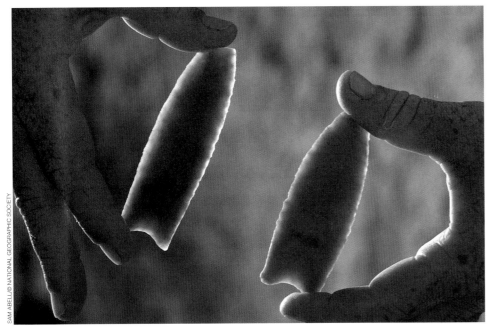

⬿ Clovis projectile points from the Murray Springs mammoth and bison kill site, in Arizona. Clovis weaponry was well designed, demonstrates superior technology, and was made from the best of raw materials.

WHO WERE THE FIRST AMERICANS ?

DAVID HURST THOMAS

THE MOST SIGNIFICANT, if least dramatic, event in the history of the Americas occurred when the first human footprint appeared in the New World. No one knows exactly when this happened, or where. We do not know what these Paleoindians wore, looked like, spoke, or thought. We do not know when they left their Asian homeland, or what conditions they experienced along the way.

And yet there remains no reasonable doubt that the first Americans did indeed travel from Asia during the late Pleistocene. Biology, language, and archaeology all point to an Asian homeland. It is the timing and conditions surrounding their arrival that remain unknown.

In this chapter, George Frison has argued that Clovis is the earliest cultural complex in the New World, established some time between 12,000 and 11,000 years ago. This relatively conservative estimate remains reasonable, because despite decades of concerted research, no undisputed evidence of pre-Clovis occupation has been uncovered anywhere in the Western Hemisphere.

Considerable nonarchae-ological evidence also supports this position. Joseph Greenberg's recent reanalysis of American Indian languages suggests that there were three waves of migrants into the New World and that the earliest took place about 12,000 years ago: these were the people of the Clovis Complex. Other investigators, independently analyzing human tooth morphology and blood genetics, have come to the same conclusion.

But considerable controversy surrounds Greenberg's broad-brush linguistic reconstructions, and numerous skeptics question the relevance of the dental and genetic evidence in this prehistoric context. Moreover, although it is still controversial, archaeological evidence emerging from a number of sites suggests that people arrived considerably earlier. Many archaeologists have begun to acknowledge, if sometimes only privately, that people might well have arrived in the New World as early as 40,000 years ago.

TOM D. DILLEHAY

☞ This pressure flaker made of antler, a flintknapping implement used to remove channel flakes, was found in the Woodland occupation level at Meadowcroft Rockshelter.
MERCYHURST ARCHAEOLOGICAL INSTITUTE, ERIE, PENNSYLVANIA

☉ Finds at the Monte Verde site include wooden pegs tied to an adjacent floor timber, remnants of junco-reed knots, and flattened pegheads.

MERCYHURST ARCHAEOLOGICAL INSTITUTE, ERIE, PENNSYLVANIA

☞ The Meadowcroft Rockshelter before excavation in 1973, looking to the west. This remarkably well-stratified site in southwestern Pennsylvania has yielded radiocarbon dates as old as 19,000 years ago, and the oldest stone artifacts appear to date from between 15,000 and 14,000 years ago.

Hints of Pre-Clovis Occupation

Numerous sites throughout North and South America have provided tantalizing suggestions of pre-Clovis occupation, but none has yielded ironclad proof acceptable to all archaeologists. Some of the best evidence comes from excavations at Meadowcroft Rockshelter, a remarkably well-stratified site in southwestern Pennsylvania. Here, James Adovasio and his colleagues have documented a sequence of more than 40 radiocarbon dates in near-perfect stratigraphic order. The oldest cultural date is a little more than 19,000 years ago, and the oldest stone artifacts appear to date from between 15,000 and 14,000 years ago. Evidence of early human habitation found in the various occupation levels consists of fire-pits, stone tools and by-products of tool-making, a wooden foreshaft, a piece of plaited basketry, and two human bone fragments.

Although many archaeologists consider the evidence from Meadowcroft to be conclusive, others remain unconvinced. The stone implements are scarce and small, and don't tell us much. They are also disturbingly similar to much later artifacts. Surprisingly, there are no remains of the giant animals known to have existed in the Pleistocene era, and the plant remnants recovered are clearly of types that grow in temperate zones, whereas, for part of this time, the ice front should have been less than 75 kilometers (47 miles) to the north.

Another leading pre-Clovis candidate is Monte Verde, an open-air residential site in southern Chile. Excavator Tom Dillehay and his colleagues have unearthed four distinct zones of buried cultural remains. The foundations and fallen pole-frames of close to 12 residential huts have been excavated, with fragments of skin (perhaps mastodon) still clinging to the poles. Abundant plant remains have been found in the deposits, as well as numerous shaped stone tools, including several grooved *bola* stones.

Dillehay argues that the upper layers at Monte Verde contain "well-preserved and clear, conclusive evidence" of human habitation about 13,000 years ago. Even more controversial are the deep layers, where remains associated with possible cultural features and several fractured stones have been radiocarbon-dated to 33,000 years ago.

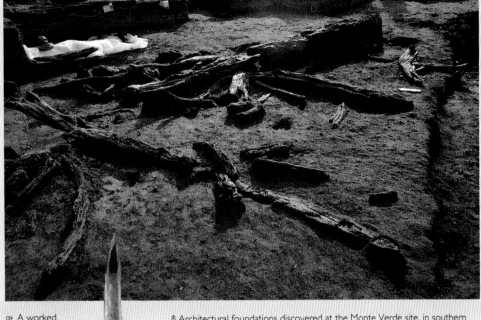

⊛ A worked bone awl from the Late Archaic occupation level at Meadowcroft Rockshelter.
MERCYHURST ARCHAEOLOGICAL INSTITUTE, ERIE, PENNSYLVANIA

⊛ Architectural foundations discovered at the Monte Verde site, in southern Chile, indicate that about 12 semirectangular huts once stood here. Fallen pole-frames were also excavated, with fragments of skin (perhaps mastodon) still clinging to them.

⊛ Tortoiseshell bowl fragment from the Woodland occupation level at Meadowcroft Rockshelter.
MERCYHURST ARCHAEOLOGICAL INSTITUTE, ERIE, PENNSYLVANIA

⊛ A Paleoindian projectile point (Miller Lanceolate type) from Meadowcroft Rockshelter.
MERCYHURST ARCHAEOLOGICAL INSTITUTE, ERIE, PENNSYLVANIA

⊛ Modified mastodon tusk and burned rib fragments from Monte Verde.

Big-game Hunters or Foragers?

These controversial findings suggest not only that humans arrived in the New World much earlier than previously thought, but also that the earliest Americans were not the glamorous big-game hunters associated with the sophisticated Clovis Complex and its elegant stone tools. Rather, the plant and animal remains from Monte Verde suggest that they were hunter-gatherers who lived mainly on wild plant foods and shellfish. They may also have scavenged, and hunted slow-moving mammals such as seals, but these would have been secondary activities.

Yet, despite the findings from Meadowcroft, Monte Verde, and numerous other sites, we have no unequivocal, indisputable archaeological evidence that the New World was inhabited before Clovis times. The debate rages on, and until more substantial evidence comes to light, claims as to the identity of the first Americans are likely to be based, as one skeptic has put it, as much on psychological as on archaeological grounds.

☗ A device made of mammoth bone found at the Murray Springs site, in Arizona, thought to be a shaft-straightening tool, was probably used like this. The shaft, also of mammoth bone, was found at the Anzick site, in Montana.

A site close to the Mexican border discovered in 1951, Naco, contained a single mammoth and 8 Clovis projectile points. Further down in the valley, the Lehner site has yielded the remains of several mammoths and 13 Clovis points, 3 of which are fairly small and made of quartz crystal. In the same valley, at Murray Springs, evidence was found in the 1960s of both a mammoth and a bison kill of Clovis age lying immediately under a geological feature known as the "black mat"—a dark layer several centimeters (about an inch) thick believed to have been derived from organic materials. The Clovis occupation surface was so well preserved that it has even been suggested that depressions in part of the site area are mammoth tracks. An artifact of carved mammoth bone found here, thought to have been a device used to straighten shafts, is almost identical to at least one recorded from northeast Asia.

In the 1970s, another mammoth kill site was found at Colby, in northern Wyoming. In this case, the animals had been driven into the cul-de-sac formed by the steep walls of a dry arroyo to be killed. Two piles of mammoth bones found here provide clear evidence of human activity. One pile was made up of the left front quarter of a mammoth, with the long bones of several other mammoths stacked around it, and was capped by the skull of a juvenile male mammoth. A fluted projectile point was found at the bottom of the left part of the ribcage. Because of the northerly location of the Colby site, it has been suggested that this pile of bones is the remains of a frozen meat cache that was never used. Nearby is a dispersed pile of mammoth bones, also containing the partial remains of several animals. This second pile is thought to be a similar meat store that had been opened up and used.

The piles are similar to caches of caribou meat that arctic people of more modern times are known to have kept. Long bones were stacked around the meat that had been stripped from the carcasses and stored for future use. The skull was placed on top of the pile, which was then packed with slush to freeze the contents and protect them from scavengers and carnivores. These were short-term winter caches, and meat that was not used would have spoiled with the coming of spring. For the Clovis people, such stores of frozen food were necessary to provide for the long, intensely cold winters on the Northwest Plains. If not needed, the meat was simply allowed to spoil.

Other mammoth kill sites containing only one or two animals have been found, including the Domebo site, in Oklahoma, and the Lange-Ferguson site, in western South Dakota. At the

Kimswick site, in Missouri, Clovis weapons were found together with mastodon remains. Sites without mammoth remains but containing characteristically fluted Clovis projectile points include the Debert site, in central Nova Scotia, the Lamb site, in New York, the Vail site, in Maine, the Bull Brook site, in Massachusetts, and the Thunderbird and Williamson sites, in Virginia. Together they show that Clovis hunters ranged widely throughout the northeast of the United States and southeast Canada.

Fluted projectile points and cylindrical-shaped, carved ivory objects found in rivers in northern Florida are almost identical to a specimen from a Clovis site in the extreme east of Wyoming. At least two stone flaking sites in western Kentucky cover more than 40 hectares (100 acres) each and are located alongside sources of high-quality chert. Clovis fluted projectile points are common finds in plowed fields in Ohio and Illinois, and further south, in the lower Mississippi Valley, fluted points are regularly found where Clovis-age landforms are exposed. They are also found in the southwest, in California, and in the Great Basin. Sites where the stratigraphy can be radiocarbon-dated are rare, however, and are largely confined to the Plains and the southwest, where conditions of erosion and deposition are most likely to have left the cultural materials in good stratigraphic sequence with other Paleoindian cultural complexes.

In Texas, at the Pavo Real site, near San Antonio, Clovis stone artifacts were found in an undisturbed context buried underneath younger cultural layers and separated from them by nearly a meter (3 feet) of noncultural deposits. Cores, blades, and blade tools are very similar to those found in Upper Paleolithic sites in Europe and Asia. Similar evidence has been recovered from the large surface sites mentioned in western Kentucky, and at least two Clovis blade caches have been found in the southwest of the United States. Together, these finds suggest that the Clovis tradition was closely linked to the Upper Paleolithic tradition of the Old World.

Clovis Tool and Weapon Caches

In 1961, rancher William Simon was operating a large earthmover on the Big Camas Prairie near the small town of Fairfield, in Idaho, when something caused him to stop and look back at the area shaved by the machine's blade. Exposed but undamaged were five unusually fine examples of Clovis projectile points. Further examination revealed other stone artifacts, several of which had been damaged by the earthmover. This became known as the Simon Clovis cache and was the first of several such finds.

In 1968, workers operating an end loader near the small town of Wilsall, in Montana, exposed a cache containing more than a hundred items, including Clovis points, bifaces (chopping and cutting implements with a sharp edge formed by percussion flaking from each side), tools, carved bone, and a small amount of skeletal material from two juvenile humans. There were also several carved cylindrical artifacts made of heavy long bone, probably mammoth, which may have been foreshafts for holding Clovis projectile points. Some of these have a single-beveled, cross-hatched end, with the other end tapered to a cone shape, while others have both ends single-beveled and cross-hatched. Everything was heavily coated with red ocher. Known as the Anzick site, this is the only known example of a Clovis burial.

A cache unearthed in 1988 during trenching operations in an orchard by the Columbia River, near the town of Wenatchee, in Washington, contained cylindrical bone artifacts similar to those found at Anzick, as well as exceptionally large Clovis projectile points, bifaces, and tools. A further cache found at about the same time in northeast Colorado contained 13 Clovis points, most of which were made from Alibates dolomite, a distinctive material found only in the Texas Panhandle, north of Amarillo, while others were made of a local material known as Flat Top chert. There were also some ivory fragments.

The publicity that surrounded the Wenatchee finds brought to light a cache of 56 Clovis artifacts discovered many years earlier, now known as the Fenn cache. We will never know exactly where it was discovered, as the person who made the discovery died many years ago, but it was somewhere in the area where Utah, Idaho, and Wyoming join. It included complete and reworked Clovis points, bifaces, a single blade tool, and a crescent. Three quartz crystal points were made of material similar to that of several bifaces from the Simon site. Several items were made of obsidian (a type of volcanic glass) that has been traced to a source in southeast Idaho. One of these is a projectile point with longitudinal scratch marks on the flute (the smooth area on each side of the point where the channel flakes were removed) that are identical to those found on obsidian Clovis points from California and Oregon. The crescent-shaped object is identical to crescents found on the surface in the Great Basin and long thought to be of Clovis age. All items were heavily coated with red ocher, reminiscent of the Anzick cache, but unfortunately we will never know if human skeletal remains or ivory or bone artifacts were also present.

Many of the bifaces and projectile points are made of a type of stone found only in a narrow strip of land stretching from northwest Utah, across the southeast corner of Wyoming, and into western Colorado. Other items are made of an extremely high-quality chert that comes from the Bighorn Mountains of northern Wyoming. One specimen from each of the Simon and Anzick

caches and two from the Fenn cache were made of the Bighorn Mountain material.

We can learn a lot about the Clovis tradition from these caches. Now that several have been found, they can be seen as an integral part of the Clovis cultural system rather than as anomalies. The Anzick cache gives us an insight into Clovis burial practices. If platform burials—where the dead are exposed for some time before burial—were the norm, this would help to explain the scarcity of Paleoindian burials. The use of red ocher in three of the caches strongly suggests ritual activities and a possible relationship with those associated with human burials among

Remains of what was possibly an unused frozen meat cache at the Colby site, in Wyoming. A protective cover of mammoth long bones was stacked around the left front quarter of a mammoth, and the skull of a five-year-old male mammoth placed on top.

GEORGE C. FRISON

CLOVIS WEAPONS: A MODERN EXPERIMENT

George C. Frison

The archaeological record leaves no doubt that the North American High Plains Paleoindians hunted several species of large animals very successfully, including mammoths. Although archaeologists will never be able to reproduce the hunting conditions of this period, nor acquire the expertise of these Paleolithic hunters, experiments with African elephants can give us an insight into both the weapons they used and the animal behavior they would have encountered. The main limitation of such experiments is that there are bound to be some differences between elephants and mammoths and also differences in the natural environment between then and now.

Clovis projectile points from mammoth kills have survived, however, and we can compare the physiology of elephants with that of frozen mammoths recovered from Siberia. We know that mammoths and African elephants have hides of similar thickness, although elephant hides have a more armor-like surface, probably because elephants inhabit regions characterized by thorny vegetation. Mammoth hide is covered with long hair and short, thick fur that would have offered little resistance to an expertly propeled Clovis projectile point.

← This replica of a Clovis projectile point, mounted on a foreshaft inserted into the end of the mainshaft, was used in the elephant experiments.
GEORGE C. FRISON

In the national parks of Zimbabwe, elephant herds have multiplied beyond the carrying capacity of the ecosystem, and a program of controlled killing, or culling, has been instituted. The Zimbabwe Division of Wildlife agreed to allow experiments with Clovis weapons to be carried out, provided that only dead or dying animals were targeted.

The strategy used to cull African elephants is to kill an entire family— the oldest female, all of her offspring, and her family's offspring, except for males beyond puberty. Because elephants have a matriarchal social structure, random killing is ill advised. Animals from one family are not accepted by other families, and those lacking a matriarch leader become outcasts, which are a danger to national park visitors.

An internationally known flint-knapper, Dr Bruce Bradley, has made replicas of Clovis projectile points from several different kinds of raw-stone flaking materials. The points were mounted on short wooden shafts (foreshafts) which could be used with either a thrusting or throwing spear, or an atlatl—a type of throwing stick—and long shaft. The thrusting or throwing spear is either held in both hands at the time of impact or thrown with one arm from a distance. The purpose of the atlatl is to add length to the throwing arm. It has a hook on one end which engages with a shallow cup on the end of the long shaft, allowing the shaft to be propeled.

The best part of the animal to aim at is probably the lung cavity, halfway between the bottom of the ribcage and the top of the back. On the average young adult elephant, the hide here is 8 to 10 millimeters (a quarter to half an inch) thick, and the ribs are rounded, which usually allows the projectile point that hits a rib to

♂ A dart launched by an atlatl from a distance of nearly 20 meters (22 yards) penetrated the hind quarter of this juvenile African elephant to the end of the foreshaft.

slide around it and penetrate the ribcage. Lower down, the ribs are wider and flatter, making it difficult to penetrate the heart, which lies close to the bottom of the ribcage. Higher up, the hide is thicker. If the spear penetrates the flesh at the top of the back, this produces a painful wound that will eventually prove fatal only if the spear has penetrated the interior of the ribcage.

It requires considerable strength to penetrate an elephant's hide with a thrusting spear. A spear thrown from a distance is effective, but a great deal of practice is needed to throw it accurately. An atlatl and dart were found to be the most effective method, the dart having a combined weight—shaft, foreshaft, and projectile point— of 478 grams (16 ounces) and a combined length of 220 centimeters (7 feet 2 inches). But each hunter needs to experiment to find the length and weight that suit him personally.

During the culling operations, a mature female elephant that was mortally wounded and left for dead managed to climb to her feet, thus allowing a throw at a standing elephant using an atlatl

and darts. From a distance of 20 meters (22 yards), an elephant's body is much higher off the ground than, for example, a bison's, and the first shaft passed just under the animal's belly. But the second shot, into the lung cavity, was lethal, although it was difficult to get a sharp enough angle of elevation on the spear shaft to allow for the height of the animal.

Several things rapidly became apparent in these experiments that would not have been evident simply from the archaeological record. Hunters must spend a considerable amount of time in making and maintaining their weapons. For example, the shaft must be straight, or the force will not be properly applied to the base of the projectile point. Similarly, hidden flaws in a piece of stone flaking material can cause a projectile point to break at the critical moment, allowing the animal to escape or even causing serious injury to the hunter. Weapons become an extension of the hunter, and careful maintenance and continual practice are required if hunting is to be a successful strategy for survival.

Upper Paleolithic hunters and gatherers in the Old World.

Some of the stone items in these caches represent the finest efforts of Clovis flintknappers and are made of the finest available materials, while others are broken and somewhat carelessly reworked. If these collections were, in fact, burial offerings, then the term cache is probably inappropriate, since there would have been no intention of recovering the materials for use at a later date. In this case, some of the best flaked stone artifacts would have been lost for future use. Some of the raw materials found in the caches had obviously been brought from far-off sources, indicating trade or other contacts between widely dispersed groups.

Clovis flintknappers were masters of percussion flaking—that is, shaping stone materials with stone and antler hammers. Unless new discoveries prove otherwise, the Clovis hunters were the first to exploit North America's stone resources, and it can be assumed that there were adequate surface supplies of all materials for their purposes. Clearly, Clovis flintknappers recognized and sought out stone with exceptional flaking qualities, and when they acquired it, crafted it into objects of exceptional quality, such as their projectile points. There are many highly accomplished flintknappers today, and they find that it requires considerable effort to acquire the kind and

quantity of flaking materials, and to develop the technology, necessary to duplicate the artifacts found in the Clovis caches. Quarrying of stone has been documented at the Knife River flint sources, in central North Dakota, between 11,000 and 10,000 years ago, suggesting that the best surface materials had been depleted by the end of Clovis times.

Mammoth Hunting in Clovis Times

Mammoth hunting has captured the imagination of students of human hunting strategies more than the hunting of any other large animal. Unfortunately, most modern illustrations of mammoth hunting—as, indeed, of most forms of big-game hunting in prehistoric times—are highly misleading. A more pragmatic approach to this question is needed, based on a knowledge of animal behavior and human hunting ability.

We know from studies of frozen mammoths recovered from Siberia that the hide covering a mammoth's ribcage was as much as 12 millimeters (half an inch) thick. Clearly, well-designed weapons were needed to penetrate it. Either by design or accident, Clovis weapons were aesthetically pleasing as well as functional. The Clovis projectile point is an example of good structural design that minimizes breakage under stress. Flutes extending distally from the base allow the point to be easily inserted and bound into a notched foreshaft, and rough edges of the point were ground smooth for some distance distal to the base to prevent the blade edges from cutting the shaft bindings upon heavy impact.

Moreover, if the point snaps off, it can be repaired with simple tools in a matter of minutes. The point was attached to either a thrusting spear or an atlatl (a spear-thrower) consisting of a long, heavy mainshaft and a foreshaft. Since a flaw in the stone can render the point useless and put the hunter in danger, all points would have to have been carefully tested before use, particularly before hunters set off on a large-scale kill.

This fluted projectile point from the Fenn Clovis cache is an example of highly controlled diagonal percussion flaking. The point is made of a red, opaque chert found in Wyoming. GEORGE C. FRISON

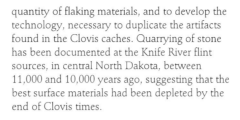

A fluted Clovis point of high-quality chert from the Anzick cache, in southwest Montana. GEORGE C. FRISON

This fluted Clovis point from the Simon cache, in south central Idaho, is one of the finest examples of Clovis lithic technology known. The same cache contained incomplete points of quartz crystal. GEORGE C. FRISON

➤ Paleoindian weaponry components, including a throwing stick (atlatl), a wooden foreshaft with a stone projectile point attached with sinew, and the forward end of a long mainshaft wrapped with sinew. The tapered end of the foreshaft is inserted into a hole in the mainshaft carefully designed for an exact fit.

JOSEPH H. BAILEY/© 1979 NATIONAL GEOGRAPHIC SOCIETY

⚱ One of four fluted Clovis points from the Colby mammoth kill site, in Wyoming. They were found in association with the partial remains of eight mammoths scattered along the bottom of an arroyo for nearly 100 meters (about 110 yards).
GEORGE C. FRISON

Morphologically, mammoths are similar to modern elephants, although mammoth hide is not quite as tough as that of African elephants in the wild. Experiments on African elephants have shown that Clovis weapons are effective, and we can assume that Clovis hunters would have been skilled hunters. (See the feature *Clovis Weapons: A Modern Experiment*.) The family structure of African elephants, based on a strong matriarch to protect the family, places certain limits on their procurement, since any attempt to harm a family member brings instant retaliation by the matriarch. It would seem likely that mammoths had a similar family structure, but this is something we will never know.

The evidence is too limited to allow us to say whether the Clovis people hunted mammoths opportunistically or in seasonal campaigns, or both. Finds of the remains of one or two animals around a water source suggest opportunistic hunting, while the Lehner and Colby sites seem to represent the remains of kills made over a period of time, possibly as the result of a more systematic and predictable hunting strategy. It has been suggested that the mammoths found in the Lehner site may represent a whole family killed on one occasion, but this seems unlikely in view of the fact that this would have created a surplus of meat

far beyond the means of a small hunting group to process and store.

Most modern artists' depictions of mammoth hunting show an animal incapacitated in a bog or pit, surrounded by hunters, some with spears and darts, others throwing rocks. Dogs are barking, a dead or maimed hunter is being dragged from the scene, women and children are in the background, and the whole operation appears to be one of noise and confusion. This goes against the rules of intelligent hunting. If a healthy mammoth were submerged in a bog to the extent that it could not extricate itself, a hunting band would not have been able to extract it either. Butchering the animal would have been an even bigger problem. A far better strategy would be to kill the animals on solid ground, and Clovis hunters had both the weapons and the hunting expertise to do this.

The Folsom Cultural Complex

The hunting groups known as the Folsom Cultural Complex appeared about 10,900 years ago, close on the heels of Clovis, and survived for about 600 years. Folsom remains are not found over such wide areas as Clovis, being confined to the Great Plains, the southwest, the central and southern Rocky Mountains, and several intermontane basins partly or entirely within the Rocky Mountains. These people did not hunt mammoths but mainly targeted a now-extinct species of bison, along with occasional pronghorn and mountain sheep. A few camel bones, usually in the form of tools, have been found in some Folsom sites, but there is little evidence to suggest that camels were hunted.

In 1934, amateur archaeologists discovered fluted projectile points identical to those found earlier at the Folsom site, in New Mexico, at a site in northern Colorado now known as the Lindenmeier site. To this day, Lindenmeier remains the largest and most complex Folsom site known. The large number and variety of tools, weapons, and other artifacts found here shows that the Folsom groups were very skilled at making and using stone tools. A small but significant number of bone tools and decorative items show that they were equally adept at working bone. Their flake tools, made from carefully selected materials, exhibit a wide variety of skillfully prepared edges, points, and corners that equal or surpass those of any other Paleoindian cultural complex in the archaeological record of the New World. Microscopic analysis of wear patterns on tool edges suggests that these tools were used to work bone, wood, hide, and possibly other materials as well.

Folsom projectile points are crafted extremely skillfully, and reflect a knowledge of flake technology equal to that known anywhere else in the world. The fluting is a refinement of that found on Clovis points, although many of today's most skillful flintknappers find it difficult to accept that Clovis stone technology was a direct precursor of Folsom technology. Whether Folsom fluting should be considered an aesthetic rather than a functional feature is open to question. The fluting process required high-quality flaking stone and also carried a high risk of failure, which inevitably would have meant that much of this prized raw material was wasted. On the other hand, experiments on modern bison show that fluting is of little, if any, benefit in the hafting process. Therefore it has no effect on the point's ability to produce a lethal wound.

Much has been written about the fluting process because of the difficulty of replicating it. However, many present-day flintknappers have been able to produce very close approximations, using a variety of methods. The key factors are to understand the principles of flaking, to be able to recognize and acquire stone of adequate quality, and, finally, to be able to control the amount and direction of the pressure needed to remove the channel flake that forms the flute. Numerous devices, some simple and some more complex, can be used to remove the channel flakes. Two

An outstanding example of a Folsom projectile point. The flutes on each side were removed as a single flake.
GEORGE C. FRISON

PHOTO ARCHIVES, DENVER MUSEUM OF NATURAL HISTORY

Two ribs of an extinct subspecies of bison and a Folsom point in their original position in a block of matrix from the Folsom site, in northeast New Mexico. This confirmed the association of human weaponry and extinct bison in North America.

☛ A Folsom bison kill site in eastern Wyoming's Agate Basin. The partial remains of at least eight bison were found here, along with those of at least four pronghorn (*Antilocapra americana*). The animals were probably killed in the arroyo adjacent to the bone bed, and the Paleoindian group would have camped alongside the meat supply during the winter months.

♀ Topography of the Agate Basin bison kill site. The animals were driven up arroyos (from right to left of the photograph), where natural and/or artificial barriers formed traps.

punches, one made of elk antler and the other from the rear leg bone of a bison, were excavated from a Folsom level at the Agate Basin site in the midst of a scatter of channel flakes and projectile points broken at various stages of manufacture. These are believed to have been used, in conjunction with some sort of simple leverage device, to remove channel flakes.

The Evidence of Paleoecology

The Folsom level at the Lindenmeier site was buried in sediments up to several meters (10 feet) thick, and was exposed in the banks of an eroding, or downcutting, arroyo. Radiocarbon dating had not been invented at that time, and

since the site is located on a dry tributary of the Cache La Poudre River, which originates in the Colorado Front Range of the Rocky Mountains, a geological project was set up to try to date the Folsom deposits in relation to river terraces that could be correlated with glacial events in the mountains during the late Wisconsin Period. These efforts met with some success, and this encouraged an interdisciplinary approach to investigating archaeological sites. As with the Lindenmeier site, many important Paleoindian sites, particularly those on the Plains and in the southwest, are found in stratified geological deposits. If we are to reconstruct the ecological conditions of the late Pleistocene and early Holocene periods as accurately as possible, and to understand how humans and animals would have fitted into this environment, we need to draw upon the expertise of many different specialists, including geologists trained in quaternary studies, soils specialists, palynologists (who study fossil pollen), paleobotanists, paleoclimatologists, and others. Interdisciplinary studies are continually being refined in ways that help archaeologists to interpret their finds in cultural terms.

Killing Fields and Bone Beds

Bone beds resulting from the killing, butchering, and processing of bison in prehistoric times are the most visible of Paleoindian archaeological sites. The location of these kill sites is largely determined by topography. Arroyos are common landscape features throughout the Great Plains. They changed continually through time as a result of geological processes, and from time to time a combination of landforms occurred that formed a natural bison trap. Sometimes the prehistoric hunters may have added a fence or drive line—stone lines believed to have been used to strengthen wooden fences often remain.

Continuing geological activity has destroyed most archaeological evidence of arroyos used for large-scale bison kills, but sometimes these same processes act to preserve such sites. Arroyos continually undergo cycles of erosion and deposition. The bone bed at the bottom of an arroyo that is aggrading (or filling up) may be temporarily protected and preserved by a layer of sediments. Later on, during the degrading (or downcutting) cycle, the bone bed is usually destroyed. But in rare cases, the arroyo may take a different course during the downcutting cycle, and the bone bed, or parts of it, may be preserved intact.

A bone bed results from the activities of human hunters and is therefore a valuable source of cultural information. The investigation of bone beds falls under a branch of science known as taphonomy, which deals with the study of animal remains between the time the animals were killed and the time the bones are exhumed. Archaeologists use many kinds of taphonomic data. For example, changes to bones that result from human activity can usually be distinguished from those caused by carnivores and scavengers, and bones stacked and piled by humans can be distinguished from piles of bones washed together by floods. Stages of bone weathering can often tell us for how long and under what conditions a bone bed was exposed in the past. Where large numbers of animals were involved, we can often determine whether the bones resulted from a single mass kill or accumulated gradually over a longer period from a number of hunting episodes.

Paleontologists alerted archaeologists to the fact that the teeth of animals such as bison erupt at particular stages, allowing the age of young animals to be determined to within a few weeks. Not only are teeth more likely to be preserved than other animal parts, but especially during Paleoindian times, mandibles were usually discarded intact when carcasses were butchered and processed, because they were of little use as food. If a bison kill included young animals, we can work out fairly accurately at what time of year it took place by adding the animal's age to the time of its birth—which we know from the fact that the young are born within a short period during spring. By contrast, if bison or other animals were taken throughout the winter, rather than in a single kill, we can establish this, too, by examining the teeth to see which had erupted and/or the stages of development of fetal remains. Bone beds can also give us information about butchering methods and the amount of meat Paleoindian hunters acquired. When drawn together, all this information helps us to reconstruct the Paleoindian way of life.

Bison Hunting in Folsom Times

Many other Folsom sites have been located throughout the Great Plains and intermontane basins in the Rocky Mountains since the Lindenmeier site, and most show evidence of bison hunting. The Lipscomb Bison Quarry, in the northeast Texas Panhandle, contained the carcasses of at least 14 (and probably more) extinct bison, along with Folsom fluted projectile points and stone tools. At the Folsom site itself, in northeast New Mexico, are the remains of about 30 extinct bison, which may or may not represent a single kill. One area of the Lindenmeier site, known as the "bison pit", contains the bones of 9 or more extinct bison. (See the feature *The Paleoindian Bison Hunters*.)

The Hell Gap site is topographically similar to the Lindenmeier site, having a permanent water source and opening onto a plain that would have been ideal for the grazing megafauna of the late Pleistocene and early Holocene periods. Bison bone and carcass remains found here indicate that Paleoindian hunters killed small groups of bison over a period of nearly 3,000 years, using a natural barrier or an artificial trap made of logs (or a combination of both) located in the arroyo.

For at least a thousand years since Folsom times, Paleoindians have trapped bison in arroyos around the Agate Basin site in east central Wyoming, to the north of the Hell Gap site. One winter kill made during Folsom times contains the partial remains of eight bison. The hunting group

apparently camped alongside the butchered animals, using the meat, which was probably frozen, as needed. The arrangement of activity areas, artifacts, and other features suggests that they lived in small, above-ground structures very similar to Plains Indian tipis. The site is located on the arroyo floodplain, a good place to live in winter but one that would have flooded and become uninhabitable with the approach of warm weather and spring runoff.

🔆 Looking up Wild Horse Arroyo at the location of the Folsom site before excavation in 1926. The bison bone bed is exposed near the arroyo bottom. The arroyo becomes much narrower and the gradient increases sharply immediately beyond the bone bed, creating ideal conditions for a natural trap.

THE PALEOINDIAN BISON HUNTERS

George C. Frison

PALEOINDIAN BISON HUNTERS on the plains of North America were familiar with their hunting territory and the day-to-day habits of the animals, and they had developed the best weapons known anywhere in the world during that period. The communal hunt was an important social event as well as a means of acquiring food. The entire band, or even several bands, gathered at a designated location not only to provision the group with meat but also to perform numerous social obligations and related activities that served to reinforce the solidarity of the group and helped to ensure its continued existence.

Communal bison hunts were events in which the chances of failure were always present, so the supernatural was called upon to reinforce the chances of success. The religious leader, or shaman, performed the necessary rituals involved in calling in the animals and ensuring that the spirits of the dead animals were properly treated. In this way, future hunting success would not be imperiled, since the general belief among hunting societies such as these was that the animals made themselves available for the benefit of humans, but only as long as they were accorded the proper respect through the performance of established rituals. Repeated failures could be blamed on the shaman, but he could protect himself by claiming that the failure was due to someone in the group neglecting to observe the proper rituals.

Many Paleoindian sites on the plains bear witness to as much as 2,000 to 3,000 years of repeated use, owing to topographic features that in their natural form or with slight modification formed traps for animals. Since the teeth of bison are known to erupt at certain ages, especially in young animals, and the calving season is restricted to a short time in early spring, we know from the fossil evidence that many Paleoindian bison kills were carried out in late autumn and winter. Evidence from some kill sites on the Northern Plains indicates that surplus meat was temporarily frozen and placed in protected caches for use as needed.

GEORGE C. FRISON

⊕ Skull and other bones of butchered bison at the Casper site, in Wyoming.

⊕ A modern model of the parabola-shaped dune used to trap bison at the Casper site.

GEORGE C. FRISON

⊕ The spectacular Olsen-Chubbuck site, in eastern Colorado, has revealed the carcasses of more than 200 large Pleistocene bison, killed when they were stampeded into a deep, narrow arroyo about 10,000 years ago. Stone projectile points among the bones indicate that some animals were dispatched by the hunters. The herd included males and females of all ages. Many animals at the bottom were so deeply buried under other animals that they could not be retrieved. This was an unusual situation, since in other known Paleoindian bison kills there was little waste.

♟ Bones of bison butchered 10,000 years ago lie in the trench of a parabolic sand dune at the Casper site, in Wyoming. At the time of the kill, the trench was several meters deep and at least 150 meters (160 yards) long. Animals driven into the trap would have had to reverse direction in order to escape, during which time they would have been extremely vulnerable.

♟ These remains of bison carcasses have been preserved in the same position as they were after butchering in the sand dune trap at the Casper site.

Further north, in the Powder River Basin in northeast Wyoming, the burning of coal beds more than 30 meters (100 feet) thick, estimated to have occurred several million years ago, caused an area of land more than a kilometer (half a mile) wide and several kilometers (almost 2 miles) long to subside. This eventually collected water to form a shallow lake. Tall grasses growing along the lake margins would have attracted grazing megafauna, and, with time, arroyos formed as runoff water drained into the lake. One of these became a major bison trap and is now known as the Carter/Kerr-McGee site. It very nearly duplicates the Paleoindian cultural record of the Hell Gap site. The location and configuration of the arroyo would have made it an ideal trap for large animals during Paleoindian times.

One of the larger of the known Folsom sites is the Hanson site in the Bighorn Basin, in north central Wyoming. Once again, it is near the head of an arroyo that opens up into a large area where bison would have grazed in Folsom times and so would have been an ideal bison trap. Bison would have moved naturally or been driven along the arroyo to a point where there was a natural or artificial trap. The number of bison bones found in the Folsom level of the site strongly indicates that there was a kill area nearby.

The Sand Dunes National Monument, in the San Luis Valley of southern Colorado, was formed when sand moving across the eastern part of the valley was stopped by steep mountain slopes. Several Folsom bison kill sites were found on the margins of the dunes. One of these, known as the Cattle Guard site, is very close to the surface but nonetheless contains a collection of artifacts in an undisturbed context. This was undoubtedly a favorable area for killing bison in Folsom times, although we cannot be sure which hunting strategy was used. A U-shaped sand dune was

used as a bison trap 10,000 years ago in central Wyoming, and similar features may have been present and used during Folsom times in the San Luis Valley.

The Goshen Cultural Complex

For nearly two decades after the Hell Gap site was investigated, nothing appeared in Paleoindian sites to kindle any interest in the Goshen Complex. This changed in the early 1980s with the discovery of the Mill Iron site, in southeast Montana. Projectile points and tools eroding out of a steep rocky slope near the crest of a flat-topped butte were strikingly similar to those recovered from the lowest level at the Hell Gap site and given the name of Goshen. As the Mill Iron site had evidence of only one Paleoindian culture, there was no possibility of stratigraphic comparisons with Clovis and Folsom layers, but radiocarbon dating indicates that the artifacts are about 11,000 years old. Although two mammoth rib fragments—one used as a tool or the haft of a weapon—were recovered from the Mill Iron site, there is no evidence to indicate that mammoths were killed there. Mammoth bones would undoubtedly have been present and used for some time after the animals became extinct.

A bison bone bed at the Mill Iron site contained the partial remains of at least 31 animals that were killed in mid or late winter. Extreme erosion in the area has removed so much of the landforms that would have been present when the site was occupied that no clue remains as to the hunting strategy used at the time. Nor is it possible to determine if the bone bed represents more than a single kill.

Many Folsom sites have been found in the San Luis Valley, in southern Colorado. Deep sand deposits have collected at the eastern side of the valley, and Folsom bison kills have been found at the edge of the dunes. The floor of the valley lies at an elevation of about 2,400 meters (8,000 feet), and the mountain peaks in the background rise above 4,250 meters (14,000 feet).

A Goshen projectile point from the Mill Iron bison kill site, in southeast Montana.
GEORGE C. FRISON

Excavations in the poorly preserved bison bone bed at the Mill Iron site revealed the partial remains of at least 31 animals, killed in late winter or early spring. They were probably killed close by, but erosion has removed all evidence of nearby landforms suitable for a trap.

At the Carter/Kerr-McGee site mentioned earlier, in the central Powder River Basin in northern Wyoming, a small remnant of a cultural level with Goshen-style projectile points was found underneath a Folsom level. This is another case where the stratigraphic evidence suggests that Goshen is older than Folsom. Judging by its location, the Carter/Kerr-McGee site must have been used as an animal trap, but in the Goshen level, only a metatarsal bone of a late Pleistocene camel was found, along with several unidentified fragments of heavy long bone. As was the case at Hell Gap, this was first thought to be a Clovis level, but a closer look at the projectile points revealed that they are more likely Goshen.

The technology represented by Goshen projectile points is very similar to that of Folsom except that Goshen points are not fluted. Instead, several pressure flakes extend distally from the base—presumably to make the base thinner as an aid to hafting—but there is nothing that can be called a flute. The tools found are similar to both Clovis and Folsom tools. Taking all this evidence into account—types of tools and projectile points, stratigraphy, and hunting strategies—it seems reasonable to conclude that Goshen may have been the immediate precursor of Folsom.

Current archaeological investigation of a small basin within the Rocky Mountains near the headwaters of the Colorado River, known as Middle Park, has yielded both Folsom and Goshen sites. Goshen projectile points have been found at a kill site containing at least 13 bison, located at an elevation of about 2,620 meters (8,600 feet). In a nearby camp site, Goshen and Folsom artifacts are found together. It is clear from this evidence

that bison frequented higher elevations during the late Pleistocene and early Holocene periods. Since the bison remains are located where a major game trail reaches the crest of a steep hill, it seems likely that hunters forced the animals up the trail, to be killed when they were winded after the steep climb and less alert to danger by other hunters waiting at the crest of the slope.

Although sites such as these are still being discovered, we do not yet have enough information to be sure of the relationship between the Clovis, Goshen, and Folsom cultures. The evidence to date, however, based on both radiocarbon dates and stratigraphy, indicates that the Clovis hunters arrived in North America about 11,000 years ago, and that both the Goshen and Folsom cultures followed very soon afterward.

The Great Animal Extinctions

What happened to the giant animals of the late Pleistocene period that were present, but apparently on the verge of extinction, when the Clovis hunters arrived? This is a fascinating question. Unless evidence is uncovered showing that highly efficient hunters were present in North America in pre-Clovis times, we cannot attribute their demise to human predation alone. Although the Clovis culture was widespread in North America, there is very little to suggest that these people could have hunted these animals to extinction—although they may well have delivered the *coup de grâce* in some cases, in particular to mammoths. Nor does it seem likely that either horses or camels were seriously hunted by humans in North America, while bison survived as the main prey of Paleoindian hunters on the Plains for at least 3,000 years after the Clovis hunters disappeared. The large-scale animal extinctions at the end of the Pleistocene period have yet to be satisfactorily explained and probably resulted from several contributing factors. (See the feature *The Fate of North America's Early Animals*.)

Beyond Bones and Stones

Paleoindian studies involve many and varied disciplines, but in the final analysis, the surviving evidence must be interpreted within a framework of human behavior. The archaeological record shows that Paleoindians developed the ability to make different types of stone tools and weapons. However, weapons (especially projectile points) changed in form over time, and it is on the basis

of these changes that archaeologists are able to identify different cultural complexes. Tools do not show as much change, and are therefore a less reliable guide to time. Because of this, the enduring stone projectile point has become the "guide fossil" for North American archaeologists. This, along with stratigraphy and radiocarbon dating, has allowed us to establish a chronology for the various Paleoindian groups that inhabited North America.

We cannot project ourselves back in time and observe Paleoindian groups at first hand, but we can use our knowledge of recent hunter-gatherer societies at a similar cultural stage in different parts of the world to shed light on the past. For example, Inuit (or Eskimo) groups who hunt caribou and sea mammals and the historic record of the bison hunters of the North American Plains provide good bases for comparison and allow us to look at the Paleoindians as human societies rather than archaeological sites. We must remember, however, that we can compare such groups only in general terms.

On this basis, we can conjecture that Paleoindian communities consisted of small groups of nomadic *Homo sapiens sapiens* concerned with problems of day-to-day survival. They lived in close harmony with a harsh and unforgiving environment, where a single mistake in the everyday quest for food could mean death or disablement and even result in the family starving to death. They had to compete directly with large predators and scavengers for food, and they had to protect stored surpluses from these and other dangers. For example, rodents burrowing into a food cache from below could have the same end result as a grizzly bear tearing the cache apart from the outside.

The mainstay of the Paleoindian economy was hunting, which was a male-centered activity. Women butchered the meat from the kill, prepared it for consumption, and gathered plant foods. While the latter was a less prestigious activity than hunting, plants were an important part of the everyday food supply. Paleoindians lived in small bands, the only political leadership being provided by the male who claimed the greatest charisma by virtue of being the most accomplished hunter and provider. Bands ranged in size from 20 to 50 individuals made up of 4 to 10 nuclear families. For most of the year, the band fragmented into smaller single or multiple family groups to exploit the available food resources more efficiently. Communal hunting or a windfall in the form of surplus food would have brought the entire band or even several bands together. The wide-ranging sources of the stone used to make the flake tools found at the Lindenmeier site, in northern Colorado, suggest that more than one band may have gathered there to take part in communal bison hunting.

Mule deer (*Odocoileus hemionus*) grazing the lush grass away from the edge of the sand dunes in the San Luis Valley. Trees at the base of the sand dunes indicate that conditions would have been ideal for bison in the past, with running water.

Bands were territorial, and resources within the territory were exploited systematically, although boundaries were less distinct than those defining modern-day states or countries. Bands were exogamous—that is, members took partners from outside the band—and this involved crossing territorial boundaries. In hunting societies such as these, it was the women who moved to the husband's residence, since it was vitally important to survival that the intimate knowledge of the hunting territory be passed on from father to son.

Hunting groups such as these had a special relationship to the animal world. Hunting magic and ritual dominated most animal hunting activities, especially where the chances of failure were high, as in the case of a communal bison kill. These people believed that animals made themselves available to humans, but that a well-defined measure of respect was expected in return. The animal spirits had to be treated appropriately at every stage of the hunting process, and if this was not done, the animals would no longer make themselves available. The shaman, or medicine-man, was present at communal hunts to ensure that the proper rituals were observed. Shamans also had a role in curing sickness, which was generally believed to result from breaking taboos, rather than from natural causes.

These Paleoindian hunting societies survived for thousands of years, and one of the secrets of their enduring success was cooperation. No matter who killed the animal or gathered the food, all members of the group shared, since not every hunter or gatherer could be successful at every attempt. When food was in short supply, sharing was even more important. It was considered reprehensible to hoard food, and in these kinds of societies it was next to impossible to do this without being found out. The people most admired were those who were the best providers and who shared the most. Storing food in caches was quite different from hoarding and was strictly a short-term measure to provide for periods of extreme cold or other times when it was not possible to go out and search for food. Caching may also have been more common in the Arctic, and was not as necessary for groups living in warmer areas.

It is difficult to imagine humans, however acclimatized they may have been, surviving the winter in the colder regions without adequate clothing and shelter. The archaeological record tells us very little about this aspect of Paleoindian life, and very few sites offer clues to the nature of winter living quarters. What evidence there is suggests that they lived in simple structures, perhaps similar to the tipis of the North American Plains Indians, consisting of hides of large animals stretched over a conical framework of poles. Such shelters are, in fact, remarkably warm in winter when well insulated with snow and heated with small fires. Even so, it is difficult to imagine them surviving subzero temperatures without adequate clothing, especially footwear, and we know that they possessed the tools to make such clothing. For example, eyed bone needles not unlike the metal ones of today have been recovered from Folsom sites.

Ideally, the archaeologist hopes to find sites with undisturbed cultural levels, containing characteristic projectile points along with organic material that can be radiocarbon-dated. Unfortunately, this rarely happens. But we should never lose sight of the fact that Paleoindian archaeology deals with people, much like ourselves, who managed to survive under very difficult environmental conditions, to raise families, and to maintain the continuity of human populations from one generation to the next. It is much more than the mere study of artifacts of stone and bone.

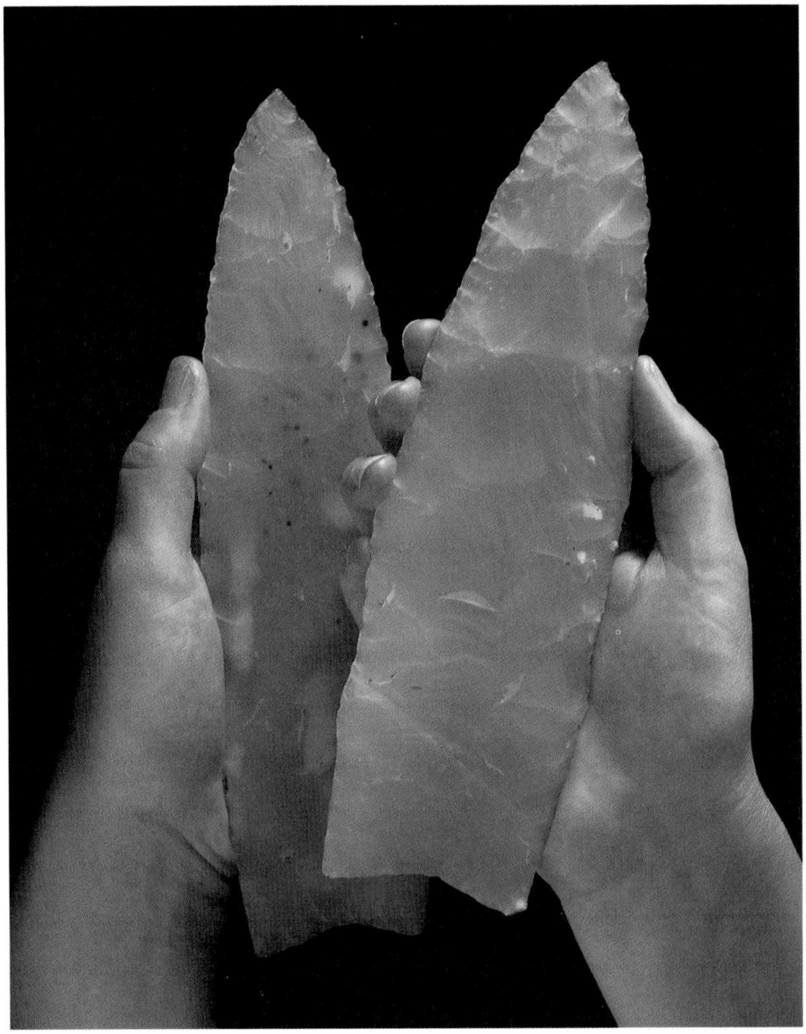

WARREN MORGAN

⇧ Two Clovis points from the Richey-Roberts cache at Wenatchee, Washington, along the Columbia River—the first Clovis cache to be excavated by professional archaeologists. Other items included blades, blade tools, unfinished projectile points, and carved cylindrical items of mammoth bone similar to those from the Anzick site.

THE FATE OF NORTH AMERICA'S EARLY ANIMALS

Donald K. Grayson

Towards the end of the Pleistocene era, some 35 genera of mammals became extinct in North America—in the sense either that they no longer existed anywhere on Earth (29 genera), or that they disappeared from North America while continuing to exist elsewhere (6 genera). Large herbivores were prominent among the losses, including mastodon, mammoths, musk oxen, horses, camels, huge ground sloths, and giant beavers. Many others were carnivores that probably preyed upon the herbivores, such as the sabertooth cat, the American cheetah, the American lion, and the dire wolf.

The archaeological and paleontological records leave little doubt that virtually all of these mammals were extinct by the end of the Pleistocene era, 10,000 years ago. What is far from clear is when the extinctions began—and what caused them.

◄ The Great American Mastodon.
H.S. RICE/COURTESY DEPARTMENT OF LIBRARY SERVICES, AMERICAN MUSEUM OF NATURAL HISTORY

♀ Lion-sized predators, sabertooth cats were widespread in North America during the Pleistocene era.

Nearly all of the extinct mammals appear to have survived the glacial maximum that occurred between about 22,000 and 18,000 years ago. Indeed, since the mid-1960s, it has been generally assumed that virtually all the extinctions occurred between about 12,000 and 10,000 years ago, but this is not borne out by recent detailed investigations of the available radiocarbon dates. Of the 35 extinct genera, only 9, including horses, camels, mammoths, and mastodon, can be reliably shown to have existed later than 12,000 years ago. The remaining 26 may have become extinct during this period, but we cannot be sure: they may have started to die out thousands of years before the end of the Pleistocene era.

Until we know a lot more about the timing of the extinctions, we can only conjecture as to what may have caused them. Two main explanations have been put forward. The best-known theory is that developed by paleoecologist Paul S. Martin, who points out that the extinctions seem to have coincided with the appearance of Clovis hunters in North America. He argues that these Paleoindian hunters emerged south of the glacial ice about 11,500 years ago, where they came upon a great variety of what they saw as large game mammals. Because these herbivores had never before encountered human predators, they had not developed any form of defensive behavior. Taking advantage of this massive, naive, and accessible food supply, the human hunters multiplied and spread southward very rapidly. Behind them, they left a trail of extinct populations—and, ultimately, extinct genera—of mammals. As their prey disappeared, so, too, did such carnivores as the sabertooth cat, the American cheetah, and the American lion.

Although intuitively appealing, the "overkill hypothesis" has fallen

CHIP CLARK/NATIONAL MUSEUM OF NATURAL HISTORY, SMITHSONIAN INSTITUTION

out of favor in recent years. To begin with, there is evidence to suggest that Paleoindians ate a far more varied diet than this hypothesis assumes. Moreover, only mammoth and mastodon remains have ever been found in a context indicating that the animals were killed by humans.

Although our knowledge of how Paleoindians subsisted is very limited, the fact that no kill sites have been found for mammals other than mammoths and mastodon appears to be compelling. In the continental United States, the most frequently found fossils are those of horses (followed by mammoths), but there are no kill sites for horses. Similarly, the third most commonly found fossils are camels (followed by mastodon), and, again, none of the camel sites appears to be a kill site.

As the overkill explanation has lost support, climatic explanations have become more widely accepted. These have been developed in detail by paleontologists Russell W. Graham, R. Dale Guthrie, and Ernest L. Lundelius. While they are complex, they are all based on the fact that massive environmental changes took place in the period during which the extinctions occurred, including, in many areas, changes in the seasonal distribution of temperatures and dramatic alterations in the nature of the vegetation. As a result, the distribution of small mammals changed tremendously, and the larger mammals, which were not as numerous and made greater demands on their environment, could not survive. While the proponents of the climatic explanations do not exclude the possibility that humans may have had a role in making some of the mammals extinct—perhaps delivering the *coup de grâce* to some species—they maintain that the ultimate cause is to be found in the dramatic environmental changes that marked the end of the Pleistocene era in North America.

Reaching a height of some 5.5 meters (18 feet) and with an estimated body weight of just over 3 tonnes (3 tons), Harlan's ground sloth was the largest of the four genera of ground sloths that existed in North America towards the end of the Pleistocene era.

PIONEERS OF THE ARCTIC

2 5 0 0   B C   –   A D   1 5 0 0

The Last of the Habitable Lands

MOREAU MAXWELL

T HE ARCTIC, the last of the habitable lands, was occupied quite late in human history, about 4,500 years ago. Survival in this most harsh and bitter of environments depended ultimately on people's ability to kill animals for food, clothing, and fuel. This was an almost unbelievably awesome task. It could require, on occasion, a solitary hunter, armed with only a flimsy spear, to face and defeat a polar bear standing twice his height, knowing that with one blow of its great paws it could break him in two.

Drinking water, that most basic of human requirements, was extremely difficult to obtain. In the frozen Arctic, fresh water is locked away in rock-hard ice and must be melted for use. In many parts of the region, the only firewood is driftwood. As this is too scarce to rely on for fuel, early Arctic people burned the fat of sea mammals instead.

◄● Towards spring, the ice packs of the eastern Arctic break into drifting fields, with open-water leads between. Hunters on the ice may drift away from shore, to be lost forever. Rough hummocky ice is formed when drifting ice fields collide. These hummock ridges may rise 5 meters (15 feet) or more above the flat surface of the ice.

🔥 Wooden mask with carved bone eyes from an Old Bering Sea culture burial. The mask probably covered the face of the skull.

NORTH POLE

● Independence Fiord

GREENLAND

● Bache Peninsula

● Port Refuge

● Sarqaq sites

Lancaster Sound

● Pond Inlet

Baffin Bay

● Cape Denbigh

ALASKA

● Kapuivik

● Ekulluk sites

● Igloolik

Davis Strait

● Naknek

● Great Bear Lake

● Lake Harbour sites

Hudson Strait

Atlantic Ocean

Pacific Ocean

● Great Slave Lake

● Arnapik

CANADA

● Saglek

Hudson Bay

Labrador

Quebec

CARTOGRAPHY: RAY SIM

♟ ARCTIC SMALL TOOL TRADITION SITES
Some early prehistoric sites occupied between 2000 BC and AD 500.

⚲ THULE CULTURE SITES
The ultimate distribution of the Classic Thule culture from AD 1200 to AD 1500.

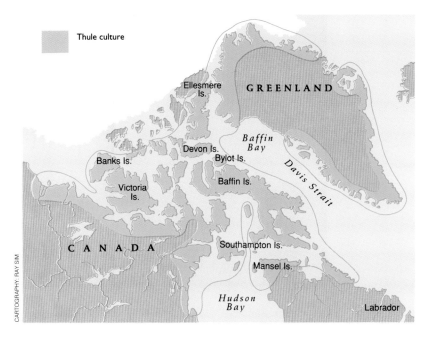

Thule culture

Ellesmere Is.

GREENLAND

Devon Is.

Baffin Bay

Banks Is.

Bylot Is.

Davis Strait

Victoria Is.

Baffin Is.

CANADA

Southampton Is.

Mansel Is.

Hudson Bay

Labrador

CARTOGRAPHY: RAY SIM

As well as providing fat for fuel, seals were the main source of food and clothing. Hunting was a difficult and dangerous task, especially in winter. At that time of the year, seals are best hunted in the strip of open water between the sea-ice and the wide expanse of ice frozen fast to the shore. Here, the hunter had to wait patiently for a seal's head— smaller than a volleyball—to surface, presenting a fleeting target for his harpoon. Throughout the often long wait, he had to remain constantly alert for a low roar from the ice he was standing on, signaling that it was breaking away from the shore, carrying him out to sea with it. Even today, hunters at the ice edge sometimes drift away, never to return.

Days of labor were required to make a single harpoon. The hunter would first collect scarce and precious bits of driftwood, which he would join skillfully to make the shaft. He would then spend many hours carving the head out of hard ivory and flaking a flint point for its tip. Finally, he faced the perilous task of finding and killing seals and other prey. A successful hunter, returning with a small seal carcass, would have barely enough to feed his family for a week. Then the task would have to be repeated.

What Is the Arctic?

The Arctic is the northernmost region on Earth, extending right up to the North Pole. It can be defined in terms of degrees of latitude or distance from the equator. The southern boundary of the Arctic—the Arctic Circle—girdles the Earth at about 66 degrees 30 minutes North, running through the far north of Alaska, Canada, and Scandinavia and crossing Siberia. Here, on one day of the year, about 21 June, the sun does not set, and about 21 December, it does not rise. At the northern limit of land, there is no sunlight from about the middle of February to the middle of March, and few daily hours of darkness until early October. This dramatic fluctuation between sunlight and darkness has marked effects on both biological growth and human behavior.

As our interest here is in how early humans adapted to life in the Arctic, it is useful to consider the region in terms of its low annual "heat budget", or lack of heat energy. This does not mean that the Arctic has the lowest maximum temperatures: in many inland regions of Siberia and the Yukon, winter temperatures sometimes drop to levels never reached in the Arctic. Rather, it is the relative absence of heat energy throughout the year that distinguishes the Arctic and creates a unique environment. Scientists sometimes define the limits of the Arctic environment in terms of the average July temperature. An isothermic line connecting all regions of the north where the average July temperature does not exceed 10 degrees Celsius (50 degrees Fahrenheit) provides a useful boundary.

Two other lines that can be plotted on the Earth's surface, the permafrost line and the tree line, are also used to define the Arctic region, corresponding roughly to the isothermic line. The permafrost line marks regions where, except for a thin active surface, the ground remains permanently frozen. The more visible tree line, to the north of which forests cannot grow, is related to the permafrost region, because the frozen ground prevents tree roots from penetrating deeply and inhibits the subsurface drainage of meltwater. The tree line marks the border between boreal taiga to the south—the coniferous forests that extend across much of the subarctic—and treeless tundra to the north.

Adapting to Life in the Arctic

Although many species of mammals and birds wander back and forth across the tree line, certain animals have adapted specifically to this environment and are considered to be Arctic species. The polar bear is the best known of these. It sometimes spends the summer below the tree line, waiting for the sea-ice to freeze so that it can resume its hunting activities. (See the feature *Arctic Animals*.) Other Arctic animals include white arctic wolves, foxes, and hares; seals and walruses; arctic char

WAYNE LANKINEN/BRUCE COLEMAN LTD

⚓ An erect polar bear standing some 3.5 meters (11 feet) or more tall would be a fearsome beast to a hunter armed with only a spear.

➤ Razor-sharp microblades of chert and quartz crystal barely 10 millimeters (three-eighths of an inch) wide were pressed from carefully prepared cores. These artifacts, frequently found in Arctic Small Tool Tradition sites, were utility knives. Their sharp edges were especially useful for cutting seal and caribou skin patterns for clothing.

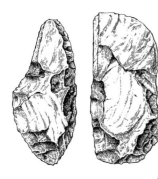

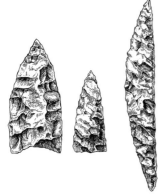

⚓ Stone tools from the Denbigh Flint Complex. The top two are burins. The second row, left to right, are two harpoon endblades and a sideblade for hafting in the side of an arrow.

ILLUSTRATIONS: KEN RINKEL (AFTER MOREAU MAXWELL)

(a type of sea trout that travels from the sea up a river or into coastal waters to spawn); caribou; and migratory ducks and geese. These were all prey for early people of the Arctic.

Humans adapted to Arctic conditions in a number of ways. They developed specialized techniques—in particular, various types of harpoons—for hunting animals on land, sea, and sea-ice. As well as food, animals provided skins and feathers for clothing and fat for fuel. People also learned to build shelters that offered them protection from the extreme cold. The evidence of these activities that has been preserved in the archaeological record is sufficiently clear to allow us to distinguish between Arctic people and the people of the boreal taiga, to the south. In more recent times, we know these two groups as Inuit (or Eskimos) and Indians.

The First Paleoeskimos

The first inhabitants of North America are thought to have crossed the broad land bridge of Beringia, between eastern Siberia and Alaska, as early as 20,000 years ago. At this time, the sea level was much lower, and this region was exposed as a broad plain of tundra and artemisia bush. In pursuit of the giant animals that roamed the American continent during the Pleistocene period, including mammoths, mastodon, and bison, these early hunters penetrated first southwards, into the northern American plains, and then beyond, on into South America. These ancestors of present-day Indians continued to live in the unglaciated interior of Alaska until about 6000 BC.

This Paleoarctic tradition, its distinctive stone tools grouped by experts into such cultural entities as Akmak, Anangula, Chindadn, and Denali, may have had its origin deep in the Aldan River region of Siberia as early as 30,000 years ago. These early people fished in the rivers and hunted land animals, particularly caribou, but did not develop the techniques of sea-ice hunting that were characteristic of later Arctic peoples.

The culture generally considered to be the fore-runner of the first North American people to adapt to the Arctic was named the Denbigh Flint Complex, after Cape Denbigh, in Alaska, where the oldest flint tools belonging to the western Paleoeskimo tradition were found. It appears in the archae-ological record several thousand years after the Akmak and Anangula cultures. Radiocarbon dating is less reliable in the Arctic than elsewhere, because the different types of organic materials available for analysis, such as bone, antler, and ivory tusks, seem to take up the carbon isotope at varying rates that are not yet well understood. It suggests, however, that Denbigh emerged not much earlier than 2000 BC. Denbigh's origins are unclear. It may have evolved from Akmak, or it may be related to some later Siberian tradition brought by hunters across Bering Strait.

The Arctic Small Tool Tradition

All that has survived of the Denbigh culture in Alaska is a distinctive set of stone tools found in a number of sites north and east along the Alaskan coast, from the base of the Alaska Peninsula to the Canadian border. The tools include burins (or gravers) only 2.5 centimeters (1 inch) long, used for carving bone, antler, and ivory; delicately flaked, bipointed endblades used to tip bone and antler arrowheads; sideblades of flint and quartz crystal for inserting into bone arrowheads and spearheads (to increase the loss of blood in land prey such as caribou and musk oxen and thus bring them to ground faster); triangular endblades, probably used to tip harpoon heads; and tiny blades of flint or quartz crystal known as micro-blades, no more than 10 millimeters (three-eighths of an inch) wide, used for such purposes as cutting skins and carving wooden handles. Other, less distinctive, tools include endscrapers and side-scrapers for working hard materials and dressing skins, and a few examples of polished adzes.

Except for the adzes, these tools and weapon tips are so small that they have become known as the Arctic Small Tool Tradition, which can be traced through several cultural complexes along the Arctic coast eastwards to Greenland. It is because the tools and weapons of these various complexes are so similar that the Denbigh Flint Complex is seen as the ancestral North American Arctic culture.

The earliest Denbigh sites are inland on the Kobuk and Brooks rivers, at the base of the Alaska Peninsula. Both sites have yielded evidence of caribou hunting and riverine fishing. Settlements consisted of clusters of two or three shallow pit houses 60 centimeters (2 feet) deep, each with a sloping entryway and a central fireplace. Early Denbigh hunters appear to have used coastal sites only during the short summer. Later sites seem to have been used throughout the year, perhaps because by then hunters had developed the skills necessary to kill sea mammals along the frozen coast.

The Denbigh Complex appears to be the only logical ancestor of the Arctic Small Tool Tradition, which spread eastwards from Alaska to Greenland. However, there is a problem with the dating of Denbigh that has yet to be resolved. Radiocarbon dates from the initial site on Cape Denbigh and several Brooks River sites suggest that the complex goes back to about 2000 BC. Equally reliable dates from the easternmost sites where the Arctic Small Tool Tradition is found, in Greenland, also go back to about 2000 BC, or even a few centuries earlier.

It is highly unlikely that early hunting bands would have migrated the 4,800 kilometers (3,000 miles) from western Alaska to northern Greenland in less than a century. Even four or five centuries would be rapid for such a migration. In addition, there is no obvious impetus for it.

JOHNNY JOHNSON/BRUCE COLEMAN LTD

FRANCOIS GOHIER/AUSCAPE

Some small herds of caribou remained in arctic valleys throughout the winter, but most migrated from southern forests in huge herds in the spring, retreating to the south in late autumn.

The killer whale was too dangerous to be hunted frequently from kayaks. Bones from sites as early as Sarqaq, however, indicate that these whales were occasionally killed or the bones scavenged from dead animals washed ashore.

ARCTIC ANIMALS

PEOPLE WHO LIVE IN THE ARCTIC are far more dependent on animals for food and clothing than other hunter-gatherers. Today, supplies—even watermelons—can be flown in to isolated settlements, but before the advent of European explorers meat constituted 90 percent of the diet.

Seals of many species—ringed, bearded, harp, gray, and bladder-nosed—were the main source of food, and their layers of fat blubber provided fuel for cooking lamps. The skins of caribou killed in the autumn had hollow, air-filled hair, providing good insulation for winter clothing, and the meat was a welcome change from seal. Bear meat, loaded in spring and summer with trichinosis, was dangerous to eat then, and to eat the liver, with its concentration of vitamin A, was lethal. In winter, bear steaks were good, and the skin useful for trousers and mittens.

NORBERT ROSING/BRUCE COLEMAN LTD

Even today, large numbers of polar bears congregate at Churchill, on Hudson Bay, to wait for the sea-ice to freeze, so that they can hunt seals again. Here, two young males spar with each other in establishing dominance. They are more a marine than a terrestrial animal, living most of the year on sea-ice and capable of swimming long distances in the open-water leads between ice fields.

In spring, when sea-ice and open-water hunting was difficult and caribou meat thin, the appearance of migrating geese and ducks was a welcome sight.
VARIN-VISAGE/JACANA-AUSCAPE

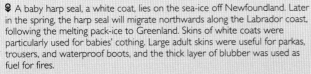

A baby harp seal, a white coat, lies on the sea-ice off Newfoundland. Later in the spring, the harp seal will migrate northwards along the Labrador coast, following the melting pack-ice to Greenland. Skins of white coats were particularly used for babies' clothing. Large adult skins were useful for parkas, trousers, and waterproof boots, and the thick layer of blubber was used as fuel for fires.

DR ECKART POTT/BRUCE COLEMAN LTD

ERWIN AND PEGGY BAUER/BRUCE COLEMAN LTD

JEFF FOOTT/AUSCAPE

Musk-ox meat tastes like good beef, but the thick, woolly hides of these animals were more useful for sleeping skins than for clothing. Horns could be carved, steamed, and bent for use as spoons.

Walrus meat and blubber were used, but the ivory tusks were especially valued for making weapons and tools. The 2.5 centimeter (1 inch) thick hide was split and used as covering for umiaks.

Indians moving north into Alaska during the period of global warming that occurred between about 2500 BC and 1600 BC may have put pressure on Arctic people. Moreover, 4,000 years ago, to the east, Hudson Bay and Hudson Strait were free of glacial ice. Their unoccupied shorelines, with few animal predators, may have been so rich in prey that they lured people onward.

The most likely explanation of this seemingly conflicting evidence is that some of the dates from both Denbigh and Greenland are inaccurate, but the fact that very few sites have been found between Alaska and Greenland suggests that these early people did indeed migrate eastwards within fewer than 500 years.

Greenland, the Earliest Eastern Settlement

The earliest evidence of the eastward spread of the Arctic Small Tool Tradition comes from a complex named Independence I, after a fiord in northeast Greenland. According to radiocarbon dates derived from local willow remains, the people of this complex moved into the unglaciated Arctic desert of Peary Land between 2050 BC and 1700 BC. The complex extended west and south through Ellesmere Island to Devon Island and south along Greenland's east coast to at least as far as Dove Bay.

Independence I was uniquely a High Arctic culture (north of 75 degrees North latitude), adapted to one of the Arctic's most inhospitable regions. Food resources were scarce, since the fiords were free of ice for only a few months during the summer, and hunting was curtailed by nearly three months of total darkness. Unlike most Arctic people, the people of Independence I did most of their hunting inland, except during the short summer, when they harvested a few ringed seal and arctic char from the coast and coastal rivers. Their main prey was musk oxen, along with hare, ptarmigan, and geese. Fuel, in this icy inland desert, was limited to occasional pieces of driftwood, tiny stems of willow, and the greasy bones of the musk ox.

Their stone tools were those of the Arctic Small Tool Tradition: burins, microblades, and a variety of endscrapers and sidescrapers for dressing skins and working hard materials. Their weapons included bipointed endblades for arrow tips, and sideblades for arrows or lances. Larger, bifacially flaked blades that are tapered and notched at the blunt end have also been found, and may have been lance tips or knives. Bone needles with tiny, drilled eyes are among the few artifacts recovered from Peary Land made of materials other than stone, and indicate that skins were sewn to make clothing.

An Independence I site at Port Refuge, on Devon Island, has yielded harpoon heads made of ivory and antler that differ significantly from most harpoon heads found in the eastern Arctic. One

By June, the sea-ice has broken into a few drifting pans, and kayak hunting by weaving around the ice chunks is again possible. Polar bears, whose natural domain is the solid sea-ice, are forced onto land, where their only source of food is the tiny lemming. They are particularly dangerous at this time.

The ptarmigan, here in winter plumage, remains in the Arctic throughout the winter. It is a useful survival food in these lean times.

Meat of the arctic fox is strong in ammonia and barely edible. Fox fur was used for babies' clothing and to trim parkas.

☉ A round, soapstone oil lamp from a Sarqaq site. A small core of soapstone would be placed in the middle to hold a moss cotton wick.

☉ A typical Sarqaq non-toggling harpoon head. The pointed base would fit into a round socket, and the slotted tip would hold a stone blade.

end is tapered to fit into a hollow socket, and the position of the line holes does not allow the head to act as a toggle—that is, to open outwards after penetrating the prey. Instead, it held the prey with only two side barbs, making it less efficient for hunting sea mammals than the harpoon heads found from later cultures, such as Canada's Pre-Dorset culture. The latter fitted into a blade-like foreshaft and toggled beneath the skin, providing a secure hold for retrieving the prey.

Independence I summer sites are often marked only by stone fireboxes, indicating that shelters were little more than simple tents. The most distinctive shelters were probably the winter dwellings. As evidenced by the rocks still in place that were used to anchor tent edges, tents were elliptical and occupied an area of 3 meters by 4 meters (10 feet by 13 feet). A structure of parallel, vertical stone slabs was set in the center, divided into storage sections for food and a central firebox for heating—to be fueled by such scanty materials as were available. A family would spend the dark winter wrapped in musk-ox skins in the shelter of their smoky skin tent, sleeping as much as possible and limiting food and water to the bare minimum needed for survival in order to reduce the need to go outside the tent—much as Arctic travellers trapped in a storm still do.

The Sarqaq to the South

A period of increasing cold may have brought an end to northeast Greenland's Independence I culture about 1700 BC. To the south, along the relatively ice-free west coast from Upernavik to Julianehaab, archaeologists have found sites with artifacts similar to, yet significantly different from, the Arctic Small Tool Tradition. The stone tools and weapons of these people, known as the Sarqaq (or, in Greenland, the Saqqaq), are similar to those of both Denbigh and Independence I—

burins and burin spall tools (the latter made of chips of stone); arrow, lance, and harpoon tips; microblades and scrapers—but are smaller and more delicately flaked than those found in Independence I sites. Unlike Independence I artifacts, many of the burins and endblades are polished. The few Sarqaq harpoon heads that have been found are of the non-toggling type found in Independence I sites rather than the open-socketed type found in later Paleoeskimo sites. Small, round, soapstone oil lamps, not found in Independence I sites, are also common in Sarqaq sites.

Both the coastal seal-hunting sites and inland caribou camps of the Sarqaq appear to have been more densely populated than the Independence I sites, probably because of a readier supply of food and improved hunting technology. Nonetheless, summer hunting in the open waters was fraught with danger. Evidence from Sarqaq sites indicates that narrow, kayak-like boats were in use from early times. Throwing a harpoon from these inherently unstable craft was highly dangerous, and represented a feat of remarkable skill. Even up to recent times, drowning was the most common cause of death among men in the Arctic. An additional hazard faced by hunters waiting for seals on still water is a form of vertigo that commonly occurs when the sea and sky merge to form an expanse of light and no horizon is visible. In these conditions, the kayaker often senses, incorrectly, that the craft is tipping, and in trying to right it, overturns it.

The first Sarqaq sites discovered were dated at no later than 1900 BC, which led to the theory that Sarqaq people were descendants of an Independence I community driven south by increasing cold. More recent radiocarbon dating of local willow remains indicates that these sites go back to at least 2200 BC. This suggests that, while Independence I people were entering Greenland via a northern route over Ellesmere Island and Smith Sound, other people, whose artifacts more closely resembled those of the Canadian Pre-Dorset culture, might have entered from the south. This would have meant crossing the wide expanse of Baffin Bay, which consists of open water or drifting ice for much of the year, or the ice fields of Davis Strait.

Few organic materials remain from most Sarqaq sites. A notable exception is Qeqertasussuk, on Disco Bay, the earliest site known to date, where a surprising collection of organic artifacts was found. Near a fireplace formed of small stones lay a carved spoon of whalebone, the side-prong of a fish spear, and fragments of wooden bowls. Close by were the shoulder blade of a killer whale, fragments of a wooden bow, wooden arrows, fragments of a slender boat, and the bones of the earliest domestic dog yet found in the Arctic. More than 60,000 bones of birds and animals used for food were recovered, indicating that these early people had adapted to their harsh environment more successfully than might have been expected.

The Pre-Dorset People of Northern Canada

The third of the earliest Paleoeskimo cultures in the eastern Arctic region, called the Pre-Dorset, was restricted to northern Canada, extending from Ellesmere Island, along the coasts of several intervening islands, to the middle of Labrador, and west to Banks and Victoria Islands. Radiocarbon dates suggest that the Pre-Dorset culture goes back to at least 1800 BC and possibly even to 2000 BC. In a late stage of the culture, about 1000 BC—perhaps because of increasingly colder climates—it extended south into the Keewatin Barren Grounds and onto the edge of the boreal taiga. Pre-Dorset stone tools are similar to those of the Arctic Small Tool Tradition, with a variety of burins (some polished at the tip), drill bits, many microblades, several types of endscrapers and sidescrapers, and sideblades for inserting into antler lanceheads. A few polished slate knives and small soapstone lamps have been found in later sites dating to about 900 BC.

Artifacts made of organic materials—bone, antler, and ivory—seldom survive from the more southerly sites. In the colder, drier conditions north of the Arctic Circle, harpoon heads of antler and ivory, antler lances with sideblades, bow parts of antler and wood, bone arrowheads, fish spears, and needles with tiny, round, drilled eyes have been found. A few bones of domestic dogs have also been found, suggesting that dogs may have been used for hunting.

This stone Sarqaq knife inserted in a wooden handle wrapped with whale baleen was found in a Qeqertasussuk dwelling radiocarbon-dated to 2200 BC to 2300 BC.
NATIONAL MUSEUM OF DENMARK, DEPARTMENT OF ETHNOGRAPHY

A Pre-Dorset chert burin. The left-hand corner has a chisel-like edge for carving ivory and caribou antler.
MOREAU MAXWELL

By mid-June, most of the snow cover has melted from the land—a view of Baffin Island from near the coast.

NORMAN TOMALIN/BRUCE COLEMAN LTD

EARLY ARCTIC CULTURES

MOREAU MAXWELL

ROM THE EARLIEST periods to modern times, carved antler and ivory artifacts have been characteristic of Arctic cultures. Harpoon heads, foreshafts, needlecases, and combs carved at first with flint burins and later with burins of meteoric or European iron all had distinctive regional shapes and designs. Changes to individual features of harpoon heads through time provide us with the most reliable method of dating them relative to each other. Much Arctic carving was in the form of weapon decoration, but Dorset people in particular often carved three-dimensional human and animal figures that had magical and artistic significance.

BIRNIRK

This prehistoric western pottery decorated by impressing the soft clay with curvilinear designs only rarely spread to eastern Thule sites.

IPIUTAK

Ipiutak ivory carvings, including elaborate open spirals, single-piece linked chains, and swivels, were probably made possible by tools of imported Siberian iron.

IPIUTAK

Masks of ivory segments covered the faces of some Ipiutak dead.

PUNUK

Possibly representing a bowhead whale, this ivory carving may have been a fetish to sew on a whaler's clothing for luck.

OLD BERING SEA

With walrus in ready supply, most Old Bering Sea carvings were of ivory and elaborately engraved. This bear is one of the few naturalistic carvings.

DENBIGH

Denbigh flint weapons were more precisely flaked than most other blades of the Arctic Small Tool Tradition. With their careful rows of parallel flakes, they are almost art forms.

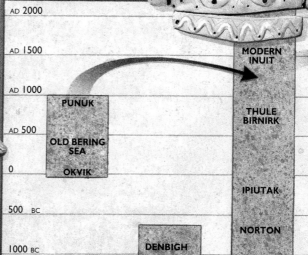

AD 2000		
AD 1500		MODERN INUIT
AD 1000	PUNUK	
AD 500	OLD BERING SEA	THULE BIRNIRK
0	OKVIK	
500 BC		IPIUTAK
1000 BC	DENBIGH	NORTON
1500 BC		
2000 BC		

WEST

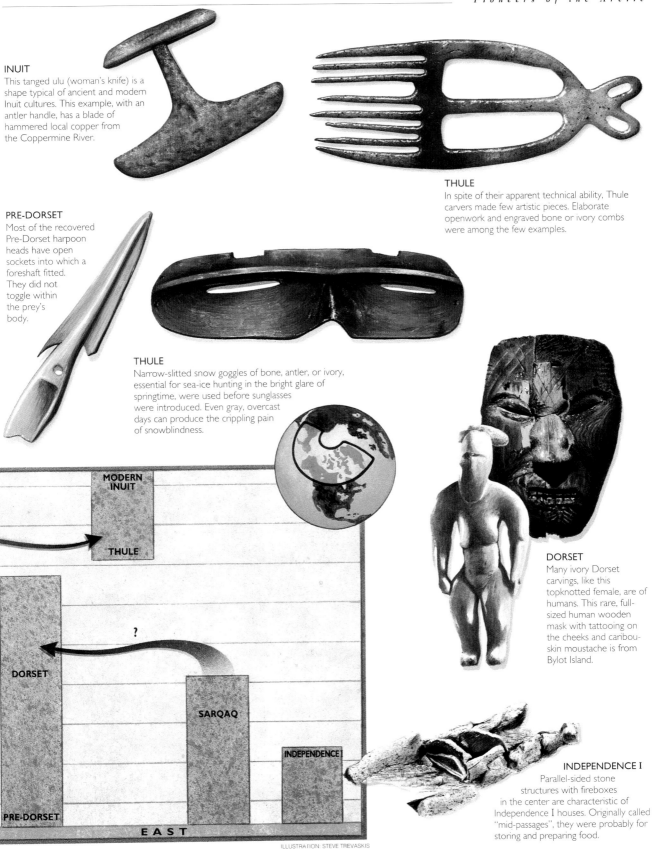

INUIT
This tanged ulu (woman's knife) is a shape typical of ancient and modern Inuit cultures. This example, with an antler handle, has a blade of hammered local copper from the Coppermine River.

THULE
In spite of their apparent technical ability, Thule carvers made few artistic pieces. Elaborate openwork and engraved bone or ivory combs were among the few examples.

PRE-DORSET
Most of the recovered Pre-Dorset harpoon heads have open sockets into which a foreshaft fitted. They did not toggle within the prey's body.

THULE
Narrow-slitted snow goggles of bone, antler, or ivory, essential for sea-ice hunting in the bright glare of springtime, were used before sunglasses were introduced. Even gray, overcast days can produce the crippling pain of snowblindness.

DORSET
Many ivory Dorset carvings, like this topknotted female, are of humans. This rare, full-sized human wooden mask with tattooing on the cheeks and caribou-skin moustache is from Bylot Island.

INDEPENDENCE I
Parallel-sided stone structures with fireboxes in the center are characteristic of Independence I houses. Originally called "mid-passages", they were probably for storing and preparing food.

MODERN INUIT
THULE
DORSET
SARQAQ
INDEPENDENCE I
PRE-DORSET
EAST

ILLUSTRATION: STEVE TREVASKIS

221

Remains of animals used for food indicate that these Pre-Dorset people hunted all of the available prey, with the probable exception of beluga and narwhal whales, which would have been too large for their hunting equipment. Faint traces of tent rings, often surrounding a flat rock on which seal fat was burned for heat, are generally the only remaining indications of shelter. On the Labrador coast, however, several sites have remains of houses with central structures built of parallel stone slabs resembling those found at Independence I sites.

Radiocarbon dating of Pre-Dorset sites is difficult. Dates of about 2000 BC, much the same as those from Independence I and Sarqaq sites, have been derived from the remains of sea mammals, but these do not give accurate ages, because the fossil sea water they appear to have ingested can result in dates several centuries older than they should be. More reliable dates derived from wood are no earlier than 1800 BC. Whether this means that the Canadian Pre-Dorset culture represents a later immigration from the west, or simply that we have not recovered adequate earlier materials for dating, is a problem yet to be solved.

From Sarqaq/Pre-Dorset to Dorset

The cultural transition from the Pre-Dorset to the Dorset periods—and, in Greenland, from Sarqaq to Dorset—presents an equally knotty dating problem. While some scholars see a smooth continuation of artifact types from one culture to the next, occurring somewhere between 900 BC and 500 BC, others see Dorset artifacts as being sufficiently different as to indicate a major cultural change. A group of sites discovered in the more southern areas of Labrador and Newfoundland complicates the problem. The stone artifacts found here are distinctly different from, yet still within, the Arctic Small Tool Tradition. Known as Groswater Dorset, this complex appears from radiocarbon dates to overlap both the late Pre-Dorset and early Dorset cultures.

Early Dorset sites are found on Baffin Island and in northern Labrador from the onset of permafrost, about 600 or 700 BC. Artifacts useful for hunting on sea-ice appear here at the same time. These include small sleds, sled shoes made of ivory, snow knives (for cutting blocks of snow to make igloos), and so-called ice creepers, consisting of pieces of antler fastened to boot soles for walking on sea-ice. The fact that these antler and ivory artifacts, as well as bone and wooden objects, have been found at these sites may, however, tell us nothing more than that organic materials are preserved in permafrost, whereas before the onset of permafrost they would have disintegrated. Because permafrost preserves even skin and feathers, we know much more about Dorset than about preceding cultures.

The Dorset culture—named after Cape Dorset, on Baffin Island—presents an interesting contrast to the Pre-Dorset. Dorset people occupied the same coasts as did those of Pre-Dorset times, but from Dorset times, the same style of harpoon head is found throughout this vast region. Whenever it changed, the new style appears simultaneously in sites throughout the region, providing us with our most reliable means of distinguishing between Early, Middle, and Late Dorset phases. Although the line holes in Dorset harpoon heads often appear to be round, they were not drilled, as in Pre-Dorset times, but scratched in with fine flint tips.

Dorset stone tools are generally typical of the Arctic Small Tool Tradition, with numerous microblades and scrapers. In several regions, however, early Dorset culture is marked by the appearance of various types of slate knives notched on the sides near the base, allowing them to be bound to wooden handles, and burin-like tools made of polished flint, chalcedony (a type of translucent quartz), and nephrite (a type of jade), which replaced the earlier spall burins. We do not know why, but bows and arrows, drills, and hunting dogs, all so widespread in Pre-Dorset times, completely disappeared in the Dorset period.

Dorset artifacts made of organic materials include a variety of ivory and antler harpoon heads for hunting seals and walruses, antler 'anceheads for hunting caribou and polar bears, and handles made of bone, antler, wood, and ivory for knives, burin-like tools, and microblades.

Caribou skin was essential for winter clothing, but hunting caribou was both difficult and dangerous. These wary animals have excellent hearing, and to stalk them over the treeless landscape and get close enough to kill one with nothing but a handheld lance, as Dorset people did, required exceptional hunting skill. Women in the camp then had the long and arduous task of scraping and tanning the skins, cutting patterns with razor-sharp microblades, and sewing the material with stitches tiny enough to ensure water-tight seams.

A typical Early Dorset ivory toggling harpoon head with a chert endblade. An internally carved basal socket (not visible) would have fitted over a blade-like foreshaft of caribou antler.
MOREAU MAXWELL

An ivory fish spear from a Dorset site on northern Baffin Island. Such spears were used for arctic char, which swim upstream from the sea to spawn in the late spring.
MOREAU MAXWELL

Typical Middle Dorset harpoon heads of ivory and antler. The small ivory hunting fetish would probably have been hung on a hunter's clothing.
MOREAU MAXWELL

NATIONAL MUSEUM OF DENMARK, DEPARTMENT OF ETHNOGRAPHY

On the coasts of Labrador and Newfoundland, Dorset houses were well-defined structures, often with the central passage of stone slabs found in Independence I and some Pre-Dorset houses. North of Hudson Strait, a few small, shallow pit houses have been found, some of them with a roof framework of driftwood, but most shelters were simply skin tents, of which the only surviving evidence is the boulders used to hold down the flaps. In Late Dorset times, "longhouses" were built of rectangular rows of boulders. These structures, which could be as much as 45 meters (148 feet) long, enclosed a number of individual family tents when local communities gathered in the spring. (See the feature *A Dorset Camp*.)

Dorset Art

The most fascinating aspect of Dorset culture is its art. Hundreds of miniature ivory, antler, and wood carvings have been recovered, particularly from later Dorset sites. These range from naturalistic to impressionistic and schematic images of local animals and birds. Humans and bears are the most common subjects, and are usually depicted with skeletal engravings—like X-ray paintings—on the surface. Often the belly or throat of both the human and bear carvings is slit and filled with red ocher, suggesting a form of sorcery against enemies. Occasionally, humans are represented by small wooden dolls with removable arms and legs. The only life-size carvings known are one complete and two fragmentary wooden masks from the Button Point site on Bylot Island.

Cultural Developments in the West

While the sequence from Independence I, through Sarqaq and Pre-Dorset, to Dorset was occurring in the eastern Arctic, similar cultural changes were taking place in Alaska and on islands to the west, in the Bering Sea. The Denbigh Complex changed little throughout most of its region until about 700 BC, except that stone artifacts from Late Denbigh times tend to be less delicately flaked than those of the "classic" Denbigh period. Coastal sites were used only during the summer, inland hunting and fishing still being the main means of subsistence.

To the north of Bering Strait, from Kotzebue to the Firth River, a new complex, known as Choris, appeared about 1600 BC. Its artifacts of chipped stone are generally continuations of Denbigh types, but larger. New types of projectile points, designed for the tips or sides of antler arrows and lances, have been found here, and a few types of stone tools are noticeably absent. Clay pottery, decorated with linear stamping, and stone labrets—ornaments worn in a slit in the lower lip—appear for the first time. Choris seems to represent a more flexible approach to life in the interior and on the coast, with a number of regional variants. Slate knives for separating seal blubber from meat are common finds in coastal sites, whereas large flint knives for butchering caribou are more common in the interior. In the settled communities on the coast, houses were large, measuring 12.5 meters by 7 meters (42 feet by 24 feet), whereas tents were used in the hunting camps in the interior.

⚱ Female figurines like this group of carved wooden Thule figures from a site at Angmagssalik, East Greenland, are typically found in Thule sites.

SISSE BRIMBERG

⚱ This crudely carved Dorset human figurine is from the Knud Peninsula, Ellesmere Island. The pierced chest was filled with red ocher.

In the late stages of the Norton culture, at about the beginning of the Christian era, a distinct and fascinating culture appeared to the north of Bering Strait. This was the Ipiutak, best known from a site at Point Hope. It owed some of its stone tool ancestry to Norton but, unlike Norton, lacked pottery, ground slate tools, oil lamps, and houses with tunnel entries. Surprisingly, in view of its location on the migratory route of the baleen whale, the Ipiutak site at Point Hope shows no evidence of whale hunting. Some seals and walruses were taken, but the evidence suggests that these people had not really adapted to a coastal way of life. Rather, the abundance of animal bones and caribou-hunting weapons found here indicates that they survived mainly on caribou. If a substantial number of the more than 600 small, square house pits at Point Hope were ever occupied simultaneously, the site would have been the largest prehistoric settlement in the Arctic.

One hundred and thirty-eight Ipiutak graves have been excavated, and they provide strong indications of status distinctions and the power of shamans in the culture. Many weapons, carvings, and tools were buried with the dead, more than 100 arrows sometimes being found in single graves. Some skulls were covered with elaborate bone masks, with ivory eyeballs, pupils of jet, ivory nose plugs in the shape of birds' heads, and ivory lip covers representing the sewing together of lips. Other graves contained collections of ivory chain-links, swivels, and pretzel-shaped objects, all apparently made for the purpose of demonstrating carving skill. Ivory carvings of animals and humans are elaborately engraved in what has been called a Scytho-Siberian style. Iron tools imported from Siberia—which gave Ipiutak artists much greater scope than stone carving tools—are found here for the first time in the Arctic. After AD 800, Ipiutak people deserted the coast and moved to smaller hunting camps around lakes in the interior.

In contrast, during the same period, the people who inhabited St Lawrence and Punuk Islands, in the Bering Sea, were successfully hunting large marine mammals—walruses and baleen whales—among the drifting ice floes. Two distinct styles of artifacts, known as Old Bering Sea and Okvik, also appeared towards the beginning of the Christian era in St Lawrence Island sites. Although Old Bering Sea and Okvik artifacts were first described by scholars in 1937, there is still dispute as to whether they represent new cultural complexes or are simply stylistic variants of a single culture.

The artifacts found, mainly harpoons, are richly engraved with complex designs. Harpoon heads, wings for harpoon shafts, harpoon sockets, and a number of other objects whose use has not been identified are decorated with geometric,

🔱 Intricately carved segments of bone and ivory covered the skeletal faces of some Ipiutak burials. Eyes would have been ivory disks, with pupils of black jet.
A. ANIK AND J. BECKETT/COURTESY DEPARTMENT OF LIBRARY SERVICES, AMERICAN MUSEUM OF NATURAL HISTORY

⟳ This Ipiutak ivory swivel would have been screwed into a socket of wood or antler. The elaborate Ipiutak ivory carvings were probably made possible by tools of imported Siberian iron.
RAINEY, 1940/COURTESY DEPARTMENT OF LIBRARY SERVICES, AMERICAN MUSEUM OF NATURAL HISTORY

Choris, as a cultural complex, disappeared about 700 BC. There then appears to have been a cultural hiatus. Both Choris to the north and Late Denbigh to the south were separated from Norton, the succeeding complex, by some 200 years.

Extending from the Alaska Peninsula to the Firth River, Norton existed at the same time that the shift from the Pre-Dorset to the Dorset culture was taking place in the east, but there is no evidence of contact between the Dorset and Norton peoples. Rather, Norton was an amalgam of characteristics from the south and west, with oil lamps and check-stamped pottery from Siberia (created by patting wet clay with wooden paddles carved with checkered or curvilinear designs) and stone vessels and ground slate tools from other cultures south of the Alaska Peninsula. Compared with the preceding cultures, Norton settlements were larger and more stable, and the people exploited the sea to a greater extent. Coastal pit houses were large, and 1 to 2 meters (3 to 6 feet) deep, with a central hearth and a tunnel entry extending 2 to 3.5 meters (6 to 11 feet). Many types of stone tools are continuations of Denbigh types, although they are larger and more often ground and polished. Drills, not found in Dorset, are common. Specially designed spears for birds and fish suggest that these were becoming more important sources of food.

curvilinear, and circular designs, which may have had some ideological significance. The Old Bering Sea style is more Asiatic in its orientation than Okvik. Graves excavated on the Chukchi Peninsula of Siberia contain materials identical to those found on St Lawrence Island. In a later cultural complex, known as Punuk—after the island in the Bering Strait where it was found—sea mammals were hunted even more intensively. As a result, settlements were bigger and more densely populated, some having as many as several hundred people.

Ancestors of the Present-Day Inuit

Between AD 500 and AD 800, a culture known as the Birnirk emerged. Best known from excavations near Point Barrow, it is clearly at least one of the ancestors of the modern Inuit (Eskimo) culture— if, indeed, we cannot trace their ancestry back to the Denbigh culture. Birnirk appears to represent a combination of Ipiutak traditions and hunting techniques derived from people of the Bering Sea, and it spread along the Alaskan coast and as far west as the Kolyma River. By AD 1000, the Birnirk and Punuk cultures had merged and developed into the fully Arctic-adapted Thule culture. Thule carried into the eastern Arctic the skin kayaks and umiaks, the dog sleds, and the techniques of hunting on sea-ice that today we associate with traditional Eskimos. One of the most important of these techniques was that of hunting ringed seal through the breathing holes they maintain in the sea-ice. This technique, probably developed about AD 1200, made it possible to take more game during the long winter months. The hunter had to keep a long, patient watch at the hole until the fluttering of a wisp of duck down he had placed over it indicated that a seal was breathing in the water below, whereupon he would make a swift thrust with his harpoon.

As the Thule whale hunters moved into the eastern Arctic between about AD 1000 and AD 1200, the preceding Dorset culture disappeared. Thule technology, with its more efficient hunting weapons, may have displaced the Dorset culture, but it has also been suggested that Dorset people may have died out a century or two before the Thule culture appeared.

Although there is still much to be learned about how early humans adapted to the Arctic, one conclusion is clear: surviving the dangers and difficulties of this extraordinarily harsh environment was undoubtedly one of humankind's most remarkable achievements.

⚲ An ivory hat ornament from the Old Bering Sea period, with jet eye inlays and lateral holes for hair and wooden plugs. Such ornaments, signs of superior hunting skill, were fastened to wooden peaked hats used to shield the eyes when kayak hunting.
SMITHSONIAN INSTITUTION/ COURTESY MUSEUM OF ANTHROPOLOGY AND ETHNOGRAPHY, ST PETERSBURG

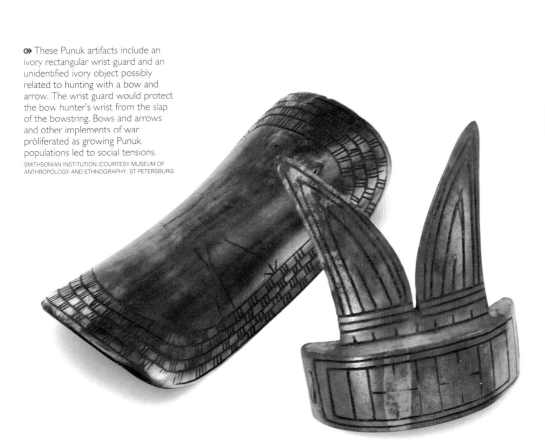

↪ These Punuk artifacts include an ivory rectangular wrist guard and an unidentified ivory object possibly related to hunting with a bow and arrow. The wrist guard would protect the bow hunter's wrist from the slap of the bowstring. Bows and arrows and other implements of war proliferated as growing Punuk populations led to social tensions.
SMITHSONIAN INSTITUTION /COURTESY MUSEUM OF ANTHROPOLOGY AND ETHNOGRAPHY, ST PETERSBURG

A rectangular wall
5 meters (16 feet) wide and
45 meters (148 feet) long enclosed
approximately 18 individual family
tents used for sleeping and eating.
Across a narrow bay, a row of hearths
and food-storage platforms provided
cooking areas for each family.

A DORSET CAMP

MOREAU MAXWELL

THIS 1,200-YEAR-OLD DORSET CAMP on the Knud Peninsula, just south of the Bache Peninsula, on Ellesmere Island's east coast, is unique, although others like it may exist in the Dorset realm. Here, Dr Peter Schledermann and assistants excavated a late spring gathering site for Dorset people coming together after a winter spent isolated in hunting camps on the sea-ice. The location was ideal. It is near a polynya, an open-water pond in the sea-ice, which acted as a magnet in the spring for air-breathing sea mammals. On one occasion, the excavators counted 300 walrus congregated in the open-water polynya.

The surplus of food animals available at this time enabled the whole band of some 100 people to assemble for social and religious purposes. Here, mates could be chosen, marriages performed, and kinship obligations strengthened. Many of the beautiful Dorset ivory carvings appear to have magical–religious significance, and this gathering was undoubtedly a time for some religious ceremony—possibly in celebration of the coming short, warm period of summer.

Here, on a flat beach, the people have built a rectangular enclosure of waist-high rocks. Inside this enclosure, 5 meters (16 feet) wide and 45 meters (148 feet) long, the distribution of recovered artifacts and animal bones suggests that each family had its own skin tent for sleeping and eating. All of the cooking was done across a narrow bay on a row of individual hearths 32 meters (105 feet) long. Adjacent to each low hearth was a rock platform for storing food (such as seal carcasses). On shore, several men are shown struggling to drag ashore a walrus, which may have weighed a tonne or more (about a ton).

At this time of the year, the arrival of migratory birds—ducks and geese—would have increased the food supply. Some caribou might have been taken in the hills inland, but in spring the animals are thin and their hides of little use for clothing. The band might have stayed together, if food were available, through the summer until the collective caribou drives in the autumn. At that time, the hides would be thick and ideal for clothing. There is some evidence that Dorset people—as did the later Thule people and the still later modern Inuit—drove the caribou through V-shaped fences of rock piles shaped like men. Standing behind each rock pile, a man armed with a lance would have killed the animals as each ran through.

☞ Radiocarbon dating of wood excavated from cooking hearths by Dr Karen McCullogh suggests a date of AD 800 to AD 900.

⚲ Dr Peter Schledermann and assistants excavate the area within the enclosure. Recovered artifacts and animal bones suggest that the site was occupied by people of the Late Dorset culture in the late spring and early summer.

ILLUSTRATION: JOHN RICHARDS

MARTHA COOPER/NATIONAL GEOGRAPHIC SOCIETY

MARTHA COOPER/NATIONAL GEOGRAPHIC SOCIETY

228

THE GREAT TRANSITION

1 0 , 0 0 0 B C – 4 0 0 0 B C

First Farmers of the Western World

LENNART PALMQVIST

THE PERIOD FROM 10,000 BC to 4000 BC witnessed the most important single innovation in the history of humanity before the Industrial Revolution: the seemingly simple change from acquiring food entirely by hunting and gathering to producing it through cultivation and stockbreeding. The beginnings of this momentous change can be traced to what is known as the Neolithic period—and it was the food-producing cultures that evolved in Southwest Asia during this time that eventually gave rise to Western civilization.

The area referred to as Southwest Asia comprises the modern-day states of Turkey, Iran, Iraq, Syria, Lebanon, Jordan, and Israel. The territory along the eastern coast of the Mediterranean Sea is sometimes called the Levant, and the region that now includes Israel and the western portion of Jordan is often referred to as Palestine.

An Iranian farmer tills the land with a simple wooden plow of a type known since ancient times, from as early as the fifth millennium BC.

Dating from the seventh millennium BC, this mask made of hard limestone from Kh Duma, near Hebron, in Israel, is 22 centimeters (about 9 inches) long.
ISRAEL MUSEUM, JERUSALEM

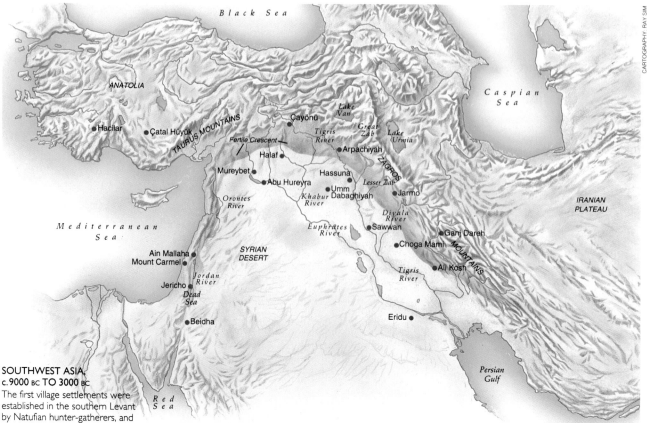

CARTOGRAPHY: RAY SIM

SOUTHWEST ASIA,
c. 9000 BC TO 3000 BC
The first village settlements were established in the southern Levant by Natufian hunter-gatherers, and also in Palestine and on the central Euphrates, where the earliest evidence of cereal cultivation is found. Later, the first pottery appeared simultaneously in several places in the Zagros Mountains and Anatolia, and on the central Euphrates.

RALPH SOLECKI/TEXAS A & M UNIVERSITY

⬆ Tools from the Zawi Chemi settlement and Shanidar Cave, in the Zagros Mountains. On the right is a curved bone sickle handle, and beside it, a bone reaping knife with a flint blade.

Southwest Asia can be roughly divided into three major vegetation zones. The first is known as the Mediterranean zone, extending in a narrow band along the eastern shore of the Mediterranean Sea and the southern and western coasts of Turkey. The vegetation here consists largely of evergreen trees, plants, and shrubs—species that are not adapted to withstand cold temperatures.

The second is the desert and desert–steppe zone, consisting of the deserts of Syria, Jordan, and Iraq and the bordering steppe region, including Mesopotamia—the area around the lower reaches of the Tigris-Euphrates river system. Rainfall is low, plant cover is sparse, and the contrast between summer barrenness and early spring vegetation is striking.

The third is the highland zone, which partly lies between the other two zones and partly surrounds them. This zone includes the Lebanon Mountains of the Levant, the mountains of eastern Turkey, and the Zagros Mountains, which extend the length of Iran's western border and into northern Iraq. To the west of this arc of mountains lies the Anatolian plateau, with an average altitude of 1,370 meters (4,500 feet). The characteristic vegetation of this highland zone is temperate forest of oak, cedar, pine or fir, pistachio, and juniper. Edible fruits, nuts, and wild cereals abound, and sheep, goats, cattle, and pigs are found in large numbers.

Within these broad zones, there are considerable local variations in natural resources. In most areas, the rainfall is insufficient to support perennials, but rain is more plentiful in the uplands that sweep from the Levant to the Zagros Mountains, which form the backbone of the so-called Fertile Crescent: the broad arc of territory curving from the head of the Persian Gulf, around the northern edge of the Syrian Desert, to Palestine and the Egyptian border.

The proximity of these zones to one another and the localized nature of certain resources encouraged the movement of people and the exchange of goods, and it is likely that farming became established in several places at more or less the same time. Archaeological evidence suggests that farming began on the hills and grasslands that flank the arid Syrian steppe and on the southern Mesopotamian floodplains. Just as they did thousands of years ago, these slopes still harbor the wild ancestors of the cereals and animals that became the basis of the region's agricultural economy—wild barley, two forms of wild wheat, plant foods such as legumes, and wild cattle, sheep, goats, and pigs.

The Beginnings of Settled Life

The warmer and wetter climate that developed in Southwest Asia at the end of the Pleistocene era, about 12,000 years ago, brought about great environmental changes. Open woodlands flourished, with nuts that could be harvested and grasses that had the potential to be domesticated, and the warmer winters enabled communities to move from caves in mountainous areas to regions where wild cereal grasses, such as barley and emmer, grew, and could be gathered. The harvesting of grain, in turn, stimulated the development of such tools as sickle blades and grinding stones, and the building of storage facilities—developments that paved the way for the emergence of agriculture.

Probably the single most important factor in the transition from a hunter-gatherer economy to a food-producing economy was the establishment of settled communities. Plants and animals were originally domesticated as a minor part of a general subsistence strategy, but they soon became so important that farming became an almost universal way of life.

The earliest Neolithic settlements were confined to the Levant and the western foothills of the Zagros Mountains. In these regions, and on the uplands of Anatolia, there was sufficient rainfall for wild wheat and barley to grow. As long ago as 9000 BC, people in these areas ate a wide variety of plants, and with time, cereal grains,

pulses, and nuts made up an increasing proportion of their diet.

The current method of investigation used by paleoethnobotanists and archaeologists to establish where each plant species was first domesticated is to determine the genetic ancestors of early domestic plants and then to chart the present-day distribution of these wild species. The distribution of these plants, adjusted for changes in climate over time, together with details obtained from plant remains recovered from archaeological sites, provides the necessary information.

Similarly, by analyzing the remains of bones in such sites, archaeologists can determine whether animals that were eaten were hunted in the wild or kept in domestic herds. The archaeological record suggests that each of the five species characteristic of Neolithic animal husbandry (sheep, goats, cattle, pigs, and dogs) was initially domesticated in a different region.

By the end of the Neolithic period, after cereals had been domesticated and cultivated, and stock-breeding was established, people in Southwest Asia had developed farming methods geared to open landscapes. This, in turn, gave rise to urban settlements in the floodplains of the Tigris and Euphrates rivers, in ancient Mesopotamia.

⚱ A large pottery storage jar from the Jordan Valley, dating from the fourth millennium BC.

⚲ The landscape near Diyarbakir, in southeastern Turkey, not far from the remarkable Neolithic site of Çayönü.

➦ A human skull from Jericho, dating from the eighth millennium BC, with molded plaster features and cowrie shells set into the eyes.

➦ *Opposite:* Plaster head of a human figurine, carved in bas-relief and painted, found in Jericho. It dates from the seventh millennium BC.

♀ This massive circular stone tower, about 9 meters (30 feet) high, is built against the inside of the town wall of Jericho. It dates from the Pre-Pottery Neolithic period, during the eighth millennium BC. The entrance is at the bottom.

The Natufian Culture

The transitional phase, during which people lived a settled existence based on the intensive collection of wild cereals, is best documented in Palestine. One of the most ancient settlements known to date was built in Jordan at Tell es-Sultan, Jericho, near the Dead Sea. Today, the site of ancient Jericho is marked by a great settlement mound—*tell* being the Arabian name for a mound formed from the accumulated remains of human occupation.

Jericho is one of a series of archaeological sites in the Levant and southern Turkey that are connected to the Natufian culture, named after a cave site in the Wadi en-Natuf, in the Judean hills, in Israel. Other well-known sites are El Wad, in the Mount Carmel area, and Ain Mallaha, in the Jordan Valley. Some of these sites date back to 12,500 years ago.

The Natufian culture is characterized by small villages of circular, stone-walled huts and relatively large populations. Artifacts include numerous mortars and grinding stones, apparently used for grinding grains and seeds, and many-toothed sickle blades of flint, which often still bear what is known as a sickle sheen along their cutting edges, indicating that they were used for harvesting wild

cereals. No domestic plants or animals have been identified at Natufian sites, although the bones of many hunted animals have been found, and wild emmer wheat was once native to the area. The largest Natufian sites and cemeteries contain considerable evidence to suggest that Natufian society was hierarchical and that such commodities as seashells, obsidian, and stone bowls were widely exchanged between communities.

Situated beside a perennial spring, the ancient site of Jericho is today marked by a settlement mound. Jericho began as a camp of Natufian hunters and food gatherers about 9000 BC. Archaeologist Kathleen M. Kenyon re-excavated the site in the 1950s, with remarkable results. By 8000 BC, a massive stone wall enclosed the settlement. On the bedrock that lies below the accumulated debris of Neolithic settlements and later civilizations, Natufian implements have been found, along with traces of a stone structure dating from about 7800 BC. This structure had sockets for massive poles—possibly totem poles—which suggests that it was a sanctuary or shrine. It would appear that Natufian hunters were accustomed to visiting the spring, and recognizing its importance, established a holy place beside it.

Muddy land watered by the spring provided excellent conditions for cereal farming in an otherwise arid environment, and by 7500 BC, Jericho had grown to a size of 1.6 hectares (4 acres). The people of early Jericho lived in mudbrick huts clustered within the stone wall, but they did not make clay vessels. The huts were circular, with floors of beaten mud, and their walls inclined inwards, suggesting that they were once domed. They may have been roofed with plastered branches, as there are many traces of wattle and daub in the walls.

It is unlikely that early Jericho's economy was based solely on agriculture. Imports found in the area include obsidian from Anatolia, turquoise from Sinai, and cowrie shells from the Red Sea.

THE NATUFIAN PERIOD: THE BEGINNINGS OF SETTLED LIFE

KATE DA COSTA

THE NATUFIAN CULTURE, one of several Levantine cultures that appeared towards the end of the Paleolithic period, dates from 12,500 to 10,300 years ago. This was roughly the end of the last Ice Age, a time when the climate in the Levant became warmer and moister. Natufian material has been found from southern Turkey to the Sinai, although to date the overwhelming amount of evidence has come from the southern Levant—modern-day Israel and Jordan.

The Natufian culture has been recognized since Dorothy Garrod defined it in 1932 and proposed naming it after the Wadi en-Natuf, in Israel—a wadi being the channel of a watercourse that is dry except during periods of rainfall. The culture is of particular interest, because it may have been during this time that people started to settle in villages. While it is known that some groups had adopted a sedentary way of life before agriculture developed, living all year round in the same settlement, it is unclear whether this happened in the Early Neolithic or the Natufian period.

Some Natufian sites are obviously temporary camps, used by people collecting seasonally available plants or animals, or on special journeys to acquire other resources, such as basalt for grinding stones.

♀ The walls of Natufian houses were made of rough stones, reeds, and mud. Here, the foundation stones of a circular house are being uncovered during excavations at Wadi Hammeh.

The larger sites—of more than 1,000 square meters (3,280 square feet), with deposits up to 3 meters (10 feet) thick—were not necessarily year-round settlements but may simply represent the accumulated debris of communities that used the same site for part of the year over several years. Different groups were almost certainly living in a variety of ways at this time—for instance, some may have been semisedentary, others mobile—depending on the local environment, the resources available, and each group's preferences. Certainly, most Natufian settlements were used more intensively than sites from earlier periods, and the Natufian culture was more elaborate and varied than any before it.

Circular Houses

The few complete Natufian houses that have been excavated are circular or elliptical and up to 10 meters (30 feet) in diameter. At some sites, there is evidence of houses having been rebuilt on the same alignment as many as three

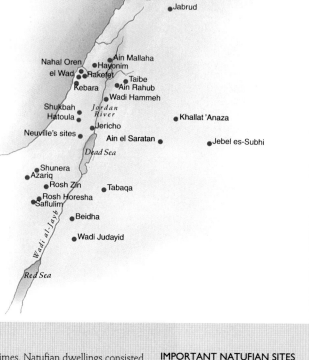

times. Natufian dwellings consisted of a circle of stones only one course high, with an opening in part of the wall spanned by posts. The walls must have been made of some perishable material, probably a combination of reed matting and mud. Internal postholes indicate that the houses had roofs. Most have several features within them, mainly fireplaces surrounded by stones and a raised rectangular area made of stones or tamped earth, which may have been a food preparation area. Shallow pits, roughly plastered with mud, and stone-lined basins have also been found, and have often been identified as grain storage bins or silos. None has been reported as containing grains, however, and there are many examples of these pits being used as graves.

IMPORTANT NATUFIAN SITES IN THE LEVANT

Shukbah is in the Wadi en-Natuf, after which the culture was named.

Although we have no idea what clothing was worn, we do know that, at least in death, body ornament was considered appropriate. Necklaces, headdresses, and belts made of mollusk shells or the toe bones of gazelles were found with many skeletons. Other animal bones were also found, but less frequently, and some skeletons were marked with colored ochers. There was no pattern to the burials, some being primary, others secondary; some individual, some multiple. One remarkable grave contained the skeletons of a child and a puppy. Many sites have graves of adults and children within the

◆ These bone sickle hafts and lunate blades, together with a handful of smooth agate pebbles, were found lying on the floor of a house in Wadi Hammeh, exactly as they had been left more than 10,000 years ago.

PELLA EXCAVATION PROJECT/J. CARTER/ J.HALFHIDE

boundaries of the site, and often within houses. We have no way of knowing whether houses were abandoned after they had been used for burials.

The Natufian Toolkit

The characteristic stone tools of the Natufians are blades and bladelets, microlithic tools being the most common. Some microliths were mounted in wood or bone handles, and it seems likely that some were used for hunting, although no weapons specifically designed for hunting have been found. The most remarkable of the composite tools are sickles, which have been discovered lying on floors, some with their tiny bladelets still in grooves in the handles. The sheen on the cutting edges shows that they were used to gather plants, but whether cereals, vegetables, or reeds is not known. Artifacts were clearly produced on a large scale: more ground stone tools—in the

form of mortars, pestles, hand mills, shaft straighteners, and shallow bowls—are found on a typical large Natufian site than have been recovered from all the sites known from the immediately preceding periods put together. In contrast with earlier periods, most stone tools have been found within houses or other structures. It has been commonly assumed that the mortars and pestles were used for processing plant foods, but the only recorded residues on the pestles are of ocher.

Some of the mortars have linear decoration incised around the outer rim, and this practice of decorating utilitarian objects marks a dramatic change from earlier periods. While art is known from quite early times,

portable art and the decoration of tools such as mortars and sickle handles became much more common in the Natufian period. Sculptured objects that are not tools have also been found, but perhaps what speak most eloquently from the past are the collections of what appear to be souvenirs—river-smoothed agate pebbles, fossils, odd-shaped or pretty colored stones—found within Natufian dwellings. These are the kinds of souvenirs we ourselves might collect when wandering about the countryside.

Food Sources

These ancient people had a varied diet, but probably relied mainly on plant foods. The numerous finds of sickles, mortars, and hand mills imply that either the types of plants they ate or the way food was processed had changed from earlier periods. Their favored prey were the larger animals, such as gazelles, cattle, pigs, deer, and members of the horse family, but they also ate migratory birds; small animals, such as hares; and aquatic animals, such as turtles, fish, and shellfish.

◆ A fine example of Natufian decorative work, this bone sickle haft from Kebara Cave has a deer or gazelle head carved on the handle.
ISRAEL ANTIQUITIES AUTHORITY

◀ These mortars and pestles were ground from basalt at a time long before metal tools were in use.
PELLA EXCAVATION PROJECT/R. WORKMAN

ISRAEL ANTIQUITIES AUTHORITY

⚓ This animal carved from limestone was found in a Natufian cave dwelling at Umm es-Zuitina, in the Judean desert.

JOEL DAY/THE PHOTO LIBRARY, SYDNEY

⚓ A field of maturing wheat. The use of wheat in Southwest Asia goes back to the eighth millennium BC. Emmer is one of the oldest varieties of domesticated wheat and is thought to have been the principal species grown in prehistoric and early historic times.

Being an oasis, strategically situated on the trade routes between the Red Sea and Anatolia, its early prosperity probably resulted from extensive trading activities.

Farming in Northern Syria

The next phase in the development of agriculture in Southwest Asia occurred when, instead of just collecting wild cereals, people began to sow the seeds of these plants outside their natural habitat. Two recently explored sites in northern Syria—Mureybet and Tell Abu Hureyra, on the banks of the Euphrates River, near the modern-day town of Aleppo—have yielded materials dated to the earliest period of farming, between 7600 BC and 6000 BC. Mureybet is of particular interest, being the earliest village site from which remains of a domesticated plant have been recovered, in the form of einkorn. Since in its wild state this variety of wheat grows far away, in the foothills of the Taurus and Zagros mountains, it must have been cultivated here.

Abu Hureyra lies outside the area where wild cereals grow today, but between 9500 BC and 8000 BC, when the site was first occupied, the climate here was somewhat warmer and moister, and the village lay in a well-wooded steppe area, where animals and wild cereals were abundant.

The Hureyra people initially built a semi-permanent settlement here and harvested wild cereals as part of their subsistence strategy. They also had access to a reliable source of meat in the form of the Persian gazelles that arrived from the south each spring. About 7600 BC, a new village rose on the site of the earlier settlement, extending over nearly 12 hectares (30 acres). At first, the inhabitants hunted gazelles intensively, but about 6500 BC, they switched to herding domestic sheep and goats and to growing pulses, einkorn, and

other cereals. Their rectangular, single-storied, multi-roomed mudbrick houses were linked by narrow lanes and courtyards and had black, burnished plaster floors, sometimes decorated with red designs. Each house was probably occupied by a single family.

The Switch to Farming

Why did the hunter-gatherers of Southwest Asia give up a way of life that had been successful for tens of thousands of years? What caused them to become reliant on domesticated animals and plants for their food? With the emergence of the village-based farming life these developments made possible, great cultural changes must have been set in train.

The eminent Australian archaeologist V. Gordon Childe saw the change to agriculture and an assured food supply as analogous to the change that attended the Industrial Revolution. In his epoch-making synthesis of prehistory, *Man Makes Himself*, published in 1936, he accordingly labeled it the Neolithic Revolution. Some years later, Childe advocated the so-called Oasis Theory to explain this phenomenon, a theory based on the climatic change that took place at the end of the last glacial period. He proposed that increasing aridity throughout Southwest Asia forced people and animals to gather at a few, dwindling oases, where close association led to the domestication of animals and plants.

This explanation was challenged by Robert Braidwood, of the Oriental Institute of Chicago, who advocated the so-called Hilly Flanks Theory. According to this theory, humans "settled in" to their environment—that is to say, people developed increasingly efficient means of exploiting plants and animals as their culture evolved. To test this theory, Braidwood initiated a series of excavations at Jarmo, in the foothills of the Zagros Mountains. By focusing on the threshold of cultural change, he hoped to find traces of the beginnings of this early agricultural revolution.

Early Farming Villages in the Zagros Mountains

The earliest evidence of settlement in the Zagros Mountains is less substantial than that found in northern Syria, although there were semipermanent encampments in northern Iraq, such as those at Karim Shahir, Zawi Chemi, and Shanidar Cave, about 10,000 BC to 9000 BC. In the upper excavation levels of Zawi Chemi and Shanidar Cave, domesticated sheep account for 80 percent of the remains of the animals that were eaten, making this site the earliest known example of human control of food production in Southwest Asia. But many startling discoveries are sure to be made in years to come.

The first of the early village-based farming communities to be discovered, and probably the best known, is Jarmo, situated in the Chemchemal Valley, east of Kirkut, in northeastern Iraq. It dates from the seventh millennium BC, but more precise dates are difficult to establish, because radiocarbon datings at this site are uncertain. Braidwood is convinced that Jarmo flourished for about 300 years in the mid-seventh millennium BC.

Lying at an elevation of 800 meters (2,600 feet), and covering an area of some 4 hectares (10 acres), Jarmo has archaeological deposits 7 meters (23 feet) deep. In the upper third of these, pottery is found in quantity for the first time. The economy was based on village-style agriculture, along with hunting and gathering. Two-row barley, wheat (einkorn and emmer), and several large-seeded annual legumes were cultivated, and sheep and goats were herded. The first certain evidence of domesticated pigs has also been found in these upper levels. This is of particular interest, because pigs, like dogs, eat the same range of foods as humans and are not adapted to the nomadic herding way of life.

The site apparently never had more than 25 houses at any one time, and had a population of 150 or so. The rectangular houses, each consisting of several small rooms and a courtyard, were built of molded mud. The clay walls were often built on a stone base, and clay floors were laid over beds of reeds. Storage bins and domed clay ovens were found, and it is thought that the latter may have been used for drying grains. Tools of chipped stone were found in huge quantities, a high proportion of them of obsidian and flint. There was also a great number of ground stone objects, including marble bracelets and a variety of attractive stone bowls.

The most remarkable artifacts from Jarmo are a striking quantity of lightly fired clay figurines, representing both animals and humans, plus a variety of other clay objects, such as stamps.

WERNER BRAUN

⚙ Iranian farmers winnowing grain with wooden forks—a technique for separating the chaff that has been in use since ancient times.

JENNIFER FRY/BRUCE COLEMAN LTD

◆ The Zagros Mountains, between Hamadan and Bisitun. Many human settlements dating from the beginning of the Neolithic period have been found in the mountainous regions of Southwest Asia, possibly reflecting an environment that offered an abundant and varied supply of food.

This terracotta "goddess" excavated from the upper levels of Munhata, in the Jordan Valley, dates from the sixth millennium BC. Several of its features are common to figurines found throughout the Levant from the early seventh millennium BC: the exaggerated buttocks, the elongated back of the head, and the emphasis on the eyes. The frightening appearance is a particular characteristic of Munhatan figurines.

ISRAEL MUSEUM, JERUSALEM/ERICH LESSING/MAGNUM

Part of the prehistoric village excavated at Jarmo, in modern-day Iraq, showing the walls of two adjoining houses. The walls found in all excavation levels were built of pressed mud, packed into courses. Traces of reed matting can be seen on several of the floors.

ORIENTAL INSTITUTE, THE UNIVERSITY OF CHICAGO

The pottery, buff to orange in color, is mostly plain and handmade, although often burnished.

Archaeologists find pottery very useful as a means of dating sites relative to each other, particularly when the sites are fairly similar. In prehistoric periods, pottery was often elaborately decorated, and styles of decoration had a relatively short life. Although pots are easily broken, their sherds are virtually indestructible.

Braidwood and his team of natural scientists believed that the climate had been essentially stable during the period when animals and plants were domesticated, which would mean that Childe's Oasis Theory could be rejected. Through his work at Jarmo and other sites in the Zagros, Braidwood concluded that agriculture had arisen in Southwest Asia as a "logical outcome" of specialization and the elaboration of culture. The hunter-gatherers simply "settled in" during the Holocene period, becoming intimately familiar with their plant and animal neighbors. As their culture evolved, people developed more efficient means of exploiting their environment, and agriculture thus formed a natural link in the long evolutionary chain.

While Braidwood's work made a number of worthwhile contributions to solving the problem of when, where, and why hunter-gatherers adopted a settled way of life, subsequent information accumulated from similar investigations throughout Southwest Asia has complicated as well as enriched our picture of the Neolithic period.

Ali Kosh

The mound of Ali Kosh, in Khuzistan, on the Deh Luran plain, provides the first evidence outside Palestine and northern Syria of a farming community in a lowland area. The major food crop from the earliest period of Ali Kosh was emmer, which was not native to the area. Wild two-row hulled barley was also present, and presumably cultivated. The earliest people known here also herded goats and sheep, and supplemented their diet by hunting, fishing, and collecting wild food. No acceptable radiocarbon datings exist for this stage of occupation, but the succeeding Ali Kosh phase appears to date from some time between 7200 BC and 6400 BC, which would make it roughly contemporary with the early Jarmo and early Palestinian sites.

In the second Ali Kosh phase, there is increasing evidence that winter-grown cereals were cultivated. The villagers here harvested their cereals with flint sickles, which were set into wooden handles by means of asphalt. Grains were probably collected in the simple twined baskets found at this site. Wheat, barley, and seeds from wild herbs were ground on stone slabs in the shape of a saddle or a shallow basin, using simple disk-shaped handstones or pitted limestone. This use of a stone mortar for grinding was a notable innovation.

At this time, about 100 people are thought to have lived at Ali Kosh. External contacts seem to have increased in this phase, for obsidian had been brought from Anatolia and seashells possibly from the Arabian Gulf, while copper probably came from somewhere in Iran. Pottery appears in the next phase, about 6000 BC to 5500 BC, together with several types of artifacts similar to those found in Mesopotamia later in the sixth millennium BC, particularly at the site of Tell es-Sawwan.

ABU HUREYRA: THE WORLD'S FIRST FARMERS

Peter Rowley-Conwy

Abu Hureyra lies on the Euphrates River in Syria, 120 kilometers (75 miles) east of Aleppo. It is a huge "tell" mound, made up of the superimposed remains of mudbrick houses mixed with household rubbish. Most of the site dates from the earliest period of farming, between about 9000 BC and 7000 BC. At the bottom, however, is a much smaller settlement that dates from the final prefarming phase, perhaps 11,000 BC to 9500 BC.

The excavation of Abu Hureyra is a story of success against the odds. The discovery of the site, in 1971, caused consternation: not only is it enormous, covering about 12 hectares (30 acres), but it was about to be flooded by the construction of a dam. Only a tiny proportion of the site could be excavated in the two seasons available. The excavator, Andrew Moore, chose to use modern but time-consuming methods of data recovery, and his decision has been fully vindicated by the spectacular results. The second excavation season coincided with the October War of 1973, but despite the difficulties, Moore excavated seven trenches at different places on the site. This work has provided a rare glimpse of what life was like among both the last hunter-gatherers and the first farmers.

Gazelle Hunters

Animal bones were found in profusion. The hunter-gatherers of the first settlement hunted mainly gazelles, as well as a few wild cattle, sheep, and onagers (a type of wild ass). Young gazelles can be aged very accurately by their teeth, and a curious pattern emerged at Abu Hureyra: many jaws of newborn animals were present, as were many from animals aged 12 months, but there were none in between. As gazelles are born in May, this indicated a very short hunting season, confined to that month. Probably, entire herds were killed by being driven into a trap, and most of the surplus meat was stored by salting or drying for use through the year.

TELL ABU HUREYRA EXCAVATION

Why was the hunting season so short? Possibly, the hunters camped at Abu Hureyra only in May, but other data argue against this. Plant remains were recovered in bulk by modern flotation methods, showing that no fewer than 157 species of plants were eaten—more than is known to be eaten by any modern hunter-gatherer group, and far more than have been found in any other archaeological site. No plants were cultivated; seeds were collected from wild grasses and other plants available at various times of the year from early spring to late autumn. Clearly, Abu Hureyra was occupied for longer than just the period when the gazelle hunt took place. The gazelles must, therefore, have been migratory, moving into this area only in May.

Early Plant Foods

But were plant seeds or was gazelle meat more important in the diet? Another modern analytical method provides the answer. Many human burials were found at Abu Hureyra, and the skeletons often have peculiar pathological conditions. The state of the toe, ankle, and knee joints reveals that people spent many hours kneeling down with their toes curled under; strong development of the shoulders and upper arms indicates

labor using the arm muscles; and pathologies of the lower back show that the movement involved was one of continuously rocking the trunk backwards and forwards. The only activity that can account for all these at once is using grindstones to make flour. This must have been done on a very large scale, suggesting that plant foods were more important than meat in the diet.

After 9500 BC, there was a gap of a few centuries in the use of the site. From about 9000 BC, the story resumes with a large farming township, and the plant remains from this period are quite different. Far fewer species are present, but they include cultivated plants: barley, rye, lentils, chickpeas, two species of wheat, and several other plants. The pathologies of human bones continue to show that people spent much time grinding seeds into flour, but the seeds now came from cultivated plants. Interestingly, both male and female skeletons show these pathologies, indicating that both sexes prepared plant foods—a remarkable challenge

At Abu Hureyra, the early farming village lay above a settlement used by the last hunter-gatherers. Here, a rectangular house built by the farmers has been cut through to reveal the circular dwellings of the hunter-gatherers.

to our (usually unconscious) assumption that only women would have done this kind of work, even in the distant past.

Despite the fact that these farmers cultivated crops as the mainstay of their diet, they continued to depend largely on wild animals for meat. Gazelles still account for two-thirds of the bones at the site and, again, were killed exclusively in the month of May. From about 7500 BC, however, gazelle bones suddenly become less numerous, being replaced by those of sheep and goats. Female goats were kept into adulthood for breeding, while most males were killed at two years of age for their meat. This pattern could not have resulted from hunting, so these animals must have been domesticated. Clearly, not all species were domesticated at the same time; throughout Southwest Asia, plants were domesticated before animals.

The results achieved at Abu Hureyra show what can be achieved by modern scientific methods. Only a very small part of the site was excavated before it was flooded in 1974; but the methods have been tried and tested, and can now be used at other sites to increase our knowledge of the most important economic change the world has ever seen—the emergence of agriculture.

Grindstones such as this were essential for preparing plant foods. The farmers at Abu Hureyra used them to process cultivated crops such as wheat and barley, while the earlier hunter-gatherers used them to grind wild plant seeds.

THE BRITISH MUSEUM

⚱ The grill-plan buildings at Çayönü have a series of parallel foundation walls running the length of each building. This form of construction, incorporating passages to allow the circulation of air beneath the floor, may have been a means of keeping the building dry during the damp winter months.

➥ A view of Çayönü taken in 1972. The rolling plains that surround the site are intensively cultivated today, but when the site was occupied about 7000 BC, they were covered in forest. The mountains in the distance are part of the Tauros range.

Early Neolithic Sites in Anatolia

Anatolia provided a diverse and favorable environment for human settlement from early in the Holocene period, about 8000 BC. The settlement of Çayönü, near Diyarbakir, in southeastern Turkey, is situated on the high bank of a tributary of the Tigris, and the river terrace runs for only a few kilometers before meeting the foothills of the Taurus Mountains.

The site was occupied from about 7250 BC to 6700 BC by people who grew domesticated plants such as wheat, peas, and lentils. It is especially interesting in that the animal bones found in the different levels of this settlement show a clear shift from the hunting of wild animals to the keeping of domesticated ones.

Extensive areas of the site have been investigated since 1964 by a joint team from the University of Istanbul and the Oriental Institute of Chicago. Çayönü covers an area of about 100 meters by 200 meters (330 feet by 660 feet). Its architectural remains are fascinating, consisting mainly of residential buildings, although at least three are monumental in size, suggesting that they had a communal function and possibly indicating that there was some kind of chieftainship system. The domestic buildings include strange, so-called grill-plan buildings and more regular cell-plan buildings. The nondomestic structures have floors paved with flagstones. The substantial proportions of its buildings and the relative sophistication of their construction are what sets Çayönü apart from other early sites with fully domesticated cereals.

Almost all the excavated levels can be attributed to a cultural phase known as the Pre-Pottery Neolithic. While the people here had not yet begun to use pottery, they produced tools made of flint and obsidian, or fashioned from stone by grinding; ornaments made of polished stone; and clay figurines. Most surprising was their use of copper, presumably obtained from the nearby source at Ergani-Maden. The metal was shaped by heating and then pounded to make pins, hooks, reamers (a finishing tool for shaping holes), and beads. This is so far the earliest evidence of people intentionally using metal.

⚱ A reconstruction of the north and east walls of the so-called Second Vulture Shrine at Çatal Hüyük. The vultures have human legs and are thought to represent priests in disguise. A headless corpse lies between them. In other shrines, there are scenes of more bird-like vultures picking at corpses, possibly reflecting the practice of exposing dead bodies for defleshing.
ARLETTE MELLAART

➥ Excavations at Çatal Hüyük, showing several houses. The structure in the center is one of those thought to have been shrines, because of the unusual painted or plaster decorations on their walls.

JAMES MELLAART

Çatal Hüyük

In 1958, James Mellaart discovered another Anatolian settlement at Çatal Hüyük, situated on a small river 48 kilometers (30 miles) southeast of modern-day Konya. Çatal Hüyük covers an area of 13 hectares (32 acres) and is three times the size of Pre-pottery Jericho. A flourishing township by 6000 BC, it consisted of brick houses arranged side-by-side like a honeycomb. The most unusual feature of these houses is their highly standardized plan, each occupying some 25 square meters (30 square yards) of floor space. Access must have been by means of a wooden ladder from the courtyard onto a flat roof, and from there through a shaft and, finally, a low doorway. The living rooms had built-in benches and platforms, as well as hearths and ovens, all made of earth and plaster.

The extraordinary standardization of the estimated 1,000 houses, accommodating a population of 5,000 to 6,000, suggests deliberate planning and a high level of cohesion and cooperation within the community. Of particular interest are groups of rooms, each with a storeroom, that were apparently used as shrines. The elaborate murals and other contents of these rooms strongly indicate that organized ritual activities took place here.

⚁ A scene depicting a red-deer hunt, painted on the antechamber wall of a hunting shrine found in level III of Çatal Hüyük, dating from about 5800 BC.

⚁ This baked clay figure of an enthroned female, from Çatal Hüyük, may represent a goddess giving birth. She is supported on either side by cat-like animals, which are probably leopards. The statue was found in a grain bin.
C.M. DIXON

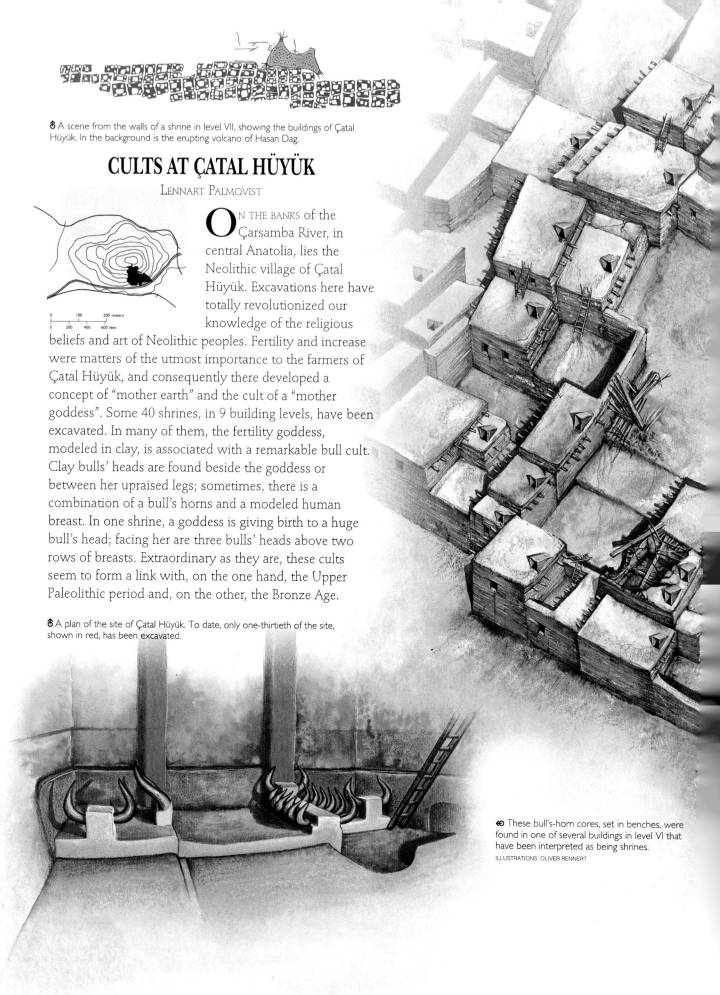

⚥ A scene from the walls of a shrine in level VII, showing the buildings of Çatal Hüyük. In the background is the erupting volcano of Hasan Dag.

CULTS AT ÇATAL HÜYÜK

LENNART PALMQVIST

O N THE BANKS of the Çarsamba River, in central Anatolia, lies the Neolithic village of Çatal Hüyük. Excavations here have totally revolutionized our knowledge of the religious beliefs and art of Neolithic peoples. Fertility and increase were matters of the utmost importance to the farmers of Çatal Hüyük, and consequently there developed a concept of "mother earth" and the cult of a "mother goddess". Some 40 shrines, in 9 building levels, have been excavated. In many of them, the fertility goddess, modeled in clay, is associated with a remarkable bull cult. Clay bulls' heads are found beside the goddess or between her upraised legs; sometimes, there is a combination of a bull's horns and a modeled human breast. In one shrine, a goddess is giving birth to a huge bull's head; facing her are three bulls' heads above two rows of breasts. Extraordinary as they are, these cults seem to form a link with, on the one hand, the Upper Paleolithic period and, on the other, the Bronze Age.

⚥ A plan of the site of Çatal Hüyük. To date, only one-thirtieth of the site, shown in red, has been excavated.

◄⊙ These bull's-horn cores, set in benches, were found in one of several buildings in level VI that have been interpreted as being shrines.

ILLUSTRATIONS: OLIVER RENNERT

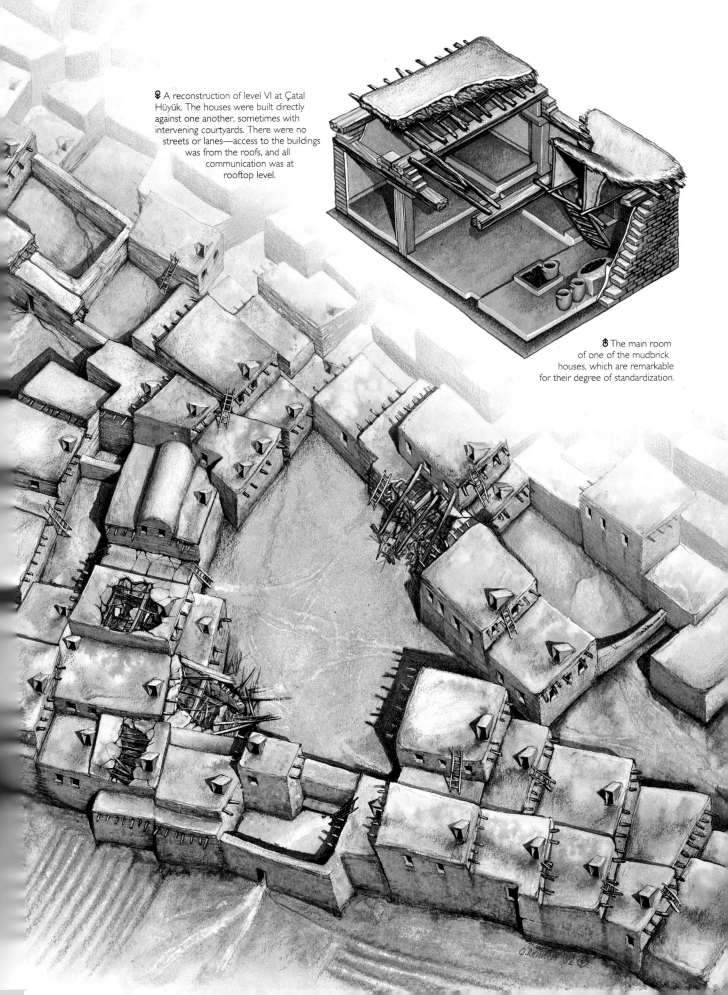

♀ A reconstruction of level VI at Çatal Hüyük. The houses were built directly against one another, sometimes with intervening courtyards. There were no streets or lanes—access to the buildings was from the roofs, and all communication was at rooftop level.

♂ The main room of one of the mudbrick houses, which are remarkable for their degree of standardization.

⊙ This female skull excavated from one of the shrines at Çatal Hüyük is encrusted with cinnabar (mercury sulfide): an example of a so-called ocher burial.

ARLETTE MELLAART

♀ A valley in the central Zagros Mountains near the modern-day town of Isfahan, in Iran. The interior slopes of the Zagros are dotted with trading centers that formed part of a wide-spread trading network dating back to Neolithic times. This network skirted the central desert to the east and west across the Zagros Mountains and extended down onto the Mesopotamian plain.

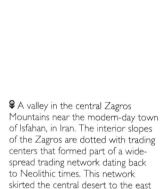

The paintings on the carefully plastered walls depict hunting scenes or women giving birth, or consist of numerous geometric patterns. The shrines also contain groups of human and animal figures chipped from stone or modeled in clay. There are groups or rows of bull's-horn cores set in benches or in stylized bull's heads. The rites performed in the shrines, undoubtedly concerned with fertility, seem to form a link with the Upper Paleolithic period, on the one hand, and with the Bronze Age (for example, Early Minoan Crete) on the other.

Çatal Hüyük's wealth was founded on agriculture and trade. Evidence of cattle breeding is found in the earliest excavation levels—the first evidence of unquestionably domesticated cattle

known in western Asia—and the inhabitants obtained obsidian for trade from the nearby volcano of Hasan Dag.

The archaeological evidence from Çatal Hüyük is fascinating in many respects. Neolithic villages in Southwest Asia do not appear to have had cemeteries or elaborate tombs comparable with those of the same period in western Europe. In early Jericho, for instance, the dead were buried under house floors, with their heads buried separately. At Çatal Hüyük, the corpses were placed beneath sleeping platforms. Wall-paintings in three of the shrines show vultures together with headless human figures, the figures often lying curled on their left side. Mellaart has interpreted these scenes as depicting part of the burial process, and a considerable amount of evidence supports this view. For instance, many of the bodies buried beneath the house floors were lying on their left side; human skulls were found on house floors separated from bodies; flesh was removed from bodies before burial—perhaps by vultures.

Undecorated pottery vessels were in general use, and well-preserved prototypes in wood or basketwork have survived, along with equally well-preserved fragments of woven fabrics. The wooden vessels show a variety of form, a mastery of technique, and a sophistication in taste that is unparalleled in the Neolithic period elsewhere in this area.

Among the specialized crafts of Çatal, the chipped stone items, exemplified by a number of ceremonial weapons and ground and polished obsidian mirrors, are by far the most elegant in Southwest Asia. High-quality woolen textiles, in a variety of weaves, were also produced.

Clearly, the crafting of specialized and even luxury items from certain materials was an important feature of Çatal's economy. The fact that many essential raw materials had to be brought from elsewhere points to a commercial basis for much of the community's wealth. The unusual size of Çatal itself strongly suggests that its people exercised some form of political control over the surrounding region.

The site appears to have been occupied from some time late in the seventh millennium BC until the latter part of the sixth millennium BC, when, for unknown reasons, it was abandoned.

Late Neolithic Mesopotamia

The reasons why an advanced, though isolated, settlement such as Çatal Hüyük came to nothing in terms of further social and economic development remain obscure. In Mesopotamia, early farming villages were established in an area that was far less viable economically than Anatolia, yet it was in this arid zone, virtually devoid of natural resources, that urban civilization first developed. From the sixth millennium BC, Mesopotamia was to be the center of the social, technological, and political progress that led to the world's first truly urban society.

THE MACQUITTY COLLECTION

Development throughout Southwest Asia had been more or less constant until about 6000 BC, and methods of producing and storing food were well developed. As there was no longer a pressing need to obtain food by hunting, fishing, or gathering, the need to settle in places that offered wild food resources gradually diminished. For the first time, it became possible to establish settlements outside previously favored areas.

During this period, increasing experience in plant cultivation made it possible to raise the yield per unit of land, and with the aid of irrigation, two or three harvests could be produced a year. Less land was needed to feed the inhabitants of a settlement, which meant that settlements could be established closer together. This was important, because the geographical proximity of settlements was a prerequisite both for the creation of settlement systems and for the division of labor within communities. The finely painted pottery of the Halaf period, named after Tell Halaf, in northern Syria, is an example of craftwork produced by specialists—clear evidence of division of labor.

Most of what we know about Southwest Asia from about 6000 BC to 3500 BC is based on styles of pottery. Little is known about other evolving technologies that changed settlement patterns or about new forms of economic organization.

The first phase of Late Neolithic culture in Mesopotamia (6000 BC to 5500 BC) is commonly

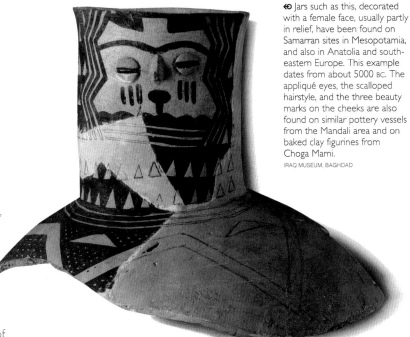

◄◉ Jars such as this, decorated with a female face, usually partly in relief, have been found on Samarran sites in Mesopotamia, and also in Anatolia and southeastern Europe. This example dates from about 5000 BC. The appliqué eyes, the scalloped hairstyle, and the three beauty marks on the cheeks are also found on similar pottery vessels from the Mandali area and on baked clay figurines from Choga Mami.
IRAQ MUSEUM, BAGHDAD

considered to be the Hassunan, named after the site of Tell Hassuna, which lies west of the middle Tigris River, about 30 kilometers (20 miles) south of modern-day Mosul. While the country is undulating and merges imperceptibly with the uplands, it is low-lying in comparison with the hilly region where nearby Jarmo is located. Other sites of the Hassuna culture are restricted to a limited region of similar terrain in northern Iraq.

In content and style, the early Hassunan artifacts—stone tools and simple pottery—were clearly a continuation of what had been produced in Jarmo, as though the Jarmo culture had spread downhill. Although construction methods improved during Hassunan times, dwellings remained simple. Settlements were, in fact, nothing more than villages of farmers.

The next phase of Late Neolithic culture in Mesopotamia (about 5600 BC to 5000 BC) is often called the Samarran, after the Islamic city of Samarra, beneath which a particularly attractive and elaborately painted style of pottery was first found. Similar pottery was found at Hassuna in levels III to VIII, and was long thought to have been imported luxury ware. Recent excavations at Tell es-Sawwan and Choga Mami, however, have confirmed that Samarra must be considered a separate culture and that its people flourished north of Baghdad, on the fringes of the floodplain, some time in the sixth millennium BC.

Perhaps the most important single discovery from these excavations relates to the Samarran economy. In contrast with Hassunan sites, Samarran sites are well to the south of the zone

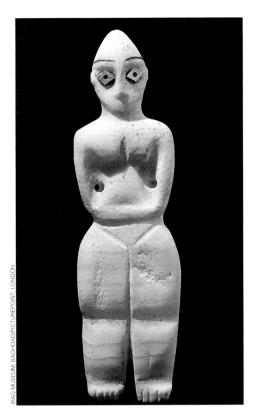

IRAQ MUSEUM, BAGHDAD/PICTUREPOINT, LONDON

IRAQ MUSEUM, BAGHDAD

⬧ This male figurine made of clay, excavated from the Samarran site of Tell es-Sawwan, dates from the sixth millennium BC. In the later excavation levels of this site, upright alabaster figures of a quite different type have been found in large numbers.

◄◉ An alabaster statuette from a grave at the Samarran site of Tell es-Sawwan, dating from the sixth millennium BC. The eyes have been emphasized by means of bitumen inlays.

☗ A Samarran bowl from Hassuna, with a centrifugal design of stylized ibexes. Pottery of this kind was first found in graves dating from the sixth millennium BC, below the Abbasid capital of Samarra.
IRAQ MUSEUM, BAGHDAD/HIRMER FOTOARCHIV

➣ A polychrome Halaf plate from a potter's workshop excavated at Arpachiyah, dating from early in the fifth millennium BC. It has a diameter of 32 centimeters (about 12 inches).
IRAQ MUSEUM, BAGHDAD

where rain-fed agriculture is now possible. Paleobotanical evidence from both Sawwan and Choga Mami suggests that irrigation was practiced in both areas in the sixth millennium BC. It has even been suggested that agriculture at Sawwan was probably based on seasonal flooding. At both Sawwan and Choga Mami, emmer, bread wheat, naked six-row barley, and hulled two-row barley have been identified, as have considerable quantities of linseed. The villages at both sites are large in comparison with those from earlier periods, occupying areas of up to 5 hectares

(12 acres). Stamp seals have been found, suggesting that private ownership was recognized, and a more conscious professionalism among Samarran craftspeople is indicated by the widespread use of potter's marks. Surplus wealth had become available for nonproductive purposes.

This is especially evident at Tell es-Sawwan. Here, beneath several unusually large buildings, numerous graves have been found, many containing the remains of infants. The graves also contained an extraordinary collection of hundreds of ground stone objects—in particular, female statuettes and a variety of elegantly shaped bowls made of alabaster. These objects indicate that Sawwan was a settlement with some special significance.

The discovery of a distinctive pottery style at Tell Halaf, on the Syrian-Turkish border, midway between the Tigris and the Euphrates, gave a name to the third phase of Mesopotamian protohistory (5500 BC to 4300 BC). Like the Hassunan, the Halafian culture was centered on northern Iraq,. but was considerably more widespread. Halafian sites are also found in northern Syria and somewhat further down the Tigris and Euphrates rivers than Hassunan sites.

Halafian settlements were still no more than villages, but construction techniques had improved, and there were cobbled streets between the houses. Although most walls were formed of packed mud, at some sites there is evidence of mudbricks—the first known in Mesopotamia. Also for the first time in Mesopotamia, structures or chambers are found that differ from dwellings or other utilitarian buildings. These consist of vaulted, circular rooms shaped like beehives, ranging from about 5 to 10 meters (15 to 30 feet) in diameter, and built of packed mud. Sometimes, rectangular antechambers are attached to them, but these buildings were seldom, if ever, lived in. They may represent the first step towards temple architecture.

Halafian pottery was the finest ever produced in prehistoric Mesopotamia. (The historic period begins with the first written sources, about 3200 BC.) Handmade from very fine clay, it had thin walls and was decorated with skillfully applied paintings of geometric motifs and, occasionally, figures of animals, birds, and flowers. Flat stamp seals of steatite or other stone, engraved.with simple geometric figures and used to impress ownership marks on lumps of clay attached to goods, were abundant in the Halafian period.

The dating of Halafian sites is controversial, but various authorities place the end of the Halafian culture well into the fifth millennium BC, as late as 4300 BC. From about 6000 BC to 4500 BC, the middle reaches of the Tigris and Euphrates river valleys in northern Mesopotamia were settled by farming peoples who had probably moved in from one or more regions of the central Zagros Mountains area to the east, north, and west. Farming techniques were established but not elaborate, and permitted

only a moderate increase in the number, size, and quality of settlements during the period. Some developments are especially notable: native copper was occasionally worked, although not for the first time in Southwest Asia; pottery was greatly improved, aesthetically and technologically; and the plow came into use as an aid to agriculture.

Early Settlement in Sumer

It is only from a relatively late stage that there is archaeological evidence of settlement in the arid southern plains of Mesopotamia. The 'Ubaid culture, which extended from 5000 BC to 3750 BC, is generally thought to be the earliest manifestation of settled farming in the southern floodplains. The earliest phase, known as 'Ubaid 1, or Eridu, was very limited geographically, but these settlers from the south soon moved up the Tigris and Euphrates rivers in search of new land. At this point, Mesopotamia became the center of civilized Southwest Asia—the place where the foundations of the Sumerian civilization were laid.

At Eridu, slightly west of the present-day course of the Euphrates, a series of small square rooms fitted with altars has been found in very early excavation levels in association with distinctive monochrome-painted pottery. These buildings represent the beginnings in the south of the long and much elaborated tradition of Mesopotamian temple architecture.

Little is known about the early 'Ubaid economy, but it seems almost certain that the 'Ubaid peoples were irrigation farmers who harnessed the destructive spring floods of the Euphrates River to improve their crop yields.

Certainly, there is evidence that settlements were becoming bigger. Eridu may have covered an area of 10 hectares (24 acres) in the later 'Ubaid periods, with as many as 4,000 inhabitants. Populations of this size must have increased the need for some form of centralized control, but evidence of social stratification, such as differences in grave goods or in houses, is extremely limited.

A number of technological innovations took place in 'Ubaid times: copper casting; the use of fired bricks for building; and the use of simple sailboats for river transport. The fine-quality decorated pottery of the Halafian and Samarran cultures gave way to technologically improved but mass-produced wares, often crudely decorated. Some pottery was manufactured on the tournette, a forerunner of the fast-spinning potter's wheel. Engraved stamp seals depicted animals and humans together, whereas in the Halafian period they had borne only simple geometric figures.

While agriculture in southern Mesopotamia must have been extremely productive, it seems likely that wealth was increasingly based on mercantile trade during this period, and that command over the organization of commerce and the exaction of tributes would have been centered in the temples. Never before had a single culture been able to spread its influence over such a vast area. So widespread was this influence that the prosperous 'Ubaid culture, on the plains of Mesopotamia, provided the basis for the cultural explosion represented by the emergence of the later historic—and first literate—civilizations.

☉ The Euphrates River flows almost due south after leaving the Turkish mountains. Downstream, after passing through agricultural lands, it cuts its way through a dry plain on either side. At intervals along its course, villages have sprung up, with orchards and crops that flourish on the alluvial soil left behind by the river. The ancient island of Ana is seen here from the river's northern bank.

☉ Beyond the hilly flanks of the Fertile Crescent—the foothills of the Zagros Mountains proper—only limited agriculture is possible, and the area is consequently given over to the herding of sheep and goats. Farming here follows traditional ways, as shown in this scene of wheat threshing.

'AIN GHAZAL: THE LARGEST KNOWN NEOLITHIC SITE

GARY O. ROLLEFSON

IN THE COURSE OF ITS 2,000-YEAR HISTORY, 'Ain Ghazal, in Jordan, witnessed a remarkable period of human cultural development. The settlement was founded as a small permanent hamlet in 7250 BC, and its residents combined farming, hunting, and herding to provide an abundant and stable food supply that allowed sustained population growth on a scale never before possible. While it grew constantly over some 750 years, 'Ain Ghazal experienced a sudden population explosion in the centuries immediately before and after 6500 BC—probably as a result of people abandoning settlements in the region as the land was exhausted. By 6000 BC, the village extended over 12 hectares (almost 30 acres) and housed about 2,000 people.

The period between 7250 BC and 6000 BC is the "classic" phase of Neolithic development—known to archaeologists as the Pre-Pottery Neolithic B (PPNB) period—which extended south from eastern Turkey to the fringes of the southern deserts of Palestine and Jordan. In the previous period, from 8500 BC to 7600 BC (known as the PPNA), a few communities in the Levant had begun to grow crops, but there is no evidence of animal domestication.

PPNB people produced long flint blades of exceptionally fine quality, using them as arrowheads and sickles as well as for a range of other purposes. They built spacious and sturdy houses, with durable plaster floors that reflect a sophisticated technology. Their agricultural crops included several species of cereals and legumes, and by 6000 BC they had domesticated sheep, goats, cattle, and pigs. But of all their accomplishments, perhaps the most impressive are the rich expressions of religious belief that have come down to us in the form of their ritual objects and burial remains.

Toys, Cults, and Amulets

Many tiny clay animal figurines, which may have served various purposes for the people of 'Ain Ghazal, have been found. A unique sitting dog, for example, may have been simply a child's toy, since nothing comparable has been found at 'Ain Ghazal or anywhere else in Southwest Asia. The vast majority of animal figurines depict cattle, which were not domesticated until near the end of the PPNB period, and it has been suggested that they may have been related to a "cattle cult".

Human figurines are less numerous, and may have been personal

Plaster was used to recreate the faces of some individuals, presumed to have been family members. As time passed and the plaster cracked, the "portraits" were buried and replaced with those of people who had died more recently.
HISAHIKO WADA

amulets. With one exception, all were found "decapitated", either as heads or headless bodies. Some figurines have grossly extended abdomens and pendulous breasts, and probably represented fertility spirits that were thought to ensure women's good health during pregnancy.

Burial Customs

The dead were usually buried beneath the floors of houses. After a waiting period long enough for the flesh and ligaments to decay, the burial pit was reopened and the skull removed. Many skulls appear to have been simply reburied elsewhere, some under the same floor.

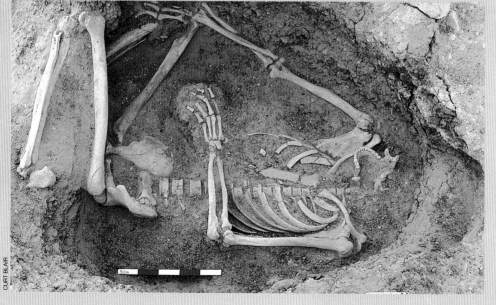

Most children and adults were buried beneath the plaster floors of houses. After a time, the burial pits were reopened to extract the skulls, and a new floor was then built.

CURT BLAIR

5cm

But others received unusual treatment: plaster was used to recreate facial features, producing what archaeologist Kathleen M. Kenyon called "portraits" of the dead. Such people may have been family or lineage members.

Infants under the age of about 15 months were disposed of with considerably less regard. Although the remains of some very young children have been found under doorways, possibly implying that they served as "foundation deposits", or in a ceremonial context, such as in a pit of plastered human skulls, most appear to have been discarded in rubbish heaps. About a third of the adult burials have similarly been found in rubbish heaps, the bodies not decapitated, suggesting that these people did not enjoy the degree of respect accorded to most other members of the community.

Ancestor Worship

The human and animal figurines represent a link with the spiritual world on an individual level, and the human burials demonstrate this link on the level of the family. Communal expressions of religion took a more overt form. So far, more than 30 plaster statues and busts have been

GARY O. ROLLEFSON

☗ Projectile points made with exemplary skill show how important hunting was to the people of 'Ain Ghazal. Half of their meat supply came from wild animals during the PPNB period; in later periods, this had declined to less than 10 percent. Large points like these were characteristic of the PPNB.

PETER DORRELL AND STUART LAIDLAW

☗ Statues and busts, made from bundles of reeds coated with plaster and decorated with red paint and bitumen, were focal points of communal activities. They were probably displayed (at least occasionally) in a special building. This statuette may have been a village's "mother goddess".

☗ One of two clay figurines of wild cattle, ritually "killed" with flint bladelets, that were found buried beneath the plaster floor of a house. This isolated find may represent an act of magic, believed to bring luck during the hunt.
CURT BLAIR

recovered from huge "burial pits". The busts, standing about 45 centimeters (18 inches) high, are clearly an elaboration of the plastered skulls, and may represent mythical ancestors of family groups. The taller statues (about 90 centimeters, or 3 feet, high) depict both men and women—the latter including fertility statuettes—and probably portray mythical ancestors believed to have founded the settlement.

More than a thousand years of intensive farming and grazing took their toll on the soils and plant life around 'Ain Ghazal and the other settlements of the southern Levant. By 6000 BC, most of the villages had been deserted. Only a few, such as 'Ain Ghazal, situated near the edge of the steppes, where goats could be herded, survived, if in somewhat reduced circumstances.

Between 6000 BC and 5500 BC (known as the PPNC period), 'Ain Ghazal continued to grow, extending over about 14 hectares (35 acres), but judging by the less dense housing in this period, the population had probably declined. Some people may have lived at the site for only a few months of the year, spending the rest of their time tending their flocks of goats in the steppes and desert.

By 5500 BC, local residents were making pottery for storage and cooking purposes, ushering in what is known as the Pottery Neolithic period. But this technical innovation could not compensate for the damage suffered by the surrounding farmland. Within a few centuries, 'Ain Ghazal had been all but abandoned, serving as nothing more than a temporary camp for nomadic pastoralists visiting the spring that lay at the heart of the original and once thriving settlement.

HUNTER-GATHERERS AND FARMERS IN AFRICA

1 0 , 0 0 0 B C – A D 2 0 0

The Transformation of a Continent

RICHARD G. KLEIN

ABOUT 12,000 YEARS AGO, there was little difference between the cultures and economies of Africa and Eurasia, and both continents remained largely unchanged from the way they had been thousands, or even tens of thousands, of years earlier. People everywhere still used Stone Age technologies, and they relied entirely on hunting and gathering wild resources for their subsistence. What marks this period out as one of the most significant in prehistory is that it was a time of profound, global climatic change—from the cooler and generally drier conditions of the last Ice Age to the warmer and generally moister conditions of the present interglacial period, known as the Holocene.

Almost everywhere, changed climatic conditions led to a radical redistribution of plants and animals, to which people had to adapt. This they did in many ways, one of the most significant being that they undertook the first serious experiments in plant and animal domestication. To begin with, hunting and gathering probably continued to be more important, but in most societies that adopted them, cultivation and herding rapidly took over as the main mode of subsistence. In some places, the larger populations and economic surpluses made possible by cultivation and herding eventually led to the development of urban centers with monumental architecture, craft specialization, social stratification, wide trade networks, and other markers of "civilization".

◄ A herd of cattle at an agricultural village in Niger, West Africa. At the end of the last Ice Age, many of the continent's hunter-gatherers took up farming and herding.

↑ This barbed bone harpoon head comes from a fishing settlement dating to about the fifth millennium BC at Lowasera, on the ancient shoreline of Lake Turkana, in northern Kenya.
DAVID PHILLIPSON

David Phillipson

☝ These microlithic tools were made by the Iberomaurusians (sometimes called the Oranians), who inhabited northwestern Africa between 16,000 and 10,000 years ago.

♀ A galloping herd of Cape, or African, buffaloes (*Syncerus caffer*) in Kruger National Park, Transvaal, South Africa.

I t may be that Africa played a smaller role in the domestication of plants and animals and in the evolution of civilization than did other regions, especially nearby Southwest Asia, but its role was far from peripheral. Cattle may have been domesticated in the deserts of North Africa as early as anywhere else, and many important crops—including yams, sorghum, peanuts, and bulrush and finger millet—were native to Africa and must first have been cultivated there. On a broader scale, in the millennia following the end of the Ice Age, Africa, like most other parts of the world, was progressively transformed from a continent of hunter-gatherers to one of mainly pastoralists and mixed farmers, some of whom built civilizations of lasting renown.

Of these, the civilization that sprang up along the Nile Valley, in Egypt, about 5,100 years ago, is by far the best known, but the indigenous civilizations that appeared much later in the savannas and forests of West Africa and in the woodlands of south central Africa were also extraordinary. This chapter summarizes what is known of the hunter-gatherers of these regions, and traces their progressive replacement by pastoralists and mixed farmers.

This process began in the northeast between 7000 BC and 5000 BC, and culminated in the extreme south of the continent between the beginning of the first century AD and AD 200—and in some places even later, perhaps only after contact with Europeans.

Africa in 10,000 BC

In a strictly archaeological sense, Africa in 10,000 BC differed little from the Africa of many thousands of years before. People everywhere still lived by hunting various large mammals, by gathering wild plants, tortoises, and other ground game, and, wherever practical, by fishing and gathering food from the beaches. They did not make pottery or work metal, and their most conspicuous stone artifacts tended to be tiny (microlithic) pieces, often trimmed or backed (dulled) along one end or edge, mainly to facilitate hafting on wooden or bone handles or shafts. These small stone tools vary significantly from region to region, reflecting the existence of numerous local cultures or ethnic groups, each with its own distinct subsistence strategy, manufacturing or hafting technology, and style. At sites where bone is preserved, the stone artifacts are usually accompanied by points, awls, and other well-made bone implements, and by bone or shell beads and pendants. The bone and shell artifacts are broadly similar to much earlier ones, and their specific forms likewise vary from place to place, reflecting regional differences in culture.

Among the people who inhabited Africa at that time, none are better known or more typical than the Iberomaurusians (sometimes called the Oranians), who occupied the Northwest African coastal plain and its hinterland between northwestern Morocco and northeastern Tunisia. They appeared in this region about 16,000 years ago, or slightly before, after a long interval when Northwest Africa had been largely abandoned because of extreme aridity. The return of moister conditions is signaled by the pollens and animal remains recovered from Iberomaurusian sites, as well as by the Iberomaurusians themselves. Somewhat ironically, their successful adaptation to these conditions is most conspicuously reflected in their prolonged use of numerous cemeteries, some of which contain more than 100 skeletons.

Like most of their contemporaries in Africa (and elsewhere), the Iberomaurusians made a wide

Anthony Bannister/NHPA

The Bushmen of the Kalahari Desert, in southern Africa, are one of the few populations of hunter-gatherers found on the continent today. Here, a group of Bushmen are collecting wild berries.

A woman of the !Kung Bushman group of the Kalahari empties her apron of the mongongo nuts she has gathered.

variety of stone and bone artifacts. Their stone tools comprised numerous small, elongated backed blades or bladelets, including pointed ones that may have been used to tip arrows or other projectiles; larger retouched pieces, including many that were probably used to scrape skins; grindstones that may have been used to crush grass seeds; and perforated stone balls like those that some Africans in historic times attached as weights to pointed wooden digging sticks. Their bone tools include a range of carefully shaped pieces that probably served as punches, projectile points, hide burnishers, and knives. Among their personal ornaments were seashells and small stones, with carefully drilled holes.

Iberomaurusian sites often contain the bones of Barbary sheep, hartebeest, wild cattle, gazelles, zebra, and other large mammals that were hunted, together with the shells of land or marine gastropods (a class of mollusks, which includes snails) that were eaten. Although no plant remains other than charcoal and pollen have been found, the grindstones and what appear to be digging-stick weights suggest that these people also ate wild plants, as most hunter-gatherers living in comparable conditions in historic times are known to have done.

From about 8000 BC, the Iberomaurusians were succeeded locally by various "cultures", of which by far the best documented is the Capsian. Capsian people appear to have been physically different from the Iberomaurusians, and this may indicate that the Capsians migrated into the area, most probably from the east, bringing their culture with them. Their stone artifacts tend to be larger than those of the Iberomaurusians, endscrapers

and backed blades being particularly abundant. At least some Capsians also manufactured large numbers of geometric microliths—small chips of stone trimmed into triangles, crescent shapes, trapezoids, and other regular forms. They produced a remarkable range of bone artifacts, and are famous for their art, which includes stone figurines and engraved ostrich eggshells, as well as more commonplace bone or shell pendants, and beads. As evidenced by the large number of shells excavated from their sites, terrestrial snails formed a major part of their diet. Like the Iberomaurusians, they also hunted Barbary sheep and other large mammals, and ate wild plant foods. As well as grindstones and digging-stick weights, Capsian sites have yielded microliths that would have been mounted in bone or wooden handles and were used to cut wild grasses, as indicated by the distinctive "sickle sheen", or polish, on the surface of the stone that can still be seen today.

About 5000 BC, the range of Capsian artifacts was augmented by pottery and ground stone tools, and at about the same time the Capsians began to herd sheep and goats, while continuing to hunt wild animals. Neither sheep nor goats are indigenous to Africa, and their appearance at this time clearly points to pastoralism. It may be that domesticated grains were introduced at the same time, but even if these arrived a little later, 5000 BC marks an important turning point in Northwest African prehistory. From this time onwards, farming and herding progressively replaced hunting and gathering as the principal means of livelihood, and by Roman times the region was better known for its granaries than for its wildlife.

Traces of vegetable mastic (or resin) remain on this backed microlith from the rock shelter of Makwe, in eastern Zambia, close to the Mozambique border, showing how such tools were hafted.

⚱ An Early Khartoum potsherd with the characteristic decoration of wavy lines. Ceramic remains such as this are the oldest known pottery in Africa and are contemporary with the earliest pottery found in neighboring Southwest Asia.
ASHMOLEAN MUSEUM, OXFORD

➥ A Kalahari Bushman digs a springhare (*Pedetes capensis*) from its burrow with a stick. Springhares are fairly large, nocturnal rodents, which inhabit open, sandy country in eastern and southern Africa.

⚱ Bored stones, like these from Kalemba, in eastern Zambia, are frequently found at hunter-gatherer sites in southern Africa. Rock art confirms that the larger stones were used as digging-stick weights.
DAVID PHILLIPSON

➥ Barbed points from Early Holocene deposits at Lowasera, on the eastern shore of Lake Turkana, in Kenya. The people here lived mainly by fishing. Wavy-line pottery found at Lowasera is very similar to that found at Early Khartoum sites.

The Earliest African Herders and Farmers

Despite what historical and environmental considerations might suggest, the oldest known farming sites in Africa have been found not in the Nile Valley, or in some equally lush environment, but in the Sahara. The explanation for this is partly that the Sahara was not always as arid as it is now: between 10,000 BC and 4500 BC—or even later in some places—it was commonly much moister. While never truly wet, it was moist enough to support seasonal stands of grass and ephemeral lakes or ponds. Some time between 10,000 BC and 8000 BC, it was extensively, if sparsely, occupied by groups that resembled their Iberomaurusian contemporaries in Northwest Africa, both in the kinds of artifacts they made and in their hunting-gathering way of life.

PETER JOHNSON/NHPA

The southern Sahara seems to have been particularly attractive, and about 7000 BC it was settled by groups who lived by hunting antelopes and other large mammals, by gathering wild grasses and other plants, and, most notably, by fishing in the widely scattered lakes and streams. The sites occupied by these groups contain a rich range of artifacts, including large flaked "scrapers" or "adzes", backed microliths, upper and lower grindstones (known as manos and metates to New World archaeologists), perforated or drilled stone digging-stick weights, grooved stones that may have been net sinkers, barbed bone points that were surely harpoon heads, and, perhaps most striking, pottery decorated with a distinctive wavy line or dotted wavy line.

Broadly similar stone, bone, and pottery artifacts have been found at sites of a similar age in parts of East Africa, which also enjoyed a far higher rainfall at that time than they have in recent times. The pottery, which has been dubbed "Early Khartoum", after a site at Khartoum, on the Sudanese Nile, where it is found in abundance, is the oldest known pottery in Africa and, it would appear, as old as any in neighboring Southwest Asia. This may even mean that ceramic technology was independently developed in the Sahara or East Africa.

In Southwest Asia, pottery seems to have been invented and adopted by farming people who lived a settled, village-based existence. But even the richest Early Khartoum sites, including Early Khartoum itself, have provided no evidence of cultivated plants or herded animals. Until recently, it could have been argued that the appearance (or development) of pottery in Africa was not connected with the emergence of food production, but discoveries in the Western Desert of Egypt now suggest otherwise.

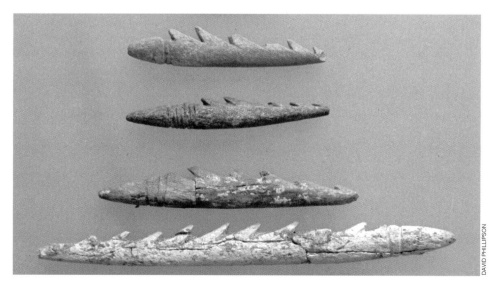

DAVID PHILLIPSON

GÖRAN BUREN-HULT

In the Western Desert, people who were making Early Khartoum-like pottery about 7000 BC lived in a harsher environment than most Early Khartoum people to the south and west, and they supplemented hunting, gathering, and fishing with cattle herding. (See the feature *The Use of Plants in the Sahara*.) By 6000 BC, these people were also cultivating barley, and may have added sheep or goats to their herds. The sheep and goats (these species cannot always be distinguished from their bones) surely originated in Southwest Asia, where their wild progenitors were domesticated some time between 9000 BC and 6000 BC. The cattle, however, may have been domesticated in North Africa, since wild cattle were widely distributed in the north in prehistoric times, and the earliest firm evidence of domesticated cattle elsewhere (in western Asia and southeastern Europe) dates from only about 6000 BC. The barley may also have been domesticated in North Africa, but is more likely to have come from Southwest Asia, where it was being cultivated by 7300 BC.

By 5000 BC, the herding of cattle, sheep, and goats, perhaps accompanied by cereal cultivation, appears to have been widespread throughout the Sahara, and it would probably have continued in the region for much longer if the climate had not started to become drier at about this time. This probably encouraged pastoralists to congregate around the relatively well-watered mountain massifs that dot the Sahara, and it may also have forced some to retreat progressively southwards into the savannas just south of the Sahara.

Possibly, the drying up of the Sahara or related climatic changes may also explain the rather sudden appearance of farming villages in the Egyptian Nile Valley between 5000 BC and 4500 BC. At this time, mixed farming based on wheat, barley, flax, sheep, goats, cattle, and pigs seems rapidly to have replaced pure hunting and gathering as the means of subsistence, and on the rich soils of the Nile floodplain, cultivation and animal husbandry allowed far larger populations to develop.

Initially, the farming villages were small and relatively simple, but as the population increased, some villages grew into towns, some of which in turn became the capitals of kingdoms vying for control of the Nile Valley. About 3150 BC, the rulers of one kingdom succeeded in unifying the entire valley north of Aswan—and Egyptian dynastic civilization was born.

♠ Tall stands of nerium grow along the shores of the partly water-filled Wadi Iherir, in Tassili n'Ajjer, southeastern Algeria. After about 5000 BC, the increasingly dry climate forced pastoral peoples of the Sahara to congregate in these relatively well-watered mountain massifs.

255

♔ A herd of Baggara goats at Musawwarat es-Sofra. The Arabic-speaking Baggara people are nomadic cattle owners who inhabit the dry savannas between the Nile and the Chad border, in Sudan. Goats and sheep are kept for their meat.

♌ These edge-ground stone axes are from the Neolithic site of Esh Shaheinab, on the eastern bank of the Nile, some 50 kilometers (30 miles) north of Khartoum, in Sudan. They date from about 4000 BC.
DAVID PHILLIPSON

Sub-Saharan Africa

Although herding, sometimes accompanied by cultivation, flourished in the Sahara and other parts of northern Africa before 5000 BC, neither herding nor cultivation seems to have spread southwards at any speed. In West Africa, the appearance of pottery and of ground stone axes or hoes between 5000 BC and 4000 BC may indicate that pastoralists or farmers were present, but so far, domestic animals are well documented only from 2500 BC onwards, and domestic plants only from about 1200 BC. Herding apparently became established in East Africa about 4000 BC, when the inhabitants of the central Sudan started to herd cattle, sheep, and goats while continuing to hunt wild mammals and fish on a large scale.

The early Sudanese herders possessed pottery, backed microliths, barbed harpoon heads of bone, and other objects that could well have been derived from local, Early Khartoum prototypes, together with ground stone axes, amulets of foreign stone, and types of pottery that indicate influences from far to the north or northwest. These herders relied heavily on sorghum and millet, possibly gathered wild rather than cultivated. Further east and south, in present-day Ethiopia, Kenya, and northern Tanzania, pastoralism—again, it would appear, without domesticated plants—seems not to have become well established until about 2500 BC. Even further south, there is no evidence of pastoralists or farmers before the beginning of the first century AD.

Among the early sub-Saharan pastoralists, none are better studied than the so-called Pastoral Neolithic peoples who appeared in the highlands of southern Kenya and northern Tanzania about 2500 BC, or perhaps a little earlier. Bones of cattle, along with those of sheep and/or goats, are found at most Pastoral Neolithic sites, but they are sometimes significantly outnumbered by the remains of wildebeest, zebra, gazelles, and other wild species. This is often the case at earlier Pastoral Neolithic sites in particular—those dated as earlier than 1000 BC—suggesting that herding may initially have supplemented hunting and gathering in a fairly minor way and that it only later took over as the main means of subsistence.

There is no unequivocal evidence that any Pastoral Neolithic people ever cultivated plants, but like herder-gatherers throughout sub-Saharan Africa in historic times, they almost certainly relied heavily on wild plant foods. Some later Pastoral Neolithic sites contain traces of comparatively substantial structures, which may mean that the people had settled in these localities or, what seems more likely, that they were extremely regular in their movements and often returned to the same place year after year. The predominance of bones of animals of breeding age at some later sites may indicate that herds were kept mainly to provide milk and blood products, like those consumed by many East African pastoralists in historic times. The latter rarely slaughtered immature animals, since the milk and blood these would provide when they were fully grown more than offset their own needs for milk and pasture.

The artifacts made by Pastoral Neolithic peoples include skillfully shaped obsidian flakes and blades, a remarkable range of pottery, and carefully crafted ground stone bowls and platters that are especially associated with grave sites. These stone bowls are so conspicuous and distinctive that the Pastoral Neolithic was originally called the Stone Bowl culture. About AD 700, or perhaps a little earlier, Pastoral Neolithic populations were replaced or absorbed by pastoralists who knew how to work iron. These people may have been ancestors of the Masai and other similar East African herding peoples known in historic times.

SOME MAJOR LATE PLEISTOCENE AND HOLOCENE SITES

The sites mentioned in the text are shown, together with some other important sites dating from these periods.
CARTOGRAPHY: RAY SIM

DAVID PHILLIPSON

⬥ A sherd of Bambata ware from southwestern Zimbabwe, dated to about 200 BC. Pottery of this type may be associated with the earliest evidence of herding in southern Africa.
DAVID PHILLIPSON

◀⊙ An example of Nderit ware from Stable's Drift, southern Kenya. Nderit ware is probably the oldest pottery made by East African Pastoral Neolithic people. As well as being decorated on the outside, the vessel is deeply scored on the inside.

CARTOGRAPHY: RAY SIM, AFTER D.W. PHILLIPSON (1985): *AFRICAN ARCHAEOLOGY*, CAMBRIDGE UNIVERSITY PRESS, CAMBRIDGE, P. 114.

PROBABLE AREAS OF DOMESTICATION OF INDIGENOUS AFRICAN CROPS

Most crops were grown near the areas where they were first domesticated, but sorghum and millet became staples throughout much of the continent.

- Yams
- African rice
- Sorghum
- Bulrush millet
- Teff
- Finger millet
- Fonio
- Peanuts
- Ensete and noog
- Bulrush millet, teff, ensete, and noog

↪ This iron blade from Muteshti, in Zambia, dates from shortly after the beginning of the Christian era, when iron-working became common over wide areas of south central Africa.
DAVID PHILLIPSON

Speculation continues as to the reasons for the late and relatively slow southward spread of pastoralism in Africa, but they may include both natural and cultural factors. Although the Ancient Egyptians and, perhaps, other groups attempted to domesticate gazelles, oryxes, and other hoofed animals found in Africa, only one—the donkey or ass—ever became important economically, and it was used mainly for draft in or near the drier parts of Northeast Africa, where its wild ancestor lived. Otherwise, pastoralism in Africa, as in most other parts of the world, centered on cattle, sheep, and goats, which were not indigenous to sub-Saharan Africa and which may at first have been poorly suited to tropical African environments.

Perhaps it was only after an interval during which new breeds were developed that economies based on the herding of cattle, sheep, and goats could compete effectively with entrenched hunter-gatherer traditions in equatorial East and West Africa. Competition may have been especially difficult under the relatively moist conditions that prevailed before 5000 BC, when it seems likely that the tsetse fly—which devastated African herds into the present century—may have ranged much further to the north and west.

Cultivation appears to have spread southwards even more slowly than pastoralism, probably at least in part because it required the domestication of indigenous plants. The principal crops on which early North African farmers depended—barley and wheat—could not be grown in tropical Africa, except in some relatively isolated highland areas. African cultivators solved this problem by domesticating a wide variety of sub-Saharan plants, of which the most important for the subcontinent as a whole

N. COHEN/COMSTOCK

are certainly sorghum and varous kinds of millet. It is difficult to document the process of plant domestication, partly because identifiable plant remains are not preserved in many archaeological sites; partly because the earliest domestic millets, sorghum, and other crops would in any case have closely resembled their wild ancestors; and partly because relatively few relevant sites have been excavated.

While the oldest date we have for a variety of millet is 1200 BC, and that for sorghum is about the beginning of the first century AD, it may be that these grains, along with other important crops, such as African rice, yams, and peanuts, were first cultivated long before this. What is clear is that

☝ A traditional container from eastern Nigeria for storing yams. Yams were one of the most important crops in precolonial Africa, but their domestication in prehistoric times has not been documented.

◂ A wooden spade and pitch-fork used to cultivate and process millet in Ethiopia. Millet became a staple of farming peoples throughout much of sub-Saharan Africa during the Christian era.

☝ About 6000 BC, barley, together with wheat, was introduced to northeastern Africa from Southwest Asia. It spread along the Mediterranean coast and down the Nile Valley to Sudan and Ethiopia, but was not cultivated in the tropics, where the climate was unfavorable.

whenever various African plants were domesticated, plant cultivation was largely, if not entirely, restricted to the northwestern and northeastern parts of sub-Saharan Africa until between 500 BC and 300 BC. At about that time, some West Africans who relied on cattle and sheep, as well as on domesticated millet, sorghum, and, perhaps, other crops, acquired the technique of iron-smelting, probably from North Africa, where it had been introduced about 800 BC. Armed with iron implements for felling trees and tilling the soil, and with iron weapons for subduing enemies, these people were able to carry their mixed farming way of life to places where before it had been impractical or successfully resisted.

Iron-aided mixed farming swept rapidly through the savannas bordering the central African rainforest, reaching the Great Lakes region of East Africa by the beginning of the first century AD, and the extreme southeastern tip of Africa no more than two or three centuries later. Almost everywhere, this type of farming tended to supplant or incorporate economies and societies based simply on herding or hunting and gathering. Its spread was halted only where climatic conditions were totally unsuitable, as in the deep tropical rainforest of central Africa and at the southwestern corner of the continent, where rainfall was insufficient or fell during the winter, the wrong season for indigenous African crops.

THE USE OF PLANTS IN THE SAHARA

FRED WENDORF, ANGELA E. CLOSE, AND ROMUALD SCHILD

🔾 Carbonized plant remains were recovered from ash deposits surrounding potholes in the floor of an 8,000-year-old house at Nabta Playa, in Egypt.

🔾 A 5,500-year-old grinding stone at the Stone Age settlement of Iheren, on the Iherir Plateau, in Tassili n'Ajjer, provides a reminder of the Sahara's verdant past. As humus does not form in the desert, Stone Age relics are often found exposed on the surface.

The eastern Sahara was without rain from before 70,000 years ago until about 11,000 years ago. At some time between 12,000 and 11,000 years ago, there was a northward shift of the summer monsoon system, and seasonal rainfall returned. Except for brief periods of aridity lasting no more than a century or two, rainfall continued until about 3400 BC, when the modern period of aridity began. Estimates of the rainfall during this period range between 50 and 200 millimeters (2 and 8 inches) per year, so even during the "wet" periods, the eastern Sahara was still a desert.

Between about 8000 BC and 3000 BC, people lived in the eastern Sahara, the earliest sites probably being short-term camps of cattle herders, who most probably came from the Nile Valley and made forays westwards to exploit the grasslands that flourished in the Sahara after the summer rains. After about 6200 BC, organized villages became established, with rows of houses and storage pits, and several sites had large, deep, walk-in wells. Cattle were still herded, although

most meat was obtained by hunting gazelles and hares, and a considerable quantity of wild plant food was collected.

The Site of Nabta Playa

Plant food remains have been recovered from several sites dating to between 7000 BC and 5400 BC, the most extensive collections coming from houses and pits at a site found partly buried under silt and clay at Nabta Playa, one of the largest erosional basins in the Sahara, about 100 kilometers (60 miles) west of Abu Simbel. With the onset of rains, temporary lakes, known as playas, would form in these basins.

At Nabta Playa, there are traces of hearths on the floors of the houses, and small hemispherical depressions, or potholes, had also been dug in the floors. Half of one house alone had at least 74 such potholes. Brown, ashy sediments had piled up around the rims of some of the potholes, and this sediment was rich in plant remains. Probably, containers of food had been placed in the potholes, and hot ash (the brown sediment) piled up around them in order to cook the food. The contents had sometimes boiled over or fallen into the ash, eventually carbonizing and thus being preserved.

A wide range of plants has been identified, the collection being dominated by *Zizyphus* stones, grass grains, legume seeds, and what appear to be seeds of the mustard and caper families. (*Zizyphus* fruits grow on a small tree or bush and are still eaten today in Egypt and elsewhere in North Africa.) Clearly, the local vegetation was varied and, in some seasons, fairly luxuriant. Sedges and some grasses that favor wet habitats grew around the lake; a more restricted range of vegetation,

including *Zizyphus* trees and perennial grasses, grew where surface or ground water was available for most of the year; and annual grasses developed after the summer rains.

All the plants in the collection are members of the natural sub-desertic (also known as the Sahelian) flora. The sorghums and millets are morphologically wild, but sorghum and millet were probably first cultivated in the African Sahelian zone. Chemical comparisons with modern wild and domestic sorghums suggest that the Nabta sorghum may have been cultivated.

A Wide Variety of Plants

Certain plant varieties were found to be associated with particular potholes. Some potholes yielded predominantly legumes (sometimes one variety, sometimes several); some yielded grasses (including sorghums and millets); some crucifers, cucurbits, sedges, or varieties of borage; some *Zizyphus* fruits; and some yielded mixtures in differing proportions. Altogether, the people of Nabta were collecting and eating at least 44 different kinds of plants.

The fact that specific plant food remains were found in individual potholes, together with the large number of potholes, suggests that each hole was probably used only once or, in some instances, several times. Probably, the food remains result from a series of very short stays of a few weeks, or even a few days. These discoveries have shown, in some detail, the way in which Neolithic plant gatherers exploited the Holocene environment in the Egyptian Sahara, how they used what was seasonally available, what they chose to eat from what was available, and the ways in which they combined various plant foods.

🔾 A trench cut through the Early Neolithic site at Nabta Playa exposed several house floors and large storage pits.

RICHARD G. KLEIN

☝ The mouth of Die Kelders Cave, on the Indian Ocean, about 120 kilometers (75 miles) southeast of Cape Town. The Later Stone Age deposits at this cave show that pottery and sheep herding reached the southern tip of Africa between the first and fourth centuries AD. The herders continued to hunt and gather extensively, and they made essentially the same kinds of stone and bone artifacts as their hunter-gatherer predecessors.

DAVID PHILLIPSON

☝ The pastoral Khoikhoi people of southwestern Africa made pots like this, the inset lugs serving as handles. The history of these people can be traced to at least AD 400, when sheep and cattle herders with characteristic Khoikhoi pottery spread widely along the western and southern coasts of the Cape Province of South Africa.

↪ A female bushbuck (*Tragelaphus scriptus*) in Hwange National Park, Zimbabwe. The appearance of bones of this and other forest-dwelling species at cave sites in southern Africa at the end of the last Ice Age reflects a considerable change in vegetation and the food supply available to humans.

Southern Africa:
The Last Hunter-gatherers

People in southern Africa continued an exclusively hunting-gathering way of life for much longer than anywhere else on the continent. While herders or mixed farmers were widely established in North Africa by 5000 BC and in East (and probably West) Africa by 2500 BC, herding and mixed farming did not appear in southern Africa until between the beginning of the first century AD and AD 200. At this time, Iron Age mixed farmers swept rapidly southwards through the moister eastern third of southern Africa, replacing or absorbing Stone Age hunter-gatherers. At much the same time, Stone Age pastoralists, with their herds of sheep and cattle, spread through the western and southern coastal regions, where summer rainfall was inadequate for indigenous Iron Age crops such as sorghum and millet.

These pastoralists used pottery, but no iron or other metals, and both physically and culturally (as reflected by the types of artifacts they made) they resembled their hunter-gatherer predecessors more than they did their Iron Age contemporaries, continuing to rely heavily on hunting and gathering. While they probably spread in response to the Iron Age diaspora, they may have absorbed rather than replaced many previous hunter-gatherers, and some hunter-gatherers may simply have grafted herding onto their established way of life.

This was the situation that prevailed in southern Africa at the time of European contact, which began with Bartholomeu Diaz's epoch-making voyage around the Cape of Good Hope from AD 1487 to AD 1488. Subsequent European travelers and explorers found Stone Age pastoralists, whom they called "Hottentots" or Khoikhoi, in the south and west; Bantu-speaking, Iron Age

mixed farmers in the east; and surviving bands of hunter-gatherers, whom they called "Bushmen" or San, in the remote mountains and the very dry regions of the interior—and assumed it had always been thus.

The Stone Age of southern Africa is unique not only because it lasted so long, but also because we are able to interpret archaeological finds in the light of historical records going back to the end of the fifteenth century. The observations of early Europeans have proved useful in deducing the functions of many types of artifacts found in prehistoric sites throughout Africa. They have also provided a record of practices, such as the collection of particular plants and insects, that were probably important in prehistoric times but that would be difficult, if not impossible, to infer from the archaeological record. In addition, a long tradition of archaeological research in southern Africa, beginning in the 1860s, combined with the presence of many rich sites, has resulted in an unusually detailed record of interrelated cultural and environmental change from 10,000 BC to the present.

Nowhere did the climatic and environmental changes that occurred at the end of the last Ice Age affect human populations more than in southern Africa, where broad expanses of coastal plain were drowned by the rising sea, and large areas that had been open grassland were transformed into bush and forest. One result of the changing coastline was that caves that had previously been up to 80 kilometers (50 miles) from the sea were now within walking distance of it. Reflecting this change in the food supply, these cave sites have yielded abundant remains of shellfish, fish, seals, and sea birds in addition to the bones of antelopes, tortoises, and other terrestrial game. Reflecting the change in the vegetation, grassland creatures such as wildebeest, bontebok, hartebeest, springbok, wart hog, and zebra were replaced by bush or forest species such as bushbuck, bushpig, and a type of small antelope known as the gray duiker.

The extent and relative speed of the change in vegetation may partly explain why some grassland species—including a huge, long-horned buffalo

ANTHONY BANNISTER/NHPA

(*Pelorovis antiquus*), a giant relative of the wildebeest and hartebeest (*Megalotragus priscus*), and a comparably large species of zebra (*Equus capensis*)—apparently disappeared from southern Africa around that time. This cannot be the sole explanation, however, since the same species survived a similar change during the transition from the previous glaciation to the last interglacial period, about 130,000 years ago. The explanation is probably to be found in the kind of hunter-gatherers who were present in 10,000 BC. These were so-called Later Stone Age people, who replaced Middle Stone Age populations between 50,000 and 40,000 years ago. It was Middle Stone

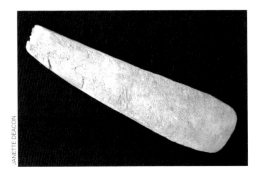

Age people who occupied southern Africa 130,000 years ago. Unlike their Later Stone Age successors, they do not seem to have used bone, ivory, or shell to make artifacts, and produced no known art or personal ornaments. They made a small range of stone artifacts, but none of the microlithic items for which Later Stone Age peoples are justly famous. What is perhaps most significant, they did not make any bone or stone objects that could be associated with the use of bows and arrows, such as are found in Later Stone Age sites from at least 10,000 BC.

Using the bow and arrow, Later Stone Age people were able to kill dangerous game, such as buffalo and wild pigs, far more often than their Middle Stone Age predecessors. With other advances in technology, such as bone gorges (double-pointed bone slivers the size of a toothpick, which could be baited and tied to a line) and net sinkers, they also became the first people to fish and hunt fowl on a large scale. This is probably why Later Stone Age populations were much larger and denser than their predecessors, as shown by the fact that Later Stone Age sites are much more numerous per unit of time, and by the small average size of the tortoises and shellfish they contain. The much larger size of these species in Middle Stone Age sites almost certainly indicates that Middle Stone Age people exploited them much less intensively, probably because there were fewer people at this time. Considering all the available information, it seems probable that Later Stone Age hunters contributed to the extinction of some prominent big-game species simply by continuing to hunt big game at a time when the game supply was rapidly being depleted by environmental changes.

These fragments of ostrich eggshell decorated with incised patterns, from the Later Stone Age culture known as Robberg, in South Africa, are between 14,000 and 12,000 years old. The largest is just over a centimeter (half an inch) wide.
JANETTE DEACON

A polished bone tool about 15 centimeters (6 inches) long, from the Albany culture in the southern part of Cape Province, South Africa, dating to about 8000 BC.

These bone gorges made by people of the Albany culture, dating to about 8000 BC, were possibly used for fishing. Consisting of slivers of bone, polished and pointed at both ends, they are 2 to 3 centimeters (about 1 inch) long.

Also made by the Albany people, these two hollow bone tubes with spiral grooving and the two flat bone pendants date to between 9000 BC and 7000 BC. The larger pendant is about 2.5 centimeters (1 inch) long.

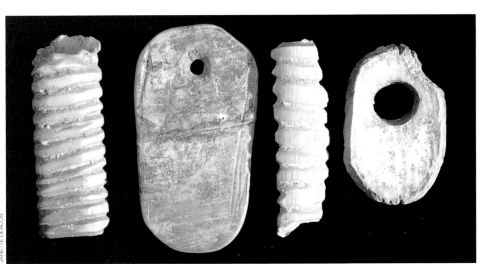

These ornaments made from seashells, dating from about 3000 BC, are from the Wilton culture, which widely replaced the Albany culture between 7000 BC and 6000 BC.
JANETTE DEACON

Stone blades such as this, about 1 centimeter (half an inch) long, were blunted, or "backed", along the curved edge and sharp along the straight edge. They were made in small numbers by the Robberg people, from 18,000 to 12,000 years ago, and in larger quantities by the Wilton people, between 5000 BC and 2000 BC. They were hafted for use as arrowheads and for cutting purposes.
JANETTE DEACON

These ostrich eggshell "buttons", about 1 centimeter (half an inch) across, were made by people of the Wilton culture about the first century AD.

The Later Stone Age people who occupied much of southern Africa in 10,000 BC are known as the Robberg people, after a locality on the south central (Indian Ocean) coast where their artifacts and food debris have been especially well described. At that time, or shortly afterwards, the Robberg culture was replaced by the Albany culture (also known as the Oakhurst, or Smithfield A, culture). Unlike their Robberg predecessors, Albany people seem to have made few, if any, microlithic tools. They did, however, make an unusual range of well-crafted bone artifacts, which may have been better suited to hunting and gathering in the bushier environments that developed in the postglacial period.

Between 7000 BC and 6000 BC, the Albany culture was widely replaced by the most famous of all Later Stone Age cultures in southern Africa—the Wilton, named after a site in the eastern part of Cape Province, in South Africa. Wilton people manufactured large numbers of

tiny convex stone scrapers and crescents (also called segments), the latter backed along the thick edge, together with larger, less formal, flaked stone tools; upper and lower grindstones; bored stones that appear to be digging-stick weights; points, awls, and other standardized bone artifacts; and a range of pendants, beads, and other objects that were probably ornaments.

The surviving food debris consists mainly of bones of small antelopes, hyraxes, tortoises, and other ground game, but at sites where conditions favor preservation, large numbers of plant remains have also been recovered. The most conspicuous plant species are members of the iris family, which the people of this region were noted to have been exploiting heavily at the time of European contact. Taken together with such evidence from the historical record, the plant remains at Wilton sites serve as a potent reminder that archaeologists have sometimes exaggerated the importance of hunting versus gathering in prehistoric times, simply because animal bones are more commonly preserved than plant tissues. In fact, it is likely that plants formed a major, possibly the predominant, part of the diet of all prehistoric hunter-gatherers in Africa, including people such as the Robberg, whose sites are especially rich in the bones of big-game animals.

Wilton people were living in southern Africa when Iron Age mixed farmers seized the eastern

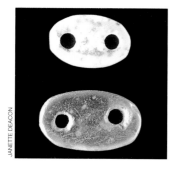

JANETTE DEACON

Small stone scrapers were hafted on bone or wooden handles by means of mastic and used to work skins. They are frequently found in Wilton sites, between 5000 BC and the first century AD.

JANETTE DEACON

ANTHONY BANNISTER/NHPA

third of this region and Stone Age pastoralists spread along its western and southern coasts between the beginning of the first century AD and AD 200. Iron Age mixed farming all but destroyed Wilton-style hunting and gathering, whereas the herding of cattle and sheep supplemented rather than replaced this way of life.

Pastoralism succeeded because it supported larger human populations than pure hunting and gathering, but southern African pastoralists continued to hunt and forage on a large scale, and their sites are commonly dominated by the bones of indigenous animals. In part, these people planned their movements to take advantage of the seasonal availability of different plants and animals. Their thriving culture was noted by early European visitors, and it was primarily to trade European goods for local sheep and cattle (to provision passing ships) that the Dutch East India Company established the first permanent European settlement in southern Africa, at what is now Cape Town, in 1652.

Unfortunately, this settlement rapidly changed from a trading post to a staging point for European colonists who brought crops such as wheat and barley that could grow where only

pastoralism had been practicable before, and who also introduced firearms and epidemic diseases that rapidly reduced the native population. The indigenous pastoralist culture disintegrated, and had all but ceased to exist by 1750. Individual pastoralists survived, but only as clients or servants of the Europeans, and the native pastoralist languages were largely lost. By 1850, European incursions into the southern African interior had similarly eradicated or displaced the last surviving Stone Age hunter-gatherers. People continued the hunting-gathering way of life in the Kalahari Desert and in some other marginal environments, but came increasingly to rely on introduced Iron Age or European technology for their subsistence, and they have shown a remarkable willingness to grow crops or tend animals when circumstances permit. Very likely, the people of this region have combined food production with hunting and gathering for various periods over the centuries, and it now seems unlikely that any southern African people known from recent times can be regarded as largely unaltered survivors of the hunting-gathering populations that dominated the subcontinent until 2,000 years ago.

⚭ These !Kung Bushmen are cutting up tsama melons, a wild species of gourd which is an important staple for many Kalahari hunter-gatherers.

F. JACKSON/ROBERT HARDING PICTURE LIBRARY

⚭ People of the Peuhl tribe, from the Falingé region, in Niger, herding their long-horned cattle. Cattle were an important symbol of wealth among African Iron Age people, and probably also among many of their prehistoric Stone Age predecessors.

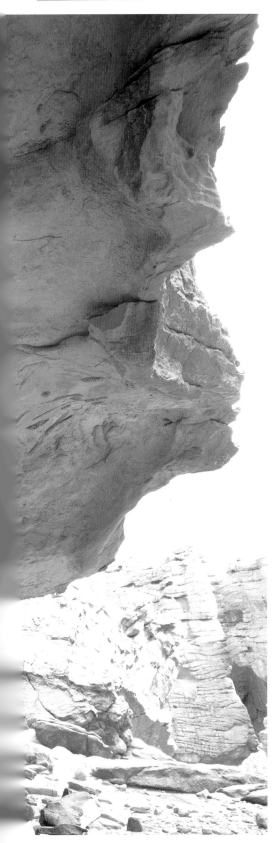

Art of the African Stone Age

No summary of African Stone Age prehistory from 10,000 BC would be complete without some mention of the art. People were clearly creating art, both portable and mural, long before that time. Painted rock slabs from excavation levels dated between 27,500 and 19,500 years ago at Apollo II Cave, in Namibia, may be the oldest paintings so far found anywhere in the world. A few later African cave sites, all more recent than 10,000 BC, have yielded painted or engraved stones buried in the ground, but throughout Africa, the art that is most abundant and most famous is in the form of paintings and engravings on exposed rock surfaces. In general, this rock art cannot be reliably dated, but the very fact that it has survived despite the harsh climatic conditions suggests that most of it is no more than a few thousand years old. Some, however—most probably the paintings of elephants, giraffes, and other sub-Saharan species on Saharan rock surfaces—may be much older.

While the style or subject matter of some paintings implies that the artists were Iron Age people, many others would appear to have been painted by Stone Age pastoralists or hunter-gatherers. It seems reasonable to assume that paintings showing herders and cattle were produced mainly by pastoralists, while many paintings depicting wild species only were probably produced by hunter-gatherers. Paintings with pastoralist themes are relatively much more common in North Africa than in southern Africa, where pastoralism appeared far later. In some remote mountain ranges of southern Africa, there are paintings depicting domestic horses, wagons, and even a mid-seventeenth-century galleon. Stylistically, these paintings resemble the paintings that portray indigenous animals or people, but their subject matter indicates a date between the seventeenth and mid-nineteenth centuries AD. The artists must have been among the last African Stone Age people to practice their age-old craft.

What motivated people to produce rock art has been a matter of intense debate among archaeologists and cultural historians, and no agreement is in sight. At different times and places, the art may have functioned to enhance hunting or herding success, to celebrate rites of passage (births, deaths, or the transition to adulthood), or to mark the territories of particular groups. Much of it, particularly in southern Africa, may have been produced by folk-doctors, or shamans, as they attempted to reproduce their experiences when in a state of trance. Based on what is known of such communities in historic times, perhaps the only firm conclusion that can be drawn is that little of the art was produced for its own sake. Almost certainly, most of it was motivated by social, economic, or religious concerns that varied somewhat from culture to culture. But even if the purpose of the art remains poorly understood, its aesthetic appeal is enduring, and it is an especially poignant reminder of Africa's Stone Age past.

Rock engravings of animals at Twyfelfontein, in Namibia.
MARY JELLIFFE/ANCIENT ART & ARCHITECTURE COLLECTION

The Stone Age hunter-pastoralists who occupied the Sahara between 8000 BC and 3000 BC often painted or engraved on exposed rock surfaces. An archer poised on a sandstone surface in Tassili n'Ajjer, in present-day Libya, is a superb example.

Herds of animals on a rock wall in Tassili n'Ajjer, central Sahara.
JAMES WELLARD/SONIA HALLIDAY PHOTOGRAPHS

ROCK ART IN THE CENTRAL SAHARA

GÖRAN BURENHULT

⚘ The Stone Age *abri* settlement and rock art site of Iheren. The strange rock formations of the isolated Iherir Plateau, in the mountain massif of Tassili n'Ajjer, southeastern Algeria, shelter some of the Sahara's most exquisite art treasures.

♀ The Iheren frieze, on the Iherir Plateau, includes a number of vivid scenes, the most spectacular being the portrayal of a lion hunt. With their spears raised, three men with elaborate hairstyles or wigs approach a lion that has attacked a sheep.

THE HEAT VIBRATES in the air between the black walls of rock, but everything is peaceful and silent—relentlessly silent. The sun's dazzling rays shine from a cloudless sky over the ocean of sand and the mountain formations, and the shadows become short and as black as night. Not a green shoot can be seen, and no breath of wind cools the dry landscape. It is hard to imagine that anything has ever been able to live here, least of all human beings.

Yet the rocks swarm with life. If you crawl into the shade under a rock shelter and let your eyes become accustomed to the darkness, you will encounter an amazing world made up of thousands of vivid images of human beings and animals. This treasure-trove of pictures, thousands of years old, lies in the heart of the Sahara, 10 days' journey from the Mediterranean coast, in a four-wheel drive, through an expanse of sterile desert that was once a region of streaming water and lush vegetation.

Rivers and Lakes

Traces of these very different climatic conditions are many and obvious. Innumerable wadis (dry water-courses) run from the mountain regions out towards the plains that were once dotted with lakes, on whose shores lived many varieties of plants and animals. In most valleys, the vegetation consisted mainly of cedars, cypresses, oaks, and walnut trees, and there were also tamarisks and acacias—species that still grow in the mountain regions of the central Sahara, particularly in Tassili n'Ajjer.

Between 9000 BC and 3000 BC, the Sahara was a very favorable place to live, both for food producers and hunter-gatherers, and there is hardly a place in the region that does not bear traces of their activities. Pottery and stone tools, grinding stones, hearths, graves, and rock art are found everywhere, and as humus does not form in the desert, these Stone Age relics are often exposed on the surface.

The earliest art may date to the final stage of the Upper Paleolithic period, before 9000 BC, when big-game hunters made monumental rock carvings in most mountain regions of the Sahara. Their carvings depict a great variety of plants and animals that disappeared from the area long ago: antelopes, buffalos, giraffes, elephants, lions, and hippopotamuses. This period was once named the Bubalus period, after the now-extinct giant buffalo, *Bubalus antiquus*, which is often featured in these carvings.

About 8000 BC, paintings—again, often very large—began to appear on rocks. The bearers of this art tradition were mainly negroid hunter-gatherers, but common finds of grinding stones show that they were becoming increasingly dependent on the gathering of wild seeds. About this time, pottery was first made in the central parts of the present-day desert area.

A Wealth of Detail

It seems likely that there was a food crisis during a period of drought about 6000 BC, which may have led to the domestication of indigenous

GÖRAN BURENHULT

animals. The dark-skinned African herders of the region were the descendants of earlier hunter-gatherers, and their cattle were short-horned. At a later stage, long-horned cattle were introduced by light-skinned immigrants from the east, people who today are found in the Sudan and Ethiopia. At the same time, sheep and goat herders were spreading southwards from the Mediterranean coastal areas.

The rock art these herders produced, between 6000 BC and 2000 BC, represents the high point of this art form in the Sahara. The rocks are covered with scenes of remarkable liveliness that abound in humans and animals rendered in splendid colors. The humans are always depicted in action, and often in groups: hunting, fighting,

dancing, or riding cattle. The paintings are extremely elegant, and rich in such details as masks, wigs, costumes, body decorations, and tattoos.

From about 2000 BC, the increasingly dry climate of the Sahara gradually drove out these cattle herders. Today, these pastoral cultures are found mainly in the southerly border areas of the Sahara: the Sudan, Chad, Niger, Mali, and Burkina Fasso. But in the intervening period, there were two more distinct phases of rock art.

Between 1500 BC and 100 BC, horses were used for transport through the Sahara, and along the routes they followed are found paintings from this period depicting mounted riders and two-wheeled carts.

The final period of rock art, which began about 100 BC and is characterized by early Tuareg script and images of camels, shows the desert as it is today. Overgrazing, first by cattle and then by goats and sheep, accelerated the natural process of desertification, and now all that is left to bear witness to a period of teeming life are the grinding stones that lie exposed on the surface, amid the silence and the trembling heat, and the rock picture galleries with their multitude of vivid images.

⟴ This elegant portrayal of a dancing male figure with elaborate body painting is at the site of Tadjelamin. The other two images, one of which represents a female figure dressed in a puffy robe, may be part of the same dance scene.

⟴ A group of giraffes painted on a rock wall in the central part of the settlement of Tin Abaniora, on the Iherir Plateau, Tassili n'Ajjer.

GÖRAN BURENHULT

STONE AGE HUNTER-GATHERERS AND FARMERS IN EUROPE

1 0 , 0 0 0   B C   –   3 0 0 0   B C

From Forager to Food Producer

PETER ROWLEY-CONWY

THE LAST ICE AGE reached its peak about 18,000 years ago. At this time, ice sheets covered most of Britain and Scandinavia, the Alps, the Pyrenees, and many smaller mountain ranges throughout Europe. Much of the rest of Europe, away from the Mediterranean, was covered by treeless tundra vegetation. The most common large animal in these tundra regions was the reindeer, but red deer, aurochs (wild cattle), bison, and horses were also to be found, in smaller numbers. Humans, during this period, were largely confined to southwestern France, the Italian and Iberian peninsulas, and parts of central and eastern Europe, away from the glaciers.

Some time after about 15,000 years ago, the climate began to grow warmer, culminating in a fairly warm spell before another, and final, period of intense cold set in 13,000 years ago. The end of the last Ice Age is put at 11,500 years ago, when temperatures rapidly increased to about their present levels.

◄● Skara Brae is an early farming village in the Orkney Islands, off northern Scotland. Shortly before 2500 BC, it was covered by a sand dune, which preserved most of the village intact.

⊕ A bone comb found in the Late Mesolithic shell midden at Meilgård, in Denmark. Archaeologists will never be able to reconstruct such things as hairstyles, but finds of this sort suggest that hunter-gatherers who lived thousands of years ago had a similar interest in personal display to modern peoples.
NATIONAL MUSEUM OF DENMARK

⚱ This stone statue, carved by hunter-gatherers at Lepenski Vir, in Serbia, is one of the earliest pieces of monumental art known in Europe.
MARIJA GIMBUTAS

↪ Bog sites provide excellent conditions of preservation for otherwise perishable items, such as this fishtrap made of withies, which was lost by prehistoric fishers at Lille Knabstrup, in Denmark, some time between 4000 BC and 5000 BC.

The most sensitive indicators of temperature we have are insects. Different species can tolerate different temperatures, and insects are able to migrate to newly habitable lands very rapidly after climatic changes, so their preserved remains are a good guide to climatic conditions of the past. In southern England, for example, insect remains dated to 11,500 years ago show that average July temperatures increased from 9 to 17 degrees Celsius (48 to 63 degrees Fahrenheit) in little more than a century. There have been climatic changes since, but none to compare with this.

Not surprisingly, the result of this global warming was massive ecological change. Trees spread north into the tundra—some much faster than others, as we know from studies of preserved pollen grains. (Trees emit huge numbers of pollen grains. These are preserved in waterlogged areas, and the plant family or species to which they belong can be identified under a microscope. As the layers build up, changing proportions of pollen provide a history of the vegetation.) The first postglacial forests of central and northern Europe were largely of birch, a species that originated north of the Alps and is a fast colonizer. Pine followed, then hazel, and finally the main forest trees—oak, ash, lime, and elm—which slowly spread northwards from their Italian and Iberian glacial refuges. Land mammals similarly moved north, reindeer migrating as far as Scandinavia, where they are still found today. Red deer and wild cattle became more numerous, and were joined by such true forest animals as elk (known as moose in North America), roe deer, and wild boar.

At the same time, another major change was taking place. When the last Ice Age was at its coldest, so much water was landlocked in the form of glaciers that the sea level was more than 100 meters (330 feet) lower than it is today. Ireland and Britain were joined to continental Europe, and much of the area now covered by the North Sea, the Bay of Biscay, the Adriatic, and seas in other parts of the world was dry land. As the glaciers melted, the sea level rose rapidly. This continued throughout the earlier part of the postglacial period, with the result that many low-lying areas were inundated. Britain, for example, was separated from Europe about 7500 BC.

This was the rapidly changing environment to which the inhabitants of Europe had to adapt. The period between the end of the Ice Age and the first appearance of farming in Europe is usually termed the Mesolithic. During this period, groups of people spread northwards into previously unoccupied areas, learning to cope with dramatically different conditions of life in terms of climate, vegetation, and resources.

New Sources of Evidence

Archaeologists will rarely admit to having enough evidence, but the Mesolithic period does have some advantages over preceding periods in terms of the amount of evidence that has survived. Like their predecessors, Mesolithic people were hunters and gatherers and made use of caves and open-air camp sites. But thanks to the warmer climate of Mesolithic times, two new sources of archaeological evidence have come down to us in the form of bog sites and shell middens. Each of these has added immensely to our understanding of the period.

Bog sites can preserve objects spectacularly well. Since the end of the Ice Age, many lakes have gradually filled up with peat, a type of soil formed by partly decomposed vegetation. Early people living on lake shores often threw their rubbish into the water, and as the peat built up

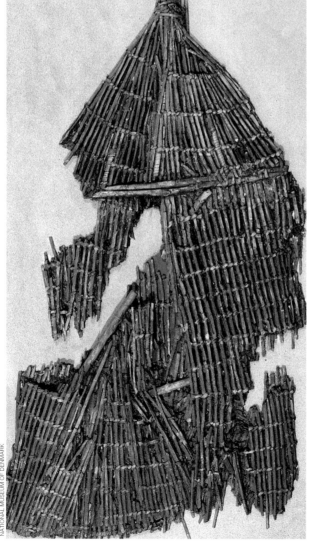

NATIONAL MUSEUM OF DENMARK

and covered the rubbish, all kinds of objects were preserved in the wet, anoxic conditions. Without oxygen, the microbes that normally attack and destroy organic objects cannot survive. As a result, lake peats sometimes preserve a remarkable range of organic items that would otherwise long since have decomposed, such as bones, wooden tools, cordage of various sorts, and plant remains. Mesolithic people probably behaved in much the same way wherever they lived, but thanks to the preservative qualities of peat, we know more of the life of those who lived in these lakeside settlements than we do of those who lived elsewhere, where the only materials to survive are often flint tools.

Shell middens can tell us a great deal about early seashore settlements and how the people of these times exploited marine resources, including fish, shellfish, mammals, and birds. (See the feature *Shell Middens: The Rubbish Dumps of History*.) The first coastal settlements known in Europe date from the later Mesolithic period, about 5000 BC, by which time the sea had risen to near its present level. Any evidence of coastal occupation from earlier periods has, of course, long since been drowned by the rising seas.

The extent of coastal settlement during the earlier Mesolithic period has long been a matter of debate among archaeologists. In the middle of this century, many researchers believed that people did not occupy coastal areas to any significant extent until the Late Mesolithic period. At this time, deciduous forests, mainly of oak and lime, were widespread, and it was believed that these would have supported few game animals or edible plants, thus forcing people to make more use of coastal resources instead.

More recently, new evidence has emerged to suggest that people have always exploited coastal resources and also that game and plant foods were plentiful in the Late Mesolithic forests. First, Late Mesolithic sites are still being discovered in inland areas, some of which have yielded the bones of such game as red deer and wild boar. Secondly, seashells have been found in Early Mesolithic sites near the present-day coast in areas such as northern Spain, where the steeply sloping terrain shows that these sites would have been only a few kilometers inland during the late Ice Age and early postglacial period—not in large quantities, but enough to show that marine resources were being exploited at this time. This raises the intriguing possibility that Early Mesolithic shorelines lying many meters below the present-day sea level may still have shell middens on them. Perhaps one day it will be possible to locate and study them.

Life during the Mesolithic

Modern hunter-gatherers live in many different ways. Many, like the Bushmen of the Kalahari, are mobile, living in small groups and moving from

camp to camp according to the availability of food. Such people have an intimate knowledge of their environment and monitor resources closely, showing great skill in the way they plan their movements so that food is available in all seasons of the year. Other groups, such as the Tsimshian and Tlingit people, who occupy the coast of British Columbia, live in a base camp all year, sending out hunting and fishing parties to satellite camps in appropriate seasons. This more sedentary way of life, of course, is possible only in areas where a variety of food resources is available in the immediate vicinity, and even these groups usually have to store food to get through the bad seasons. Other present-day groups of hunter-gatherers do both, staying put in the good seasons, and moving in the bad. This is perhaps the most common pattern.

🔹 Amber was used by hunter-gatherers for ornaments, such as this pendant from Holme, in Denmark.
NATIONAL MUSEUM OF DENMARK

SOREN H. ANDERSEN/UNIVERSITY OF AARHUS, DENMARK

Enough is known of the Mesolithic period in Europe to suggest a similar picture. Many of the known sites are small, indicating that they were temporary camp sites, and some are sufficiently well preserved to reveal quite a lot about the way their inhabitants lived. Finds of animal bones are particularly valuable in this respect, as they can indicate not only what people ate but, in many cases, in which season the prey was killed.

The bones of migratory species are one source of such evidence. Many European birds migrate; for example, the whooper swan (*Cygnus cygnus*)

🔹 At Ringkloster, in Denmark, Late Mesolithic people lived close to a lake shore. Little survives of their original settlement, but the rubbish they threw into the lake has been well preserved. The people hunted mainly red deer and wild boar, and trapped pine martens for their pelts. Bones of these three species are common finds, as are wooden artifacts and many other items.

SHELL MIDDENS: THE RUBBISH DUMPS OF HISTORY

PETER ROWLEY-CONWY

A midden is a rubbish dump, and a shell midden is exactly what the words imply: a mound consisting predominantly of the discarded shells of edible shellfish, along with other refuse. Accumulated over the years, these rubbish heaps mark sites of prehistoric human habitation.

There was nothing special about shell middens to the people responsible for them—rubbish would have been dumped at every camp site the group occupied, and if shellfish were eaten, their shells would have formed part of the rubbish. There is, therefore, no fundamental distinction between shell midden sites and any other type of site. The quantity of shells found in middens depends simply on how frequently shellfish were eaten.

This bulk is the result of one particular attribute of shellfish: what you throw away takes up more space than what you eat. One red deer supplies as many kilojoules (or calories) as about 50,000 oysters, but its butchered and broken remains, even if they were all preserved, would take up only a fraction of the space that the oyster shells would occupy. At camp sites where shellfish were an important part of the diet, middens can accordingly be very large. Some found in Europe are as much as 100 meters by 40 meters (330 feet by 130 feet) in area, and between 2 and 3 meters (6 and 10 feet) deep. Not surprisingly, these are by far the largest Mesolithic sites known, but shellfish probably formed a smaller part of Mesolithic people's diet than the huge bulk of shells might imply.

To archaeologists, shell middens are a virtual treasure trove of information. In the first place, they are relatively easy to find, both by virtue of their bulk and because they tend to be predictably strung out along the prehistoric shorelines from which the shellfish were collected. Secondly, the calcium

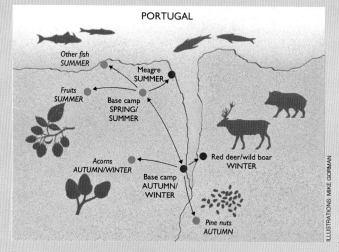

⚓ Generalized settlement patterns in Late Mesolithic Denmark and Portugal, based on the combined evidence from a number of separate areas. The foods obtained at each site and the season of occupation are shown. Normal text indicates settlement sites for which there is evidence. *Italics* indicate settlements that probably existed but for which we have no evidence.
● Settlements with shell middens   ● Settlements without shell middens

in the shells provides a nonacidic environment for all the other objects that ended up in the midden. As a result, organic items such as bones are preserved when they might otherwise not have been, and features such as cooking hearths and even dwellings and burials may also be well preserved within middens, built on the midden as it accumulated. In a sense, because of its volume and its preservative qualities, a shell midden provides a three-dimensional view of a site that might otherwise consist only of a layer of charcoal and preserved flints 5 to 10 centimeters (2 to 4 inches) deep.

Shell middens can tell us a great deal about the people who accumulated them. The settlements at which they are found served various purposes. Two of the best-researched midden groups in

Europe come from the Late Mesolithic period of Denmark (the Ertebølle culture) and Portugal.

In Denmark, seasonality studies indicate that some of the settlements were occupied for most or all of the year. As is to be expected, these are usually the sites with the largest shell middens, and they are often in attractive sheltered locations on bays or estuaries. It appears that these were base camps occupied by at least some of the people for most of the time. Many smaller shell middens have also been found. Unlike the larger ones, they were occupied in particular seasons and usually have evidence of some specialized economic activity, such as hunting dolphins and porpoises.

When the evidence from various sites is combined, a general picture starts to emerge. During the winter, hunting parties headed inland, hunting deer and wild boar for their meat and animals such as pine martens for their pelts. Meanwhile, other groups stayed on the coast and hunted migrating sea mammals and birds, eating the shellfish that eventually formed the middens. In summer, fish was probably a major part of the diet. Because the central base camp was occupied all year, it is likely that food was brought in from the special-purpose camps, but such things are difficult to prove.

Research is less advanced in Portugal than in Denmark, but again, by combining the evidence from various areas, we are starting to get a different picture. Groups spent the winter at base camps near the inland ends of large estuaries, hunting deer and wild boar and supplementing their diet with shellfish. In spring and summer, people moved to camps nearer the open coast. As well as hunting large mammals, they caught rabbits, and they also set up fishing camps, a common catch being meagre (*Argyrosomus regius*—a large sea fish that comes inshore during the summer).

CARTOGRAPHY: RAY SIM

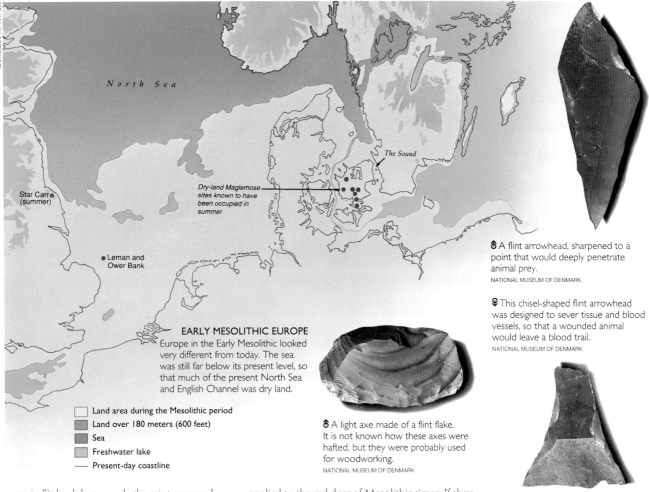

EARLY MESOLITHIC EUROPE
Europe in the Early Mesolithic looked
very different from today. The sea
was still far below its present level, so
that much of the present North Sea
and English Channel was dry land.

☐ Land area during the Mesolithic period
▨ Land over 180 meters (600 feet)
▨ Sea
▨ Freshwater lake
— Present-day coastline

North Sea

The Sound

Dry-land Maglemose
sites known to have
been occupied in
summer

Star Carr
(summer)

Leman and
Ower Bank

⚅ A flint arrowhead, sharpened to a
point that would deeply penetrate
animal prey.
NATIONAL MUSEUM OF DENMARK

⚵ This chisel-shaped flint arrowhead
was designed to sever tissue and blood
vessels, so that a wounded animal
would leave a blood trail.
NATIONAL MUSEUM OF DENMARK

⚅ A light axe made of a flint flake.
It is not known how these axes were
hafted, but they were probably used
for woodworking.
NATIONAL MUSEUM OF DENMARK

⚅ Heavy axes made of flint, such as
this specimen, were probably used
by hunter-gatherers to make dugout
canoes and other large wooden items.
NATIONAL MUSEUM OF DENMARK

nests in Finland, but spends the winter around
the western Baltic and North Sea. Many bones
of these swans have been found at the Late
Mesolithic sites of Aggersund and Sølager, in
Denmark, indicating that these sites must have
been occupied in winter. Fish can provide similar
evidence: the Late Mesolithic shell midden of
Arapouco, in Portugal, contains many bones of
fish that come inshore only during the summer
and must, therefore, have been eaten then. The
bones of migratory marine mammals such as seals
and porpoises, and of the various land mammals
that sometimes migrated in postglacial Europe,
can tell a similar story.

But in most of Europe, large land mammals did
not migrate over long distances, and the mere
presence of their remains does not tell us when
they were hunted. In these cases, archaeologists
need to call upon more specialized techniques. If
the jaws of young animals are found among the
remains, we can work out fairly accurately from
their stage of tooth development how old the
animals were when they were killed. Modern red
deer, for example, lose their milk teeth at about 24
to 26 months of age, and the same probably

applied to the red deer of Mesolithic times. If they
were born in June, like their modern counterparts,
a deer that had lost its milk teeth and was
developing adult teeth in their place would have
been killed some time during June, July, or
August, when it was 24 to 26 months old.

When a number of sites are found in a region,
we can start to see the overall pattern of settlement. The classic British bog site of Star Carr, on
England's eastern coast, has yielded jaws of young
red deer, roe deer, and elk, indicating that this
Early Mesolithic site was a summer camp. Across
the North Sea from Star Carr, Denmark has many
bog sites that have preserved evidence of the so-
called Maglemose culture. (The Danish place
name Maglemose means "great bog".) These sites
also date from the Early Mesolithic period,
although from a little later than Star Carr, and
several have yielded enough jawbones to indicate
that they, too, were occupied in summer.

So where did these people spend the winter?
While many other sites have been found, they
have not yielded enough animal bones for firm
conclusions to be drawn. Some of these may have
been winter settlements, but there is another

⚓ At Lepenski Vir, on the River Danube, in Serbia, archaeologists have excavated the remains of many trapeze-shaped houses. The reconstruction above shows the most likely method of construction. The inset plan shows the layout of the village. People would have been encouraged to settle here because of the abundant fish in the river.
ILLUSTRATION: RAY SIM

Central house

Meeting place

River Danube

➲ Remains of a hut floor at the Early Mesolithic bog site of Ulkestrup, in Denmark. The outer edges of the floor were formed by large split planks, and the interior by a layer of small twigs. Thin poles formed the walls and roof. Only a small number of poles have survived, but they would have been more numerous and much longer, and probably supported a single ridgepole. No trace of any covering material has survived, but reeds and rushes were most likely used as thatch.
ILLUSTRATION: RAY SIM

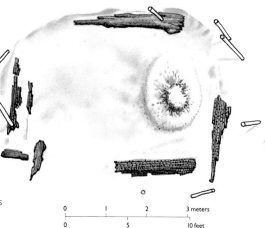

```
0        1        2        3 meters
0                 5        10 feet
```

possible explanation. At this time, the sea was still far below its present level: the modern Baltic Sea was a freshwater lake, drained by rivers into the North Sea across lowlands that are now flooded. If people had wintered near these rivers, their camp sites would now be under water, and this would explain why there are no known sites indicating winter occupation. While far from conclusive, other evidence also points to this.

Flint artifacts of the Maglemose type have been recovered by divers in The Sound (the strait between Denmark and Sweden) at depths of between 5 and 23 meters (16 and 75 feet). A more remarkable find is that of an antler point, probably a spearhead, picked up by chance in a trawl net from a depth of 39 meters (128 feet) on the Leman and Ower Bank, off East Anglia. Similar to finds from Star Carr, it dates from the same period. We do not, of course, know whether these submarine finds come from winter settlements, but they may. The only thing we know for certain is how little we know of coastal life during the Early Mesolithic period, given that so much of the Maglemose shorelines have now been lost.

If we compare what is known of the Early Mesolithic Maglemose culture with finds from a Late Mesolithic Danish culture (which extended to southern Sweden) called the Ertebølle, after a major shell midden, we find considerable differences. As we have seen, all the surviving evidence of Maglemose times points to seasonal camps. By the Late Mesolithic, a different pattern had emerged in these coastal areas, and it is not difficult to see why. At this time, the sea had risen close to its present level, and marine resources, including fish, shellfish, seals, and waterbirds, would have become more plentiful, making it attractive for people to settle there all year round. With food in ready supply, they clearly had no need to move camp. And because the sea level has changed little from that time, the shell middens that bear witness to this change in the way of life—unlike so much of the evidence from Maglemose times—have been preserved.

Mesolithic Dwellings

Although many Mesolithic sites are known, traces of dwellings are rare. Many of the structures would have been lightweight and temporary, perhaps inhabited for only a single visit to a camp site, and little would remain after thousands of years. Sometimes traces of postholes survive, providing a ground plan, although it is often difficult to be sure what is a posthole and what is not. If a structure was altered or reconstructed during subsequent visits, the result can be very difficult to interpret. Even less is known about the sides and roofs of such dwellings, so any reconstruction can be nothing more than a "best guess".

When the remains of more than one structure are found at a site, the first question that arises is whether all the dwellings were occupied at once. If three huts are found next to each other, for example, this could indicate that three families lived there at the same time. Alternatively, one

family might have built a new hut every few years, but not on exactly the same spot. Dating methods such as radiocarbon are not precise enough to tell us which is the case. But if flint tools are found, together with the waste pieces that result from working flint, they can provide a vital clue. If the pieces found within a single hut can be fitted back together to form a single nodule, then that nodule was clearly worked there. If, on the other hand, pieces from two huts fit together, both huts must have been in use at the same time.

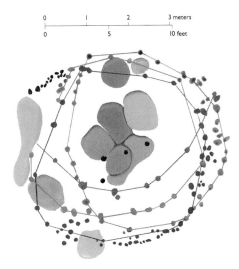

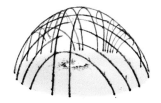

⚐ The angle of the postholes at Mount Sandel shows that the posts leaned inwards, suggesting that long, thin poles may have been bent over to form a hooped structure—although other interpretations are also possible.
ILLUSTRATION: RAY SIM

⬳ At Mount Sandel, huts were sometimes rebuilt several times, as the overlapping circles of postholes reveal. In the center lay several hearths, one belonging to each building phase.
ILLUSTRATION: RAY SIM

⚘ Mount Sandel, on the Bann River, in Northern Ireland, was an Early Mesolithic settlement, where people caught (and probably smoked) salmon, hunted wild boar, and collected hazel nuts. Animal skins may have been used to cover the huts, but no trace of this survives.
ILLUSTRATION: RAY SIM

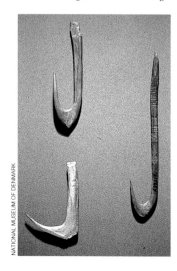

NATIONAL MUSEUM OF DENMARK

🔱 Bone fishhooks recovered from Early Mesolithic sites in Denmark are well made. At lakeside sites, bones of pike and other fish are very common, indicating that fish were an important source of food for the inhabitants.

Mesolithic Tools and Weapons

Mesolithic people used a wide variety of tools and other equipment, but the characteristic stone tool of this period is the microlith—the word simply meaning "small stone". Microliths are commonly found, and come in many types. They were apparently mass-produced as components of composite tools, including weapons, and are usually assumed to have been mounted as tips and barbs on arrows and spears. While they have occasionally been found still in position on hunting weapons, they may well have been used for a range of other purposes. They have been found mounted as sickle blade segments in Southwest Asia, but such tools are not known from the European Mesolithic.

Judging by the large numbers of animal bones found at well-preserved sites, these weapons must have been very effective. Mesolithic people were evidently capable of killing such dangerous quarry as wild boar and aurochs. A few bows from this period have been preserved in bog sites, including impressive specimens from Tybrind Vig, a Late Mesolithic site in Denmark, made of elm and measuring 160 centimeters (5 feet, 3 inches). The first evidence of domestic dogs dates from this period, and men armed with powerful bows and accompanied by dogs to track wounded animals would have been very effective hunters.

Other types of flint tools from this period include scrapers and burins for working wood, bone, and hide; larger blades, used as knives; and heavier items, such as axes and adzes. Bone and antler were also fashioned into a wide variety of tools. Being long, straight, and hard, cannon bones from the lower limbs of red deer and elk were often used, sometimes as mounts for microliths to form spearheads or daggers. Although wood must have been commonly used, wooden artifacts rarely survive, except in bog sites. These have sometimes

yielded quite large items, such as bows. Further finds of paddles, some of them beautifully decorated, and, occasionally, of canoes, show that water transport and water resources were important in Mesolithic times, while a sledge runner recovered from the bog site of Sarnate, in Latvia, has given us a rare glimpse of another early form of transport.

Precious little cordage has survived. The German bog site of Friesack, not far from Berlin, has yielded many fragments of netting, along with a float made of birch bark, strongly suggesting that these fragments come not from a dip net on a handle but from something much larger. This was certainly the case with a find from the bog site of Antrea, in Karelia, where a collection of net fragments, floats, and sinkers indicate a net that hung vertically in the water and was about 30 meters (100 feet) long. The nets from both these sites were made of bast (the inner bark of certain trees). Plaiting and basketry must also have been common, but finds are rare. Fish traps of plaited twigs have occasionally been found—probably lost during use in streams and lakes, and preserved as sediments built up around them.

The hunting of land mammals leaves many traces in the archaeological record, in the form of animal bones and weapons and other technology. Fishing and related

🏹 Arrowheads are occasionally found still attached to parts of the arrow shaft. Sometimes, two microliths were used, one forming the tip and one the barb. Chisel-ended arrows are known from the Late Mesolithic period of Denmark. Bolt-headed arrows, carved entirely from a single piece of wood, were used to stun or kill small animals, so that their fur would not be damaged by the impact.

ILLUSTRATIONS: RAY SIM

activities leave far fewer traces, although occasional finds of major pieces of equipment, such as boats and nets, indicate that they were equally or more important in some areas.

The third main food source is even less visible in archaeological terms: hardly any evidence of plant foods has come down to us, although early people must have eaten many types of fruits, nuts, roots, and tubers, and in considerable quantities. Vegetable matter survives only if charred or continuously waterlogged in anoxic conditions, and tools and other equipment can rarely be shown unequivocally to have been used to collect or process plants, although studies of wear patterns and organic residues on the edges of tools

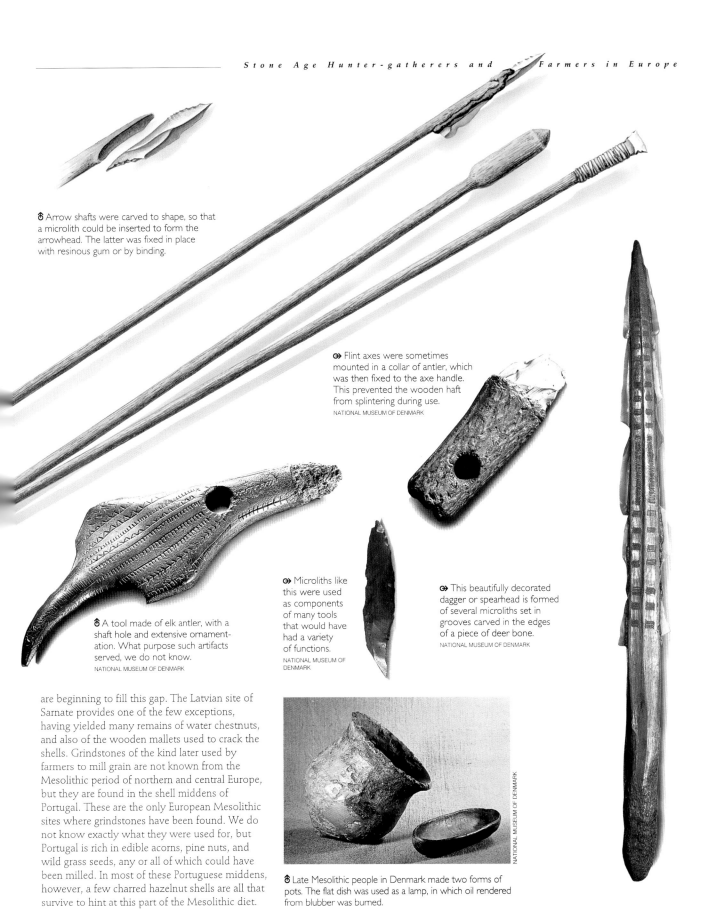

⬆ Arrow shafts were carved to shape, so that a microlith could be inserted to form the arrowhead. The latter was fixed in place with resinous gum or by binding.

⬂ Flint axes were sometimes mounted in a collar of antler, which was then fixed to the axe handle. This prevented the wooden haft from splintering during use.
NATIONAL MUSEUM OF DENMARK

⬆ A tool made of elk antler, with a shaft hole and extensive ornament-ation. What purpose such artifacts served, we do not know.
NATIONAL MUSEUM OF DENMARK

⬂ Microliths like this were used as components of many tools that would have had a variety of functions.
NATIONAL MUSEUM OF DENMARK

⬂ This beautifully decorated dagger or spearhead is formed of several microliths set in grooves carved in the edges of a piece of deer bone.
NATIONAL MUSEUM OF DENMARK

are beginning to fill this gap. The Latvian site of Sarnate provides one of the few exceptions, having yielded many remains of water chestnuts, and also of the wooden mallets used to crack the shells. Grindstones of the kind later used by farmers to mill grain are not known from the Mesolithic period of northern and central Europe, but they are found in the shell middens of Portugal. These are the only European Mesolithic sites where grindstones have been found. We do not know exactly what they were used for, but Portugal is rich in edible acorns, pine nuts, and wild grass seeds, any or all of which could have been milled. In most of these Portuguese middens, however, a few charred hazelnut shells are all that survive to hint at this part of the Mesolithic diet.

NATIONAL MUSEUM OF DENMARK

⬆ Late Mesolithic people in Denmark made two forms of pots. The flat dish was used as a lamp, in which oil rendered from blubber was burned.

THE DOMESTICATION OF ANIMALS

RONNIE LILJEGREN

The domestication of animals has been one of most crucial things humans ever accomplished. In conjunction with the cultivation of cereals, it accounts for much of the increase in human numbers over the last 10,000 years. Not surprisingly, therefore, animal domestication has been a major area of archaeological study.

Taming and domestication are two very different activities. Individual animals of most species can be tamed, and hunter-gatherers without domesticates sometimes tame the occasional animal—usually a newborn or very young individual found during hunting. The reasons for this vary from curiosity, or the desire for a pet, to fattening the animal for a few weeks or months before eating it. All human groups are probably aware that individual animals can be reared in this way in a human society.

Domestication, on the other hand, involves not one but a group of animals, controlled and selectively bred by humans, usually with little or no interbreeding with wild animals. There are only two core areas where herd animals were domesticated: Southwest Asia (sheep, goats, cattle, and pigs) and the Andes (llamas and alpacas). Other herd animals, such as horses, camels, and various East Asian types of cattle, were domesticated in particular regions, but only after agriculture had been established nearby.

Identifying Domesticated Animals

Taming is very difficult to recognize archaeologically, but once separate domestic populations came into existence, genetic changes took place that can sometimes be seen. In addition, the age at which animals were killed can be determined from their teeth and bones. Thus, if animal remains are found of an age that is characteristic of killing for domestic purposes,

Cheviot

Four-horned Jacob

Merino

Mouflon

Lincoln

Syrian fat-tailed sheep

ILLUSTRATION: PETER SCHOUTEN

then the animals were probably domesticated.

The first animal to be domesticated was the dog. A grave at Ain Mallaha, in Israel, dating from about 13,500 years ago, contained the body of an old woman and the skeleton of a puppy some three to five months old. Whether this was a tamed wolf or a domestically bred dog is unknown, but domestic dogs are known by 9500 BC to 8000 BC from sites as far apart as Seamer Carr, in England, and Danger Cave, in Utah. Evidently, the wolf/dog was domesticated in a number of places, most probably for hunting purposes.

In Southwest Asia, genetic changes indicate that sheep and goats were domesticated before 8000 BC. Among goats, for example,

the horns change from scimitar-shaped to corkscrew-shaped, which is usually thought to result from domestication. At some sites, kill patterns related to domestication have been found, with many female goats surviving to old age but most males being killed at about two years of age. This shows that herders kept the females for breeding, but slaughtered the males when they reached their maximum weight. Cattle and pigs were domesticated rather later—before 7000 BC.

Breeding to Meet the Growing Demand

The need for a ready source of meat and hides is probably a sufficient explanation for the domestication of sheep, goats, cattle, and pigs. In Southwest Asia, cereals were

Animal domestication is a continuous process. It takes place over many generations, different races being developed to suit different environments. Sheep, with about 400 breeds, are a good example. Wild sheep, such as the mouflon, have a hairy outer coat and a woolly undercoat, and both sexes have horns. Modern sheep, such as the Lincoln, are often polled, or only the rams have horns, as in the case of the merino. Among Jacob sheep, animals with four, or even six, horns are common—a genetic defect, probably caused by inbreeding, which has been preserved as a decoration. Syrian fat-tailed sheep are adapted to a hot, dry environment, and use their fat as an energy supply. Wool differs considerably from one breed to another. It is long, coarse, and lustrous in the Lincoln; dense, with very fine fibers, in the merino; and quite coarse, and with little luster, in the Cheviot.

cultivated before sheep and goats were domesticated. Farmers were more numerous than hunter-gatherers, and the increased need for meat would have put pressure on local populations of wild animals. Breeding from tamed animals would have been an effective way of making up for the decreasing number of wild animals. Secondary products such as milk, blood, and wool, and the use of animals for traction, are usually thought to have been exploited only later. In some cases, this was certainly so.

Wild sheep have a hairy outer coat covering a woolly undercoat. Thick wool suitable for spinning and weaving resulted from long periods of selective breeding by farmers, which could only have been undertaken using domesticated sheep.

Milk, perhaps made into cheese, may have been exploited much earlier. Milking a goat for a year provides more energy than a goat carcass, and provides that energy by degrees, over a long period, rather than all at once: two good reasons why dairy products may yet turn out to have been utilized very early indeed.

As agriculture spread, other animals were domesticated, but remarkably little is known about them. Horses were probably domesticated in the grassy steppes north and east of the Black Sea. At the site of Dereivka, in Ukraine, which dates to a little before 4000 BC, there are more than 2,000 horse bones. For many years it was thought that these horses were domestic animals, but the kill ages do not support this assumption. Most of the horses were killed between five and eight years of age, just when they would have been most useful for both breeding and working if they had been domesticated. They were therefore probably hunted for meat—except for one animal, whose teeth had the characteristic beveling that results from long use of a bit. Perhaps humans used a few tamed or domesticated horses to assist them when hunting.

Even less is known about camel domestication. The earliest claim comes from Shahr-i Sokhta, in Iran, dating to about 2700 BC. The evidence here is burned camel dung found in a pottery vessel—circumstantial, but not conclusive, evidence that the camel was domesticated!

Small Animals

Grain stores attract rodents, so it is not surprising that the first evidence for the domestication of the cat—at Khirokitia, in Cyprus—goes back to 7000 BC. The island has no native wildcats, so the cats must have been introduced in domesticated form.

Ferrets are useful when hunting rabbits, and the use of tame or domestic ferrets is mentioned in the writings of the Roman author Strabo at about the beginning of the first century AD.

Other small animals were domesticated for food—for example, guinea pigs in Peru, rabbits in Europe, and ducks and goldfish in China. All these animals were raised by societies that also kept larger herd domesticates. In Mexico, there were no larger herd domesticates, so smaller domesticated species were of considerable importance. The turkey was domesticated in this region, and specially bred fat dogs were the other source of meat, apart from that from hunted animals.

Sheep, goats, pigs, cattle, llamas, and alpacas are of vital importance to the cultures that herd them. Why, then, did people in the other early centers of cereal cultivation, such as Mexico, China, and West Africa, not domesticate local species such as deer and antelope?

While many species can be tamed, few are suited to being herd domesticates. Males in most deer and antelope species are territorial during the mating season and try to keep a group of females in their territory while fighting off other males. Herd structure is consequently weak or nonexistent, and the difficulties of domesticating such species are immense. In just a few species, however, there are a number of units within a herd, each consisting of a male with a number of females. Such herds do not range over the landscape during the mating season but are much more cohesive. All the major herd domesticates are of this second type: as we would expect, early farmers did not domesticate species at random but made effective use of those with the most potential.

THE ANCESTRY OF DOMESTICATED ANIMALS

DOMESTICATED ANIMAL	TIME	WILD ANCESTOR	PLACE
dog	>11,000 BC	wolf	many places?
sheep	8000 BC	wild sheep	Iraq, Iran, Levant coast
goat	8000 BC	bezoar (wild goat)	Zagros Mountains, Iraq
pig	7000 BC	wild boar	Southwest Asia (Anatolia)
cattle	8000 BC	aurochs	Southwest Asia and possibly Europe
horse	4000 BC	wild horse	southern Ukraine
one-humped camel	3000 BC	wild camel	southern Arabia
two-humped camel	2500 BC	wild camel	Turkmenistan/Iran
gayal or mithun	?	gauar	possibly India
bali cattle	3500 BC	banteng	Java or India
cat	7000 BC	wild cat	Southwest Asia
reindeer	?	wild reindeer	arctic Eurasia
ass	3500 BC	wild ass	Northeast Africa
yak	?6000 BC	wild yak	the Tibetan highland
water buffalo	>2500 BC	Indian wild buffalo	Indus Valley (Mesopotamia?)
llama	4000 BC	guanaco	Andean plateau
alpaca	4000 BC	guanaco	Andean plateau
guinea pig	>1000 BC	wild cavy	Peru?
rabbit	AD 1000	wild rabbit	southern Europe
duck	1000 BC	mallard	Southeast Asia
goose	3000 BC	greylag	southeastern Europe, Northeast Africa
domestic fowl	2000 BC	red jungle fowl	Indus Valley
peafowl	1000 BC	wild peafowls	India
turkey	500 BC	wild turkey	Mexico
budgerigar	AD 1840	wild budgerigar	Australia
canary	AD 1500	wild canary	Canary Islands
goldfish	AD 1000	Crucian carp?	China
mulberry silkworm	>2000 BC	wild silkworm	China
honeybee	>2400 BC	wild bees	Southwest Asia, Europe, Africa?

Cemeteries

While individual graves—and the occasional cemetery—are known from the Paleolithic period, it is not until the Mesolithic that we find evidence of the widespread use of cemeteries. About 20 cemeteries have now been found in Europe, some containing more than 100 graves. Disposal of the dead varied widely from place to place, reflecting regional variations in culture.

Cemeteries linked to the Ertebølle culture have been found in Denmark and southern Sweden, and several cemeteries have also been found beneath Portuguese shell middens. Thanks to these shell middens, we know quite a lot about the way of life of these two groups, but we know much less about that of the people of Brittany, England, the Baltic States, and Russia, where cemeteries dating from this period have also been found.

One striking aspect of these cemeteries is that most are in coastal areas. This has led some archaeologists to speculate that cemeteries were one of the means by which particular groups of people laid claim to certain territories. The presence of dead ancestors in a cemetery could legitimize such a claim and strengthen a group's sense of identity with its land. Clearly, this would be more likely to happen in areas where food resources were plentiful and stable, encouraging people to adopt a more settled way of life—such as along the coasts. The evidence from shell middens indicates that in Portugal, coastal people regularly moved from summer to winter camps within a limited area, while in Denmark, they seem to have lived in permanent settlements.

People living in the interior, without access to marine resources, would most likely to have moved further, more frequently, and less predictably than coastal groups. They would, therefore, have been less likely to have identified with a fixed territory, and this may be why cemeteries are rarely found away from the coast. Significantly, the few exceptions have been found in places where resources would have been unusually plentiful and predictable, such as at

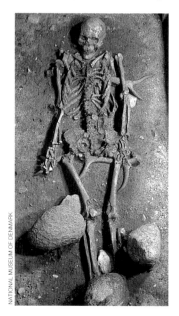

🔼 Cemeteries from the Late Mesolithic period are fairly common in coastal regions of Europe. Bodies were sometimes placed on red-deer antlers to be buried, and accompanied by various tools and pieces of jewelry.

↪ One young woman was buried in the Vedbæk cemetery, in Denmark, with a group of teeth, mostly from red deer, stitched or tied to the back of her belt or dress as a decoration. When her skeleton was excavated some 7,000 years later, the teeth were found still in place below her pelvic bone.

↪ *Opposite*: A grave in the Vedbæk cemetery, in Denmark, bears witness to a probable tragedy. The adult skeleton is that of a young woman aged about 18, and next to her lies the skeleton of a newborn child. We may speculate that they died in childbirth. The child was buried with a flint blade at its waist. Adult males in the same cemetery were similarly equipped, so perhaps the child was a boy. (It is very difficult to determine the sex of very young skeletons.) The red coloring is from ocher placed in the grave. The animal teeth near the woman's head were probably sewn as decoration onto a piece of clothing. The boy was lying on the bones of a swan's wing.

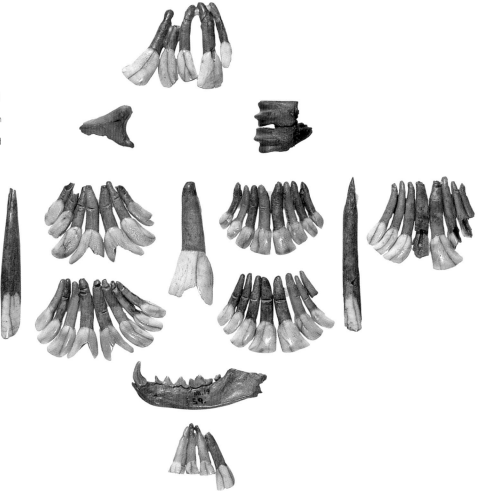

⚓ Lepenski Vir, in Serbia, lies where the River Danube flows through a gorge. This part of the river is particularly rich in fish, including sturgeon, which was a very important source of food in this area.

⚓ The sites of villages established by the earliest agriculturalists in southeastern Europe are marked by so-called tell mounds, formed by the repeated rebuilding of mudbrick houses.

MIKE ANDREWS/ANCIENT ART & ARCHITECTURE COLLECTION

Lepenski Vir, a prime fishing location in Serbia, on the River Danube. Fewer cemeteries are known from the Early Mesolithic and Paleolithic periods, but if most had similarly been in coastal regions, they would obviously have been flooded by the rising seas along with the settlements.

Whatever the truth of this, cemeteries are the only places where we can encounter individuals from these times. Limited though it is, the Danish and Swedish evidence indicates that these hunter-gatherers were quite tall and robust, comparable to modern Europeans, and very different from the shorter farmers of later prehistoric and Medieval times. Judging from this, Mesolithic diets, at least on the coast, must have been considerably better than those of these later peoples.

Ornaments are commonly found in graves in all these cemeteries. As the number of ornaments varies from grave to grave, it would seem that some people enjoyed a higher social status than others, but we know very little of the social structure of this time. Rich ornaments are occasionally found in children's graves, and it has been suggested that this may indicate that wealth and high social status were inherited. This could mean that there were hereditary chiefs. While this is certainly possible, burial customs are so varied

and difficult to interpret that it is very difficult to prove such a proposition one way or the other.

The First Farmers of Southern and Eastern Europe

Hunter-gatherers would probably have continued to pursue their various ways of life throughout Europe, with little change, but for one thing: the development of farming. How this development came about is an issue that is still hotly debated.

Most of the early crops and domesticated animals (such as wheat and barley, and sheep and goats) did not live wild in Europe, and so must have been introduced at some stage. Wild cattle and pigs, on the other hand, were found throughout postglacial Europe. These could have been domesticated locally, although current evidence suggests that they, too, came from outside Europe. All these species live wild in Southwest Asia, which is also where the earliest evidence of farming has been found.

The big question is, then, did immigrant peoples take farming to Europe with them, or did local Mesolithic groups somehow acquire the plants and animals and take up farming themselves? Obviously, there can be no single answer, since various combinations of immigrants and local people would have been involved in different places. Opinions remain sharply divided as to which was the more important overall.

Some areas offer better clues than others as to the sequence of events. In southern Greece, for example, Franchthi Cave has yielded evidence of human occupation spanning thousands of years, so the sudden appearance there of wheat, barley, lentils, sheep, and goats, in layers dated to 7000 BC, could mean either that these things were introduced by immigrants or that local hunter-gatherers rapidly adopted practices and species that were passed between communities along existing contact routes. The island of Crete, on the other hand, was unoccupied during the Mesolithic period, so farming can only have arrived there with immigrants.

Throughout southeastern Europe, the way of life of the earliest farmers differed little from that established earlier in Southwest Asia. Numerous so-called tell mounds—mounds formed when houses made of sun-dried mudbricks collapsed, and new houses were later built on top of them—have been discovered throughout these areas, and have proved to be the sites of villages occupied by between 50 and 300 people. These communities were clearly too big to have been supported by hunting, gathering, and fishing, and lived quite close to one another. It was farming that supported populations of this size and density and made this pattern of life possible.

While the evidence from the eastern Mediterranean region tends to favor the immigration theory, that from the western region presents quite a different picture. More Mesolithic settlements have been found in the western basin than in the eastern, reflecting the more abundant resources in the west. This would suggest that the population in the west was larger. The earliest farming settlements here do not take the form of villages. The earliest sites have been found mostly in caves, many of which had previously been occupied by hunter-gatherers, as shown by the often abundant fish bones in these sites. Here, it looks much more as though local people took up elements of farming, while continuing to exploit coastal resources.

This proposition gains some support from the fact that not all elements of the farming economy spread from the eastern to the western basin at the same time. Instead, it appears that only sheep and wheat spread rapidly round the coastal fringe of the western Mediterranean. Perhaps Mesolithic hunter-gatherers found sheep easier to integrate into a part-farming, part-fishing economy, but the details remain obscure. The earliest bones of sheep found in northwestern Italy have been dated to about 6000 BC; those from southern France and Spain, to 5500 BC (earlier dates are claimed in both countries, but not generally accepted); and from Portugal, to 5200 BC. Goats

in northwestern Italy followed some 500 years later, and domestic pigs later still, but the dates for the introduction of these species elsewhere in the western Mediterranean are still debated. Wild animals and fish were caught in much greater numbers in the west, probably because they were more abundant. The fact that the earliest evidence of farming is found along the coast, as well as the difficulties of overland travel in those times, make it likely that farming spread by boat, whether or not migration was involved to any extent.

NEOLITHIC EUROPE

Farming did not spread across Europe at a slow and even rate. Sometimes it spread very fast indeed, but in between such periods, there were long pauses. Farming spread particularly fast in southeastern and central Europe and around the Mediterranean coasts, while it took longer to penetrate the coastal regions.

CARTOGRAPHY: RAY SIM

☛ The simplest form of plow is the ard, which scratches a shallow furrow in the soil. An ox-drawn ard can cultivate a field much faster than a person using a digging stick, but it is a more complex tool to make, and the oxen take a considerable time to train. An ard therefore represents a much bigger investment of human resources.

HISTORICAL-ARCHAEOLOGICAL RESEARCH CENTRE, DENMARK

All European farmers made pottery, whereas very few hunter-gatherers did. The earliest farmers in Greece and south-eastern Europe produced well-made vessels in a variety of forms, often with geometric designs painted in several colors—mainly red, buff, and black. The pottery found in the western Mediterranean is different: it was not painted, and decorative bands were impressed or incised into the clay. Different styles of pottery cannot be used to distinguish different tribes, but they do suggest that there were major cultural differences between the two regions.

The Forest Farmers of Central and Northwestern Europe

Farming had not yet spread north of the Mediterranean, and most plants and animals, as well as farming methods, were adapted to the Mediterranean climate. Crops, for example, would probably have been planted in autumn. They would have grown throughout the cool, wet winter, and been harvested in May or June before the hot summer drought set in. This cycle mimics the natural cycle of wild grasses in the area.

Farmers moving out of this climatic zone and into central Europe faced a major challenge in that they had to turn the agricultural year on its head. In the colder regions, it was winter frost, not summer drought, that was the main threat to crops. Crops had to grow through the moist summer and be harvested in the autumn, so new crop strains and new agricultural techniques had to be developed. For farmers to have carried through these changes in less than a thousand years was a remarkable achievement indeed.

But farming did not spread across Europe at an even rate. Sometimes it spread quickly, and at others there were long periods when it did not spread at all. The unevenness of its advance is particularly marked in southeastern Europe. Farming spread through areas with a Mediterranean-type climate in just a few centuries—and then came to a halt in Hungary, where the climate is different and the wet, heavily forested soils of temperate Europe begin.

Farming reached the northern edge of the Mediterranean climate zone in southern Hungary

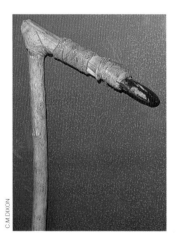

C.M.DIXON

⚒ A polished stone adze and reconstructed haft. Tools like this were used to fell trees and work timber. They would have been vital to early farmers for clearing forest for agriculture, for building houses, and for making all kinds of wooden tools.

☛ The longhouses built by the first farmers in central Europe were substantial structures of considerable size. From the evidence of postholes, archaeologists can reconstruct the main timber elements with considerable accuracy. Finds of burned clay with impressions of sticks show that the walls and internal partitions were often made of wattle and daub—screens made of interwoven sticks covered with wet clay or cow dung, which hardened as it dried. Split planks were also used. The roofs were most probably thatched. We do not know whether there was an upper floor, as shown in this reconstruction, but it seems likely. The structure could certainly have supported one, and the farmers would have needed a place to store harvested grain and animal fodder for the winter.

ILLUSTRATION: OLIVER RENNERT

by 6000 BC, but only in 5300 BC did it spread any further into the cooler and wetter climates of central Europe. The next great leap took farming right across central Europe to the borders of Scandinavia and the North Sea in the space of just a few generations. Farmers had to make massive changes in their economy to be able to do this: wheat and barley were now almost the only crops grown, perhaps because pulses such as lentils and peas did not adjust so readily to the colder climate. Sheep and goats (the most common animals in the Mediterranean) were not well suited to the central European forests and so became less important. The animal bones found in settlement sites of this period are most often those of pigs and cattle, and animal products in general may have become a more significant part of the diet. It has been suggested that dairy products came into use at this time, and this seems likely.

These economic changes were accompanied by major social changes. No longer did settlements consist of compact villages made up of small houses. Instead, massive timber longhouses up to about 50 meters (164 feet) in length appeared all across central Europe, from Hungary to Poland and from the Netherlands to Ukraine. These longhouses were not grouped in villages but were spaced some way apart. We do not know how many people lived in these buildings, nor what activities went on inside them. Unlike later longhouses, there is no evidence that one end was used for stalling animals, but this does not necessarily mean that the whole of the interior was used as human living space.

After the rapid spread of this longhouse forest-farming culture, there was once again a pause. It was another thousand years before farming spread into southern Scandinavia. This, of course, was the area of the Late Mesolithic Ertebølle shell middens, which would explain the delay. Given the rich marine resources in this area, which were supplemented by other sources of food such as land mammals and plants,

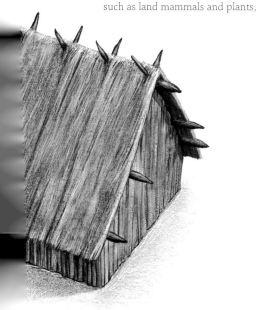

there would have been little incentive for these coastal people to abandon their hunting-gathering way of life. A similar situation prevailed in Portugal, where hunter-gatherers living at the sites marked by their shell middens continued their traditional way of life for several centuries after farming had become established in the surrounding countryside. The attractions of coastal life in these areas would seem to be the most likely reason why farming spread into the Atlantic coastal fringes of Europe in a much more piecemeal way than it did into the interior of Europe.

These new farming groups, of course, developed vastly different technical skills from those of the Mesolithic hunter-gatherers. As noted, only a few hunting-gathering groups (the Ertebølle among them) made pottery, while all the farmers did. Farmers would obviously have to have cleared areas of forest, and the heavy stone axes they used for this purpose are commonly found. Less is known about the implements they used for cultivation. Only limited areas can be worked with a digging stick, and soon after 3000 BC, there is evidence that ards (simple scratch ploughs without wheels) were in use. Ards are sometimes found in bog sites, but the earliest evidence of them has come down to us in the form of furrows preserved as dark lines on the old soil surface beneath burial mounds. As farming began several centuries before people started to build these mounds, any earlier evidence of such furrows has not survived. Ards may be very old.

The development of agriculture was one of the most momentous changes that Europe has ever seen. It brought about a massive increase in population density, and this has continued ever since, as new farming methods and crops have been introduced. Without farming, the social and economic structures we call "civilization" could never have developed, and the Industrial Revolution is inconceivable. Europe was never the same again.

⚘ Experiments have shown that substantial trees can be felled with stone axes in a remarkably short time. Bronze axes do not speed up the process. It was not until the coming of iron axes that farmers found a more efficient way to clear land of trees.

⚘ Grain was ground into flour with smooth grindstones. A handful of grain was placed on a large stone, and then ground with a small stone. Hunter-gatherers in some areas probably ground nuts by this method, but grindstones become much more common in early farming societies.
C.M. DIXON

⊕ The mummified body was initially partly uncovered by the Alpine gendarmerie. It lay on its front on a large slab in the rock cleft.

THE ICE MAN OF THE TYROL

ANDREAS LIPPERT

⊕ A view of the site from the north, with the Ortler mountains in the background.

Similaun glacier

MORE THAN 5,000 years ago, a man was crossing a remote pass in the mountains of the Tyrol. As a storm approached, he sheltered in a hollow in the rock, some 3,200 meters (10,500 feet) above sea level, where he apparently froze to death. For several weeks his body was exposed to the wind and sun; as it dried out, it became mummified. The body was then covered by snow and finally entombed within the ice of a glacier that covered the site. There it lay, undisturbed, until September 1991, when it was discovered by hikers.

Pollen analyses in the alpine valleys and occasional finds of stone axes high up in the mountains have long indicated that people frequented the mountains and made use of the high pastures during the last stages of the Neolithic period. But the discovery of the remarkably well-preserved body of the "Ice Man", near the Tisenjoch pass, in the Otztal Alps, has permitted the kind of detailed investigation of life during this period that would otherwise never have been possible.

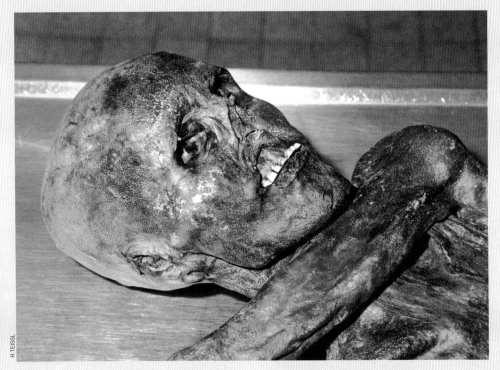

⚲ On the left side of the Ice Man's back, three groups of vertical lines are tattooed. These markings may have indicated his tribe or status.

◀⦿ The mummified head. Although considerably shrunken, the eyeballs and their pupils are still preserved.

◀⦿ The remains of a fur shoe still surround his right foot. His roughly fashioned boots were lined with hay, obviously as insulation against the cold, and tied with laces made of grass and leather.

The Ice Man—also known as Similaun Man, after the glacier in which he was found—was about 30 years old. He was dressed for the climate in fur and leather, patched together with thread made from sinew. A large, mat-like item woven from long grass may have been a shawl. His fur shoes were lined with hay and tied with laces made of grass and leather. On his knees, feet, hands, and back, groups of lines and crosses were tattooed in dark blue. These may have indicated his tribe or status.

A Neolithic Tool Kit

This Neolithic traveler was well equipped for his journey, with an axe, a bow and quiver, a backpack, a leather case containing several items, a firelighter and tinder, and a dagger. Before he settled down for refuge in his rocky hollow, the man had carefully deposited his quiver and axe, his bow and backpack, in two different places.

The shaft of the axe was made from a piece of yew wood about 80 centimeters (30 inches) long, with a short fork at one end, to which a very early type of copper-flanged axe, 9 centimeters (almost 4 inches) in length, was attached. The unfinished bow, roughly made of yew wood and unpolished, was about 1.8 meters (5 feet, 11 inches) long. The quiver was a fur bag stitched with leather and stiffened with hazelwood. It contained 14 arrow shafts, about 85 centimeters

(33 inches) long, and made of dogwood and guelder rose. Two were notched and feathered ready for use, with arrowheads made of flint. The quiver also contained a pointed object made of bone or antler, possibly a tool for skinning animals. Finally, there was an animal sinew, the raw material for bowstrings or threads.

The frame of the backpack consisted of a thin piece of hazelwood bent in a U-shape and two small boards of larch tree with peg-

shaped ends. Nearby remnants of thick grass cord suggest that this was how the pack was attached. In the longish leather case was a flint scraper and a piece of tree-bark resin. On this resin were tiny fragments of pyrite. Together, these served as a firelighter. X-rays have revealed two flint points inside the container. These items obviously made up a repair kit for the arrows.

In addition, the Ice Man carried a tool used for sharpening flint artifacts, consisting of a small piece of bone set into a thick wooden peg. Two small tree fungi threaded onto a leather thong were evidently used as an antibiotic medicine. A dagger-like flint blade with a wooden hilt was probably a tool rather than a weapon; an oval bag of the same size, made of woven grass, presumably served as a sheath.

The earliest preserved prehistoric body ever found, the Ice Man is of immense significance for our understanding of the past. By studying his body and equipment, scientists have been able to provide answers to many questions about the social status, cultural level, health, and nutritional status of a native of the Alps in the Late Neolithic.

THE MEGALITH BUILDERS OF WESTERN EUROPE

4 8 0 0 B C – 2 8 0 0 B C

Stones, Tombs, and Temples
along the Atlantic Coast

GÖRAN BURENHULT

THE GIANT STONE TOMBS that stand along the shores of the Atlantic have fascinated people for centuries. We know almost nothing about them, apart from their age and, in some cases, their ceremonial functions. Why were they built? What role did they play in society? Were they solely places in which the dead went to their final rest, or did they symbolize the life to come? Should they be regarded as dwelling places for dead ancestors? What role did astronomical observations play in the building of the monuments and in the ceremonies that took place at them? Why were most of them built in coastal areas of western Europe? Did they perhaps mark territories occupied by particular communities? The people who could have answered these questions vanished long ago, but recent excavations and research have brought us some way towards solving this enigma, surely one of the most intriguing of all archaeological puzzles.

✆ The Ring of Brogar, a huge stone circle in the Orkney Islands, north of Scotland, consists of gigantic, erect stone slabs. The function of this impressive monument is still unknown, but it may have served as a religious meeting point for a large number of settlements throughout the Orkney Islands, among them the famous Stone Age village of Skara Brae.

⚓ A decorated stone slab from Antelas, at Oliveira de Frades, in the Viseu Valley, Portugal.

REPRODUCED BY PERMISSION OF OXFORD UNIVERSITY PRESS FROM ELIZABETH SHEE TWOHIG (1981): *THE MEGALITHIC ART OF WESTERN EUROPE* [AFTER ALBUQUERQUE E. CASTRO *ET AL.* (1957): *COMM. SERV. GEOL.* 38].

FABRICE ROULAND/RAPHO

☙ Life was easy for the Mesolithic hunter-gatherers of western Europe. Abundant coastal resources, including oysters, mussels, fish, and seals, as well as beached whales, supplemented by hunting and a rich supply of forest products, allowed these people to become more or less sedentary.

GÖRAN BURENHULT

☙ Thick heaps of prehistoric leftovers, such as this one at Culleenamore, in northwestern Ireland, dot the coasts of western Europe. These so-called kitchen middens consist mainly of oyster shells, and bear witness to the enormously rich food supply available to Mesolithic peoples.

More than 6,000 years ago, the Stone Age peoples of western Europe started to erect stone monuments over their dead—as tombs or as ceremonial places—and thereby introduced the megalithic tradition of the Neolithic period. Initially, archaeologists generally regarded these monuments as late offshoots of the monuments of Near Eastern civilizations, such as the pyramids of Egypt and the ziggurats of Mesopotamia. They were thought to have been introduced by the first farmers, who would then have spread along the Atlantic coast. Later on, it was suggested that a religious cult lay behind the appearance of these megaliths, and that Stone Age missionaries of some kind had spread by sea among the early farmers. Migration and the spread of ideas were key terms in this discussion.

In the 1960s and 1970s, however, excavations and a series of remarkably early radiocarbon datings at megalithic sites in western Europe finally threw these theories overboard. The oldest known megalithic tombs in France and Ireland were found to have been built about 4700 BC—2,000 years before Egypt's pyramids were erected. Every form of outside influence could therefore be ruled out. Today, we know that the idea of erecting megalithic tombs, and the need to do so, developed within the Stone Age societies of western Europe during the fifth millennium BC, but the meaning and function of the monuments still remain one of the great enigmas of archaeology. The megalithic tradition died out 5,000 years ago, so there is no traditional continuity, or "living link", in Europe that can answer our questions, and we know almost nothing of the social, psychological, and religious background that gave rise to them.

In Europe, the megalithic tradition reached its peak just before 3000 BC. Magnificent monuments—such as Stonehenge, in England, Newgrange, in Ireland, and the famous stone alignments a kilometer (more than half a mile) long at Carnac, in Brittany, France—were all built at this time. But what happened nearly 2,000 years earlier to give birth to this tradition?

A Land of Plenty

As a result of the dramatic improvement in the climate that occurred after the last Ice Age, people's living conditions changed entirely. As the forests advanced, hunting techniques altered, requiring new tools and hunting equipment. The axe, as well as the bow and arrow, came into use for the first time. For the most part, these developments occurred simultaneously over a vast area, from North Africa, in the south, to Scandinavia, in the north. But in one respect, the people along the Atlantic coasts of Ireland, France, and Portugal differed from their kinsfolk: they were the first people in the world to build megalithic tombs over their dead.

The climatic shift brought about sweeping changes in vegetation and landscape, and the so-called Atlantic period began about 6000 BC. As the average annual temperature rose, the open, boreal forests of pine and hazel gave way to dark, dense forests of deciduous species such as linden, oak, and elm, and the sun-loving undergrowth was replaced by ferns and ivy. This did not suit grazing animals, which in many places decreased markedly in numbers—some, such as the giant deer (*Megalocerus giganteus*), becoming extinct. Other animals, such as the wild boar, flourished. Europe boasted a much warmer climate 7,000 years ago than it does at the present time. Species such as the water chestnut and the European pond tortoise thrived as far north as Scandinavia, whereas today we have to go as far south as southern central Europe to find them in their wild state.

At the same time, much of the ice sheets, which had been several kilometers thick, melted away, leading to a dramatic rise in the sea level. The North Sea was drowned, and the English Channel and the Irish Sea were created, turning England and Ireland into islands. Over a period of 2,000 years, almost half of western Europe was submerged. One might expect that such a dramatic reduction in land would have made it more difficult for humans to survive, but in fact, the countless newly created bays, inlets, and brackish lagoons provided one of the richest ecosystems on Earth for human subsistence.

Along the entire Atlantic coast, thick rubbish heaps, consisting primarily of mussel and oyster shells, bear witness to the importance of seafood for Mesolithic societies at this time. These heaps, known as kitchen (or shell) middens, are often more than 50 meters (164 feet) long, 20 meters (66 feet) wide, and sometimes more than 5 meters (16 feet) thick.

The people living along the coasts of Portugal, northern Spain, France, Ireland, western England, Holland, and southern Scandinavia all adapted to the changed conditions in the same way. The rich environment led to many of these societies becoming more or less sedentary, and while most groups in Europe's interior soon had to supplement the gathering of plants with farming, it took nearly a thousand years before the coastal peoples along the Atlantic were forced to do the same. This was in spite of the fact that inland and coastal societies were in close contact with each other: the appearance of pottery and polished stone axes among the coastal hunter-gatherers clearly demonstrates that they were influenced by the farmers of central Europe.

It is in the light of these facts that we may perceive the subsequent developments. As a result of their secure food supply and settled way of life, the coastal hunter-gatherers soon developed cultural practices typical of advanced farming societies. About 5000 BC, the first burial grounds appeared in southern Scandinavia. Sites such as Barum and Skateholm, in Sweden, and Bøgebakken, north of Copenhagen, in Denmark, have become legendary. A few centuries later, the first boulders were pulled into position over the dead on the west coast of Ireland and on the south coast of Brittany, in France. The megalithic tradition had begun.

The Social Revolution

When a group of people becomes sedentary, their way of life and mutual relations soon change considerably. The reason for increased sedentism within the Stone Age societies along the Atlantic coast is to be found in the presence of a wide range of foodstuffs that varied with the seasons and could be reached from the settlements in less than a day. In summer, the deciduous forests were filled with plants, fungi, roots, bulbs, and fruits; small game, larvae, and other edible insects abounded. Birds, birds' eggs, and fish supplemented this richly varied and nutritious diet. In the autumn, nuts and berries were eaten, whereas seafood and big-game formed the major part of the winter diet. Mussels, oysters, fish, and seals were vital foods for groups living in the year-round settlements.

In mobile societies, all members of a group probably performed the same activities. But as societies became sedentary, individual group members began to specialize in such skills as tool-making, food production, hunting, or fishing. At the same time, there was a growing need for greater social organization, and groups began to lay claim to resource areas in which other groups were not allowed to operate. Instead

of roaming freely, without territorial boundaries, more and more groups came to occupy specific regions, and the risk of conflict arose for the first time, although as long as populations remained small and resources were rich, there were probably few disputes. The first acts of aggression that can be traced in the archaeological record belong to the early, sedentary farming societies in central Europe: fortified settlements, battle-clubs, and ceremonial axes tell their own story.

The determining factor in this process of change was population growth. In present-day or historically known mobile societies, groups are not allowed to increase in size unless there is enough for all the members of the group to eat, even during the hardest of times; and in any case, it is impossible to carry more than one child during long migrations. Long periods of breast-feeding (which automatically reduces female fertility), abortion, and infanticide all serve to regulate population levels. As a result, starvation and

⇧ An infrared photograph showing Ballysadare Bay and the southern part of the Knocknarea Peninsula, in County Sligo, northwestern Ireland, in the middle of which lies the megalithic grave field of Carrowmore. The arrow indicates the kitchen midden area at Culleenamore. Infrared photography makes it possible to locate prehistoric remains that are not visible to the naked eye.

MEGALITH SITES IN EUROPE

BC	BRITTANY	IRELAND	BRITAIN	IBERIA	N. EUROPE
1500					
2000			Stonehenge III	Praia das Marcas	
2500					
3000	Gavrinis	Sliabh Guillion / Poulnabrone	Stonehenge II / Avebury / Giant's Hill / Skara Brae	Los Millares / Santa Cruz	Tustrup
3500	Carnac / Kerléven	Newgrange / Knowth	Stonehenge I / Stones of Stenness / West Kennet		Grønhøj / Carlshögen / Karleby / Drenthe
4000		Carrowmore 7	Fussell's Lodge / Lambourn	Orca das Seixas / Fragoas	Gladsax
4500	Ile Carn / Ile Bono				
5000	Barnenez / Ile Gaignog / Kercado	Carrowmore 4			

293

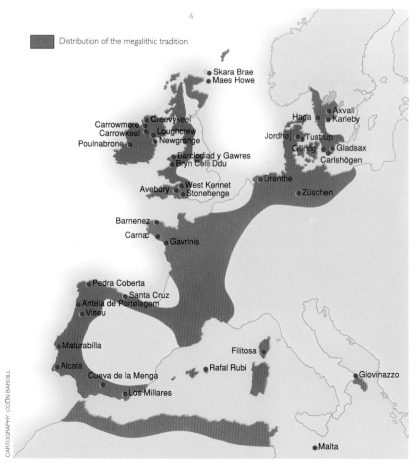

Distribution of the megalithic tradition

CARTOGRAPHY: COLIN BARDILL

**MEGALITHIC SITES OF
WESTERN EUROPE**

The distribution of the megalithic tradition in western Europe, showing major monuments and sites. Very similar monuments were erected from Portugal, in the southwest, to Scandinavia, in the north.

GÖRAN BURENHULT

☝ A type of megalithic tomb known as a dolmen, at the grave field of Carrowmore, in northwestern Ireland. Together with some of the monuments in Brittany, France, this area has produced some of the earliest megalithic datings so far known.

4000 BC, that the first megalithic tombs were erected in western Europe.

Mobile hunter-gatherers seldom have permanent burial grounds, so grave fields, where a society's dead are all buried inside a defined area, are a sure sign of a population with a high degree of sedentism. While all known hunter-gatherers perform certain rituals or ceremonies in connection with burials, the burials generally take place wherever the group happens to be at the time, and such people rarely inter the dead below ground or erect lasting monuments above ground. Instead, the dead are often placed on platforms in the wilderness, and scavenging birds of prey restore the remains to the earth. It goes without saying that this kind of burial is seldom found in the archaeological record, and this explains why few graves have been discovered dating from the greater part of the time of the European Mesolithic hunter-gatherers. The first grave fields, which appeared about 5000 BC, thus testify to a considerable change in settlement patterns. The first megaliths are obvious examples of the same process.

The First Megaliths

In the Knocknarea Peninsula, in County Sligo, northwestern Ireland, about 40 stone monuments today overlook the Atlantic Ocean: dolmens, passage tombs, and stone circles. Clustered together in the interior of the peninsula, these monuments are all built of crude boulders torn loose from the surrounding mountains during the last glaciation and spread all over the area like meteors. The place is called Carrowmore, a Celtic name meaning "field of many stones". Originally, there may have been as many as 200 tombs, but during the past 100 years quarrying has destroyed many of them. Today, the area is protected against further destruction.

Between 1977 and 1982, a series of large-scale excavations was carried out at four of the undestroyed tombs at Carrowmore, and at a number of Stone Age settlements along the coast and on nearby Knocknarea Mountain. Many of these were kitchen midden settlements containing huge numbers of shells, predominantly of oysters. The dates of the grave field were startling. Carrowmore turned out to be one of the world's oldest known megalithic grave fields, its earliest monuments erected by about 4700 BC. The excavated settlements, as well as the large quantities of unopened mussels and oysters, the magnificent bone needles made from deer antler, and the ornaments made from sperm-whale teeth that were found in the graves, show that the monuments were built by people who were mainly hunter-gatherers but were increasingly turning to cattle breeding.

The situation in northwestern Ireland was far from unique. During the fifth millennium BC,

malnutrition are almost unknown among mobile hunter-gatherers, despite the fact that they often inhabit areas with poor food resources.

When hunter-gatherers adopt a settled way of life, the balance changes. Tasks such as building houses, cultivation, and herding are done more easily by a large group. Large numbers of people are also an advantage when dealing with competing or even hostile groups. As a result, sedentism is closely connected with a heavy increase in population growth.

Paradoxically, the lavish coastal resources of the Atlantic coast forced the hunter-gatherers to engage actively in food production. Groups were tempted to settle in one place, and as time passed, the growing population could not support itself solely on what nature had to offer within the settlement area. A reduction in the salt content of sea water—which reduced oyster numbers, for example—accelerated this inevitable development. By about 4000 BC, most hunter-gatherer societies along the Atlantic coast had adopted a Neolithic way of life and had become part-time herders, although marine resources were still the main source of food for a long time. It was during this period of transformation, between 5000 BC and

similar social changes occurred more or less simultaneously in France, Spain, and Portugal. Some of the stone-built tombs in Brittany are among the oldest monuments known anywhere in the world. On the French Mediterranean coast, a farming economy was introduced into the Mesolithic Tardenoisian culture (named after the site of La Fère-en-Tardenois) during the sixth millennium BC, whereas the oldest known Neolithic settlements on the Atlantic coast did not appear until the beginning of the fifth millennium, about 4850 BC. The oldest layers of a settlement excavated at Curnic, in Guissény, have provided this early dating.

There are close similarities between the resource areas of the French regions, where megalithic traditions were first established, and those of Carrowmore. The populations along the Atlantic coast had access to a variety of apparently inexhaustible food resources, especially in the form of marine life. It is no coincidence that the central area of the megalithic tradition in France, the Bay of Morbihan, continues to be one of western Europe's best areas for oysters and other shellfish.

In addition, rivers abounded with fish, and the surrounding swamps teemed with birds. Further inland, the Atlantic deciduous forest offered an abundance of animal and plant foods. If farming was a part of a group's subsistence, it took place within a small enough area to allow megalithic traditions to develop. It has been argued that stone-built tombs served as territorial markers, and it cannot be ruled out that the monuments, apart from serving as graves and cult centers, also signaled a group's right to occupy a particular area.

An important find, showing that a pure hunting-gathering economy of the Mesolithic Tardenoisian tradition survived well into megalithic times, has been uncovered in a stone-built tomb at Dissignac, in St Nazaire. It consists of large numbers of microliths, small flint points, and barbs in the form of triangles, lancets, and microburins, found together with about 800 microliths of the Tardenoisian type. As at Carrowmore, large deposits of mussel shells have also been found in several graves. Whereas the Irish burials were always cremations, the communal burials of the French passage tombs took a different form.

⚲ Grave no. 4 at Carrowmore, during excavation. Erected about 4700 BC, it is the earliest known megalithic construction in Ireland.

⚲ The portal tomb of Poulnabrone, situated in the barren landscape of Burren, in County Claire, western Ireland, is one of Ireland's best-known and most impressive megalithic tombs. It was erected about 3000 BC. Originally, the roof-block was much larger, but recently part of it broke off, and now only two-thirds remain.

IMAGES OF OLD EUROPEAN RELIGION

Marija Gimbutas

THE PERIOD KNOWN as Old Europe—from about 6500 BC to 3500 BC—is characterized by a continuity of theme and style in its artifacts that represents an enduring view of the world. The richest materials come from southeastern and central Europe—present-day Greece, Bulgaria, Romania, Moldova, western Ukraine, Serbia, Bosnia, Croatia, Hungary, the Czech Republic, and Slovakia.

This terracotta bear, from the Greek island of Syros, carries a basin that opens into the animal's hollow body. The vessel may have been used in ceremonies connected with the worship of the birth-giving goddess.

Female statuettes proliferated, and have been found in what were temples, courtyards, and burial sites. Associations between objects and symbols painted or incised on these statuettes, and on shrine walls, ritual vases, and other cult objects, tell us much about the beliefs that prevailed in Old Europe. Connected with the cycles of nature and the female body, many of these symbols were adapted by farming societies from symbols developed by earlier hunting and gathering cultures. They indicate a matrilineal, custom-bound form of village life. Broadly, these symbols are associated with the giving and protection of life, fertility, death, and regeneration.

Life-giving and Life-protecting Symbols

As in the Upper Paleolithic period, a wide range of water symbols is linked with the giving of life, including zigzags, wavy or serpentine bands, and rows of vertical lines. There are also associations between the goddess and waterfowl, and the goddess is sometimes shown in the form of a waterfowl.

When this type of symbolism was first used, copulation was probably not known to cause pregnancy.

The face of a goddess, surrounded by meandering lines, peers from a stylized vulva on what was either an altar or a throne. This was found at Szegvár-Tüzköves, in southeastern Hungary, and dates from the fifth millennium BC.
HUNGARIAN NATIONAL MUSEUM

Since it was the female who gave birth, she was seen as the life-giver, and the breasts, buttocks, and belly were thought to be endowed with the power of procreation. The moisture in the goddess's uterus and internal organs was seen as the source of life, and breast milk was considered to be the substance that sustained life.

The goddess in a birth-giving pose is common in Paleolithic and Old European art, and she is sometimes symbolized solely by a vulva. The major animal forms she assumes are a deer, an elk, and a bear. In her madonna or nurse form, she wears a bear mask and carries a pouch for a baby or holds a child on her lap. She may also appear in such a pose as a snake or a bird.

The bird-goddess appeared, sculptured and painted on pottery vessels, from the Early Neolithic period—the seventh millennium BC. Vases in the form of birds and bird-women have also been found, as have models of temples topped with the image of the bird-goddess. She has a beak or a pinched nose, a long neck, an elaborate hairstyle or crown, breasts, wings, and, sometimes, protruding buttocks. She is symbolized by streams and rainwater, in the form of horizontal or vertical parallel lines

A clay model of a temple from a Macedonian shrine. It has T-shaped openings on each side and is topped by a bird-goddess mask standing on a cylinder in the roof. The goddess's necklace is shown in relief.

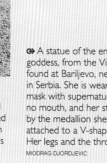

A statue of the enthroned bird-goddess, from the Vinca culture, found at Bariljevo, near Priština, in Serbia. She is wearing an oversized mask with supernatural eyes and no mouth, and her status is shown by the medallion she is wearing, attached to a V-shaped necklace. Her legs and the throne are broken.
MIODRAG DJORDJEVIC

respectively; V-shapes probably derived from the pubic triangle; and meandering lines.

The snake-goddess sits in a yogi-like position and has curved arms and legs, and a long mouth. She wears a crown, and her emblem is the snake coil. Thought to guarantee the continuity of life, she was worshipped in house shrines, and images of her continue into the Bronze and Iron Ages. In European folklore, snakes and birds are thought to be incarnations of ancestral spirits, a belief that goes back to Neolithic times.

🔵 This burnished clay figurine of a Neolithic snake-goddess comes from Crete. She has snake-like legs and a human face.
C.M. DIXON

Symbols of Fertility

The pregnant goddess, symbol of human and animal fertility, is portrayed as a nude with her hands on her enlarged belly. She predominates in the Early Neolithic period, and images of her are usually found on oven platforms and courtyard altars. She is associated with designs in the form of lozenges, triangles, snakes, and either two or four lines. With the advent of agriculture, she also became the deity that ensured soil fertility, and the sow became sacred to her.

There are also two male figures associated with plant regeneration and fertility: one is youthful and

🔵 One of the famous Cycladic figurines, this stiff nude, or white lady, from the island of Syros is carved from marble. Her arms are folded, and she wears a mask with a large beak-like nose and no mouth.
NATIONAL MUSEUM OF ATHENS/SCALA

Throughout prehistory, symbols of death are found combined with symbols of regeneration. In the shrines at Çatal Hüyük, dating from the seventh millennium BC, breasts are shown enclosing boar tusks and vulture skulls. Megalithic graves, stelae, and burial urns carry images of the owl-goddess decorated with breasts, or with her body shown as a life-creating labyrinth, with a vulva at its center.

Symbols of Regeneration and Energy

The goddess of regeneration is shown as a bee; a butterfly; a triangle; an hourglass shape with human head and feet, or with hands in the form of bird claws; a fish; a frog; and a hedgehog. A bull with crescent horns, or a bull's head alone, was also one of the earliest and most common symbols of regeneration and energy. The egg, another universal symbol of rebirth, has been associated with the beginning of the universe since Paleolithic times.

The ideology that gave rise to this extraordinary range of symbols appears to have ultimately disappeared in the wake of the far-reaching social and economic changes that

strong and has an erect phallus; the other is ancient and peaceful. Both men are shown seated on stools. The old man sits quietly, his hands resting on his knees or supporting his chin. He is the god of dying vegetation—a major Bronze Age god in Southwest Asia and universally known throughout European history.

Symbols of Death

The goddess of death is shown as a rigid nude, her folded arms pressed tightly to her bosom and her legs together or tapering. She either has no face, her face being represented by a nose alone, or is masked, and her pubic triangle is supernaturally large. Sometimes she is shown as a finger-like object made of bone or bone-colored material that is either undecorated or has round, owl-like eyes. Her image is present from the Upper Paleolithic through the period of Old Europe, and extends to about 2500 BC in the Aegean area.

occurred during the fourth and third millennia BC, which I believe are linked to successive waves of Indo-European pastoralists from the South Russian steppes. By degrees, the Old European world view, with its focus on the mother, gave way to an emphasis on the father.

MARIJA GIMBUTAS

🔵 White lady statuettes such as this one found near Sparta, in the Peloponnese, are always associated with death and are often found in Neolithic graves in southeastern Europe. The figure stands rigidly, with folded arms, and has an enormous pubic triangle.

🐸 The frog goddess is a major Old European archetype of birth-giving and regeneration. This black stone amulet from Thessaly is perforated, suggesting that it was intended to be attached to something else.
MARIJA GIMBUTAS

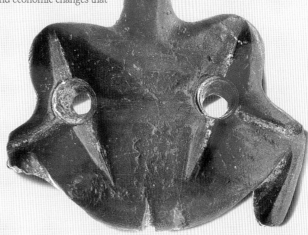

⚘ The famous mound of Barnenez, in northern Brittany, France, contains a tomb consisting of 11 chambers, which are reached by long, narrow passages. The earliest parts of the mound were built about 4500 BC.

C. CUNY/EXPLORER/AUSCAPE

⚘ Reconstruction of a long-barrow at Fussell's Lodge, in Wessex, England. The barrow was 51.5 meters (170 feet) long and was built about 3900 BC to 3800 BC.

ILLUSTRATION: KEN RINKEL, AFTER PAUL ASHBEE (1970): *THE EARTHEN LONG BARROW IN BRITAIN*, DENT, LONDON.

They were inhumations (burials of uncremated bodies), and the grave goods consisted mainly of necklace beads, stone axes, and pottery. Some of the oldest dated stone-built monuments in Brittany are the passage tombs of Barnenez, Ile Gaignog, and Kercado, which were all erected between about 4800 BC and 4500 BC. The material from Kercado comes from an early excavation, but its date closely corresponds with those of the other two. Like most megalithic monuments in western Europe, the French tombs were often rebuilt and enlarged a number of times, or were at least used continuously for long periods of time.

From Tomb to Temple

Almost all the European megalithic monuments were erected during the fourth millennium BC in what were by then well-established farming societies. Later, a handful of regions along the Atlantic coast developed into important ceremonial centers, which probably served ritual purposes for sizeable surrounding areas, far beyond the immediate territories. These early farming societies were characterized by rapid population growth, made possible by the production and storage of food. At the same time, a smaller number of food sources led to greater risks when fluctuations occurred in food production: bad harvests and sudden diseases among animals could have devastating effects on the population. Once the virgin forests of Europe had been occupied by farmers and herders and no further population expansion was possible, pressure on resources increased, forcing people to make better use of existing territories. Improved agricultural technology became necessary, resulting in the appearance of the plow and, during the Late Neolithic period, the two-wheeled cart. Pressures on resources apparently led to conflicts between

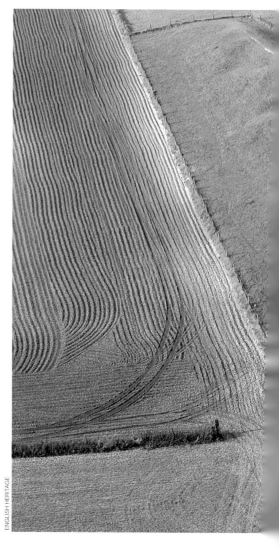

ENGLISH HERITAGE

neighboring groups of people. Many archaeological finds, such as fortified settlements of different kinds and ceremonial battle-axes, reflect increasing levels of aggression.

Jobs such as clearing new land and constructing fences are often beyond the abilities of a single family, and a considerable number of people would have been needed to build the large fortifications and ceremonial centers that early on became part of the first farming societies. During the fourth millennium BC, massive henges and palisades were erected across the continent, in England (in the form of causewayed enclosures), and through to southern Scandinavia—a henge being a circular monument built for ceremonial purposes, generally surrounded by a ditch. As a rule, groups of sizeable burial monuments were situated close to such constructions. The graves often consist of long mounds, a type of structure that is well known across Europe—from Kujavian graves in Poland

◄● The long-barrow of West Kennet, in Wiltshire, southern England, is part of the ritual complex of Avebury. It is about 100 meters (330 feet) long and was built about 3500 BC.

♀ The wall of stones in the eastern end of the West Kennet long-barrow blocks the entrance to a passage that leads into five burial chambers, where the remains of some 46 people have been found.
RONALD SHERIDAN/ANCIENT ART & ARCHITECTURE COLLECTION

♀ The eastern end of the West Kennet long-barrow consists of a concave wall of huge sandstones, blocking an earlier entrance.

to English long-barrows. In western Europe, particularly in the English long-barrows, there is evidence of the practice of secondary burial after removal of the flesh, and the megalithic tombs thus served as ossuaries. Similar constructions have also been found in southern Scandinavia, and from about 3800 BC long-barrows and, occasionally, houses for the dead were erected in Denmark. Recently, however, an entirely new type of Scandinavian monument from this time has come to light: large fortified constructions of a ceremonial character.

At Sarup, on the Danish island of Funen, lies one of these imposing Early Neolithic structures. It consists of a system of moats or pits, each 20 meters (66 feet) in length, which together constitute a formation hundreds of meters long. Close by, a system of earthworks has been found on which a 3 meter (10 foot) high palisade of gigantic oak logs was erected. The whole site

ENGLISH HERITAGE

Stonehenge, in Wiltshire, is undoubtedly one of the world's most famous prehistoric sites and the most striking megalithic monument in Europe. For a long time, it was a major ritual center for megalithic western Europe. The oldest building phase has been dated at about 3300 BC, when the site consisted of a circular wall with ditches, along which ran a series of sacrifical pits, the so-called "Aubrey Holes". During the second phase, which occurred about 500 years later, the inner stone circle, the "Bluestone Circle", was erected. Today's magnificent stone circle with lintels was built during the early phases of the Bronze Age, about 1800 BC. During all of its long period of use, Stonehenge probably served as a temple that received the first rays of the summer solstice, on 21 June.

covers an area of about 4 hectares (10 acres) and dates from about 3400 BC. All the Danish ceremonial centers known today lie on spits of land in marshes and water systems, and groups of nearby stone-built tombs have been documented. A similar construction has also been found at Stävie, in southern Sweden.

These grand constructions, like the contemporary megalithic graves and temples, must have required joint efforts that would have demanded considerable social organization. Farming societies under the leadership of village chiefs were probably already in existence during the early phases of the European Neolithic period; probably, too, the farming societies behind the large megalithic centers were chiefdoms, with all that this implies in terms of paramount chiefs, specialization, social differentiation, and the redistribution of goods and services. In historically known chiefdoms, the subordinated village chiefs are often members of the royal family, or at least closely related to the paramount chief, and this creates close ties.

The paramount chief often serves as a religious head as well—a master of ceremonies or even a high priest—and in these societies there are objects and regalia that can be linked directly to official positions and duties, as well as temples and ceremonial centers. It is in this connection that we may be able to understand the reasons behind the erection of those remarkable megalithic monuments at that time, especially in England, Ireland, and France.

The Sun and the Stones

In Wiltshire, in southern England—one of the main areas for stone-built tombs in Europe—there are a number of huge circular monuments. The earliest constructions were causewayed enclosures, such as the one on Windmill Hill, where a system of ditches and earthworks with transverse passages provides the basic structure. Most characteristic, however, are the henges, which are the most common kind of construction in the area and are often equipped with circular ditches and one or more inner circles built of stone or wood.

The biggest and most remarkable of these circular monuments is Avebury, in the middle of which now lies a whole village complete with church, pub, and petrol station; Woodhenge and Stonehenge are others.

The actual megalithic tomb at each of these sites is most often built into the short side of a magnificent long-barrow, and an almost complete lack of ornamental decorations on the graves and ceremonial monuments is characteristic of the region. The exception is Stonehenge, which boasts a series of carvings of bronze axes dating from early metal times, the period when the monument was last in use.

Modern excavations at Avebury have shown that polished stone axes were deposited there during religious ceremonies. By studying the shapes of these axes and the kinds of rock from which they were made, it is easy to determine where they came from, and it has been shown that they originated from practically every known megalithic area in southwestern England—from Cornwall, in the south, to Liverpool, in the north. Interestingly, no axes have been found that can be shown to have originated from the rich Neolithic districts further east, the reason being that megalithic burial and ceremonial traditions

⚷ The huge site of Avebury, in Wiltshire, with a diameter of more than 400 meters (1,300 feet)—in the middle of which lies a whole village— is the biggest henge monument in the region. It was used between about 3000 BC and 2000 BC, and forms part of a major ritual complex that also includes the West Kennet long-barrow, Windmill Hill, and Silbury Hill.

↩ The stone circle that surrounds Avebury originally consisted of more than 100 stones, many of which weigh about 40 tonnes (39 tons).

CAUSEWAYED ENCLOSURES

RICHARD BRADLEY

Farming communities in Europe first appeared mainly in two areas. On the fertile soils of central Europe and the Rhineland, we find evidence of large settlements with a productive agricultural economy; and here it seems as if people were moving into a largely unused environment. In the western Mediterranean, along the Atlantic coastline, and in southern Scandinavia, farming was adopted more gradually, and there is evidence of stable populations of hunter-gatherers. Each of the two areas is associated with one distinctive kind of monument: megalithic tombs originated along the Atlantic coastline and in Scandinavia; earthwork enclosures first developed among the Rhineland settlements and in neighboring areas.

The contrast goes even further. Some of the earliest burial monuments along the coastline copy the form of the longhouses in the agricultural heartland, and in these areas the houses of the living are rarely found. Where the large settlements of central Europe are discovered, especially those in the Rhineland, they are sometimes enclosed by earthworks consisting of between one and three banks and ditches. These can form continuous barriers, but in certain cases the ditches are interrupted at regular intervals by narrow causeways—hence the term "causewayed enclosures".

The earliest enclosures are poorly understood. They date from about 4800 BC and were built towards the end of the first period of farming expansion in central Europe. Often they were constructed near substantial settlements, and sometimes they occupy open spaces in between the main groups of houses and emphasize an area of ground that had already been important for some time. They were usually constructed towards the end of the period in which the settlement was in use, and sometimes even after any houses had been abandoned. These enclosures seem to have been used for a variety of communal activities,

including preparing food and making flint artifacts. On a few sites, new settlements have been built on old enclosures, and in these cases the earthworks were sometimes rebuilt on a larger scale. Sites that began as specialized enclosures within a heavily settled landscape sometimes themselves became fortified settlements. Among these were settlements whose inhabitants specialized in making fine pottery.

By about 4000 BC, there are signs of a more fragmented pattern of settlement. Major groups of longhouses no longer appear, and there are fewer signs of an expanding agricultural economy. While settlement sites are harder to discover, causewayed enclosures continue to be built, and their distribution extends to France. More of them adopt an extremely stereotyped ground plan. A few of these earthworks and ditches still enclose houses, but alongside these there is a range of quite new kinds of archaeological deposits. Some of the enclosures contained special kinds of artifacts, including unusual types of pottery normally found only with the dead. Meat joints, or even entire animals, have been found buried either within the filling of the ditches or in specially excavated pits inside the enclosure. Some appear to be the

remains of feasts, while others may be sacrificial deposits. There are also human burials. Although whole bodies are sometimes found, isolated bones are more common. This is consistent with the discovery of defleshed human remains, sometimes in elaborate formal arrangements, inside Neolithic funeral monuments. Some parts of the body are underrepresented in the monuments, suggesting that ancestral relics may have been circulated amongst the living. Human skulls are frequent finds and were often deposited in the ditches.

Causewayed enclosures were most widely distributed between about 3800 BC and 3200 BC. They extended from central Europe as far west as the Atlantic coast of France, as far south as Languedoc, and as far north as Britain, Denmark, and Sweden. As they did so, we find two major developments. Some enclosures were built in areas where there is little evidence of intensive farming. At the same time, the causeways in the ditches became the focus for more and more extravagant deposits of artifacts and human and animal bones. A growing proportion of the objects deposited were of nonlocal origin. The circulation of human remains became even more important, and it

◄ Hambledon Hill, in England, where the earthworks of a late prehistoric hill-fort overlie a complex of Neolithic causewayed enclosures and burial mounds. One enclosure was ringed by human skulls and may have been used for exposing the dead, while another was a defended settlement.

is only in this period that we find earthwork enclosures in the same areas as megalithic tombs—human bones may even have been moved between these monuments. Some enclosures were still constructed in the heart of the settled landscape, but in other areas they were in remote locations, sometimes in small woodland clearings. They took on important roles as communal meeting places, and there is still greater evidence that they were used for the exchange of exotic objects and for large-scale feasting.

Finally, in Britain and western France, a few of these monuments were reconstructed as defended settlements. Their earthworks were rebuilt without any causeways, and inside we find the remains of houses. Sometimes these defenses were not effective: a small number have been discovered that were attacked and destroyed. In Denmark, we find a similar sequence, but there the earthworks were abandoned and replaced by open settlements. In a sense, the history of enclosures turns back on itself. Some of the earliest sites had been enclosed settlements; so, too, were some of the last to be built. In between, they played a variety of more mysterious roles in prehistoric society, including the celebration of the dead.

The fact that the same kind of enclosure was built for considerably more than a thousand years, and across such large areas of Europe, is testimony to the strength of beliefs that we cannot understand in any detail today. But we do know that a basic continuity of ritual architecture has been maintained over a similar period in more recent societies—we might think, for example, of the stereotyped ground plans of mosques and Christian churches.

were not adopted in those regions. The area of origin of the axes found at Avebury thus corresponds exactly with the area of distribution of megalithic tombs in southwestern England. This gives an important dimension to the contemporary religious and social systems, in which an advanced religious organization apparently reached far beyond the borders of the individual megalithic farming economies scattered throughout this vast area. Furthermore, a very marked boundary line can be shown to have been drawn against societies that for some reason did not adopt the tradition of building megalithic monuments.

The sheer size of the megalithic structures in Wiltshire suggests that they were erected by a work force that could not have been called in from the immediate vicinity alone. The ditch and the large stone circle at Avebury boast a diameter of more than 400 meters (1,300 feet), and the circle originally consisted of more than 100 stones, many of which weigh about 40 tonnes (39 tons). Inside the circle were two smaller stone circles, each measuring about 100 meters (330 feet) in diameter, and from the southern part of the monument a system of stone alignments almost 2 kilometers (a little over a mile) long—the Kennet Avenue—leads in the direction of a huge mound known as Silbury Hill.

Silbury Hill is Europe's largest prehistoric mound. It is 40 meters (130 feet) high and covers an area of 2.2 hectares (5 acres). This huge hill is probably not a burial mound—the partly terraced hillside and the flat crest suggest that it once formed the foundation of a temple building. It may have been used in the cult ceremonies at Avebury

and Kennet Avenue. During the 1970s, a tunnel was cut into the middle of the mound. No grave was found, but it was established that the entire hill was man-made, and radiocarbon datings of peat found inside showed that it was built during megalithic times and was partly contemporaneous with Avebury. It has been calculated that if 500 men were to have been constantly engaged in building Silbury Hill, it would have taken more than 10 years to construct. A central leadership, or at least a concentration of religious power, would have been essential to ensure such a long-term effort. To a great extent, this also applies to the building of Stonehenge, where it is thought that the building material for the bluestone circle was transported to Wiltshire from the Preseli Mountains, in southern Wales, some 400 kilometers (250 miles) away.

It is likely that a similar religious "super-organization" existed, along with traditional tribal societies, in another important megalithic region in western Europe: Carnac, in France. The huge structures concentrated in the area around Carnac and Locmariaquer, in Morbihan, southern Brittany, are among Europe's most distinctive megalithic monuments. The most conspicuous are the menhir (standing stone) alignments erected in three main complexes: Le Ménec, Kermario, and Kerlescan, where some 3,000 menhirs still stand in rows. Most of them are colossal—up to 6 meters (20 feet) high—and together the alignments are nearly 4 kilometers (more than 2 miles) long. The complexes of erected stones are all composed of parallel alignments—at Kerlescan, no fewer than 13—and each complex is about 100 meters

The passage grave of Les Pierres Plates, at Locmariaquer, in Brittany, France. A large number of stones in this monument, notably the orthostats, are decorated with carvings.

Silbury Hill, in Wiltshire, is 40 meters (130 feet) high and 160 meters (525 feet) in diameter, making it the largest man-made mound in Europe. It was built some time during the third millennium BC. It contains no burial remains, and it is thought that it once served as the foundation of a temple building.

(330 feet) wide. Connected with these rows of stones are stone altars, stone circles, and a long series of megalithic tombs.

Many suggestions have been made as to the ceremonial function of the alignments, but no conclusive explanation has yet been given. Perhaps the individual stones represented deceased ancestors. Le Grand Menhir—a huge menhir at Locmariaquer, which today is broken into five pieces but was originally 21 meters (nearly 70 feet) high—may once have been used for astronomical observations or simply as a clearly visible center for the cult, as on clear days it could have been seen from many places around the Bay of Morbihan, including the stone alignments at Le Ménec, Kermario, and Kerlescan. Le Grand Menhir, probably the world's biggest menhir, is partly shaped and has an even, smoothed surface. It consists of a kind of granite that is not native to the area and must have been transported from the interior of Brittany to its final position by the water's edge—a remarkable feat, considering that it weighs 350 tonnes (345 tons).

In terms of megalithic ornamentation, Carnac is one of Europe's most important regions. At present, we know of 250 decorated stones from 75 different sites, mainly passage tombs, in Brittany alone. The earliest passage tombs, such as Ile Gaignog, date from the period between 4800 BC and 3700 BC. They contain simple depictions, such as yoke-like figures, sickles (or "hooks"), and axe blades with handles, and various kinds of anthropomorphic motifs— so-called "bucklers", which appear to represent divine figures.

The later passage tombs date from the period between 3700 BC and 3100 BC. By that time, megalithic monuments had become considerably

◄○ The Le Ménec alignments, at Carnac, in Brittany, France, consist of 11 parallel lines of stones more than a kilometer long. We do not know what ceremonial function these alignments may have served, but it has been suggested that the individual stones may represent dead ancestors.

CHARLES WALKER COLLECTION, LONDON

⌖ A large number of megalithic tombs, stone altars, and stone circles, such as this one, are found in association with the remarkable stone alignments of Carnac.

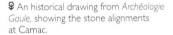

⚲ An historical drawing from *Archéologie Gaule*, showing the stone alignments at Carnac.

LOUIS BERTRAND/EXPLORER/AUSCAPE

◉ The large passage grave of Gavrinis, situated on an island in the Bay of Morbihan, near Carnac, is one of the large megalithic monuments in western Europe that contain decorated stones. The orthostats in both the chamber and the passage are decorated. Clear similarities can be seen between this site and Newgrange, in Ireland.

⚢ The carvings of Gavrinis are characterized by large groups of U-shaped patterns, snake figures, and zig-zag lines, as well as triangular axe blades in relief.

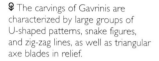

P. PLISSON/EXPLORER/AUSCAPE

P. PLISSON/EXPLORER/AUSCAPE

⚢ The passage grave of Antelas, at Oliveira de Frades, near Viseu, Portugal. This grave contains magnificent megalithic decorations in the form of schematic paintings in red and black.

GÖRAN BURENHULT

bigger, the tombs' interiors had been enlarged, and the passages extended. It was during this period that well-defined, inner compartments were constructed. The ornamentation, which originated from the earlier period, went through a remarkable development during this later phase, and it was at this time that some of the most splendid decorations in megalithic western Europe were created—equaled only by the art of the passage tombs in the Boyne Valley, in Ireland. There are close similarities between some elements of the decorations in the two regions, and contact between the two regions at this time of artistic perfection cannot be ruled out.

The peak of megalithic composition is represented by a passage tomb on Ile de Gavrinis, an island in the middle of the Bay of Morbihan. Here, both the stones in the chamber and those in the passage are decorated, and U-shaped images are boxed inside each other and placed in groups of differing sizes and in a variety of positions.

The anthropomorphic figures, which were among the original images in the early passage tombs in Brittany, developed from symbolic images into more and more marked, visual parts of the cult ceremonies. From very simple, frame-like images, these bucklers gradually became figures with marks indicating eyes and breasts, and in spite of their austere style, they appear to depict a divine figure. In megalithic monuments dating from the end of the Stone Age, these images appear to represent a female goddess. In gallery graves, which are the latest of the megalithic tombs, she is represented by a pair of breasts in relief, often with a necklace of beads placed either above or below the breasts. The worship of this female deity is also reflected in freestanding anthropomorphic stelae (upright slabs) or menhir statues in western France,.which have eyes, a nose, and marks clearly indicating breasts: there is no doubt as to their sex. Some of these figures, usually those with necklaces, also have stylized hands, usually placed below the breasts.

Along with the magnificent stone-built tombs in Brittany, the Irish passage graves represent some of Europe's most imposing and grandiose monuments. Most of them are clustered in groups in the northern and, especially, the eastern parts of the island, and they are often dramatically situated high on mountain ridges. Loughcrew, in County Meath, and Carrowkeel, in County Sligo, are among the important grave fields, and there are also magnificent constructions at Tara and Fourknocks, in County Meath, and at Baltinglass, in County Wicklow. The most outstanding, however, are Newgrange, Knowth, and Dowth, in the Boyne Valley, County Meath.

Some 25 kilometers (16 miles) from its mouth at Drogheda, by the Irish Sea, the Boyne River makes a sharp bend, in the middle of which lie three giant 5,000-year-old mounds. Two of them, Newgrange and Knowth, have for many years been the subject of systematic excavations. Newgrange has been reliably dated at about 3200 BC to 3000 BC, and thus represents the end of a 1,500-year-old megalithic tradition in Ireland. Knowth is somewhat older and has been dated to about 3700 BC to 3500 BC.

Newgrange is gigantic. It measures 85 meters (279 feet) in diameter and covers an area of almost half a hectare (1 acre). A passage 19 meters (62 feet) long leads into the cruciform chamber, which has a corbeled roof and a ceiling 6 meters (20 feet) high. Almost every stone in the kerbstone circle, as well as in the passage, is covered with ornamentation. The people who built this monument clearly had a sophisticated knowledge of astronomy: the entire grave is constructed to receive the first rays of the winter solstice on 21 December through a separate roof-box above the long passage. Newgrange is a gigantic observatory that was erected to serve a megalithic cult. (See the feature *Newgrange: Temple of the Sun.*)

Cannibals in the North

The stone-built tombs in northern Europe are known for their rich finds of burial deposits. These consist mainly of splendidly decorated pottery of many different shapes, but there are also large numbers of amber amulets in the form of miniature clubs or battle-axes. Often, these finds have been made outside the entrances to the chambers, and it was once assumed that they were the remains of grave goods that had been removed before later burials had taken place. In the 1930s, however, it was shown that most of these finds had never been placed inside the chambers but were simply the remnants of sacrificial food offerings made in connection with burials and

other recurring ceremonies. That an ancestor cult predominated is clearly indicated by these megalithic rituals.

The burials always took the form of inhumations. Large numbers of bodies were placed on the floor of the chamber, with space often being left for later burials. During the time they were in use, the graves must have been filled with bodies in varying stages of decomposition. In some places, the burial chambers were divided into smaller units separated by stone slabs. As a rule, these compartments are too small to accommodate a body lying prone, yet the bones of complete individuals have been found within them. It is possible that the flesh was removed from the bodies before they were buried, as in long-barrow burials in England, perhaps by boiling or decomposition. However, since there are no traces of cutting on the bones, and since not even the smallest bones of the feet are missing, it seems likely that the bodies were placed in a sitting position in the compartments, with their arms and legs tied together, and that they were left to decompose.

Cremated human bones have often been found during excavations of dolmens and passage graves, particularly outside the entrances to the chambers, and this has been taken as clear evidence that human sacrifices took place in connection with megalithic burial ceremonies, as cremation was never practiced in northern Europe during the Stone Age. Furthermore, the excavation of a dolmen at Fosie, in southernmost Sweden, has shown that a series of cremated human bones, which were all placed beneath separate stone slabs, was the result of cannibalism. Probably only the brains were eaten, as the bones consisted of the deliberately broken cranial parts of 22 people.

⚤ The megalithic decorations in the Viseu region, in Portugal, as well as those in Galicia and Cantabria, in Spain, consist mainly of paintings, which are often on stones in the chambers. Fortunately, many of these 5,000-year-old works of art are very well preserved, including this one in the passage grave of Antelas.
REPRODUCED BY PERMISSION OF OXFORD UNIVERSITY PRESS FROM ELIZABETH SHEE TWOHIG (1981): *THE MEGALITHIC ART OF WESTERN EUROPE* [AFTER ALBUQUERQUE E. CASTRO *ET AL.* (1957): *COMM. SERV. GEOL.* 38].

♀ The first signs of aggression and war in northern Europe appeared as people began to adopt a settled way of life and to take up farming. This 35-year-old man from Porsmose, outside Naestved, in Denmark, was pierced by two bone arrows, One of them had pierced his breastbone, the other had gone through his nose and into his brain. The man lived about 3000 BC, during the time of the megalithic tradition.
NATIONAL MUSEUM OF DENMARK, DEPARTMENT OF ETHNOGRAPHY

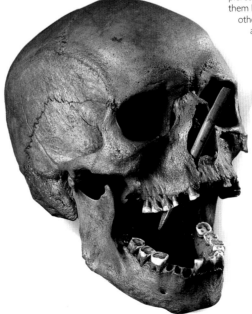

NEWGRANGE: TEMPLE OF THE SUN

GÖRAN BURENHULT

JUST ONCE EVERY YEAR, at 9.54 am on 21 December, a growing light spreads gradually in the pitch-dark burial chamber. Six minutes later, the sunbeam is at its broadest and bathes the chamber, situated 22 meters (72 feet) from the entrance, in a dazzling light. Then the light starts to fade, and by 10.15 am it has disappeared altogether.

This amazing scene lasts for 21 minutes, and after that the burial chamber remains in total darkness for a further 364 days, until the next winter solstice. The place is Newgrange, in the Boyne Valley, in Ireland, one of the most splendid megalithic monuments in Europe—a passage grave with a cruciform chamber, situated deep in a magnificent mound. Newgrange and the nearby mounds of Knowth and Dowth are grand monuments of a Stone Age society in western Europe and bear witness to an astonishing knowledge of technology and astronomy.

The graves represent the peak of an almost 2,000-year-old megalithic tradition in Ireland, and have been dated at about 3200 BC, making them more than 500 years older than the Pyramid of Cheops, in Egypt. It is well known that the sun played an important part in the cult ceremonies of the Stone Age, the best example being Stonehenge, in southern England, which was designed to predict the summer solstice. But it was not until Michael J. O'Kelly's excavation of Newgrange at the end of the 1960s that it became clear that the winter solstice, the rebirth of the year, had also been of great importance in cult ceremonies and rituals among Ireland's Stone Age farmers.

The chamber has a corbeled roof, and is thus held together by the weight of the soil above. Each roof-stone is pushed in a little more than the one below, so each layer of stones reduces the diameter of the roof. During construction, the roof must have been supported from within by stanchions. Neither the

☞ Once a year, on 21 December, at 9.54 am, the burial chamber of Newgrange is illuminated by the rising sun. At 10.15 am, this dwelling of the dead once again rests in total darkness for a further 364 days.

♀ The excavator, Michael J. O'Kelly, beside the entrance stone at Newgrange, which is considered by many to be the most exquisite example of megalithic art known. The stone slab to the right of the passage entrance is the sealing stone that once blocked the entrance and thus separated the world of the living from the world of the dead. The roof-box, through which the first rays of the winter solstice penetrate, is clearly visible above the entrance.

chamber nor its vaults has ever been rebuilt or even repaired, so the construction has withstood the ravages of time for more than 5,000 years.

In 1963, during the excavation of the monument, a notable discovery was made above the passage entrance. There is a rectangular opening, 90 centimeters (about 3 feet) high, on top of the passage roof-block, and this roof-box runs the entire length of the first passage and leads into the chamber. An elegant triangular pattern is carved on the front of the first roof-block. On the ground below the opening, two quartzite cubes were found, both of which were scored horizontally on the underside. These cubes fitted exactly into the opening, and furthermore, the first roof-block had the same kind of horizontal scores. It was obvious that the quartzite cubes had been used to seal the opening of the upper passage, and judging from the scoring, this passage had been opened and resealed frequently.

When Newgrange was completed at the end of the fourth millennium BC, the chamber and passage were sealed with a stone block, and at subsequent cult ceremonies no one was admitted to the monument's interior. Clearly, the opening and the narrow tunnel above the passage served as a "channel of communication" between the living, outside the sealed chamber, and the dead, inside.

Professor O'Kelly made some calculations relating to the function of the roof-box. These showed that the summer solstice could not have had any significance at Newgrange, but that the winter solstice, on 21 December, could possibly explain the complicated construction above the passage. In the early morning of 21 December 1969, O'Kelly made his way into the dark chamber to see if his calculations were correct. He sealed the entrance of the monument with a black cloth, just as the sealing stone had once blocked the opening, but the narrow tunnel above the passage was left open.

With his camera ready, he sat down in the middle of the floor of the chamber and waited for the sun to rise. He switched off his torch, and everything turned pitch-black. The rest is best described in O'Kelly's own words:

"At exactly 9.54 a.m. (BST) the top edge of the ball of the sun appeared above the local horizon and at 9.58 a.m. the first pencil of direct sunlight shone through the roof-box and right along the passage to reach across the tomb chamber floor as far as the front edge of the basin stone in the end-chamber. As the thin line of light widened to a

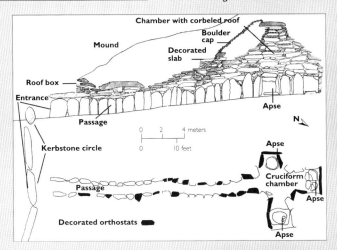

🜂 Plan and profile drawings of the passage and chamber of Newgrange. The stones marked in black are decorated. The passage that leads into the chamber extends for 19 meters (60 feet) and is lined with more than 40 monoliths, 15 of which are decorated with carvings.
AFTER O'KELLY, 1975

or only animals? Which individuals in society went to their final rest in Newgrange? Many small megalithic tombs in Ireland contain the bones of hundreds of cremated people, but only a small number have been found in Newgrange. These few may have been chiefs who also served as priests, but it is also possible that the bones are those of people sacrificed at the inauguration of the monument and that Newgrange was never used as a burial chamber. Clearly, it was primarily a cult center—not a burial place.

Newgrange provides a splendid example of the intellectual sophistication of our illiterate, Stone Age ancestors. Advanced social systems probably existed in many regions in Europe as early as 5,000 years ago. Certainly, there were powerful chiefdoms that maintained close contacts with each other over wide areas. There is evidence in southern England that the stone circles at

17 cm [7 inch] band and swung across the chamber floor, the tomb was dramatically illuminated and various details of the side and end-chambers as well as the corbelled roof could be clearly seen in the light reflected from the floor. At 10.04 a.m. the 17 cm band of light began to narrow again and at exactly 10.15 a.m. the direct beam was cut off from the tomb. For 17 minutes, therefore, at sunrise on the shortest day of the year, direct sunlight can enter Newgrange, not through the doorway, but through the specially-contrived narrow slit which lies under the roof-box at the outer end of the passage roof."

So the roof-box was opened before sunrise on 21 December every year to let the first sunbeams of the year into the chamber, but what happened then? Were the spirits of the dead consulted about the coming year? Or did the living report on what had been done during the past one? Were people sacrificed—

🜂 Newgrange has a diameter of between 79 and 85 meters (260 and 280 feet). It is bordered by a kerbstone circle consisting of 97 boulders, each more than 3 meters (about 10 feet) long, and almost all of them are richly decorated with megalithic carvings.

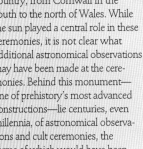

🜂 A majority of the weight-bearing monoliths in the burial chamber and the apses are exquisitely decorated, mainly with spirals and zigzag patterns, the finest ornament of all being the famous triple spiral.

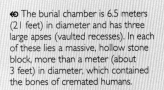

🜂 The burial chamber is 6.5 meters (21 feet) in diameter and has three large apses (vaulted recesses). In each of these lies a massive, hollow stone block, more than a meter (about 3 feet) in diameter, which contained the bones of cremated humans.

Avebury were used for cult ceremonies that were common to the whole southwestern part of the country, from Cornwall in the south to the north of Wales. While the sun played a central role in these ceremonies, it is not clear what additional astronomical observations may have been made at the ceremonies. Behind this monument—one of prehistory's most advanced constructions—lie centuries, even millennia, of astronomical observations and cult ceremonies, the forms of which would have been transmitted orally from generation to generation.

GÖRAN BURENHULT

⚜ The stone-built tombs in the district of Drenthe, in northern Holland, are some of the most impressive in Europe, both in terms of length and the size of the stones used. This dolmen at Borger, on the road between Assen and Emmen, is one of the most outstanding examples in the region.

GÖRAN BURENHULT

⚜ A well-preserved, stone-built tomb at Drouwen, north of Borger, in the district of Drenthe.

Remains of people from megalithic times who were sacrificed and eaten have also been found in bogs. One such find was made in a bog at Sigersdal, in Zealand, Denmark, consisting of the remains of two naked young girls (probably sisters) who had been strangled, clubbed, and drowned about 3500 BC. A clay pot, the bottom marked by the imprints of emmer grains, was found with them. The pot had probably contained food offerings, a common type of sacrifice during Neolithic times. Further out into the bog, 13 magnificent polished flint axes had been lowered into the water as well.

It seems likely that some form of fertility cult was behind the sacrifice at Sigersdal. By making such an offering, people believed that they would secure the right conditions for continued existence and for the return of the seasons, with new crops and new human and animal offspring. These rituals were probably linked to the winter and summer solstices, a connection that, in megalithic Europe, is clearly seen in monuments such as Newgrange and Stonehenge, whose main function was related to these important annual events.

There are several examples of cannibalism from the period around 3500 BC, when the sisters were sacrificed at Sigersdal. At Troldebjerg, in Langeland,

Denmark, the remains of at least three people have been found, together with votive offerings in the form of flint axes, battle-axes, and pottery containing food. The human offerings included a 13-year-old child and a 40-year-old woman, both of whom had been killed by violent blows to the head. Sacrificial animals, including five young steers, four pigs, a goat, and a dog, show traces of having been killed in the same way.

The Surviving Evidence

Megalithic traditions have survived in many societies in various parts of the world, and in some places stone-built tombs are still erected over the dead. Studying these more recent cultures can help us understand some of the elements that gave rise to megalithic traditions, the beliefs of megalithic people, and the function of the monuments. For a start, it is clear that such tombs were never built by mobile hunting-gathering societies. While this may seem self-evident, the building of the tombs themselves can be related to many factors, such as social ranking, group size, and a degree of territorial control, which would often have led to increased aggression.

In all such peoples studied, all members of a society are well aware of which person or family has built and uses a certain monument, and the social rank of an individual is generally reflected in the size, appearance, or placing of the tomb or the erected stone. Another distinctive trait of most of these societies is the fact that many people or families are not entitled to erect any monument at all over their dead. In some societies, every man, or at least a majority of the men, can, by way of complicated and costly ceremonies, work his way up to a sufficiently high rank for this to become possible. In other societies, however, this is not possible, because the traditional hereditary lines cannot be broken.

It is clear, therefore, that megalithic monuments are erected only by settled societies with a relatively high population density, and the right to such a monument is associated with high social rank, either inherited or acquired. Without exception, the leaders of those societies are chiefs. In addition, human sacrifices, and sometimes the eating of individuals from enemy tribes, played a crucial role in all historically known megalithic societies. This corresponds with the archaeological record of the European Neolithic period, and suggests a society in which aggressive actions were thought necessary to ensure continued existence, and in which these actions were part of religious ceremonies. Outside pressure and warfare demand powerful leaders, and it is perhaps unsurprising that all known megalithic societies are dominated by men. This does not necessarily imply that women have a low status, but only that the men hold the political power and perform the cult ceremonies.

In historically known megalithic societies, monuments never serve primarily as territorial markers, nor do they depend on the society's technological level, as they appear in societies resembling those of the Stone Age, the Bronze Age, and the Iron Age. But societies that depend on stone-built tombs for their cult ceremonies have many features in common. The cult is almost always associated with the worship of ancestors. In some heavily stratified societies, including most of the Polynesian chiefdoms in the Pacific, some megalithic monuments were associated with the worship of gods, but these are the exceptions that prove the rule. Usually, the different graves and menhirs represent ancestors whose spirits are considered to be always present and to take part in the ceremonies. Sacrificial offerings are made to appease ancestors and secure admission to the kingdom of the dead, where the final reunion takes place. In societies that erect tombs with entrances, similar to the European dolmens and passage graves, the entrance generally represents the gates of the kingdom of the dead. Clearly, people's motives in erecting megalithic monuments seem similar, irrespective of time and place.

The reasons for the decline of the megalithic tradition in Neolithic western Europe are not well understood. Economic and social collapse has been suggested as a possible explanation, but a religious upheaval probably also played a crucial part in the social changes that occurred across the continent about the middle of the third millennium BC. The changes were also partly a consequence of the appearance of metal and other innovations, such as the wheel, the cart, and possibly also the use of horses for riding. Behind this change in tradition lies the appearance of the so-called Battle-axe cultures, which were once thought to have been a part of the Indo-European migrations. It can be shown, however, that these new societies had their beginnings in the old, megalithic ones because of the continued and widespread use of the old burial grounds and, above all, because of the continuity of settlement that has been revealed by modern excavations.

From about 2800 BC, no new stone-built monuments were erected in Europe. The megalithic priests had had their day.

The world's oldest monumental entrance, the entrance to the Hagar Qim temple, on the island of Malta, is a magnificent example of early megalithic architecture.

The megalithic temple of Mnajdra, which lies on the south coast of Malta, is characterized by a complicated inner construction and the presence of high altar stones of different kinds.

NEW LIGHT ON DEATH IN PREHISTORIC MALTA:
THE BROCHTORFF CIRCLE

DAVID TRUMP, ANTHONY BONANNO, TANCRED GOUDER, CAROLINE MALONE, AND SIMON STODDART

⏺ A large, headless, standing statuette from the temple of Hagar Qim, carved from soft limestone. Although they are often referred to as "mother goddesses", the sexuality of these stone figures from Malta is ambiguous.
RONALD SHERIDAN/ANCIENT ART & ARCHITECTURE COLLECTION

THE SMALL MEDITERRANEAN ISLANDS of the Maltese archipelago are famous for their temples built between 3500 BC and 2500 BC, which are some of the earliest free-standing stone buildings in the world. These complex, lobed structures, with altars, doorways, and a great deal of decorated, carved stone, bear witness to the elaborate rituals and beliefs of prehistoric peoples.

Rituals connected with the dead were carried out in one of the most impressive of all prehistoric sites, the Hal Saflieni hypogeum. This extraordinary underground chamber was once the burial temple of an estimated 6,000 to 7,000 people. Carved out of soft limestone, it has many elements in common with the other temples, including megalithic doorways, and has steps leading into some 30 major rooms, arranged on three main levels. Salvage excavations undertaken in the early 1900s resulted in most of the skeletal material within the hypogeum being discarded and lost, and few records survive even of the layout of the finds.

An Underground Burial Monument

Recently, however, excavations have been carried out on the Brochtorff Circle, a monument on the island of Gozo similar to Hal Saflieni, and this work is providing valuable information about prehistoric burial customs, enabling researchers to fill in many details that were lost at Hal Saflieni. The Brochtorff Circle was first excavated in the 1820s, but, fortunately for posterity, these excavations were not completed. The only useful

⏺ The innermost excavated area of the Brochtorff Circle, showing the limestone cave system, embellished by architectural features.
CAROLINE MALONE/SIMON STODDART

⏵ The details of this reconstruction of the Brochtorff Circle are based on recently excavated evidence. Many of the cavities would originally have been roofed.
AFTER STEVEN ASHLEY

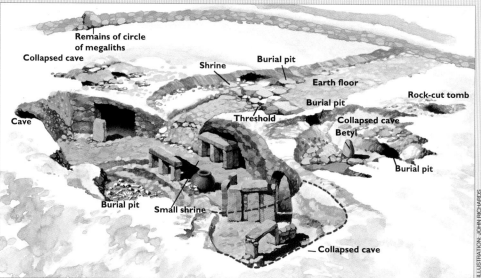

Remains of circle of megaliths
Collapsed cave
Shrine
Burial pit
Earth floor
Rock-cut tomb
Cave
Burial pit
Threshold
Collapsed cave
Betyl
Burial pit
Burial pit
Small shrine
Collapsed cave

ILLUSTRATION JOHN RICHARDS

CAROLINE MALONE/SIMON STODDART

◄● Eight limestone figures found in a bundle at the small shrine—perhaps the tools of trade of a ritual specialist. Some appear to be at varying stages of manufacture.

records of this early work are two watercolours by a local artist.

The Brochtorff Circle was first used about 4000 BC, and stands on a plateau of rough coralline limestone. A vertical shaft opened into a rock-cut tomb consisting of two chambers about 2 meters (6 feet, 6 inches) in diameter. This tomb contained the partial remains of at least 63 people, deposited in a burial rite in which many of the long bones and skulls of earlier occupants were removed and disposed of to make room for new arrivals. The bodies were placed in the chambers together with shell necklaces, pots of ocher, and small stone and bone pendants. A curious carved stone figure of type known as a statue menhir stood in the entrance of one chamber, and a large seashell in a jar of ocher stood in the other.

The Ceremonial Heart

In time, these small-scale burial tombs, which were possibly used for individual families, were superseded by a much larger communal cave cemetery. This cemetery was established in a natural cave system that was transformed through the use of blocks of softer stone, improving its appearance and adding to its architectural qualities. A circle of megaliths was set up surrounding the site, two larger, upright stones flanked the entrance, and a large temple-structure filled a roofless cave at the center of the circle. This temple was the ceremonial and ritual heart of the site. The excavations have recently un-

covered a small shrine, flanked by a standing megalithic screen, where someone, perhaps a shaman, appears to have left the tools of his trade: a bundle of figures with flat, schematic bodies, a pottery strainer, a small pot of yellow ocher, a large stone vessel and, most remarkable of all, a stone sculpture representing a pair of obese figures sitting side-by-side on a wicker couch.

These seated figures are unique in the Maltese islands and quite distinct from other forms of Mediterranean sculpture. The figures had distinctive hairstyles, with pigtails. The surviving head shows an elaborate "bob", with a pigtail at the back. One holds what may be a smaller representation of itself, and the other holds a small vessel. The attractive honey-colored stone was originally painted in many colors, and traces of black, red, and yellow can still be made out today. What was the significance of these two figures? Only by analyzing the context of the shrine in the course of future excavations can we hope to answer this question.

Immediately next to this shrine, a natural pit full of bones shows that the site was primarily a place of burial. Small "mother goddess" figurines of baked clay accompanied these burials. Bodies were not interred complete, but were evidently the subject of a series of rites that have left their traces throughout the caves and niches on the site. Bundle burials (bundles of bones), scorched burials (partly burned bones), partly articulated bodies, stacks of skulls, and numerous other configurations have been recorded, some of them buried alongside domestic animals, including pigs, sheep, and even a small puppy.

This burial site appears to have been the focus of an entire community, and preliminary analysis of the human bones suggests that people of all ages, both male and female, were buried here. Whereas there are several temples on the plateau, there is only one monumental cemetery, situated strategically on slighly higher ground between two temples.

◄● Seated side-by-side on a couch, these limestone figures (one with the head broken off) were found together with the figures shown above. The one on the left holds a smaller figure; the other, a small cup.

BRONZE AGE CHIEFDOMS AND THE END OF STONE AGE EUROPE

4 5 0 0   B C   –   7 5 0   B C

The Rise of the Individual

ANTHONY HARDING

THE AGE OF BRONZE in Europe was, in truth, a kind of Golden Age— an age in which a number of major advances occurred that were to transform the Neolithic world of "Old Europe" into the home of the Celts, the Italians, the Etruscans, the Thracians, and the Dacians, along with all the other people of the region known from historic times. The years between 3000 BC and 700 BC therefore represent a crucial transitional stage of development for society, technology, and the economy.

Although the alloys used in copper metallurgy may seem a relatively minor matter compared with the other important developments that took place during this period, metalworking for the production of tools and weapons became a major preoccupation for the people of those times. The changes that occurred in this technology over time have enabled archaeologists to develop a chronological framework for the period, and to see the period within the broader context of human development between the last Ice Age and the rise of the Greek and Roman civilizations.

⊷ Sheet bronze body-armor molded to the contours of the human torso, and decorated with bosses. This fine cuirass was found at Marmesse, in France, and dates from the Late Bronze Age—the ninth or eighth century BC.

⬥ This beaten sheet gold ornament in the form of a cross with spiral terminals, from the Moigrad Treasure, Romania, is from the Late Neolithic period, about 5000 BC to 3000 BC.

BRONZE AGE SITES

The major Bronze Age sites mentioned in the text are shown, together with mining areas. There were major Bronze Age centers in many other areas as well.

CARTOGRAPHY: RAY SIM

✿ Mine sites

Two gold earrings from Boltby Scar, Yorkshire, England. The use of gold to adorn the head and hair is a sure sign that this metal was highly valued.
BRITISH MUSEUM

The entrance to one of the Bronze Age mine shafts at Mount Gabriel, County Cork, in southwestern Ireland.

WILLIAM O'BRIEN

The Quest for Metal

Metals came into regular use, in the sense that ores were mined and smelted, back in the Neolithic period. By 4000 BC, technology had advanced to the stage that large numbers of tools were being made by the technique of smelting and hammering. The casting of copper tools became common practice after 3000 BC. Gradually, various substances, notably tin and lead, were added to the copper to harden it and so make it easier to cast; sometimes this appears to have been done simply to extend the quantities available. True bronze—copper with an admixture of about 10 percent tin—came into popular use about 2000 BC and was from then on the commonest alloy of copper. The history of gold exploitation was comparable, although alloys were much rarer. Sheet gold was more commonly used than solid gold, and was often used to cover everyday objects, such as buttons—a sure sign that this metal was regarded as something special.

The quest for metal ores must have been a major preoccupation for Bronze Age industrialists. Once sources were found, their mining methods were efficient and exhaustive. In the Austrian Alps (such as the Mitterberg area, near Bischofshoven), on the Great Orme's Head, in North Wales, and elsewhere, deep shafts and adits some hundreds of meters long were cut into solid rock to reach the veins of ore. Fires were lit to crack open the rock, and the ore was prized out with wedges and picks. At Mount Gabriel, in southern Ireland, there is also evidence of Bronze Age mining—albeit sketchy, because the miners of those times removed every trace of ore.

These early mines were predominantly worked between about 3000 BC and 750 BC. Although the methods used to date these sites have been questioned, techniques derived from the natural sciences, together with archaeology, can provide a consistent chronological framework.

The traditional approach—relying on the evidence of artifacts that link Europe with Greece, and Greece with Egypt—provides a chronology that is generally agreed upon, with certain exceptions, and in many instances the timber used in construction can be dated by means of tree-ring analysis. It is an extraordinary achievement to be able to date the building of a settlement to an exact year in the remote past: for instance, the major part of a settlement discovered in Switzerland at Mozartstrasse, near the Opera House, in central Zürich, was built about 1600 BC. Much of the timber used came from trees felled between 1604 BC and 1573 BC, but an especially large number of trees were felled in 1602 BC and between 1599 BC and 1598 BC. It is rare that artifacts themselves can be dated so precisely, but the techniques of tree-ring dating are now so well developed that they will very likely have been perfected by the year 2000.

Burial Rites and the Individual

Had you entered a burial chamber in Neolithic Europe, you would have found an extraordinary and frightening scene of disarray, with bones scattered about and newly arrived corpses lying in compartments or on shelves on either side. Burial was collective in the sense that the same space was used again and again. When one body was reduced to bare bones, it was swept aside to make room for another. One of the most remarkable changes that heralded the arrival of new beliefs and practices after 2500 BC, and marked the beginning of the Bronze Age, was the shift to individual burial throughout much of central and western Europe. Just as the nature of the new culture varied from place to place, so, too, did the timing of this change in burial practices.

Across much of continental Europe, the characteristic pottery found with these individual burials is known as corded ware, being decorated by impressing cord into the wet clay, and is most commonly in the form of tall drinking cups. Often, a stone battle-axe, so called because these axes apparently had a military and/or ceremonial function, is found with the pots. (See the feature *The Battle-axe People: Europe's First Individualists*.)

↥ The grip of a solid-hilted, Late Bronze Age sword from Switzerland. The metal grip has been cast onto the blade and secured by a set of rivets.
SWISS NATIONAL MUSEUM

⚲ A large burial mound on Overton Hill, near Avebury, Wiltshire, in southern England. Such barrows covered individual burials of the Early Bronze Age in many parts of Europe, and were clearly intended to be highly visible monuments to the dead.

ROGER VLITOS/JANET AND COLIN BORD

THE BATTLE-AXE PEOPLE: EUROPE'S FIRST INDIVIDUALISTS

MATS P. MALMER

In the first centuries of the third millennium BC, a surprising change occurred in Europe. Most people appear to have begun to follow a single religion, and a new social system seems to have evolved, giving greater freedom and rights of personal ownership to the individual. The preceding thousand years had been very different, with the European peoples favoring a collective approach. At the same time, Europe's cultural map had been extremely diverse.

A variety of megalithic tombs built from heavy boulders were constructed for communal burials, offerings, and worship on the Iberian peninsula and in France, the British Isles, the Netherlands, and Scandinavia. In Germany, Poland, and Hungary, the first farmers built villages comprising communal houses up to 45 meters (148 feet) long. In the Alpine region and northern Italy, villages and other extensive wooden structures were built on moors or lake shores. In eastern Europe, hunters and fishers also lived in large villages. Although pottery was being produced all over Europe, every region seems to have had its own types of pots. They were often extremely well made, in many different shapes, and were, so archaeologists believe, of symbolic significance. It is thought that each region, with its own pottery, monumental graves, and distinctive type of village, constituted a social unit of some kind, perhaps with its own language.

In the third millennium, the situation changed radically. No more megalithic tombs were built. Instead, we find individual burials, usually in pits or wooden coffins, which were either left as flat graves or were covered by a low earthen mound. The body was always placed in a crouched position, as if sleeping. Thousands of such graves have been excavated in many parts of Europe, from Spain in the west to Ukraine in the east, and from Sicily in the south to central Norway in the north.

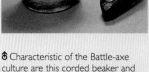

⚒ Characteristic of the Battle-axe culture are this corded beaker and stone battle-axe, recovered from a man's grave.

◁ In graves of men from the Bell Beaker culture, a bell beaker is sometimes found with a copper dagger. The grave find shown here also includes amber beads and a bowman's wrist guard made of stone, with gold studs to fasten it to a leather strap.

EUROPE AT THE TRANSITION FROM STONE AGE TO BRONZE AGE

The continent was dominated by two mutually related cultures, the Bell Beaker culture and the Battle-axe culture. Remains of one or both will probably be found in the future in most areas that now seem empty. We do know, however, that they did not extend to the Balkan peninsula.

- ■ Bell Beaker culture
- ■ Battle-axe people/Corded Beaker culture
- ☐ Overlap of Bell Beaker and Corded Beaker cultures

The houses, too, changed. They are as wide as before, about 6 to 7 meters (20 to 23 feet), but they are much shorter, usually 10 or 12 meters (33 to 39 feet), being suitable for a single family rather than a group.

Beakers and Battle-axes

As grave goods, we now usually find only one type of clay pot, a gently S-curved beaker, obviously intended for drink. This is in sharp contrast to the preceding age, with its variety of pottery shapes. There are, however, two slightly different types of beakers, one found mainly in western Europe and the other in eastern Europe. The former is called a bell beaker, because it looks like an upside-down bell, and the latter a corded beaker, because a cord was often used as an instrument for decoration. Both are well made and neatly decorated with horizontal lines or bands. It may seem strange that archaeologists have bothered to distinguish between the two, for the main difference between them is that the bell beaker is decorated from rim to base, whereas only the upper part of the corded beaker is decorated. But, in fact, they have been thought not only to have come from two different cultures, but from two entirely different ethnic groups.

In a man's grave, a bell beaker is sometimes found with a copper dagger, while a corded beaker is often discovered with a stone battle-axe. This is why archaeologists refer to the people who lived in those parts of Europe where corded beakers are found—from central Russia and Ukraine to the Rhine— as the Battle-axe people. The Bell Beaker people are found throughout western Europe, while in the border zones, and especially the Rhine area, the two cultures were mixed. The Bell Beaker culture appeared a little later than the Corded Beaker culture, but the two coexisted for a long period.

A Man, a Woman, a Dog, and the Rising Sun

One example of the many thousands of graves from this period was found in Linköping, in southern Sweden. It contains two skeletons, one of a man, the other of a woman, both of them in a crouched position. Double graves such as this are sometimes found in Battle-axe cultures, but no evidence has been found to indicate that either of the people was sacrificed. Possibly, both died of the same disease.

The woman is at the northeastern end of the grave, lying on her left side, and the man is at the southwestern end, lying on his right side. Thus, both are looking to the southeast, towards the rising sun. The man is 25 to 30 years old and about 180 centimeters (5 feet, 9 inches) tall; the woman is 18 to 20 years old and about 162 centimeters (5 feet, 4 inches) tall. They are racially similar to modern Swedes.

In front of the man's face lies his stone battle-axe. It is a very beautiful weapon, but not very practical, since it would easily break at the shaft-hole; a wooden cudgel would be much more reliable. There is also a fine dagger of deer antler and a bone needle for fastening his dress.

The woman's grave goods are even richer. By her head are two low beakers—a typical Swedish variant—with bell beaker decoration. So the Battle-axe culture is represented in this grave by the man's axe, and the Bell Beaker culture by the woman's beakers. Near the beakers are sheep bones—the remains, no doubt, of a piece of mutton. Sheep were typical livestock during the third millennium, whereas cattle predominated in the fourth. Three small adzes, suitable for carpentry, are also near the woman. Adzes have been found in many women's graves, so there can be little doubt that women did woodwork. Near the woman's feet is a lump of brown paint, and behind her back there are a few small objects, which were probably originally contained in a small skin bag. There are two small copper spirals, most likely very costly items. Copper objects are occasionally found in the Battle-axe culture, but occur more commonly in the Bell Beaker culture. The woman's skin bag also contains an amber bead, a fine needle for fastening her dress, and a few other household items. At her back there is the skeleton of a dog—a medium-sized spitz—obviously buried together with his master and mistress.

The Linköping grave provides a "snapshot" of the Battle-axe people. We see a young couple. They are tall, noble, and rich. Since they are living in one of the best agricultural regions of Scandinavia, they are probably landowners. He has an exquisitely worked battle-axe, but it is more a status symbol than a weapon. We may guess that he

The double grave from Linköping, in southern Sweden. The man's skeleton is on the left. In front of his chest are his stone battle-axe and a dagger made of deer antler. The woman's skeleton is on the right. On each side of her head, there is a pot; and at her back, the skeleton of a dog.
ÖSTERGÖTLANDS LÄNSMUSEUM

likes hunting and has refined manners. She is well dressed and paints her body, but she is also accustomed to doing practical work.

Possession Becomes Personal

How is the massive change in Europe at the beginning of the third millennium to be explained? Many scholars think that the Bell Beaker culture originated on the Iberian peninsula and spread to Britain, Scandinavia, and Ukraine. The idea has been put forward that these people were prospectors, looking for copper and tin ores. The Battle-axe cultures are thought to have come from Russia or eastern Germany and to have spread as far as Scandinavia and the Rhine, but cord-decorated beakers are also found in the Bell Beaker culture of England, France, and Spain.

Many scholars maintain that the Battle-axe people introduced Indo-European languages and conquered the whole of Europe. But to do this they would have needed a warlike spirit and military skill and technology surpassing that of the Romans, and this was certainly not the case.

One of the pots found in the Linköping grave, with bell beaker decoration.
ÖSTERGÖTLANDS LÄNSMUSEUM

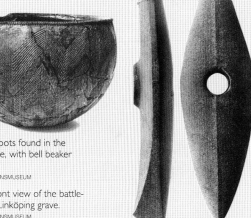

Side and front view of the battle-axe from the Linköping grave.
ÖSTERGÖTLANDS LÄNSMUSEUM

The encounter in the Rhine area of eastern Battle-axe people and western Bell Beaker people could hardly have occurred peacefully. No doubt, the megalith builders and other peoples of an earlier age would also have defended themselves against the Battle-axe invaders.

A more reasonable explanation seems to be that the change in Europe occurred when people became acquainted with metal and realized its economic importance. Before metal entered their lives, there was no reason for them to possess a piece of land; land was

probably owned by the village or the tribe, and both houses and graves were communal. But when a man could hold a piece of metal in his hands that was worth as much as a large field, then the moment for personal ownership had arrived. And since, in a primitive society, economics, social relations, and religion are very closely connected, it is likely that the economic change had exactly those effects that we can observe in the Battle-axe and Bell Beaker peoples. They were the first individualists in the civilization of temperate Europe.

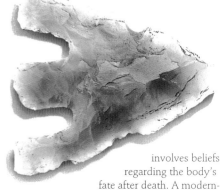

This barbed and tanged flint arrowhead of the Early Bronze Age is typical of many found with burials of the late third and second millennia BC, indicating the importance of the bow and arrow for hunting and warfare.

B. WILSON/ANCIENT ART & ARCHITECTURE COLLECTION

An Early Bronze Age bell beaker pot and several metalworker's tools—two cushion stones, an awl, and a wrist guard—from Lunteren, in Gelderland, Holland. The find also included six flint arrowheads, a flint axe, a stone hammer, and a whetstone, and represents a typical set of tools from the earliest stages of the Bronze Age. The triangular, flat copper dagger is from a different site.

RIJKSMUSEUM VAN OUDHEDEN, LEIDEN

By contrast, in western Europe and parts of central and southern Europe, individual burials coincided with the appearance of bell beakers—drinking cups shaped like an upside-down bell. These beakers are often accompanied by arrowheads and stone or bone rectangular plates that are perforated at the corners. The plates are believed to be guards worn to protect an archer's wrist from the slap of the bowstring.

In central Europe, people were usually buried in a simple pit or a stone-lined grave in the ground, but in the west, it was more common to bury the dead under a great mound of earth or stones, known as a barrow or tumulus. Cemeteries containing dozens of such graves are to be found in many parts of Europe; and in some areas of south central England and Denmark, prominent mounds litter the landscape. Not all of these mounds date from the period when corded ware or bell beakers were in use, for the custom of building them became a trend that extended over hundreds of years. Sometimes, the dead were richly provided for, as evidenced by several graves in central Europe, including Leubingen, in Sachsen-Anhalt, Germany, and the graves associated with the Wessex culture, in England; sometimes they were given little or nothing. What is important is the fact that an identifiable individual was buried in his or her own purpose-built space.

Individual interment was not the only major change in burial customs during the Bronze Age. While burial in a pit or under a mound was standard practice throughout most of Europe until about 1300 BC, after that date it became increasingly common to burn the dead and deposit the ashes in an urn, which was then buried in the ground—hence the term urnfields to describe these cemeteries. The period of the urnfields continued down to the start of the Iron Age, about 750 BC. The change from burial to cremation has been interpreted as evidence of a major shift in beliefs. In most societies, treatment of the dead is imbued with symbolic significance and involves beliefs regarding the body's fate after death. A modern-day example of this is the wide-spread opposition to the reintroduction of cremation in Britain voiced in the nineteenth century: only after a number of well-publicized court cases did it become evident that cremation was not an illegal practice, merely a socially unacceptable one.

From the time of the urnfields, both burials and cemeteries are much more numerous, cemeteries commonly containing several hundred graves. It therefore seems likely that Europe's population increased dramatically during the urnfield period—the Late Bronze Age. Whether this came about as a result of improved agricultural methods is unclear. From an archaeological point of view, however, the urnfields present a problem, in that the practice of cremating the dead destroyed much of the evidence that would enable us to reconstruct the society and population of the period.

Nevertheless, much has been learned from the detailed study of certain cemeteries, such as that at Przeczyce, in Poland, where 874 graves were found. Most of these were burial sites, only about 15 percent containing cremated remains. Because of this, grave goods had usually survived intact (whereas in cremations they are often destroyed or damaged), making it possible to correlate an individual's age and sex with the richness of the grave goods. At Przeczyce, such status distinctions were minimal, but this does not mean that they did not exist in Przeczyce society. The production of fine metal products during the Late Bronze period indicates that significant wealth was attainable, but this wealth was not often displayed in death. Only in rare cases can we confidently identify a burial as that of a local chieftain or princeling—such as the great mound of Seddin, in Mecklenburg, Germany, which contained a rich find of gold and bronze objects. Elsewhere, we can only speculate.

Thus, although Bronze Age burials have provided a large quantity of material, they have often provided little information. In such cases, we need to turn to other sources of information, such as settlements, evidence of warfare, exchange of goods, industry, ritual, and belief, in order to construct a picture of the times.

Lakeside Settlements

Life in the Bronze Age, as in all traditional societies, revolved around the common needs of subsistence, production, and shelter. People worked, ate, slept, socialized, and died within the environment of a simple agricultural village. Since most of these villages were built with organic materials, few traces of them are left. Our knowledge of Bronze Age housing is therefore limited, and only where stone was used regularly can we confidently reconstruct the form and function of these buildings. Fortunately, in several areas settlements have been found that are surprisingly rich in archaeological remains.

It is on lakes in the Alps that traces of settlement are most apparent. Numerous well-preserved villages have been found in their shallow waters, especially in Switzerland. There are two reasons for this. First, periodic flooding resulting from high rainfall, or rapidly melting snow in spring, caused water levels to fluctuate, which meant that these settlements were periodically occupied and abandoned. Secondly, the house timbers have been well preserved in the waterlogged ground. This occupation pattern recurred regularly at many lake sites from the Early Neolithic to the end of the Bronze Age. During the Bronze Age, there were phases of occupation during the corded ware period

(about 2700 BC to 2500 BC), during the late Early Bronze Age (between 1650 BC and 1500 BC), and during two periods of the Late Bronze Age (1050 BC to 950 BC, and about 850 BC).

Piles were driven into the soft mud of the lake shores, creating a platform on which super-structures could be erected. The precise way in which this was done varied; indeed, there is controversy about how and where along the lake edges the houses were built. Certainly, the ground was wet and would have to have been stabilized. The thousands, even millions, of wooden posts that were used for this purpose strongly suggest a highly organized effort. Since trees were felled in large numbers, the environmental effects must have been drastic.

Auvernier, on Lake Neuchâtel, was a typical settlement, with rows of rectangular houses ranged within a surrounding palisade. The houses probably had a timber framework, with wattle-and-daub infilling. Each house had a hearth, and no doubt other standard fittings as well, although in most cases it has been impossible to identify individual pieces of furniture.

Similar houses may well have been built on dry-land sites along the Swiss alpine valleys. In these regions, a series of glacially formed knolls and hillocks—either on the valley floor or, less commonly, high on the valley sides—were chosen for high-density, long-term settlement. A site such as Padnal, near Savognin, in the Engadin, was occupied more or less continuously from the Early Bronze Age to the start of the Late Bronze Age, the form of the houses changing very little throughout this period. Occupation of the same site for hundreds of years led to a build-up

The site of Padnal, near Savognin, in the Engadin, southeastern Switzerland. The flat top of the mound is the result of people leveling off accumulated debris each time new buildings were erected on the site.

A reconstruction of the Late Bronze Age settlement at Zedau, in eastern Germany. The houses are framed by upright posts, and have wattle-and-daub walls and thatched roofs.
ILLUSTRATION: JOHN RICHARDS

⚱A gold disk from a burial at Kirk Andrews, on the Isle of Man, Britain.
TOWNLEY COLLECTION/BRITISH MUSEUM

of debris, which significantly raised the surface level, not unlike the tell sites of Southwest Asia or eastern Europe. Among these rare stratified sites are some on the Hungarian plain, which are typically 150 to 200 meters (500 to 650 feet) in diameter and up to 10 meters (33 feet) high. Excavation of one of these sites at Tószeg, near Szolnok, in central Hungary, has revealed a dense succession of rectangular houses, built from daub on wooden frames, which filled the interior of the mound.

Sites such as these, however, represent a minority of those known to have existed in Bronze Age Europe. Much more common is the simple open site, usually occupied once or twice only, with a scatter of post-built houses, the sole remains of which are traces of wooden uprights. A Late Bronze Age site (from the urnfield period) at Zedau, in eastern Germany, illustrates the pattern well. Here, no less than 78 small rectangular and square post-built houses were constructed. Most had six or four posts, wattle-and-daub walls, and a thatched roof. Hearths and ovens lay outside. There is little evidence of planning, the structures appearing to have been built by individual social groups with the requirements of day-to-day living in mind.

These structures took various forms, according to local economic and social circumstances. On the downlands of southern England, a character-istic formation was a group of round, post-framed houses, often built on platforms, with a number of stock pens nearby. The earthen banks surrounding these enclosures merge with the fields stretching between one site and the next. A site such as Black Patch, near Newhaven, in Sussex, is a good example. Several hut platforms were located on the slope of a hill, each supporting two to five round huts. The excavator of this site has

🌼 A reconstruction of Bronze Age life at Tanum, Bohuslän, in western Sweden, with post-framed, thatched-roof houses.

JENS RYDELL/BRUCE COLEMAN LTD

suggested that the size of the huts indicates that each was probably occupied by only one person. It is likely, therefore, that a group of huts was occupied by a family, including, perhaps, retainers or other dependants.

Most of the sites described so far were open, undefended farming hamlets. At times, however, there was a need for defense. Defended sites occur only at particular times in particular areas. Presumably, their existence indicates a need

to retreat into relatively inaccessible areas for protection, perhaps against organized groups of marauders from neighboring territory. We can see this trend developing most clearly during the Late Bronze Age, and in some places even earlier. Ram's Hill, in Berkshire, southern England, for instance, was protected first by a palisade and later by a fully developed wooden rampart. Complex ramparts were built during the Late Bronze Age at many German sites, although

these sites seem to have been occupied only briefly. Little is known about the nature of the houses inside such hill-forts, but at the Wittnauer Horn site, in northern Switzerland, what looks like a main street is faced on both sides by rows of rectangular houses. At Ram's Hill, the remains of round houses were found inside a palisade, and it seems likely that when other sites are excavated extensively enough, comparable remains will come to light.

Ϭ Numerous settlements were established along lake shores such as this, at Neuchâtel, beside the Jura Mountains, in western Switzerland. Their foundations were secured by driving wooden piles into the mud.

OAK COFFIN GRAVES IN DENMARK

GÖRAN BURENHULT

A SERIES OF EARLY BRONZE AGE mounds in southern Jutland, in Denmark, holds a very special position in the history of European archaeological research. The remarkably well-preserved finds from these burial sites, notably clothes and wooden artifacts, are unique for this period, providing a detailed picture of everyday life and death in northern Europe nearly 3,500 years ago.

These great mounds are those of Muldbjerg, Egtved, Skrydstrup, Borum Eshøj, Trindhøj, and Guldhøj. They were usually built of turf, which formed a massive, wet cover over the grave site. Iron salts, which occur naturally in turf, leached and soon turned into a layer of iron sandstone. This protective cover prevented air from entering the mound's interior. The oak coffins and their delicate contents were thus enclosed within a preservative environment very similar to that of bogs.

The degree of preservation of the skeletal remains varies greatly from mound to mound. In some cases, the grave is empty, nothing being left of the mortal remains. In others, even the brain and heart are preserved. The hair is often very well preserved, even in the armpits and around the genitals, and sometimes even facial features can be discerned.

In one man's grave at Guldhøj, some remarkable wooden artifacts were unearthed, including bowls and a folding chair made of ash-wood and otter fur. The folding chair is very similar to chairs found in contemporary Egyptian tombs. In the man's belt was a dagger in a wooden sheath. As in most of the other graves, the body had been placed on a cow's hide.

Male Fashion before the Age of Trousers

It is the well-preserved clothes, however, that make the Danish oak coffin graves one of the most notable Bronze Age finds in Europe. The graves of two men discovered in Muldbjerg and Trindhøj have provided detailed information about the clothes and ornaments worn by men at that time. Both were dressed in long loincloths held in place by leather straps. Trousers were not yet being worn. These plain-weave clothes consist of nine pieces of cloth sewn together with whipstitch. Both men carried a kidney-shaped cloak over their shoulder and wore a round cap. Swords, fibulas, double buttons, and belt adornments completed their outfit.

Two burials of women are particularly interesting, because they provide information not only about the clothes and ornaments of the time, but also about the social structure of northern Europe 3,500 years ago.

◐ A drawing of the burial of an old man from Borum Eshøj, as he was found during an excavation in 1875. This giant mound contained three oak coffins with the well-preserved remains of an old man, a young man, and an old woman. These people were probably members of the same family.

◐ The well-preserved skin of the young woman from Skrydstrup reveals beautiful facial features. She has a unique hairstyle, with a net of black horsehair. Rings of gold were placed by her ears.

GÖRAN BURENHULT

Married or Unmarried Women?

The Egtved mound contained the remains of a slender 20 to 25-year-old woman about 1.6 meters (5 feet, 3 inches) tall. The well-preserved facial skin revealed a beautiful profile. Her hair was short and light blond, her teeth were in perfect condition, and her nails were neatly trimmed. She wore a poncho-like sweater and a knee-length skirt held by a woven belt. Flowers found in the grave indicate that she was buried in summer. A rolled-up piece of cloth by her feet contained the burned bones of an 8 to 9-year-old child—possibly the remains of a human sacrifice. A birch-bark container with the remnants of an alcoholic drink made from wheat and cranberries, flavored by bog-myrtle and honey, was found nearby.

The girl from Skrydstrup had died at the age of 18. She was slender, and about 1.7 meters (5 feet, 6 inches) tall. Her hair was about 60 centimeters (24 inches) long, elaborately arranged, and held with a hairnet and a headband. Gold earrings were placed in her hair, by her ears, and from her facial features we can guess that she was very pretty. Unlike the woman from Egtved, she was dressed in a remarkably long skirt measuring 1.45 by 4 meters (about 4 feet, 9 inches by 13 feet).

The finds from Egtved and Skrydstrup have provided evidence of two different kinds of female clothing during the Bronze Age. It has been suggested that the different styles reflect differences in the dress of married and unmarried women.

Braids of hair found in Danish bogs may indicate that young Bronze Age women sacrificed their hair when they married. The complicated hairstyle of the Skrydstrup woman possibly indicated her social status and that she was unmarried. Judging by its size, the cloth she wore as a skirt may have served as a dowry. The short hair and elegant skirt of the Egtved woman would then represent the outfit of the married woman. Together, these finds from Jutland allow us an unparalleled, if tantalizingly brief, glimpse into Bronze Age society.

The well-preserved outfits provide detailed information about Bronze Age clothing in northern Europe 3,500 years ago. Trousers had not yet come into use. Instead, the men wore loincloths and wide, kidney-shaped cloaks.
NATIONAL MUSEUM OF DENMARK

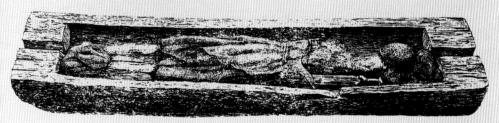

Many of the Danish oak coffin graves, like these two from Trindhøj, were plundered soon after the burials had taken place—an interesting sign that this Bronze Age society was not able to exercise total control over antisocial elements.
NATIONAL MUSEUM OF DENMARK

⚷ This unique sheet gold cape from Mold, in North Wales, dates from the Early Bronze Age. The cape is decorated with bosses of several different shapes.
BRITISH MUSEUM

➲ The solid, cast-on grip and swelling, leaf-shaped blade of this sword from Switzerland are characteristic of certain weapon types from the Late Bronze Age.
LAUROS-GIRAUDON

♀ This sheet bronze helmet from southern France is decorated with large bosses, and has a prominent crest of sheet bronze running from side to side.
MUSEES DE NICE/LAUROS-GIRAUDON

➲ *Opposite*: Gold from a grave at Varna cemetery, near the Black Sea coast of Bulgaria. The numerous objects include sheet metal bulls, horn symbols, disks, beads, an armring, and a solid gold axe with a shaft.

Warfare: Shining Armor and Deadly Weapons

The picture that emerges is one of people carrying on a centuries-old agricultural tradition whose peace is periodically shattered by the attacks of marauders. This impression is reinforced by the trappings of war that are so prevalent in Bronze Age sites. Weaponry is found at all stages of the period, both in graves and in hoard finds. In the earlier years of the Bronze Age, the standard weapon was the bow, supplemented by the dagger for those few who could gain access to this weapon. People presumably fought first with bow and arrows, followed by hand-to-hand combat when the need arose.

Nothing is known about the defensive armor used in the Early Bronze Age. In the Middle Bronze Age, daggers evolved into rapiers and, eventually, swords. The spear was also invented at this time and rapidly became widespread. These weapons continued to be used, with refinements, throughout the Late Bronze Age and into the Iron Age, with the main addition being defensive armor. The history of the sword is of great importance in understanding how Bronze Age combat developed. At first, the sword seems to have been used entirely as a thrusting weapon, and it was therefore slim and light. As the demand arose for it to deliver cutting or slashing blows as well, it became much heavier, with a broad, leaf-shaped blade. Great attention was given to the method of attaching the handle to the blade. This was one of the weak points in the design of early swords, and improvements were constantly sought.

Armor was then required to ward off the blows of the heavier weaponry. Although the armor that survives is made of sheet bronze, it is more likely that the functional armor of the day was made of leather or, in the case of shields, wood. Experiments have shown that sheet bronze is easily penetrated by arrows or by sword blows. Body armor consisted of the cuirass (covering the torso), greaves (over the shins), and helmet, with side pieces to cover the cheeks. A magnificent cuirass found at Marmesse, in France, illustrates the care that went into these creations. The sheet bronze is molded to the shape of the torso, and the musculature and other features are shown schematically. Early helmets were basically conical, with a knob at the top for the addition of a plume.

One can well imagine that the Bronze Age warrior, when fully dressed in high-quality armor of this sort, was an impressive and fearsome sight—no doubt the aim of the exercise. Shining armor, fearful war-cries, and deadly weapons—as we can imagine from the description of Achilles in *The Iliad*—were intended to be an irresistible combination. It is doubtful, however, whether such warriors ever attacked fortified sites. Perhaps, instead, they challenged their enemies to single combat on open ground.

Industry and the Exchange of Goods: The World beyond the Village

For most people, life in the Bronze Age consisted of agricultural labor to ensure the provision of daily bread, but they were aware of a world beyond their own. During the period, many commodities in raw or finished form were transported over short and long distances, to service the needs of those who had no local access to them. This movement had both economic and social implications. We need only consider the distribution of raw materials across Europe, and it is immediately evident that access to these materials varied considerably. Thus, gold was obtained from well-known deposits such as the Wicklow Mountains of Ireland or the Muntii Metalici in the Carpathians, in Transylvania, and moved to Britain and western Europe; amber came mainly from the Baltic area and western Jutland;

⚭ An Early Bronze Age necklace of jet beads from Scotland, consisting of six spacer beads, perforated longitudinally, and a larger number of spindle-shaped small beads. The necklace imitates the decoration on crescent-shaped neck ornaments made of sheet gold.

tin came from Cornwall, Brittany, Spain, and perhaps from distant Turkey and Afghanistan; and copper itself came not only from major sources such as the Austrian Alps, Cyprus, and Transylvania, but also from many small sources in the British Isles, the Alps, Iberia, and the Balkans.

Advances in methods of determining the composition patterns of copper and other metals, of amber, and of manufactured materials such as glass and its primitive form, faience, have enabled archaeologists to reconstruct the movement of goods across large distances within Europe—although, of course, many goods were moved only a short distance. (The word "trade" has connotations that may not be appropriate for a period of whose economic organization we know little or nothing.) This kind of analytical approach has to be combined with typological studies (relating to the form and function of objects) if a true picture is to emerge. Where artifacts are specifically and unambiguously different in form, such methods can be decisive. If we examine the pattern of bronze production and distribution, for example, we can reconstruct something of the mode of operation of Bronze Age smiths from the ways molds were formed and reused. In addition, the distribution of objects from their presumed points of origin sheds light on the location of smithing workshops. We are thus well placed to determine how and when goods were moved, and to advance reasonable theories about why they were moved.

One of the most striking pieces of evidence for long-distance contact is provided by amber. Amber is a resin, derived from fossil pine trees. While it is found quite widely across the world, by far the greatest quantities in Europe come from what are called Baltic sources, although not all Baltic amber actually comes from the shores of the Baltic Sea. Baltic amber can be identified by analysis, and was present in Bronze Age Greece, Italy, Hungary, and the Balkans, as well as in the countries north of the Alps. What is more, the amber found in Greece, almost exclusively in high-status graves, includes flat, rectangular beads known as "spacer-plates" (designed to keep the strands of a multiple-stranded necklace in position) that are perforated in a curious V-shaped pattern found on amber in central, northern, and northwestern Europe. In all likelihood, these beads were manufactured in Britain or Germany and transported to Greece—a journey of several thousand kilometers.

This is not as far-fetched as it might seem, as we can also point to the example of Greek Bronze Age pottery, which was taken to many parts of Italy, to Sardinia, and also, it seems

(from a single certain identification), to Spain. It has not yet turned up north of the Alps, in France, or on the shores of the Black Sea, but it would come as little surprise if it did, since the Mediterranean was the scene of much international exchange of goods between east and west. A number of spectacular finds, including several shipwrecks, graphically illustrate how far imperishable goods, at least, traveled. From these cargoes, we can be sure that metals were one of the main items to be moved about the Mediterranean in the Bronze Age, and that the people of Cyprus were significantly involved in this process. Scientists have been less successful in tracking down the movement of goods in continental Europe by analytical means, but the distribution of so-called ring ingots—copper alloy neck rings, thought to be a means of transporting copper—indicates that Alpine copper was transported around large areas of central Europe. It is likely that Irish copper and gold also had a wide circulation.

But simply to identify the sources of such commodities is to ignore another critical factor: how desirable particular commodities were for the communities that used them. Although we may take it for granted that gold was a desirable resource, this has not always been the case. It was only when the need developed to express status differences by specially created wealth divisions, and objects and commodities were used to express those divisions, that gold became a prestige item. It has been suggested that gold was not at first regarded as being especially valuable, but by the time of the Copper Age cemetery at Varna, in Bulgaria, about the middle of the fifth millennium BC, this view had presumably changed. Here, gold was the preferred adornment for the parts of the body associated with power: the head, hands, and genitalia. Certainly, by the time the great gold neck ornaments known as lunulae, and the ornamental collars known as gorgets, which are found somewhat later in Ireland, were created, gold was prized. There are grounds, too, for thinking that all kinds of exotic materials—such as seashells, boars' tusks, and glass and faience beads—came to acquire a special cachet in the eyes of Bronze Age craftspeople and their patrons.

Of course, not all goods were exchanged over long distances. It is likely that most of this activity took place between neighboring communities and involved locally available materials. The movement of metal and pottery objects can be tracked in this way, but it is not always easy to say what this movement might represent. A recent study has shown how particular types of female ornaments moved freely within a radius of 100 kilometers (60 miles) from their sources, suggesting the existence of a series of communities that favored similar styles of objects. A striking

⚭ A necklace of faience beads from a cemetery at Košice, in eastern Slovakia, dating from the Early Bronze Age. Bronze Age faience is a primitive form of glass.

MICK SHARP

feature is that objects found outside their own immediate area of distribution are found only within neighboring communities. It seems likely that they belonged to women who married into these communities.

Ritual and Belief: Stone Rings and Carved Ships

What did Bronze Age people believe about life, death, the supernatural, and the place of humans in the natural world? Although we cannot answer these questions directly, we can look at a range of sites that reflect the influence of their beliefs. Stonehenge, for example, attained its developed form during this period, although it had been begun many years earlier, in the Neolithic period. During the Bronze Age, people brought massive stones to the site—both local sarsens and imported bluestones (probably from the Preseli mountains of southwestern Wales)—and erected them in a variety of shapes and patterns, culminating in the present arrangement of rings and horseshoes.

Judging from the number and richness of the barrow groups around it, Stonehenge was a major center, and it remained unique even though its basic elements—a circular bank and ditch—are repeated many times across the length and breadth of Britain. Whatever else it was, Stonehenge undoubtedly served as an important center of ritual and ceremonial activity. Although it is popularly associated with the Druids, we know nothing specific about the rites that were practiced there or the ethnic background of the people who constructed it. The same is true of the cup and ring marks carved onto exposed rock surfaces in various parts of Britain, mainly in the north and west.

Equally remarkable, and more informative of aspects of Bronze Age ritual life, are the many carvings that adorn rock faces in parts of Scandinavia and the southern Alps. Unlike British examples, many are of recognizable forms—people, animals, and ships, and artifacts such as plows, axes, and lures (trumpets)—although there are also many kinds of symbols that cannot be directly interpreted. Great panels of rock bearing such art have been found, especially in western Sweden. As they have no apparent utilitarian purpose, the carvings are believed to

↑ A rock art panel at Ormaig, near Kilmartin, Argyll, in Scotland. As well as numerous cup marks, the panel includes the rare ringed rosette design, which is also known from Galloway (southwestern Scotland) and Ireland.

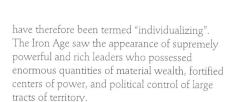

⊕ Rock art in Argyll, western Scotland: part of the panels at Achnabreck, near Lochgilphead. On the left is a cup with two rings; and on the right, a rare example of a horned or double-ended spiral.

MICK SHARP

reflect belief systems, and possibly people's preoccupation with the daily tasks of subsistence, including contact with other groups by means of water travel.

There are numerous carvings of ships, and because Scandinavia has since been uplifted as a result of geological processes, they are often in places that are now far from the sea. Originally, they would have been created within sight of creeks and bays. Such carvings, a regular part of Bronze Age life in the area, may have been undertaken as a propitiatory act before people set out on a voyage. The main means of communication between neighboring communities was by sea, and these journeys are unlikely to have been very long ones. The images raise the interesting question of who owned the ships, since it would have required a good deal of valuable labor to build them. It has been suggested that this was one of the means by which some individuals sought to obtain power over others, and that such boats were the tangible expression of this power.

The Individual Comes of Age

We have looked at the bare bones of the period that we call the Bronze Age. What inferences can we draw about society in that period? To understand the changes that occurred, we must remember that in the preceding Neolithic period, an individual's death was hardly ever marked by the provision of special grave goods, even though the resting place itself was often large and elaborate. The Neolithic period in western Europe saw the construction of large numbers of great stone monuments that demanded enormous amounts of labor and great architectural skill, and it is unlikely that they could have been erected without leadership in the form of chiefs. In the absence of any direct evidence for individual chiefs, the chiefdoms have been termed "group-oriented", meaning that they relied upon and reflected the abilities of a whole group. By contrast, the Bronze Age recognized the contributions of individuals, and the leaders of that period

⊕ Stone molds for casting double-winged bronze pins, from eastern Switzerland.

SWISS NATIONAL MUSEUM

have therefore been termed "individualizing". The Iron Age saw the appearance of supremely powerful and rich leaders who possessed enormous quantities of material wealth, fortified centers of power, and political control of large tracts of territory.

Chronologically and, presumably, socially, the Bronze Age falls between the extremes of the Neolithic period and the Iron Age. It is unfortunate that the material evidence does not give us a better idea of the conditions that Bronze Age leaders inherited and developed, but there is some evidence to show that even in the earliest

phases of the period, definite, if simple, social divisions existed. The remarkable developments in agricultural technology, and the massive increase in industrial production, enabled the powerful to maintain and enhance their position by exploiting people who relied on these occupations for their livelihood. Such a system was self-perpetuating, and it is not surprising to find it had been carried to extreme lengths by 500 BC. But we must not forget that climatic and environmental deterioration would also have played a major role in bringing about economic and social change.

The Bronze Age was a period of remarkable technical mastery and great technical advances— a time when the foundations were laid for the Iron Age world, which, in turn, brought forth the great civilizations of the Classical period. The Bronze Age impressed itself on the landscape of parts of western Europe, and its monuments remain visible to this day. Shadowy though this period may at times appear, the shadows are from time to time dispersed by shafts of sunlight glancing off the gold and bronze its warriors wore, and the Bronze Age emerges as a true harbinger of the spectacular developments that took place in Europe after 800 BC.

☥ Dating from the early first millennium BC, this rock art at Emelieborg, near Tanum, in Bohuslän, western Sweden, depicts figures in horned helmets, probably engaged in ritual fighting, together with animals.

VALCAMONICA: A CENTER OF CREATIVITY

EMMANUEL ANATI

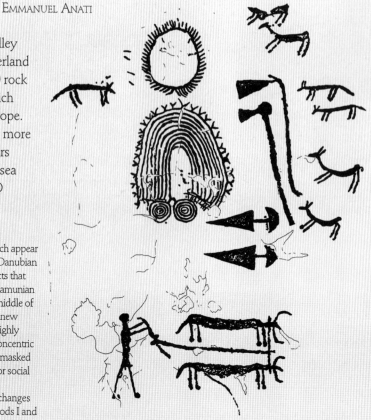

Valcamonica, in the Italian Alps, is a narrow valley 70 kilometers (45 miles) long, between Switzerland and Lake Iseo, north of Brescia. More than 300,000 rock engravings have been discovered there to date, which makes it the richest concentration of rock art in Europe. The areas of rock art are spread along the valley for more than 25 kilometers (16 miles) and are from 20 meters (660 feet) to about 1,400 meters (4,600 feet) above sea level. These areas have been classified by UNESCO as "World Cultural Heritage".

The earliest rock art in Valcamonica was produced by hunters in the Proto-Camunian period, some 12,000 years ago. This art is characterized by large animals drawn in contour, spears, fishing traps, and some symbols. The elk, which became extinct in this region at the beginning of the Holocene period, is the main animal depicted. The art relates to hunting rituals and practices and indicates that the peoples of Eurasia had traditions in common.

In the sixth millennium BC, a change occurred in both the style and content of the rock art, and compositions of the Proto-Camunian type were no longer produced. Stylized human figures in a praying position, with upraised arms, featured during the Neolithic period (5500 BC to 3300 BC) and were often combined with symbols and such subjects as sun disks, axes, and dogs. Depictions of

plows, hoes, and idols, which appear to have been derived from Danubian prototypes, testify to contacts that influenced the now-stable Camunian community. Towards the middle of the fourth millennium BC, a new iconography, based upon highly abstract symbols, such as concentric circles, zigzag patterns, and masked images, foreshadowed major social and ideological changes.

Several compositional changes took place in Neolithic periods I and II. In period I, the human praying image was associated mostly with single depictions such as a sun disk, an axe, an animal, or another human being. The first domestic animal to be represented was the dog. Oxen and goats were added in period II, and the number of items per composition increased, with symbols and representations of ceremonies and collective social, economic, and cult activities. Weapons and tools included spears, boomerangs, bows and arrows, spades, and agricultural objects.

☉ A tracing of the stele known as Bagnolo II from Valcamonica, showing triangular copper daggers of the Remedello type, axes, animals, a sun disk, spectacle-spirals under a necklace-like element of parallel lines, and a plow scene. The carving can be dated to the Chalcolithic period, 3200 BC to 2500 BC.

Periods I and II are also characterized by images of technological acquisitions, such as plows, bows, traps, and weaving looms. The main economic activities of hunting and fishing are represented, in conjunction with agriculture and animal-rearing and objects suggesting that organized trade was developing. Religious beliefs included a sun cult, a cult of the dead, and a cult of dogs and other animals; and towards the end of the period, anthropomorphic "idols" appeared. Symbols and patterns engraved during these periods, such as masked faces, zigzags, concentric circles, meandering lines, and axes, are similar to the decorations of megalithic cultures.

During the Chalcolithic (the beginning of period III), from the end of the Neolithic to the beginning of the Bronze Age (3200 BC to 2500 BC), new figurative patterns appeared on menhir statues and in monumental compositions in Valcamonica, including double-spiraled pendants (spectacle-spirals), sun disks, triangular copper daggers, and perforated axes and halberds, accompanied by human and animal figures. The sun is shown as the head of a cosmological being, and the river is its belt. Such compositions, more than 5,000 years old, are the earliest known that can be attributed to a typically Indo-European world view.

Apparently originating in eastern Europe, these symbolic–religious elements reached the European Alps along with economic and technological innovations that resulted in profound cultural change. The most important of these innovations

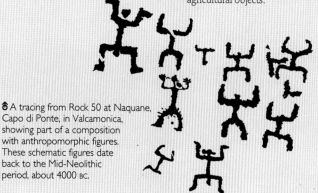

☉ A tracing from Rock 50 at Naquane, Capo di Ponte, in Valcamonica, showing part of a composition with anthropomorphic figures. These schematic figures date back to the Mid-Neolithic period, about 4000 BC.

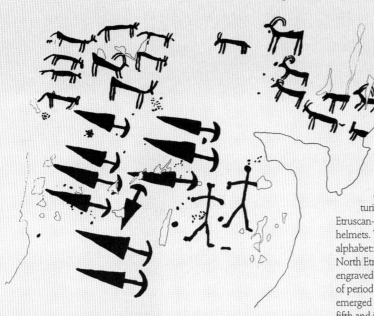

⬧ This section of the Chalcolithic carvings at Massi di Cemmo no. II, Capo di Ponte, in Valcamonica, shows triangular copper daggers, animals, and human figures.

were metalworking (with the first copper tools), the introduction of the wheel, and the use of wheeled vehicles. In the European Alps, the first evidence of metal tools and wagons occurs in the form of images depicted in rock art and on menhir statues, about 3200 BC. At this time, there is also evidence of socio-economic changes: a hierarchy with chiefs and priests, and more complex commercial production by artisans.

During the Early and Middle Bronze Age (2500 BC to 1200 BC), there was a consolidation of the changes bought by the Chalcolithic revolution. Mining, metalworking, and centers of specialized production evolved, and became integrated within a commercial network that covered large parts of Europe and the Mediterranean basin. These changes were reflected in the rock engravings of Valcamonica: new, increasingly complex compositions that represented a way of life based on economic production. Axes and daggers predominated for a long period, being replaced during the final phases by scenes of warriors engaged in duels and other warlike activities.

Weapons, other objects, and topographical maps were typical of

the Early and Middle Bronze Age (the middle and end of period III). Mythological scenes and anthropomorphic figures became more numerous in the Middle Bronze Age, and the horse appeared, along with other domestic animals. Metalworking and weaving were shown, and religious beliefs related to a cult of objects and weapons. During the Late Bronze Age, there is evidence in the engravings of a growing cult of spirits and heroes.

In the second and first millennia BC, political entities emerged from tribal societies, and this eventually led to the formation of nations. Societies became more complex as economic structures and relationships among various groups evolved. Towards the end of the second millennium BC, in the Final Bronze Age (the beginning of period IV), the Camunians depicted figures and objects that related to the urn-field cultures of central Europe. In the first half of the first millennium BC, economic and cultural contacts with the area encompassed by the Hallstatt culture became increasingly evident. The subject matter and figurines from bronze and pottery

objects find many parallels in the rock art of the Early Iron Age.

From the seventh to the fifth century BC, Villanovian and Etruscan influences were apparent. It is likely that Etruscan traders reached Valcamonica during this period and introduced a new style of rock art featuring muscled warriors with Etruscan-style daggers, shields, and helmets. They also introduced the alphabet: more than a hundred North Etruscan inscriptions were engraved on the rocks in the middle of period IV. Celtic characteristics emerged somewhat later, in the late fifth and in the fourth century BC, and

period IV ended with the Roman occupation of Valcamonica in 16 BC.

Period IV is characterized by realistic scenes of daily life and magical–mythological figures. A range of engravings that is very useful in establishing chronology shows people holding shields, helmets, spears, axes, and items of personal adornment; and numerous engravings of structures, huts, and temples provide much information relating to the history of architecture. Agricultural tools such as plows, scythes, sickles, hoes, and pickaxes are shown, and there are scenes of metalworking and wheel-building. The domestic animals depicted are those found on a modern farm: dogs, oxen, horses, pigs, goats, ducks, chickens, and geese.

In the Post-Camunian period, after the Camunians' territory had been incorporated into a Roman province, there were sporadic expressions of rock art. There are some Roman engravings, including a few Latin inscriptions, and a large number of medieval and later scribblings. Unlike the prehistoric engravings, these did not have a religious motivation, and appear to have been the games of shepherds. They are mostly personal impressions, ranging from depictions of hangings to heraldic emblems.

The rock art of Valcamonica is characterized by continuously changing style and subject matter over the course of 10,000 years, and this enables us to use the engravings as historical documents. They form one of the largest known archives of European history, and art history, stretching from the end of the Ice Age to the Roman conquest and beyond.

◄⬤ Some of the youngest examples of rock art in Valcamonica show Etruscan influence, probably through traders from the south. In this carving from Naquane, the warriors are dressed in Etruscan helmets and can be dated to between 550 BC and AD 450.

STONE AGE FARMERS IN SOUTHERN AND EASTERN ASIA

6 0 0 0 B C – A D 1 0 0 0

Farmers, Potters, Fisherfolk, and Navigators

PETER BELLWOOD AND GINA BARNES

TODAY, SOUTHERN AND EASTERN Asia are home to more than half of the world's population. The biological and cultural patterns that make this region such an ethnic kaleidoscope owe a great deal to the achievements of its earliest agriculturalists, whose first major settlements can be traced back to before 5000 BC.

The prehistories of the various regions of southern and eastern Asia followed different, if overlapping, courses. For example, much of the cultural development of Southeast Asia, Japan, and Korea was linked to that of China. India's culture, on the other hand, developed partly under the influence of western and central Asia. Despite this, both India and Southeast Asia shared many aspects of language and culture because of communication between northeastern India and the Southeast Asian mainland.

◄◼ Rice terraces in Bali, Indonesia. In much of monsoonal Southeast Asia, rice is grown in lowland areas in bunded fields, often fed simply by summer rainfall. Hillside terraced and irrigated systems such as these are found especially in Java, Bali, and the northern Philippines.

◼ A Taiwan jade earring from a grave in Peinan in the form of a human figure. Numerous jade earrings in a variety of styles were recovered from graves at this Neolithic site in Taiwan, together with many other finely crafted items.
CHAO-MEI LIEN

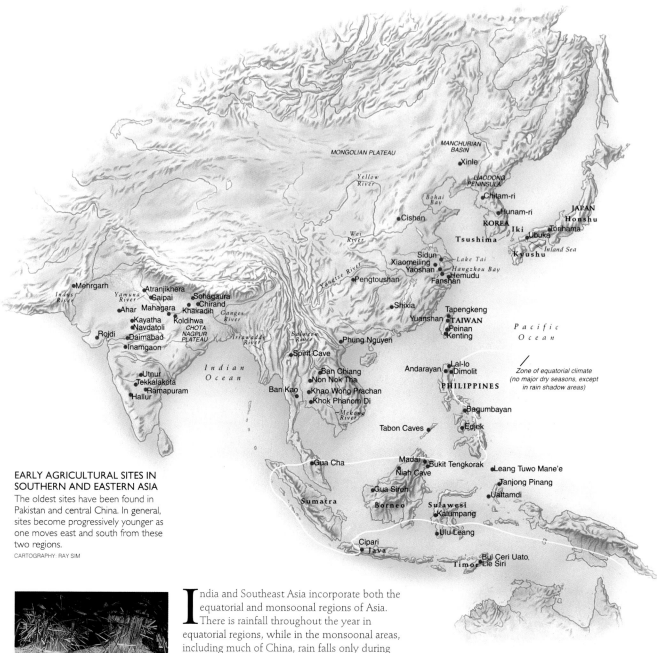

EARLY AGRICULTURAL SITES IN SOUTHERN AND EASTERN ASIA

The oldest sites have been found in Pakistan and central China. In general, sites become progressively younger as one moves east and south from these two regions.

CARTOGRAPHY: RAY SIM

☝ Bundles of harvested rice panicles stored for drying before being threshed, in Bali, Indonesia. Evidence of rice cultivation in prehistoric times comes from impressions or husks in pots and bricks, from charred grains in hearths, and, occasionally, from waterlogged deposits.

India and Southeast Asia incorporate both the equatorial and monsoonal regions of Asia. There is rainfall throughout the year in equatorial regions, while in the monsoonal areas, including much of China, rain falls only during summer. The agricultural prehistory of this huge and diverse area was dominated by summer-growth cereals such as rice and the various millets. This contrasts with the winter-growth cereals and legumes (pod-bearing vegetables) that were grown at that time in western Asia and Pakistan. In addition, Southeast Asia and neighboring Melanesia offered early cultivators a number of important tropical tubers, fruits, and other edible plants, particularly bananas, sugar cane, yams, taro, coconuts, and breadfruit.

Despite this wealth of plant food, the archaeological and linguistic records of India and Southeast Asia give no indication that early hunter-gatherer communities in these areas had independently begun to cultivate plants to any significant extent. There is evidence, however, that this occurred in two neighboring regions: western Asia and China. Both regions were to exert a considerable influence on India and Southeast Asia.

By 7000 BC, western Asian agriculture—based on winter wheat and barley, and domesticated cattle, sheep, and goats—had spread into western Pakistan, where it is particularly well documented at the site of Mehrgarh. By 2500 BC, this complex had given rise to the Harappan civilization on the plains of the Indus and in neighboring Gujarat, Rajasthan, and Haryana.

Far to the east, agricultural communities based on rice cultivation in the Yangtze Valley and millet cultivation in the Yellow River Valley were well established by 6000 BC. These people kept domestic pigs, dogs, chickens, and, perhaps, (along the Yangtze) water buffaloes. At the same time, other communities, about which rather less is known, were controlling the water levels in swamps in the New Guinea highlands, probably in order to grow taro and other native noncereal plants. These three regions—western Asia, central China, and New Guinea—can all be regarded as primary and indigenous centers of early agricultural activity.

Until 4000 BC, most of India and Southeast Asia, with the possible exception of some regions of northern Southeast Asia close to China, were still occupied by hunter-gatherers. Over much of India and Sri Lanka, these peoples developed stone tool industries featuring small blades and microliths. Similar industries developed in parts of central Indonesia (especially Java and southern Sulawesi) and the Philippines, whereas on the Southeast Asian mainland, pebble and flake tools of a type known collectively as the Hoabinhian industry were in vogue. There is no convincing evidence that any people in this region before 4000 BC lived in settled communities, systematically practiced agriculture, or made pottery.

⚓ A polished quadrangular-sectioned stone adze from Peninsular Malaysia, probably dating from the last two millennia BC.
ZALEHA TASVIB/KUALA LUMPUR MUSEUM

⚓ This stone knife from the Tembeling River valley, in Pahang, Peninsular Malaysia, is of uncertain age.

⚓ A stone bracelet from Peninsular Malaysia, probably dating from the last two millennia BC.
ZALEHA TASVIB/KUALA LUMPUR MUSEUM

⚓ A Hoabinhian biface tool from Peninsular Malaysia. This type of tool was used by hunter-gatherers in the Malay Peninsula between about 8000 BC and 2000 BC.
ZALEHA TASVIB/KUALA LUMPUR MUSEUM

BRUNO BARBEY/MAGNUM

⚓ An undated edge-ground axe from Gunung Cheroh, in Ipoh, Malaysia. Similar tools appear earlier than 20,000 years ago in northern Australia and Japan.
ZALEHA TASVIB/KUALA LUMPUR MUSEUM

⚓ The watery landscape of the Yangtze basin, in southern China, was host to experiments in the domestication of rice and other aquatic plants.

INDIA

⚱ A Malwa jar from the Chalcolithic village of Inamgaon, Maharashtra, dating from about 1500 BC. Malwa ware is the finest of the early painted pottery styles found in northwestern India.
DECCAN COLLEGE, INDIA

⚱ This pottery kiln excavated at Inamgaon has a firing chamber, clay "cushions" to support the pots, and an outer stoke-hole. It dates from the Early Jorwe period, about 1300 BC. Kiln-firing technology for pottery is known from sites in northern Iraq as early as 6000 BC, and spread into India via the Harappan culture.

B etween 4000 BC and 2000 BC, a number of important developments took place that heralded significant cultural changes on the Indian subcontinent. By about 3000 BC, there are indications that a cattle-based pastoral economy was spreading southwards from Rajasthan into the western and central Deccan. For example, the site of Utnur, in northern Karnataka, incorporated an oval enclosure surrounded by a palm-trunk stockade big enough to accommodate perhaps 500 cattle. Huts were constructed between the corral and a separate outer stockade. The inhabitants made pottery, some of which was painted. Accumulated cattle dung was periodically burned, forming large ash mounds, which are still visible today. On present evidence, this pastoral way of life seems to have been restricted to only a few regions in western and south central India.

Agricultural Beginnings

Hard on the heels of these early pastoralists appeared the earliest agricultural societies of northwestern India and the Deccan. By about 2500 BC, as agriculture expanded out of the Indus region into Gujarat, a major change had occurred. The Harappan culture here had come to depend

⚱ Harvested sorghum. A type of millet, sorghum was grown by the early agriculturalists of the Deccan Peninsula, along with other monsoon crops. It was probably brought to India from sub-Saharan Africa, via southern Arabia, about 2000 BC.

less on winter-growth crops such as wheat, barley, and legumes as summer-growth cereals such as millets and sorghum were introduced. This change is especially well documented at the Mature and Late Harappan site of Rojdi, in central Gujarat. Although some sites well south of Rojdi show that the people here retained an economy based on western Asian crops until after 1000 BC, the partial shift to millets and sorghum undoubtedly advanced the process of the agricultural colonization of the Deccan.

Two of the plants involved in this process, finger millet (*Eleusine coracana*) and sorghum (*Sorghum bicolor*), are believed by some archaeologists to have originated in Africa, although certain botanists dispute this in the case of finger millet. The two cereals could have been spread by trade contacts—extensions, perhaps, of the historically documented trade between the Indus civilization and the inhabitants of the Persian Gulf area during the late third millennium BC. Two other millets, *Panicum miliaceum* (common millet, perhaps domesticated in northern India) and *Setaria italica* (foxtail millet, which may have been first domesticated in eastern Europe or central China), also played a part in this spread of agriculture.

Millets never became as important on the Ganges plains as in the Deccan. On the Ganges plains we see, after 3000 BC, a mix of wheat and barley, with rice at many sites. As early as 4500 BC, rice may have been cultivated at Koldihwa, in Uttar Pradesh, but the evidence for this has not been confirmed. The oldest confirmed dates for rice in India are from about 2500 BC at Chirand and Khairadih, in Bihar. Rice was also known to the Harappans well before 2000 BC.

The cultural materials associated with the oldest farming settlements in India are extremely varied—there is certainly no single cultural source. The spread of agriculture from the northwest towards Maharashtra and the Deccan was

DECCAN COLLEGE, INDIA

associated from the start with a number of artifacts and activities that may reflect Harappan antecedents. For example, these people produced painted wheel-made pottery fired in true firing chamber kilns, and copper and bronze axes. They carried on a stone blade industry and made clay figurines of humans and animals, particularly cattle. Their economy was based on various combinations of summer and winter cereals, along with domesticated cattle and, to a lesser extent, sheep, goats, pigs, buffaloes, and fowl. Cotton and flax were used to make woven fabrics and cordage. Houses were rectangular, with walls of wattle and daub or stones set in clay, lime-plastered floors, clay ovens, storage pits, and storage platforms. A few circular structures have also been found, probably used for storage.

Excellent examples of such sites, dating from about 2600 BC onwards, are found at Ahar, in Rajasthan; Kayatha and Navdatoli, in the Malwa region of Madhya Pradesh; and Inamgaon and Daimabad, in Maharashtra. At Inamgaon (about 1400 BC), an area of 5 hectares (12 acres) was partly fortified by means of a bank of earth and stones, with the houses laid out on a roughly rectangular grid and separated by lanes. One area of the site was fed by an irrigation ditch, which suggests that crops (mainly barley and legumes in this instance) were probably cultivated all year round.

Further to the south, in Karnataka and Andhra, the oldest agricultural sites, dating from the late third millennium BC, contain circular houses, some of which have stone foundations and mud-plastered floors. While copper tools were used from the time of the earliest agricultural expansion, stone axes and blade tools were still being produced. At sites such as Hallur and Tekkalakota, in Karnataka, and Ramapuram, in Andhra Pradesh, the economy was firmly based on cattle husbandry and the cultivation of millets (including pearl millet, *Pennisetum typhoides*, which may also have originated in Africa). Surprisingly, little is known of early agricultural developments in the far south of India. In Sri Lanka, the first cultivators do not appear to have arrived until the Iron Age, between 1000 BC and 500 BC.

The Ganges Plains

During the late third millennium BC, a north-westerly (possibly Harappan) influence is found in the form of red-slipped (ocher-colored) and black-on-red painted pottery at sites on the Ganges plains. These pottery finds extend from the Yamuna River eastwards toward Bihar and, ultimately, Bengal. Contemporaneous with these red wares (and excavated together with them at Saipai, in Uttar Pradesh) are a number of hoards of copper implements—axes, swords, harpoons, spearheads, and human-shaped plaques (so-called anthropomorphs)—found since 1822 in the Ganges–Yamuna interfluve zone and in Chota

Nagpur. Ocher-colored pottery was also found with both barley and rice at Atranjikhera, in Uttar Pradesh, but by 1000 BC, rice had become the dominant crop in most of the Ganges basin.

The importance of rice suggests that early agriculturalists with a cultural tradition derived from the northwest were not the only settlers in this region. At many sites in Uttar Pradesh and Bihar, there are signs of earlier occupation by settlers who grew rice, made the cord-marked and rice-husk-tempered pottery typical of Southeast Asia, and built circular huts of wattle and daub. They had already colonized the plains before 2000 BC, and their traces, usually also associated with western-type crops and domestic animals, can be seen at Koldihwa, Mahagara, Sohagaura, and Chirand.

Many of these early agricultural settlements in the Ganges basin, especially those showing northwesterly influences, probably mark the arrival of Indo-European-speaking peoples from a linguistic homeland in western or central Asia. Similarly, Neolithic finds in the Deccan are probably associated with early Dravidian languages, traceable to a joint homeland with the Elamite language, in Iran or Pakistan. The early spread of both these language families within India may not have occurred completely independently. Elements of both, for instance, may have been represented in the Mature and Late Harappan civilization, just as the contemporary Mesopotamian civilization incorporated at least three ethnolinguistic elements: Sumerian, Akkadian, and Elamite. Both groups, especially the Dravidians, intermarried and ultimately assimilated with the numerous hunter-gatherer communities that preceded them on the subcontinent.

The Indo-Europeans and the Dravidians, however, did not determine the whole course of Indian prehistory after the development of agriculture. As noted, peoples with cultural and linguistic affinities with the Southeast Asian mainland also played a part.

Peter Bellwood

🜨 This anthropomorphic figure of cast copper from Shahabad, in Bihar, probably dates from the second millennium BC. Such figures are often found in hoards with copper implements. They may have served as ritual axes, as some show signs of sharpening around the head and shoulder regions.

BO-GIRAUDON

♀ A carinated pot from the Peninsular Malaysian Neolithic period, which lasted from about 2000 BC to 500 BC. It was excavated from the Neolithic cemetery in the cave of Gua Cha, in Kelantan, Malaysia.
ZALEHA TASVIB/KUALA LUMPUR MUSEUM

PEINAN: A NEOLITHIC VILLAGE

CHAO-MEI LIEN

THE IMPORTANCE OF the Peinan site, in Taiwan, is twofold. First, it may help us to better understand the Neolithic culture of the island. Secondly, it may shed light on links between this culture and the forebears of the Austronesian peoples of today.

The Peinan site is located in southeastern Taiwan. It was identified as a site of archaeological importance at the end of the nineteenth century, but was not fully investigated until 1980, when graveling operations began in preparation for the construction of a new railway siding at Peinan. A series of intensive archaeological salvage excavations was then carried out from 1980 to 1989. These revealed that Peinan was the largest prehistoric site in Taiwan, measuring more than 80,000 square meters (95,000 square yards).

A carved jade earring from Peinan, in southeastern Taiwan, in the form of two human figures and an animal. More than 13,000 finely crafted objects have been recovered from graves at this Neolithic village.
CHAO-MEI LIEN

The archaeological finds excavated from within an area of 10,000 square meters (12,000 square yards) included an enormous number of artifacts, at least 50 units of architectural foundations, 1,530 burials and graves, and more than 13,000 items of beautifully crafted objects recovered from graves, which together provide us with a clear picture of village life in eastern Taiwan between about 3000 BC and 1000 BC. This collection of finds is known as the Peinan culture.

A Village Life

The people of the Peinan culture lived a settled village life. On the evidence of the stone tools found in the habitation levels of the site,

This woman was buried wearing jade earrings and slate bracelets. Examination of her upper jaw showed that her lateral incisor and canine teeth were missing, owing to the custom of extracting these teeth at puberty.

In the left foreground is the cover of one of the slate-lined graves. The surrounding ground floor is paved with slate slabs, showing that the grave is 20 to 30 centimeters (8 to 12 inches) beneath.

associated from the start with a number of artifacts and activities that may reflect Harappan antecedents. For example, these people produced painted wheel-made pottery fired in true firing chamber kilns, and copper and bronze axes. They carried on a stone blade industry and made clay figurines of humans and animals, particularly cattle. Their economy was based on various combinations of summer and winter cereals, along with domesticated cattle and, to a lesser extent, sheep, goats, pigs, buffaloes, and fowl. Cotton and flax were used to make woven fabrics and cordage. Houses were rectangular, with walls of wattle and daub or stones set in clay, lime-plastered floors, clay ovens, storage pits, and storage platforms. A few circular structures have also been found, probably used for storage.

Excellent examples of such sites, dating from about 2600 BC onwards, are found at Ahar, in Rajasthan; Kayatha and Navdatoli, in the Malwa region of Madhya Pradesh; and Inamgaon and Daimabad, in Maharashtra. At Inamgaon (about 1400 BC), an area of 5 hectares (12 acres) was partly fortified by means of a bank of earth and stones, with the houses laid out on a roughly rectangular grid and separated by lanes. One area of the site was fed by an irrigation ditch, which suggests that crops (mainly barley and legumes in this instance) were probably cultivated all year round.

Further to the south, in Karnataka and Andhra, the oldest agricultural sites, dating from the late third millennium BC, contain circular houses, some of which have stone foundations and mud-plastered floors. While copper tools were used from the time of the earliest agricultural expansion, stone axes and blade tools were still being produced. At sites such as Hallur and Tekkalakota, in Karnataka, and Ramapuram, in Andhra Pradesh, the economy was firmly based on cattle husbandry and the cultivation of millets (including pearl millet, *Pennisetum typhoides*, which may also have originated in Africa). Surprisingly, little is known of early agricultural developments in the far south of India. In Sri Lanka, the first cultivators do not appear to have arrived until the Iron Age, between 1000 BC and 500 BC.

The Ganges Plains

During the late third millennium BC, a north-westerly (possibly Harappan) influence is found in the form of red-slipped (ocher-colored) and black-on-red painted pottery at sites on the Ganges plains. These pottery finds extend from the Yamuna River eastwards toward Bihar and, ultimately, Bengal. Contemporaneous with these red wares (and excavated together with them at Saipai, in Uttar Pradesh) are a number of hoards of copper implements—axes, swords, harpoons, spearheads, and human-shaped plaques (so-called anthropomorphs)—found since 1822 in the Ganges–Yamuna interfluve zone and in Chota

Nagpur. Ocher-colored pottery was also found with both barley and rice at Atranjikhera, in Uttar Pradesh, but by 1000 BC, rice had become the dominant crop in most of the Ganges basin.

The importance of rice suggests that early agriculturalists with a cultural tradition derived from the northwest were not the only settlers in this region. At many sites in Uttar Pradesh and Bihar, there are signs of earlier occupation by settlers who grew rice, made the cord-marked and rice-husk-tempered pottery typical of Southeast Asia, and built circular huts of wattle and daub. They had already colonized the plains before 2000 BC, and their traces, usually also associated with western-type crops and domestic animals, can be seen at Koldihwa, Mahagara, Sohagaura, and Chirand.

Many of these early agricultural settlements in the Ganges basin, especially those showing northwesterly influences, probably mark the arrival of Indo-European-speaking peoples from a linguistic homeland in western or central Asia. Similarly, Neolithic finds in the Deccan are probably associated with early Dravidian languages, traceable to a joint homeland with the Elamite language, in Iran or Pakistan. The early spread of both these language families within India may not have occurred completely independently. Elements of both, for instance, may have been represented in the Mature and Late Harappan civilization, just as the contemporary Mesopotamian civilization incorporated at least three ethnolinguistic elements: Sumerian, Akkadian, and Elamite. Both groups, especially the Dravidians, intermarried and ultimately assimilated with the numerous hunter-gatherer communities that preceded them on the subcontinent.

The Indo-Europeans and the Dravidians, however, did not determine the whole course of Indian prehistory after the development of agriculture. As noted, peoples with cultural and linguistic affinities with the Southeast Asian mainland also played a part.

Peter Bellwood

BO-GIRAUDON

⚒ This anthropomorphic figure of cast copper from Shahabad, in Bihar, probably dates from the second millennium BC. Such figures are often found in hoards with copper implements. They may have served as ritual axes, as some show signs of sharpening around the head and shoulder regions.

♀ A carinated pot from the Peninsular Malaysian Neolithic period, which lasted from about 2000 BC to 500 BC. It was excavated from the Neolithic cemetery in the cave of Gua Cha, in Kelantan, Malaysia.
ZALEHA TASVIB/KUALA LUMPUR MUSEUM

NEOLITHIC JADES OF THE LIANGZHU CULTURE

TSUI-MEI HUANG

IN THE 1970S AND 1980S, a large number of Late Neolithic sites, now known collectively as the Liangzhu culture, were discovered in the Lake Tai area of the Lower Yangtze Valley, in China. These sites have been radiocarbon-dated to between about 3400 BC and 2000 BC. More than 5,000 pieces of jade, including a large number of perforated disks known as *bi* and tubes known as *cong* have been found in graves here.

According to the ancient Chinese text *Zhou Li (Rites of Zhou)*, which dates from about 400 BC or 300 BC, *bi* and *cong* were widely used by the court in the Zhou dynasty (which lasted from about 1000 BC to 221 BC). Little is known of how they were used, but they were described as ritual objects given by the king to his subjects. They were associated with homage paid to Heaven and Earth, from which came the king's mandate to rule.

Jade Grave Goods

In October 1982, the tomb of a man of about 20 years of age was unearthed in a field to the east of an oval earthen mound called Sidun, in Wujin, Jiangsu province. The tomb was profusely furnished, containing 4 pottery vessels, 14 stone and jade implements, 49 jade ornaments, 24 *bi*, 33 *cong*, and 3 jade *yue* axes that showed no signs of wear. (*Yue* axes are broad-bladed and were usually used as weapons.) The two largest and most highly polished *bi* were resting upon the man's abdomen and chest; the remainder had been placed above his head, and beneath his head, body, and feet. Twenty-seven large *cong* surrounded the body; others rested above the man's head and next to his feet. Such an arrangement of *bi* and *cong* corresponds with descriptions given in the *Zhou Li* of how these jades were arranged on and around the corpses of the elite.

In 1986, more than 3,200 pieces of jade—constituting more than 90 percent of the grave goods—were found in 11 grave mounds arranged in two lines on an artificial hill at Fanshan, in Yuhang county, Zhejiang province. The next year, another 1,000 jade objects were excavated from 12 graves scattered

in two tiers within a rectangular earthen platform on the top of Yaoshan (Mount Yao), 5 kilometers (3 miles) northeast of the Fanshan site. The platform, about 400 square meters (4,300 square feet) in size, consisted of three layers. The inner layer, at the eastern end, formed an altar, and was built of red earth. The second was a ditch filled with gray earth surrounding the altar. The third layer (the foundations), to the west, north, and south of the ditch, consisted of yellowish brown earth scattered with pebbles. The goods found in the graves partly built into the red soil of the altar were more lavish than those in the more distant graves.

The structure of the platform and the way the graves had been grouped show that as well as being a cemetery, Yaoshan was used for ceremonial purposes. In addition, the positioning of the graves, and the way they differ from each other, show that there were privileged social groups within the culture.

Monster-like Creatures

Most of the Liangzhu jades consist of nephrite, a type of jade that is extremely hard and tough. All the *cong* and various other jade objects are decorated with designs of monster-like creatures. In addition, some are carved with human and animal images in the form of intaglio, relief, and openwork, and decorated with exquisitely incised spiral patterns. Since there is no evidence that metal was in use at the time these jades were made, it is thought that they may have been carved with sharks' teeth.

◄ Carved from jade, *cong* are circular inside, square outside, and vary in length. They are thought to have been ritual objects used by the court to symbolize the Earth. *Cong* and *bi* are also described in ancient Chinese texts as symbols of rank.
WENWU PUBLISHING

⬧ A *bi* is a flat jade disk, ranging from about 10 to 30 centimeters (3 to 9 inches) in diameter, with a small hole in the center. *Bi* are thought to have been used to symbolize Heaven.
WENWU PUBLISHING

These jades were both ritual symbols and symbols for legitimating social differentiation and political relationships, but nothing is known about how they were distributed. The monster-like motif constantly reinforced the social structure, reiterating a supposedly divine message of social and political inequality.

The manufacture of such technically sophisticated jades strongly suggests that there was a social hierarchy, with the rulers having a monopoly of the supply of jade and control over a group of specialized craftspeople. The recent discovery of a deposit of tremolite—a stone resembling nephrite—in the village of Xiaomeiling, in Liyang county, not far from Lake Tai, suggests that there may have been nephrite mines in the region.

The Liangzhu excavations are significant. By showing the importance of jade along the southeastern coast of China in the Late Neolithic period, they challenge the orthodox view that civilization developed in the north of the country.

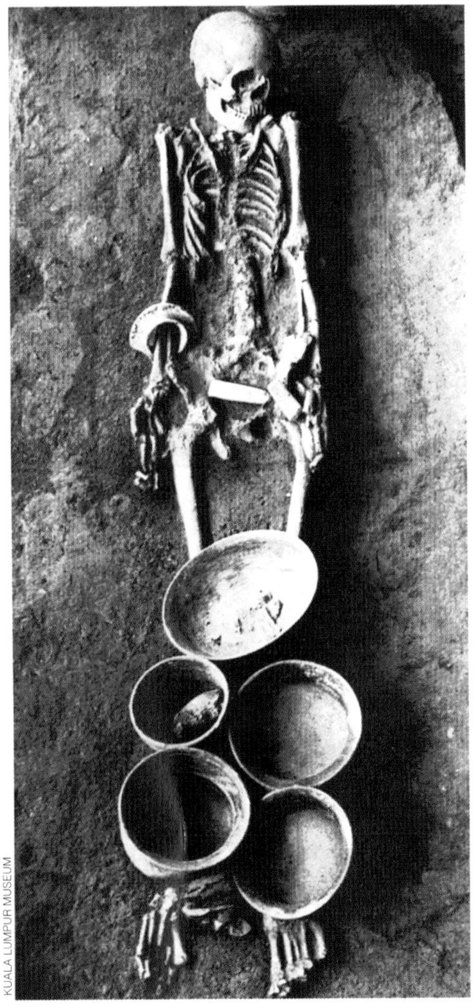

KUALA LUMPUR MUSEUM

The skeleton of a young woman buried at Gua Cha, central Peninsular Malaysia, about 1200 BC. A single pot had been placed above her head and five pots over her legs (one of which contained a rat skull). She was wearing a polished nephrite bracelet, and two stone adzes were buried with her.

SOUTHEAST ASIA

The agricultural prehistory of Southeast Asia is inseparably linked to that of China. Indeed, until the southward conquests and colonizations of the Chinese after 1000 BC, there was no marked cultural separation between Southeast Asia and what is now China. Both regions were home to culturally related people who spoke the Tai, Austroasiatic, and Austronesian languages. The Yangtze River formed the northern boundary of Southeast Asia.

By the sixth millennium BC, societies with an economy based on rice cultivation and domesticated pigs, dogs, and chickens (plus, perhaps, cattle and water buffaloes) already existed in the Yangtze basin of China. By 3000 BC, this way of life had spread over the coastal regions of southern China and into Vietnam and Thailand, and by 2500 BC, into northeastern India.

Sites of this period in Southeast Asia are best known in Thailand, although claims of evidence of agriculture as early as 7000 BC in Spirit Cave, in the far northwest of the country, are now being questioned. Certainly, rice agriculture was established at Ban Chiang, in northeastern Thailand, by 3000 BC, along with domesticated pigs, dogs, fowl, and cattle. This culture was also characterized by the production of cord-marked, burnished, and incised pottery placed in graves. Similar collections of items, less well understood, have been found in Vietnam.

Thai Burials

Unfortunately, unlike India, there are no detailed settlement plans for early agricultural sites anywhere in Southeast Asia, but a number of burials with considerable collections of offerings have been unearthed in the region, such as at Ban Chiang and Non Nok Tha, in northern Thailand, and at Khok Phanom Di, to the east of Bangkok. At this latter site, a cemetery dating to between 2000 BC and 1500 BC has been excavated within a massive 5 hectare (12 acre) occupation mound. The bodies were mostly wrapped in barkcloth (a felted fabric beaten out of the inner bark of trees, weaving apparently being unknown this far south at this time), dusted with red ocher, and buried with a range of items including pottery, shell ornaments, bone fishhooks, stone adzes, and, possibly, rice offerings. One wealthy woman, thought to have been a potter, was buried under a large pile of the clay cylinders from which pots were made, together with more than 120,000 shell beads, which had probably been sewn onto a barkcloth jacket. Her grave also contained numerous finely incised and burnished pottery

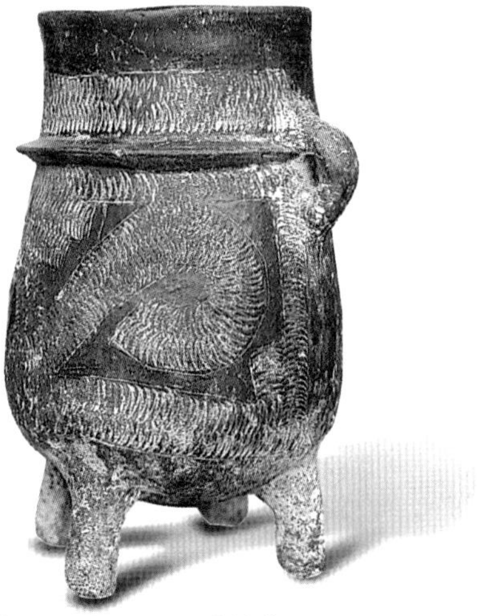

The surface design of this four-legged vessel from the Early Period at Ban Chiang (third millennium BC) was made using a technique known as rocker stamping.

LUCA INVERNIZZI TETTONI/PHOTOBANK

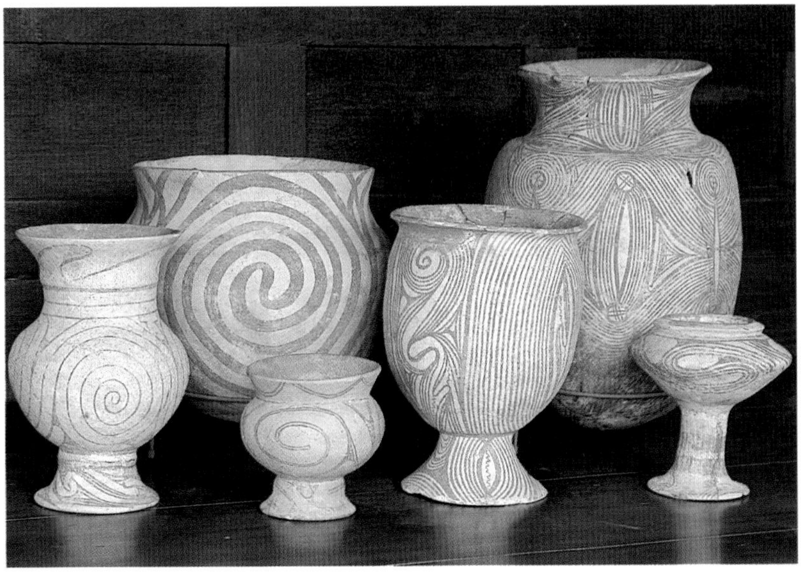

Red-on-buff painted pots from the Late Period at Ban Chiang, about 200 BC to AD 200. With their intricate curvilinear patterns, these pots are world renowned.

LUCA INVERNIZZI TETTONI/PHOTOBANK

☞ These glass ornaments from Ban Chiang are undated, but are presumably later than 400 BC. Glass does not appear in Southeast Asia until after that date.

CHARLES HIGHAM

♠ The burial of a 35-year-old woman at Khok Phanom Di, in central Thailand, dated to about 2000 BC to 1500 BC. More than 120,000 shell beads were found around her upper body, and had probably been sewn onto a jacket. She had shell disks at her shoulders, a shell bangle on her left wrist, and about 10 pottery vessels were placed over her legs. Clearly a person of high status in the community, she was evidently a potter.

☞ A tripod pot from Ban Kao, dated to about 1800 BC. The legs are cord-marked, and perforated to allow air to escape during firing.

LUCA INVERNIZZI TETTONI/PHOTOBANK

vessels. A 15-month-old child was buried with similar items nearby, possibly indicating that this was a hierarchical society, in which wealth was inherited. Graves were placed in fenced enclosures reserved for family groups and maintained over many generations.

Khok Phanom Di yielded no metal artifacts, although people living in the Khao Wong Prachan Valley, near Lopburi, in central Thailand, knew how to cast bronze to make socketed axes and

bracelets as early as 1500 BC. In central Thailand, as in much of India, the technology for copper and bronze working appeared soon after the beginnings of agriculture. Strangely, however, metalworking did not spread to Indonesia for another thousand years.

Agriculturalists spread down the peninsula of southern Thailand into Malaysia after about 2500 BC, but there are no signs of metalworking in the region until about 500 BC. These peninsular agriculturalists made a distinctive type of burnished or cord-marked pottery, often with pedestals or hollow tripod legs. Pottery of this sort has been widely found in sites from Ban Kao, in Thailand, southwards into Malaysia.

The Move South

In the islands of Southeast Asia (Indonesia, the Philippines, East Malaysia), as on the mainland, the record of agricultural societies begins later the further southwards one moves. Between 3000 BC and 2000 BC, early agriculturalists from southern China settled Taiwan. By 2000 BC, some of their descendants in eastern Indonesia came into contact with western Melanesian horticulturalists, with whom, in time, they assimilated. By 1500 BC, their descendants, in turn, were poised to colonize the Pacific islands, beyond the Solomons.

The early agricultural record in the islands of Southeast Asia is restricted mainly to small collections of pottery and stone tools from rock shelters and caves; dense vegetation and heavy erosion in this region make it difficult to find open sites with clear evidence of agriculture. In some upland regions, though, the start of agriculture has been dated by analyzing pollen and charcoal in core samples taken from lake and swamp sediments. The results show that forests had been cleared, presumably for agriculture, by at least 3000 BC in Taiwan, and some time before 2000 BC in Sumatra and Java. The available archaeological, linguistic, and ethnographic data suggest that the crops grown in this region in prehistoric times included rice, yams, taro, sugar cane, bananas, coconuts, other fruits and tubers, and, in rare instances, millet. It is likely that rice cultivation was less important in the equatorial regions and never extended as far as the Pacific islands beyond western Micronesia.

Taiwan Transition

The early agricultural archaeology of Taiwan reveals a transitional phase between southern China, on the one hand, and the islands of the Philippines and Indonesia, on the other. The early cord-marked pottery of the Tapengkeng culture was soon partly replaced by the plain or red-slipped wares of the Yuanshan and Peinan cultures. Other artifacts found in Taiwan's Neolithic sites include stone adzes and barkcloth beaters, slate reaping knives (probably used to harvest rice and millet), and slate spear or arrow points. Rice was certainly grown. At the site of Peinan, near Taitung, in southeastern Taiwan, recent excavations have uncovered more than 1,500 graves lined with slate slabs associated with a settlement consisting of dry-stone–walled houses and storage pits laid out in lines. The jade grave goods from this site, most of which dates to about 1000 BC, reflect an astonishing level of stone-working skill. (See the feature *Peinan: A Neolithic Village*.)

Southwards from Taiwan, approaching the equatorial zone, a number of sites have been found in the Philippines and in central and eastern Indonesia (Lal-lo, Andarayan, Dimolit, Leang Tuwo Mane'e, Uattamdi). Dated to between about 2500 BC and 1500 BC, they have yielded collections of red-slipped pottery, perhaps derived from that in Taiwan, with occasional shell or stone adzes. In the rock shelter site of Bukit Tengkorak, in Sabah, red-slipped pottery dating to 1000 BC has been found together with obsidian from New Britain, which lies far to the east in the Lapita homeland region of western Melanesia. Unfortunately, this region has not produced much direct evidence of agriculture owing to the relatively poor conditions for preservation and the lack of good sites for settlements. There is, however, evidence that pigs were introduced into Timor about 2500 BC.

Elsewhere in the islands of Southeast Asia, the oldest pottery in Sarawak, also dated to about 2500 BC in the Niah Caves and Gua Sireh, is quite different from the red-slipped wares of eastern Indonesia. It was impressed with a carved wooden paddle and sometimes tempered with rice husks, resembling the pottery of Malaysia and Thailand. Virtually nothing is known of early agricultural archaeology in Kalimantan (southern Borneo), Java, Bali, or Sumatra, but agriculture was presumably introduced to these regions at about the same time as to the other Indonesian islands.

Agricultural Colonizations

As in India, the early agricultural record of Southeast Asia tracks the colonizations of agricultural peoples and the concomitant spread of their distinctive languages, rather than the simple spread of agricultural techniques between settled communities of hunter-gatherers. (See the feature *The Austronesian Dispersal and the Origin of Language Families*.) It is probable that before 2000 BC, most of the languages of mainland Southeast Asia were Austroasiatic, extending into northeastern India and the Ganga plains, and possibly even into Borneo and Sumatra. These languages probably spread with the beginnings of rice agriculture from an area spanning much of southern China and northern Southeast Asia, from Burma across to Vietnam. Since 2000 BC, other speakers of Tai and Tibeto-Burman languages have replaced some of these Austroasiatic populations as they spread out of their linguistic homelands in southern China.

In the islands of Southeast Asia, the Austronesian speakers colonized southwards from Taiwan after 3000 BC, finally settling the whole of the Philippines and Indonesia and assimilating the people who lived in the areas west of Timor and the Moluccas. This expansion came to a halt in and around New Guinea, but continued after 1500 BC into the previously uninhabited islands of the Pacific. Ultimately, during the first thousand years AD, this migration extended as far as Madagascar and Easter Island.

Peter Bellwood

♂ This elaborately incised and red-slipped pottery from Bukit Tengkorak, in Sabah, northern Borneo, dates from about 1000 BC. It was found with obsidian imported from the Pacific island of New Britain, 4,000 kilometers (2,500 miles) to the east.

♀ A stone cist grave at the megalithic cemetery of Cipari, on the eastern slopes of Mount Ceremai, near Kuningan, in West Java, Indonesia. Neolithic dates at an age of 4,000 years have been claimed for the earliest constructions at this site, although megalithic traditions in island Southeast Asia are generally thought to have developed much later, during the Iron Age.

PEINAN: A NEOLITHIC VILLAGE

CHAO-MEI LIEN

THE IMPORTANCE OF the Peinan site, in Taiwan, is twofold. First, it may help us to better understand the Neolithic culture of the island. Secondly, it may shed light on links between this culture and the forebears of the Austronesian peoples of today.

The Peinan site is located in southeastern Taiwan. It was identified as a site of archaeological importance at the end of the nineteenth century, but was not fully investigated until 1980, when graveling operations began in preparation for the construction of a new railway siding at Peinan. A series of intensive archaeological salvage excavations was then carried out from 1980 to 1989. These revealed that Peinan was the largest prehistoric site in Taiwan, measuring more than 80,000 square meters (95,000 square yards).

◄◙ A carved jade earring from Peinan, in southeastern Taiwan, in the form of two human figures and an animal. More than 13,000 finely crafted objects have been recovered from graves at this Neolithic village.
CHAO-MEI LIEN

The archaeological finds excavated from within an area of 10,000 square meters (12,000 square yards) included an enormous number of artifacts, at least 50 units of architectural foundations, 1,530 burials and graves, and more than 13,000 items of beautifully crafted objects recovered from graves, which together provide us with a clear picture of village life in eastern Taiwan between about 3000 BC and 1000 BC. This collection of finds is known as the Peinan culture.

A Village Life

The people of the Peinan culture lived a settled village life. On the evidence of the stone tools found in the habitation levels of the site,

⚤ This woman was buried wearing jade earrings and slate bracelets. Examination of her upper jaw showed that her lateral incisor and canine teeth were missing, owing to the custom of extracting these teeth at puberty.

◄◙ In the left foreground is the cover of one of the slate-lined graves. The surrounding ground floor is paved with slate slabs, showing that the grave is 20 to 30 centimeters (8 to 12 inches) beneath.

they appear to have relied mainly on the cultivation of hill rice and millet for their subsistence; and the stone tools and animal remains indicate that they also hunted wild boar and deer quite intensively. The site was repeatedly occupied, which may be related to a system of shifting cultivation. They were skilled in procuring slate slabs, which they used to build houses and graves and to make various kinds of tools.

Village Layout

The village was located at the foot of the Peinan Hills, on the southern terrace of the Peinan River. Within the village, houses were built side-by-side in a line following the direction of the hill. The houses were rectangular, and built directly on the ground surface. The average size was about 11.5 meters by 5.5 meters (38 feet by 18 feet). Doorways could not be identified with certainty, but they most likely faced east, towards the delta of the Peinan River. Front yards and most house interiors were paved with slate slabs or split boulders. Each house was adjacent to one or two outside storage structures, which adjoined those of neighboring houses. Graves were located underneath the house floors rather than in a separate village cemetery, and had the same orientation as the houses.

Graves and Burials

A total of 1,530 burials and graves were found in the excavated area. The graves were lined with slate slabs, and the burials ranged from fetuses to the elderly. Most of them were single burials, but about 21 percent of the graves held more than one skeleton, usually because they had been opened at a later date and reused. In most cases, the bodies were buried in an extended posture, with the head towards the southwest. The burials revealed a high fetal and infant mortality rate.

Analysis of the skeletal remains provided evidence of several customs, including chewing betel nut, tooth extraction, and headhunting. These practices are common to almost all other Neolithic cultures in the region.

About 75 percent of the adult graves and 23 percent of the infant graves yielded beautifully crafted grave goods, the most abundant and refined being made of a local material called Taiwan jade, or tremolitic nephrite. The items included necklaces made of tubular pieces of varying lengths; other items of adornment such as earrings, hair ornaments, and bracelets; and delicate examples of blades and adzes. Some of the ornaments were decorated with unique zooanthropomorphic and/or geometric designs, among them being earrings that would impress any connoisseur of jade.

⊷ Fifteen grave pots were found in this grave, indicating that at least that number of people had been buried here. Most burials at Peinan were single burials, but about 21 percent of the excavated graves had been opened and reused.

CHAO-MEI LIEN

⚜ Tools such as this Taiwan jade arrowhead were made with great skill. Fine examples of blades and adzes, made from the same stone, were also found in graves.

CHAO-MEI LIEN

☞ An example of Peinan grave pottery.
CHAO-MEI LIEN

☞ The graves at Peinan were densely distributed and lined with slate slabs. The bodies were usually buried with their heads towards the southwest.

CHAO-MEI LIEN

CHINA

❂ Fields terraced into the yellow soils of the loess plateau of northern China. The oak forests that once grew here were cleared for millet cultivation.

hina's two great river basins nurtured the development of two very different types of agriculture. In the north, millet was grown in the Yellow River basin, while in the south, in the Yangtze River basin, rice was cultivated. These crops provided China's staple food for thousands of years, although today rice is the more important. This division of the agricultural landscape was the result not of custom and culture but of climate and geography, combined with the constraints of a primitive agricultural technology.

❂ In southern China, abundant water is available to irrigate fields for wet-rice cultivation. This scene, in Jiangsu province, in the Yangtze River basin, shows the sculptured landscape characteristic of rice-growing regions.

Agricultural Contrasts

The northern mainland consists of loess—fine particles of soil, blown in from the central Asian deserts during the Ice Age. This soil settled like a mantle, hundreds of meters thick in places, over the region drained by the upper reaches of the Yellow River. Although rainfall is sparse in the north, in the course of time erosion riddled the loess plateau with gullies and gorges, and sediments have been carried eastwards and deposited across the great plains of northern China. It is this sediment that gives the Yellow River its name. Pollen analysis suggests that the plateau was once forested, mainly with oaks, but the plains were subject to large-scale seasonal flooding which continuously deposited new sediment. Flooding not only discouraged settlement of the area, but also deeply buried whatever early occupational remains there may have been.

With an annual rainfall limited to 250 to 500 millimeters (10 to 20 inches), falling only in summer, and no irrigation technology to raise river water to field level, the earliest agricultural methods used in the loess country were designed to conserve moisture. Millet, a drought-resistant plant, was the ideal crop, and foxtail millet (*Setaria italica*) and common millet (*Panicum miliaceum*) were both grown in Neolithic times. Forests were probably cleared to permit cultivation, but judging from early writings on agricultural methods, it appears that the typical slash-and-burn techniques of burning the forest cover to create ash fertilizer and long fallowing to restore fertility were unnecessary. The capillary action of loess soils brought both moisture and nutrients up from the depths. This process was encouraged by turning the soil with plant matter intact, and then leaving it to lie fallow for a year, allowing the plant matter

◀● The Yellow River picks up its load of yellow sediments in the loess lands of northern China. These sediments are later deposited by floodwaters, which were more feared than welcomed by early farmers, across the great central plains.

🌷 The earliest evidence of farming in China reveals the presence of domestic animals. Early on, cattle were harnessed to work in the fields. V-shaped stone implements dating from the Middle Neolithic period are thought to have been plowshares. From this time, draft animals were important to agriculture in both the north and south.

🌷 Within historic times, land has been terraced to grow both millet and rice. As population growth put pressure on land resources, terracing brought increased areas of land under cultivation but required a greater investment of human labor, both to construct and to maintain the terraces.

to decompose and form a cover under which moisture could collect. Crops were planted only in the second and third years of a three-year cycle.

In contrast, the agriculture practiced in the south was based on an abundance of water. The lower Yangtze River winds through flat alluvial plains past numerous marshes and lakes. Rice was at home in this watery landscape, needing to be inundated for several months during its growing period. Because rice also needs dry conditions for ripening, early agriculturalists drained their rice fields by digging ditches. The construction of drainage works was probably the first step in altering the environment; later, canals were dug for irrigation purposes. This led to the creation of specialized field systems for growing rice outside its natural, seasonal, marshy habitat. Because the water depth must be kept constant, which is difficult over large areas, paddy fields have been,

347

MUSEUM OF FAR EASTERN ANTIQUITIES, STOCKHOLM, SWEDEN

⚓ Dating from 2500 BC, this rare anthropomorphic jar lid from Banshan, in Gansu province, measures only about 20 centimeters (8 inches) in diameter.

⚓ This Late Neolithic hardstone blade may have been a hoe used both vertically and horizontally, as indicated by the perforations made to fit different hafts.

RONALD SHERIDAN/ANCIENT ART & ARCHITECTURE COLLECTION

until modern times, necessarily small—40 square meters (430 square feet) or less. With the development of terracing, which radically transformed the natural landscape, much greater areas became available for rice cultivation.

Thus, the patchwork of small paddy fields in the south and the extensive unstructured fields in which millet was cultivated in the north were both designed to maximize the amount of water available for growing crops. Each system influenced the local culture. For example, rice growing required a significant investment in the field system, and demanded a degree of cooperation between the various groups living along the irrigation network to ensure that the rice was adequately watered. The development of small, dispersed landholdings spread the risk. As the census conducted during the Han period (206 BC to AD 220) shows, the population of the rice-growing south grew much more rapidly than the population in the north.

The Early Chinese Neolithic

Unlike other areas of the world, China has not yet yielded the secrets of its transition to an agricultural society. Recent excavations have pushed back the earliest dates for crops far beyond the traditional Yangshao period (about 4200 BC to 2900 BC), which now has the status of Middle Neolithic only for northern China. The earliest agricultural sites known belong to full-scale agricultural societies, but no evidence has yet emerged regarding the processes of domestication, except, perhaps, in the case of the chicken.

Sites with evidence of the earliest millet farming in the north are generally attributed to the Peiligang culture. These sites are scattered in clusters along the eastern foothills of the loess highlands, to the north and south of the Yellow River, and on terraces of the Wei River flowing into the Yellow River from the west. Dated to between 6500 BC and 5000 BC, the sites consist of villages with cemeteries and storage pits. Millet remains have been excavated from the pits and found in storage jars. Remains of a jungle fowl found at the site of Cishan suggest that it is an ancestor of the domestic chicken. Pigs and dogs were also domesticated, but the many remains of various kinds of deer that have been found indicate that people continued to hunt wild game. The artifacts associated with these early villages are of an extremely advanced type, including highly crafted, polished stone hand mills with legs, serrated stone sickles, several functional ceramic items, and numerous bone implements, some of which have engraved decorations. Clearly, these belonged to a fully developed agricultural village society. What remains to be explained is how this culture developed out of the microlithic, nonceramic cultures known from the early postglacial period in northern China, where wild millet varieties are assumed to have originated.

In southern China, fewer village sites have been discovered, chief among them being Hemudu, dating to about 5000 BC. A mysterious layer of rice remains, 50 centimeters (20 inches) thick, consisting of stalks, leaves, grains, husks, and chaff, was found covering this site. Judging by the architectural finds, these rice remains may have resulted from granaries collapsing. Hemudu stood at the edge of a marsh on the coast of Hangzhou Bay, and waterlogging has preserved both the rice remains and the remains of a number of wooden buildings. These buildings had been constructed using sophisticated techniques, including mortise and tenon joints, and raised above the marshy ground on stilts.

This area would have been ideal for growing rice. Remains of aquatic plants used as food were also found, suggesting experiments in aquaculture. As at the Peiligang sites in the north, the remains of wild game, both from the forest and the water's edge, suggest a continued reliance on hunting. An elaborate range of artifacts was also found at Hemudu, with carved and engraved bone implements, wooden objects for a variety of purposes, and distinctively shaped ceramics often incised with decorations. The main agricultural tool was a bone spade made from a water buffalo's shoulder blade, the water buffalo having been domesticated locally, along with dogs and pigs.

The discovery and excavation of Hemudu in the 1970s dealt the final blow to the idea that agricultural societies originated in the north and spread southwards (the so-called "nuclear hypothesis"). Remains of rice in the south have now been dated to between 7000 BC and 8000 BC at Pengtoushan, in Hunan province. Both Hemudu and Pengtoushan are in the region where the wild ancestors of rice are assumed to have grown. It is now thought that rice was probably domesticated at several times and places within this region in the early Holocene period, about 8000 BC.

The Spread of Rice Agriculture

Since rice originated in the south, rice grain impressions on northern Yangshao pottery, first identified in the 1920s, can be considered as evidence that rice was introduced to this region. But it is still not clear how far north rice was cultivated during the Neolithic period. Rice grains are compact, nutritious, and store well. Though heavy, they also travel well, and have been used in bulk as currency in historic times. For this reason, it cannot be assumed that rice discovered in an archaeological deposit was grown in that region. Although field systems are the best documentation of rice growing, as yet none have been excavated in northern China. Nevertheless, historical literature suggests that by the Han period rice was being grown by ethnically distinct groups in the swampy coastal lowlands of Bohai Bay. A major research problem today is to determine how and when the practice of rice growing was transmitted further east to the Korean peninsula, although its arrival and spread in the Japanese islands is relatively well documented.

Gina Barnes

⚘ Even within the Yangshao tradition, painted pots are less numerous than unpainted ones decorated only with surface finishing techniques, such as cord-marking, pricking, or paddling. This pot is painted in vertical sections that do not entirely cover the surface.
RONALD SHERIDAN/ANCIENT ART & ARCHITECTURE COLLECTION

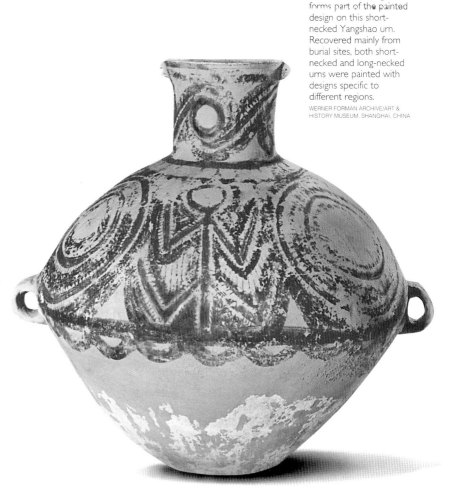

⚘ A human stick figure forms part of the painted design on this short-necked Yangshao urn. Recovered mainly from burial sites, both short-necked and long-necked urns were painted with designs specific to different regions.
WERNER FORMAN ARCHIVE/ART & HISTORY MUSEUM, SHANGHAI, CHINA

THE AUSTRONESIAN DISPERSAL AND THE ORIGIN OF LANGUAGE FAMILIES

PETER BELLWOOD

COMPARATIVE LINGUISTS divide the majority of the world's languages into families, some of which extend over huge geographic areas. For instance, in the Old World, the Indo-European, Afro-Asiatic, Niger-Kordofanian, Sino-Tibetan, Elamo-Dravidian, Austroasiatic, and Austronesian language families have spread over enormous distances, reaching more than halfway around the world in the case of Austronesian.

The known history of the spread and replacement of languages indicates that societies can sometimes assimilate their neighbors in a linguistic sense, particularly if they have expansive tendencies or aspire to conquest or to control by an elite. Such processes, however, cannot explain the spread of the great language families just listed. They can only have reached their present extents through thousands of years of linguistic diversification combined with large-scale population growth and dispersal.

LANGUAGE FAMILIES IN THE OLD WORLD

Areas of early agriculture are outlined in black. The African region outlined represents the postulated homeland region for the Niger-Kordofanian and Nilo-Saharan language families. That in western Asia represents the homeland region for Indo-European, Caucasian, Sumerian, Elamite, Dravidian, and, possibly, Afro-Asiatic. That in eastern Asia represents the postulated homeland region for Austroasiatic, Tai, Austronesian, Hmong-Mien, and, possibly, Sino-Tibetan. New Guinea was the homeland of many diverse families of Papuan languages.

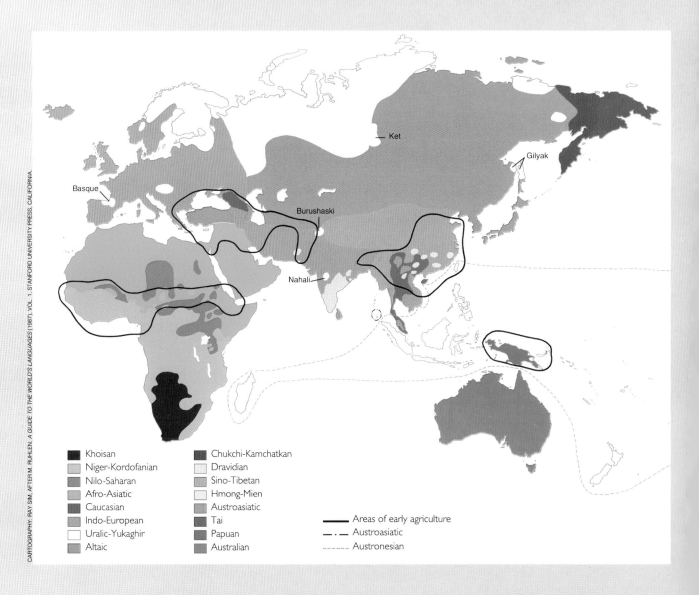

Ket

Gilyak

Basque

Burushaski

Nahali

Khoisan
Niger-Kordofanian
Nilo-Saharan
Afro-Asiatic
Caucasian
Indo-European
Uralic-Yukaghir
Altaic

Chukchi-Kamchatkan
Dravidian
Sino-Tibetan
Hmong-Mien
Austroasiatic
Tai
Papuan
Australian

⸺ Areas of early agriculture
⸺·⸺ Austroasiatic
------ Austronesian

CARTOGRAPHY: RAY SIM, AFTER M. RUHLEN, *A GUIDE TO THE WORLD'S LANGUAGES* (1987), VOL. 1, STANFORD UNIVERSITY PRESS, CALIFORNIA.

Language Homelands

Because the component languages of families such as Indo-European and Austronesian have so many features of grammar, vocabulary, and sound in common, it is thought that they must be derived from an ancestral form of those languages, a so–called "protolanguage", that originated in a specific and quite circumscribed homeland. On the basis of comparative studies, linguists can suggest likely areas for these homelands.

One of the key features of such homelands is that they are areas where there is evidence of the language family in question having developed over a longer period of time than is the case in peripheral regions. In general, a language family becomes more diverse with time, so the greater the degree of diversity to be found within a language family in a given region, the longer the period over which that family of languages has developed in that region.

The homeland regions currently favored by linguists for many major language families coincide with regions that the archaeological record indicates were early centers of agriculture. Such centers include New Guinea; central and southern China; western Asia; the southern borderlands of the Sahara, in Africa; central Mexico; and the northern Andes, in South America. In these areas, linguists have traced not only the greatest internal degree of diversity within the major language families, but also unusually large numbers of language families existing in close proximity. The picture suggests a pattern of outward spread in several

directions, much as the petals of a flower spread from their central point.

Such movement, and the overall spread of these major language families, cannot be explained simply by linguistic diffusion through contact between different populations or by people switching, for whatever reason, to a secondary language and, in time, abandoning their own. We are left with only one sensible conclusion. Early populations must have spread the "protolanguages", and the most likely time in prehistory for this to have taken place is at the interface between hunter-gatherers and early agriculturalists. This is not to claim that all language expansion occurred at this interface—clearly, this would fly in the face of history. But the extent to which languages spread in the early phases of agricultural development appears to have been unparalleled until the period of European colonialism after AD 1500.

Agriculture, even in the earliest phases, would always have supported substantially higher population densities than did hunting and gathering, and given the chance, agriculturalists would generally have sought new land to cultivate. More recently, as the

world has become more "packed" with people, such pancontinental spreading of languages and populations has become more difficult, as the historical record indicates. Not even the mightiest empires known in historic times have been able to spread their language permanently over a wide area, replacing all previous languages, unless they colonized substantial parts of those areas. The history of Latin, Mongol, Spanish, Dutch, and English bears eloquent testimony to this.

The Spread of Austronesian Languages

If this perspective is applied to the Austronesian language family, to take an example that is of great significance for Southeast Asian prehistory, the linguistic and archaeological evidence suggest that, in essence, the Austronesian languages originated in southern China before 3000 BC, in a zone of early rice agriculture that was also the homeland of the Austroasiatic and Tai languages. The early Sino-Tibetan languages probably evolved to the north, in the Yellow River basin, in an adjacent region of millet agriculture.

During the two millennia after 3000 BC, the early Austronesian speakers continually colonized areas away from those regions of the Asian mainland populated by early Austroasiatic, Sino-Tibetan, and Tai speakers who were similarly expanding. This expansion— through regions occupied by small forager groups only, according to the archaeological record—took them first into Taiwan, then into the Philippines, then into Indonesia, and eventually, via Melanesia, into the uninhabited islands of the Pacific. Austronesians, in general, skirted New Guinea, where separate agricultural populations (the ancestral speakers of the Papuan language families) were already in occupation.

Ultimately, by AD 1000, the Austronesian languages had spread throughout the islands stretching from Madagascar to Easter Island— more than halfway around the world. This was achieved by people moving into new areas and colonizing them. While language diffusion as a result of contact and interaction between peoples can explain localized linguistic variations, only colonization can explain the very widespread distribution of major language families.

INITIAL EXPANSION OF AUSTRONESIAN SETTLEMENT

Archaeological and linguistic evidence indicates that early Austronesian speakers spread out from southern China and Taiwan, generally skirting the large island of New Guinea, whose interior was already occupied by agricultural populations. While current finds suggest that there was a gap of 1,000 years between their reaching western Polynesia and their subsequent spread into central Polynesia, some archaeologists believe that this gap will be eliminated as research proceeds. Madagascar, not shown here, was settled in the first millennium AD.

▨ PAPUAN LANGUAGES

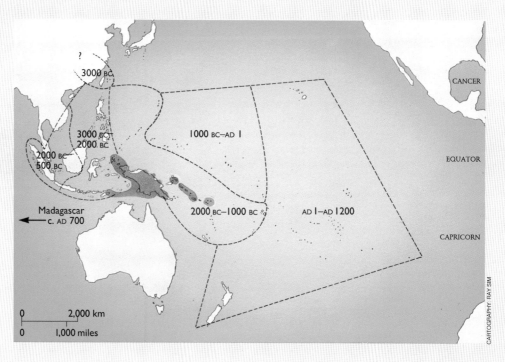

KOREA AND JAPAN

E arly farmers of the Korean peninsula and
Japanese islands grew millet, barley, wheat,
and rice. Of these cereal crops, only millet
was native to the region. Barley and wheat were
brought from the west through the Chinese
mainland, and rice spread towards the northeast
from the Yangtze delta. The introduction of wet-
rice agriculture from 1000 BC was a clear departure
from other subsistence methods. Growing an
irrigated crop requires scheduling and regular
maintenance, as well as a sophisticated
technology—all of which had a significant social
impact. How was this technology transmitted,
and how did its introduction change society?

Chulmun and Jomon

While there is no debate as to the methods of rice
cultivation used in Korea and Japan, where rice
was an introduced crop, this is not the case with
millet and a range of vegetable crops. There are
numerous questions as to how communities in
this region domesticated these plants, and how
this process was coordinated with the hunting and
gathering of wild food resources before wet-rice
technology was adopted. The people of the

postglacial Chulmun culture, who occupied the
Korean peninsula from 6000 BC to 1500 BC, and
those of the Jomon culture, who occupied the
Japanese islands from 10,000 BC to 300 BC, were
hunter-gatherers. Red deer, wild boar, salmon,
shellfish, and nuts were the main food items.
Not only was the environment generally rich,
but these people had developed reliable storage
facilities in the form of underground pits and
ceramic containers, enabling them to live a settled
existence. Both Chulmun and Jomon societies
were characterized by the construction of
substantial pit houses, although burial remains
from either culture are rarely found.

Perhaps because of the richness of the forests,
salmon runs, and coastal shellfish grounds of
northeastern Honshu, the first evidence of
domesticated vegetable crops comes from western
Honshu, an area that was poorer in natural food
resources. Red beans and gourds have been
recovered from the Torihama site (dated to
between 5000 BC and 3500 BC), and buckwheat
pollen has been recovered from Ubuka bog (dated
to about 6500 BC). Charred layers have been
identified in western Jomon excavations. These
unrelated data have stimulated theories that slash-
and-burn agriculture may have been practiced.
The main slash-and-burn crop, however, is
thought to have been millet rather than
buckwheat, and no certified remains of either of
these crops have been recovered from Jomon sites.

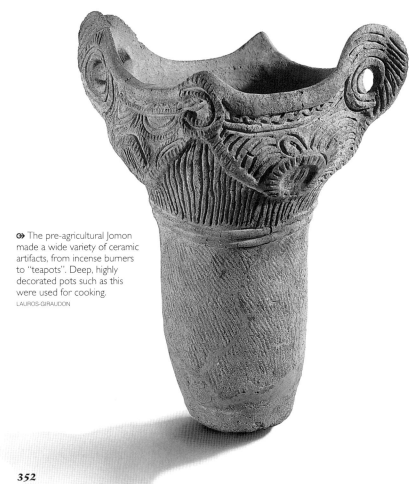

❧ Excavations continue year-round in
Japan, shedding light on such pre-
agricultural subsistence practices as
collecting shellfish, as well as on early
methods of rice cultivation.

MARK J HUDSON

❧ Jomon fisher-peoples living on the
rocky northeastern coast of Honshu
did not take up rice cultivation until
two centuries after it was introduced
to Japan, in 500 BC.

❧ The pre-agricultural Jomon
made a wide variety of ceramic
artifacts, from incense burners
to "teapots". Deep, highly
decorated pots such as this
were used for cooking.
LAUROS-GIRAUDON

ALBERT NORMANDIN/THE IMAGE BANK

The Chulmun sites of the Korean peninsula tell a similar story. Most sites are on river banks or the coast and have yielded considerable evidence of fishing and shellfish collecting as well as of hunting deer and boar and gathering nuts. Only from the site of Chitam-ri, in the north, has a grain, tentatively identified as millet, been recovered in clear association with Chulmun pottery. This raises the question of the relationship between the northern Chulmun societies and the millet agriculturalists of the Chinese mainland. An important link between them is the Xinle culture of the Liaodong peninsula, in the southern Manchurian basin.

The Xinle Culture

Dates for the Xinle culture range between about 5500 BC and 2500 BC, and the Xinle site itself was occupied between 5500 BC and 4500 BC. Although carbonized millet has been found at Xinle, other sites in the vicinity have yielded evidence related to fishing. Thus, the Xinle culture was not only diversified, but represents a true halfway house between the fully agricultural societies of the North China plain and the hunter-gatherer societies of Korea and Japan. This description fits, because Xinle has textured pottery that is very similar to the Chulmun and Jomon ceramics and totally unlike the painted pottery of the Yangshao millet agriculturalists on the Chinese mainland. The Xinle people used flint tools, as did the people of the postglacial cultures of the Manchurian and Mongolian regions. Their range of polished stone tools, including mortars and pestles, and polished axes or adzes, resembles that associated with the Chulmun and Jomon cultures.

Who Was First?

From 1500 BC, there is increasing evidence of the use of agricultural products in Korea and Japan. The earliest date for rice is 1300 BC, coming from what is now North Korea. Millet has been recovered from several Korean sites, including Hunam-ri, in the south, dating to between about

1500 BC and 250 BC; foxtail millet was stored in jars together with rice, sorghum, and barley. With all these grain finds in archaeological sites, however, it is not always clear whether the crops were grown in the region or traded in, through some process of exchange. The Korean finds are associated with Mumun pottery, which succeeded Chulmun and continued on into the Bronze and Iron Ages, from 1000 BC.

In the Japanese islands, sporadic evidence of different types of grains has been recovered from Jomon sites as early as 3500 BC. We know, therefore, that peoples of the Late and Final Jomon cultures were familiar with certain grain crops and perhaps grew some themselves. Nevertheless, there is little archaeological evidence that they relied on cereals until the beginning of wet-rice agriculture about 1000 BC. Most of this evidence—in the form of paddy field systems— is found in Japan, although similar remains are expected to be found in Korea. (See the feature *Wet-rice Cultivation*.)

⚓ Amsadong is a village consisting of reconstructed Chulmun pit houses near Seoul, in South Korea. The people who once lived here fished in the river and processed nuts, but the find of a stone "plowshare" suggests that they may also have grown millet, as was done in northern China.

◄ Chulmun fisher-peoples used notched pebbles to weight their nets, but from Mumun times, in the Korean Bronze Age, clay cylinders were specially made for this purpose. These are still used today.

◄ The first millennium BC in Korea is usually called the Bronze Age, and is marked by dolmen burials, such as this. The dolmen tradition is thought to have started among the Chulmun peoples of the north at the time they began to cultivate millet.

Thus, the first people to engage in farming in Korea and Japan were Chulmun and Jomon villagers who learned about cereal grains, perhaps through trade and exchange with their neighbors on the Chinese mainland and maybe even through migration. But heavy reliance on such cereal crops emerged only with the bronze-using and iron-using cultures that succeeded Chulmun and Jomon between 700 BC and AD 300 on the Korean peninsula and between 300 BC and AD 300 (the Yayoi period) in the Japanese islands. Information about the agricultural practices used by these peoples on the Korean peninsula is extremely scarce: one engraving on a bronze object shows a person wielding a forked foot plow, and some historical documents mention crops and domestic animals. Remains of actual field systems are confined mainly to the Japanese islands, where the Yayoi people constructed substantial paddy fields in the western coastal lowlands.

Island-hopping to Japan

The northwestern half of Kyushu Island, in westernmost Japan, is dotted with mountain clusters separated by large stretches of alluvial plains. From the northern coast, one can see the island of Iki, then the Tsushima islands; and from Tsushima, the southern coast of the Korean peninsula is visible on a clear day. Wet-rice technology is thought to have reached Kyushu by island-hopping across these straits. Perhaps migrating rice farmers from the Yangtze delta region of China brought it to the Jomon people. Perhaps Jomon seafarers visited the southern coast of the Korean peninsula, where they learned about rice growing.

There is no doubt that Kyushu rice technology came directly from the peninsula, because with it came characteristic peninsular artifacts: beveled adzes made from peninsular rock, polished stone daggers and arrowheads, and cylindrical beads—all previously unknown in the Japanese islands. The new technological "package" included such implements as stone reaping knives and wooden rakes for preparing the fields.

In northern Kyushu, the local Jomon people took up rice farming. These people used Yamanotera and Yusu-style ceramics. Deep, wide-mouthed bowls typical of this kind of pottery have been found in excavations of paddy fields and canals. The alluvial flats were well suited for conversion to rice fields, although people continued to collect plants and shellfish in the traditional way, as well as to hunt and fish. Harvested grain was kept in a style of storage jar inspired by peninsular ceramic traditions. Gradually, the range of artifacts of the Final Jomon farmers in northern Kyushu was transformed by the requirements of grain production. The population also expanded considerably. By 300 BC, the period of "incubation" in northern Kyushu had ended. A new pottery style—the Yayoi, combining the peninsular and local styles—emerged, and the populace exploded out into the Inland Sea area.

Within a hundred years, rice farming and its attendant Yayoi culture spread throughout the western Japanese islands, and migrants even made "spot" landings on the northern Honshu coast. This rapid transformation is very similar to the expansion of the Early Neolithic farmers of Europe's Linear Bandkeramik culture.

In both cases, it is not yet known exactly how the migration occurred and what happened to the existing hunter-gatherer communities in the areas that were taken over. Were they converted to an agricultural way of life? Were they eliminated through warfare and disease? How many people actually migrated out of Kyushu, and were they of a different ethnic composition owing to their long contact with the Korean peninsula?

These questions lie at the center of current scholarly debate on the earliest farmers of the eastern Eurasian fringe. The outcome of this debate is sure to shed light on how the Asian people made that momentous transition from mobile hunters to farmer settlers.

Gina Barnes

☖ The Yayoi people of Japan were once thought to have been peaceful, rice-growing villagers, but it is now recognized that warfare traditionally played an important part in their life. Within 600 years of their adopting agriculture, about AD 300, the Yayoi spawned an elite who controlled the resources necessary to make such elaborate artifacts as this gilt-bronze sword pommel.
COURTESY OF THE FREER GALLERY OF ART, SMITHSONIAN INSTITUTION, WASHINGTON, DC

♬ Bronze and iron arrived in Japan with wet-rice technology, so the Yayoi were not mere Stone Age farmers. Intricately decorated bronze bells such as this would not have been personal possessions but may have played a role in seasonal agricultural rituals performed by the whole community.
COURTESY OF THE FREER GALLERY OF ART, SMITHSONIAN INSTITUTION, WASHINGTON, DC

MARK J. HUDSON

☖ Yayoi villages consisted of thatched pit houses and granaries raised on stilts. A wide ditch is often found around the settlements, as a form of protection, while nearby cemeteries housed jar burials, coffin burials, and precincts for important families marked off by moats. The house shown here is a reconstruction.

WET-RICE CULTIVATION

Mark J. Hudson

Japan is so far the only country in East Asia where paddy fields have been identified archaeologically. About 500 such sites have been excavated, a fifth of them dating to the Yayoi period (300 BC to AD 300), which saw the emergence of Japan's first full-scale farming culture. Since wet-rice cultivation did not begin in Japan until this time, we cannot be sure when the technology represented by these field systems was first developed. However, many of the problems posed by growing rice in paddy fields are the same today as they would have been in the Early Neolithic period throughout East Asia, and the Japanese sites afford us a unique insight into how those problems were resolved.

In wet-rice cultivation, water supply is more important than soil type or climate. Rice can be cropped continuously on the same land if the field is kept inundated until shortly before harvest. Water is usually retained through a careful process of leveling and bunding (or embanking) fields. The water supply can come either from flood, ground, or rain water, or else via irrigation channels. Although its origins are unclear, this basic paddy technology has existed in East Asia for thousands of years. The photographs show the seasonal round in modern Japan.

⚬ Rice seedlings are transplanted into flooded fields. In Japan, this method, which has several advantages over direct seeding, probably dates to the Yayoi period.

⚬ After the rice is transplanted in May or June, it is left to ripen. Careful attention is given to weeding over the summer months.

⚬ Harvesting in the late autumn is now done by machine in Japan, but more traditional iron tools are still used in some parts of Asia.

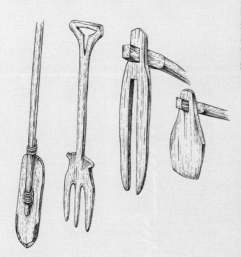

⚬ Wooden agricultural tools from Yayoi sites. Although iron tips were added to some tools in later centuries, the basic shape of many implements remained more or less unchanged until early this century.
ILLUSTRATION: DAVID WOOD

☞ Stooks of rice left to dry in the field after harvest.

355

356

PACIFIC EXPLORERS

10,000 B C – 0 B C

Highlanders and Islanders

J. PETER WHITE

TWELVE THOUSAND YEARS AGO, only the larger islands of the western Pacific knew the tread of human feet. People lived in the Bismarck Archipelago, on the Solomon Islands, and on the great island of New Guinea—from which one could still walk across Torres Strait to Australia and, ultimately, Tasmania.

People had lived on these lands, through all the climatic changes of the last Ice Age (here most noticeable through the lowering of sea levels, as sea water was frozen into the ice sheets of the northern hemisphere), for 30,000 years or more. And even after the end of the Ice Age, until about 2000 BC, they remained confined to these larger islands, which we now call Near Oceania. The smaller islands of the Pacific, or Remote Oceania—from the modern countries of Vanuatu, New Caledonia, and Kiribati eastwards—were explored only after that date.

Three aspects of human history in this part of the Pacific are sufficiently well known to allow at least the outlines of a story to emerge and problems to be recognized: the development of agriculture and the production of stone axeheads in the New Guinea highlands, and the spread of Lapita pottery in the islands. Much of the rest of Pacific prehistory can still only be glimpsed through the finds from a few excavations. This is the case particularly with both Irian Jaya and the Solomon Islands. Parts of Papua New Guinea are better explored, but a coherent story is still being pieced together. For instance, the origins, age, and real uses of stone figurines, as well as mortars and pestles, found in both highland and lowland areas are still not known.

◄❍ Intensively cultivated gardens of root and tree crops mingle with patches of managed forest throughout much of Papua New Guinea's central highlands.

❺ A rim sherd of Lapita pottery. The characteristic geometric decoration is made with toothed stamps—like combs with short teeth—applied in horizontal bands.

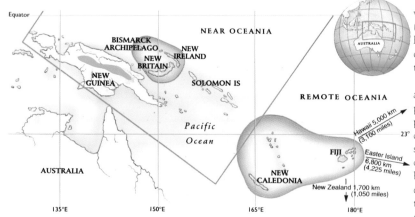

NEAR AND REMOTE OCEANIA

Near Oceania comprises the islands of the Southwest Pacific that are relatively large and close together. Most consist of continental rocks and host a diverse range of plants and animals. The islands of Remote Oceania are further apart, mostly small, and have simpler environments.

CARTOGRAPHY: RAY SIM

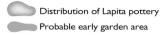

Distribution of Lapita pottery

Probable early garden area

One major theme emerges from the research discussed in this chapter. This is that change and development in this part of the world are not the result of innovations brought by waves of migrants. Although contacts with Southeast Asia have brought some new things to the area, most of the changes have developed internally. Near and Remote Oceanic cultures today are the creations of the people whose ancestors have been there for tens of thousands of years.

The New Guinea Highlands

The central mountain range of New Guinea is formed by the edge of the Pacific plate crumpling as the Indo-Australian plate pushes north and beneath it. Running northwest-southeast, the mountains rise to a maximum height of some 5,000 meters (16,500 feet), so there is snow and ice on the highest peaks. Between the mountains, in both the central highlands of Papua New Guinea and parts of Irian Jaya, there are wide, flat

valleys at altitudes of about 1,500 meters (5,000 feet). It is here that more than a million highlanders live, people whose existence was completely unknown to the Western world until the early 1930s.

At the time of this first contact with Europeans, all these highlanders were agriculturalists. Their primary crop was sweet potato, grown in carefully prepared garden mounds, often with water-control ditches. While the form of gardens varied somewhat from area to area, especially in respect of the shape and size of garden mounds, their basic structure did not, and their produce fed dense populations of people and pigs. The tools these highlanders used were simple—wooden digging sticks and spades shaped like canoe paddles, as well as stone axes—but they nonetheless succeeded in controlling their environment, especially in steep, swampy, or frosty areas, to a considerable extent. They used drains to take away excess water or cold air (both of which flow downhill), terracing to prevent soil creep, and, in some areas, wooden irrigation pipes to carry water to dry areas.

In their essentials, these highlands gardens of roots, vegetables, and tree crops were similiar to gardens found throughout the Pacific and in many parts of tropical Southeast Asia at that time—indeed, such gardens are still common today. There are no grain crops, and people rarely store harvested crops, year-round harvesting being the norm. Many theorists have seen this form of agriculture as a "simpler", and therefore earlier, form of cultivation. It may well possess a longer history than do grain crops such as rice, but recent research shows that it is far from simple. In the New Guinea highlands and many other parts of the Pacific, the main crop today is sweet potato

NEW GUINEA

The island of New Guinea is comprised of Papua New Guinea and Irian Jaya (Indonesia). It lies at the edge of the Pacific Indo-Australian plates, which accounts for its high and steep topography. Nearly all our knowledge of the region's prehistory comes from research carried out on the eastern half of the island.

CARTOGRAPHY: RAY SIM

◀◉ The Wahgi Valley is the largest valley in the New Guinea highlands, with fertile soil on both the floor and the surrounding slopes. At an altitude of 1,600 meters (5,200 feet), there is little malaria, and the valley is densely populated.

(*Ipomoea batatas*), a plant undoubtedly of American origin, which arrived in the region only within the last 1,200 years. Most other crops are local domesticates—including taro, bananas, and sugar cane—with the occasional import, such as yams, from Southeast Asia.

Early Agriculture at Kuk

The site that has told us most about the history of highlands agriculture is situated in the Wahgi Valley. Known as Kuk, it is part of a very large swamp that has preserved evidence of a 9,000-year-long tradition of gardens and drainage systems, along with some evidence of vegetation changes over this period. Long-term research by Jack Golson of the Australian National University has yielded some important results.

First, although the swamp can be very productive, some form of water control has always been necessary for agriculture to be possible here. This has been achieved by digging ditches up to 2 kilometers (one and a quarter miles) long and 3 meters (10 feet) deep to channel water from its inlet point across the swamp to a river outlet. Radiocarbon dating shows that the first of these ditches was dug about 7000 BC.

Secondly, the form of gardens was not always as described by Michael Leahy in the 1930s (see opposite). Golson has been able to identify six major periods when swamps were used for agriculture, and it is only during the last 2,000 years or so that people have made square garden beds. Before that, the pattern of garden mounds and small ditches was much less regular, suggesting that the area was used less intensively.

Thirdly, during the later part of the Pleistocene period, until some 12,000 years ago, much of the valley floor was forested, whereas it is now entirely covered with grass. The gradual environmental change over this time has been caused by generations of people clearing the land

Michael Leahy, with his brothers and Jim Taylor, were the first white people to visit the Wahgi Valley, in 1931. The photograph above was taken on an early visit.

The gardens we saw west of the Chimbu were laid out in neat squares, each bed being eight or ten feet square and surrounded by drainage ditches from one to two feet deep. Soil taken from the ditches had been heaped up on the beds, so as to raise them above the general ground level. The gardens were fenced mainly with wooden slabs. We saw some of them on steep hillsides that showed evidences of laborious terracing, rows of slabs being driven in the ground to keep the soil from washing away... The level valley floor between the gullies was intensively cultivated, all the land being covered with neatly fenced gardens, or deeply scored with the drainage ditches of former years.

The green garden patches were a delight to the eye, neat square beds of sweet potatoes growing luxuriantly in that rich soil, alternating with thriving patches of beans, cucumbers and sugar cane. Some of the gardens had picket fences, the pickets being made of straight branches two inches thick, neatly hacked off to the same height. Others were stoutly fenced with rails, each section of the fence consisting of eight or ten rails laid horizontally between stakes driven in the ground.

There were no villages, the whole valley as far as we could see being one continuous settlement, with groups of oblong houses spaced every few hundred yards. Each group of houses had a clump or two of the beautiful, feathery bamboo, a few banana trees and a grove of casuarinas, and invariably flowers and ornamental shrubs.

From M. Leahy and M. Crain, *The Land That Time Forgot*, Hurst & Blackett, London, 1937.

SIMON HABERLE/THE QUALITY IMAGE

⚘ Taro is an edible root native to Southeast Asia, Near Oceania, and, probably, northern Australia. It requires careful cooking to remove bitterness, but people have been eating it for at least 25,000 years.

⚘ A native of America, sweet potato has been grown in Near Oceania for perhaps the last 1,200 years. Today, it is the staple food for millions of people in the region.

for gardens and using the timber to make fences, houses, and fires. The casuarinas Leahy mentions are still regularly planted to provide timber—a practice that goes back at least 1,200 years.

Fourthly, evidence of one crop grown from about 4000 BC until the present has been found in the ditches in the form of phytoliths characteristic of one kind of banana. (Phytoliths are plant cells filled with opaline silica deposited from ground water, which survive in the ground for thousands of years.) Remains of other crops have so far proved elusive, but this is not surprising, given that the root crops grown in the highlands—including sweet potato, taro, and yams—produce none of the hard evidence in the form of phytoliths, pollen, seeds, or shells that might survive in the archaeological record. We can, however, be reasonably sure that the main crop was taro, a root crop native to the western Pacific and Southeast Asia.

The history of agriculture at Kuk is partly paralleled elsewhere in New Guinea. Other swamps in the same area were cultivated in a similar way, although, as far as we know at present, only from about 3500 BC. At the eastern edge of the highlands, where the climate is more

seasonal, people near Arona made their gardens in the flat shores of very old lakes, now dry, modifying them by digging ditches to retain water during the dry season. This technique was used from before 1000 BC, probably to grow taro. Nowadays, sweet potato is grown in these areas, and because it tolerates drier conditions, the gardens overrun these old systems, the ditches no longer serving any purpose. In the upper Sepik Valley, in the Yeni swamp, at an altitude of only 500 meters (1,600 feet), an increase in the quantity of grass relative to tree pollen has shown that forest clearance had started by at least 3000 BC. At the same time, the people in this lowland area also hollowed out small basins and built low ridges suitable for wet and dry crops. Today, the area is uncultivated grassland, perhaps abandoned during the last century because of a disease epidemic or warfare, both of which are frequent causes of local depopulation.

From Forest Cultivation to Gardens

Any discussion of New Guinea highlands prehistory must take account of the probability that people living in these areas had cultivated

CLAIRE LEIMBACH

wild food plants for tens of thousands of years. For at least as long as *Homo sapiens* has existed, people living in tropical areas have tended particular kinds of plants that were useful for food, tools, medicine, or decoration, rather than just foraging opportunistically. Thus, what we are seeing at Kuk is not a sudden recognition by wandering hunters and gatherers that plants could be cultivated (sometimes called the "Aha!" theory of agricultural origins). Rather, Kuk shows the transition from tending useful plants where they grew naturally, or had been planted, in areas scattered throughout the landscape to grouping them in a convenient location and preparing the ground for them. The evidence for this, dating from 7000 BC, occurs at about the same time as that of similar agricultural developments elsewhere in the world. These highlands gardeners may also have fenced their plots.

Like many made at present in highland areas where the population is less dense, these early gardens are likely to have mimicked the diversity of the local environment, with a range of plants growing in close proximity. In this, they differed from the gardens Leahy describes, most of which were devoted to a single crop and were located in areas of high population. That change came later, in the last 5,000 years, as the population increased and larger crops were required.

In considering why people started to grow crops in gardens, we must start from what we know to have happened: the fact of people grouping together the plants they cared for. One obvious explanation of this change is that it was to protect plants, which represented people's livelihood, from some threat. Threats may have included other people, animals such as pigs, and such natural occurrences as floods and cold weather. Pigs are native to Southeast Asia, not New Guinea, and were probably brought by boat. Very limited archaeological evidence—a mere handful of teeth in dated sites—suggests that they may have been imported as early as 8000 BC, although some radiocarbon dates for the teeth themselves suggest that they may be much younger. If pigs were present, however, they could have been significant competitors for the fruits and roots people ate, thereby encouraging the development of fenced gardens.

An alternative view is that the changes occurred for more positive reasons, such as to create a more regular food surplus to provide for ceremonies or to exchange with neighbors for other goods. Population increase is likely to have played a part, as may a change in the climate, such as increased rainfall.

Our problem lies in testing these proposals. Some, such as whether pigs were present at this time, or whether the climate changed, can be tested; others rely more on comparative studies of similar societies from the more recent past.

CLAIRE LEIMBACH

◄● Stone axes were the major tools used to clear forest for gardens and to cut timber for fences and houses. In the extensive Baliem Valley (in the Irian Jaya highlands), axes were hafted by inserting them into a carefully shaped hole in a handle made of solid wood. Elsewhere, handles took on a more complex form, and axeheads were bound in with flexible cane.

J. PETER WHITE

⚬ Gardens on the edge of Kuk swamp. Squared-off beds growing sweet potato are in different stages of production. Bananas and tall casuarina trees (for timber) are also cultivated.

PETER FOX/THE QUALITY IMAGE

◄● Forest has to be cleared to make gardens, and the timber is often used to fence the gardens against feral pigs. Some useful trees are left standing—here pandanus, the leaves of which are used for house thatch—and the rest of the litter burned to return nutrients quickly to the soil.

THE LAPITA SITE AT NENUMBO, IN THE SOLOMON ISLANDS

ROGER C. GREEN

MORE THAN A HUNDRED sites with sherds of the distinctive Lapita pottery—pottery made by the first people to settle the smaller islands of Remote Oceania, dating from 1300 BC—have now been identified by archaeologists, but less than half of them have been tested by excavation. Major investigations have been carried out at a dozen sites, of which Nenumbo, on the low-lying coral island of Ngaua, in the Outer Eastern Islands of the Solomons, is one of the most thoroughly examined so far.

The distribution of potsherds at 36 Lapita sites shows that hamlet-sized settlements ranged in size from 500 square meters to 4,500 square meters (5,400 square feet to 48,500 square feet). Nenumbo, being about 1,000 meters (3,300 feet) square, is among the smaller of these hamlets.

At Nenumbo, the distribution of potsherds was analyzed, and excavations made in areas where sherds were most concentrated. The discovery of large postholes confirmed that there had been a structure 7 meters by 10 meters (22 feet by 33 feet) in the center of the hamlet, and smaller postholes showed that there had been several post and thatch structures nearby.

Radiocarbon tests carried out on charcoal from several fireplaces, supported by tests made on a number of obsidian artifacts, show that the hamlet was occupied for a relatively short time about 1100 BC. The site was then covered by ash from the nearby (and still active) volcano of Tinakula to a depth of about 30 centimeters (1 foot), and was subsequently used for gardening.

The people of Nenumbo fished and gathered shellfish on the inshore reef and in the lagoon, and caught the occasional bird. They also caught two kinds of rats, one of which was a Polynesian variety, and raised domesticated pigs and chickens. Given the presence of these domestic animals, pots and earth ovens for cooking, storage pits, implements for food preparation, and a relatively small amount of debris from meat and shellfish consumption, it seems likely that they also grew root and tree crops.

Imported Items

The sophistication of the Nenumbo people's economy and their voyaging skills are also reflected in numerous imported items. They imported obsidian from their Lapita homeland in the Bismarck Archipelago, some 2,000 kilometers (1,250 miles) to the northwest; and a few pieces of glittering micaceous rock, one piece of obsidian, and some sedimentary sandstone came from the D'Entrecasteaux Islands, a similar distance to the west. Numerous chert pieces, finished adzes, and the occasional pot came from islands in the south central Solomons, several days' sailing northwest. Most of the pots, additional pieces of chert, and a number of volcanic ovenstones came from islands within a day's sailing (in several directions); and a few obsidian items were brought from the Banks Islands, several days' sailing southwards.

Specialized chert and obsidian tools were found at the site of the large building, along with a considerable quantity of decorated sherds, many of which formed flat-bottomed dishes or open or carinated (shouldered) vessels. In the area where the post and thatch structures stood, excavations revealed cooking ovens, storage pits, a well, and pots with restricted necks.

Decorations on the more complex of the pots range from a human mask face to rectangular and curvilinear patterns in panels repeated around the upper portion of the carinated vessels. More than a hundred motifs are found on these pots, similar to motifs found on pottery at sites further west and, to a lesser degree, to the east. Nenumbo has proved a key site in furthering our understanding of the Lapita culture.

☝ Several potsherds making up a portion of an anthropomorphic face design, found at the hamlet site of Nenumbo, on the coral island of Ngaua, in the Solomons.
MATTHEW SPRIGGS

◄ A reconstruction of the complex face design that decorates some of the Nenumbo pots, as shown in the sherds above.
MATTHEW SPRIGGS

Powerful Axes

Another aspect of highlands archaeology that has been extensively researched is the manufacture and distribution of stone axe blades. Stone axeheads are found in sites from Late Pleistocene times onwards. They range in length from 4 to about 35 centimeters (one and a half to 14 inches), with the smaller ones usually being the result of much resharpening. Axeheads are oval or rectangular in cross-section and were hafted in short wooden handles. Most prehistoric Pacific axeheads are made of river pebbles of tough stone, flaked and ground into shape. Quarries in areas of high-quality stone were developed during the last 3,000 years, and finds of axes from these sources can be used to determine trade routes and other links between people. The development of quarries in itself points to changes in social organization at this time.

In the early twentieth century, nearly every highlands man owned a stone axe, and some owned several. Women used axes and had rights to them, but whether they owned them is less clear. Axes were used to chop trees and for other gardening tasks; to make wooden tools, fences, and houses; and to split firewood. But some were also regarded as being valuable objects that could only be used in exchanges involving such valued items as women, pigs, and imported seashells. In some areas, each man made his own axehead from local river stone, but in others the finished product was imported. At Lake Kopiago, near the Strickland River, for example, axeheads came from a quarry several days' walk away. Each head changed hands several times on the way and ended up costing a pig or a large container of salt. Because they were socially distant from the process of axe production, local Duna people did not know how axes were made, or where they came from.

In the central highlands, around the Wahgi Valley, many axeheads were produced at a small set of quarries along the Tuman River. John Burton's extensive research into early twentieth-century practices has shown that these quarries were particularly important to the clans who owned them as a source of large axeheads—20 to 30 centimeters (8 to 12 inches long)—which were considered to be a sign of prestige and commonly formed part of so-called bride prices. In the course of mining these out of a band of stone some 2 meters (6 feet, 6 inches) thick lying some 8 to 15 meters (25 to 50 feet) underground, clansmen also produced quantities of smaller pieces of stone. Unlike the larger axeheads, which were ground into shape by the mining clans, these smaller pieces of stone were traded with neighbors, who ground them down into everyday work axes.

Quarrying expeditions, Burton suggests, took place every three to five years, on average, and involved up to 200 men for a period of several months. Each expedition may have produced 10 to 25 axeheads per man—a total of 2,000 to 5,000. If this seems a small return for the investment of time and labor—and only a few of these axes would have been large—it must be realized that not only did the rock seam dip into the mountain, which meant that much overburden had to be cleared away to expose a rock face, at which only a few men could then work, but all the axe stone was extracted by heating the seam with fires and then hammering it with handheld stone hammers until it cracked and chunks of stone could be wedged out. In this way, 40,000 to 100,000 axeheads per century were produced, to be exchanged within the wider community. (This scale of production was probably achieved only in the last few centuries.)

A few axeheads from these quarries, usually small ones resulting from larger ones breaking during use or resharpening, traveled as far south as the southern coast of New Guinea, well beyond the highlands; but the majority were used within a radius of some 50 kilometers (30 miles) by the half-million people who lived there.

Axeheads, or chips off them, from the Wahgi Valley quarries are not found in archaeological excavations, even at nearby sites, earlier than 500 BC. Quarrying began, in fact, at

M.J. LEAHY COLLECTION/NATIONAL LIBRARY OF AUSTRALIA

In many parts of the New Guinea highlands, large stone axes were carefully bound into wooden handles with elaborate decorative bindings. Such axes were used for display and so-called bride prices rather than as a chopping tool—as shown in this photograph, taken at a sing-sing in the 1930s. (A sing-sing is a ceremony that includes dancing and singing.)

The axehead in this axe from Simbu Province is some 30 centimeters (12 inches) long, and the whole tool is designed to be a valuable item, fit only for display.

C. BENTO/AUSTRALIAN MUSEUM

⊕ Clubheads are made in the shape of disks, stars, triangles, and even "pineapples". They were shaped by sawing and grinding and were then mounted on a straight handle, being held in place by carefully woven fiber bindings. They were in widespread, though not common, use within the last century, and a few were still being made in the 1930s.

C. BENTO/AUSTRALIAN MUSEUM

⊕ *Opposite:* This carving of a woman is unusual in depicting a complete human form. The hands and legs are crossed, and she appears to be wearing a head covering. The figure is about 40 centimeters (16 inches) high and was acquired in the Ramu Valley, in the lowlands of Papua New Guinea.

R. BOLZAN/AUSTRALIAN MUSEUM

♀ Some pestles are highly elaborate in form, but what is portrayed is open to interpretation. This one, from southwestern Papua New Guinea, has been likened to a bird, a reptile, a penis, and a woman!

R. BOLZAN/AUSTRALIAN MUSEUM

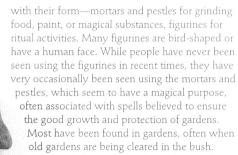

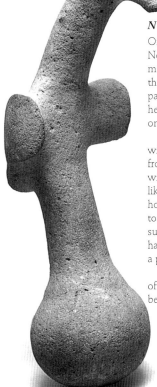

about the same time as square garden beds—representing a more intensive form of soil tillage and, presumably, a growing population—came into use at Kuk. The archaeological evidence from rock shelter sites suggests that it was only after these developments had taken place that people started to raise and eat pigs to any extent. Axe quarrying, that is, can be seen as one aspect of increasing economic intensification within central highlands societies. Other, social, changes would have accompanied such developments. The social dominance of "big men", for example, who achieved their eminence by hard work, many marriages, and managing increasing quantities of exchangeable goods rather than by birth, may well date from this time. Larger-scale societies usually develop some more visible form of hierarchy.

New Guinea Stone Carvings

Only four types of stone carvings are found in New Guinea, all of them quite small objects: mortars, pestles, figurines, and clubheads. On the main island, the first three have been found particularly in parts of the highlands, but clubheads are more common and have been found on most islands within Papua New Guinea.

Stone-headed clubs were used in some areas within the last century. In shape, they vary widely, from a flat disk, through a flat star shape, usually with four or five points, to something that looks like a knobbed hand grenade. All, however, have a hole through the center to allow them to be bound to a long handle. Mostly made of a tough stone such as basalt, they were pecked (with a stone hammer), ground, and drilled into shape over a period of some weeks.

More puzzling are the other three kinds of carvings, which have never been seen to be used in a way that seems compatible

⊕ Mortars are usually made of a tough volcanic or metamorphic rock such as basalt or hornfels. They may be plain bowls, or have a fluted shape—like this one from Siane, in the Papua New Guinea highlands—or even be mounted on a pedestal.

JENNY MILLS

with their form—mortars and pestles for grinding food, paint, or magical substances, figurines for ritual activities. Many figurines are bird-shaped or have a human face. While people have never been seen using the figurines in recent times, they have very occasionally been seen using the mortars and pestles, which seem to have a magical purpose, often associated with spells believed to ensure the good growth and protection of gardens. Most have been found in gardens, often when old gardens are being cleared in the bush.

None of these carvings have been made since the time of European contact. New Guineans today usually regard these objects as being natural rather than having been made by humans. A few fragments have been found in archaeological sites dated between 3000 BC and 1000 BC, but whether most are as old as this is unclear.

Archaeology in the Lowlands

We know much less about the prehistory of coastal New Guinea. On the north side of the island, recent excavations in caves and shell mounds have shown, as expected, that settlement dates back into the Late Pleistocene period. Pottery was being made from at least 3000 BC. People continued to live in the area when the Sepik River basin was flooded by the sea about 4000 BC and subsequently refilled with sediment washed down from the highlands. No sites of similar age have been found on the south side of the island, not because people did not live there, but most likely because these early sites have been destroyed by erosion of the hills or buried deeply by soil filling the river valleys.

In the recent past, pottery was made and exchanged over much of lowland New Guinea, especially along the coasts. While older pottery has been found in parts of the north coast, most of this lowland pottery was made after 1300 BC, and its source is sometimes traced to the widespread style known as Lapita.

THE SEPIK RIVER PEOPLE OF PAPUA NEW GUINEA: CULTURE AMID CATASTROPHES

PAUL GORECKI

The Sepik basin is one of the most culturally diversified regions in the world. Ever since the mighty Sepik River was first explored by Europeans, in 1887, both the art and the material culture of the Sepik people have attracted enormous interest from museum and private collectors all round the world. Many have wondered how old this "primitive" art is, but no one can yet offer a definitive answer. Serious archaeological research in the Sepik started only in the 1980s, and the results so far indicate that the region has undergone far-reaching environmental changes over the past 10,000 years—changes that must have had a considerable impact on the people living there.

Earthquakes, Floods, and Volcanoes

The Sepik and north coast of the island of New Guinea can aptly be described as regions of catastrophes. Prehistoric coastal societies clearly had to cope with major and sudden changes in their immediate surroundings, as people in these areas still have to today. We know that the coast is constantly uplifting through tectonic activity, with the result that coral reefs and their fish and shellfish resources are periodically destroyed. In the Vanimo region, substantial uplifts

occurred in 1600 BC, 500 BC, and AD 700—at an average rate of 1.5 meters (5 feet) per 1,000 years. Coastal and inland regions are also affected by severe earthquakes from time to time. An earthquake recorded in 1907, for example, changed the Sissano lagoon from fresh to salt water. Another, in the Torricelli mountains in 1935, caused large-scale landslides and loss of life, as well as destroying garden and forest resources. In addition, the coast has regularly been hit by the aftermath of volcanic eruptions, and a number of volcanoes are still active today.

This pottery sherd from Seraba Cave, decorated with incised parallel wavy lines, is dated to 700 BC.
PAUL GORECKI

PAUL GORECKI

Located behind Fichin village (shown here) in equatorial rainforest, Lachitu Cave has evidence of human occupation dating back to 35,000 years ago.

PAUL GORECKI

The coral fringe reef on New Guinea's northern coast is constantly being uplifted through tectonic activity. The section of coast shown here is near Musu village.

Prehistoric people living in the Sepik River basin have also had their share of major catastrophes. In fact, it seems that the basin itself may have been formed only recently. Although results are still preliminary, there is growing evidence that a large part of what is now the Sepik River basin may once have been a huge marine inlet. In 4000 BC, the sites of such townships as Angoram and Pagwi may have been on the coast; while the sites of present-day Ambunti and Amboin would have been on islands surrounded by the sea, and those of all present-day river villages, including Timbunke, would have been under the sea. Assisted by tectonic uplift, the basin may have been gradually formed after the last rise in sea level about 4000 BC. It would have started out as a brackish, mangrove-dominated environment, becoming a vast freshwater swampland perhaps less than 2,000 years ago. Even today, the Sepik River and all its southern tributaries are still searching for a permanent bed to settle in and in the process causing regular large-scale flooding—another natural disaster affecting people's way of life.

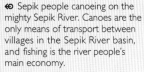

Sepik people canoeing on the mighty Sepik River. Canoes are the only means of transport between villages in the Sepik River basin, and fishing is the river people's main economy.

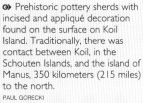

Prehistoric pottery sherds with incised and appliqué decoration found on the surface on Koil Island. Traditionally, there was contact between Koil, in the Schouten Islands, and the island of Manus, 350 kilometers (215 miles) to the north.
PAUL GORECKI

GERRY ELLIS

Ancient Sepik Cultures

Despite these clearly hostile conditions along the coast and in the basin, people have lived here for more than 35,000 years, developing a number of cultures that have culminated in what can be seen today. Lachitu Cave, near Vanimo (on the northern coast, near the Indonesian border), has evidence of human occupation going back 35,000 years. Deposits from this cave have shown that by 14,000 years ago these coastal people were relying heavily on shellfish from reef areas for food, the dominant species harvested being *Turbo argyrostoma*.

By 4000 BC, more extensive areas of the Vanimo coast seem to have been inhabited. Deposits in Lachitu and nearby Taora Cave dating from this time indicate that local people were still relying mainly on marine foods, supple-

mented by a few land mammals. A specific, notched type of stone tool appears in these caves at this time, which, according to studies of wear patterns and organic residues, may have been used specifically to make bows and arrows. Strange slate artifacts dating from about 3400 BC have also been found in these caves. While their function is still unknown, they seem to be ceremonial rather than utilitarian. Similar, but undated, artifacts have been found elsewhere in New Guinea, including in the Sepik River basin.

Melanesia's Earliest Potters

At about the same time, pottery makes its first appearance not only along the Vanimo coast but also in the Lower Ramu and Middle Sepik basins. In both Lachitu and Taora caves, near Vanimo, it first appears between 3600 BC and 3400 BC in the form of undecorated vessels, with coral sand added to the clay to prevent cracking during firing. In the Lower Ramu, the earliest pottery has been found in the open sites of Beri and Akari, also dating to about 3600 BC. Some of the vessels found here have decorations incised into them or notched into their lips. In the Middle Sepik, pottery has been found in Seraba Cave in layers dating from 4000 BC, and by 700 BC pottery-making was clearly a flourishing tradition in the Middle Sepik region. The dominant decoration on these Seraba vessels consists of two parallel wavy incisions around the circumference. What all this means is that

pottery—one of the traditional arts for which the Sepik people are world famous—has a much longer history in New Guinea than in any other part of Melanesia.

An Early Exchange Network

Another remarkable aspect of Sepik prehistory is the complex network of exchange these early people set up. It seems that over the past 10,000 years Sepik people not only established an exchange network within the region but also extended it to areas far afield. For instance, the tiny island of Koil, off Wewak, near the mouth of the Sepik River, was visited by long-distance sea traders from the island of Manus within the last few thousand years. These traders introduced the volcanic glass known as obsidian into the local exchange systems, and we know that more than 1,000 years ago it was already regarded as a valuable commodity by those living along the Vanimo coast, more than 700 kilometers (430 miles) from its source. All the obsidian flakes so far found between the mouth of the Sepik River and the Irian Jaya border come exclusively from Manus.

Archaeological research in the Sepik has just begun, and yet it is already yielding fascinating results that have a significant bearing on the prehistory of Melanesia in general. There is no doubt that Sepik societies, with all their complexity and their remarkable kaleidoscope of traditional art, have roots that go back deep into the remote past.

THE SEPIK REGION
The Sepik basin is regularly flooded, while the northern coast and the adjacent islands are subject to periodic earthquakes and volcanic eruptions.

CARTOGRAPHY: RAY SIM

Taora
Lachitu • Vanimo
Bismarck Sea
TORRICELLI MOUNTAINS
KOIL IS
Wewak
SEPIK BASIN
Pagwi
Seraba • Angoram
Sepik R
Ambunti
Timbunke
Beri
Akari
Amboin
CENTRAL HIGHLANDS

⚓ The precision of the geometric designs characteristic of Lapita pottery was often accentuated by an infill of powdered lime.

H. GALLASCH/JIM SPECHT

Lapita Pottery

Lapita pottery is central to much of the research that has been carried out in the Pacific islands, at least as far east as Tonga and Samoa. It is important for several reasons.

The first is that the people who made this pottery were clearly the first to settle the smaller islands of Remote Oceania—and probably the earliest inhabitants of any Pacific island east of the Solomons. They almost certainly voyaged as far as South America, for which the presence of the sweet potato is the only evidence. Their descendants eventually reached Hawaii, Easter Island, and New Zealand, while some moved north and west into what are now the central and eastern island nations of Micronesia.

Secondly, an extensive region was settled in a very short time. This implies both that exploration was purposive, not accidental, and that voyagers had good sailing canoes and navigation skills. The settlement of Remote Oceania is the earliest large-scale maritime colonization to have occurred anywhere in the world.

Thirdly, despite some intensive investigations over the last two decades, there is still major disagreement among researchers about the origin

NATIONAL MARITIME MUSEUM, GREENWICH

⚓ The artists who sailed with Captain Cook and other European explorers showed the islands of Oceania to be beautiful, and life in these parts to be generally carefree. Some of the Pacific island vessels they portrayed were faster and more maneuverable than those of the Europeans. This view of Tahiti was painted by William Hodges on Cook's second voyage in 1773.

of Lapita pottery and associated cultural materials such as shell ornaments, the central issue being whether they were of local origin or made by migrants from Asia.

Lastly, the story of this research tells us much about how Westerners, both scientists and laypeople, have interpreted the history of the Pacific Ocean peoples over the years.

Lapita pottery was first discovered on Watom Island, just off New Britain, in 1909. How it came to be named after a site on the west coast of New Caledonia, is something no one seems to know. It has since been found over an area ranging from near the Irian Jaya border, in the west, to Samoa, and possibly even the Marquesas, in the east (the sherds here being few, small, and not highly

characteristic)—a distance of some 8,000 kilometers (5,000 miles).

Lapita ware is characterized by being coarsely handmade and poorly fired, but very finely decorated with bands of geometric designs impressed into the clay by stamps consisting of a single row of teeth—probably like short combs with short teeth (although none have ever been found). This decoration can be extremely elaborate, sometimes incorporating stylized faces and decorative plugs fitted into ear lobes. Geometric decoration is found on a range of pot shapes, including round-based, narrow-necked bowls and flat platters. Other pots have similar geometric designs incised rather than stamped into the clay, although this form of decoration is never as fine.

The significance that has been attached to the distribution of Lapita pottery needs to be understood in the context of Pacific history in general. The early northern European sailors, such as Captain James Cook, who brought news of the Pacific islanders to Europe in the eighteenth century, described Remote Oceania in glowing terms—the wonderful climate, easy way of life, and beautiful, friendly islanders—an image that many Europeans, Americans, and Australians still cherish. These explorers contrasted the tall, fair, friendly Polynesians with the inhabitants of the larger islands such as the Solomons further west, who were shorter, dark-skinned, and much less friendly towards unknown intruders. They were also surprised at the similarity of language and customs between many islands, from Hawaii to New Zealand, attributing this to the inhabitants' evident ability to sail between these islands. From these and other observations, the idea took root among Europeans that these islanders could not be the descendants of islanders living further west and must, therefore, have migrated into the Pacific from somewhere else. Where that somewhere else might be has never been entirely clear. Guesses have included India, China, South America, and everywhere in Southeast Asia; one of the lost tribes of Israel has also been considered. Within the last few decades, however, Southeast Asia has become the favored area, largely because language studies have pointed in this direction.

All Remote Oceanic languages are of Austronesian stock. Other Austronesian languages are spoken in Taiwan, the Philippines, throughout Indonesia, in some coastal areas of New Guinea, on the smaller islands of Near Oceania, and even in Madagascar, far away across the Indian Ocean. Austronesian languages are quite similar to each other, and linguists have accordingly argued that they must have developed in one part of this area quite recently (otherwise they would be more different) and spread as people migrated to other regions. It is difficult to date these migrations, as there are no written records and there is as yet no general agreement among scholars as to the

PAUL GORECKI

linguistic methods that might be used for this purpose. But it is generally agreed that the original Austronesian language (proto-Austronesian) originated between 6000 BC and 3000 BC—probably, most linguists believe, in Taiwan.

Within Remote Oceania itself, the relative closeness of the languages of different islands has been paralleled, in recent decades, by the relationships demonstrated through archaeology. Radiocarbon dates show, for example, that Hawaii was settled well before New Zealand, and we know that the Hawaiian language has diverged more from that of the central Pacific than the Maori language has. It is this demonstrated link between archaeology and language history that has become a model for the rest of Pacific history. Lapita pottery, it has often been argued, provides tangible evidence that Austronesian speakers from Southeast Asia migrated through the islands of Near Oceania and out into the Pacific.

There are some problems with this view, the main one being, perhaps, that Lapita pottery has not been found in any quantity west of the islands of Near Oceania. Only a handful of sherds has

been found on the main island of New Guinea, for example. Nor has any pottery been found that is clearly its ancestor.

More tellingly, although Lapita was long thought to be the oldest form of pottery in Near Oceania, pottery recently found on the north coast of New Guinea has been dated to about 3000 BC—making it about 1,700 years older than the earliest Lapita pottery. Unlike Lapita ware, this early New Guinean pottery has almost no decoration on it, and increasingly, researchers are coming to the view that the geometric designs characteristic of Lapita ware may be derived from designs already being used on contemporary barkcloth (used for clothing) and in tattooing, for example. Moreover, the generally rough quality of Lapita ware, which is often made with large amounts of coarse shell temper and poorly fired, is not what would be expected if it derived from Southeast Asian pottery. While the craft of pottery-making may originally have come from Asia, it seems unlikely that Lapita pottery did so, and its distribution is therefore unlikely to reflect the migratory routes of early Austronesian speakers.

⚱ Nearly half of this pot (later reconstructed) was dug up at Lamau, on the west coast of New Ireland, in 1985. The design is geometric, but the decoration is not as fine or as elaborate as the dentate-stamped form of Lapita pottery. Lapita bowls commonly take this shape.

PAUL GORECKI

⚱ The decoration on the Lamau pot is incised—cut into the damp clay with a sharp shell or stone—rather than stamped into the clay.

☝ The first recorded find of Lapita pottery was made in 1907 by Father Otto Meyer, on Watom Island, near Rabaul. His specimens, including these four sherds, were sent to the Basel Museum, in Switzerland. The next two finds were made in Tonga, in the 1920s, and in New Caledonia, in the 1950s.
MUSEUM FÜR VÖLKERKUNDE/J. SPECHT

♀ Rings, beads, and armbands from the Talepakemalai site, Papua New Guinea. Made of *Conus* and *Spondylus* shells, they were found on an old lagoon floor, where they had been dumped, along with broken Lapita pottery, shells, and animal bones, from houses built on stilts over the water.

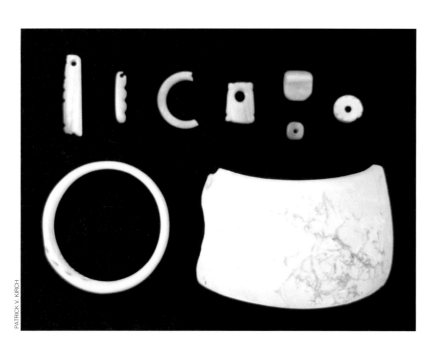

PATRICK V. KIRCH

Lapita Sites and Early Exchange Systems

Excavations in Near Oceania within the last decade have revealed small quantities of Lapita pottery in most New Britain and New Ireland sites occupied between 1300 BC and 0 BC. In some sites, however, including the small offshore islands of Eloaua, Watom, and Ambitle, and several islands of the Arawe group, it has been found in considerably larger quantities. The Talepakemalai site on Eloaua, in particular, has preserved not only quantities of pottery but also a wide range of stone and shell artifacts, the latter including fishhooks, bracelets, rings, armbands, beads, and pendants. It has also yielded evidence that these Lapita potters commonly fished in lagoons and gathered shellfish, were engaged in agriculture,

and kept domestic pigs, dogs, and chickens. The bases of some house posts have also been found. The site appears to have been a village built on stilts over a tidal lagoon, and radiocarbon dates suggest (as do those from some other sites) that people lived here continuously for some hundreds of years. Analyses of clays, tempers, and decorative motifs suggest that pottery or clay was moved between some sites, but research as to the extent to which this occurred is still under way. The clearest evidence of the transport of materials comes from the presence of obsidian. (See the feature *Obsidian Tools: A Study in Prehistoric Melanesian Trade.*)

Obsidian is a volcanic glass, usually black. It is known to occur in only three areas of Near Oceania—on Lou and Fergusson islands, and on the Willaumez Peninsula of New Britain—with several possible sources in each area. Some progress has been made in distinguishing obsidian from different sources, and material from both the Willaumez and Lou quarries has been found in Lapita sites. It is found not only in Near Oceania, but as far east as Fiji, although only in small quantities in these Remote Oceanic sites. Willaumez obsidian has also been identified far to the west, in sites on the small Talaud Islands, in Indonesia, and on the northeast coast of Sabah. The finds from the eastern islands of Near Oceania and in the west date to within the Lapita period, but not—as we might expect if the traffic in obsidian had been initiated by Southeast Asian migrants—to its earliest stages.

Obsidian was clearly important to the people who made Lapita pottery, but why they wanted obsidian is not well understood, since locally available stones or sharp-edged shells could have been used in its place. However, they evidently valued it, flaking it into very small pieces once it was away from its source, using some of these pieces for cutting and scraping vegetable foods and making a few into points and engraving tools.

It may be that the sites that have yielded quantities of Lapita pottery were centers of distribution networks. They were often located on deep-water bays, with good but protected sea access, although the inhabitants of these villages drew most of their food supply from the land nearby. In some ways, they seem very like the settlements of traditional traders in these regions, who until the early twentieth century made their living largely by moving a wide range of goods—pottery and feathers, pigs and axes—around local areas. What distinguishes the Lapita period is the fact that such similar pottery is found over such enormous distances, suggesting that it was the physical expression of some as yet unknown ideology. How obsidian was distributed—whether through one large-scale trade network that linked Lapita potters, or through a series of such networks, or through some other mechanism such as small-scale, hand-to-hand trade—remains to be determined.

The People Who Settled Remote Oceania

We can also look to biological evidence, both modern and ancient, for clues to the identity of the first people who settled Remote Oceania. The modern evidence includes such studies as finger and palm prints, tooth size and shape, the genetics of various blood groups, and mitochondrial DNA analysis, all of which have a component of inherited characteristics and can therefore be used to establish relationships. Ancient evidence comes from burials and consists mostly of the shape and size of various bones and teeth, which can be compared with each other and with those of different modern groups.

The modern evidence faces the difficulty that evolution (random biological changes acted on by selective forces), genetic drift (random changes that become established by chance), and mixing between different populations, as well as the small size of original founding populations, must be assessed and their effects excluded before long-ago links can be proposed. The main problem with the prehistoric evidence is simply that so little of it has survived. There are, for instance, fragmentary remains of only about 15 people from sites that contain quantities of Lapita pottery, and that is too few to enable us to draw any firm conclusions.

None of these problems has prevented researchers from putting forward carefully qualified interpretations, but it is not surprising that workers in the two different fields have come up with rather different results. A recent survey by geneticists Sue Serjeantson and Ron Hill concluded that although Pacific islanders showed unmistakeable evidence of Near Oceanic forebears, some genetic markers linked them quite closely also with Asian ancestors. On the other hand, anatomist Phil Houghton points out that the large, muscular bodies of many Polynesian people are physiologically well adapted to ocean voyaging, and that people of similar build have been found in burials associated with Lapita pottery. Houghton further claims that this physiological type is unsuited to living on tropical landmasses such as Southeast Asia or New Guinea, is therefore unlikely to have evolved there, and is, moreover, not found there. He believes that such people can only have evolved in the island environment of Near Oceania. In part, such differences result from the fact that different researchers use different methods and different theoretical frameworks—the usefulness of which will become more apparent as further research is carried out.

Pasts Yet to Be Written

As our knowledge of Pacific history and prehistory unfolds, two things become clear. The first is that large-scale changes have occurred in the Pacific world, for the most part independently of what was happening elsewhere in the world at that time. Until recently, histories of Pacific peoples have been written largely in terms of waves of migrants. Each wave was thought to have brought with it some cultural attributes that are still found in the area, such as agriculture, pottery, and axes. By contrast, current studies of Pacific prehistory show that many developments originated locally. Highlands agriculture, for example, was based on locally developed techniques and predominantly local crops and supported populations as dense

◀ A woman and child of Tanna Island, Vanuatu, drawn by William Hodges in 1774. The woman is wearing earrings, probably of shell, and a necklace made of shell disks and a whole shell. Her cap is made of barkcloth, and the child is carried in a kind of bag made of the same material and slung over her shoulders.

NATIONAL LIBRARY OF AUSTRALIA

as in any other rural society of the time. Lapita pottery evolved in the islands of Near Oceania, and its makers carried it far afield in the Pacific, colonizing on a scale unmatched until the European voyages of the last 500 years. People in the newly independent countries of Near Oceania can lay claim to a long and vigorous history of cultural independence.

But the recognition that Near Oceania has an independent history is also important to the rest of the world. In Western accounts in particular, there has been a strong tendency to see traditional Near Oceanic cultures as "living fossils", examples of what the whole world must have been like before cities and industrial societies developed. But no society has been static. The past is not exactly like the present: everywhere it is a foreign country, to be explored through history and archaeology.

OBSIDIAN TOOLS: A STUDY IN PREHISTORIC MELANESIAN TRADE

ROBIN TORRENCE

EUROPEANS TRAVELING in the Pacific islands about 200 years ago observed elaborate trading networks operating throughout Melanesia. In some places, specialist traders distributed a broad range of utilitarian goods and foodstuffs, as well as ceremonial items, such as shell necklaces and armbands of various types, between widespread settlements. In other areas, large groups of men left their village for months at a time to undertake long-distance trading expeditions, carrying large cargoes across dangerous seas.

A Noncommercial Economy

Melanesian trade had a very different character from the commercial and market-based economies we know in modern times. In Melanesia, there was no "money" or universal medium of exchange: exchange rates varied from place to place, but at any one point they were fixed, so that, for example, a certain amount of fish was always given in return for a particular quantity of sago, or a special kind of shell ornament was exchanged for another of a particular type. Value was determined by arbitrary cultural rules and not by scarcity or the amount of labor invested in goods. An important aim of Pacific archaeology is to trace the history of trading systems, in order to better understand the development of these noncommercial economies, so different from our own.

The task is not an easy one. Many items that were probably traded—such as fish, garden crops, feathers, and baskets—are perishable and would leave few traces for archaeologists to discover. Fortunately, however, tools made from a black, glassy volcanic stone called obsidian are commonly found at prehistoric sites in Melanesia. Obsidian occurs naturally only in a few, very restricted localities, but it has been found over a wide area, in sites far from its source. Trade seems a likely explanation for this distribution. Certainly, in recorded history, specialist traders carried obsidian nodules and tools along established trade routes.

Prehistoric Trade

Archaeologists study prehistoric trade by looking at both the distribution and production of items. Since obsidian from each of the five source areas known in Melanesia has a slightly different chemical composition, obsidian artifacts can be readily traced to their geological source. Distribution patterns are studied by making maps showing where obsidian tools derived from each source area have been found. By about 18,000 years ago, obsidian from outcrops around Talasea and Mopir, on New Britain, had found their way to Matembek Cave, on New Ireland. Between about 1500 BC and AD 500, obsidian from Talasea is found in sites stretching from Malaysia in the west to Fiji in the east, the most extensive distribution of a good known anywhere in the prehistoric world.

The second approach to study-ing trade is to look at production—that is, how obsidian artifacts were made. Research being conducted in the province of West New Britain by archaeologists from the Australian Museum provides a useful case study of this kind of analysis. The first stage of the research focused on the obsidian outcrops themselves. Exploration in the Talasea region revealed that sources of obsidian are scattered over an area of at least 100 square kilometers (38 square miles) and so would have been within easy reach of anyone living in the area. No one group of people could have held a monopoly over supplies of the raw material. But not all potentially use-able sources were exploited. People

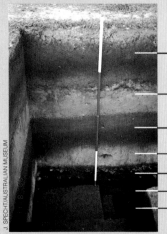

J. SPECHT/AUSTRALIAN MUSEUM

PHASE 4

Volcanic eruption c. 1,100 years ago

PHASE 3

Volcanic eruption c. 3,500 years ago

PHASE 2

Volcanic ash undated

PHASE I

◊ Stratigraphic layers excavated at Bitokara Mission. The darker layers, representing different phases of obsidian tool manufacture and use, are separated by yellow layers composed of volcanic ash from two major eruptions.

always preferred outcrops where large nodules of obsidian could be obtained with little effort, but they selected different locations at vari-ous times during at least the past 5,000 years. The choice of sources, therefore, cannot completely be explained by economic reasons, as would be the case in a commer-cially based economy. It seems likely that social factors have long played a role in establishing rights of access to obsidian sources.

Changing Patterns of Use

The second stage of the Australian Museum project has concentrated on how obsidian artifacts were made and used in the period from somewhere before 1500 BC up to the present day. An exciting site was discovered in 1981 at Bitokara Mission, near Talasea, when an archaeologist noticed abundant quantities of obsidian artifacts at the base of a freshly dug toilet pit. The Mission is perched on top of a cliff containing obsidian deposits and overlooks the nearby harbor. The setting was created by a very

thick and viscous volcanic lava that flowed slowly down the slopes of a volcano and stopped at this point. A team returned in 1988 and carried out systematic excav-ations. The Bitokara Mission excav-ations revealed a sequence of levels containing abundant quantities of waste by-products from artifact production, as well as discarded, used tools. Layers representing four periods of manufacturing activity are neatly separated by layers of volcanic ash, which have sealed the material beneath them.

In the earliest two phases, which have not yet been precisely dated but are earlier than 1500 BC, blocks of obsidian were dug up or collected from obsidian flows located on slopes just slightly uphill

RICHARD FULLAGAR

◊ When viewed under very high magnification, fragments of plants cut or scraped about 1500 BC can be observed still adhering to the edge of an obsidian stemmed tool found at Bitokara Mission.

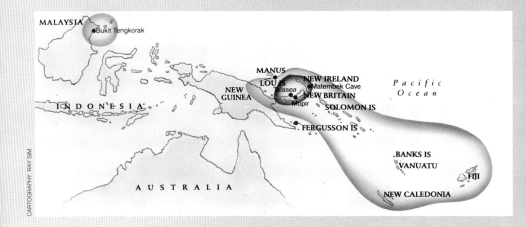

CARTOGRAPHY: RAY SIM

PREHISTORIC OBSIDIAN
The widespread distribution of obsidian from Talasea and Mopir demonstrates regular contact among seafaring peoples. The different patterns reflect different trading systems in these two periods.

Known distribution

about 1000 BC

about 8000 BC

HISTORIC TRADE ROUTES
Obsidian traveled overland between trading partners in adjacent villages, and by sea with specialist traders.

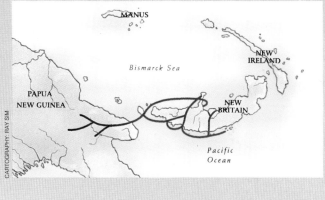

CARTOGRAPHY: RAY SIM

from the Mission. Large flakes were struck off them and were carried downhill to a level spot for the final stages of manufacture. The artifacts made at Bitokara varied greatly in shape and size, but many had a protrusion, or stem, which was probably wrapped with plant material and used as a handle. Microscopic analysis of wear patterns and residues preserved on their edges show that the stemmed tools were mainly used to cut plants, possibly root crops.

In the second of these two periods, as well as stemmed tools, many small flakes were made by hitting an obsidian cobble repeatedly and turning it over several times during the process. The resulting "rotated core" has a very distinctive shape. Analysis has revealed that most of the flakes were used for cutting and scraping plant material, but a few were used on animal tissues. The cores were not used as tools but are merely a waste product.

The division of labor between quarrying on the hillside above Bitokara Mission and the manufacture of tools lower down the slope, combined with the evidence that large quantities of stemmed tools were made, suggests that production in these two earliest periods was at least partly geared toward exports. Unfortunately, sites elsewhere in island Melanesia dating to before 1500 BC are extremely rare, so we do not yet know much about where the obsidian artifacts were going.

About 1500 BC, the entire area was completely devastated by ash from a major volcanic eruption. It seems likely that it would have been abandoned for at least a generation. When people once again began to exploit obsidian at Bitokara Mission, in the third period, they no longer quarried on the hillside or made stemmed tools. Only small flakes were made, using the technique of rotated cores from the previous period. From the fact that quite a few flakes can be fitted back together on their core, it seems that many of these small tools were made and used at the same spot, therefore suggesting that few, if any, tools were exported.

These results are puzzling, since it was during this third period at Bitokara that obsidian from Talasea is most widely distributed. Possibly, the hillside outcrops at Bitokara Mission were abandoned because they had been buried by the ash, and people chose instead to gather lumps that had eroded out and could be found in stream courses or on beaches. At this stage of research, however, we do not know why people stopped making stemmed tools for export. It seems likely that unworked pieces of obsidian were traded during this period. This change in exports from Talasea suggests that the nature of trade during the third period also differed from earlier times.

About AD 900, another volcanic eruption occurred. In the subsequent, fourth period of occupation, rotated cores are no longer found. The greatly reduced number of artifacts present indicates that production had declined considerably at this site, and, again, there is no evidence of quarrying on the hillside. It seems that in the fourth period the site at Bitokara Mission was used only occasionally. Since it is known from observations made by Europeans during the past hundred years that unmodified pieces of obsidian from Talasea were systematically being traded throughout West New Britain and across to mainland New Guinea, other outcrops in the area may have been exploited at this time. Old people living in the region today do not remember obsidian from Bitokara Mission being traded, but they do know of other places where obsidian is said to have been collected for trade.

A Key to the Past
The Australian Museum project at Talasea shows that the processing of obsidian at one source area has

changed several times in the past. The variations observed at Bitokara in how obsidian was acquired (quarried or collected) and exported (in the form of tools or raw material) suggest that prehistoric economic systems operated in a different way from the trading systems seen at the time of European contact. These initial results are exciting, but a great deal more needs to be learned before archaeologists can reconstruct how these early trading systems worked.

Already, further excavations are in progress at other source areas in the Talasea region to find out if the patterns that have emerged at Bitokara are repeated more widely. Studies of how obsidian was used at sites where it had to be imported are also under way. Finally, archaeologists are studying the trading system of the last several hundred years both by talking to people who remember how it worked and by comparing their stories with contemporary archaeological remains.

FARMERS OF THE NEW WORLD

10,000 BC – AD 1492

An Enduring Native American Gift to the World

DAVID HURST THOMAS

By the time Europeans began exploring the Americas, all but a handful of the indigenous societies relied, to some degree, on domesticated plants for their livelihood. The list of New World domesticates includes a diverse range of grains, root crops, vegetables, spices, nuts, and fruits. Although initially wary of new foods, the European interlopers soon learned first hand the potential of Native American agricultural products. The new crops were quickly exported to European ports, and from there, the New World bounty reached around the globe.

Today, the result is amazing. Sixty percent of the food that now supports the world's population was originally domesticated by Native Americans—maize, potatoes, manioc, beans of several varieties, squash and pumpkins, sweet potatoes, vanilla, tomatoes, chili peppers, pineapples, avocados, gourds, sunflowers, and amaranths. American cottons paved the way for all modern commercial varieties—and, for better or worse, Native Americans were also responsible for domesticating the still-sought-after stimulants of tobacco and coca (the source of cocaine).

◄Ө An Anasazi ruin inside a sheltered cave, overlooking the Green River and Canyonlands National Park, in Utah. The canyon walls offered countless flat surfaces for prehistoric artists to paint their pictographs and peck their petroglyphs. Much of this rock art survives today.

⬧ Maize (Indian corn) was developed through thousands of years of experimentation. So extensive was the genetic manipulation that today, modern maize requires human intervention to spread its own seeds.

D. DONNE BRYANT STOCK

MIDDLE AMERICA

The area known as Mesoamerica was one of the first regions in which plants were domesticated. From their early agricultural base, the Mesoamerican people forged one of the New World's two great civilizations.

⚱ The earliest people in Mexico's Tehuacán Valley cooked seed pods from the screwbean mesquite (*Prosopis pubscens*) into a rich syrup. Later, the Cahuilla Indians of California carefully pruned the thorny wild mesquite trees to make it easier to harvest the pods.

⟿ Chili peppers have a high tryptophan content. Used as a condiment, they complement maize, which provides little of this important amino acid.

Clues from the Tehuacán Valley

Our modern understanding of American agriculture draws heavily on the innovative archaeological investigations of Richard "Scotty" MacNeish in the 1960s. After years of searching for early evidence of maize in places like Mexico's Sierra de Tamaulipas, MacNeish was finally drawn to the caves and rock shelters of the arid and mountainous Tehuacán Valley, in central Mexico. Having investigated 38 of the Tehuacán caves, MacNeish dug several test pits into the deposits of Coxcatlán Cave, where the remains of six tiny corncobs had been preserved, all more primitive than any discovered previously. Radiocarbon dating put their age at about 3600 BC, older than any domesticated corn yet discovered. Even earlier remnants of maize have been found since.

Buoyed by his results, MacNeish launched a major interdisciplinary project in the Tehuacán Valley. After excavating 9 sites intensively and testing 18 others, he was able to trace a sequence of cultural developments from about 9500 BC to the arrival of Europeans in AD 1531. This research still forms the basis of our understanding of early American agriculture. More recent excavations, by Kent Flannery and his colleagues, at Guilá Naquitz, in the Mitla area of the Oaxaca Valley, in Mexico, have corroborated the early part of the Tehuacán sequence.

The earliest people of the Tehuacán Valley lived in small, mobile family groups which probably consisted of between four and eight people. Familiar with the range of local environments and with the foods seasonally available in each area, they survived by hunting the native American horse, antelope, and deer, and by gathering the fruits, seeds, and nuts that grew around them. They roasted century plants, cooked up syrup from mesquite pods, and leached tannic acid from bitter acorns to make them palatable. These early foragers sometimes lived in caves, and sometimes camped in the open—fanning out when food was scarce and converging on favored camp sites when times were better.

When these first Tehuacanos arrived, at the end of the Pleistocene period, the climate was colder and drier than it is today. But as central Mexico became warmer, both the grasslands and the water supply began to shrink, ultimately driving some animals, including horses and antelopes, to extinction. In time, smaller game, such as deer and cottontail rabbits, became more important as a source of food, as did gophers and even rats.

About 7000 BC, the Indians of central Mexico, while continuing to range widely in search of food and other resources, began to collect plants more intensively, particularly those that were eventually domesticated—such as squash, beans, and the wild ancestor of maize (probably teosinte).

Some time before 5000 BC, the people of the Tehuacán Valley started to make use of a considerably wider range of plant foods. Bottle gourds may have been the first plants domesticated in the New World, but people also began to plant and tend squash, amaranths, chili peppers, and, perhaps, avocados. These initial gardens required minimal care and contributed little to the food supply. Neither seasonal foraging trips nor settlement patterns were much affected.

Agriculture may have arisen in response to the changing climatic conditions during the Late Pleistocene period that culminated in the end of the last Ice Age and the beginning of the period we know as the Holocene. With the changes in vegetation this brought about, supplies of important plant foods would have become less predictable.

Later, as the population grew, hunter-gatherers became increasingly less mobile and more territorial. Plant cultivation proved to be a good way to increase the food supply, and food storage a logical way to even out the differences between good and bad years.

Tiny maize cobs like the ones MacNeish discovered at Coxcatlán Cave appeared in Tehuacán Valley gardens some time before 3400 BC, along with beans, chili peppers, squash, gourds, and amaranths. By about 2500 BC, agriculture provided perhaps 25 percent of the Tehuacán food supply. A thousand years later, this proportion had increased to about 40 percent. The evidence from Tehuacán and Oaxaca indicates that permanent villages may have been established by 2500 BC. MacNeish believes that people may have been living in villages all year round by this date, although other archaeologists suggest that the earliest permanent villages did not appear in Middle America until about 1700 BC.

The Maize Debate

Considerable debate also surrounds the introduction of maize into South America. (See the feature *On the Trail of Maize: Mother of Corn.*) Although evidence of maize existing before 4000 BC occasionally turns up in South America, maize finds continue to be sparse for the next 2,500 years, until about 1500 BC.

Robert McC. Bird, who has examined most of the prehistoric maize recovered in South America, suggests that maize arrived in Middle America about 3000 BC. Numerous varieties of maize developed and gradually moved southwards. With an extremely wide range of maize types in existence, the rate of both evolution and dispersal had accelerated by 1000 BC. Rapid hybridization took place, making maize an even more adaptable and versatile plant and increasing its yield. This also accounts for the complex mosaic of maize varieties found across South America.

Bird also stresses that after a period of localized evolution and differentiation, certain varieties of maize were taken north, back into Middle America. This process may have been repeated many times, producing new genetic varieties that often resulted in specialized kinds of maize adapted to local conditions.

MICHAEL S. THOMPSON/COMSTOCK

☝ Amaranths were among the earliest wild plants to be domesticated in the Americas.

⚘ These three large ceramic figures from Nayarit, in western Mexico, depict Native American women making tortillas from ground maize. They date to between about 200 BC and AD 600.

AMERICAN MUSEUM OF NATURAL HISTORY

Relying heavily on new data from Ecuadorian plant phytoliths —microscopic silica particles contained in plants—Deborah Pearsall argues that because early maize is so varied, it must have been introduced to South America some time before 5000 BC. At this early date, however, maize was neither widespread nor an important part of the diet. Evidence from Peru indicates that maize did not become widespread until about 1500 BC, or slightly later.

Many archaeologists, such as Pearsall, have come to rely heavily on the evidence provided by the distribution and analysis of microscopic plant phytoliths. Distinctive silica phytoliths occur in

plants of the grass family and are also found in groups such as rushes, sedges, palms, conifers, and deciduous trees.

Although phytoliths have been identified in archaeological sites for decades, it was rare for archaeological deposits to be systematically analyzed for phytoliths before 1970. Since then, interest in this unusual technique has exploded, and today the identification and analysis of phytoliths recovered from archaeological sites hold great promise for reconstructing paleo-environments and for tracking the process of plant domestication.

The difficulties of basing taxonomy (plant classification) on phytoliths have meant that phytolith analysis is still not widely accepted as a valid method of archaeological research. Considerable progress has recently been made in the area of taxonomy, however—in particular, Pearsall's breakthrough in identifying maize phytoliths, which pushed back the date for the introduction of maize to Ecuador by several thousand years. The next step is to develop reliable criteria for identifying teosinte phytoliths, which would represent a major advance in our understanding of how maize was domesticated.

Apart from such systematic problems, some archaeologists remain reluctant to accept phytolith data when they conflict with more traditional evidence, such as kernel impressions, maize motifs that appear on ancient ceramics (as at Valdivia, in Ecuador), actual maize parts, and traces of maize on metates (grinding slabs).

Plant Domestication: The Beginning of Agriculture

Plants were domesticated at many different times and in many areas throughout South America. Although much remains to be learned, it seems clear that the range of plants cultivated in South America did not evolve in isolation. Cultivars (plant varieties produced from a naturally occurring species) were exchanged across large regions almost from the time they originated.

Regardless of when they first arrived—surely some time before 14,000 years ago—the earliest South Americans followed a Paleoindian way of life, hunting now-extinct Pleistocene animals and smaller game, and gathering wild plants. Then, about 8000 BC, a shift occurred. Evidence from a number of Andean sites shows that a new way of life was adopted: the so-called Archaic adaptation, based largely on hunting llama, alpaca, and deer, and gathering a range of wild plants.

This period also saw the beginnings of plant domestication in South America. Domesticated potatoes were present in northern Bolivia by 8000 BC; beans and chili peppers in highland Peruvian valleys by about 8500 BC. By 6000 BC, the list of domesticated plants had expanded to include squash, gourds, and guavas. These earliest

♀ Painted by renowned artist Diego Rivera, this mural at the Palacio National, in Mexico City, shows the importance of maize to ancient Mexican communities.

ULRIKE WELSCH/PHOTO RESEARCHERS

finds are still in question, mainly because of the nature of the archaeological sites where they were found. Most of the early cultigens have been recovered from dry caves, many of which, unfortunately, had been disturbed by later burials. The deposits in such caves also attract rodents, which tend to scatter food remains, mixing them with other material.

Coastal and lowland cultivars, including cotton and squash, appear in central sierra sites between 4200 BC and 2500 BC. From about 4000 BC to the end of the Peruvian Preceramic period (1800 BC to 1200 BC), there is increasing evidence, from sites such as Huaca Prieta, that plants were extensively cultivated, including many that had been domesticated previously (such as beans, gourds, squash, chili peppers, and, of course, guavas). New crops also appear about this time, particularly cotton, avocados, sweet potatoes, peanuts, and manioc. Despite this diversity, root crops were the main source of carbohydrates in the diet until maize spread through the mid-altitude and low-altitude zones.

How Were Plants Domesticated?

Such are the apparent facts of the initial domestication of plants in Middle and South America. But how do we explain the processes that were involved?

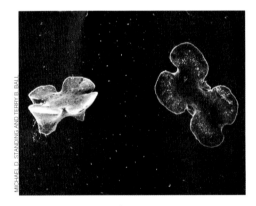

One cogent explanation has been offered by archaeologist Kent Flannery. Survival of the earliest human communities in the Mexican highlands depended upon certain key food resources—maguey, cactus fruits, mesquite pods, wild grasses (such as *Zea*), white-tailed deer, and cottontail rabbits. Many of these plants and animals were available for only a few months of the year, and when more than one resource was available at one time, hunter-gatherers had to decide which had priority. Since these two factors—seasonal availability and what is often referred to as scheduling—meant that no particular resource predominated, this

way of living proved flexible and relatively resistant to change.

Flannery argues that the origin of agriculture can be traced to genetic changes in only one or two of the many plants that humans exploited. For example, the wild ancestor of maize might have undergone genetic alteration as a result of natural crossbreeding and subsequent evolution, with some assistance in the form of human intervention. Whatever the reason, the upshot was an increase in the size and number of cobs and the number of kernel rows, and the loss of the outer leaves—known as glumes—that enclosed the individual kernels.

Beans, on the other hand, might have evolved independently from maize, becoming larger and more permeable to water and therefore easier to process as food. They may also have evolved limper, less brittle pods that did not disintegrate when mature, making harvesting easier. These minor genetic changes would have set further changes in motion, for as these plants began to provide better harvests, they would have become the preferred source of food. This, in turn, would have helped along the process of genetic change. People would have begun to alter their way of life to take advantage of these cultigens.

Biologist David Rindos has suggested another explanation, emphasizing evolutionary processes independent of human enterprise and initiative. His theory, the so-called coevolutionary perspective, plays down any linear, cause-and-effect relationship.

☙ Ecuadorians harvesting potatoes, which were first domesticated about 8000 BC.

☙ The identification and analysis of phytoliths (microscopic silica particles occurring in plants) is providing new information about early plant domestication. This scanning electron photomicrograph shows the morphology of the phytoliths characteristic of maize.

☙ The Hopi Indians of eastern Arizona used wooden tweezers to collect the edible fruit of the prickly pear, and rolled the fruit in sand to remove the spines. They also collected prickly pear joints. The large thorns were burned off; then the joints were boiled, dipped in a rich syrup made from baked sweet corn, and eaten.

ON THE TRAIL OF MAIZE: MOTHER OF CORN

David Hurst Thomas

Wild perennial
teosinte

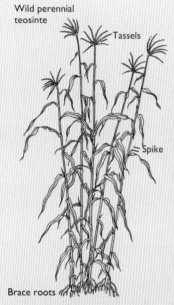

Tassels

Spike

Brace roots

Modern maize (*Zea mays*, below) and wild perennial teosinte (above) are closely related. They have the same number of chromosomes and hybridize freely. The main difference between the plants is in their seed-bearing female organs: whereas teosinte has numerous small, brittle spikes that shatter when they mature, maize has two or three large ears, enclosed by husks. Teosinte also has numerous side stalks (tillers). The tassels are the male flower clusters.

⬧ These drawings of Aztec methods of planting, tending, and harvesting maize, attributed to sixteenth-century native artists, were published in the *Codex Florentino*.

Of the more than 100 plant species domesticated by Native Americans, none is more familiar or widespread than maize (*Zea mays*), also called Indian corn. Maize was the staff of life for much of pre-Columbian America, from Argentina to Canada, from sea level to the slopes of the Andes. For more than 7,000 years, the people of the Americas domesticated hundreds of kinds of maize, from the ancient thumbnail-sized wild cobs to the formidable ears of corn sold today throughout the world.

The combination of maize, beans (*Phaseolus*), and squash (*Cucurbita*) is commonly considered to be America's agricultural triumvirate. Not only can all three crops be grown together in the same field, but they complement one another nutritionally. Although rich in starch, maize is deficient in lysine, an essential amino acid. Beans are rich in protein, and contain large amounts of lysine. Eaten together, beans, maize, and squash combine to create especially valuable plant protein.

Modern maize

Ear

Brace roots

↪ Important stages in the evolution of teosinte to maize, resulting from selective harvesting and planting of transitional stages of teosinte.

Stage 1: In wild teosinte, long canes are borne near the base, terminating in an all-male tassel. The upper spikes are predominantly male, while the lower spikes tend towards a female state.

Stage 2: As branches become shorter, the degree of femaleness increases.

Stage 3: The branches continue to condense. (Stages 1 to 3 are still found in wild populations growing in Guerrero, Mexico.)

Stage 4: A husk begins to enclose the fruit cases.

Stage 5: The husk fully encloses the ear. The form of teosinte shown here was ancestral to Tehuacán soft-cob maize.

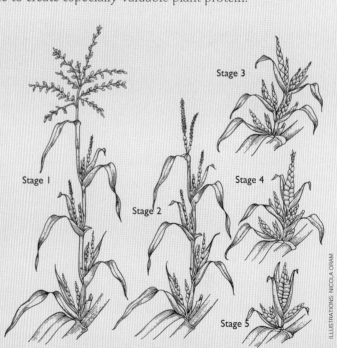

Modern ears of maize (com) exhibit a fantastic degree of diversity in size, shape, and color, as a result of centuries of selective breeding and crossbreeding. Because domesticated maize also hybridized with wild teosinte, a huge gene pool became available to Native American farmers. The maize ear in the lower right-hand corner is US Corn Belt dent, the world's most productive maize. To the left is an ear of Cuzco Gigante, a Peruvian race with the world's largest kernels. Above the Cuzco is a tiny Lady Finger popcorn, and above that is the whitish ear of a Brazilian pod corn, its kernels enclosed in chaff.

The precise origin of maize is controversial: the literature on this subject is vast and sometimes contentious. The prevailing view is that modern maize evolved through natural mutation and hybridization (or interbreeding) and frequent backcrossing with its nearest wild relative, teosinte (*Zea mexicana*). This explanation is supported by several lines of evidence. For example, frequent hybridization occurs between maize and teosinte under natural conditions; maize and teosinte have the same number of chromosomes; there are several key anatomical similarities between the two; and there is an overlap in the size range of pollen spores found in the two species. Teosinte derives from the Nahuatl word *teocintli*, which means "God's ear of maize". In many parts of Mexico, teosinte is still called *madre de maiz*, "mother of maize".

A little-supported alternative view, championed in particular by botanist Paul Mangelsdorf and his colleagues, is that cultivated maize is descended from a now-extinct form of wild pod popcorn, which bore individual kernels enclosed and protected by chaff. These botanists hold that wild teosinte resulted from the hybridization of maize with *Tripsacum*, a type of wild grass.

⚘ Gourds (*Cucurbita*) are among the oldest cultivated plants in the New World. Archaeological specimens dating from 8800 BC to 7250 BC have been recovered from Guilá Naquitz Cave, in Oaxaca, Mexico.

Instead, he sees domestication not only as an evolutionary stage, but as a process resulting from coevolutionary interactions between humans and plants.

The process of plant domestication began when people started to disperse and to protect key wild plant resources. For example, by favoring larger seeds over smaller ones, people have, over the centuries, brought about significant genetic changes. Assuming that people also planted these larger seeds, such economically desirable genetic traits as superior size would have been encouraged, leading to total domestication of the species. In other words, the relationship between plants and human beings both promoted and preserved a "conservative" ecological liaison.

Specialized domestication took place as new types of relationships between plants and people developed. Plants being used as food became increasingly common in areas where people lived, and so population movements were to indirectly benefit domesticated plants.

Over time, people came to rely on the plants they needed for food to such an extent that people and plants became interdependent. People also selectively destroyed various plant species in the vicinity of their communities, setting the stage for the development of complex agricultural systems. Full-blown agriculture began when practices such as weeding, irrigation, and plowing created new opportunities for plant evolution, thereby increasing the rate at which domesticated plants evolved.

⚘ Beans (*Phaseolus*), an important source of protein, on sale in a modern Ecuadorian market. Cultivated in the Peruvian Andes at least 8,000 years ago, American beans reached the Old World during Columbus's second voyage of 1493, and then rapidly spread across Europe, Africa, the Mediterranean basin, and Asia.

Not all archaeologists are comfortable with the Rindos model. Darwin's evolutionary theory holds that living things evolve by means of natural selection. Although Darwin's principles have been further developed by geneticists, plant ecologists, and, more recently, molecular plant biologists, Rindos rules out human intervention, considering it to be irrelevant. Many others, Flannery included, feel uncomfortable about excluding human intentions from early agricultural enterprise. Understandably, anthropologically oriented scholars seek cultural explanations for cultural behavior, and become concerned when human behavior is reduced to biology. Flannery puts it this way: "… anthropologists know that human hunter-gatherers are mammals, primates and predators, but that is not what anthropologists find most interesting about them."

Highland and Lowland Systems of South America

The agricultural system of the high-elevation Andes—from just below 3,000 meters (10,000 feet) to slightly above 3,500 meters (11,500 feet)—is ancient. Remains of domesticated potatoes—the only high-elevation crop also found to any extent

SOUTH AMERICA
Key archaeological sites yielding evidence of the early domestication of plants in South America. Botanical remains recovered from Ayacucho and Guitarrero Cave provide evidence that maize, beans, gourds, squash, and potatoes were being cultivated by the fifth millennium BC.
CARTOGRAPHY: RAY SIM

in lower zones—have been recovered from archaeological deposits as old as 8000 BC.

Paleobotanical evidence is more sporadic in the mid-elevations of the Andes— between about 1,500 meters and 3,000 meters (5,000 feet and 10,000 feet). It is clear, however, that agricultural activity extends back to between 8000 BC and 7500 BC at Guitarrero Cave, where people grew chili peppers and two species of beans. Even at this early date, people in the mid-elevations were in contact with farmers from other areas.

The Guitarrero Cave site also contains a number of legumes, including peanuts, common beans, and lima beans. Apparently, these plants did not evolve in the area, but were probably introduced from lower elevations, along with squash and gourds. Fruit trees, including guava, were also important at the mid-elevations. The use of coca can be traced archaeologically to an ancestral form that grows wild on the eastern Andean slopes. Coca was probably first cultivated on the Peruvian montaña, and then spread to the Amazon.

The lowland agricultural systems of South America pose many problems for archaeologists. Most of the crops were initially domesticated in the tropical forest, where sites are difficult to find and even more challenging to excavate. In addition, plant remains are usually poorly preserved. As a result, most of the archaeological evidence comes from elsewhere, such as the deserts of coastal Peru, where plants cultivated earlier in the lowlands were incorporated into floodplain (and later irrigation) agriculture.

The starchy dietary staple of most Amazonian and Caribbean tribes at the time of European contact was manioc or cassava (*Manihot esculenta*), the source of tapioca and without doubt one of the dozen most important food plants in the world today. Both bitter and sweet forms of manioc contain various levels of prussic acid, the source of cyanide. Removing the poison requires a substantial effort—peeling, grating, washing, squeezing, and toasting—but flour from bitter manioc can be stored for months, as can bread made from the flour.

Current research suggests that manioc originated as a domesticated plant in northeastern Brazil and was introduced into Middle America from South America. Because manioc is grown from cuttings, however, little direct evidence of its cultivation has survived in the archaeological record, and the dates for both its initial domestication and its later distribution across the continent remain in dispute.

Some argue that the first evidence of the domestication of manioc can be traced archaeologically through the appearance of small stone flakes set as blades in early grater boards, used to convert the manioc tubers into pulp, and pottery griddles (*budares*), used to roast the processed manioc. These griddles have been tentatively dated to about 2100 BC along the Middle Orinoco River, and they become common after 1000 BC. Other archaeologists believe manioc was domesticated much earlier—perhaps by 5000 BC—in the tropical forests of lowland Colombia, Venezuela, and Ecuador.

Despite the antiquity and importance of manioc, archaeological evidence indicates that sweet potatoes may have been cultivated even earlier, at least in Peru. Apparently, these two tuber crops were not introduced to the coast together, which probably means that they were initially domesticated in different places.

⬆ Agricultural terraces at the Inka citadel of Machu Picchu, in Peru, perched some 2,400 meters (8,000 feet) above sea level. These astonishing stone terraces were so skillfully constructed that it seems they will last forever. Laborers added layers of rock and clay as subsoil, and then hauled up rich alluvial soil from the river far below, over steep embankments 800 meters (half a mile) deep. At the time of the Spanish conquest, Native American farmers were producing 3,000 kinds of potatoes in the Andes.

◄ A manioc (*Manihot esculenta*) plantation near Loreto, in Peru. Also known as cassava, manioc is the source of tapioca.

⚡ Cotton bolls beginning to open in the San Joaquin Valley, California. Cotton was probably first domesticated in western South America about 3100 BC, with a secondary center of domestication in Amazonia.

Evidence is particularly sparse for the domestication of the numerous tree fruits important to lowland agriculture. Avocados can be traced to the Late Preceramic or Initial period of Peru, with guanabanas (soursops), pineapples, and papayas appearing somewhat later. Cotton was probably domesticated in western South America, either in the northern coastal region or in southwestern Ecuador. Amazonia was a secondary center of domestication. The earliest cotton has been found in the Ayacucho caves, dating from 3100 BC to 1750 BC; finds later than 2000 BC are commonplace.

Maize arrived in the tropics from Mexico some time before 4000 BC, as food-producing populations expanded into Amazonia, moved down into the eastern slopes of the Andes, and then spread westwards across the Andes.

The Domestication of Animals

Although a wealth of plant foods was domesticated in the Americas, domesticated animals were of little importance, except in the central Andes. In this region, the domestication of camelids—llamas and alpacas—is particularly interesting. The hides were made into clothing and rope; the wool was woven to make warm clothes; the meat was eaten fresh, or sundried as *charki*; the entrails and bones were stewed; and the tallow was used to make candles.

The earliest evidence of animal domestication comes from sites at elevations above 4,000 meters (13,000 feet), where the altitude makes the cultivation of food crops much less effective. This evidence raises an intriguing question about the relationship between the domestication of plants and animals in the High Andes. At Panaulauca Cave, Pearsall found evidence dating back to the second millennium BC linking the corralling of camelids with the increased use of *Chenopodium* and *Lepidium*, both plants that thrive on disturbed soil, such as the

◈ High-altitude pastoralists in the central and southern parts of the Andes relied heavily on domesticated camelids. The alpaca was kept mostly for its wool, and llamas were used primarily as beasts of burden Of the domesticated animals, only the guinea pig seems to have been a significant food source. This handsome silver long-haired llama dates from the Inka period.

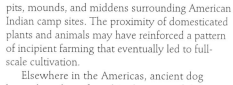

pits, mounds, and middens surrounding American Indian camp sites. The proximity of domesticated plants and animals may have reinforced a pattern of incipient farming that eventually led to full-scale cultivation.

Elsewhere in the Americas, ancient dog bones have been found in the caves of the Junín region of the Peruvian Andes, dating back to about 6000 BC. In fact, it may be that domesticated dogs accompanied the first Americans across the Bering Strait. Archaeological and documentary evidence also suggests that, at times, dogs were eaten, providing an important source of protein.

The guinea pig, domesticated from its wild Andean ancestor, provided another food source, and in Middle America, people supplemented their largely vegetable diet with muscovy duck and turkey.

and permanent wetlands. This method, called drained field agriculture, was a sophisticated form of intensive wetland agriculture carried out on specially designed fields. The construction of these fields varied tremendously, from the sunken fields and canals found in arid areas along the Peruvian coast to the *chinampas* (incorrectly called "floating gardens") built in shallow lakes near Mexico City. The overriding objective was to produce patches of well-drained, aerated, well-structured, and fertile soil that would produce high crop yields over long periods of time. Indeed, some of the highland Mexican fields in use during the time of the Spanish conquest are still being cultivated today.

The earliest examples of these fields may be as old as 1000 BC, but most date to between AD 300 and AD 1000, a time of major population growth. It was during this time, when food was in high demand, that the largest number of terraced and drained fields were being cultivated.

The simplest, and apparently the most ancient, practice was simply to cut canals from a wetland area into an adjacent swamp, with the intervening field only slightly raised. This style of construction was eventually modified by piling up nutrient-rich muck from the canal beds to create raised fields of extremely rich soil, in which multiple crops could be grown year after year. Because the fields were elevated above the floodplain, crops were not flooded out during the rainy season.

Drained field technology became a critically important aspect of New World agriculture, providing sufficient food for the dense populations that lived in areas such as the Maya lowlands. On the basis of archaeological evidence from Pulltrouser Swamp, in Belize, Middle America, B.L. Turner estimates that the construction of raised fields took between

⚲ These freshly harvested cocoa pods are the fruit of the cacao, or chocolate, tree (*Theobroma cacao*). Chocolate is made from the beans.

◄● An early stage of archaeological excavations at Coxcatlán Cave, in the Tehuacán Valley, Mexico. This extraordinary site contained 28 stratified zones, with 42 distinct cultural occupations that yielded abundant artifacts, animal remains, and botanical specimens spanning the period from 10,000 BC to the present.

⚲ Aerial view of Pre-Columbian raised fields near Lake Titicaca, Peru. Some 80,000 hectares (198,000 acres) of the lakeside marshes surrounding Lake Titicaca were reclaimed for agriculture. Between 400 BC and AD 1000, potatoes and other crops grown in these artificially drained fields supported from 20,000 to 40,000 people living at the nearby city of Tiahuanaco.

Mayan Engineering: Raising the Fields

Plants were domesticated in places such as the Tehuacán Valley over thousands of years, but elsewhere, under very different circumstances, agricultural change came about much more abruptly.

The Maya began cultivating maize some time before 2000 BC, presumably in dry-land fallow (plowed land that has remained unsown) and orchard gardens. Early fallow practices ranged from forest and bush rotations, with slash-and-burn techniques, to short, annual rotations which probably involved weeding, tilling, crop mixing, mulching, and so forth. Dry-land fallow required only 19 to 25 working days per hectare per year.

But like many other Native American people, the Classic Maya (AD 300 to AD 900) of the Yucatán Peninsula, in Mexico, eventually developed a method for cultivating seasonal

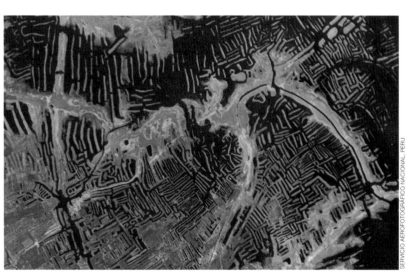

⊕ One of the Hohokam irrigation canals excavated at the Snaketown site, in Arizona. Such major canals were interlinked with vast networks of lateral ditches and diversion areas. Although corn was the most common crop to be irrigated, archaeological excavations have shown that beans, squash, bottle gourds, cotton, possibly barley, and amaranths were also widely grown in these systems.

ARIZONA STATE MUSEUM

♀ Aerial view of Anasazi fields and gardens, located in the central Rio Grande Valley of New Mexico. These were solar gardens of sophisticated design. The lines and grids are formed of aligned stones of various sizes. The dark stones retained the sun's heat into the night, warming nearby plants and extending their growing time. The squares were commonly filled with gravel, which helped to trap rainwater and runoff. The interspersed "waffle gardens" were usually enclosed by clay adobe ridges or walls, and then irrigated.

833 and 3,116 work days per hectare. Clearly, the output from the fields must have justified this considerable effort.

This ancient system of intensive, year-round cultivation sustained high-yield crops such as maize, beans, squash, cacao, and cotton. In modern Mexico, these fields support such diverse crops as manioc, cabbages, squash, rice, corn, watermelons, alfalfa, chili peppers, carrots, turnips, and salad vegetables. A newly constructed canal system near Villahermosa, in Mexico, is being used for intensive fish

TOM BAKER

farming, and it is likely that the ancient canals of Middle America that were built to drain the fields were similarly used to add vital protein in the form of fish to the pre-Columbian diet.

After AD 900, the Maya went through a period of social upheaval, during which they suffered major population losses throughout much of their territory. As the demand for agricultural products declined, the higher-cost systems were abandoned, and dry-land fallow agriculture once again prevailed.

Agriculture Comes to North America

As in highland Mexico, the evidence from North America clearly indicates that the domestication of plants was a long-term process. For thousands of years, nonagricultural Native Americans had a varied impact on wild plants without actually domesticating them. For instance, before the arrival of Europeans, Californian foragers modified the natural environment in a variety of ways. The people of the interior commonly torched underbrush, directly improving the habitat for the valued acorn crops they depended on. Further south, the Cahuilla, another Californian group, carefully pruned thorny mesquite trees to facilitate harvesting the edible pods. The Paiute, who lived in the Owens Valley, irrigated large stands of Indian ricegrass and other wild plants, even though most of the plants they ate grew completely wild. Although the oak tree, mesquite, and Indian ricegrass were never domesticated in California, practices such as these set the stage for the development of complex agricultural systems elsewhere in the Americas.

Plant macrofossils have been recovered from various rock shelter sites, leading many archaeologists to believe that maize first appeared in western North America about 1000 BC. Others, citing as their evidence maize pollen detected in Chaco Canyon sediments, suggest that cultigens arrived in the Southwest a thousand years earlier.

Despite the tremendous amount of research that has gone into establishing such "first dates", the question is less important than it may first appear. Whichever date ultimately proves to be accurate, organized farming did not develop overnight in the American Southwest. For at least a thousand years, the cultivation of maize and other plants was combined with the traditional hunting and gathering way of life.

This is perhaps best illustrated by the Western Apache of east central Arizona, where some of the earliest examples of plant cultivation in the American Southwest can be found. The Western Apache had a balanced economy. Men hunted large game animals, but meat was not eaten to the extent that game were driven from their territory altogether. They farmed, but not to the extent that they depended on crops alone to

GEORGE H H HUEY

TOM TILL

⚑ Anasazi farmers of the American Southwest built intriguing cliff dwellings and multiroom apartment structures, called pueblos. Here, at Spruce Tree House, in Mesa Verde National Park, Colorado, the ladders coming up through the floor mark the entrances to two subterranean kivas (ceremonial rooms).

↩ A modern pathway leads visitors through the circular ruins at Tyuonyi (Bandelier National Monument, New Mexico), one of the most impressive Anasazi pueblos in the Rio Grande drainage area. Tree-ring dating shows that the 400 rooms were built between AD 1383 and AD 1466. When the population was at its peak, Tyuonyi was three stories high.

↪ This original Anasazi ladder still stands in place, leading into a Utah kiva.

TOM TILL

🐾 An Anasazi petroglyph from southeastern Utah, dated to between AD 700 and AD 800, depicting a prehistoric bear hunt.

🐾 Manos (hand stones) and metates (grinding slabs) were used to process maize in these Anasazi grinding bins at Betatakin (Navajo National Monument, Arizona).

👉 A chilly winter morning at Spruce Tree House, a well-preserved Anasazi cliff dwelling in Mesa Verde National Park, Colorado.

sustain them throughout the year. They gathered wild plant foods and small game, but not enough to obviate the need for big-game hunts.

The Western Apache moved regularly. Their winter camps were in the south, and in spring they moved higher up into the mountains to the north to plant, hunt, and collect food from the wild. From late August until October, they also harvested piñon nuts, acorns, and juniper berries, before moving back to their winter homes.

For the Western Apache, farming provided a buffer against a possible shortage of naturally available foodstuffs. Because maize could be stored, it was readily available in such times of shortage. The earliest varieties of corn were not very productive and required relatively little effort to cultivate, which meant that traditional hunting and gathering activities were not disrupted. Perhaps 25 percent of the Western Apache diet came from domesticated plants, hunting supplying another 35 to 40 percent.

During the late nineteenth century, the basic social unit among these Western Apache farmers was the relatively autonomous household. Individual households could move from one group to another at will, although members of each group tended to be from the same clan. In some years, such groups lived almost entirely by hunting and gathering; in others, they relied almost exclusively on farm products. The same applied to the Hopi of eastern Arizona. When crops failed, as they did occasionally, Pueblo communities broke up into smaller family foraging groups, which were capable of living off foodstuffs available in the wild.

Farming in the Southwest Comes of Age

By 1000 BC, casual agriculture was well established in the Mogollon Highlands of the American Southwest. At sites such as Bat Cave, New Mexico, we can see that people had come to rely on agriculture for a significant part of their food supply. By about AD 200 to AD 700, the ecology of the Southwest had changed forever, for both farmers and nonfarmers.

In arid regions, people would have needed a strong incentive to persist in cultivating maize. The adoption of agriculture was by no means an inevitable process, and the archaeological record shows that populations expanded and contracted in cycles over a period of 2,000 years. When a population outgrew its territory, people migrated to other areas. Sometimes, the migrants succeeded in establishing stable farming societies that lasted for centuries. At other times, they failed, and the land was temporarily abandoned. But once agriculture took a firm hold in the Southwest, hunting and gathering became less important.

Although maize, settled village life, and ceramics were once thought to have arrived as a "package" from Mexico, it is now clear that

Zuni people have farmed their homeland, just west of the continental divide in western New Mexico, for centuries. Here, Zuni farmers tend their "waffle gardens": small agricultural plots for growing fruit and vegetables such as melons, herbs, chili peppers, and onions. Enclosed by ridges of clay earth, the rectangular compartments retain water diverted from the nearby river.
THE BETTMAN ARCHIVE

Although it is difficult to establish continuities between archaeological complexes and modern Pueblo people, some archaeologists think that the ancient Anasazi of Chaco Canyon can be linked to the modern Zuni people. This large Zuni jar from the late nineteenth century is decorated with numerous stylized plant, bird, and deer motifs, together with repeated geometric units, painted on a white slipped background. The "heartline" extending from the deer's mouth to its heart is a distinctively Zuni motif.
AMERICAN MUSEUM OF NATURAL HISTORY

these characteristic features of the local culture arrived separately. Taken together, they greatly enhanced an already rich Native American heritage in the Southwest. Archaeologists conventionally divide this late pre-European period into three major cultures: the Mogollon, the Hohokam, and the Anasazi, each occupying a distinctive ecological niche within the mosaic of Southwestern environments.

The highland Mogollon farmed the forests and upland meadows along the border between Arizona and New Mexico. They are best known as the makers of the legendary Mimbres pottery, painted with complex geometric designs and intricate human forms, birds, bats, bighorn sheep, rabbits, and insects. The earliest Mimbres pottery, in the classic black-on-white tradition, dates from about AD 750 to AD 1000. Then, between about AD 1050 and AD 1200, the tradition shifted to more colorful designs, featuring, in particular, different shades of black and red.

The early Mogollon people lived in villages of randomly spaced pit houses (in which the floor is dug down to a depth of half a meter, or about 18 inches, to facilitate sealing the walls against wind and rain). After a time, they shifted to apartment-like structures built above ground, with interconnected storage and living rooms, similar to Anasazi pueblos. The Mogollon culture began to decline in AD 1100, and had been completely eclipsed by AD 1250.

The scorching Sonoran Desert to the west was home to the Hohokam. Archaeologists originally thought that the Hohokam migrated from Mexico about 300 BC, but it is now believed that they

were native to the area. The Hohokam were accomplished desert-dwelling farmers who constructed hundreds of kilometers of irrigation canals throughout central Arizona. Today, more than 2,000 years later, a canal system that has been virtually superimposed on the early Hohokam plan diverts water from the Salt River for the city of Phoenix, Arizona.

By about AD 1450, the classic Hohokam culture had declined, perhaps as a result of drought or increased soil salinity. Many believe that the modern O'Odham (Pima and Papago) people are descended from Hohokam pioneers.

The Anasazi homeland lay to the north, in the high deserts of the Colorado Plateau. Although the earlier Anasazi lived in pit houses, between AD 700 and AD 1000 their descendants began constructing the distinctive multiroom apartment (pueblo) complexes that were to give their descendants, the Pueblo Indians, their name. About AD 900, the Anasazi people of northwestern New Mexico experienced a sustained burst of cultural energy, giving rise to what is known as the Chaco Phenomenon. (See the feature *The Chaco Phenomenon.*)

Farmers of the North American Plains and Woodlands

Traditional textbooks on the history of Western civilization often suggest that primary agricultural inventions originated independently in three places—in the so-called Fertile Crescent of Southwest Asia, in Southeast Asia, and in highland Mexico. Now, archaeologists recognize that plants were domesticated many times, in many places—including an important and newly discovered center in northeastern America. Although early explorers recorded extensive maize cultivation throughout eastern North America, new archaeological evidence makes it clear that the full-blown cultivation of maize began only five centuries before Europeans arrived.

The transition from foraging to farming along the rivers of the eastern woodlands involved three key steps: first, native North American seed plants were domesticated about 2000 BC; second, horticultural economies based on these local crops began to emerge between 250 BC and AD 100 (maize arriving on the scene about AD 100); and third, maize finally became a major crop between AD 800 and AD 1100.

From 6000 BC to 700 BC, the foraging people of eastern North America followed the same basic seasonal pattern, moving from one part of their home range to another in pursuit of grasses, fruits, nuts, fish, and game, as they became available. They traveled in small bands, which gave them the flexibility needed to respond quickly to fluctuations in the local food supply.

After about 4000 BC, the changing climate enriched many river valley environments. Shoals and lakes developed, and the abundance of wild seed plants, shellfish, fish, and animals such as deer and raccoons encouraged people to form permanent settlements. Men hunted; women collected wild plants. Shellfish, so abundant in shallow waters, were available to all.

Over countless generations, people had become familiar with the life cycles and habits of the nut trees and seed plants so important to them, and in the rich soils of their settlements the women began the great experiment that would ultimately produce domesticated plants. They probably tried out many types of plants, but, in the end, it was weeds from the floodplains that produced results. Sunflower and its distant cousins marshelder, goosefoot, and a wild gourd (the ancestor of summer squash) became the success stories. These aggressive, weedy plants, which colonized the areas swept clean by spring floodwaters, all produced highly nutritious seeds and were important sources of food. They readily invaded the rich soils surrounding human settlements and were the subject of early experiments aimed at increasing yield and dependability. There is evidence that these seed crops were being deliberately planted in 2000 BC, at which time they were beginning to yield a dependable, managed food supply that could be stored for use in late winter and even into early spring.

People and plants became interdependent to the point that human groups began to reoccupy certain areas because they offered favorable farming conditions. Despite this, however, current archaeological evidence shows that domesticated crops were not a substantial source of food before 500 BC, and that agriculture did not play a major role until about AD 100, a full thousand years after the first plants were domesticated.

The First Farmers of Eastern North America

So it was that Native Americans began domesticating plants in eastern North America. Local crop plants became important economically during the so-called Hopewell period, which extended from 100 BC to AD 400. This period is named after a huge Ohio mound that was excavated in the nineteenth century. These people—some of the earliest of North America's Mound Builders—built large, impressive geometrical earthworks and conical burial mounds for what must have been elaborate burial ceremonies. Hopewell became the "umbrella" name for a Pan-Indian religion, to describe a situation in which linguistically and culturally distinct people shared the same basic beliefs and symbols. For centuries, Hopewell was a dominant force across eastern North America.

Because both burial mounds and domesticated plants are found earlier in Mexico than in southeastern North America, archaeologists once thought that the practice of mound building and

agriculture must have arrived together from Middle America. But, as in the American Southwest, there is no direct evidence that any group ever moved north from Mexico. Maize and beans arrived in the east from the American Southwest at different times, so it seems unlikely that they were introduced directly from Mexico.

For years, most archaeologists considered the Hopewell economy to be strictly based on maize. Now, however, with more precise dating methods available, we know that the earliest maize in eastern North America dates from only about AD 100. These new insights are important, because they make it clear that neither the development of Hopewellian society nor the rapid shift towards agriculture that took place in eastern North America can be attributed to the importation of corn from Mexico. For centuries, maize was only a minor, almost negligible, addition to already well-established food resources. The extraordinary Hopewellian accomplishments in the areas of agriculture, religion, and culture must have been solely the result of local ingenuity and inventiveness—the culmination of thousands of years of human experience.

How did such a remarkable agricultural system evolve? The use of any particular plant crop was extremely localized, depending on the ecology of the local area. In some places, foragers relied little

EASTERN NORTH AMERICA
Key archaeological sites of eastern North America. The massive earthworks at Poverty Point date to about 200 BC. The earliest burial mounds were raised by the Adena culture, after about 500 BC. The remaining sites date from the Mississippian tradition (AD 700 to AD 1500).
CARTOGRAPHY: RAY SIM

☙ The sunflower (*Helianthus annuus*) was domesticated in eastern North America by 2000 BC.

SUPERSTOCK

households located along a stream or river valley. In some parts of the fertile floodplains, such as those surrounding the lower Illinois River, small settlements formed loosely knit villages.

But the cultivation of food plants that could be stored simply provided a buffer against food shortages. Foraging and the hunting and gathering way of life remained important and were by no means replaced by agriculture.

At the time that Hopewellian societies began to extend the boundaries of their river valley fields, their horizons expanded dramatically in other ways. Across the eastern woodlands, small farming settlements were clustered around centrally located ceremonial sites, where various seasonal rites took place. These sites varied considerably in form. Today, the only archaeologically visible clues to the location of such places are the low earthen domes built over the graves of revered people.

☥ The flawlessly modeled Serpent Mound, an earthen religious effigy extending for 210 meters (690 feet) in Adams County, Ohio. The serpent is wriggling northwards, mouth agape, trying to swallow a massive egg.

☛ A carved stone animal effigy from the Hopewell period, found in Ohio.
HILLEL BURGER/ROBERT S. PEABODY MUSEUM OF ARCHAEOLOGY

☥ A Hopewell snake effigy made of mica, from Hamilton County, in Ohio.
HILLEL BURGER/ROBERT S. PEABODY MUSEUM OF ARCHAEOLOGY

on cultivated plants, but in general the broad mid-latitude riverine zone, stretching from the edge of the Appalachian Mountains west to the prairie margin, became a homeland to these early food producers, who cultivated several high-yield, highly nutritious local crops. These people grew squash, marshelder, sunflower, and goosefoot, as well as erect knotweed, maygrass, and a little barley. Modern experiments have demonstrated the economic potential of these indigenous eastern North American crops.

From about the beginning of the first century AD to AD 200, Hopewellian settlements remained small, generally comprising one to three

But these sites were not just places of death. They were also the scenes of lavish feasts and other activities that brought together families scattered across the countryside. Along the rivers of northern Mississippi and northern Alabama, people built and maintained flat-topped earthen mounds that elevated the ceremonial above the everyday world. These mounds foreshadowed the later and much larger Mississippian pyramids. Elsewhere, earthen embankments, often very large and testifying to remarkable engineering skill, surrounded such ceremonial platforms, setting them apart. In south central Ohio, elaborate earthen banks extended for hundreds of meters, forming octagons, circles, and squares, at once defining and protecting these sacred precincts.

The Ascendancy of Maize

The centuries between AD 800 and AD 1100 saw a dramatic shift in American agriculture. The Mississippi people began to look beyond the traditional cultivation of native plant crops and to focus on a single, nonindigenous species— maize. In time, corn would come to dominate both their fields and their lives at such places as Etowah, Moundville, Angel, Hiwassee Island, Spiro, and Cahokia.

Across eastern North America, this concentration on growing corn led to the emergence of more complex sociopolitical structures. Maize would support the evolving Oneota peoples of the Great Lakes, the Iroquoian confederacy of the Northeast, and the Fort Ancient settlements along the middle Ohio River Valley, as well as the diverse range of Mississippian chiefdoms that emerged along the river valleys of the Southeast and Midwest. It would be maize that later sustained the Creek and Choctaw to the south, the Mandan and the Pawnee of the Plains.

Maize had dominated agriculture in the Southwest from the time it was introduced via Mexico, but in the east, more than six centuries elapsed between the time that maize was introduced as a minor cultigen and its becoming a major crop. This lag can be partly explained by genetic modifications to the plant itself. About AD 1000, a new variety of corn, known as eight-row maize, was developed in eastern North America. Frost-resistant and specifically adapted to the short growing seasons, this new breed of corn quickly spread to the northern latitudes, and by the time of European contact, it dominated Native American agriculture across the Northeast, the Ohio Valley, and the Great Lakes.

Imported or Homegrown?

One critical question remains: was agriculture in the New World invented completely independently, or was the idea in some way imported from the Old World?

Most archaeologists would agree that New World farmers developed in relative isolation from Old World influences. With two exceptions, all New World cultigens were domesticated from native American species, which strongly suggests that American agriculture developed independently. These two exceptions—gourds and cotton—are important and instructive. Possibly Old World imports, they became extremely important in the Americas.

The bottle gourd is one of the most ancient cultivated plants in the New World, perhaps because of its usefulness as a container for transporting food and water during preceramic times. The problem lies in identifying the wild ancestor of bottle gourds. Many botanists argue that gourds are native only to Africa. Specimens that were either gathered from the wild or cultivated have been found in very early Mexican and Peruvian sites, so it may be that gourds arrived in South America with African explorers in very early times. Alternatively, because gourds can float in sea water for nearly a year, they may have drifted across the Atlantic from Africa.

The archaeological evidence reveals that cotton was domesticated in Mexico some time before 3000 BC, and cotton textiles were being produced along the Peruvian coast by 2500 BC. Mexican and Peruvian cottons are different species, and were probably domesticated independently from local varieties. But there is a genetic complication: both Mexican and Peruvian cottons can be explained only as hybrids of local varieties and African cotton. To some investigators, cotton provides clear-cut evidence of deliberate trans-Atlantic contact. Others, seeking more "independent" explanations for Old World and New World agriculture, point out that African wild cotton could have drifted across the Atlantic and hybridized with New World species without human intervention, perhaps even before humans arrived in South America.

Setting aside bottle gourds and cotton as possible exceptions, current evidence clearly indicates that American Indian agriculture was an indigenous New World achievement, in which outside influences played no significant part.

An autumn assortment of squash and gourds from New England. Recent research has shown that some of today's cucurbits were domesticated in Mexico. Others, including virtually all the summer and acorn squashes, were first domesticated in eastern North America, about 2000 BC.

Looking across the prehistoric landscape at Mound City Group National Monument, near Chillicothe, Ohio. This is the most famous Hopewell site, where ancients buried their dead beneath these earthen mounds, often accompanied by fine pottery, elegantly carved stone pipes, and opulent jewelry. The 5 hectare (13 acre) compound is surrounded by a rectangular earthen embankment.

THE CHACO PHENOMENON

DAVID HURST THOMAS

Ｎ EARLY A THOUSAND YEARS AGO, the Anasazi people living in the Chaco Canyon of northwestern New Mexico developed one of the most progressive and prosperous social systems in prehistoric North America. By means of a complex ritual and economic network, dozens of formerly autonomous communities united to pool their strengths in this precarious environment.

Black-on-white ladles from Pueblo Bonito.

P. HOLLEMBEAK/J. BECKETT/ AMERICAN MUSEUM OF NATURAL HISTORY

Archaeologists now estimate that perhaps 6,000 Anasazi people lived in Chaco in AD 1100. For six generations, this now-remote region was the heart of the Anasazi world. By AD 1130, nine towns, each containing hundreds of rooms, dominated a 15 kilometer (9 mile) stretch of Chaco Canyon. The largest of these, Pueblo Bonito (Beautiful House), was once five stories high and could house a thousand people. America would

From the twelfth century, Chaco architects had tried to shore up the cliff behind Pueblo Bonito. But on 21 January 1941, a massive limestone slab known as Threatening Rock tumbled downwards, the rubble crushing 65 excavated rooms in the northeastern section of the site.

THE SOUTHWEST
Important archaeological sites and culture areas in the southwestern United States. The three major cultural traditions, Anasazi, Hohokam, and Mogollon, can each be subdivided into numerous time periods, and several local variants have also been identified.

CARTOGRAPHY: RAY SIM

This black-on-white pitcher, about 18 centimeters (7 inches) high, was found at Pueblo Bonito. Pitchers such as this were produced between AD 1075 and AD 1200.

P. HOLLEMBEAK/J. BECKETT/AMERICAN MUSEUM OF NATURAL HISTORY

GEORGE H.H. HUEY

Construction of this unusual triple-walled, circular structure behind Pueblo del Arroyo has been tree-ring-dated to AD 1109. Some archaeologists think that it may have been built by migrants from the north, who brought Mesa Verde-like architecture to Chaco Canyon.

TOM TILL

Farmers of the New World

♠ Although Chacoan society lacked money, turquoise beads probably served as status symbols and items of portable wealth. These are some of the 2,300 beads and small pendants recovered from a single room at Pueblo Bonito.
P. HOLLEMBEAK/J. BECKETT/AMERICAN MUSEUM OF NATURAL HISTORY

STEVE MULLIGAN

☞ One of the 12 kivas (ceremonial rooms) at Chetro Ketl, just down the road from Pueblo Bonito. The great curving wall had special niches, each filled with strings of stone and shell beads and then sealed with masonry. In the center of the floor is a raised square firebox flanked by a pair of rectangular masonry vaults (perhaps foot drums). Constructed between the early eleventh and early twelfth centuries AD, Chetro Ketl, at its peak, had several stories, with 200 to 225 ground-floor rooms and a total of 550 rooms.

AMERICAN MUSEUM OF NATURAL HISTORY

not witness a larger apartment building until the Industrial Revolution of the nineteenth century.

The Chaco people built arrow-straight roads running hundreds of kilometers into the surrounding desert, the longest and best-defined of which—probably built between AD 1075 and AD 1140—are more than 80 kilometers (50 miles) long. In places, the Chacoans constructed causeways, and elsewhere they cut stairways into sheer cliffs. The

☜ The ages of these black-on-white pitchers, all found in a single room at Pueblo Bonito, vary considerably.

generally straight bearings of these constructions suggest that the works were carefully planned and engineered.

Because the Chaco Anasazi did not use wheeled carts or draft animals, one wonders why the roads were so wide and straight, and what they were used for. Although some of the shorter roads connect Chaco Canyon with quarries and water sources, the function of the longer roads—whether for trade, processions, hauling building materials, defense, carrying food, or simply ease of travel for what must have been a great deal of traffic—remains unknown.

More than 600 kilometers (400 miles) of well-built roads connected Chaco to outlying settlements, probably reflecting extensive regional alliances. Several related mesa-top signal stations have been found, which provided line-of-sight communication, presumably by smoke, fire, or reflected light.

Archaeologists believe that the Anasazi systematically packed up their possessions and left Chaco Canyon about AD 1150. Various reasons for this have been put forward, but it probably resulted from a complex interaction between such factors as drought, soil erosion, crop failure, human overpopulation, disease, and low-level warfare.

Modern Pueblo people believe that the Anasazi left Chaco because the serpent deity—the god in charge of rain and fertility—mysteriously abandoned them. Helpless without their god, the people followed the snake's trail until they reached a river, where they once again built houses.

Four centuries later, the incursions of the Spanish explorers were witnessed by 50,000 Pueblo people living in more than a hundred towns along the margins of the San Juan Basin and the Rio Grande drainage area. These Pueblo people were the descendants of the Chaco Anasazi.

⬆ The frog was a symbol of water in Anasazi culture. This jet effigy is 8.5 centimeters (about 3 inches) long.
AMERICAN MUSEUM OF NATURAL HISTORY

GEORGE H.H. HUEY

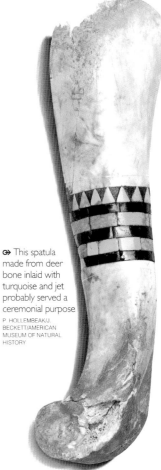

↪ This spatula made from deer bone inlaid with turquoise and jet probably served a ceremonial purpose
P. HOLLEMBEAK/J. BECKETT/AMERICAN MUSEUM OF NATURAL HISTORY

↞ Doorways in Pueblo Bonito, with the original roof beams still in place. More than 200,000 such support timbers were used in buildings throughout Chaco Canyon, each beam having been carried by hand from the mountains, a distance of at least 65 kilometers (40 miles).

398

WHY ONLY SOME BECAME FARMERS

1 1 , 0 0 0 B C – A D 1 5 0 0

A Global Overview

NOEL D. BROADBENT, GÖRAN BURENHULT, AND MOREAU MAXWELL

THE TRANSITION FROM hunter-gatherer to farmer was one of the most sweeping events in the history of humankind. Most experts today agree that the impetus for this transition came from need rather than desire. Such a fundamental shift in the way of life led to major changes in social structures, and to the development of new religious systems—farmers' gods were different from those of hunter-gatherers. Increased sedentism created entirely new settlement patterns, and at the same time, population growth increased. Mobile hunter-gatherers have to restrict their group size, both for practical reasons—you cannot carry more than one child at a time during long journeys— and in order to be able to survive when times are harsh. In a farming economy, on the other hand, as long as virgin land is available, more hands mean that more crops can be grown and more cattle raised, thus starting an endless circle of population growth leading to a demand for more food.

◄● The people along the mighty Sepik River, in Papua New Guinea, are one of the few New Guinean populations that do not depend on farming for their livelihood. Instead, these settled riverine people subsist by gathering plants, fishing, and hunting, sago being their main source of food.

☝A Sub-Neolithic flint arrowhead from Finland.

The developing farming tradition was accompanied by a number of new phenomena. With increased population pressure came the need to control personal territory, and this created the risk of conflict. For the first time, evidence of aggression appears in the form of fortified settlements and ceremonial combat weapons—symbols of power and dominance. With this new emphasis on strength and aggression, women's status declined. In many places, inequality between the sexes had its roots in the social organization of the established farming societies.

With large numbers of people living in the same area for long periods, problems of hygiene arose that were unknown to mobile hunter-gatherers. As time went on, the farming way of life also led to a far less balanced and less nutritious diet than that enjoyed by hunter-gatherers. The quality of stored food deteriorated as a result of infestation by rats and other vermin, creating a breeding ground for new, deadly strains of bacteria. Epidemic disease appeared for the first time.

☝ A Mesolithic ice pick made of elk bone, from Kirkkonummi, in southern Finland.
NATIONAL BOARD OF ANTIQUITIES, FINLAND

♀ Traditional hunter-gatherer societies still exist on the remote Andaman Islands, in the Bay of Bengal. Here, a man of the Onge tribe, on Little Andaman Island, is fishing with bow and arrow. The ocher paste on his face serves as both a decoration and an insect repellant. At the turn of the century, there were 672 Onge; now, they number only about 100.

At the Crossroads

Farming communities were much more vulnerable to climatic fluctuations than were hunter-gatherers. The possibility of storing grain and keeping domesticated animals led to a false sense of security. There was, of course, a reserve if crops failed; but this meant drawing on next year's seed for sowing, thus depleting stocks and paving the way for future catastrophe. Being dependent on a limited range of foodstuffs, farming communities found it difficult to withstand times of adversity. Farming and herding

were also vastly more labor-intensive than hunting and gathering. Why, then, did people become farmers at all? And why did a number of peoples around the globe never adopt any form of farming? Only by understanding why people in certain parts of the world became farmers, can we understand why others didn't.

At the end of the nineteenth century, it was thought that farming emerged as a way of life during the period known as the Neolithic for the simple reason that it was in every respect a superior way of life to hunting and gathering. Some individual, so it was believed, hit upon the brilliant idea of planting a seed in the ground in order to avoid having to wander around to find food. In the 1930s, the Australian archaeologist V. Gordon Childe put forward what appeared to be a more credible explanation in his so-called Oasis Theory, which postulated an event of such profound significance that he called it the Neolithic Revolution. He suggested that a period of extreme drought in Southwest Asia at the end of the last glacial period forced people to gather at the few oases and river valleys that remained, where their close association with animals and plants led to the process of domestication. Thus agriculture was born.

But Childe's theory was not supported by later studies of Neolithic settlements, which were established in a range of different climatic and environmental settings. Robert Braidwood's work during the 1940s paved the way for a less rigid approach. He suggested that farming emerged largely in response to the ever-increasing cultural differentiation and specialization within different populations—in short, it was a matter of people adapting to local conditions. The oldest farming communities known are found in the so-called Fertile Crescent of Southwest Asia (the region stretching from the Levant, through the present-day states of Syria and Iraq, to the Zagros Mountains). In the early stages of these settlements, Braidwood found clear signs that people had specialized in hunting aurochs and wild sheep, and in gathering the wild grasses that were the prototypes of the later cultivated cereals, as far back as glacial times.

Barbara Bender, on the other hand, has argued that it was predominantly social factors that lay behind the changes characteristic of the Neolithic period, such as the development of more complex, hierarchical societies with a wide-ranging network for the exchange of goods between different regions. Parallel to the rise of food production, status symbols and other artifacts came to play a crucial role in these societies.

In various places throughout the world, a series of farming communities developed independently of each other, according to local conditions. In Southwest Asia, for example, wild prototypes of barley and wheat provided

RAGHUBIR SINGH/JOHN HILLELSON AGENCY

ANTHONY BANNISTER/NHPA

the basis for an emerging agricultural economy. Corresponding developments in North Africa were based on millet; in South and East Asia, on rice, and in central America, on corn. Similarly, different types of animals were domesticated in different parts of the world.

The Crisis That Never Was

The fact that the transition from hunting and gathering to farming took place at roughly the same time in many parts of the world indicates that similar factors lay behind the process. But one thing is certain: the late glacial and Mesolithic hunter-gatherers had a much more complex social system (one that had its roots in the Upper Paleolithic period), and engaged in much more specialized subsistence activities, than was previously assumed. It was in these Mesolithic hunting-gathering communities, with their relatively limited tribal territories, that the conditions for developing a system of food production were most favorable. Their knowledge of local food resources was very sophisticated. For example, there is evidence that Mesolithic hunter-gatherers in western Europe cleared forests

to facilitate the hunting of deer as early as about 6000 BC. At the same time, the dog was domesticated, and even different species of deer may have been kept as domestic animals.

It is a common misconception that hunter-gatherers must live in straitened circumstances, on the brink of starvation and malnutrition. One should keep in mind that present-day hunter-gatherers are restricted to regions such as semideserts and arctic areas—the least hospitable regions on Earth. Modern studies of such societies have shown that the opposite is the case, and that they normally have a very stable supply of food, often with a large surplus. The !Kung Bushmen of the Kalahari Desert, in Botswana, whose technology is similar to that of the Mesolithic hunter-gatherers of Europe, provide a good example. In this dry desert area, they not only successfully manage their food supply, but can also afford to be very selective when gathering edible plants. It has been estimated that the !Kung collect and eat only about one-quarter of the plant species available, and that they spend only two or three hours a day searching for food—less than 20 hours a week.

A Bushman aiming his poisoned bone arrow at an animal in the dry grass stands of the Kalahari Desert, in southern Africa. The Bushmen, sometimes called the San, live in small, scattered, mobile bands. Their most common prey are antelopes, including gemsbok, springbok, wildebeest, and eland.

JOHN DOWNER/PLANET EARTH PICTURES

In front of a dome-shaped grass hut, a Kalahari Bushman collects plants. Bushman bands number between 30 and 60 people.

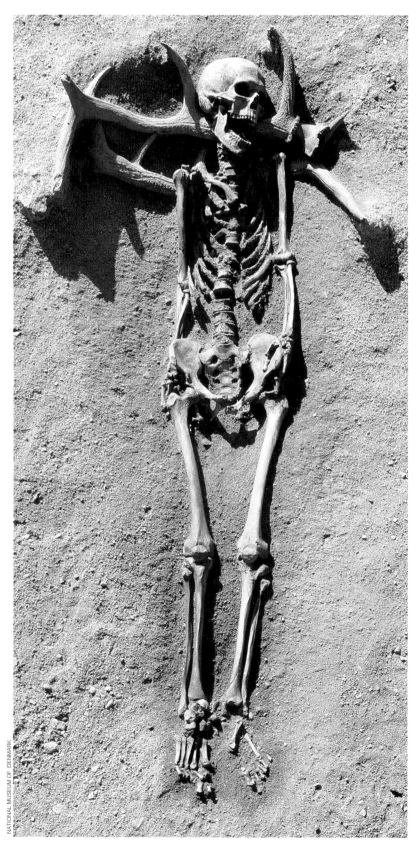

It is clear that the changed climatic and environmental conditions at the end of the last glacial period were one of the main reasons for the rapid development of new economic systems all over the world. In most cases, this process was probably not voluntary. A combination of many different factors gradually forced people to actively produce food to meet the demands of growing populations. In particular, the Mesolithic hunter-gatherers who lived along the coasts of northwestern Europe can give us an insight into the reasons why people left their hunting, fishing, and gathering way of life, and became farmers.

From Mesolithic to Neolithic

About 6000 BC, the so-called Atlantic period began in western Europe. This was the warmest period after the last glacial, with average temperatures reaching several degrees above those of today. Dense deciduous forest covered the land. There was an abundance of big game, including boar, deer, and bears, as well as smaller animals. Lakes and rivers teemed with fish, and in coastal regions, fish, seals, mussels, and shellfish were plentiful. These were some of the richest resource areas on Earth. Having such a rich and varied supply of food, these people were less vulnerable to fluctuations in the availability of any one foodstuff.

The territory within which these Mesolithic societies moved shrank in size once they no longer needed to cover great distances in pursuit of big game. It has been estimated that the population density during this period was about 1 to 20 individuals per square kilometer (less than half a square mile). Contrary to earlier beliefs, then, the shift to farming did not represent an improvement in people's living conditions. A few hours of gathering per day was replaced by perhaps 10 hours of toiling in hard soil. In addition, gathering food for domesticated animals demanded a great deal of work. As supplies of food became uncertain, people began, for the first time, to suffer from starvation and disease. Yet within 2,000 years, these Mesolithic peoples had become farmers.

◀ One of the spectacular Mesolithic burials at Vedbæk, near Copenhagen, in Denmark, dating back some 7,000 years. An old woman, aged about 50, had been placed on her back, with her head and shoulders resting on two red-deer antlers—possibly reflecting an association between age and high status in the Mesolithic communities of northern Europe.

Paradoxically, it was mainly in resource-rich areas of the world that farming communities developed. Arctic regions were obviously unsuitable for farming and herding, as were desert areas and tropical rainforests. The only way to survive in these areas is to adapt to the existing environment. As a rule, this requires people to live in groups small enough to be sustainable, and to undertake long seasonal migrations.

The abundant food supply enjoyed by European Mesolithic communities usually led them to adopt a completely settled way of life, a combination that always leads to population growth. By about 5000 BC, the first farming communities had been established all over central Europe, with the exception of coastal western Europe. In spite of close contacts between farmers inland and hunter-gatherers on the coast—as evidenced, for example, by the latter's adoption of pottery and polished stone axes—it was almost another thousand years before these coastal

☝ Numbering between 150,000 and 200,000, Pygmies live in small bands scattered across the rainforests of equatorial Africa. They subsist by hunting and gathering, but have developed a close system of cooperation with their farming neighbors.

↩ Members of a Bushman band on the move through the Kalahari Desert, carrying their few belongings with them.

☗ Dating from about 2800 BC, this Pitted-ware grave at the settlement of Ajvide, on the island of Gotland, in Sweden, contained the remains of a 20-year-old woman. She was dressed in a skirt that had been decorated with seal teeth. Five left sides of hedgehog mandibles were found on her chest, together with the leg bones of cormorants.

peoples started to cultivate their land and herd animals. Until then, they clearly had not needed to exert themselves in time-consuming farming activities. By about 4300 BC, however, the Neolithic era was firmly entrenched, bringing to an end the agreeable life of the Mesolithic.

The same scenario was repeated in many parts of the world. Lending support to the ecological explanation is the fact that some farming communities, for ecological reasons, actually reverted to a hunter-gatherer economy. For instance, the first farming community in eastern Sweden, the so-called Vrå culture, was established shortly after 4000 BC. About 3000 BC, a cooler and moister climate (known as the subboreal period) led to a marked increase in the supply of marine foods, especially seals, in the Baltic Sea. The early farming economy that had been established in this region disappeared, and its practitioners instead founded a rich hunting-gathering community, known as the Pitted-ware culture, after their distinctive pottery. This was based mainly on fishing and seal hunting, but some elements of the earlier farming economy were retained, notably domestic pigs.

This very clear-cut Scandinavian example shows how rapidly people adapted to changing ecological conditions in order to secure their food

☗ Seals, mainly harbor and gray seals, were the mainstay of the Pitted-ware economy. Enormous amounts of seal bones have been unearthed in the settlements, along with quantities of pig, fish, and wildfowl bones.

☗ As the name implies, Pitted-ware pottery is characterized by deep pits in the surface. Some researchers have suggested that these pits had some practical purpose, while others think that they were simply decorations.

☞ The limestone cave of Stora Förvar ("Great Repository") on the island of Stora Karlsö, off the coast of Gotland, in the Baltic Sea. During Pitted-ware times, some 5,000 years ago, the cave was used as a seasonal settlement, where seals, fish, and birds' eggs were the main sources of food.

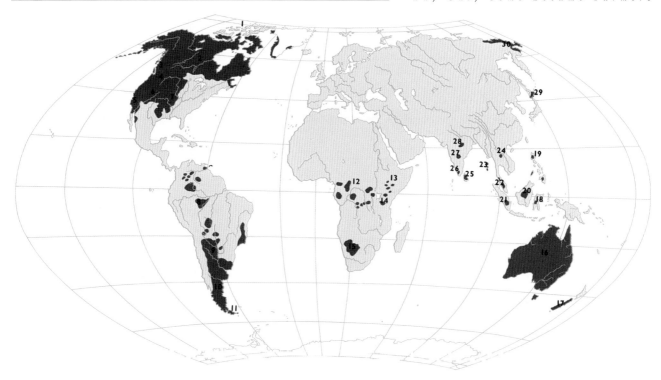

supply. We are thus able to understand not only the complex and richly varied Neolithic process that took place throughout the world, but also the survival of those hunter-gatherer communities that managed to live in a state of ecological balance, not expanding beyond the land's capacity to support them in their traditional way of life—a situation that at the same time fostered social stability.

The majority of the hunting-gathering peoples that have retained their original way of life are to be found in isolated marginal areas, where climatic conditions are extreme. What characterizes all these societies is that they have adapted to their particular environment in highly specialized and often sophisticated ways. Such peoples include the Bushmen of southern Africa and the Pygmies of the central African rainforests, as well as a number of peoples on the Indian subcontinent and in Southeast Asia, such as the Birhor, the Andamanese, and the Semang.

Two regions, where hunter-gatherers with richly varying economies have existed into modern times, stand out as exceptions within this scattered picture: Australia and North America. For thousands of years, the Australian Aborigines have adapted both to some of the world's most arid deserts and to resource-rich coastal areas, notably in northern Australia. Similarly, the North American Indians and Inuit (Eskimos) have shown a remarkable ability to adapt to a range of different environments, from coastal areas in the Pacific northwest to forests, deserts, and arctic tundras.

GÖRAN BUREENHULT

☝ The aboriginal populations of the Malay Peninsula include the Semang, the Senoi, and the Jakun. They still subsist mainly by hunting and gathering, but in recent times, the Jakun, in particular, have partly adopted agriculture. The main hunting weapon is a wooden blowpipe, such as this one used by a Jakun hunter at Tasek Chini, in Peninsular Malaysia.

HUNTER-GATHERERS

The areas marked are those where hunter-gatherer populations have existed in historic times—generally in extreme environmental conditions.
CARTOGRAPHY: RAY SIM

1 Eskimos
2 Subarctic Indians
3 Northwest Coast Indians
4 Plateau Indians
5 California Indians
6 Great Basin Indians
7 Plains Indians
8 Amazon basin hunter-gatherers
9 Gran Chaco Indians
10 Tehuelche
11 Fuegians
12 Pygmies
13 Okiek
14 Hadza
15 Bushmen
16 Australian Aborigines
17 Maori
18 Toala
19 Agta
20 Punan
21 Kubu
22 Semang
23 Andaman Islanders
24 Mlabri
25 Vedda
26 Kadar
27 Chenchu
28 Birhor
29 Ainu
30 Chukchi

POPPERFOTO/SPORTING PIX

☗ Ainu men in front of their settlement in Hokkaido, Japan. The vanishing Ainu have followed their traditional hunting-gathering way of life until recent times. Some anthropologists believe them to be the descendants of Jomon peoples who lived in Hokkaido and northern Honshu, while others have suggested that they constitute an independent Paleoasiatic ethnic group.

The Jomon: Fishers and Potters

The comparatively late arrival of farming along Europe's Atlantic coast, where the climatic changes at the end of the last glacial period ensured an abundant supply of marine foods for the taking, has direct parallels in many other parts of the world. The salmon-fishing Indians along North America's northwestern coasts developed a complex system of chiefdoms (which is uncharacteristic of hunter-gatherer societies, most of which are not hierarchical), and never adopted any form of farming or herding. In northern Japan, an abundance of marine resources shaped one of the earliest and most distinctive fishing cultures known.

The people who crossed the Beringia land bridge during the last glacial period and settled the New World originated from the eastern Siberian hunter-gatherer communities that roamed the harsh tundras around the valley of the Aldan River. Between 18,000 and 12,000 years ago, the so-called Dyukhtai tradition evolved there. But not all of these Siberians made their way northeast towards the Chukchi Peninsula and Alaska. About 13,000 years ago, when the melting ice sheets raised the sea level, drowning many coastal areas, a number of peoples settled along coasts and lakes

☛ Dating from the late Jomon period, this elaborately ornate clay mask may have had some ritual significance.
UNIVERSITY MUSEUM/UNIVERSITY OF TOKYO

further south, in eastern Asia. As the land area shrank, coastal regions became more important, and the warmer climate also allowed deciduous forests to spread, providing additional sources of food. As in Europe, in areas where food resources were abundant, people settled within limited territories. The Jomon were one of these peoples.

The Jomon communities, including those on the island of Honshu, largely depended on the abundant local supplies of shellfish and salmon, supplementing their diet with animals such as red deer and wild boar, and plant foods such as nuts, acorns, and edible seeds. This hospitable environment led them to adopt a settled way of life as early as 13,000 years ago. As a result, the Jomon were the first people to make pots—and somewhat later (about 11,000 years ago), also figurines and masks—of burned clay. The tiny clay figurines usually depict female figures, so-called *dogu*, and were probably used in some kind of fertility cult.

To date, more than 10,000 Jomon settlements have been discovered. Most are in Honshu, and such sites as Fukui, Kamikuroiwa, and Sampukuji have yielded some of the oldest finds of pottery. All of the settlements bear witness to similar cultural traditions, but there is also a marked degree of regional adaptation to different environments. Subsistence was tightly linked to the changing seasons. The earliest settlements are found beneath rock shelters or consist simply of pit houses. These were replaced after about 5000 BC with larger wooden houses, which were well built and had elaborate fireplaces.

During the course of the long-lasting Jomon tradition, plants were cultivated to a limited extent in some areas, primarily different species of *Echinochloa* and *Perilla*. Other kinds of domesticated plants, such as bottle gourds and mung beans, were probably introduced from the south. These Neolithic introductions mainly occurred in western Honshu, whereas the communities in the richer coastal regions of the northwest maintained their original way of life.

About 3000 BC, the colder climate of the subboreal period began to affect Japan. Coastal resources once again became increasingly important, and cultivation in western Honshu declined. About 1500 BC, the Jomon people of Kyushu, in the south, started to cultivate wet rice and buckwheat, whereas the original Jomon tradition survived until as late as about 300 BC in northern Honshu and Hokkaido. In Hokkaido, some populations continued their 14,000-year-old way of life until about AD 800.

Göran Burenhult

← This Jomon clay figurine, or *dogu*, dates from the third or fourth century BC. Most of these *dogu* depict female figures, and it has been suggested that they were used in some sort of fertility cult.
WERNER FORMAN ARCHIVE

→ A late Jomon ritual site at Tabara, in Tokyo, Japan

MARK J. HUDSON/AUSTRALIAN NATIONAL UNIVERSITY

ARCTIC HUNTERS AND FISHERS OF EURASIA

♨ A drawing of a rock carving at Zalavruga, near Belomorsk, in Karelia, Russia, showing three men on skis. Settlements in the vicinity of this rock art site have been dated to about 2000 BC to 1500 BC.
GÖRAN BURENHULT

FENNOSCANDIA, c. 8500 BC TO 3500 BC
➷ The arrows indicate the earliest migration routes into northern Norway, Sweden, and Finland. The early sites mentioned in the text are shown, and the shaded areas indicate cultures.
CARTOGRAPHY: RAY SIM

♀ Early settlers favored sites such as this shallow lake in Finnish Lapland, where waters rich in oxygen and nutrients provided a reliable supply of fish, one of the Arctic's most important food sources.

H uman cultural adaptation to arctic conditions developed during the Paleolithic period, more than 20,000 years ago. Vast numbers of Pleistocene (Ice Age) animals supported human populations at the southern margins of the continental ice sheets in Europe. From Siberia, which was largely untouched by these ice sheets, there was an open route to North America across the Bering land bridge—the gateway to the New World.

The Arctic Environment

The key to survival in arctic regions was not merely obtaining food, but being able to withstand temperatures as low as minus 46 degrees Celsius (minus 50 degrees Fahrenheit) for weeks at a time. Without minutely sewn, watertight, and insulating clothing made from animal skins, humans could never have done this. This kind of clothing was made possible by the invention of the bone sewing needle during the Paleolithic period. Technology in general (housing, transport, heating, and so on) also had to be adapted to treeless environments that were covered by snow and ice for most of the year. The Arctic is, in fact, a vast desert surrounding a frozen ocean, and for these reasons arctic cultures are among the most specialized that humans have ever developed.

Arctic regions have low temperatures throughout the year, with average summer temperatures of no more than 10 degrees Celsius (50 degrees Fahrenheit). Under such conditions, the ecosystem is characterized by low

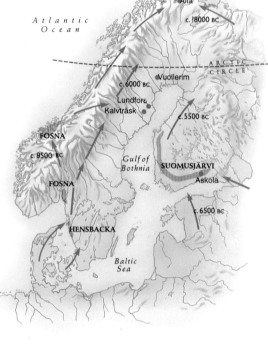

productivity, with few species of plants and animals. People settled where supplies of fish and game were good, close to rivers and estuaries rich in oxygen and nutrients, and along coasts that were free of ice for part of the year. The most important sources of food in the Arctic were fish, seals, whales, and reindeer (caribou in North America). In the Subarctic, elk (moose in North America), beaver, and birds were more important, although reindeer, which migrated into the forests after grazing on the tundra or in the high mountains during the summer, were also hunted.

Remarkably, farming was introduced to a limited extent as early as 2500 BC in areas with maritime climates, such as northern coastal Norway, Sweden, and Finland. But hunting, fishing, trapping, and berry collecting remained the economic mainstays in these regions well into the twentieth century.

Early Settlement in Scandinavia and Finland

Scandinavia and Finland, which were deglaciated less than 10,000 years ago, became the last stronghold of European hunters who depended on arctic and subarctic resources. While these hunting societies were in some respects similar to those that had disappeared thousands of years earlier in Europe, it must be kept in mind that these northern cultures coexisted with, and were influenced by, the Neolithic, Bronze Age, Iron Age, and Medieval cultures evolving in western Europe and European Russia at that time.

🔸 Mesolithic spearheads or knives from Finland made of polished slate. Flint does not occur naturally in northern Scandinavia and Finland, so quartz and slate were utilized instead.

The earliest settlements in Scandinavia are found along the western coasts of Sweden and Norway. These cultures—known as Hensbacka in Sweden, and Fosna and Komsa in Norway—go back as far as 9000 BC to 8000 BC. Although reindeer were hunted in the highlands of southern and northernmost Norway, the people who lived in these settlements depended largely on marine resources, such as seals, whales, fish, and sea birds. In this regard, they were similar to the Paleoeskimo societies that spread across arctic areas of North America some 3,000 years later.

By 6000 BC, hunters had penetrated the interior of the Scandinavian peninsula as far north as the Arctic Circle. The remains they left behind in the archaeological record are similar to those of the Mesolithic peoples of northwestern Europe. They made microliths and small axes of flint and flint-like stones, and larger tools of bone and elk (moose) antler, including fishing harpoons and fishhooks, as well as wooden and bark equipment, such as net floats, bows, traps, and dug-out canoes.

The Nordic region was also settled from the east and southeast. As in Norway, the oldest sites in Finland are associated with ancient beaches. In southern Finland, the Askola and Suomusjärvi cultures were based primarily on seal hunting, which became the economic foundation of coastal societies throughout the Baltic region.

In northern Sweden, indigenous inland and coastal cultures developed during the period from 5500 BC to 2000 BC. Communities of 60 or so people lived all year round on the coasts, combining seal hunting with fishing and the hunting of elk and beaver. At the Lundfors site, by the Skellefteå River estuary, burned bones and thousands of net sinkers indicate that ring seals were caught by means of extensive seal-netting systems. At a well-preserved settlement at Vuollerim, the remains of four semisubterranean (pit) houses, 11 meters (36 feet) long and 4 meters (13 feet) wide, have been excavated. These were winter houses, which provided shelter for three or more families each season.

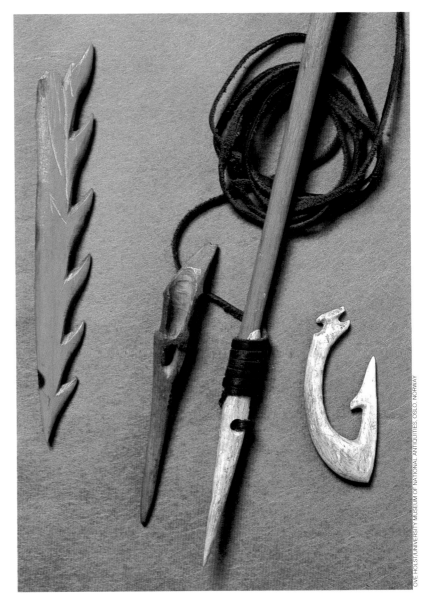

🔸 Much hunting and fishing equipment, including harpoons, points, and fishhooks, was made of wood or bone, but these materials are rarely preserved in archaeological sites. Such artifacts are best preserved in peat bogs, clay, or limestone-rich soils. Here, one of the points has been reconstructed as a harpoon head.

🔹 Sub-Neolithic net sinkers made of stone, juniper, and birch bark from Kangasala, in southern Finland. Nets were used to catch both fish and seals.

⚓ This polished black slate knife from the Lundfors site, in northern coastal Sweden, dates from about 3500 BC.
NOEL D. BROADBENT

NATIONAL BOARD OF ANTIQUITIES, FINLAND

⚓ Stone sinkers and bark floats from a wicker fishing net dating from about 9000 BC that was preserved in clay at Antrea, in Finland.

⚱ Flint arrowheads from Finland, dating from about 3000 BC.

In the inland areas, dwellings were built partly of mounds of burned and cracked stones and clustered in groups of between two and five huts, each cluster inhabited by a single hunting band. The main winter food was elk, which were captured by means of hunting pits.

The cutting tools these people used were made of polished slate and flaked quartz. The same local materials were used in Finland, although unusually beautiful red and green slate tools from northern Sweden and Norway were widely circulated.

Coastal sites in northern Norway from about 4000 BC to the beginning of the first century AD are marked by rows of depressions that once formed the floors of pit houses—up to 80 at a single site. Permanent villages grew up in succession on the same sites. Later villages were built on beaches at lower elevations and closer to the changing shoreline. These differences in elevation have provided archaeologists with a means of dating prehistoric settlements throughout the north. Because northern shorelines were displaced at the end of the last Ice Age as the deglaciated land rebounded, we know that the higher the elevation of a coastal site, the older it must be.

Recently discovered rock carvings from Alta, in northern Norway, have been dated in this way. These carvings depict the animals the people of the time valued and the rituals associated with them. The subject matter of this rock art, which includes rock paintings in other areas, is remarkably similar to that of the Paleolithic cave artists of France and Spain, 32,000 to 12,000 years ago. Shamanism—human mediation with nature and animal spirits by special individuals, known as shamans—is the most characteristic belief system among northern peoples, from the Saami of Scandinavia to the Greenlanders.

N. BURENHULT

Domestication of Reindeer

Farming cultures influenced the northern hunters and fishers in various ways. The Finnish groups, for instance, began to make pottery as early as 4200 BC, using large vessels to prepare and store food. But they did not farm or raise animals, and are therefore referred to as sub-Neolithic. By about 2500 BC, true farmers had moved up the Scandinavian coasts to above the Arctic Circle. Although probably only marginally successful at farming, they did introduce the concept and techniques of animal domestication. Similar contacts took place between herders and northern hunters in Siberia about the same time. This contact probably led to the domestication of reindeer, which was to become one of the most characteristic aspects of northern cultures in Eurasia. It is interesting to note that the oldest skis in the world, from Kalvträsk, in northern Sweden, also date from about 2500 BC. Without skis, reindeer herding would have been practically impossible.

NATIONAL BOARD OF ANTIQUITIES, FINLAND

NOEL D BROADBENT

These images of deer at the isolated rock art site of Vingen, in Sogn og Fjordane, western Norway, are usually thought to date from about 1000 BC, but could be much older. In these northerly areas, people continued to follow a hunting-based, Mesolithic way of life until well into the Bronze Age.

The rock carvings found at Alta, in northern Norway, depict both the animals important to the people of the time and the rituals associated with them—subject matter remarkably similar to that of the Paleolithic cave art of France and Spain.

A Lapp herder tends a reindeer flock in Norway. Reindeer were probably tamed about 2500 BC, perhaps under the influence of Scandinavian herders who had migrated above the Arctic Circle by this time.

Reindeer can be tamed and bred like sheep and goats. Tame reindeer were primarily used, however, as decoys to attract wild reindeer, for pulling sleds, and for milking. Large herds of semidomesticated reindeer were not kept for their meat until late Medieval times. Until then, the indigenous people of Lappland, the Saami, were still hunters and fishers, not unlike their Stone Age forebears. Siberian people such as the Nenets, the Evenki, the Yakuts, and the Chukchi also combined traditional hunting and fishing with the benefits of domesticated reindeer.

To this day, reindeer are one of the Arctic's most productive land resources. Northern seas, likewise, are among the richest fishing waters on Earth. It is therefore not surprising that indigenous peoples living today throughout the circumpolar North are very protective of their right to continue to exploit these resources, which have under-pinned their way of life for thousands of years.

Noel D. Broadbent

BRYAN AND CHERRY ALEXANDER/NHPA

⚲ These Thule artifacts were among those recovered from a site on the east coast of Ellesmere Island, northwest of Greenland. In the center are two small female fetishes carved from ivory, and to the left is a harpoon head.

⚲ This ring of stones held down a skin tent at a Thule camp site at Cape Copeland, on Shannon Island, north-eastern Greenland. A sleeping platform can be seen at the back of the ring, on the right.

⊙➤ This small Thule pit house excavated on the south shore of Baffin Island has been partly reconstructed by retying the ten pairs of bowhead whale ribs that formed the roof rafters.

THE THULE CULTURE

The Arctic culture known as Thule emerged from the Birnirk culture of northern Alaska about AD 900. Centered on the hunting of huge bowhead whales, which weigh between 30 and 40 tonnes (about 30 to 40 tons), it appears to have spread rapidly eastwards, reaching the sea coasts of the Canadian Arctic, Greenland, and Labrador by the fifteenth century.

This migration took place during a warm period, when Norse settlers were also moving through ice-free waters into Iceland and on to settlements in southern Greenland. The warmer temperatures may have reduced the ice in Beaufort Sea and opened gulfs and channels to the east that allowed whales to migrate. Warmer winters would also have meant that fewer snow caves were available in the west as birthing dens for ring seals, on which the Birnirk people depended. No evidence of whale hunting has emerged from Birnirk sites, and whale-hunting technology may have come from the Punuk Islands, in the Bering Sea, where people had hunted whales for nearly a thousand years.

The earliest appearance of the Thule culture in the eastern coastal regions, during the middle to late eleventh century, may have overlapped with the occupation of the region by people of the indigenous Dorset culture. Because the latter disappeared suddenly, it was thought that the

Thule culture displaced it. More recent evidence, however, suggests that this culture may have collapsed, for unknown reasons, a century or two before the Thule arrived.

The most useful means of determining the relative ages of Thule sites has proved to be examining the progression in the style of harpoon heads. The distinctive decorated type known as Sicco, frequent in Punuk sites and rare in Birnirk sites, has been found in some eastern sites, suggesting a route for what may have been the earliest eastward migration. Whale hunters would have traveled across western waters to Barrow Strait and Lancaster Sound, and then north through Smith Sound to the east coast of Ellesmere Island and northwestern Greenland. Finds from sites in the middle of the eastern shore of Ellesmere Island, from the so-called Ruin Island Phase, tend to support this hypothesis. Named after a small island between northern Greenland and eastern Ellesmere Island, these predominantly Thule sites have yielded Sicco harpoon heads and a few other types of artifacts with Punuk characteristics, together with woolen cloth, boat rivets, and links of chain mail armor, the latter items suggesting the presence of Viking explorers. Radiocarbon dating places these finds in the late twelfth and early thirteenth centuries, a period consistent with Norse accounts of northern voyages from settlements in southern Greenland.

To the south, finds from earlier Thule sites seem more characteristic of the Birnirk-derived Thule culture. This suggests a migration from the Point Barrow region of northern Alaska about the late eleventh century, and a second wave a century later (characterized by the Ruin Island Phase) from regions of western Alaska strongly influenced by the Punuk culture.

A typical Thule dwelling—a pit house 3 meters by 3.5 meters (10 feet by 12 feet), dug 2 meters (about 6 feet) deep into the earth on the side of a hill—was lined with large boulders, whale skulls, and bones, rather than the driftwood so common in the west. Roof rafters of whale jaws would have been covered with walrus skins, sods of earth, and rocks. A sleeping platform of flat rock slabs was raised about 46 centimeters (18 inches) above the floor, for warmth. Since cold air flows downwards, a tunnel 3 to 6 meters (10 to 20 feet) long, sloping up the hill and ending in a deeper cold trap, gave access to the stone-paved living area through the floor. Large soap-stone lamps, with cotton-grass wicks fueled by seal oil, provided light, as well as heat for cooking in soapstone bowls.

On the evidence of a few scenes engraved on ivory tools, whale-hunting teams probably consisted of three or four kayakers, plus a harpooner and paddlers traveling in a large, skin-covered umiak. Once a detachable harpoon head was sunk into a whale, lines attached to inflated sealskins were thrown out to prevent the whale from sounding, and the creature was then dispatched with lance thrusts to its vital organs.

But whales were probably seldom taken. Seals, walrus, caribou—and virtually all of the other animals, birds, and fish of the region—were more common prey. The Thule used a wide range of hunting equipment, including disarticulating harpoons, thrown by hand or by means of a throwing board, with the head and line attached to floats. Caribou were stalked with weak, sinew-backed bows, or driven between the converging sides of rock piles shaped like human figures (called inuksuit). Sleds drawn by four to six dogs extended the Thule hunting grounds onto snow-covered sea-ice. Familiar headlands and mountain peaks provided aids to navigation.

The Thule people made a vast range of tools and implements with specific functions. There were knives for butchering, carving, and cutting blocks of snow; the characteristic crescent-shaped woman's knife (ulu); and needles, thimbles, and needlecases. Most useful was the bow drill, a tool still in use well into historic times.

In the cooler thirteenth century, sea-ice reduced breathing space for the great whales. The Thule abandoned their deep, winter pit houses for snow houses built on the sea-ice, where seals could be hunted at their breathing holes. The homogeneous whale-hunting Thule culture was replaced by more specialized regional variants, from which emerged the traditional "tribes" of the Inuit (or Eskimos) of historic times.

Moreau Maxwell

Thule hunters drove caribou between drift fences called inuksuit, made from piles of rocks. The inuksuk (singular) shown here is on Kulusuk Island, in southeastern Greenland.

The bow drill was a bow-shaped piece of ivory or antler tied at each end by a thong wrapped around a wooden spindle tipped with a piece of stone. The opposite end of the spindle was set in a socket, held in the teeth. The sawing action rotated the spindle. Hard walrus ivory was drilled with a series of holes to allow segments to be broken off and made into harpoon heads and foreshafts.
MOREAU MAXWELL

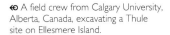

A field crew from Calgary University, Alberta, Canada, excavating a Thule site on Ellesmere Island.

THE INUIT MUMMIES FROM QILAKITSOQ

C. Andreasen and J.P. Hart Hansen

Close to the old and abandoned settlement of Qilakitsoq, in northwest Greenland, a stunning discovery was made in 1972: two graves were found containing eight mummified Inuit clothed in animal skins. They were buried about AD 1475, making them the oldest and best-preserved find of people and garments from the Thule culture, the immediate ancestors of the present-day Inuit population in the eastern Arctic.

There were two children—a child of 6 months and a boy of about 4 years—and six women, ranging in age from about 18 to 50. All wore two layers of clothes of similar design and materials: the jacket, trousers, and boots are of sealskin, while the warm inner jacket is made of bird skin from five different bird species, and the stockings are of caribou skin. Inuit people's ability to survive in the harsh Arctic climate is primarily due to their skilful use of fur for clothing, a material that provides excellent insulation by preventing loss of body heat in the cold while allowing excess body heat generated during physical activity to be dispersed.

Most seemed to have been healthy, the adults having an average height of about 151 centimeters (4 feet, 10 inches). Some diseases were present, including an extensive cancer of the nasopharynx, a kidney stone, a few fractures, parasites, and a case of hip disorder and, probably, Down's syndrome. The cause of death could not be established in all cases, and it was impossible to determine with certainty whether the bodies had been interred at the same time. Tissue typing indicated that the group was probably closely related and consisted of three generations.

The adults' faces were finely tattooed with curved lines on the forehead, cheeks, and chin. These tattoos closely resemble those on 2,000-year-old figurines from northern Alaska—providing a tantalizing glimpse of a thousand-year-long spiritual tradition not evident from the Inuit material culture.

☸ This 6-month-old baby and a boy of about 4 years were found lying on the belly of their presumed mother, who was about 25 years of age. The sealskin jacket and trousers are sewn together at the waist. The hood can be tied with the cord that ends at the top of the head, thus preventing the child from accidentally strangling itself.
JOHN LEE/NATIONAL MUSEUM OF DENMARK

THE GREENLAND NATIONAL MUSEUM AND ARCHIVES

THE GREENLAND NATIONAL MUSEUM AND ARCHIVES

Around the site, about 40 stone graves were built on bedrock. Only the two mummy graves were built on a slope of loose stones under an overhanging rock, thus providing protection from the sun, rain, and snow as well as good drainage. Combined with the arid and cold High Arctic climate, these factors kept the bodies dry and well preserved. One grave contained three adults and two children; the other contained three adults. The adults were wrapped in sealskins and were lying on top of each other. Apart from 26 pieces of skin and garments, no other grave goods were found.

The sand beach in the sheltered bay provided excellent landing facilities for the fragile skin boats of the Thule culture. Several ruins of houses made of local turf and stone indicate that the site was primarily used in winter. At this time of year, ring seals were caught at their breathing holes in the ice. In the summertime, people hunted the seals, whales, and birds that were abundant in the area. The mountainous areas to the south of the settlement were caribou hunting grounds.

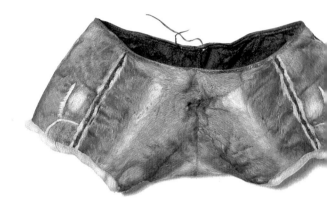

♀ The front of a pair of shorts elaborately made of 48 pieces of caribou skin joined together in a symmetrical pattern. This pair is very worn at the back, above the buttocks. Like other Inuit trousers, they are tied at the back by cord in a casing at the waist.

THE GREENLAND NATIONAL MUSEUM AND ARCHIVES

♂ The front of a very handsome pair of sealskin shorts, made of two symmetrical halves with a center seam; each half consists of 20 pieces. Unlike the caribou shorts, these show no signs of wear. The leg openings are remarkably narrow.

THE GREENLAND NATIONAL MUSEUM AND ARCHIVES

♀ Wrapped in a sealskin, this 25-year-old woman—presumably the baby's mother—wears an inner bird-skin jacket with a very long edging of caribou skin, an outer jacket, short trousers, sealskin boots, and caribou-skin stockings. Her thighs are naked. The caribou edging of the inner jacket covers the exposed flesh between the very low-sitting shorts and the outer jacket.

THE GREENLAND NATIONAL MUSEUM AND ARCHIVES

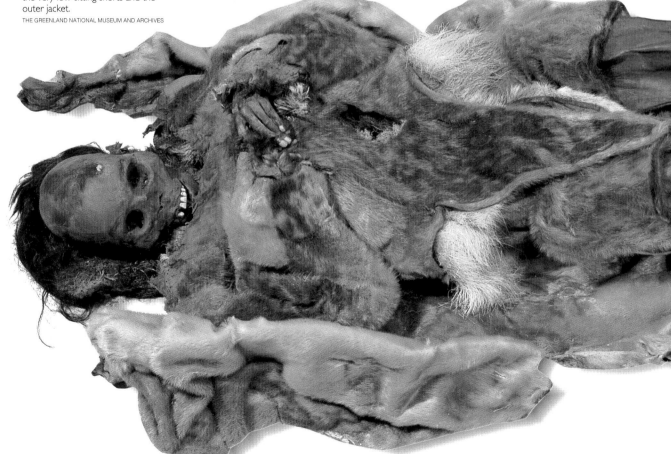

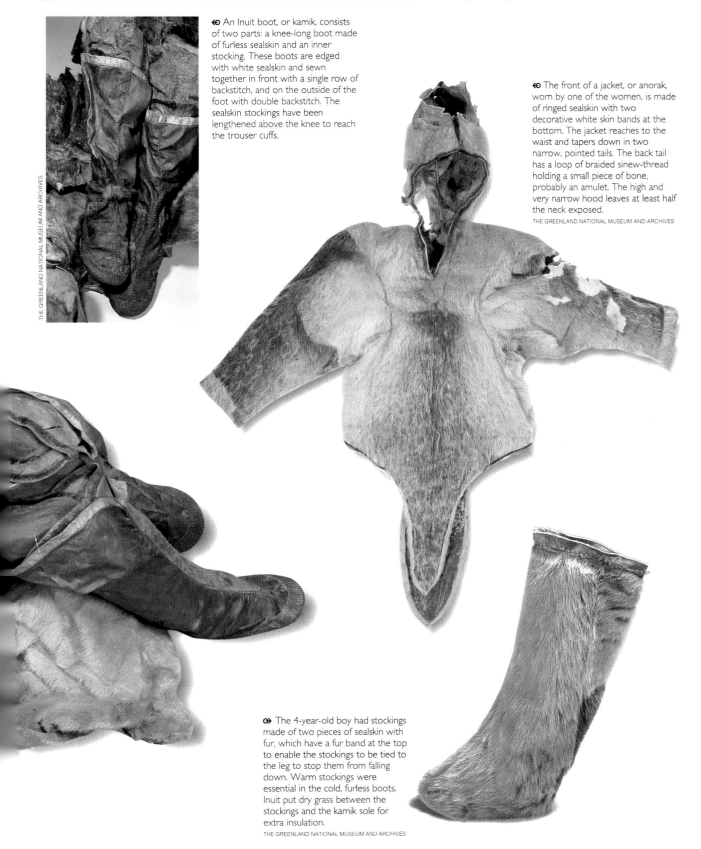

An Inuit boot, or kamik, consists of two parts: a knee-long boot made of furless sealskin and an inner stocking. These boots are edged with white sealskin and sewn together in front with a single row of backstitch, and on the outside of the foot with double backstitch. The sealskin stockings have been lengthened above the knee to reach the trouser cuffs.

THE GREENLAND NATIONAL MUSEUM AND ARCHIVES

The front of a jacket, or anorak, worn by one of the women, is made of ringed sealskin with two decorative white skin bands at the bottom. The jacket reaches to the waist and tapers down in two narrow, pointed tails. The back tail has a loop of braided sinew-thread holding a small piece of bone, probably an amulet. The high and very narrow hood leaves at least half the neck exposed.

THE GREENLAND NATIONAL MUSEUM AND ARCHIVES

The 4-year-old boy had stockings made of two pieces of sealskin with fur, which have a fur band at the top to enable the stockings to be tied to the leg to stop them from falling down. Warm stockings were essential in the cold, furless boots. Inuit put dry grass between the stockings and the kamik sole for extra insulation.

THE GREENLAND NATIONAL MUSEUM AND ARCHIVES

AUSTRALIA: THE DIFFERENT CONTINENT

1 0 , 0 0 0   B C   –   A D   1 8 0 0

An Aboriginal History

J. PETER WHITE

IN MANY PARTS of the world, it is useful to draw a sharp distinction between the Pleistocene and Holocene periods. In northern Europe, for instance, the last Ice Age ended rapidly about 10,000 to 12,000 years ago, and the major environmental changes that took place at this time had a significant impact on human life.

Throughout most of Australia, this boundary cannot be drawn as sharply, and the effects of environmental changes on human behavior can be seen only over longer time periods. Only in Tasmania and the highlands of New Guinea did extensive cold grasslands and shrublands give way to forests. The change that affected most people was the rise in sea level, but in most places the sea rose steadily over thousands of years—dramatic events like the formation of Bass and Torres straits, which separated first Tasmania and then New Guinea from Australia, were rare. It was not until about 4000 BC that the sea reached its present level, drowning much earlier evidence of coastal life. Even after the "end" of the Ice Age, about 8000 BC, climatic change continued. Some areas of southern Australia, for example, were a little warmer and wetter from 6000 BC to 3000 BC than they are today, allowing more people to occupy some inland lake areas.

Natural fire is endemic to much of Australia, and many plants depend on it for regeneration. Aborigines capitalized on this, using fire for thousands of years to "clean up the country", killing off dangerous animals and cooking edible ones in their burrows and nests.

Grindstones were used to convert the seeds of wild grasses into flour throughout many drier parts of the Australian continent.

A. FARR/AUSTRALIAN MUSEUM

MODERN AUSTRALIA

Australia has had its modern-day shape only since the sea reached its present level about 4000 BC. The majority of Aboriginal people lived around its well-watered eastern and northern margins, as Europeans do today.

CARTOGRAPHY: RAY SIM

⇨ *Opposite:* The shells in a midden usually reflect the immediate environment, since people nearly always eat shellfish close to where they are caught. The Lizard Island middens, in the Great Barrier Reef, are made up of the shells of shellfish that live on rocks and in coral crevices.

The area discussed in this chapter covers a range of environments, from subtropical to subtemperate (10 to 44 degrees South) and from rainforest to arid desert. We know that the societies that recently inhabited these 7.6 million square kilometers (almost 3 million square miles) spoke a variety of languages and lived their lives within a wide range of economic, political, and social structures. This suggests that Australian prehistory of the last 12,000 years should be looked at on a regional or even a local level in order to encompass this variety, but there is no space for that here. There is also a broad view to be obtained by focusing on particular aspects of the Australian past, and on some puzzles.

The Present and the Past

For the last 400 years, since the first European, Willem Jansz, landed on the western coast of Australia, white people have continually remarked on the fact that no Aboriginal people seemed to be farmers, gardeners, or pastoralists. Their apparent lack of defined fields, edible domestic animals, or settled villages allowed Europeans to see Aboriginal country as unproductive and unowned, available for whites to claim and colonize.

The European belief that Australia was a continent of wandering hunters and gatherers, inferior people who did not own or use their land, is still widespread. This is quite simply wrong. There is clear evidence that different territories had well-defined owners, who nurtured the plants and animals within them in different ways and to varying degrees. European misconceptions arise because Aboriginal ways are not the same as those of Europeans. Many Aboriginal methods of using the land and its products are known only from relatively recent accounts—of early European visitors, anthropologists, and Aborigines themselves—since they are not of the kind that leave clear traces in the archaeological record.

The use of fire is a good example. In AD 1788 (the date of the first European settlement), Aborigines were observed to use fire in many parts of the country to "clean it up", to open pathways, to burn off dry vegetation to encourage new growth, to kill animals that were either food or vermin, and to prevent more destructive fires later. Their extensive knowledge of local environments allowed Aborigines to predict and control the extent, direction, and effect of these burn-offs. Thus, over time, these fires were used to create a mosaic of various vegetational environments that encouraged some plant and animal diversity. The Aborigines' use of fire was, and in some areas still is, widespread and frequent enough to constitute a land-management program—but a very different program from that of European Australians, most of whom view all fires as dangerous and a threat to life and landscape.

Aborigines had different ways of looking after useful plants, too, which in some areas occurred in such profusion that they resembled orchards or gardens. For example, it is hard to read explorer George Grey's statements about the western coast of Australia having, in 1841, "well marked roads, deeply sunk wells and extensive warran [yam] grounds" without concluding that Aborigines practiced organized gardening without fences. Other practices included the transplanting of useful trees, diverting small streams to irrigate areas of edible grasses, and digging to encourage roots to spread. It is such patterns of behavior that have led many scholars to argue that Aborigines in some parts of the country, at least, depended on agriculture for their livelihood.

How far back in time did these forms of behavior occur? This question is not easy to answer, because such things leave few traces in the archaeological record. It is difficult to trace the use of fire back very far—how are we to distinguish fires lit by Aborigines from those that occur naturally, often as a result of lightning strikes? There is at present no convincing evidence of the long-term or large-scale alteration of habitats as a result of firing. This does not mean it did not occur, especially in localities where Aboriginal firing would have enhanced naturally occurring trends towards the fire-dependent environments that are quite widespread in southern Australia. And, given that Aboriginal people knew how to make fire and that they had

GRAHAME L. WALSH

a very long-term relationship with particular areas of country, it seems very likely that they began to manage their environment many thousands of years ago, possibly from the time of their arrival, although the methods used probably became more sophisticated over the years.

Similar problems arise in trying to trace the history of plant use. Aboriginal methods of managing edible and useful plants do not substantially alter the local environment in the long term. As with the use of fire, a long history of refined techniques of management is to be expected, but is hard to prove.

The recognition of these problems is particularly important in relation to Australian prehistory, where the absence of large-scale changes in technology and the material culture encourages us to think of Aborigines as living off the land without owning or affecting it. Such beliefs are incorrect.

KATHIE ATKINSON/AUSCAPE

Harvesting the Sea

The continent of Australia gradually took on its present form as the sea rose towards today's level. As it did so, it flooded Bass Strait, separating the people of Tasmania from their close Australian relatives by many kilometers of stormy ocean. Tasmanians remained isolated from the rest of the world for more than 8,000 years. The rising sea had other effects as well. The most visible to us is that it drowned some of the commonly used resources in certain areas. In the far southwest, for instance, artifacts made from a distinctive fossil-bearing rock known as chert are widely found in sites dating to about 4000 BC, and only in a recycled form after that time. Cores drilled into the seabed off the western coast of Australia in the search for oil have revealed a chert seam that would have been exposed in the earlier Holocene period.

Since the sea level stabilized about 4000 BC, evidence of early coastal life has survived in the form of shell middens, which are found around much of the coast. People certainly ate shellfish in earlier periods, but most of the evidence of this has been destroyed by the rising seas. Several sites in both Australia and New Guinea show that people were gathering and eating marine shellfish during the Pleistocene period, as far back as 30,000 years ago. All these sites are close to the sea today and in locations where deep water is close to the present shore, so that changes in the sea level would not have greatly affected their distance from shellfish beds. (People rarely carry

◆ Shell middens litter Australian coasts and are often the most visible signs of Aboriginal occupation. This one, at Princess Charlotte Bay, in northern Queensland, is on a large tidal mudflat.

GRAHAME L. WALSH

◆ This midden at Princess Charlotte Bay is some 20 meters (63 feet) high, and is the relic of thousands of visits to a favored shellfishing area. Radiocarbon dates show that such mounds can be formed in less than a thousand years.

ARCHAEOLOGY IN THE SELWYN RANGES

IAIN DAVIDSON

A S THE EXPLORERS Robert O'Hara Burke and William John Wills struggled through the summer heat to the south of the Selwyn Ranges in 1861, in their attempt to cross the Australian continent from south to north, Wills observed that "we found here numerous indications of blacks having been there, but saw nothing of them". This was the first recorded archaeological observation of the people who lived in the region. A few months later, the explorers themselves were dead of starvation, ignorant of how to survive there.

Exploratory parties sent to search for the missing Burke and Wills brought back favorable reports of this area of northwestern Queensland, and pioneer pastoralists and gold prospectors lost little time in moving in. Twenty years after the event, so many Aborigines had been wiped out by the murderous attacks of the pioneer pastoralists that tribal structures had been all but destroyed, but in the late 1890s the Queensland Protector of Aborigines, Dr Walter Roth, was able to record some surviving information about the material and social life of the various tribes of the region, such as the Kalkadoons. Although they contain a wealth of detail, his studies are, inevitably, an impoverished account of the rich currency of life in northwestern Queensland before the coming of Europeans. They provide a valuable framework for understanding some of the archaeological discoveries in the Selwyn region.

Roth describes much of the equipment used in daily life: stone tools, along with the wooden tools they were used to make; string bags and nets; pearl shells and necklaces; and much more—items that rarely survive in the archaeological record. He also describes the network of trade and exchange that crisscrossed the region, still operating at that time but completely broken down within 20 years. Of the many items exchanged or traded, four stand out: axes (probably traded as axeheads), the nicotine-based drug pituri, ochers, and ceremonies. These

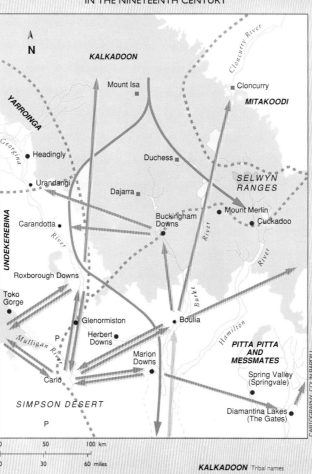

DISTRIBUTION OF TRADED GOODS IN NORTHWEST QUEENSLAND IN THE NINETEENTH CENTURY

KALKADOON
Mount Isa
Cloncurry
MITAKOODI
YARROINGA
Georgina
Headingly
Duchess
Urandangi
Dajarra
SELWYN RANGES
Carandotta
Buckingham Downs
Mount Merlin
Cuckadoo
UNDEKEREBINA
Roxborough Downs
Toko Gorge
Burke
Glenormiston
P
Boulia
Hamilton
Herbert Downs
Mulligan River
PITTA PITTA AND MESSMATES
Marion Downs
Carlo
Spring Valley (Springvale)
SIMPSON DESERT
P
Diamantina Lakes (The Gates)

0   50   100 km
0   30   60 miles

CARTOGRAPHY: COLIN BARDILL

KALKADOON Tribal names
☐ Land above 200 meters (650 feet)
☐ Land above 500 meters (1,600 feet)
● Station
■ Town
● Recorded exchange center
P Known pituri sources
⋯ Tribal boundaries (from Roth, 1897)
→ Movement of axes
→ Movement of pituri
→ Movement of ocher

☝ This finely woven bag was once used to carry pituri from the edge of the Simpson Desert to trading destinations. Such bags were often decorated with ocher.

☝ A pituri tree, *Duboisia hopwoodii*, on a dune on the northern margins of the Simpson Desert.

trading systems were essential to Aboriginal life in the region before that society was destroyed by the pastoralists. The challenge for archaeologists is to find out how trading systems emerged through the course of prehistory, and how the earlier inhabitants of the region managed without a trading system.

Axes made of stone mined from quarries near the present-day site of Mount Isa were traded to people all over a region extending from the Gulf of Carpentaria to the Great Australian Bight.

Pituri, made from the leaves and twigs of the shrub *Duboisia hopwoodii*, which grows in groves in sand dunes on the eastern

☝ Men painted with feathers for the Molonga ceremony at Boulia, 1895.

margin of the Simpson Desert, particularly around the Mulligan River, was traded in all directions over an area of 500,000 square kilometers (188,000 square miles). The trade was carefully regulated, the precious narcotic drug packed and carried in special pituri bags, finely woven and often elaborately decorated with ocher.

Roth notes that the Kalkadoons obtained ochers at markets held along the Georgina River. We cannot tell from his account whether the reciprocal trade was because of different properties of ochers in different regions or because the social act of trade was more important than the items traded. Roth also describes how yellow ochers (goethite) were roasted to turn them red. As he records it, painting was mainly used for body decoration and to decorate portable items. He scarcely mentions the rock paintings and engravings that now are the most visible signs of Aborigines' presence in the region long before 1861.

Roth also records how a cermony, the Molonga, originating to the northwest of the Selwyn Ranges, was traded year by year, ultimately making its way as far south as Adelaide, in South Australia, and as far north as Alice Springs, in central Australia. Roth's account provides much more detail than archaeologists can ever expect to find

archaeologically, but it also points to the need for archaeologists to look beyond mere utility in seeking to understand the prehistory of trade and exchange.

The Archaeological Evidence

The Selwyn Ranges mark the watershed between the creeks and rivers that drain into the Gulf of Carpentaria and those that drain south towards Lake Eyre (although few of their waters reach the lake). People have long made use of the rock shelters and overhangs formed by these ancient, weathered cliffs. Aborigines lived in this region many thousands of years before the Kalkadoons of Roth's time, and archaeological investigations are gradually revealing the antiquity and nature of prehistoric Aboriginal trading systems and the nature and associations of Aboriginal rock paintings and engravings.

Cuckadoo 1 is a rock shelter in an isolated block of heavily weathered granite. Fourteen radiocarbon dates relate to various periods of human occupation. These suggest that the site was first used more than 15,000 years ago, close to the period of maximum aridity in this region; that the site was again used about 12,000 years ago; that it was then used intermittently between 4000 BC and 1000 BC; and that there has been a series of recent occupations in the past 2,000 years. The dates also indicate that the site was not used during four periods, each lasting more than a thousand years. This is what might

be expected in Australia's unpredictable climate, with its rapid oscillations between drought and flood.

There is no evidence of painting or engraving in Cuckadoo 1, but fragments of yellow ocher were found at the lowest levels, and a pit for the heat treatment of stone artifacts, dated to 2300 BC, also contained red ocher possibly resulting from roasting goethite. As well as changing the color of ochers, heating made them more suitable for use as paints by destroying the mineral structure of the clays in the raw ocher.

The only guide to ancient trading networks that usually survives in the archaeological record is the movement of axeheads. Because they are usually made of raw materials that are easy to identify geologically, they can be traced to particular sources. Axeheads made of Mount Isa metabasalt have been found 250 kilometers (155 miles) away, hidden on the floor of a cave near Cuckadoo 1, but there is no way of dating them. Fragments of Mount Isa axes were found at Cuckadoo 1 in layers less than 1,000 years old. We have shown, therefore, that Mount Isa axes were not only traded in the Selwyn Ranges, but also used there. The dating of these fragments is consistent with other evidence suggesting a recent development of the trading systems.

Rock Paintings and Engravings

Few engravings in the Selwyn Ranges represent humans or other specific objects. Most motifs are geometric, often being based on circles and spirals, although some signs may represent animal tracks. The paintings, on the other hand, include more of what are called "figurative" signs, although it would be misleading to describe some of these signs as representational. At a few sites, engravings filled in with paint are found, and sometimes engravings and paintings are found together. There are also large numbers of hand stencils and non-figurative designs, including circles and meandering lines.

Several motifs are widely encountered throughout the region. Animal tracks, including those of macropods (kangaroos and wallabies) and birds (the latter in the form of tridents) are common in both paintings and engravings. It is clear that not all the bird tracks commonly called emu tracks should be interpreted in that way. Tom Sullivan, one of the Aboriginal men who is heir to traditional knowledge of the Selwyns, has identified some as nightjar tracks, others as brolga tracks.

The most distinctive motifs are called "Kalkadoon" figures. Some of these appear to represent ancestral beings, but others are unlikely to do so. Most have the appearance of a pair of broad "shoulders" and a rather featureless "head". The figures at some sites have no more features than this, while others are wearing headdresses.

Walter Roth photographed people, with feathering painted on their bodies and feathery headdresses, performing the Molonga ceremony at Boulia in 1895. These have some resemblance to these supposedly figurative rock paintings.

As Burke and Wills, conscious, perhaps, of their own place in history, observed the signs of the local inhabitants without seeing these inhabitants, they probably little realized that it was precisely those sorts of signs that would one day help to reveal the unwritten history of the land.

☝ A typical "Kalkadoon" figure from south of the Selwyn Ranges.

🐚 Freshwater shellfish, especially the mussel *Velesunio ambiguus*, flourish in the lakes and rivers of southeastern Australia. People have collected them for at least the last 30,000 years.

➤ *Opposite:* The East Alligator floodplain, Kakadu National Park, in Arnhem Land, northern Australia. Plant foods were the staple diet of most Aboriginal communities, and in the freshwater lagoons formed in the wet season, there grew a variety of plants with edible roots.

🔱 A shell midden on the Wudbud floodplain, in Arnhem Land. The present-day floodplains of Arnhem Land have evolved during the last thousand years, and the middens on them are the results of shellfish collecting since then.

shellfish very far before eating them.) They are all also cave sites, where environmentally fragile shells have lain protected until excavated by archaeologists. Freshwater shellfish were also commonly gathered in earlier times, and their remains are found around old lake and stream shores.

Although shell middens become common from about 4000 BC, they are not found in all coastal areas: in some cases, they were never there, and in others, they have been destroyed. In some areas, notably around the southwest of Australia, Aboriginal people did not eat shellfish (which caused explorer Nicholas Baudin to write a surprised note in his journal in 1803). Probably, shellfish were of no interest to people living around King George Sound, since other resources, including fish, were more readily available.

In other parts of Australia, people collected shellfish at some times and not others. One of the clearest examples of this is to be found at Princess Charlotte Bay, in northern Queensland. This shallow bay has been slowly filling up with mud and sand since about 4000 BC. By about 2000 BC, there was sufficient mud to support relatively large populations of the bivalve *Anadara granosa*, and from time to time some of these were pushed by exceptional cyclonic waves into mounds

(known as cheniers) on the southern shore. The largest cheniers were created first, with later ones being longer, narrower, and not continuous. This process ceased about 500 years ago, not because there were fewer storms, but because there were fewer shellfish. Aboriginal people collected *Anadara* from at least 2500 BC until recently, but large middens perched on top of cheniers are only about 2,000 to 500 years old, with the biggest about 1,000 years old.

The largest middens were not created at the same time as the biggest cheniers, as we might expect, but later. The conditions in Princess Charlotte Bay that made Aboriginal shellfishing easiest were not precisely the same as those favoring the creation of cheniers. The Princess Charlotte Bay case demonstrates that resources are not permanent and that Aborigines made use of what was available from time to time.

In other areas, there is good reason to believe that middens that used to exist no longer do so. Discovery Bay, for example, on the southwest coast of Victoria, has 80 kilometers (50 miles) of sandy beach backed by an extensive swamp and dune system. The present coast, however, is well inland of the coastline of 4000 BC. Paleo-environmental evidence has shown that the dunes, with swamps between them, were built up from 4000 BC to 2000 BC. After that, erosion began, possibly as a result of drier conditions, with dunes moving inland and one chain of swamps being destroyed by the sea. Peat that formed in these former swamps is exposed on the present beach at low tide.

In terms of their dates, shell middens at Discovery Bay nearly all fall into two groups. The smaller group comprises middens found on soils that were formed before 4000 BC, and nearly all middens on those soils date to that time. The larger group consists of younger middens dating to within the last 2,000 years; they lie on the dunes and swamps closest to the sea. Nearly all those from the intervening period have obviously been destroyed. Because of this, it is clear that middens are not a reliable guide to the human population in these areas at different times.

In Arnhem Land, on the other hand, the shoreline is advancing rather than retreating. The middens here, including those around the mouth of the Blyth River, are not more than 1,500 years old; many hectares of land, including favored camping places of the Anbara people today, have been above sea level for only this period.

A similar, but more complex, story, which has major implications for the history of local Aboriginal groups, has been traced in the floodplains of western Arnhem Land, especially along the South Alligator River. Here, as at Princess Charlotte Bay, the story is one of a river valley first filled by the rising sea and then reclaimed by floodplain muds. Middens

↪ *Opposite*: Canoes were common on the rivers, billabongs, and lakes of the interior. Small ones were made of a single section of tree bark cut out with stone hatchets and wedges and tied at the ends. The cut on this tree, in western New South Wales, has been partly covered by regrowth.

☿ Camps and dwellings were never permanent. Wooden frames covered with bark or grass were sufficient protection against the cold nights of interior Australia. These frameworks are probably about 150 years old.

composed of different varieties of shellfish occur throughout the period, but the major change in the area occurred since about 2000 BC, when extensive freshwater wetlands were first formed. The resources of these wetlands, including waterbirds and swampy plant roots, became the focus of many Aboriginal economies, with successive dry-season camps established along the edges of the wetlands and intensive production of stone tools for hunting and making numerous wooden artifacts. There is evidence that people transferred more and more of their activities from nearby rock shelters to the richer, open plains within the last thousand years.

Another example of how resources available to people could change has become apparent in the archaeological record of the last 2,000 years along the New South Wales coast. The common mussel, *Mytilus planulatus*, is found in shell middens in southern Australian and Tasmanian waters during the last 6,000 years, but represents only a very small percentage of middens north of 37 degrees South, except during the last 1,200 years or so. By the time of European settlement, it is found in quantity at some sites as far north as Sydney (34 degrees South).

Mussels are among the shellfish that have a free-floating stage in their life history; the chance distribution of young by the sea can play a major role in establishing new populations. Along the New South Wales coast, it seems likely that

mussels were established by chance over the last 2,000 years. Thickly clustered and easily gathered at low tide, they became a favored food of some Aboriginal people. The alternative explanation is that mussels were there all along, but were simply not collected, even though many other kinds of shellfish, some of them harder to gather, were collected. It is difficult to believe that this behavior would have been common to all the people living along this coast over a period of 1,200 years. There is, of course, a possible test: are mussels found in natural deposits, such as fossil beaches, in this area more than 2,000 years ago? We do not know, because this elaborate and expensive research has not yet been undertaken.

The final, and a most puzzling, situation involving the sea and its resources comes from Tasmania. Early Europeans there noted that the Tasmanians did not eat fish, although they did eat shellfish and crayfish. Several of the journals kept on Captain Cook's third voyage (AD 1777) record the Tasmanians reacting with "horror" or running away when fish that the Europeans had caught were offered to them. But Tasmanians had eaten fish until about 1500 BC: archaeological deposits dating from earlier times contain hundreds of fish bones. At least 31 types were caught then, including those that lived in both rocky reef and open-water (bay) habitats, although the former predominate. Most, perhaps all, could have been caught in traps in the form of a baited

J. PETER WHITE

box or a stone-walled basin filled by the tide.

This change in the Tasmanian diet occurred throughout the island over the span of a few hundred years or less, and suddenly at every site. It was clearly not caused by a shortage of fish, since colonies of fish-eating birds and seals continued to exist and be hunted by Tasmanians. No researchers have yet put forward a convincing environmental explanation, and it seems the answer must lie with the Tasmanians themselves. Whether the issue was one of simple dietary change (there was better food more easily obtainable elsewhere) or of religious belief is difficult to test. Many societies and religions have dietary restrictions, but both the suddenness of the change and the fact that it occurred throughout the island are surprising in the Tasmanian case.

How Many People?

Not all people lived along the sea coast, of course, although the richness and concentration of marine resources meant that population densities were high in these areas. Elsewhere, population density at the time of European contact, and probably in prehistoric times, was usually related to rainfall, with exceptions occurring along some major river systems such as the Murray. Like the Nile, this river flows in a fertile trench through very desolate surroundings for much of its length, and people living along it depended on rainfall in its headwaters rather than where they lived.

Determining population numbers of the past, especially among societies that do not settle in one location and do not build permanent houses, is difficult. Archaeological evidence is of limited use—while it can indicate the number of people who used a particular site over a certain period, it generally cannot reveal whether these people were all living at the same time. Nor are the number and distribution of stone and other artifacts much of a guide, since their presence in any area is related more to the availability of raw materials, the uses to which tools were put, and the chances of their survival than to the number of people. More useful are the remains of people themselves, although this evidence may be harder to interpret. For example, Steve Webb has recently shown that human bones from burials in the Murray River area have a much higher incidence of stress lines and other bone diseases related to a poor diet than do those from other sites. Elsewhere in the world, this is a feature associated with overcrowding in the early stages of communities settling in a particular area. This suggestion is lent some support by the fact that it is only along the Murray River that cemeteries are common, having been used, although not continuously, for the last 13,000 years. Groups of people often use cemeteries as a means of defining long-term ownership of an area, and such

KATHIE ATKINSON

overt markers of ownership become more important as population density increases.

On a different scale, we might ask what the Aboriginal population of Australia was at the time of European settlement and work back from there. The difficulty here is that during the early years of contact, Aboriginal societies were rapidly destroyed, both deliberately and through diseases, such as smallpox, to which people had no resistance. Estimates of the total Aboriginal population just before European settlement—about AD 1780—range from 300,000 to well over a million, with perhaps 600,000 being the best figure on current evidence. But should we think of this many people living in Australia for many thousands of years, or was this number reached only quite recently?

How we answer this question depends on our views as to how human populations grow and as to whether there have been any events in Australian prehistory that might have caused significant changes in population numbers.

Tools of the Past

Although they are not a guide to population density, the nature and distribution of stone tools can tell us several things about the prehistory of Australia. For example, they allow us to order sites chronologically, tell us something of the distribution of raw materials, indicate links between areas, and show how technology changed. Many researchers believe that they

🔱 Hatchet head from Gunbalunya (formerly Oenpelli), in Arnhem Land, northern Australia. Hatchets with stone blades ground to a sharp edge were made over most of the continent, although not in Tasmania. Sometimes, the blade was made from a suitably shaped river pebble, but stone was also quarried, and hatchet heads were traded for hundreds of kilometers.
C. BENTO/AUSTRALIAN MUSEUM

🔱 For a time, stone points were used as spearheads over a wide area of northern and central Australia. Many are made of silcrete, a rock that sparkles with tiny quartz crystals.
A. FARR/AUSTRALIAN MUSEUM

also hint at broader changes in Australian society from about 3000 BC on.

Throughout Australian prehistory, most tools consisted of flakes and pieces of stone with sharp edges appropriate to a variety of tasks. Tools were not formally shaped into regular patterns. An important exception to this was the manufacture of ground-edged hatchet heads, but these were found only in the tropical north, from at least 25,000 years ago.

At least three major changes in stone tools have occurred within the Holocene period. First, hatchets with ground stone heads came into use throughout continental Australia. The heads—all that survives—are found only in association with the two other changes described below, and their spread is thus dated from about 3000 BC. Why they spread at all, and only at this late date, is

✏️ Backed blades, shaped like a penknife blade, were probably used as the points and barbs of spears. In a few sites, they have been found in their thousands, suggesting frequent retooling.
A. FARR/AUSTRALIAN MUSEUM

a puzzle. Hatchets seem to have been used for similar purposes throughout the country—wood-working, including making wooden artifacts; collecting honey and possums by enlarging holes in trees; and similar lightweight tasks. They were not suited to heavier work such as chopping down trees, even if this had been desirable. It is unlikely that people were not engaging in these activities earlier than 3000 BC, so there must be other reasons why hatchets spread. Since in the recent past they were frequently painted and exchanged with neighbors, and many were made of stone available from only a few quarries, elements of prestige, value, and power may have been attached to these artifacts.

The second change is that people in northern Arnhem Land started to make finely shaped spear-points from about 3000 BC. From the beginning, points were flaked on one or both sides, sometimes by pressure rather than percussion, which gives more control and produces a flatter flake. Stone points similar to these were used until the nineteenth century to tip spears, being replaced by metal in the twentieth century, when glass specimens were also made for sale to tourists and collectors. Once again, it is hard to find a simple functional explanation for the existence of these tools, since effective spears were certainly in existence before stone points were made. Whether the new points were more effective for hunting is hard to test, as is the idea that they developed as a component of more precisely balanced spears that could be thrown further and more accurately with the aid of a woomera (the Aboriginal name for a spear-thrower, a common weapon among hunter-gatherers that extends the power and length of the throwing arm). In some Arnhem Land sites, different raw materials, especially quartzite, became more common at about the same time as points start to appear. Some of this new stone came from specific quarries, which again suggests that exchange systems were developing, with associated concepts of prestige and exchange value playing an important part in the making and spread of these points.

Stone points have been found throughout northwestern Australia, being common for several

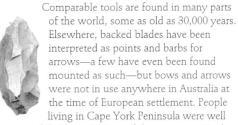

Comparable tools are found in many parts of the world, some as old as 30,000 years. Elsewhere, backed blades have been interpreted as points and barbs for arrows—a few have even been found mounted as such—but bows and arrows were not in use anywhere in Australia at the time of European settlement. People living in Cape York Peninsula were well aware of their cousins' use of these weapons in the Torres Strait islands and New Guinea, but they never adopted them. In Australia, backed blades were probably used as points and barbs on spears. This is confirmed to some extent by the resin found on the back or base of some tools, used to haft them in wood, as well as by the many discarded blades with broken tips found at some sites.

◄ Australian adzes are heavy stone flakes (left), usually about 5 centimeters (2 inches) across, set in resin on the end of a slightly curved wooden handle. With use, they chip, and then need to be resharpened. When one side becomes too blunt and steep for use (center), the stone is taken out of the resin and reversed. When that side likewise becomes too blunt, the adze "slug" (right) is discarded.
A. FARR/AUSTRALIAN MUSEUM

hundred kilometers inland. They are also found in smaller numbers through the center of the continent almost as far as the south coast, but only from 2000 BC to 1000 BC. It looks very much as if they were initially popular, being distributed

P.G. FOX/THE QUALITY IMAGE

◄ In much of interior Australia, stone tools, along with the debris that results from making them and local stones collected for hearths, comprise most of the archaeological record of Aboriginal societies. Little is preserved of bones and shells in such environments. This site is at Mootwingee, in western New South Wales.

♀ Grinding stones used for seeds, sharp-edged flakes and the cores from which they were struck, adze slugs, and a few points constitute the range of stone artifacts found in central Australia. The items shown here are from the Amadeus basin, near Uluru (formerly Ayers Rock), in the Northern Territory.

and copied over a wide area, and subsequently became restricted to the original area. This makes it unlikely that they were designed specifically for use with spear-throwers, since spear-throwers were widespread.

The third major change was the development of backed blades—long thin flakes that are blunted (or backed) by chipping away one edge—which are today found over the southern two-thirds of Australia. They are small tools, less than 5 centimeters (2 inches) long, the oldest, dating to between 2000 BC and 2500 BC, having been found in south central Queensland. Like points, they are found right across the continent within a very short time, but unlike them, they are found in their thousands at some sites.

Backed blades come in a variety of shapes, from long, thin points to squat geometric forms.

REG MORRISON

ART OF THE ESCARPMENTS: IMAGE-MAKING IN WESTERN ARNHEM LAND

Paul Tacon

Aboriginal people believe that image-making has always been central to their way of life. Whether it be through rock painting, body painting, or the decoration of portable objects, the process of painting allowed these people to tap into the power of their ancestral past. As well, the painting process reaffirmed their links and affinity with the landscape and, through the use of specialized clan designs, with each other. The resulting "sense of being" helped them in making decisions and formulating plans of action. More importantly, images could be used to pass on complex cultural knowledge from one generation to the next.

🔹 In western Arnhem Land, hand stencils of important people who had died were often filled in with clan designs as a mark of honor. This stencil is from Kakadu National Park.

The Antiquity of Image-making

The Aborigines of western Arnhem Land believe that their ancestors, the first people, were taught the skills and techniques of painting on rock by Mimi spirits. They believe that the Mimi also produced the earlier, monochrome styles of rock painting in the area, including the dynamic figures. These paintings differ from the more complex polychrome forms produced most recently, in the past few centuries. Archaeological research shows that the basic pigments used for image-making have been in use for possibly 50,000 years. Ground pieces of red ocher (hematite) have been found in every level of stratified deposits located in large rock shelters. This does not mean that the practice of rock painting dates from such early times or that paintings were executed at a constant rate. It does show, however, that ochers were consistently used and that some form of image-making or painting activity, the results of which have not survived, has taken place throughout the period this region has been occupied by humans.

The earliest rock paintings in western Arnhem Land are believed by many archaeologists to be at least 18,000 years old, but there is still considerable debate. Most of the art, however, can more confidently be placed in the Holocene period. Research is now being directed towards dating the art more precisely, and within a few years we will be able to assess its antiquity more

🔹 "X-ray" fish, such as this saratoga from Nourlangie Rock, are the most common subject found in the recent rock art of western Arnhem Land, produced over the past 3,000 years.

➤ This dynamic figure from Deaf Adder Gorge, Kakadu National Park, is more than 10,000 years old. The figure is holding boomerangs, and the dashes near its mouth are possibly one of the earliest depictions of sound. Early forms and styles of painting such as this are believed by Aborigines to have been created by Mimi spirits in the ancient past.

accurately. The important point to note is that there have been many changes in rock painting over time—more so than in other forms of rock art found elsewhere in the world—in terms of form, style, and subject.

"X-ray" Paintings

The most widely known Holocene rock art has been called "X-ray" art, because it often depicts internal features of creatures. This form of art has been produced between a couple of thousand years ago and the present, much of it in this century. It has wide appeal for Europeans because of its detail and complexity, but it is also meaningful for various groups of Aboriginal people.

One should not really talk of an "X-ray" style, however, because the paintings with internal features are part of a much larger regional style as well as of a number of substyles associated with particular language groups. For instance, solid infill figures, various forms of stick figures, stencils, prints, and beeswax compositions were also made. The range of subject matter is large and varied, with new subjects continually being discovered. Although humans, animals, and mythical beings predominate, a variety of objects, activities, and abstract designs were also illustrated. Indeed, western Arnhem Land stands out from other rock art regions of the world because of this diversity.

Contemporary Practices

The last rock artist to paint prolifically in the region, Najombolmi, died in 1964. But rock paintings have also been done in the 1980s, and much of the tradition continues on bark or, more often, fabric and large sheets of paper. Rock paintings still hold considerable meaning for Aboriginal elders, and they are used in a variety of ways to pass on knowledge. "X-ray" paintings are particularly important in this regard, as their layered nature makes them especially suitable for conveying ideas about the different levels of meaning inherent in every aspect of existence. Western Arnhem Landers emphasize that theirs is a living tradition that changes with circumstance. Because of this, we should not be surprised or concerned that subjects and media derived from European traditions have been incorporated in Aboriginal images in recent years. What is most important is that the process continues.

PAUL TACON

♂ Beeswax compositions, such as this example in Kakadu National Park, western Arnhem Land, are often found in association with rock paintings produced within the past few hundred years.

♀ Large polychrome "X-ray" paintings were commonly placed on shelter walls and ceilings in western Arnhem Land during the past 2,000 to 3,000 years. This one is in Kakadu National Park.

PAUL TACON

For many years, there have been suggestions that both points and backed blades were introduced to Australia from elsewhere, although from where has never been specified. Tools in Indonesia that are even generally similar are not old enough to be their ancestors, and such tools are rare in other areas of Southeast Asia. Two more likely explanations of these tools have been put forward. One is that they were more efficient hunting weapons, perhaps allowing different kinds of game to be hunted. The other—which would also apply to hatchets—is that they were invented and adopted as part of a growing exchange system, perhaps involving the use of selected, quarried stone, which also developed from about 3000 BC. The first is in theory able to be tested through the animal remains in archaeological sites, although it has proved difficult to find enough sites with sufficient remains for this purpose. The second explanation could be tested through more work on tracing the sources of raw materials used to make these artifacts. Interestingly, although Tasmanians were isolated from the mainland and made none of these new tools, raw materials are more widely distributed there, too, over the last 3,000 years or so. What this might indicate, we do not at present know.

Paintings and Engravings

The other prehistoric remains found throughout Australia are what can broadly be called art. A few paintings and engravings on rocks have been dated back to the Pleistocene period, but it is clear that nearly all are less than 5,000 years old. They range in style from the highly naturalistic X-ray paintings of Arnhem Land to the stylized figures found in western New South Wales and stencils of boomerangs, hands, and other objects found in the Carnarvon Ranges area, in Queensland, and, less commonly, in some other areas. Paintings made in the last 200 years are known to have had a wide range of social functions, from serving as elements of sacred and secret ceremonies to illustrating everyday events and common stories. While we cannot categorize prehistoric art in the same way, it seems very likely that some of it, at least, served similar functions.

In seeking to interpret Aboriginal art, it is important to note that regions in which similar art is found are often quite different in other important respects, such as technology (for example, types of weapons and dwellings), social organization (for example, marriage practices—which are usually governed by very complex rules in Aboriginal society—and whether or not circumcision is practiced), and

In western New South Wales, white paintings are often the most recent. This panel, at Gundabooka, may portray a dancing group, all of whom seem to be men, with the leader carrying significant objects.

KATHIE ATKINSON

COLIN KERR

language. In a few cases, a pattern of local variations can be identified. This is sometimes related to the environment—for example, among the engravings in the sandstone of the Sydney region, fish are more common in rock carvings nearer the sea—and sometimes to small-scale social or linguistic boundaries known from the recent past. For example, differently sized human figures or slight differences in the way kangaroos are painted can be linked to particular Aboriginal groups.

Research into Aboriginal art has largely centered on establishing the chronology of different styles. In the Arnhem Land area, it is clear that the X-ray style has been in use only during the last 2,000 years. Several other styles have been identified in the same area, and some are clearly older than others, since they are always found beneath them. In time, their exact age and relationships may be revealed by a new radiocarbon-dating technique known as the accelerator mass spectrometry (AMS) method. This uses a cyclotron to isolate the radioactive carbon atoms, which are then counted. It can be used on even the tiniest of organic samples, but it is an expensive process at present and therefore not widely used. Since many of the paintings contain organic material of some kind (such as saliva, blood, urine, or charcoal), many should be dateable by this method.

In the meantime, one of the best methods of establishing chronology is to examine the way in which images have been superimposed on each other. In an extensive study carried out in the Carnarvon Ranges, Mike Morwood was able to show a three-stage sequence consisting of designs made by pecking and rubbing, probably unpainted, followed by stenciled, painted, and drawn designs in a variety of colors, with white paint being used only within the last few centuries. The sequence may have started in Pleistocene times, but no definite dates have yet been established.

Some current research on dating is attempting to link paintings with coloring materials of various kinds found in archaeological deposits in the same site. This has been useful where a particular material is absent; for example, it has shown that the "Lightning Brothers" (large, paired, striped human figures) in a shelter near Delemere, in the Northern Territory, almost certainly date to within the last 200 years, because no older ochers occur in the deposit immediately below them. However, this method has been of less use where ocher is found throughout levels dating from both the Holocene and Pleistocene periods, as has often been the case.

Because of their exposed locations, it seems likely that the paintings in all these regions have been made in recent times, but this cannot readily be proved.

⚓ The male and female human-like figures at Ubirr Rock (formerly Obiri), in Arnhem Land, represent beings who are involved with the continuous re-creation of the land, including its animals, plants, and people. Paintings such as these usually have many meanings, only some of which are known to any individual.

⚲ These "Lightning Brothers", at Yiwarlarlay, in northwestern Australia, were seen in a dream there by a Wardaman Elder in the 1940s and painted there soon afterwards, when European settlement prevented Wardaman people from visiting the shelter the Brothers originally inhabited.

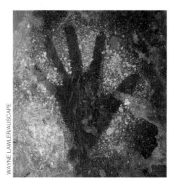

⚲ Hands mark many Australian rock shelters. This one, at Wuttagoona, near Cobar, in northwestern New South Wales, has been stenciled by paint being spat or blown around a left hand held against the wall. Women's and children's hands are sometimes featured.

⚯ The rivers and swamps of Arnhem Land provide many significant food resources for Aboriginal people, among them the barramundi fish, here depicted at Nourlangie Rock, and painted and repainted in many other rock shelters.

GRAHAME L. WALSH

⬧ Fish traps, such as this one on Goold Island, in the Great Barrier Reef, Queensland, are commonly made in shallow tidal waters in Australia's tropics. Fish swim over the stone walls of piled-up rocks at high tide, to be trapped there when the tide falls.

⬧ Along the east coast, fishhooks without barbs were cut and ground from shiny shell. They were used as lures, without bait, and are usually regarded as women's tools.

A. FARR/AUSTRALIAN MUSEUM

Social and Economic Elaboration

In the 1980s, a number of researchers argued that the changes that can be observed in stone artifacts and rock art dating to after about 2000 BC, along with other changes, indicate that Aboriginal societies in many parts of Australia had become more "complex" in this period. The cases for and against this proposition are themselves too complex to be set out in detail here, but they are an interesting example of the ways in which archaeological data and how they are interpreted affect our understanding of prehistoric societies.

The idea that there had been significant increases both in levels of productivity and in production of goods and services was first suggested by Harry Lourandos some 15 years ago. Basing his work on one anthropological view of the way traditional societies were organized, he examined the archaeological record of southwestern Victoria and found most of the evidence there to be less than 5,000 years old. He considered that the demands of a changing society, including increased competition along with a growing population, would produce such changes. In particular, he pointed to three new features found in the archaeological record from this time: artifically constructed habitation mounds—up to 6 meters (20 feet) across and 1 meter (between 3 and 4 feet) high—large fish traps, and the extensive distribution of hatchet heads made of a greenstone available from only a few quarries. He also noted the dense populations and evidence of very large-scale social groups (which the early Europeans called

"nations") recorded at the time of European settlement. Lourandos rightly saw that if production and productivity could be shown to have intensified, then climatic, environmental, or technological changes were insufficient to account for this.

Similar, but less wide-ranging, evidence has been adduced subsequently by other researchers from different parts of Australia. In particular, sites containing backed blades, which date from about 3000 BC, are 10 times more common than earlier sites; and, per thousand years, the number of backed blades found greatly exceeds the number of other artifacts found in the older sites. This has been seen as evidence of population increase, although how this might have come about (whether through lowered death rates or higher birth rates or both), and why, has not been explained. An increasing complexity in social networks has been inferred on the basis of the exchange systems in operation over the last few thousand years, by means of which stone for hatchet heads, sandstone grindstones, pituri (a narcotic), seashells from the northern coasts, songs, ceremonies, and other social phenomena were carried over distances of hundreds of kilometers and sometimes right across the country— for example, shells from northern coasts have been found in sites close to the Southern Ocean. The development of regional art traditions throughout Australia has similarly been seen as evidence that societies were becoming more complex.

Taken together, such evidence does indeed seem to suggest that "something happened" in Australia about 2000 BC. But when each piece of evidence is examined individually, the apparent pattern becomes blurred. For example, in a detailed study of one area where many rock shelter sites have been found, Mangrove Creek, near Sydney, Val Attenbrow showed that, per thousand years over the last 11,000 years, there is no common pattern of increase between the number of rock shelter sites in use, the number of newly established rock shelter sites, and the numbers of stone artifacts found in all these sites—such as we would expect to find if the population were increasing and developing more elaborate forms of social organization involving, among other things, exchange systems.

Similarly, other researchers have pointed to evidence of social elaboration occurring in earlier periods—such as the establishment of cemeteries along the Murray River Valley (the present-day border between the states of Victoria and New South Wales) from 13,000 years ago—and to the fact that some apparent changes in production over the last 4,000 years—such as variations in the pattern of shellfishing, as reflected by the middens at Princess Charlotte Bay—may simply represent changes in the natural environment in certain periods.

There is no doubt that changes did occur in Australia in the Late Holocene period, but these do not point as clearly to the development of complex societies as has been suggested. It must be remembered that the mere fact that more archaeological evidence has come down to us from more recent times is not of itself evidence of social change. We would always expect to find more evidence from more recent times, since with every year all sites face another year's possibility of destruction.

Uncovering the Past

This chapter has touched on only a few aspects of recent Australian archaeology, but there are many others of interest. Returning boomerangs, for instance, are the most widely known Australian artifact but were made only in certain parts of eastern Australia. They were only one of many varieties of curved throwing sticks, many of which were not designed to return to the thrower. All kinds of boomerangs were used for hunting, but the returning ones were also for play. Fragments of boomerangs, probably of the returning form, have been found at Wyrie Swamp, in South Australia, dated to about 8000 BC, but this technology may be much older.

Contact with the outside world is another theme of interest. The native Australian dog, the dingo, has been on the continent for only about 4,000 years, and its closest relatives known so far are in India. The dingo is the only direct link yet

shown between these two areas, but it surely did not migrate to Australia on its own. How did it get here, and what else came with it?

Fishhooks were made along the coast of New South Wales from about AD 800. Were these copied from New Guinean forms? If so, how did this come about, given that they are not found along much of the Queensland coast, which is closer to New Guinea? The best evidence of outside contact we have is that with Macassans, who collected trepang (sea slugs), pearl shell, and other valuables from the northern coast from about AD 1700, according to Macassan and Dutch records. Slim archaeological evidence in the form of shell copies of metal fishhooks suggests that outside contact extends back to at least AD 1000, but whether it occurred even earlier than this, in any form, is anyone's guess.

When Europeans arrived in Australia, they encountered societies as different from their own as any on Earth. Reconstructing the past through archaeology allows us to understand how these Aboriginal ways of life became uniquely suited to Australia's unique environment.

◄● A boomerang stenciled onto a rock wall in the Carnarvon Ranges, Queensland. Returning boomerangs were used in this area, but the one shown here is a throwing stick that probably bounced end-over-end along the ground towards the prey.

J. PETER WHITE

♀ Dingoes belong to the same species as modern dogs and are found throughout Australia, except for Tasmania. Wild pups were often reared by Aboriginal people and kept as pets. They were occasionally used in hunting.

JUTTA MALNIC

SALTWATER PEOPLE OF THE SOUTHWEST KIMBERLEY COAST

SUE O'CONNOR

THE PREHISTORY OF THE KIMBERLEY coast since 10,000 BC is as rich and diverse as the landscape in this far northwestern corner of Australia. The coastal region today supports vegetation ranging from lush rainforest thickets to open savanna. Dense mangroves fill the estuaries, whose tidal reaches stretch inland up to 70 kilometers (45 miles).

The people who traditionally lived in this area referred to themselves as "saltwater people", an apt description of their way of life. Along this part of the Australian coast, spring tides can be higher than 10 meters (33 feet), and fast currents and whirlpools are common. Despite this, the water-craft the southern Kimberley people used until early this century were simple double rafts made from two sections of lashed and pegged mangrove poles. While flimsy, these rafts did not easily overturn and sink in the precarious waters, and they could carry several people and their dingoes. They were not propeled, the people relying instead on their knowledge of the tides to travel between the offshore islands. Because of this, the Kimberley people are sometimes known as the "tide riders".

At the time of European contact, people were living permanently on some of the small islands offshore of the Kimberley coast. Most of these islands are too small to support land-dwelling vertebrates, and the inhabitants relied instead on the bountiful reefs for shellfish, fish, dugong, and turtle. They also collected the eggs of sea birds and a variety of fruits, seeds, and tubers. Such use of islands by coastal people in Australia seems to have been unique to the north.

Archaeologists have long wondered how far back this way of life goes. In many areas of Australia, shell middens date to between about 2000 BC and 1000 BC, whereas the sea reached its present level about 4000 BC. Because of this, some researchers have concluded that the Aborigines did not exploit marine resources intensively until well after the sea reached its present level.

Evidence from two Kimberley rock shelters, Widgingarri Shelter and Koolan Shelter, has made a unique contribution to this debate. These sites show that people were living in this region at least 28,000 years ago, when the sea was 20 to 50 kilometers (12 to 30 miles) distant. They then abandoned it during an arid phase that occurred between 25,000 and 13,000 years ago, when the sea had retreated to perhaps 200 kilometers (120 miles) from its present position and a vast coastal plain was exposed. As global climates warmed at the end

of the Ice Age, the sea level rose again, drowning this coastal plain.

At this time, Koolan shelter sat high on a rocky mainland promontory, with a steeply sloping offshore contour. Rising seas therefore reached this site early, and radiocarbon dating of its upper shell midden layer shows that people returned here about 11,000 years ago. At Widgingarri Shelter, on the other hand, the offshore contour has a gentle declination, which means that the rising seas reached this shelter only shortly before the sea reached its present level, about 4000 BC. The earliest layers in the midden here date to about

5000 BC. The fact that the reoccupation of the shelters coincides with the rise in the sea level suggests that people had been pursuing a coastal economy in Pleistocene times, but any evidence is now drowned.

Sea and Land Resources

At both Koolan and Widgingarri, animal remains dating from the early Holocene period show that the people of the Kimberley drew on both sea and land resources for their diet, eating fish, dugong, turtle, shellfish, and a variety of land mammals, such as kangaroos, rock wallabies, and bandicoots. Outside the rock

☝ The Kimberley coast supports a range of vegetation, from high rainforest to open savanna. Spring tides can reach as high as 10 meters (33 feet), and estuarine tidal reaches stretch inland up to 70 kilometers (45 miles).

⚲ The view from inside the Koolan Shelter, looking out towards the bay. People first lived in this shelter 28,000 years ago, and abandoned it when arid conditions set in between 25,000 and 13,000 years ago. They returned at the end of the Ice Age.

☝ These women are using metal "wires", the modern equivalent of the traditional digging stick, to collect shellfish.

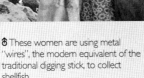

☝ The Kimberley island people relied mainly on coastal resources for their food. Here, a man is butchering a turtle on High Cliffy Island.

♀ Burning off spinifex on High Cliffy Island. Aboriginal people still carry out this traditional activity on offshore islands.

shelters, shell middens are rare in this region, probably because conditions do not favor their preservation.

Tools and Artifacts

A range of artifacts has been found in the rock shelter sites, including shell, bone, and stone tools. In the early midden levels, the stone tools are very similar to those found in the Pleistocene levels, the most common being simple retouched flakes. In the midden at Koolan Shelter, shell tools formed from large mud clam shells (*Geloina coaxans*) have been identified. The damage and residues evident on the edges of the tools indicate that they were used as handheld scrapers for working plant materials.

Between 3000 BC and 2000 BC, quite different types of artifacts are found. Points appear for the first time, the oldest dated to about 2500 BC. Most appear to have been mounted as tips at the end of wooden spears. Bone artifacts are also found, but only in the upper, more recent, layers of the middens. They may have been used as pressure-flaking tools to produce finely fluted stone points. Until recently, the people of this region used fire-hardened spears for fishing, and sometimes poisoned rock pools at low tide with certain plants. There is no evidence of the use of fish nets or fishhooks.

☝ A stone house base on High Cliffy Island. The walls are up to a meter (more than 3 feet) high.

Coastal fishing here appears to have required only simple technology.

Early Use of Offshore Islands

The first evidence of the regular use of offshore islands in this region dates from about 4000 BC. Because the wet season is so severe, little surface evidence of prehistoric occupation is preserved on most of the islands, but there are several striking exceptions.

High Cliffy Island is one of these. Situated about 8 kilometers (15 miles) off the coast, it was cut off from the mainland by rising seas about 6000 BC. Many stone structures have been found here, some of which seem to have served ceremonial functions, while others were used as house bases. The walls of the house bases stand up to a meter (just over 3 feet) high and have a small entrance. According to the Aboriginal elders who use this region today, these structures were roofed with spinifex and paperbark, the latter brought by raft from the mainland. Although these stone structures have not yet been dated, evidence from a dated rock shelter on the island suggests that High Cliffy Island has been used most intensively since 1000 BC. It is possibly only from this time that people have occupied the island permanently, as they were observed to be doing at the time of early European contact.

REFERENCE

A portal tomb in the Ox Mountains, in County Sligo, northwestern Ireland. Portal tombs are one of several types of stone-built monuments characteristic of Ireland.

abri

French word meaning "shelter", used to refer to the Paleolithic natural rock shelter sites characteristic of the limestone region of southern France.

absolute dating

Dating that can be expressed in calendar year ages on the basis of measurable physical and chemical constants or historical associations such as coins and written records. See also *relative dating*.

Acheulean

An industry of the Lower Paleolithic period, linked to the erectines, the first to use regular bifacial flaking, producing hand axes along with flakes and other cores. The culture is named after the site of St Acheul, in northern France.

adze

A heavy, wide-bladed cutting tool which is attached at right angles to a wooden handle. It was used for trimming and smoothing timber and for such tasks as hollowing out a dug-out canoe.

Anasazi

A culture found in southwestern North America in the late prehistoric era (about AD 200 to AD 1600). The Anasazi were agricultural people known for their pueblo-style architecture and finely painted ceramics. Although exact linkages are uncertain, it is clear that modern Pueblo

Indian people are descended from Anasazi ancestors. The name Anasazi is derived from a Navajo word meaning "enemy ancestors".

anthropomorphic figure

A figure or object with a human shape or character.

Archaic adaptation

Throughout the Americas, archaeologists use the term Archaic to refer to post-Paleoindian people who subsist by hunting, gathering, and fishing. Initially, the term was used to designate a non-ceramic-using, nonagricultural, and nonsedentary way of life. Archaeologists now realize, however, that ceramics, agriculture, and sedentism are all found, in specific settings, within contexts that are clearly Archaic. In eastern North America, Archaic defines a specific period of time

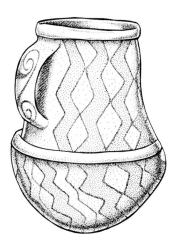
Anthropomorphic figure

between the earlier Paleoindian cultures and the later Woodland cultures. Where such Woodland adaptations did not develop, Archaic refers to a more generalized, nonagricultural way of life, which in some places lasted for 10,000 years.

Arctic Small Tool Tradition

A distinctive set of stone tools and weapon tips from the early Arctic Denbigh culture, recovered from sites along the Alaskan coast and eastwards to Greenland. All but the adzes are of a small size—hence the name.

ard

A plow-like tool, drawn by animals, that scratched a groove in the ground but did not turn over the soil.

arroyo

A steep-sided dry gully. Such geomorphic features were used by Paleoindians as natural traps to capture mammoths and bison.

Atlantic period

In Europe, the climatic period immediately following the last Ice Age, beginning about 6000 BC, when the average temperature rose. Melting ice sheets ultimately submerged nearly half of western Europe, in the process creating the bays and inlets along the Atlantic coast that provided a new, rich ecosystem for human subsistence. The Atlantic period was followed by the subboreal period.

atlatl

A New World version of a spear-thrower or throwing stick. A hook at the distal end fits into a depression at the proximal end of the spear, in effect extending the throwing arm.

Aurignacian

The earliest Upper Paleolithic technological phase in western Europe. It occurred between 38,000 and 22,000 years ago, and is characterized by the use of bone tools and a blade flint technology, with scrapers and burins. Aurignacian peoples produced the earliest art. Industries of Aurignacian type are found across Europe and western Asia, and sites are often in deep, sheltered valleys. The culture is named after the site of Aurignac, in southern France.

australopithecine

An evolutionary stage of extinct hominid (including *Australopithecus* itself) with a small cranial capacity, huge, protruding jaws, and upright

Anasazi pitcher

gait that existed in Africa between four and one million years ago. The word *Australopithecus* means "southern ape", and these hominids were so named because their fossils were found first in southern Africa.

Austroasiatic language family

Austroasiatic is a major language family of north-eastern India and the Southeast Asian mainland, comprising about 150 languages spoken by about 60 million people. It has two major groupings: the Munda languages of north-eastern peninsular India, and the Mon-Khmer languages of the Southeast Asian mainland. The Mon-Khmer languages include modern Vietnamese and Khmer (Cambodian), as well as many fairly isolated languages from southern China to as far south as Malaysia and the Nicobar Islands. The Austroasiatic language family appears to be the most ancient in its area, having been superseded in places by Indo-European, Tai, and Austronesian languages.

Austronesian language family

Austronesian is a major language family to which the languages of Taiwan, the islands of Southeast Asia, the Pacific (excluding much of New Guinea), Madagascar, and parts of the Southeast Asian mainland belong. Although all Austronesian languages are related, they are not necessarily mutually understandable.

Azilian

The final Upper Paleolithic culture in southwestern France and northern Spain, from about 9000 BC to 8000 BC, characterized by flat harpoons, carved spear-throwers made from deer antlers, and stone pebbles painted with red dots. The culture takes its name from the massive cave of Le Mas d'Azil, in the French Pyrenees.

backed blade

A small, blade-like flake, one side of which has been blunted by chipping, so that it can be fitted snugly into a haft or used while held in the hand without cutting the fingers.

barrow

A large mound built over a prehistoric burial place. Round barrows are known as tumuli; elongated mounds are known as long-barrows.

Battle-axe culture

A term applied to a number of Late Neolithic cultural groups in Europe that appeared between 2800 BC and 2300 BC. The Battle-axe culture is named after a characteristic type of polished stone axe.

Bell Beaker culture

A Late Neolithic culture from the third millennium BC in central and western Europe. The name is derived from the characteristic vessel form, which resembles a bell. The Bell Beaker culture belongs to the so-called Battle-axe cultures in Europe.

Beringia

The part of the continental shelf that connects Northeast Asia with present-day Alaska. When exposed at the time of the last glacial maximum, 18,000 years ago, it was a large, flat, vegetated landmass.

betel nut

The fruit of the betel palm, *Areca catechu*, which is chewed in New Guinea and in many parts of tropical Asia.

betyl

A sacred stone, often a standing stone, that has been fashioned into a conical shape.

bi disk

A flat jade disk with a small hole in the center, made in ancient China for ceremonial purposes. *Bi* disks were described in ancient Chinese texts as a symbol of rank, and were used as ritual objects in the Liangzhu culture of Neolithic China. They have been found in graves, arranged with cong tubes around the corpses of the elite. *Bi* disks are thought to have symbolized Heaven.

bifacial

A term used to describe a stone tool shaped on both faces. The technique is typical of the hand-axe tradition of the Lower Paleolithic period.

billabong

In Australia, a body of water, such as an anabranch or waterhole in a watercourse, that fills when flooded during the rainy season, and dries up in the dry season.

bipedal

Walking upright on two legs. For early humans, it had the advantage of leaving the hands free.

blade

A long, narrow flake struck from a stone core (often flint) selected for its flaking properties. The blade was either used as a tool in itself or became the blank from which other tools were manufactured. In Europe, blades and blade tools appear at the start of the Upper Paleolithic period, and are first associated with the Aurignacian culture and the arrival of modern humans.

BP

An abbreviation of "Before Present", BP is used in radiocarbon dating to mean "before AD 1950", the standard radiocarbon-dating reference year.

Bronze Age

A prehistoric period in the Old World, defined by the use of bronze as a new material for tools, weapons, and ornaments. In Europe, the Bronze Age proper spans the second and early first millennia BC.

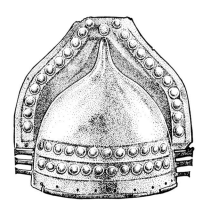

Bronze Age helmet

Bubalus period
The earliest phase of rock art in northern Africa, represented by large-scale carvings of animals, which appeared between 12,000 BC and 8000 BC. The period is named after the now-extinct giant buffalo, *Bubalus antiquus*.

buckler
A schematic motif that is found mainly in the megalithic tombs of Brittany, in France. It has been interpreted as a protective symbol.

burin
A short, pointed blade tool with a chisel end, used to carve and engrave wood and bone (particularly antlers, which were made into spearheads and harpoon tips). The most common form has a sharp tip, formed by the intersection of two flake scars. The burin is associated with Upper Paleolithic cultures, especially the Magdalenian.

burin spall tool
Small cutting tools made from chips or splinters of stone driven or pressed from the edges of burins.

C14
The radioisotope carbon-14. Its known rate of decay is the basis of radiocarbon dating.

candelabra model
One of the theories of human development, also known as the regional continuity theory. Modern humans are seen as descending from *Homo erectus* in Africa, Europe, and Asia. The opposing theory, known as the Noah's Ark model, holds that modern humans originated in one single area of Africa.

Chalcolithic period
Literally, the "Copper Stone Age". The Chalcolithic period is the transitional phase between Stone Age technology and the Bronze Age, when copper was used for tool-making and jewelry in cultures that otherwise were Neolithic in character.

channel flake
A long, thin blade of stone removed by percussion or pressure from the center line of either face of a projectile point. The smooth depression it leaves behind is known as a flute or channel.

Chatelperronian
A cultural phase of the Upper Paleolithic period, between 36,000 and 32,000 years ago, characterized by bone tools and weapons (made of ivory or reindeer antler) and flint knives. The culture is named after the site of Châtelperron, in France.

chinampas
A system of cultivation on artificial islands built of vegetation and mud in shallow freshwater lakes. These remarkably fertile fields were created by massive Aztec reclamation projects in the Valley of Mexico.

coevolutionary perspective
A relatively recent theory in cultural evolution that contends that changes in social systems are best understood as resulting from mutual selection among components, rather than as a linear, cause-and-effect sequence. Accordingly, the multiple origins of agriculture can be best understood by exploring the evolutionary forces affecting the development of domestication systems. When viewed in this way, domestication is not seen as an evolutionary stage, but as a process, and is the result of coevolutionary interactions between humans and plants.

***cong* tube**
A tubular, jade object, square on the outside and circular on the inside, made in various sizes and used for ritual purposes in ancient China. *Cong* were described in ancient Chinese texts as symbols of rank and were used as ritual objects in the Liangzhu culture of Neolithic China. They have been found in graves, arranged with *bi* disks around the corpses of the elite. The *cong* is thought to have symbolized Earth.

corbeled roof
A simple form of roofing where successive courses of overlapping stones finally meet in the center and form a "false vault" when a capstone is placed at the top. The technique was used within the megalithic tradition in Europe.

Corded Beaker culture
A Late Neolithic culture in central Europe from the third millennium BC, named after a characteristic cord-marked decoration found on pottery. The Corded Beaker culture belongs to the so-called Battle-axe cultures in Europe.

Cordilleran ice sheet
The ice mass that covered the coastal mountains along the Pacific Ocean coast of North America from northern Washington state into southern Alaska. At its maximum extent, about 20,000 years ago, it connected with the aurentide ice sheet to the east and with the Pacific Ocean to the west, and reached a thickness of some 3 kilometers (1 mile).

core
A lump of rock used in the manufacture of stone tools. Blades and flakes are struck from the core by hitting it accurately with a pebble or bone. The core may also be fashioned into an implement, such as a chopper or scraper.

Cro-Magnon
The earliest known modern humans in Europe, who were characterized by a long head, a tall, erect stature, and the use of blade technology and bone tools. They were associated with the Aurignacian culture, which produced the earliest European art. The name comes from a rock shelter in southwestern France where, in 1868, *Homo sapiens* remains were first found in association with Upper Paleolithic tools.

cruciform chamber
A megalithic tomb, characteristic of the passage-tomb tradition in Ireland, in which a passage, a chamber, and three apses together form a cross-shaped structure.

cuirass
A piece of armor to protect the torso, both front and back, and often molded to the contours

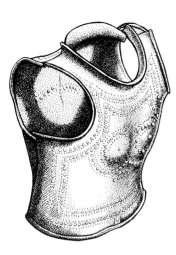

Cuirass

of the body. Although the cuirasses that survive from the Bronze Age are of sheet bronze, this material can be easily pierced by an arrow or sword, and it is likely that the functional armor of the day was made of leather.

cultural complex
An assemblage of artifacts and other physical evidence that regularly occur together within a restricted area, and are thought to represent the material remains of a particular group of people, perhaps over several generations.

cultural layer
Deposition of materials from settlements or other prehistoric areas of activity that accumulate over a relatively continuous time. Several such layers create a stratigraphic and chronological sequence.

dendrochronology
The construction of chronologies from tree-ring sequences. The annual tree-rings on timber recovered from a site are compared with an

established sequence of ring patterns that extends back to about 9000 BP.

diaspora
The dispersion of people, either forced or voluntary, from a central area of origin to many distant regions.

diprotodon
A large Australian herbivorous marsupial, now extinct, of the group that includes kangaroos, koalas, and wombats. It was characterized by two prominent incisors on the lower jaw.

DNA
The basic material of chromosomes, which includes the genes. Analysis of the DNA of different primate groups has been used to determine the evolutionary line of modern humans, and DNA techniques have also been used to show for how long the various regional human populations have been separated from each other. DNA analysis of blood residue, both human and animal, on prehistoric tools and weapons may one day provide fresh information on the evolutionary relationships between a range of animal species, and between prehistoric and modern humans.

dogu
A type of clay figurine, most often depicting a female, made in Japan during the Jomon period. The function of these figurines is unknown, but it is generally believed that they were some kind of fertility symbol.

dolmen
The French term for a megalithic tomb with a single capstone carried by orthostats, or standing stones.

Dyukhtai tradition
A Siberian cultural group of the Upper Paleolithic period. It existed along the Lena and Aldan rivers, between about 18,000 and 12,000 years ago. The people who first migrated into North America were probably from this cultural group.

einkorn
A variety of wheat with pale kernels, *Triticum monococcum*, which was cultivated in Neolithic times. It probably originated in southeastern Europe and southwestern Asia, and is still grown in mountainous parts of southern Europe as grain for horses.

emmer
A variety of wheat, *Triticum dicoccum*, which has been cultivated in the Mediterranean region since Neolithic times, and is still grown in the mountainous parts of southern Europe as a cereal crop and livestock food. It is thought to be the ancestor of many other varieties of wheat.

endblade
A small blade tool. Bipointed endblades were used to tip bone and antler arrow-heads; triangular endblades were probably used to tip harpoon heads.

endocast
An internal cast, as of the inside of the human skull.

endscraper
A blade tool with a steeply angled working edge on the end of the blade, used to work hard materials and to dress skins. It appeared in Europe during the Upper Paleolithic period.

Eocene
The geological epoch from 55 million to 38 million years ago. It occurred within the Tertiary period, following the Paleocene and preceding the Oligocene. During this epoch, mammals consolidated their status as the dominant land vertebrates.

erectine
A now-extinct member of the genus *Homo*, including *Homo erectus*, who lived in Africa, Asia, and Europe during the Lower and Middle Pleistocene. Erectines walked upright, may have used fire, and are often associated with the Acheulean industries, especially with hand axes.

estrus cycle
The regular reproductive cycle of female mammals, marked by a series of physiological changes in the sexual and other organs that signal a period of availability for mating.

ethnography
The collecting and study of basic research material, such as artifacts, for analysis of social and cultural structures and processes.

"Eve" theory
The hypothesis that all modern humans are descended from a common

first mother who lived in southern Africa about 200,000 years ago. The "Eve" theory is similar to the Noah's Ark model, and is based on genetic research showing that as modern humans spread throughout the world, they rarely, if at all, interbred with existing, but more archaic, humans, such as the Neanderthals. The "Eve" theory does not imply a creationist view, only that there has been a chance survival of a single line of mitochondrial DNA.

faience

Bronze Age faience is a primitive form of glass. It is made by baking a mixture of sand and clay to a temperature at which the surface fuses into blue or green glass. Faience beads of Aegean and southwestern Asian origin were traded widely in eastern and central Europe, Italy, and the British Isles in the second millennium BC.

flake tool

A tool made from a thin, sharp-edged fragment of stone struck off a larger stone (the core).

flintknapping

The technique of striking flakes or blades from a larger stone (the core) and the shaping of cores and flakes into stone implements. The most commonly used stone was flint (also called chert), a hard, brittle stone, commonly found as pebbles in limestone areas, that breaks with a conchoidal fracture rather than along predetermined cleavage planes. Obsidian, basalt, and

quartz were also fashioned into tools. Flintknapping began with the simple striking of one stone against another. Later methods include the use of antler and wooden strikers for both direct and indirect percussion, and bone and antler pressure-flaking tools.

flute

The smooth longitudinal groove left on a projectile point after the removal of a channel flake.

fluted projectile point

A stone projectile point associated with the Clovis and Folsom cultures of North America. Flutes were formed by removing flakes from the base towards the point by percussion or pressure. The sharp ridges of the flutes were ground smooth near the base of the point, to prevent them from cutting the bindings when the point was inserted into a notched foreshaft.

foramen magnum

The hole at the base of the skull where the spinal cord enters. Its position is an indication of posture. If the foramen magnum is far forward on the skull base, it indicates an upright posture, like that of humans, with the head balanced on top of the spine.

genome

The complete set of genetic material—the chromosomes and the genes they contain—that makes up any cell and determines hereditary features.

glacial maximum

The peak of an Ice Age, when

the ice sheets are at their greatest extent and temperatures at their lowest. The last glacial maximum occurred between 22,000 and 18,000 years ago.

graver

A stone tool used for engraving stone, bone, and wood, also referred to as a burin.

Gravettian

A cultural tradition of the Upper Paleolithic period, between 29,000 and 22,000 years ago, which follows the Aurignacian and is characterized by the appearance of Venus figurines, small pointed blades, burins, and bone spear-points. Gravettian-type industries are found from France and Spain, across central Europe, to southern Russia. The culture is named after the site of La Gravette, in southern France.

Hand stencil

greave

A piece of armor designed to protect the lower part of the leg.

grinding stone

A stone used to grind to powder foodstuffs (such as grains), medicines, and

pigments for decorating rock walls and bodies.

habiline

An early member of the genus *Homo*, including *Homo habilis*, known from fossils in Africa dating from 2.4 million to about 1.5 million years ago. Habilines made simple stone tools and are the precursors of *Homo erectus* and the erectines.

haft

The handle part of an implement such as an axe, knife, or adze.

hand axe

A type of stone tool that is typical of the Acheulian tradition and linked mainly to the erectines of Africa, Europe, India, and Southwest Asia. Hand axes consist of a nodule that has been bifacially worked. They vary in size and shape, but usually one end is pointed. The hand axe probably had a wide range of uses, such as cutting, digging, and scraping.

hand stencil

The impression of a hand produced by spraying thick paint (made from white clay or red or yellow ocher) through a blowpipe around the edges of a hand placed against a rock surface.

harpoon

A spear-like missile with backward-pointing barbs, loosely hafted, and attached to a line. When hurled at marine mammals, such as seals, the point, if it finds its mark, is separated from the shaft, and the barbs prevent it from being dislodged. The line is used to retrieve the

Harpoon

catch. The appearance of the harpoon is associated in particular with the agdalenian culture, which is known for finely carved single-barbed and double-barbed harpoon heads made of antler or bone.

henge monument
A circular, prehistoric religious site constructed of wood or stones and enclosed by ditches and walls. Henge monuments are characteristic of the megalithic period in southern England in particular.

Hohokam
A prehistoric cultural tradition of southwestern North America, dating from about AD 0 to AD 1450, generally correlated with the Sonoran Desert biotic province and centered on the well-watered river valleys of central and southern Arizona. Many Hohokam sites are characterized by extensive networks of irrigation canals.

Holocene
The present geological epoch, which began some 10,000 years ago. It falls within the Quaternary period and followed the Pleistocene. The Holocene is marked by rising temperatures throughout the world and the retreat of the ice sheets. During this epoch, agriculture became the common human subsistence practice.

hominid
A member of the Hominidae, the family that includes both extinct and modern forms of humans and, in most modern classifications, the Great Apes.

hominoid
A member of the primate family that includes both humans and the apes, and their extinct evolutionary precursors.

hypogeum
A chamber tomb cut into rock.

ibex
A wild goat with large, recurved horns, common in European and central and West Asian mountain systems. They were often depicted by Upper Paleolithic artists.

iconography
The art of representing or illustrating by means of pictures, images, or figures.

intaglio
Incised carving (as opposed to relief carving), in which the design is sunk below the surface of hard stone or metal.

interglacial
A period of warmer temperatures and diminished ice sheets occurring between periods of glaciation. The last 10,000 years (the Holocene) is probably an interglacial, since its temperatures and the distribution of vegetation are similar to those of earlier interglacials.

Iron Age
A late prehistoric period in the Old World, defined by the use of iron as the main material for tools and weapons.

isothermic line
A line on a map linking places of equal temperature at a given time or period.

kerbstone circle
A circle of stones bordering a burial mound.

kiva
A large underground or partly underground circular or rectangular room in a Pueblo Indian village where religious and other ceremonies are conducted.

labret
A decorative plug of shell, bone, ivory, metal, or pottery inserted through a hole in the lip.

lancehead
A large, flat missile point of stone, bone, or ivory. It was mounted on a long shaft to form a lightweight lance or javelin-like weapon for war or hunting. A lancehead is larger than an arrowhead, but smaller than a spearhead.

Lapita
A distinctive type of pottery with finely made bands of decoration in geometric patterns that appeared throughout much of the western Pacific about 3,000 years ago. In some sites, Lapita pottery is associated with elaborate shell tools and ornaments, the use of obsidian, and long-distance trade, so that it appears to represent a culture, although this is not yet clear.

Laurentide ice sheet
The ice mass that covered most of Canada and parts of the United States, including the Great Lakes area and northern New England. At its maximum extent, about 20,000 years ago, it was connected to the Cordilleran ice sheet to the west.

Levalloisian flake technique
A technique that produced flakes of a predetermined form by means of trimming the core to a certain shape before the flakes were struck off. The core was then discarded. A Levalloisian flake shows scars of the preparatory work on one side and is flat on the other. The technique is associated with the Middle Paleolithic period in Europe.

loess
A loamy deposit consisting of fine particles of windblown soil, laid down during the Ice Age. Loess forms a fertile and easily worked soil.

long-barrow
An elongated mound covering a burial chamber, typical of the Early and Mid-Neolithic periods in Europe. In southern England, the burial chamber consists of a megalithic tomb.

longhouse

An elongated wooden post house that appeared in central Europe with the first farming communities within the Early Neolithic Bandkeramik cultures, about 4500 BC.

Lower Paleolithic

The first part of the Paleolithic, beginning about two million years ago. The era of the earliest forms of humans and of tool-making.

lunula

A crescent-shaped neck ornament of sheet gold, characteristic of the Early Bronze Age in Europe.

macrofossils

Large-scale floral or faunal remains recovered from an archaeological excavation (as opposed to microfossils, which cannot be seen without magnification).

macropod

A grazing Australian marsupial with short forelimbs, long hind limbs adapted for hopping, and a long, muscular tail, such as the kangaroo, the wallaby, and the tree kangaroo.

Magdalenian

The last major culture of the Upper Paleolithic period in Europe. It was adapted to the cold conditions of the last Ice Age and based on the specialized hunting of deer. Characteristic artifacts are barbed harpoons and carved spear-throwers of reindeer bone and antler decorated with naturalistic carvings of game animals. It is also the period when cave art reached its peak. The culture lasted from 18,000 to 12,000 years ago and is named after the rock shelter of La Madeleine, in southwestern France.

maguey

The fleshy-leafed agave plant of tropical America. American Indians ate both the flowerhead, which they harvested after it had bloomed, and the heart of the maguey, which they prepared by digging up the entire plant and roasting it in earth ovens for 24 to 72 hours.

Lunula

manioc

Also called cassava, manioc (*Manihot esculenta*) is a starchy root crop that can be processed into an important food. It was the staple diet throughout most of Amazonia and the Caribbean at the time of European contact. Manioc is the source of tapioca.

mano

The Spanish term commonly used by American archaeologists for the smoothed, hand-held stone used to grind seeds, pigments, or other relatively soft material against the concave surface of a larger, usually immobile lower grindstone or metate. It is also known as the upper grindstone.

mastodon

Any of various now-extinct species of large, elephant-like mammals. The American mastodon (*Mammut americanum*), an extinct form of the family Mammutidae, is classified as a browser from its low-crowned teeth, as opposed to the woolly mammoth (*Mammuthus primigenius*), of the family Elephantidae, which, because of its high-crowned teeth, is classified as a grazer.

megafauna

The large, now-extinct animals of the Late Pleistocene period—including mammoths; mastodon; giant bison, sloths, and camels; and diprotodons. The term also covers extinct larger species of quite small animals.

megalithic tomb

A chambered tomb built of large stones. Its name comes from the Greek words *megas* (large) and *lithos* (stone).

Megalithic tomb

menhir

A standing stone, most often referred to in a megalithic context.

Menhirs

Mesolithic

Literally, the "Middle Stone Age". A transitional period between the Paleolithic and the Neolithic, marked by the retreat of the Pleistocene glaciers and the appearance of modern forms of plants and animals. Its peoples were hunter-gatherers whose flint industries were characterized by microliths. The term Mesolithic is limited to Europe.

mesquite pod

The edible, bean-like seed vessel harvested from the mesquite tree (genus *Prosopis*) of arid Central America. Native Americans cooked the sugary pods into a syrup; the seeds could also be roasted and eaten.

metate

The Spanish term commonly used by American archaeologists for a smoothed, usually immobile, stone with a concave upper surface on which seeds, pigments, or other relatively soft material can be ground with the aid of a hand-held upper grindstone, or mano. The metate is also known as a lower grindstone, or concave quern.

microblade

A very small, narrow bladelet, less than 10 millimeters (half an inch) wide, shaped by pressure-flaking a prepared core. Microblades were often retouched into various forms of microliths.

microlith

A very small arrowhead, barb, or other implement, most commonly of flint, made by removing a triangular, trapezoidal, or parallelogram-shaped section from a microblade. Microliths were mounted in wooden or bone shafts as arrow tips, or along one or both sides of a shaft to form a barbed spear or harpoon, or set in rows on sickles. Microliths were characteristic of the Mesolithic period in the Old World.

midden

An extensive deposit of settlement refuse, which may include the remains of shells, bones, ashes, and discarded implements. Middens are commonly built up over many years and mark the site of previous human habitation.

Middle Paleolithic

The middle part of the Paleolithic, starting some 150,000 years ago and ending with the extinction of the Neanderthals, about 33,000

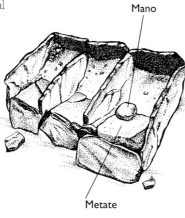

Mano

Metate

years ago. It was the era of the Neanderthal peoples and flake tools. The Middle Paleolithic is equivalent to the Middle Stone Age in sub-Saharan Africa.

Miocene

The geological epoch between 7 million and 2.6 million years ago. It occurred within the Tertiary period, following the Oligocene and preceding the Pliocene. During this epoch, many mammals of modern form, such as dogs, horses, and human-like apes, evolved.

mitochondrial DNA

A particular kind of DNA that is inherited only through the mother, enabling the tracing of accurate genetic links.

mobile

The settlement pattern of social groups who move from place to place within a given territory, building camps at each site.

Mogollon

A prehistoric culture of southwestern North America. Unlike the Anasazi culture, the Mogollon culture did not survive as a recognizable group of modern Native Americans. Remnants of the Mogollon

may have merged with Anasazi peoples to become what is known as the Western Pueblo people.

molecular clock

A method of tracing evolutionary lines based on the changes in the protein structure and DNA of living organisms that take place over long periods of time. By establishing the degree of difference between the proteins of two species, it is possible to calculate how long ago they shared a common ancestor.

Mousterian

A culture of the Middle Paleolithic period that appeared throughout Europe from the last interglacial through to about 33,000 years ago. It is characterized by the appearance of flint scrapers and points and is associated with the Neanderthals. Mousterian peoples lived in cave mouths and rock shelters. The culture is named after Le Moustier, a rock shelter in southwestern France.

Neanderthals

An extinct form of humans that appeared during the Upper Pleistocene era, some 100,000 years ago, and is known to have existed throughout unglaciated Europe and as far east as Uzbekistan. Neanderthals had prominent brow ridges, a receding forehead, and a brain of similar size to that of modern humans. They made flake tools in the form of scrapers and points. In Europe, they are associated with the Mousterian culture.

The Neanderthals persisted into the Upper Paleolithic period, some 33,000 years ago. The name comes from the Neander Valley, near Düsseldorf, Germany, where skeletal remains of this type of human were first found in 1856.

Near Oceania

Those islands of the Pacific that can be reached by water-craft without going out of sight of land. Basically, Near Oceania comprises the Indonesian archipelago, the Philippines, New Guinea, and the Solomon Islands.

Neolithic

Literally, the "New Stone Age". The term refers to the final phase of the Stone Age, when farming became an essential part of the economy.

neutron activation analysis

A method of determining the origin of flint artifacts by matching the trace element concentrations with those of flint from various known sources.

Noah's Ark model

The theory that modern humans originated in one single area of Africa and spread throughout the world, replacing other, more archaic, human types. It is also known as the replacement hypothesis. This view is supported by the so-called "Eve" theory, which postulates that all modern humans are descended from a common mother. The opposing hypothesis is often called the candelabra model.

nomadic
A term used by ethnographers to describe the movement of whole social groups of cattle breeders who utilize different parts of a given territory in different seasons, usually summer and winter pastures, and build camps for those periods.

obsidian
A black, glassy volcanic rock often used to make sharp-edged tools.

Oldowan
A term used to refer to the oldest known Paleolithic artifacts of South and East Africa, consisting of simple chipped pebble tools. The word comes from Olduvai Gorge, an important Paleolithic site in Tanzania, where fossil remains of early humans were found in association with such artifacts.

Oligocene
The geological epoch between 38 million and 28 million years ago. It occurred within the Tertiary period, following the Eocene and preceding the Miocene. During this epoch, many of the older types of mammals became extinct and the first apes appeared.

orthostat
A standing stone in a megalithic tomb, supporting one or more capstones.

ossuary
A house containing depositions of multiple human skeletons.

paleoanthropology
The study of prehistoric humans as revealed by fossil remains.

paleobotany
The study of ancient plants from fossil remains and other evidence, such as vegetable materials, preserved by charring, desiccation, or in water-logged deposits. Paleobotany provides information about the climate and environment and about materials available for food, fuel, tools, and shelter.

Paleocene
The geological epoch from some 65 million to 55 million years ago. It occurred within the Tertiary period and preceded the Eocene. During this epoch, there was great development of primitive mammals. The earliest known primates date from the Paleocene.

paleoclimatology
The study of past climates, using information such as vegetation and sedimentary records, geomorphology, and animal distribution.

Paleoeskimo
The earliest prehistoric Eskimo people, before the beginning of whale hunting. Later whale-hunting people are called Neoeskimo.

Paleoindians
The big-game hunters of the Americas from the earliest known, about 10,000 BC, to about 6000 BC. Some investigators regard the term as referring to all hunting groups involved with now-extinct mammals, in which case the peoples who hunted the species of bison that became extinct about 4500 BC would also be classified as Paleoindians.

Paleolithic
Literally, the "Old Stone Age". It began some two million to three million years ago with the emergence of humans and the earliest forms of chipped stone tools, and continued through the Pleistocene Ice Age until the retreat of the glaciers some 12,000 years ago. The Paleolithic is equivalent to the Stone Age in sub-Saharan Africa.

paleontology
The study of life forms present in previous geological periods as represented by plant and animal fossils.

palynology
The analysis of ancient pollen grains and the spores of mosses and lichens to reveal evidence of past environments.

Panaramitee style
Rock engravings featuring circles and tridents (possibly kangaroo and emu tracks) found in many parts of Australia. Many probably date to Pleistocene times.

passage tombs
A megalithic tomb in which access to the chamber is obtained through a passage.

Pastoral Neolithic
A complex of cultures that appeared in southern Kenya and northern Tanzania about 3500 BC. The term pastoral refers to abundant evidence that the people herded domestic animals. It remains unknown whether they also cultivated plants. About 1,300 years ago, they were absorbed or replaced by iron-using pastoralists and mixed farmers.

percussion flaking
The reduction of a stone core by hitting it with a hammer of stone or bone.

permafrost line
A line demarcating regions where the subsoil is permanently frozen. It is related to the tree line, because the frozen ground prevents tree roots from penetrating deeply and inhibits the subsurface drainage of meltwater.

petroglyph
A picture or symbol engraved, pecked, or incised into a rock.

phytolith
The tiny silica particles contained in plants. Sometimes, these fragments can be recovered from archaeological sites, even after the plants themselves have disappeared.

pit house
A dwelling with the floor dug down below ground level to make it easier to weatherproof against wind. Often all that remains on an archaeological site is a large, shallow pit.

platform burial
The practice of placing a corpse on an artifical, above-ground structure; the body was sometimes retrieved at a later date for interment.

playa
The sandy, salty, or mud-caked floor of a desert basin with interior drainage, usually occupied by a shallow lake during the rainy season or after prolonged, heavy rains. The word also refers to the lake itself.

Pleistocene
The first epoch of the geological period known as the Quaternary, preceding the Holocene (or present) epoch and beginning some two million years ago. It was marked by the advance of ice sheets across northern Europe and North America. During this epoch, giant mammals existed, and in the Late Pleistocene, modern humans appeared.

Pliocene
The geological epoch from some seven million to two million years ago. It occurred within the Tertiary period, following the Miocene and preceding the Pleistocene. During this epoch, modern mammals became dominant and ape-like humans appeared in Africa.

polygyny
The mating of a male with more than one female.

pressure flaking
The technique of removing flakes by means of pressure applied to a specific spot with the point of a tool made of stone or bone.

primary burial
The initial burial of a dead person.

projectile point
A weapon tip made of flint, antler, or bone.

protein sequencing
Analysis of the sequence of the amino acids that make up a protein. Comparison of the sequences in different species is one way of working out their degrees of interrelationship.

protoworld language
A single, original language, hypothesized to have been spoken by the first modern humans in Africa, from which all modern languages may descend. It has been suggested that linguistic traces of this language have survived into the present.

pueblo
A Spanish term meaning town or village, and applied by sixteenth-century explorers to the village dwellings of the American Southwest. When capitalized, Pueblo generally refers to a specific Native American group, culture, or site.

Quaternary
The most recent geological period, subdivided into the Pleistocene and the Holocene, beginning some two million years ago.

relative dating
A dating sequence that establishes which sample is older or younger than the other by means of its position in a stratified section of an excavation, or by placing it in an age sequence relative to other samples, none (or only some) of which have been

dated by absolute dating methods. Relative dating does not give exact dates in calendar years.

Remote Oceania
The small islands of the Pacific that can only be reached by sailing out of sight of land. Remote Oceania includes all the islands east of a line stretching from the Philippines to the Solomons.

sagittal crest
The crest along the top of the skull where the chewing muscles are attached, found only in very large-jawed species, such as male gorillas and orang-utans, and the *australopithecine* genus *Paranthropus*.

scraper
A core, flake, or blade with a steeply retouched edge either at the side (side-scraper) or end (endscraper). Scrapers were used to dress hides and to shape wood, bone, and ivory artifacts.

secondary burial
The practice of removing the remains of a dead person from the site of the initial burial to a grave or ossuary.

sedentism
A way of life in which people remain settled in one place throughout the year.

sexual dimorphism
The differences in shape, size, or color between males and females that occur generally in any population. Males are usually larger than females, but the reverse is sometimes the case.

shaman
A person believed to have supernatural powers. In times of sickness, shortage of game, or any other threat to a community's survival, the shaman is called upon to mediate with the spirit world on the community's behalf. The shaman presides over rituals, and may also be responsible for the keeping of laws and the continuity of traditions. Shamanism is the dominant element in the religion of most known arctic and subarctic hunter-gatherers. Most shamans are male.

sherd
A small piece of broken pottery.

Sherd

sideblade
A narrow flake with a sharp edge on one side, often inserted into bone arrowheads and spearheads to increase loss of blood and thus bring prey to ground faster.

sidescraper
A flake tool having a steep, retouched edge on one side of the flake, used for working hard materials and dressing skins.

slash-and-burn agriculture
A method of agriculture in which vegetation is felled, left to dry out, and then burned. Seeds are later planted in holes poked into the ashes.

Stamp seal

Solutrean
A culture of the Upper Paleolithic period which precedes the Magdalenian in western Europe and flourished from some 22,000 to 18,000 years ago. It is characterized by the use of pressure flaking to make large, thin, leaf-shaped bifacial points, in particular the laurel leaf point, for use as lanceheads. Some, however, are so finely tapered and delicate that it seems likely that they were made for ornamental purposes rather than for use in hunting or warfare. Bone needles with eyes appeared in this period. The culture is named after the site of Solutré, in southeastern France.

spear-thrower
A stick with a notch at one end into which the butt of a spear is fitted, thus giving increased leverage in throwing and making it possible to bring down animals from a distance. Spear-throwers made of reindeer antler are characteristic of the Magdalenian period in Europe. Similar weapons were used in the New World, where

they are known as atlatls; in the Arctic; and in Australia, where they are often called woomeras.

stamp seal
A small, hard block that has a flat surface engraved with a design that can be transferred to soft clay or wax as a mark of ownership or authenticity. Stamp seals appear in Mesopotamia from the Halafian period, in the fifth millennium BC, when they were used to impress ownership marks on lumps of clay; these were then attached to goods.

steatite
A soft, gray stone, also known as soapstone. It was used particularly to make stamp seals.

stele
An upright slab or column of stone, often decorated with carvings or bearing inscriptions.

Stone Age
The earliest period of technology in human culture, when tools and weapons were made of stone, bone, and wood. The Stone Age comprises the Paleolithic, the Mesolithic, and the Neolithic (literally, the Old, Middle, and New Stone Age). In sub-Saharan Africa, the Stone Age is equivalent to the Paleolithic.

stratigraphy
A term borrowed from geology to describe the layers of human artifacts and other remains in successive levels of occupation as revealed in

a vertical section of an archaeological excavation. By following the principle that a deposit overlying another must have accumulated at a later time, it is possible to establish a relative chronological sequence of levels, providing there has been no subsequent disturbance.

subboreal period
A climatic period that occurred between about 3000 BC and AD 0. In northern Europe, it was characterized by a cooler and moister climate than that of the preceding Atlantic period.

tang
A long, slender projecting strip or prong of a tool, often fitted into a handle or shaft.

Stele

taphonomy
The study of the natural processes that act on the remains of a plant, animal, or human between its death and the incorporation of its remains into an archaeological or paleontological deposit.

taxonomy
The study of the general principles that regulate scientific classification. Biological taxonomists attempt to devise an orderly classification of plants and animals according to their presumed natural relationships.

tell mound
A mound formed by the repeated rebuilding of mudbrick houses on the same site. As older houses collapsed, their remains formed a raised base for houses. Such mounds also incorporate other settlement refuse, graves, and many other materials, and sometimes reach considerable depth.

Tertiary
The geological period preceding the Quaternary and comprising the Paleocene, Eocene, Oligocene, Miocene, and Pliocene epochs. It began about 65 million years ago and ended about 2 million years ago.

totem
An object from the natural world, usually an animal, with which a particular clan or tribe considers itself to have a special, often a blood, relationship.

tournette
A turntable that was rotated

Umiak

manually to assist in the manufacture of a pot. It was a forerunner of the potter's wheel. In Mesopotamia, from about 5000 BC, some pots formed by hand were finished on tournettes. The fast-spinning potter's wheel was in use by about 3400 AD.

tree line
A line marking the point in the Arctic north of which no trees grow, because the subsoil is permanently frozen. See also permafrost line.

umiak
A large, open boat used by Arctic peoples, made of skins stretched on a wooden frame.

Upper Paleolithic
The last part of the Paleolithic, starting some 40,000 years ago, during which modern humans replaced the Neanderthals. Caracterized by blade technology, human burials, and art.

Urnfield period
A group of related Late Bronze Age cultures in Europe, characterized by the practice of placing the cremated remains of a dead person in a pottery funerary urn, which was then buried in a cemetery of urns. The practice dates from about 1300 BC, when urnfield graves became

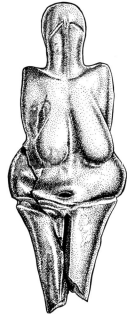

Venus figurine

increasingly common in eastern central Europe; from there, this burial rite spread west, to Italy and Spain, north, across the Rhine to Germany, and east, to the steppes of Russia. Other features of the Urnfield period include copper-mining and sheet bronze metalworking. The Urnfield period continued until the start of the Iron Age, about 750 BC, when inhumation once again became the dominant form of burial in many areas.

Venus figurines
Small carved or sculptured figurines of naked women, usually with exaggerated features, such as a large

abdomen, swelling breasts and buttocks, and marked genitals. These figurines appeared in the Gravettian phase about 29,000 years ago, and were made from a variety of materials, including antler, bone, stone, and clay. Figurines with a standardized appearance have been found across a distance of more than 2,000 kilometers (1,200 miles), from the Atlantic coast in the west to Russia in the east.

wadi
An Arabic term denoting a channel of a watercourse that is dry except during periods of rainfall.

Wallacea
The area of island-studded sea that has separated Australia from Southeast Asia for all of the last 70 million years. It marks the division between two major faunal groups: oriental animals (such as elephants, tigers, and apes) and the animals of Australia (such as kangaroos, wombats, and the monotremes). It is named after the British naturalist A.R. Wallace, who first recognized its significance.

wet-rice technology
A type of farming in which rice is grown in specially prepared flooded fields known as

paddies. Although rice can also be grown under dry conditions, wet-rice cultivation in paddy fields is much more productive, and has a considerable antiquity in Asia. The paddy fields are surrounded by low embankments, or levees, and must be continually leveled to maintain a constant depth of water, usually about 10 centimeters (4 inches). The fields can be flooded naturally or by irrigation channels, and are kept inundated during the growing season. About a month before harvesting, the water is removed and the field left to dry.

yue axe
A broad-bladed axe used as a weapon in ancient China. Jade yue axes have been found in graves from the Liangzhu culture of Late Neolithic China.

Yue axe

ILLUSTRATIONS: KEN RINKEL

453